D0744495

WILDLIFE FEEDING AND NUTRITION
Second Edition

ANIMAL FEEDING AND NUTRITION
A Series of Monographs and Treatises

Tony J. Cunha, Editor

Distinguished Service Professor Emeritus
University of Florida
Gainesville, Florida

and

Dean Emeritus, School of Agriculture
California State Polytechnic University
Pomona, California

Tony J. Cunha, SWINE FEEDING AND NUTRITION, 1977

W. J. Miller, DAIRY CATTLE FEEDING AND NUTRITION, 1979

Tilden Wayne Perry, BEEF CATTLE FEEDING AND NUTRITION, 1980

Tony J. Cunha, HORSE FEEDING AND NUTRITION, 1980

Charles T. Robbins, WILDLIFE FEEDING AND NUTRITION, 1983

Tilden Wayne Perry, ANIMAL LIFE-CYCLE FEEDING AND NUTRITION, 1984

Lee Russell McDowell, NUTRITION OF GRAZING RUMINANTS IN WARM
    CLIMATES, 1985

Ray L. Shirley, NITROGEN AND ENERGY NUTRITION OF RUMINANTS, 1986

Peter R. Cheeke, RABBIT FEEDING AND NUTRITION, 1987

Lee Russell McDowell, VITAMINS IN ANIMAL NUTRITION, 1989

D. J. Minson, FORAGE AND RUMINANT NUTRITION, 1990

Tony J. Cunha, HORSE FEEDING AND NUTRITION, SECOND EDITION, 1990

Lee Russell McDowell, MINERALS IN ANIMAL AND HUMAN NUTRITION, 1992

Charles T. Robbins, WILDLIFE FEEDING AND NUTRITION, SECOND EDITION, 1993

WILDLIFE FEEDING AND NUTRITION

Second Edition

Charles T. Robbins

Departments of Natural Resource Sciences and Zoology
Washington State University
Pullman, Washington

ACADEMIC PRESS, INC.

Harcourt Brace Jovanovich, Publishers

San Diego   New York   Boston
London   Sydney   Tokyo   Toronto

Cover photo by Charles T. Robbins.

This book is printed on acid-free paper. ∞

Academic Press, Inc.
1250 Sixth Avenue, San Diego, California 92101-4311

United Kingdom Edition published by
Academic Press Limited
24–28 Oval Road, London NW1 7DX

Library of Congress Cataloging-in-Publication Data

Robbins, Charles T.
    Wildlife feeding and nutrition / Charles T. Robbins. – 2nd ed.
        p.   cm. – (Animal feeding and nutrition)
    Includes index.
    ISBN 0-12-589382-5
    1. Animals–Food.   2. Animal nutrition.   3. Game and game-birds–
Feeding and feeds.   4. Captive wild animals–Feeding and feeds.
I. Title.   II. Series.
QL756.5.R6   1992
636.089'32–dc20   92-14273
                                                                                CIP

PRINTED IN THE UNITED STATES OF AMERICA
92   93   94   95   96   97   QW   9   8   7   6   5   4   3   2   1

To William, Shorty, Benjamin, Morty, Minnie, Bo, Blue, Lass, and the many other wild animals that have enriched my life.

Contents

Foreword

The volume of scientific literature is expanding rapidly. As this occurs, interpretation becomes more complex and thus presents a continuing need for summation in up-to-date books. This necessitates that top scientists and authorities in a given field collate much of the available information in one volume.

Dr. Charles T. Robbins, a distinguished scientist, has done an excellent job in the compilation of an enormous amount of information in this revised edition on wildlife nutrition. The text will be invaluable to wildlife biologists, to those who are interested in captive animal nutrition and management, and to those who are interested in improving the feed supply and nutrition of free-ranging wildlife. Those who are interested in wildlife as creatures of beauty that enrich their joy of nature will also find this book a source of useful information that enhances their appreciation of wildlife.

The book is extremely valuable in pointing out the many causes of poor growth, low reproduction, immobility, and deaths in wildlife due to an inadequate supply of feed, water, and nutrients. Throughout the book the author provides a myriad of examples to show that the feeding and nutrition of free-ranging wildlife is much more complex than the feeding of farm livestock and poultry.

The first edition of this book has been widely accepted. This second edition contains a great deal of new knowledge weaved into an outstanding up-to-date text. It should be very helpful to undergraduate and graduate students as well as teachers of biology and wildlife management. The book will be a useful reference for all who are interested and concerned with wildlife throughout the world.

Tony J. Cunha

Preface

Wildlife Feeding and Nutrition fills a serious gap in the wildlife and animal nutrition literature by providing a discussion of the basic principles of nutrition and their application to the broader field of wildlife ecology. This book is based on lectures presented in an upper-level wildlife nutrition course taught at Washington State University. Consequently, the needs and interests of the students in that course are reflected in the text.

Although my own research has been on the nutrition and ecology of ungulates and bears, wildlife undergraduates typically are interested in the entire natural world and all of its life forms. In order to support and expand the undergraduate's appetite for knowledge, this book is written from a very broad comparative perspective as it focuses on both wild mammals and birds. The wildlife nutritionist often does have much more of a comparative perspective than does the domestic animal nutritionist. Unfortunately, although many of the principles of nutrition could be learned by wildlife students taking the standard animal nutrition course taught in animal science departments, most of these departments have chosen to virtually ignore the nondomesticated and nonlaboratory species. Therefore, because wildlife students usually lack any nutritional background, the various chapters start at an introductory level and progress to a more advanced level that will challenge the advanced wildlife student and professional biologist.

ACKNOWLEDGMENTS

Many people have contributed to my studies and to the writing of this text. Julius Nagy of Colorado State Univesity first stimulated my interst in wildlife nutrition while I was an undergraduate. Aaron Moen of Cornell University supported and encouraged my further progress as a graduate student. While at Cornell, I thoroughly enjoyed and benefited from my association with two particularly outstanding animal scientists, Peter J. Van Soest and J. Tom Reid. Since coming to Washington State University, James King, Mary Murphy, Ann Hagerman, Tom Hanley, and Chris Servheen have been helpful in providing a stimulating exchange of ideas. Because all university research programs are dependent upon students of the highest caliber, I am indebted to those of mine who have investigated several topics contained within this book. They include Yosef Cohen, Eric Mould, Katherine Parker, Mark Wickstrom, Don Spalinger, Gary Carl, Sean Farley, Dave Hewitt, Geoff Pritchard, Eric Rominger, and Ed Reese. Their research has been supported by the National Science Foundation, Washington Department of Wildlife, U.S. Forest Service, U.S. Fish and Wildlife Service, Oregon Department of Fish and Wildlife, Chevron Oil, and National Fish and Wildlife Foundation. Finally, I wish to thank my parents and grand-parents for introducing me to the natural world and my wife, Barb, for providing me the time necessary to complete this book and for sharing with me the fun and frustrations of research.

Charles T. Robbins

1

Introduction

The physiology of wild animals is almost entirely unknown. . . . Our understanding of food and water is limited at the outset by our deficient understanding of game physiology.

LEOPOLD, 1933

Knowledge of wildlife nutrition, as a component of both wildlife ecology and management, is central to understanding the survival and productivity of all wildlife populations, whether free-ranging or captive. Although it is difficult to identify the earliest interest in wildlife nutrition, the science of wildlife nutrition is an extremely young area of investigation. The historical roots in North America largely began during the late 1870s and early 1880s when biologists, primarily ornithologists and entomologists, started investigating the food habits of wildlife in relation to the welfare of humans (McAtee, 1933). This new area of investigation was entitled *economic ornithology* because of the effort to relate the ingestion of agricultural crops or insects to the economic benefit or detriment of the farmer.

Economic ornithology officially began in 1885 in the United States when Congress instructed the Department of Agriculture to initiate "the study of [the] interrelation of birds and agriculture, an investigation of the food, habits, and migration of birds in relation to both insects and plants" (McAtee, 1933). Because of this early legislative and economic focus, studies of food habits were the major efforts of most early nutritionists (Fig. 1.1). Although techniques and emphasis on food habits research have changed over the years, food habit studies have continued to be a major percentage of all wildlife nutrition investigations. However, classical food habit studies usually tell us only what has been eaten and rarely how much, for what reason, or the physiological role or importance of the different ingested foods (Leopold, 1933). Thus, the use of only food habits information to develop management schemes is all too often destined to failure because of the absolute need to understand the much broader nutritional interaction from an ecological perspective. Unfortunately, preoccupation with food habits has reduced our investigations of other equally important areas of nutrition (Bartholomew and Cade, 1963). Similarly, early attempts to understand wildlife

1

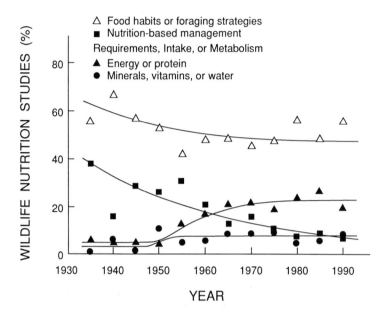

Fig. 1.1 Relative proportion of nutrition studies using wild birds and mammals published in 5-year intervals since 1935. Statistics were compiled by reviewing all titles (and abstracts if available) published in *Wildlife Review* for the appropriate years and assigning each study to one of six areas on the basis of its major contribution.

productivity based on correlations to soil fertility (Albrecht, 1944; Denney, 1944; Crawford, 1949; Williams, 1964) were not adequate to develop an understanding of nutritional interactions and, therefore, provide a base for meaningfully altering the animal–environment interaction (Jones *et al.*, 1968). Plants and the subsequent nutritional interactions are not mere passive reflectors of soil quality. Wildlife researchers were warned as early as 1937 (McAtee, 1937) that they would "do well to obtain the cooperation in their experimental work of experts in animal nutrition."

The number of wildlife nutrition studies has increased markedly since 1937, and particularly since 1960. Overall, the number of studies has doubled approximately every 11 years for the last 50 years (Fig. 1.2), which is similar to the growth of science in general (Price, 1975). The post-1960 surge presumably reflects the increased interest in the broad areas of animal biology, the environment, and ecology. The number of studies published every two years in the 1990s exceeds the total number published in the 25 years from 1935 to 1960. The increasing number of studies is indicative of a growing body of knowledge relative to all aspects of wildlife nutrition. Food habits and wildlife management

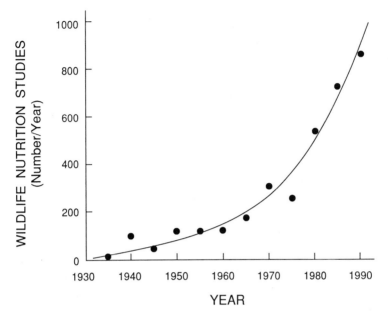

Fig. 1.2 Total number of wildlife nutrition studies per year that were cited in *Wildlife Review* in 5-year intervals beginning in 1935.

studies based on nutritional perspectives have averaged 72% (ranging from 94% to 58%) of all such inquiries. The absolute and relative number of studies in these two areas is probably underestimated because the content of papers beginning with "The ecology . . ." or "The biology . . ." cannot always be identified. Nutritional investigations, especially of food habits, may be included in many of these articles. Water requirement, intake, and metabolism investigations have averaged 3% (0–7%) of the nutrition articles in any one year, minerals and vitamins 4% (0–7%), and feed analysis or utilization studies 7% (0–12%). Research dealing with energy or protein requirements, intake, or metabolism averaged only 5% of all studies between 1935 and 1950, but increased markedly after 1950 and averaged 20% between 1955 and 1990. The increase in energy and protein studies is primarily due to the proliferation of bioenergetic investigations dating back to Brody (1945) and Scholander *et al.* (1950).

The relative decline in management programs or studies with a nutritional basis partially reflects the decline in the popularity of food plantings for wildlife. While it is certainly saddening to see such a decline, the increasing numbers of inquiries in other equally important areas will strengthen the entire field of wildlife nutrition. The pyramid of the science of wildlife nutrition must rest firmly on a base of studies of animal physiology and ecology, with management programs at the apex. Only then will efforts to maximize management returns by altering wildlife productivity through nutrition be rewarded.

Nutrition research and management of wildlife species offer many challenges not always encountered by the scientist working with domestic animals, primarily because of the need to maintain an ecological perspective in designing and implementing any wildlife nutrition research (Watson, 1973). The free-ranging animal is in a constantly changing environment, and humans have little control over many of the animal–environment interactions. For example, a survey of southern and eastern wildlife management agencies indicated that 90% or more of the total bobwhite quail production and harvest occurred without deliberate management efforts (Frye, 1961). The lack of control over wild free-ranging animals often requires that the wildlife ecologist have a greater base of knowledge to understand interactions and implement meaningful management programs than the scientist working with domestic animals. The wildlife ecologist often has a minimal incentive relative to the domestic-animal scientist to maximize meat production or economic return, but may attempt simply to understand and appreciate an ecological system. However, many nutrition results generated in such basic investigations are often essential to understanding other living systems and, as such, are the grist of applied research.

Although one might assume that our nutritional knowledge of captive animals is complete because of our long history of zoos, 60–70% of the animals dying in zoos prior to 1970 died because of poor management and husbandry, with nearly 25% dying from nutritional problems (Ratcliffe, 1966; Wallach, 1970). During this time, the primary goal of zoos was entertainment. Because zoos could obtain wild-caught specimens of virtually all living species, poor survival and reproduction were of little concern. More recently, because of the decline in wild populations of many species and the corresponding passage of laws to protect those remnant populations, the major goal of modern zoos is now conservation, including the propagation of rare species (Schmitt, 1988). The emphasis on having healthy, reproducing animals has meant that many zoos have hired staff or consulting nutritionists to understand the nutritional needs of each species and to formulate nutritious, palatable diets (Dierenfeld, 1987). Many of the recent nutrition-based, management articles focus on better dietary management of zoo animals. Because of the variety of species in zoos and the unique physical facilities, zoos are a valuable resource to the development of wildlife nutrition.

The use of captive animals in nutrition research often requires special facilities and great perseverance in handling or training the animals. Although captive and instrumented wild animals may provide the only means for answering many questions, one must always be concerned about the effects of captivity and handling on the results. The nutrition of captive primates, particularly the rhesus monkey (Harris, 1970; NRC, 1978b), and common laboratory rodents, such as the guinea pig, rat, and mouse (NRC, 1978a), has been studied the most, with the emphasis on these species as models for understanding human nutrition. While these studies are very applicable to understanding captive primate or rodent nutrition, their lack of an ecological perspective suitable for increasing our knowledge of free-ranging animals is unfortunate.

Wildlife nutrition overlaps with many other disciplines. Environmental physiology, wildlife ecology and management, conservation biology, and range and forest management often produce or implement wildlife nutrition results. Wildlife nutrition is indeed a science because the nutritional interactions between the animal and its environment are not random events but highly predictable interactions forming the basis for the science of wildlife nutrition. However, the application of much of the wildlife nutrition data to management is both an art and a science because of the lack of adequate knowledge of many control mechanisms determining the outcome of any manipulation. Many of the problems encountered by the ecologist or animal and land manager may involve basic nutritional questions about starvation, competition, winter feeding of wildlife, diet formulation, habitat manipulations such as clearcuts, fertilization, and re-seeding, predator–prey interactions, and carrying capacity estimations. Consequently, wildlife nutrition is a basic and yet broad field of investigation with many challenges.

REFERENCES

Albrecht, W. A. (1944). Soil fertility and wildlife—Cause and effect. *Trans. North Am. Wildl. Conf.* **9**, 19–28.

Bartholomew, G. A., and Cade, T. J. (1963). The water economy of land birds. *Auk* **80**, 504–539.

Brody, S. (1945). "Bioenergetics and Growth." Hafner, New York.

Crawford, B. (1949). Relationships of soils and wildlife. *Missouri Cons. Comm., Circ. No.* **134**, 10–18.

Denney, A. H. (1944). Wildlife relationships to soil types. *Trans. North Am. Wildl. Conf.* **9**, 316–322.

Dierenfeld, E. S. (1987). Zoo nutrition: A science coming of age. *Proc. Dr. Scholl Nutr. Conf.* **7**, 104–111.

Frye, O. E., Jr. (1961). A review of bobwhite quail management in eastern North America. *Trans. North Am. Wildl. Nat. Resour. Conf.* **26**, 273–281.

Harris, R. S. (Ed.). (1970). "Feeding and Nutrition of Nonhuman Primates." Academic Press, New York.

Jones, R. L., Labisky, R. F., and Anderson, W. L. (1968). Selected minerals in soils, plants, and pheasants: An ecosystem approach to understanding pheasant distribution in Illinois. *Biol. Notes (Ill. Nat. Hist. Surv.)* **63**, 8 pp.

Leopold, A. (1933). "Game Management." Charles Scribner's Sons, New York.

McAtee, W. L. (1933). Economic ornithology. *In* "Fifty Years' Progress of American Ornithology 1883–1933," pp. 111–129. American Ornithologists' Union 50th Anniversary, New York. November 13–16, 1933.

McAtee, W. L. (1937). Nutritive value of maize. *Wildl. Rev.* **9,** 36–38.

National Research Council (NRC). (1978a). "Nutrient Requirements of Laboratory Animals," Publ. No. 2767, Nat. Acad. Sci., Washington, D.C.

National Research Council (NRC). (1978b). "Nutrient Requirements of Nonhuman Primates," Publ. No. 2768, Nat. Acad. Sci., Washington, D.C.

Price, D. J. D. (1975). "Science Since Babylon." Yale University Press, New Haven, Connecticut.

Ratcliffe, H. L. (1966). Diets for zoological gardens: Aids to conservation and disease control. *Int. Zoo Ybk.* **6,** 4–23.

Schmitt, E. C. (1988). Effects of conservation legislation on the professional development of zoos. *Int. Zoo Ybk.* **27,** 3–9.

Scholander, P. F., Hock, R., Walters, V., and Irving, L. (1950). Adaptation to cold in arctic and tropical mammals and birds in relation to body temperature, insulation, and basal metabolic rate. *Biol. Bull.* **99,** 259–271.

Wallach, J. D. (1970). Nutritional diseases of exotic animals. *J. Am. Vet. Med. Assoc.* **157,** 583–599.

Watson, A. (1973). Discussion: Nutrition in reproduction—Direct effects and predictive functions. *In* "Breeding Biology of Birds" (D. S. Farner, ed.), pp. 59–68. Nat. Acad. Sci., Washington, D.C.

Williams, C. E. (1964). Soil fertility and cottontail body weight: A reexamination. *J. Wildl. Manage.* **28,** 329–338.

2

General Nutrient and Energy Requirements

The number of species whose nutritional requirements are known with any precision is relatively few. Of the mammals only about a dozen species have been studied out of the total of over 5,000; the situation with birds is worse.

EVANS AND MILLER, 1968

Wildlife nutrition provides an understanding of specific biochemical and biophysical interactions critical to the survival and productivity of individuals and populations. Nutrition is the process whereby the animal procures and processes portions of its external chemical environment for the continued functioning of internal metabolism. All animals are located somewhere on a tissue metabolism gradient (Fig. 2.1). The position of an animal along the gradient represents a dynamic balancing between cellular and organismal requirements and the rate and efficiency at which specific components of the external environment can be acquired. The wildlife nutritionist need not consider catabolism and weight loss as undesirable but rather as essential components of life strategies of many wild animals. As an indication of the importance of weight loss, many captive wildlife have seasonal gain–loss cycles even when given abundant, high quality food.

Wildlife nutritionists are primarily interested in the basic biochemical–biophysical interactions between the animal and its environment. These interactions include the nutritional requirements that all animals must acquire from their external environment. These requirements are energy, protein or amino acids, water, minerals, vitamins, and essential fatty acids. Other nutritionally related requirements must frequently be provided for captive wildlife. For example, oral health of carnivorous mammals is better if they are given bones when consuming soft diets or if they are given hard diets rather than soft diets (Vosburgh *et al.*, 1982; Haberstroh *et al.*, 1984); and birds must have access to hard, rough objects to trim their ever-growing bills (Baer and Ullrey, 1986). Similarly, there are many chemicals in plants that are not nutrients but are toxic or reduce consumption or utilization efficiencies of required nutrients (Palo and Robbins, 1991). The nutritional ecologist must frequently understand the chemical and physiological consequences when these compounds are ingested.

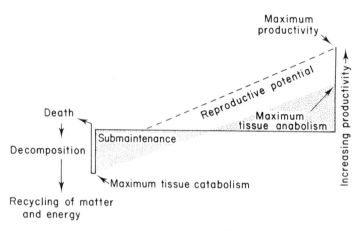

Fig. 2.1 The productivity gradient experienced by all wildlife. [From Moen (1973).]

Energy, the capacity to do work or produce motion against a resisting force, is of interest to the wildlife nutritionist since biochemical transformations, muscle contractions, nerve impulse transmissions, excretion processes, and all other active body functions require energy. Although physicists make no ultimate distinction between energy and matter, nutritionists treat energy, particularly chemical energy, as a property of matter. Energy transformations may be described by the laws of thermodynamics. The first law is that energy can be neither created nor destroyed but merely changed in form. Thus, if a specific amount of one form of energy disappears (such as chemical energy), an equal amount of another form of energy (such as heat) must appear.

The second law of thermodynamics is that energy transformations produce heat and, therefore, increase entropy within the system. Simply stated, chemical energy transformations are not 100% efficient in the production of chemical work. Although many machines can use heat to perform work, the living cell cannot. Heat is useful only in maintaining the relatively high, constant body temperature of endotherms. Fortunately, a significant portion of the chemical energy liberated during catabolic processes can be used to synthesize other useful forms of chemical energy, particularly adenosine triphosphate (ATP). The total amount of useful free energy and heat released when organic compounds are oxidized is independent of the speed of the reaction, but dependent only on initial and final states. Thus, a gram of glucose will yield the same amount of energy irrespective of whether it is burned in a flame or in the controlled reactions of the animal body as long as the end products, carbon dioxide and water, are the same. This is often referred to as Hess's law of constant heat summation.

Because of the constant summation of heat in biological systems, the mea-

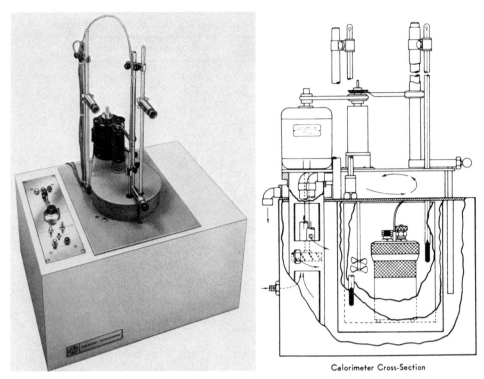

Fig. 2.2   Adiabatic bomb calorimeter used to determine the chemical energy content of plant or animal samples. (Courtesy of Parr Instrument Company, Moline, Illinois.)

surement of chemical energy as the heat of combustion is most frequently used to evaluate animal energetics. The most commonly used measures of heat in nutrition have been the calorie (1000 cal = 1 kcal) and the joule (1 cal = 4.184 joules). The calorie is the amount of heat needed to raise the temperature of 1 g of water from 14.5°C to 15.5°C. The bomb calorimeter (Fig. 2.2) is used to measure the amount of heat released when a sample of plant or animal tissue is completely oxidized. The sample is placed in a combustion chamber containing excess oxygen, which is immersed in an insulated water jacket and ignited. The temperature rise in the surrounding water is measured and is proportional to the sample's chemical energy content. For instance, when a 1 g sample is ignited and produces a temperature rise of 4°C in 1000 g of water, the chemical energy content is 4 kcal. The chemical energy content of the various organic compounds in Table 2.1 varies inversely with the carbon-to-hydrogen ratio because carbon when oxidized to carbon dioxide yields approximately one-quarter the energy of hydrogen when oxidized to water. Similarly, molecular oxygen and nitrogen

TABLE 2.1

Chemical Energy Content of Dietary Substances and Metabolic or Excretion Products

Element or substance	Energy content (kcal/g)	Composition (% weight)			
		Carbon	Hydrogen	Oxygen	Nitrogen
Carbon	8.0	100			
Hydrogen	34.5		100		
Methane	13.3	75	25		
Carbohydrates					
Glucose	3.75	40	7	53	
Sucrose	3.96	42	6	52	
Starch and glycogen	4.23	45	6	49	
Cellulose	4.18	45	6	49	
Fatty acids and fats					
Acetic acid	3.49	40	7	53	
Propionic acid	4.96	49	8	43	
Butyric acid	5.95	55	9	36	
Palmitic acid	9.35	75	13	12	
Stearic acid	9.53	76	13	11	
Oleic acid	9.50	76	12	11	
Average triglyceride[a]	9.45	75	13	12	
Amino acids and protein					
Glycine	3.11	32	7	42	19
Alanine	4.35	40	8	36	16
Tyrosine	5.92	60	6	26	8
Average protein[a]	5.65	52	7	23	16
Excretion products					
Urea	2.53	20	7	26	47
Uric acid	2.74	36	2	29	33
Creatine	4.24	37	7	24	32
Creatinine	4.60	43	6	14	37

Sources: Brody, 1945; Maynard and Loosli, 1969.

[a]The average caloric content of complex mixtures of fats, proteins, or their constituents is dependent on the concentration and caloric content of each component. Consequently, these values should not be used as constants throughout the animal and plant kingdoms.

reduce the energy content because oxygen in itself is not energy yielding and is readily available via respiration, and nitrogen, while oxidized in the calorimeter, is not oxidized in the body.

Differences in the chemical or gross energies of either plants or animals are due to the energy contents of the specific chemical compounds and their relative proportions. For example, the energy content of dried animal tissue increases as the fat content increases and decreases as the carbohydrate or mineral content increases. Plants contain many different compounds, but the gross energies of

TABLE 2.2

Average Energy Content of Plant Parts or Communities

Plant part or community	Number of samples	Average energy content (kcal/g)	Coefficient of variation
Leaves	260	4.229	0.116
Stems and branches	51	4.267	0.081
Roots	52	4.720	0.092
Seeds	22	5.065	0.219
Herb old field	35	4.177	0.096
Perennial grasses	143	3.905	0.104
Conifer forest	14	4.787	0.078
Alpine meadow	3	4.711	0.005
Tropical rain forest	15	3.897	0.060

Source: Golley, 1961.

plant tissue are often very uniform (Table 2.2). The higher energy content of roots, seeds, and evergreen and alpine communities is due to their higher content of oils, fats, waxes, and resins. Because the degree of dietary energy use may vary from 0 to 100% depending on the completeness of digestion and oxidation, gross energies must be further evaluated to understand animal energetics.

Although energy is required during all chemical transformations within the animal body, estimations of the animal's energy requirements would be an extremely tedious process if each biochemical reaction were measured. Because the oxidation of most organic compounds requires oxygen and produces carbon dioxide and heat, measurements of these parameters in the living animal indicate the energy required for all ongoing metabolic transformations. Similarly, net energy retention as growth or other productive processes is equal to the gross energies of the tissues or products. Thus, one can speak of energy requirements of the whole animal for basal metabolism, activity, thermoregulation, growth, reproduction, lactation or brooding, pelage or plumage growth, the support of parasites, and other energy-demanding processes even though each of these includes thousands of energy transformations.

REFERENCES

Baer, D. J., and Ullrey, D.E. (1986). Developing and testing a new psittacine diet. *Proc. Dr. Scholl Nutr. Conf.* **6**, 28–39.
Brody, S. (1945). "Bioenergetics and Growth." Hafner, New York.
Evans, E., and Miller, D. S. (1968). Comparative nutrition, growth and longevity. *Proc. Nutr. Soc.* **27**, 121–129.

Golley, F. B. (1961). Energy values of ecological materials. *Ecology* **42,** 581–584.

Haberstroh, L.I., Ullrey, D.E., Sikarskie, J.G., Richter, N.A., Colmery, B.H., and Myers, T.D. (1984). Diet and oral health in captive Amur tigers (*Panthera tigris altaica*). *J. Zoo Anim. Med.* **15,** 142–146.

Maynard, L. A., and Loosli, J. K. (1969). "Animal Nutrition." McGraw-Hill, New York.

Moen, A. N. (1973). "Wildlife Ecology: An Analytical Approach." Freeman, San Francisco.

Palo, R.T., and Robbins, C.T. (eds.). (1991). "Plant Defenses Against Mammalian Herbivory." CRC Press, Boca Raton, Florida.

Vosburgh, K.M., Barbiers, R.B., Sikarskie, J.G., and Ullrey, D.E. (1982). A soft versus hard diet and oral health in captive timber wolves (*Canis lupus*). *J. Zoo Anim. Med.* **13,** 104–107.

3

Protein

Proteins are major constituents of the animal's body. They are important constituents of animal cell walls and are active as enzymes, hormones, lipoproteins, antibodies, blood clotting factors, and carriers in active transport systems. Thus, *protein* is a very general term encompassing a heterogeneous group of compounds having many different functions. A continuous supply of dietary protein must be available to the animal for these functions.

The unifying principle of protein composition is that they are all composed of amino acids. Classically, proteins are mixtures of 20–25 different amino acids (Table 3.1), although over 200 nonprotein amino acids also exist (Bell, 1972; Fowden, 1974). Amino acids are linked via peptide bonds

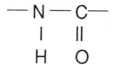

to form plant and animal proteins. Because animal and plant proteins are usually degraded during digestion to their constituent amino acids or very small peptide groups by enzymatic hydrolysis of the peptide bond, the specific kind of protein is not as important as the amino acid content and availability relative to animal requirements. Although differences in the amino acid content of animals do occur (Table 3.2) and could reflect differing amino acid requirements, many of the differences are relatively small when compared to the major anatomical differences between the species.

Some amino acids can be produced in adequate amounts by animals, and some must be ingested to meet the animal's requirements. Those that cannot be produced by the animal in sufficient amounts to meet requirements and, therefore, must come from the diet are called *essential* amino acids. Those that can be produced adequately from nonspecific precursors within the animal are called *nonessential* amino acids. Animals with simple stomachs and minimal fermentative capacity usually require 10 essential amino acids: arginine, histidine, isoleucine, leucine, threonine, lysine, methionine, phenylalanine, tryptophan, and valine. These are essential because of the inability or limited rate of the animal's metabolic pathways to produce certain ring structures and molecular

13

TABLE 3.1

Names and Structures of the Most Important Amino Acids

Amino acid and formula	Structure
Aliphatic	
Glycine, $C_2H_5O_2N$	$\begin{array}{c} NH_2 \\ \| \\ H-C-COOH \\ \| \\ H \end{array}$
Alanine, $C_3H_7O_2N$	$\begin{array}{c} NH_2 \\ \| \\ CH_3-C-COOH \\ \| \\ H \end{array}$
Serine, $C_3H_7O_3N$	$\begin{array}{c} H \quad NH_2 \\ \| \quad \| \\ HO-C-C-COOH \\ \| \quad \| \\ H \quad H \end{array}$
Threonine, $C_4H_9O_3N$	$\begin{array}{c} H \quad NH_2 \\ \| \quad \| \\ CH_3-C-C-COOH \\ \| \quad \| \\ OH \quad H \end{array}$
Valine, $C_5H_{11}O_2N$	$\begin{array}{c} CH_3 \quad\quad NH_2 \\ \diagdown \quad\quad \| \\ CH-C-COOH \\ \diagup \quad\quad \| \\ CH_3 \quad\quad H \end{array}$
Leucine, $C_6H_{13}O_2N$	$\begin{array}{c} CH_3 \quad\quad H \quad NH_2 \\ \diagdown \quad\quad \| \quad \| \\ CH-C-C-COOH \\ \diagup \quad\quad \| \quad \| \\ CH_3 \quad\quad H \quad H \end{array}$
Isoleucine, $C_6H_{13}O_2N$	$\begin{array}{c} CH_3-CH_2 \quad\quad NH_2 \\ \diagdown \quad\quad \| \\ CH-C-COOH \\ \diagup \quad\quad \| \\ CH_3 \quad\quad H \end{array}$
Basic	
Histidine, $C_6H_9O_2N_3$	$\begin{array}{c} H \quad NH_2 \\ \| \quad \| \\ CH=C-C-C-COOH \\ \| \quad \| \; \| \; \| \\ NH \quad N \; H \; H \\ \diagdown \quad \diagup \\ CH \end{array}$
Arginine, $C_6H_{14}O_2N_4$	$\begin{array}{c} H \; H \; H \; H \; NH_2 \\ \| \; \| \; \| \; \| \; \| \\ NH_2-C-N-C-C-C-C-COOH \\ \| \quad\quad\; H \; H \; H \; H \\ NH \end{array}$
Lysine, $C_6H_{14}O_2N_2$	$\begin{array}{c} H \; H \; H \; H \; NH_2 \\ \| \; \| \; \| \; \| \; \| \\ NH_2-C-C-C-C-C-COOH \\ \| \; \| \; \| \; \| \; \| \\ H \; H \; H \; H \; H \end{array}$

TABLE 3.1

Continued

Amino acid and formula	Structure

Aromatic

Phenylalanine, $C_9H_{11}O_2N$

$$\text{C}_6\text{H}_5-\text{CH}_2-\overset{\overset{\displaystyle NH_2}{|}}{\underset{\underset{\displaystyle H}{|}}{C}}-\text{COOH}$$

Tyrosine, $C_9H_{11}O_3N$

$$\text{HO}-\text{C}_6\text{H}_4-\text{CH}_2-\overset{\overset{\displaystyle NH_2}{|}}{\underset{\underset{\displaystyle H}{|}}{C}}-\text{COOH}$$

Sulfur-containing

Cysteine, $C_3H_7O_2NS$

$$\text{HS}-\overset{\overset{\displaystyle H}{|}}{\underset{\underset{\displaystyle H}{|}}{C}}-\overset{\overset{\displaystyle NH_2}{|}}{\underset{\underset{\displaystyle H}{|}}{C}}-\text{COOH}$$

Cystine, $C_6H_{12}O_4N_2S_2$

$$\text{S}-\overset{\overset{\displaystyle H}{|}}{\underset{\underset{\displaystyle H}{|}}{C}}-\overset{\overset{\displaystyle NH_2}{|}}{\underset{\underset{\displaystyle H}{|}}{C}}-\text{COOH}$$
$$\text{S}-\overset{\overset{\displaystyle H}{|}}{\underset{\underset{\displaystyle H}{|}}{C}}-\overset{\overset{\displaystyle NH_2}{|}}{\underset{\underset{\displaystyle H}{|}}{C}}-\text{COOH}$$

Methionine, $C_5H_{11}O_2NS$

$$\text{CH}_3-\text{S}-\overset{\overset{\displaystyle H}{|}}{\underset{\underset{\displaystyle H}{|}}{C}}-\overset{\overset{\displaystyle H}{|}}{\underset{\underset{\displaystyle H}{|}}{C}}-\overset{\overset{\displaystyle NH_2}{|}}{\underset{\underset{\displaystyle H}{|}}{C}}-\text{COOH}$$

Taurine, $C_2H_7O_3NS$

$$\text{HO}-\overset{\overset{\displaystyle O}{\|}}{\underset{\underset{\displaystyle O}{\|}}{S}}-\overset{\overset{\displaystyle H}{|}}{\underset{\underset{\displaystyle H}{|}}{C}}-\overset{\overset{\displaystyle H}{|}}{\underset{\underset{\displaystyle H}{|}}{C}}-\text{NH}_2$$

Heterocyclic

Tryptophan, $C_{11}H_{12}O_2N_2$

$$\text{C}-\text{CH}_2-\overset{\overset{\displaystyle NH_2}{|}}{\underset{\underset{\displaystyle H}{|}}{C}}-\text{COOH}$$

Proline, $C_5H_9O_2N$

$$\begin{array}{c}\text{CH}_2\text{—CH}_2\\ \text{CH}_2\ \ \text{CH}-\text{COOH}\\ \diagdown\diagup\\ \text{NH}\end{array}$$

Hydroxyproline, $C_5H_9O_3N$

$$\begin{array}{c}\text{HO—CH—CH}_2\\ \text{CH}_2\ \text{CH}-\text{COOH}\\ \diagdown\diagup\\ \text{NH}\end{array}$$

(continues)

TABLE 3.1

Continued

Amino acid and formula	Structure
Acidic	
Aspartic acid, $C_4H_7O_4N$	$HOOC-\underset{\underset{H}{\mid}}{\overset{\overset{H}{\mid}}{C}}-\underset{\underset{H}{\mid}}{\overset{\overset{NH_2}{\mid}}{C}}-COOH$
Asparagine, $C_4H_8O_3N_2$	$NH_2OC-\underset{\underset{H}{\mid}}{\overset{\overset{H}{\mid}}{C}}-\underset{\underset{H}{\mid}}{\overset{\overset{NH_2}{\mid}}{C}}-COOH$
Glutamic acid, $C_5H_9O_4N$	$HOOC-\underset{\underset{H}{\mid}}{\overset{\overset{H}{\mid}}{C}}-\underset{\underset{H}{\mid}}{\overset{\overset{H}{\mid}}{C}}-\underset{\underset{H}{\mid}}{\overset{\overset{NH_2}{\mid}}{C}}-COOH$
Glutamine, $C_5H_{10}O_3N_2$	$NH_2OC-\underset{\underset{H}{\mid}}{\overset{\overset{H}{\mid}}{C}}-\underset{\underset{H}{\mid}}{\overset{\overset{H}{\mid}}{C}}-\underset{\underset{H}{\mid}}{\overset{\overset{NH_2}{\mid}}{C}}-COOH$

TABLE 3.2

Amino Acid Composition (%) of Body Protein in Several Species

Amino acid	Cat	Bobwhite quail	Duck	Ring-necked pheasant	Mink	Mouse	Rabbit	Rat	White-tailed deer
Arginine	6.3	7.4	5.9	7.8	6.4	5.9	6.3	5.9	—
Aspartic acid	8.7	7.2	9.8	7.4	7.3	8.8	8.9	8.1	10.3
Glutamic acid	11.5	11.7	11.2	12.0	12.7	12.9	12.7	13.9	15.6
Glycine	10.0	7.9	8.2	7.0	8.4	10.4	8.9	10.0	10.0
Histidine	1.7	3.9	1.8	4.5	1.9	1.8	1.8	2.2	3.6
Isoleucine	3.3	3.9	4.7	4.0	3.0	3.7	3.6	3.5	3.6
Leucine	6.1	6.7	7.5	6.3	6.7	7.3	6.6	6.5	8.5
Lysine	5.6	10.0	6.0	10.1	5.7	7.9	6.6	7.6	8.0
Methionine	1.8	2.0	1.9	1.8	1.7	2.0	1.9	1.7	1.5
Phenylalanine	3.2	3.5	4.0	3.5	3.5	3.6	3.4	3.7	4.4
Threonine	3.9	3.5	4.3	3.4	3.7	3.7	4.1	3.9	4.5
Valine	4.4	4.3	5.7	4.3	4.4	4.5	4.7	5.5	4.5
Serine	—	3.7	—	3.4	3.8	—	—	—	4.1
Proline	—	6.4	—	5.0	5.9	—	—	—	5.1
Alanine	—	5.9	—	5.7	5.5	—	—	—	8.7
Cystine	—	2.8	—	2.8	2.0	—	—	1.5	0.1
Tyrosine	—	3.0	—	3.1	2.9	—	—	2.9	2.7

Sources: Dunn et al., 1949; Williams et al., 1954; Levin et al., 1973; Glem-Hansen, 1979.

linkages. While deficiencies of most essential amino acids will reduce growth and reproduction, the consumption of a single arginine-free meal by cats can produce convulsions and death within one hour. Arginine deficiency is the most rapidly induced nutrient deficiency observed in any mammal (Morris, 1985). The requirements for essential amino acids relative to necessary dietary intake are reduced or eliminated in animals that have gastrointestinal fermentation, such as ruminants, kangaroos and wallabies, rabbits, and many rodents. Bacterial modification of dietary protein within the gastrointestinal tract or the production of amino acids from other nitrogen sources, such as urea, reduces or eliminates their need as dietary constituents.

Cats require an additional sulfur amino acid, taurine. Most animals can produce taurine from methionine, cysteine, or inorganic sulfate and serine, but cats cannot. The occurrence of taurine synthesis in most animals and the loss of this ability in cats occurs because taurine does not occur in plants, but is abundant in meat. Consequently, all animals except a strict carnivore must produce taurine (Knopf et al., 1978; MacDonald et al., 1984; Ahtee et al., 1985; Pion et al., 1987). Taurine may also be required by very young infants of other mammals and, thus, should be included in milk replacers (Hayes et al., 1980; Renner et al., 1989).

Although amino acids are essential for body functioning and wildlife can select diets based on their amino acid content, very few wildlife studies have examined amino acid composition or requirements (Crawford et al., 1968; Krapu and Swanson, 1975; Parrish and Martin, 1977; Serafin, 1982; Sedinger, 1984; Murphy and King, 1987). The lack of amino acid studies may become increasingly troublesome as wildlife management intensifies and as zoological gardens increase their use of processed diets. Wildlife nutritionists have typically determined the nitrogen content of a food in order to provide an index of its protein content. Because proteins characteristically have 16% nitrogen (ranging from 18.9% for nuts to 15.7% for milk protein), the nitrogen content multiplied by 6.25 (or 100/16) is termed the crude protein content. The estimate is crude because not all plant or animal nitrogen is in the form of protein (other examples are nucleic acids and nitrates) and the exact nitrogen-to-protein ratio may not be known (Sedinger, 1984). Estimates of protein requirements of animals for maintenance and production are in many ways more difficult to make than estimates of energy requirements because dietary protein use may depend on its amino acid composition, the proportion of protein in relation to usable energy within the diet, and the total amount of food consumed (Payne, 1967; Parrish and Martin, 1977). Further, amino acids can be deaminated and used as an energy source when dietary energy is insufficient. Thus, estimations of protein requirements without consideration of energy and other dietary nutrients may be of little value.

REFERENCES

Ahtee, L., Kontro, P., and Paasonen, M. K. (eds.). (1985). "Taurine Biological Actions and Clinical Perspectives." Alan R. Liss, New York.

Bell, E. A. (1972). Toxic amino acids in the Leguminosae. In "Phytochemical Ecology" (J. B. Harborne, ed.), pp. 163–177. Academic Press, New York.

Crawford, M. A., Patterson, J. M., and Yardley, L. (1968). Nitrogen utilization by the cape buffalo (Syncerus caffer) and other large mammals. Symp. Zool. Soc. London 21, 367–379.

Dunn, M. S., Camien, M. N., Malin, R. B., Murphy, E. A., and Reiner, P. J. (1949). Percentages of twelve amino acids in blood, carcass, heart, kidney, liver, muscle, and skin of eight animals. Univ. Calif. Publ. Physiol. 8, 293–325.

Fowden, L. (1974). Nonprotein amino acids from plants: Distribution, biosynthesis, and analog functions. In "Metabolism and Regulation of Secondary Plant Products," Recent Advances in Phytochemistry, Vol. 8 (V. C. Runeckles and E. E. Conn, eds.), pp. 95–122. Academic Press, New York.

Glem-Hansen, N. (1979). Protein requirement for mink in the lactation period. Acta Agric. Scand. 27, 129–138.

Hayes, K. C., Stephan, Z. I., and Sturman, J. A. (1980). Growth depression in taurine-depleted infant monkeys. J. Nutr. 110, 2058–2064.

Knopf, K., Sturman, J. A., Armstrong, M., and Hayer, K. C. (1978). Taurine: An essential nutrient for the cat. J. Nutr. 108, 773–778.

Krapu, G. L., and Swanson, G. A. (1975). Some nutritional aspects of reproduction in prairie nesting pintails. J. Wildl. Manage. 39, 156–162.

Levin, E., Collins, V., Varner, D. S., Williams, G., and Hardenbrook, H. J. (1973). Dietary protein for man and animal. Illinois Veterinarian 16, 10–14.

MacDonald, M. L., Rogers, Q. R., and Morris, J. G. (1984). Nutrition of the domestic cat, a mammalian carnivore. Annu. Rev. Nutr. 4, 521–562.

Morris, J.G. (1985) Nutritional and metabolic responses to arginine deficiency in carnivores. J. Nutr. 115, 524–531.

Murphy, M. E., and King, J. R. (1987). Dietary discrimination by molting white-crowned sparrows given diets differing only in sulfur amino acid concentration. Physiol. Zool. 60, 279–289.

Parrish, J. W., Jr., and Martin, E. W. (1977). The effect of dietary lysine level on the energy and nitrogen balance of the dark-eyed junco. Condor 79, 24–30.

Payne, P. R. (1967). The relationship between protein and calorie requirements of laboratory animals. In "Husbandry of Laboratory Animals" (M. L. Conalty, ed.), pp. 77–95. Academic Press, New York.

Pion, P. D., Kittleson, M. D., Rogers, Q. R., and Morris, J. G. (1987). Myocardial failure in cats associated with low plasma taurine: A reversible cardiomyopathy. Science 237, 764–768.

Renner, E., Schaafsma, G., and Scott, K. J. (1989). Micronutrients in milk. In "Micronutrients in Milk and Milk Based Food Products" (E. Renner, ed.), pp. 1–70. Elsevier Publishing, New York.

Sedinger, J. S. (1984). Protein and amino acid composition of tundra vegetation in relation to nutritional requirements. J. Wildl. Manage. 48, 1128–1136.

Serafin, J. A. (1982). Influence of protein level and supplemental methionine in practical rations for young endangered masked bobwhite quail. Poult. Sci. 61, 988–990.

Williams, H. H., Curtin, L. V., Abraham, J., Loosli, J. K., and Maynard, L. A. (1954). Estimation of growth requirements for amino acids by assay of the carcass. J. Biol. Chem. 208, 277–286.

4

Water

Water is one of the most important essential nutrients because of the variety of its functions and magnitude of its requirement. Water is essential within the animal body as a solvent and is involved in hydrolytic reactions, temperature control, transport of metabolic products, excretion, lubrication of skeletal joints, and sound and light transport within the ear and eye (Robinson, 1957). Water comprises 99% of all molecules within the animal's body (MacFarlane and Howard, 1972). The very high molecular concentration of water within the body is, in part, due to the very small size of water molecules relative to protein, fat, or carbohydrate molecules. Although the actual gravimetric concentration of water within the body is lower than the molecular concentration, the neonatal bird or mammal often has a water concentration between 71 and 88% of its body weight (Table 4.1). The very high water content of young animals decreases as they grow, mature, and accumulate fat (Moulton, 1923). Water concentrations in non-obese, adult animals generally range between 50 and 65%, although water concentrations in very fat animals can be as low as 40% (Mahoney and Jehl, 1984; Ellis and Jehl, 1987; Brown, 1988). In addition to the water incorporated during growth, water requirements are dependent on many other animal–environment interactions. Water requirements are affected by ambient air temperatures, solar and thermal radiation, vapor pressure deficits, metabolic rates, feed intake, productive processes, amount and temporal distribution of activity, and physiological, behavioral, and anatomical water conservation adaptations.

Water to meet the various requirements comes from three sources: (a) *free water,* such as in streams, lakes, puddles, rain, snow, or dew; (b) *preformed water* contained in food; and (c) *oxidative* or *metabolic water* produced as a product of the oxidation of organic compounds containing hydrogen (Bartholomew and Cade, 1963). Preformed water may be as little as 2 to 3% of the weight of air-dried seeds in hot deserts or as much as 70% or more of the fresh weight of animal tissue or succulent plant parts. In relation to oxidative water, anhydrous carbohydrates typically yield 56% of their weight as water, proteins 40%, and fats approximately 107% when completely oxidized (Bartholomew and Cade, 1963). However, catabolism of protein tissue by the starving, water-deprived animal potentially yields two to three times more water per unit of metabolized energy than does body fat because of the much greater water content,

TABLE 4.1

Relationship between Body Weight (X) and the Weight of Body Water (Y) during Growth

Species	Weight range[a]	Range in body water content[a] (%)	Predictive equation	References
Mammals				
Old-field mouse	1.6–11.4 g	82.6–64.7	$Y = 0.88X^{0.89}$	Kaufman and Kaufman, 1977
Common vole	1.9–16.0 g	83.5–63.5	$Y = 0.89X^{0.88}$	Sawicka-Kapusta, 1970
Bank vole	2.1–18.4 g	84.5–60.9	$Y = 0.92X^{0.87}$	Sawicka-Kapusta, 1974; Fedyk, 1974
Brown lemming	3.5–63.1 g	83.3–53.8	$Y = 1.08X^{0.82}$	Holleman and Dieterich, 1978
Mink	274.0–750.8 g	73.5–65.0	$Y = 1.42X^{0.88}$	Harper et al., 1978
Ringed seal	3.6–45.7 kg	62.0–37.4	$Y = 0.79X^{0.83}$	Stirling and McEwan, 1975
White-tailed deer	5.4–58.4 kg	74.7–60.6	$Y = 0.92X^{0.90}$	Robbins et al., 1974
Birds				
Savannah sparrow	1.8–13.9 g	87.0–72.1	$Y = 0.94X^{0.91}$	Williams and Prints, 1986
House martin	2.0–25.0 g	87.5–61.3	$Y = 0.99X^{0.91}$	Bryant and Gardiner, 1979
Meadow pipit	4.0–19.0 g	83.0–66.1	$Y = 1.01X^{0.87}$	Skar et al., 1975
Starling	11.7–75.5 g	85.4–69.3	$Y = 1.08X^{0.91}$	Myrcha et al., 1973
Little auk	41.8–123.1 g	72.3–61.8	$Y = 1.21X^{0.86}$	Taylor and Konarzewski, 1989
Jackdaw	11.5–252.5 g	85.0–69.1	$Y = 0.96X^{0.96}$	Kaminski and Konarzewski, 1984
Lesser scaup	29.4–537.9 g	71.1–58.2	$Y = 0.87X^{0.94}$	Sugden and Harris, 1972
Lesser snow geese	0.1–3.3 kg	71.5–54.7	$Y = 0.62X^{0.98}$	Campbell and Leatherland, 1980

[a]With the exception of mink, ranges in weight and water content are from birth or hatching to peak weight.

for instance, of skeletal muscle (72%) than adipose tissue (3–7%) (Bintz *et al.*, 1979; Bintz and Mackin, 1980). Water produced by the catabolism of proteins, as opposed to fat or carbohydrate, is partially offset by the amount of water necessary for increased nitrogen excretion.

Measurements of free water intake underestimate total water requirements because of the omission of preformed and metabolic water. Many free-ranging herbivores, carnivores, frugivores, granivores, insectivores, and nectivores meet their water requirement during at least a portion of the year from preformed and metabolic water and, thus, do not need to drink water (Richmond *et al.*, 1962; Bartholomew and Cade, 1963; Taylor, 1969; Beale and Smith, 1970; Taylor, 1972; Kennedy and Heinsohn, 1974; Yousef *et al.*, 1974; Noll-Banholzer, 1976; Zervanos and Day, 1977; Byman, 1978; Morton, 1980; Calder, 1981; Alkon *et al.*, 1982; Golightly and Ohmart, 1984; Nagy, 1987; Weathers and Stiles, 1989; Tidemann *et al.*, 1989). Estimates of preformed and metabolic water can be made from fairly detailed knowledge of food intake, although such measurements are often restricted to experiments on captive animals where both food and water intake can be measured accurately.

Isotopes of water, such as tritium or deuterium oxide, have provided a simpler means than direct intake measurements for determining water flux or requirements in either the captive or free-ranging animal. This method involves injecting the experimental animal with a known amount of isotopic water that mixes with and is diluted by the animal's total water pool. The time necessary for complete mixing has ranged from less than one hour in small mammals with simple stomachs to 7–8 hours in ruminants (MacFarlane *et al.*, 1969; Mullen, 1970; Degen *et al.*, 1981; Hughes *et al.*, 1987). Dehydration increases the time necessary for equilibration (Denny and Dawson, 1975).

Once complete mixing has occurred, a blood or urine sample is taken and the isotopic water concentration determined. Because water is constantly lost in urine, feces, and evaporation and the isotopic water is further diluted by ingested water, succeeding samples will have less and less isotopic water. The loss of isotopic water following its injection, assuming that the body metabolizes the different molecular forms equally, provides an estimate of total water flux without distinguishing between free, preformed, and metabolic water. The loss and dilution of isotopic water follows an exponential decay in which the intercept of the curve at the Y axis (time 0) is an estimate of the dilution of the injected dose by the total body water pool. Total body water is estimated by dividing the total amount of isotope injected by its concentration at time 0 (Fig. 4.1). Although many authors have conducted validation experiments of the isotopic dilution method and found it an accurate indicator of water kinetics (Holleman and Dieterich, 1975; Cameron *et al.*, 1976), others have suggested that the body will differentiate in its metabolism of the differing water forms (Rubsamen *et al.*, 1979; Grubbs, 1980). The method usually slightly overestimates the water

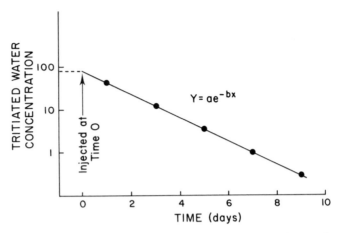

Fig. 4.1 The change in the concentration of isotopic water in the blood, urine, or other body fluid as a function of time following its injection into an animal.

pool and corresponding turnover rate (King *et al.*, 1978; Nagy and Costa, 1980; Tiebout and Nagy, 1991). Further discussions of sources of error in using isotopic water may be found in Mullen (1970, 1971), Grubbs (1980), and Nagy and Costa (1980).

The slope of the regression *b* multiplied by the body water content is an estimate of the turnover or flux rate of water. Water flux is not synonymous with water requirement. Flux rates of any nutrient reflect intake and excretion of that nutrient. Thus, if the animal has an ad libitum access to free water, flux rates will reflect an optimum level of water metabolism that is above the absolute, minimum need. For example, minimum water flux necessary for weight stasis in several captive birds and mammals ingesting dry diets is approximately 60% less than the water flux rate for the same animals having an ad libitum access to water (Thomas and Phillips, 1975; Karasov, 1983; Koerth and Guthery, 1991). Furthermore, insectivores, carnivores, nectivores and frugivores ingesting moist, low energy density diets will have water flux rates far in excess of any requirement.

Water flux in both captive and free-ranging animals increases as body weight increases (Fig. 4.2; Table 4.2). Free-ranging birds and marsupials generally have higher water flux rates than do similar-sized eutherians. However, water flux rates in each taxa differ as a function of diet and habitat. For example, water flux rates in eutherians are highest in herbivores, intermediate in omnivores, and lowest in carnivores and granivores. Both the herbivore and carnivore diets can be high in water, but the higher digestibility of the carnivore diet reduces total food intake and, therefore, water intake relative to the herbivore. Similarly,

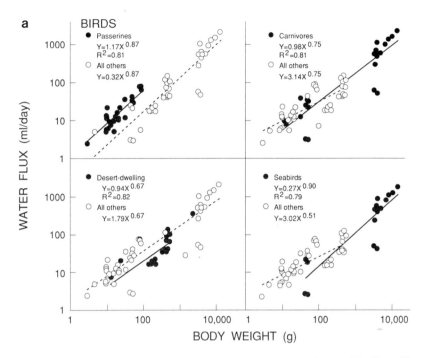

Fig. 4.2   Water flux rates of free-ranging birds, eutherian mammals, and marsupials. [From Nagy and Peterson (1988); courtesy of University of California Press.] *(Figure continues.)*

small desert-dwelling eutherians, particularly rodents, have lower water turnover rates than do those living in mesic and hydric habitats. Surprisingly, herbivorous marsupials have lower water flux rates than do carnivores. These differences relative to the eutherians may reflect the specific characteristics of the diet (such as less succulent tree leaves consumed by arboreal marsupials) or the environment (such as moist habitats of many marsupial carnivores). Passerines, hummingbirds, and seabirds have higher water flux rates and desert-dwelling birds have lower water flux rates than other birds (Bartholomew, 1972; Nicol, 1978; King, 1979; Grubbs, 1980; Hughes *et al.*, 1987; Ambrose and Bradshaw, 1988; Nagy and Peterson, 1988; Weathers and Stiles, 1989).

The above generalities will not occur in many specific cases. For example, desert-dwelling nectivores and frugivores can have very high water flux rates that reflect the diet but not the environment (Calder, 1981). Water flux rates in desert-dwelling chukars ranged from 67 ml/kg/day when feeding on dry seeds and vegetation to 420 ml/kg/day when feeding on succulent forbs (Alkon *et al.*, 1982). Because of the importance of diet and the opportunity for free-ranging animals to behaviorally adapt to stressful environments, water flux rates measured

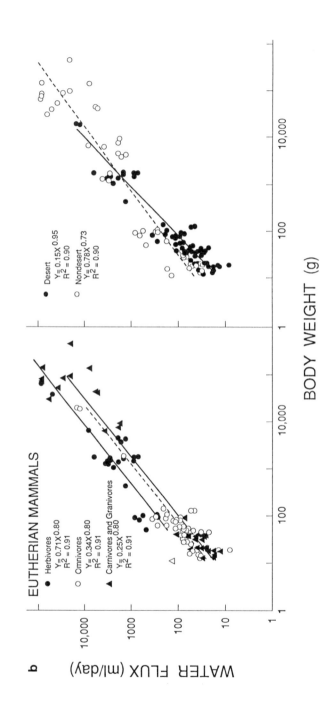

Fig. 4.2 (*Continued*)

EUTHERIAN MAMMALS

- ● Herbivores
  $Y = 0.71 X^{0.80}$
  $R^2 = 0.91$
- ○ Omnivores
  $Y = 0.34 X^{0.80}$
  $R^2 = 0.91$
- ▲ Carnivores and Granivores
  $Y = 0.25 X^{0.80}$
  $R^2 = 0.91$

- ● Desert
  $Y = 0.15 X^{0.95}$
  $R^2 = 0.90$
- ○ Nondesert
  $Y = 0.78 X^{0.73}$
  $R^2 = 0.90$

WATER FLUX (ml/day)

BODY WEIGHT (g)

b

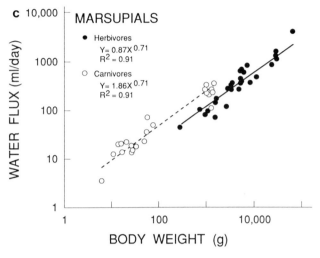

Fig. 4.2 (*Continued*)

on captive animals may have little value to our understanding of the ecology of free-ranging animals (Mullen, 1970, 1971; Boice, 1972; Alkon *et al.*, 1982).

The curvilinear regressions relating water flux to body weight indicate that small animals process and may require more water per unit of weight than do larger animals. Further evidence for this conclusion is that water consumption as a percentage of body weight increases as size of bird decreases (Fig. 4.3). These size-dependent effects are partly due to higher metabolic rates per unit of weight in small animals and higher surface-to-volume ratios which result in increased evaporative losses from small animals (Adolph, 1949; Bartholomew and Cade, 1963; Nagy and Peterson, 1988).

Several major physiological differences between birds and mammals exist

TABLE 4.2

Water Flux Rates (Y in milliliters per day) in Captive Animals as a Function of Body Weight (X in grams)

Group	Living state	Equation	r^2
Eutherians	Captive	$Y = 0.159X^{0.95}$	0.96
Marsupials	Captive	$Y = 0.547X^{0.77}$	0.91
Birds	Captive	$Y = 0.874X^{0.69}$	0.83

Source: Nagy and Peterson, 1988.

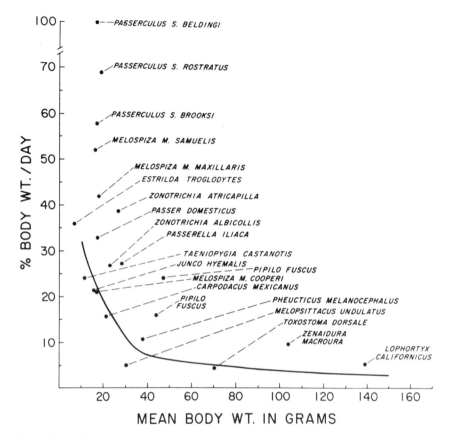

Fig. 4.3 Ad libitum water consumption by birds of various weights in the absence of thermal stress. The curve is the average evaporative water loss. [From Bartholomew and Cade (1963); courtesy of *Auk.*]

that affect water requirements. Because of their more intense metabolism and correspondingly high rates of pulmocutaneous water loss, small passerines generally dehydrate during flight at air temperatures above 7°C (Torre-Bueno, 1978). Water loss during prolonged, nonstop migrations by birds may actually limit their flight range or require flight at moderate temperatures or high altitudes (Hart and Berger, 1972). High evaporative water loss in birds is partially balanced by their reduced urinary water excretion relative to mammals. Urea excretion in mammals requires 20–40 times more water than is required to excrete a similar amount of uric acid in birds (Bartholomew and Cade, 1963). However, because of their almost universal diurnal habits, birds living within environmental conditions at or above their thermoneutral zone evaporate much more water than they produce metabolically (Bartholomew, 1972; Dawson *et al.*, 1979). Thus, unlike many fossorial and nocturnal mammals, few seed-eating birds (only several small desert or salt marsh birds) are able to meet their water requirements solely from metabolic water and very minimal preformed water (Williams and Koenig, 1980).

Many of the field studies of water metabolism have provided an understanding of the adaptations that animals have for either minimizing their water needs or for meeting their requirements. Examples of these are the storage of dry seeds in humid burrows by desert rodents to increase their preformed water content, selection of seeds by desert rodents based on their water content, and discrimination between seeds whose water content varies by as little as 6% (Morton and MacMillen, 1982; Frank, 1988); restriction of activity bouts to cooler parts of the day; selection of microclimates that reduce thermal loading (Davies, 1982); increased consumption of insects having 56 to 82% water by desert granivores and herbivores when preformed water in the normal diet decreases (Morton, 1980; Karasov, 1983; Goldstein and Nagy, 1985; Degen *et al.*, 1986); selection of succulent plants or plant parts (Zervanos and Day, 1977; Calder, 1981; Dupre, 1983; Golightly and Ohmart, 1984); production of relatively dry feces and concentrated urine; storage of heat by passively raising body temperature to restrict evaporative heat loss (Nagy, 1987); and reduction in basal energy expenditure and feed intake when water stressed (Bartholomew, 1972; Reese and Haines, 1978; Brosh *et al.*, 1986; Lautier *et al.*, 1988).

Wildlife management has been concerned with water requirements because of the opportunities to increase wildlife populations when water is limited by improving natural watering facilities or providing artificial watering facilities, such as "gallinaceous guzzlers." Many species, including mule deer (Elder, 1954), chukars (Degen *et al.*, 1984), rabbits (Cooke, 1982b), Dorcas gazelle (Ghobrial, 1970), bighorn sheep (Blong and Pollard, 1965; Jones *et al.*, 1957), elk (Delgiudice and Rodiek, 1984), and pronghorn antelope (Sundstrom, 1968) living in relatively arid conditions can be very dependent on free water. Free-ranging rabbit populations without access to free water during droughts have declined when the water content of the available vegetation dropped below approximately 50 to 60% (Richards, 1979; Cooke, 1982a, b; Nagy, 1987). The reduction in water content in more nutritious forages forced rabbits to consume less nutritious, high fiber foods that contained adequate water to meet this requirement but not their energy and nitrogen requirements. Similarly, antelope ground squirrels and Gambel's quail became dependent on other water sources when dietary water content dropped below 40% and 23%, respectively (Karasov, 1983; Goldstein and Nagy, 1985).

Even though artificial water sources often attract large numbers of birds and mammals, Snyder (1967) cautioned against their installation without very careful reviews of water requirements relative to existing supplies from all sources.

Water can increase a population only if (1) water is limiting, and (2) food and all other needs are in excess. The provision of artificial water sources has increased reproduction in some populations of small mammals and birds, but actual increases in long-term population density have been far less frequent (Nish, 1964; Gullion, 1966; Bradford, 1975; Christian, 1979; Abdellatif *et al.*, 1982). In most cases, both food and water have been limiting. When the improvement of water supplies is contemplated, water and food requirements and availability should be compared. Such analyses are necessarily species- and area-specific, but should quickly indicate whether water is limiting a population. Although building water facilities in arid areas may be worthwhile public relations efforts for conservations agencies, the rewards on a strictly biological basis may not be as apparent in all cases.

REFERENCES

Abdellatif, E. M., Armitage, K. B., Gaines, M. S., and Johnson, M. L. (1982). The effect of watering on a prairie vole population. *Acta Theriol.* **27**, 243–255.

Adolph, E. F. (1949). Quantitative relations in the physiological constitutions of mammals. *Science* **109**, 579–585.

Alkon, P. U., Pinshow, B., and Degen, A. A. (1982). Seasonal water turnover rates and body water volumes in desert chukars. *Condor* **84**, 332–337.

Ambrose, S. J., and Bradshaw, S. D. (1988). The water and electrolyte metabolism of free-ranging and captive white-browed scrubwrens, *Sericornis frontalis* (Acanthizidae), from arid, semi-arid and mesic environments. *Aust. J. Zool.* **36**, 29–51.

Bartholomew, G. A. (1972). The water economy of seed-eating birds that survive without drinking. *Proc. Int. Ornithol. Congr.* **15**, 237–254.

Bartholomew, G. A., and Cade, T. J. (1963). The water economy of land birds. *Auk* **80**, 504–539.

Beale, D. M., and Smith, A. D. (1970). Forage use, water consumption, and productivity of pronghorn antelope in western Utah. *J. Wildl. Manage.* **34**, 570–582.

Bintz, G. L., and Mackin, W. W. (1980). The effect of water availability on tissue catabolism during starvation in Richardson's ground squirrels. *Comp. Biochem. Physiol.* **65A**, 181–186.

Bintz, G. L., Palmer, D. L., Mackin, W. W., and Blanton, F. Y. (1979). Selective tissue catabolism and water balance during starvation in Richardson's ground squirrels. *Comp. Biochem. Physiol.* **64A**, 399–403.

Blong, B., and Pollard, W. (1965). Summer water requirements of desert bighorn in the Santa Rosa Mountains, California, in 1965. *Calif. Fish Game* **54**, 289–296.

Boice, R. (1972). Water addiction in captive desert rodents. *J. Mammal.* **53**, 395–398.

Bradford, D. F. (1975). The effects of an artificial water supply on freeliving *Peromyscus truei*. *J. Mammal.* **56**, 705–707.

Brosh, A., Shkolnik, A., and Choshniak, I. (1986). Metabolic effects of infrequent drinking and low-quality feed on Bedouin goats. *Ecology* **67**, 1086–1090.

Brown, C. R. (1988). Energy requirements for growth of Salvin's prions *Pachytila vittata salvini*, blue petrels *Halobaena caerulea* and great-winged petrels *Pterodroma macroptera*. *Ibis* **130**, 527–534.

Bryant, D. M., and Gardiner, A. (1979). Energetics of growth in house martins (*Delichon urbica*). *J. Zool.* **189**, 275–304.

Byman, D. (1978). Energy exchange relations and water economics of diurnal small mammals. *Am. Zool.* **18**, 632.

Calder, W. A., III. (1981). Diuresis on the desert? Effects of fruit- and nectar-feeding on the house finch and other species. *Condor* **83**, 267–268.

Cameron, R. D., White, R. G., and Luick, J. R. (1976). Accuracy of the tritium water dilution method for determining water flux in reindeer (*Rangifer tarandus*). *Can. J. Zool.* **54**, 857–862.

Campbell, R. R., and Leatherland, J. F. (1980). Estimating body protein and fat from water content in lesser snow geese. *J. Wildl. Manage.* **44**, 438–446.

Christian, D. P. (1979). Comparative demography of three Namib Desert rodents: Responses to the provision of supplementary water. *J. Mammal.* **60**, 679–690.

Cooke, B. D. (1982a). Reduction of food intake and other physiological responses to a restriction of drinking water in captive wild rabbits, *Oryctolagus cuniculus* (L.). *Aust. Wildl. Res.* **9**, 247–252.

Cooke, B. D. (1982b). Shortage of water in natural pastures as a factor limiting a population of rabbits, *Oryctolagus cuniculus* (L.) in arid north-eastern south Australia. *Aust. Wildl. Res.* **9**, 465–476.

Davies, S. J. J. F. (1982). Behavioral adaptations of birds to environments where evaporation is high and water is in short supply. *Comp. Biochem. Physiol.* **71A**, 557–566.

Dawson, W. R., Carey, C., Adkisson, C. S., and Ohmart, R. D. (1979). Responses of Brewer's and chipping sparrows to water restriction. *Physiol. Zool.* **52**, 529–541.

Degen, A. A., Pinshow, B., Alkon, P. U., and Arnon, H. (1981). The use of tritiated water for estimating total body water and the rate of water turnover in birds. *J. Appl. Physiol.* **51**, 1183–1188.

Degen, A. A., Pinshow, B., and Shaw, P. J. (1984). Must desert chukars (*Alectoris chukar sinaica*) drink water? Water influx and body mass changes in response to dietary water content. *Auk* **101**, 47–52.

Degen, A. A., Kam, M., Hazan, A., and Nagy, K. A. (1986). Energy expenditure and water flux in three sympatric desert rodents. *J. Anim. Ecol.* **55**, 421–429.

DelGiudice, G. D., and Rodiek, J. E. (1984). Do elk need free water in Arizona? *Wildl. Soc. Bull.* **12**, 142–146.

Denny, M. J. S., and Dawson, T. J. (1975). Comparative metabolism of tritiated water by macropod marsupials. *Am. J. Physiol.* **228**, 1794–1799.

Dupre, R. K. (1983). A comparison of the water relations of the hispid cotton rat, *Sigmodon hispidus*, and the prairie vole, *Microtus ochrogaster*. *Comp. Biochem. Physiol.* **75A**, 659–663.

Elder, J. B. (1954). Notes on summer water consumption by desert mule deer. *J. Wildl. Manage.* **18**, 540–541.

Ellis, H. I., and Jehl, J. R., Jr. (1987). Total body water in plalaropes and other birds: The role of lipids. *Am. Zool.* **27**, 5A.

Fedyk, A. (1974). Gross body composition in postnatal development of the bank vole. I. Growth under laboratory conditions. *Acta Theriol.* **19**, 381–401.

Frank, C. L. (1988). The relationship of water content, seed selection, and the water requirements of a heteromyid rodent. *Physiol. Zool.* **61**, 527–534.

Ghobrial, L. I. (1970). The water relations of the desert antelope *Gazella dorcas dorcas*. *Physiol. Zool.* **43**, 249–256.

Goldstein, D. L., and Nagy, K. A. (1985). Resource utilization by desert quail: Time and energy, food and water. *Ecology* **66**, 378–387.

Golightly, R. T., Jr., and Ohmart, R. D. (1984). Water economy of two desert canids: Coyote and kit fox. *J. Mammal.* **65**, 51–58.

Grubbs, D. E. (1980). Tritiated water turnover in free-living desert rodents. *Comp. Biochem. Physiol.* **66A**, 89–98.

Gullion, G. W. (1966). A viewpoint concerning the significance of studies of game bird food habits. *Condor* **68**, 372–376.

Harper, R. B., Travis, H. F., and Glinsky, M. S. (1978). Metabolizable energy requirement for maintenance and body composition of growing farm-raised male pastel mink (*Mustela vison*). *J. Nutr.* **108**, 1937–1943.

Hart, J. S., and Berger, M. (1972). Energetics, water economy and temperature regulation during flight. *Proc. Int. Ornithol. Congr.* **15**, 189–199.

Holleman, D. F., and Dieterich, R. A. (1975). An evaluation of the tritiated water method for estimating body water in small rodents. *Can. J. Zool.* **53**, 1376–1378.

Holleman, D. F., and Dieterich, R. A. (1978). Postnatal changes in body composition of laboratory maintained brown lemmings, *Lemmus sibiricus*. *Lab. Anim. Sci.* **28**, 529–535.

Hughes, M. R., Roberts, J. R., and Thomas, B. R. (1987). Total body water and its turnover in free-living nestling glaucous-winged gulls with a comparison of body water and water flux in avian species with and without salt glands. *Physiol. Zool.* **60**, 481–491.

Jones, F. L., Flittner, G., and Gard, R. (1957). Report on a survey of bighorn sheep in the Santa Rosa Mountains, Riverside County. *Calif. Fish Game* **43**, 103–111.

Kaminski, P., and Konarzewski, M. (1984). Changes of body weight, chemical composition and energetic value in the nestlings of the jackdaw, *Corvus monedula* L., during their development in the nest. *Ekol. Pol.* **32**, 125–139.

Karasov, W. H. (1983). Water flux and water requirement in free-living antelope ground squirrels *Ammospermophilus leucurus*. *Physiol. Zool.* **56**, 94–105.

Kaufman, G. A., and Kaufman, D. W. (1977). Body composition of the old-field mouse (*Peromyscus polionotus*). *J. Mammal.* **58**, 429–434.

Kennedy, P. M., and Heinsohn, G. E. (1974). Water metabolism of two marsupials—The brushtailed possum, *Trichosurus vulpecula* and the rock-wallaby, *Petrogale inornata* in the wild. *Comp. Biochem. Physiol.* **47A**, 829–834.

King, J. M. (1979). Game domestication for animal production in Kenya field studies of the body water turnover of game and livestock. *J. Agric. Sci.* **93**, 71–80.

King, J. M., Nyamora, M. R., Stanley-Price, M. R., and Heath, B. R. (1978). Game domestication for animal production in Kenya: Prediction of water intake from tritiated water turnover. *J. Agric. Sci.* **91**, 513–522.

Koerth, N.E., and Guthery, F.S. (1991). Water restriction effects on northern bobwhite reproduction. *J. Wildl. Manage.* **55**, 132–137.

Lautier, J. K., Dailey, T. V., and Brown, R. D. (1988). Effect of water restriction on feed intake of white-tailed deer. *J. Wildl. Manage.* **52**, 602–606.

MacFarlane, W. V., and Howard, B. (1972). Comparative water and energy economy of wild and domestic mammals. *Symp. Zool. Soc. London* **31**, 261–296.

MacFarlane, W. V., Howard, B., and Siebert, B. D. (1969). Tritiated water in the measurement of milk intake and tissue growth of ruminants in the field. *Nature (London)* **221**, 578–579.

Mahoney, S. A., and Jehl, J. R., Jr. (1984). Body water content in marine birds. *Condor* **86**, 208–209.

Morton, S. R. (1980). Field and laboratory studies of water metabolism in *Sminthopsis crassicaudata* (Marsupialia: Dasyuridae). *Aust. J. Zool.* **28**, 213–227.

Morton, S. R., and MacMillen, R. E. (1982). Seeds as sources of preformed water for desert-dwelling granivores. *J. Arid Environ.* **5**, 61–67.

Moulton, C. R. (1923). Age and chemical development in mammals. *J. Biol. Chem.* **57**, 79–97.

Mullen, R. K. (1970). Respiratory metabolism and body water turnover rates of *Perognathus formosus* in its natural environment. *Comp. Biochem. Physiol.* **32A**, 259–265.

Mullen, R. K. (1971). Energy metabolism and body water turnover rates of two species of free-living kangaroo rats, *Dipodomys merriami* and *Dipodomys microps*. *Comp. Biochem. Physiol.* **39A**, 379–380.

Myrcha, A., Pinowski, J., and Tomek, T. (1973). Variations in the water and ash contents and in the caloric value of nestling starlings (*Sturnus vulgaris* L.) during their development. *Bull. Pol. Acad. Sci. Cl. II Ser. Sci. Biol.* **21**, 649–655.

Nagy, K. A. (1987). How do desert animals get enough water? *In* "Progress in Desert Research" (L. Berkofsky and M. G. Wurtele, eds.), pp. 89–98. Rowman and Littlefield, Totowa, New Jersey.

Nagy, K. A., and Costa, D. P. (1980). Water flux in animals: Analysis of potential errors in the tritiated water method. *Am. J. Physiol.* **238**, R454–465.

Nagy, K. A., and Peterson, C. C. (1988). Scaling of water flux rate in animals. *Univ. Calif. Publ. Zool.* **120**, Berkeley.

Nicol, S. C. (1978). Rates of water turnover in marsupials and eutherians: A comparative review with new data on the Tasmanian devil. *Aust. J. Zool.* **26**, 465–473.

Nish, D. (1964). "An Evaluation of Artificial Water Catchment Basins on Gambel's Quail Populations in Southern Utah." Master's Thesis, Utah St. Univ., Logan, Utah.

Noll-Banholzer, U. (1976). Water balance, metabolism, and heart rate in the Fennec. *Naturwissenschaften* **63**, 202–203.

Reese, J. B., and Haines, H. (1978). Effects of dehydration on metabolic rate and fluid distribution in the jackrabbit, *Lepus californicus*. *Physiol. Zool.* **51**, 155–165.

Richards, G. C. (1979). Variation in water turnover by wild rabbits, *Oryctolagus cuniculus*, in an arid environment, due to season, age group and reproductive condition. *Aust. Wildl. Res.* **6**, 289–296.

Richmond, C. R., Langham, W. H., and Trujillo, I. I. (1962). Comparative metabolism of tritiated water by mammals. *J. Cell. Comp. Physiol.* **59**, 45–53.

Robbins, C. T., Moen, A. N., and Reid, J. T. (1974). Body composition of white-tailed deer. *J. Anim. Sci.* **38**, 871–876.

Robinson, J. R. (1957). Functions of water in the body. *Proc. Nutr. Soc.* **16**, 108–112.

Rubsamen, K., Nolda, U., and Von Engelhardt, W. (1979). Difference in the specific activity of tritium labelled water in blood, urine and evaporative water in rabbits. *Comp. Biochem. Physiol.* **62A**, 279–282.

Sawicka-Kapusta, K. (1970). Changes in the gross body composition and the caloric value of the common voles during their postnatal development. *Acta Theriol.* **15**, 67–79.

Sawicka-Kapusta, K. (1974). Changes in the gross body composition and energy value of the bank voles during their postnatal development. *Acta Theriol.* **19**, 27–54.

Skar, H.-J., Hagvar, S., Hagen, A., and Østbye, E. (1975). Food habits and body composition of adult and juvenile meadow pipit [*Anthus pratensis* (L.)]. *In* "Fennoscandian Tundra Ecosystems. Part 2. Animals and Systems Analysis" (F. W. Wielgolaski, ed.), pp. 160–173. Springer-Verlag, New York.

Snyder, W. D. (1967). Experimental habitat improvement for scaled quail. *Colo. Dept., Game Fish Parks Tech. Publ.* **19**.

Stirling, I., and McEwan, E. H. (1975). The caloric value of whole ringed seals (*Phoca hispida*) in relation to polar bear (*Ursus maritimus*) ecology and hunting behavior. *Can. J. Zool.* **53**, 1021–1027.

Sugden, L. G., and Harris, L. E. (1972). Energy requirements and growth of captive lesser scaup. *Poult. Sci.* **51**, 625–633.

Sundstrom, C. (1968). Water consumption by pronghorn antelope and distribution related to water in Wyoming's red desert. *Proc. Third Biennial Antelope States Workshop*, pp. 39–46.

Taylor, C. R. (1969). The eland and the oryx. *Sci. Am.* **220**, 88–95.

Taylor, C. R. (1972). The desert gazelle: A paradox resolved. *Symp. Zool. Soc. London* **31**, 215–227.

Taylor, J.R.E., and Konarzewski, M. (1989). On the importance of fat reserves for the little auk (*Alle alle*) chicks. *Oecologia* **81**, 551–558.

Thomas, D. H., and Phillips, J. G. (1975). Studies in avian adrenal steroid function II: Chronic adrenalectomy and the turnover of (^{3}H)$_2$O in domestic ducks (*Anas platyrhynchos* L.). *Gen. Comp. Endocrinol.* **26**, 404–411.

Tidemann, S. C., Green, B., and Newgrain, K. (1989). Water turnover and estimated food consumption in the three species of fairy-wren (*Malurus* spp.). *Aust. Wildl. Res.* **16**, 187–194.

Tiebout, H.M., III, and Nagy, K.A. (1991). Validation of the doubly labeled water method (^{3}HH^{18}O) for measuring water flux and CO_2 production in the tropical hummingbird *Amazilia saucerottei*. *Physiol . Zool.* **64**, 362–374.

Torre-Bueno, J. R. (1978). Evaporative cooling and water balance during flight in birds. *J. Exp. Biol.* **75**, 231–236.

Weathers, W. W., and Stiles, F. G. (1989). Energetics and water balance in free-living tropical hummingbirds. *Condor* **91**, 324–331.

Williams, J. B., and Prints, A. (1986). Energetics of growth in nestling savannah sparrows: A comparison of doubly labeled water and laboratory estimates. *Condor* **88**, 74–83.

Williams, P. L., and Koenig, W. D. (1980). Water dependence of birds in a temperate oak woodland. *Auk* **97**, 339–350.

Yousef, M. K., Johnson, H. D., Bradley, W. G., and Seif, S. M. (1974). Tritiated water-turnover rate in rodents: Desert and mountain. *Physiol. Zool.* **47**, 153–162.

Zervanos, S. M., and Day, G. I. (1977). Water and energy requirements of captive and free-living collared peccaries. *J. Wildl. Manage.* **41**, 527–532.

5

Minerals

Zoological Gardens: Institutes of Neglected Opportunity
RATCLIFFE, 1965

Minerals are an extremely diverse group of nutrients that have many essential functions. However, each mineral element represents a very small fraction of the total body (Table 5.1). The total ash or mineral content of the animal's body does vary but is usually less than 5%. The body's mineral content and requirements vary with age, sex, species, season, maturity, and reproductive and productive condition.

Carbon, hydrogen, oxygen, and nitrogen are usually grouped as organic constituents and are therefore not discussed as required minerals. Of the remainder, those required or represented in the animal body by relatively large amounts (milligrams per gram) are called *macroelements* (calcium, phosphorus, sodium, potassium, magnesium, chlorine, and sulfur), whereas those required in relatively small amounts are called *trace elements* (iron, zinc, manganese, copper, molybdenum, iodine, selenium, cobalt, fluoride, and chromium). When animals are consuming highly purified diets and water in dust-free environments, silicon, tin, boron, bromine, cadmium, lead, lithium, vanadium, nickel, and arsenic may be necessary for proper growth and development (Nielsen, 1984; Mertz, 1986, 1987). These are called *ultratrace elements*. However, the purity of the diet, water, and environment required to produce these deficiencies is so great that they do not cause practical problems for wildlife.

Deficiencies and imbalances of minerals are well recognized as important determinants of animal condition, fertility, productivity, and mortality (Underwood, 1977). Pathological symptoms of mineral deficiencies or imbalances have been reported by many investigators for both captive and free-ranging wildlife, although chronic deficiencies or imbalances that only marginally reduce growth, reproductive rate, and general fitness may be more important (Franzmann *et al.,* 1975). Marginal deficiencies are easily overlooked as population fluctuations are attributed to more obvious factors, such as severe weather, food shortages, parasites, and infectious agents (Underwood, 1977). As the practice of wildlife management becomes more intensive, the need for field biologists, curators, and

TABLE 5.1

Mineral Content (mg or µg/g dry matter) in the Bodies of Wild Animals

Mineral	Mammals						Birds				
	White-tailed deer	Short-tail shrew	Cotton mouse	Golden mouse	Old-field mouse[a]	Fox squirrel[b]	Blue tit	Coal tit	Goldcrest	Meadow pipit[c]	Rook[d]
Calcium (mg/g)	30.9 ± 2.6	34.4 ± 1.5	40.5 ± 5.1	37.4 ± 4.3	5.7–26.2	16.6–34.6	32.8	33.1	28.4	13.0–27.7	8.8–32.0
Phosphorus (mg/g)	22.6 ± 1.6	17.2 ± 0.5	16.7 ± 1.3	19.2 ± 0.8	17.1–20.0	16.7–19.3	20.4	20.8	18.8	14.0–19.0	13.0–22.0
Potassium (mg/g)	9.5 ± 0.5	—	—	—	8.3–15.7	8.7–12.7	5.8	6.3	5.8	8.5–17.0	7.4–11.3
Sodium (mg/g)	3.9 ± 0.2	4.2 ± 0.1	2.4 ± 0.6	3.6 ± 0.2	2.7–5.8	4.0–12.7	3.7	3.9	4.0	3.5–13.0	2.4–6.5
Magnesium (mg/g)	0.9 ± 0.1	1.4 ± 0.1	1.2 ± 0.1	1.4 ± 0.1	0.4–0.8	1.2–1.4	1.0	1.1	1.1	1.0–1.5	0.5–1.3
Iron (µg/g)	164.5 ± 10.8	500.0 ± 38.0	200.0 ± 13.0	240.0 ± 15.0	221.0–396.0	—	—	—	—	300.0–500.0	350.0–600.0
Zinc (µg/g)	68.4 ± 4.7	120.0 ± 8.0	98.0 ± 8.0	110.0 ± 10.0	108.0–142.0	—	—	—	—	94.0–120.0	71.0–122.0
Manganese (µg/g)	28.5 ± 4.0	—	—	—	3.5–17.6	—	—	—	—	10.0–17.0	10.0–52.0
Copper (µg/g)	26.1 ± 1.8	—	—	—	—	—	—	—	—	—	—
Molybdenum (µg/g)	3.0 ± 0.3	—	—	—	—	—	—	—	—	—	7.0–15.0
Iodine (µg/g)	—	—	—	—	1.9–2.4	—	—	—	—	—	—

Sources: Grimshaw et al., 1958; Beyers et al., 1971; G. A. Kaufman and Kaufman, 1975; D. W. Kaufman and Kaufman, 1975; Skar et al., 1975; Weiner et al., 1975; Havera, 1978; Pinowski et al., 1983.

[a]0–42 days of age.
[b]Range of values for embryos and adults.
[c]Range of values for juveniles and adults.
[d]Range of values from hatching to fledging.

research personnel to recognize and suggest remedies for mineral deficiencies or imbalances becomes more important.

Mineral requirements of wildlife have traditionally been evaluated in relation to deficiency symptoms and the establishment of maximum growth or reproductive rates. Wildlife ecologists have also delineated the characteristics of mineral pools (i.e., standing crops) within various communities. However, much of the very detailed information necessary for understanding mineral metabolism and requirements in relation to maintenance and production is lacking. Most of the information currently available on minerals in nutrition is on domestic and laboratory animals. Although mineral requirements determined for domestic animals can be useful starting points to evaluate wildlife diets, the assumption that wildlife will have the same quantitative requirements as domestic animals is probably false (Zervanos *et al.*, 1983; Robbins *et al.*, 1985; Samson *et al.*, 1989). Selection in domestic animals for rapid growth and efficient energy and protein utilization (i.e., economic return) and the widespread supplementation of these animals with relatively cheap minerals may inadvertently select for those animals that absorb, utilize, and conserve minerals very poorly. Studies on virtually all minerals deemed important to wildlife are needed relative to understanding efficiencies of absorption and retention, turnover rates, interactions with other minerals or dietary ingredients, effects of chronic or marginal deficiencies, requirements for various body processes, feeding strategies that may optimize mineral intake, deficiency signs, and possible routes or methods of dietary supplementation.

I. MACROELEMENTS

A. Calcium–Phosphorus

1. FUNCTIONS

Calcium and phosphorus are major mineral constituents of the animal's body and are largely associated with skeletal formation. In the mature animal, 98% of its calcium and 80% of its total body phosphorus are contained in bone (Bronner, 1964; Irving, 1964). The calcium to phosphorus concentration in bone is usually in an approximate 2:1 ratio (Morgulis, 1931; Widdowson and Dickerson, 1964). However, the composition and density of bone varies depending particularly on age and nutrition of the animal. Calcium is also important in blood clotting, excitability of nerves and muscles, acid–base balance, egg shell formation, enzyme activation, and muscle contraction, whereas phosphorus is involved in almost every aspect of animal metabolism, such as energy metabolism, muscle contractions, nerve tissue metabolism, transport of metabolites, nucleic acid structure, and carbohydrate, fat, and amino acid metabolism.

2. REQUIREMENTS

The requirements for calcium, and most other nutrients for captive wildlife, are often expressed as a percentage of the diet because of the opportunity in captivity to provide food ad libitum. Excluding economic or other constraints limiting the amounts of food offered, nutrient requirements for captive animals can be determined by feeding a diet in which consistent variation occurs in only one component. The dietary concentration of the specific ingredient is then compared to the requirement criteria, such as weight gain, reproductive success, survival, or mature weight. This technique is based on the observation that the growth rate or other criteria increase to an asymptotic level as the concentration of the limiting nutrient increases as long as toxicities or imbalances do not occur. If a second nutrient becomes limiting prior to that of the specific nutrient being studied, the regression curve will normally be shifted downward, with simply lower asymptotic growth rates (as an example) occurring at a lower nutrient concentration. Calcium and phosphorus requirements estimated with this method for growing mammals and birds range from 0.4 to 1.2% calcium and 0.3 to 0.6% phosphorus in the dry diet (NRC, 1978a, b, 1982, 1984).

Several processes, such as early growth when bone mineralization is being maximized, antler growth, and egg laying, are associated with elevated calcium–phosphorus requirements. Antlers are about 22% calcium and 11% phosphorus, with much of the remainder being protein (Rush, 1932; Chaddock, 1940; Bernhard, 1963; McCullough, 1969; Hyvarinen et al., 1977b). Egg shells are over 98% calcium carbonate and less than 1% phosphorus (Romanoff and Romanoff, 1949). The calcium and phosphorus requirements for captive, indeterminate laying birds (species such as pheasant, quail, or ducks that continue to lay large numbers of eggs if earlier ones are removed) during maximum egg production range from 2.25 to 2.75% dietary calcium and from 0.3 to 0.5% phosphorus (NRC, 1984). Ecologically, calcium and phosphorus requirements may be lower for determinate layers (such as many passerines, shorebirds, and large raptors) and indeterminate layers that successfully raise the first clutch (Cain et al., 1982). Ring-necked pheasants consuming 1.5 and 3.2% dietary calcium produced first clutches of equal size, but if the eggs were destroyed and renesting occurred, the birds consuming 3.2% dietary calcium produced significantly more eggs in the second clutch (Chambers et al., 1966).

The calcium requirements of bobwhite quail when expressed as a percentage of the diet were dependent on ambient air temperature (Case and Robel, 1974). Although such a relationship might seem incongruous, the relationship between ambient air temperature and calcium required illustrates one of the fundamental

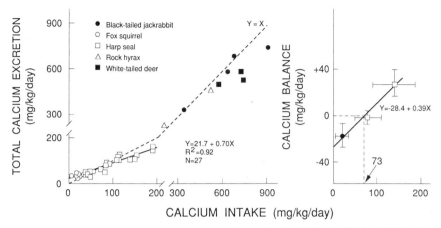

Fig. 5.1 Calcium excretion and balance as a function of intake in black-tailed jackrabbits, fox squirrels, harp seals, rock hyraxes, and white-tailed deer. (Data from Nagy, *et al.,* 1976; Havera, 1978; Leon and Belonje, 1979; Keiver *et al.,* 1984; Stephenson and Brown, 1984.)

problems of expressing a mineral requirement as a percentage of the diet. The absolute requirement for calcium was probably constant and independent of air temperature, but total feed intake was dependent on air temperature. Consequently, although a dietary calcium content of 2.3% was adequate to meet the requirements of birds housed at 5° and 15°C, this level was inadequate for birds housed at 25° and 35°C because far less food was consumed.

Requirements for maintenance of calcium balance in the nonproducing animal can be determined by comparing calcium intake to excretion. Unfortunately, calcium balances have been measured in very few wildlife, and only two of these trials (fox squirrels and harp seals) were at sufficiently low dietary calcium to be useful in estimating the minimum calcium requirement. Because these animals lost an average of 22 to 28 mg Ca/kg/day even when ingesting no calcium (i.e., *Y*-intercepts of Fig. 5.1; endogenous calcium loss) and retained 30 to 39% of ingested calcium (i.e., 1 − slope of the excretion curve or the slope of the calcium balance regression, Fig. 5.1), calcium balance occurred at a mean calcium intake of 73 mg/kg/day. At higher calcium intakes, rock hyraxes, black-tailed jackrabbits, and white-tailed deer were either at calcium balance or accumulating calcium. Maximum retention of ingested calcium in these animals was 28% and occurred in white-tailed deer that were growing antlers.

Tentative estimates of productive requirements can be made from the amount of calcium retained in new tissue divided by the net absorption efficiency. For example, if the calcium content of a live weight gain is 2%, then 100 g of new tissue would require 6.7 g of additional dietary calcium above calcium balance if the net retention efficiency is 30%.

3. DEFICIENCIES AND DIETARY SOURCES

Historically, calcium deficiencies have been the major mineral deficiency encountered in captive wildlife (Bland Sutton, 1888; Wallach, 1970; Fowler, 1986). Calcium deficiencies result in retarded growth, decreased food consumption, high basal metabolic rate, reduced activity and sensitivity, osteoporosis and rickets, abnormal posture and gait, susceptibility to internal hemorrhage, egg shell thinning, transient paralysis and tetany, retarded feather growth, reduced antler growth, elevated serum alkaline phosphatase, and death if prolonged (Rings *et al.*, 1969; Wallach and Flieg, 1969). Phosphorus deficiencies result in loss of appetite, abnormal appetite (pica), reduced antler growth and strength, rickets, reduced body growth, and weakness and death (French *et al.*, 1956; McCullough, 1969; Mahon, 1969; Krausman and Bissonette, 1977).

Excesses of other dietary components can also precipitate a calcium or phosphorus deficiency. Excesses of phosphorus or manganese, for example, form insoluble complexes with calcium, thereby reducing calcium absorption. Diets containing high levels of oils and fats may form insoluble calcium soaps in the digestive tract that reduce calcium absorption. For example, fecal calcium loss was 38% higher in harp seals consuming fresh herring with 18.4% fat relative to those consuming herring with 9.5% fat (Keiver *et al.*, 1984). Calcium in herbage frequently occurs as oxalate crystals, which are less soluble than calcium salts. The ability to absorb calcium ingested as an oxalate is dependent on bacterial fermentation and adaptation of the bacteria through previous exposure to degrade the oxalate. For example, laboratory rats with minimal fermentation cannot digest calcium oxalate; whereas the white-throated woodrat with hindgut fermentation can digest 70% (Harbers *et al.*, 1980; Justice, 1985). Excesses of iron, aluminum, and magnesium form insoluble phosphorus complexes. Dietary calcium to phosphorus ratios ranging from 1:1 to 2:1 are best for proper absorption and metabolism, although higher ratios can be handled as indicated by the extensive use of alfalfa as a single feed for many captive herbivores. Excesses of calcium have a far lesser effect on phosphorus absorption than do excesses of phosphorus on calcium absorption.

Excesses of dietary phosphorus associated with low or marginal dietary calcium levels produce an osteomalacia termed *nutritional secondary hyperparathyroidism*, or NSH. Blood calcium levels are controlled by the interaction of calcitonin (a hormone secreted by the thyroid in most mammals and the ultimobranchial glands in birds that promotes bone accretion and, thereby, a reduction in blood calcium) and parathyroid hormone that stimulates bone resorption and increased blood calcium. Thus, inadequate dietary calcium absorption produces a hyperplasia of the parathyroid, calcium resorption from the bones, and, if continued, eventual exhaustion of bone mineral stores even though intestinal and renal excretion is decreased (Arnaud, 1978). NSH has been observed

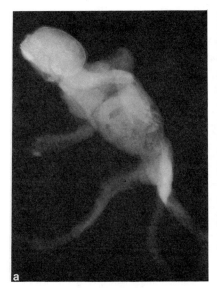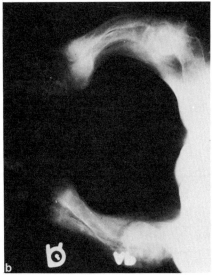

Fig. 5.2 (a) Radiograph of a marmoset fed only fruit and (b) radiograph of the front legs of a ricketic lion fed only red meat. Note the bone curvature, fractures, and poor mineralization of the bones.[Part (a) courtesy of the WSU College of Veterinary Medicine; part (b) courtesy of D. E. Ullrey, Michigan State University, East Lansing.]

in captive psittacines (parrots, cockatoos, and parakeets) fed a diet of sunflower seeds, peanuts, and oats (Wallach and Flieg, 1967; Arnold *et al.*, 1974), golden-mantled ground squirrels fed orange pulp and sunflower seeds (Rings *et al.*, 1969), and carnivorous birds and mammals fed pure meat diets (Slusher *et al.*, 1965; Scott, 1968; Wallach and Flieg, 1969, 1970; Gorham *et al.*, 1970; Dieterich and Van Pelt, 1972; Brambell and Mathews, 1976) (Table 5.2 and Fig. 5.2). Most seeds, fruits, meats, and fish fillets are very low in calcium and have calcium to phosphorus ratios ranging from 1:2 to 1:44 (Wallach and Flieg, 1969; Geraci and Aubin, 1980). Shrimp and other crustaceans having calcified exo-skeletons are good sources of calcium (Welinder, 1974) whereas insects with noncalcified cuticles are poor calcium sources (Table 5.2).

Dominance hierarchies and overfeeding of heterogeneous diets to captive wildlife can also produce calcium deficiencies via food preferences in which items inadequate in calcium are preferentially consumed even though the total diet offered is adequate (Tomson and Lotshaw, 1978; Snyder *et al.*, 1980; Tomson *et al.*, 1980). For example, one of two captive tigers offered a balanced diet became lethargic, alopecic, and anorectic while the other one remained normal. When no infectious disease could be identified, the problem was quickly identified from the feeding histories. Zoo personnel were indeed feeding a balanced commercial diet, but they also fed fresh meat. The healthy tiger ate both types of food. Because the tiger that ultimately became sick relished meat, zoo personnel had increased the meat such that this tiger no longer ate the less tasty commercial diet. When the very empathetic but ill-informed zoo personnel reduced the meat, used it only as a treat, and thereby forced the sick tiger to consume the commercial diet, this tiger quickly recovered (S. D. Farley and C. T. Robbins, unpublished).

TABLE 5.2

Calcium and Phosphorus Content and Their Relative Proportions in Food

| Feed | Content (100% dry matter basis) | | Ratio (Ca:P) |
	Calcium	Phosphorus	
Animals, invertebrates			
Cricket	0.12	0.87	1:7
Earthworm	0.95	0.95	1:1
Grasshopper	0.31	1.27	1:5
Mealworm	0.04	0.57	1:14
Wax moth larvae	0.03	0.39	1:13
Shrimp	3.40	1.50	2:1
Squid	0.11	0.36	1:3
Animals, whole vertebrates			
Newborn mice	1.60	1.80	1:1
Adult mammals	3.40	1.92	2:1
Adult birds	3.08	2.02	2:1
Fish			
Herring	1.05	1.45	1:1
Sardines	1.14	1.31	1:1
Rainbow trout	1.60	1.60	1:1
Mackerel	1.37	0.34	4:1
Animals, vertebrate flesh			
Beef	0.01	0.24	1:24
Beef liver	0.04	0.82	1:20
Horsemeat	0.07	1.06	1:15
Fish fillets			
Carp	0.23	1.14	1:5
Haddock	0.12	1.01	1:8
Mackerel	0.03	0.91	1:30
Mullet	0.11	0.80	1:7
Salmon	0.22	0.68	1:3
Forages			
Alfalfa	1.60	0.31	5:1
Orchardgrass	0.31	0.26	1:1

TABLE 5.2

Continued

Feed	Content (100% dry matter basis)		Ratio (Ca:P)
	Calcium	Phosphorus	
Red clover	1.45	0.23	6:1
Smooth brome	0.36	0.19	2:1
Spinach	0.97	0.54	2:1
Timothy	0.40	0.16	3:1
Fruits			
Apples	0.06	0.06	1:1
Banana	0.03	0.11	1:4
Grapes	0.06	0.04	1:1
Pineapple	0.14	0.07	2:1
Nuts and seeds			
Barley	0.08	0.45	1:6
Corn	0.05	0.35	1:7
Nuts (oak, hickory, walnut)	0.08	0.27	1:3
Oats	0.10	0.37	1:4
Peanuts	0.06	0.45	1:8
Soybeans	0.25	0.60	1:2
Sunflower seeds, hulled	0.17	0.94	1:6
Wheat	0.09	0.39	1:4

Sources: NRC, 1971, 1982; Havera, 1978; Allen and Oftedal, 1982; Bird *et al.*, 1982; Shearer, 1984; Strzelewicz, *et al.*, 1985; Bernard and Ullrey, 1989; Table 5.1.

Free-ranging wildlife can also suffer from NSH. Osteoporosis has been reported in wild-caught red fox and arctic fox kits in Alaska (Van Pelt and Caley, 1974; Conlogue *et al.*, 1979). The red fox kits had apparently been consuming snowshoe hare meat retrieved by the parents, and the arctic foxes had consumed seal meat without an adequate ingestion of bones. The kits were thin and unthrifty, with extensive bone porosity. Small rodents or birds, which could have been consumed whole and thereby provided adequate calcium, were apparently an insignificant part of the diet. The red fox kits recovered when fed a balanced commercial dog food. Serum calcium concentrations of reindeer consuming lichens during late winter and early spring were below levels associated with tetany in domestic livestock, even though classical tetany signs were absent (Hyvarinen *et al.*, 1977a).

Calcium and phosphorus deficiencies in captive wildlife can easily be corrected by the addition of bone meal, calcium phosphate, or calcium carbonate (limestone or oyster shells) to the diet, depending on the existing dietary calcium to phosphorus ratio and assuming adequate vitamin D availability. Limestone is readily eroded in the gastrointestinal tract of birds and either absorbed or excreted (Korschgen *et al.*, 1965; Trost, 1981). Invertebrates that do not normally accumulate calcium can either be dusted with calcium salts prior to feeding or maintained on high calcium diets (Allen and Oftedal, 1982; Strzelewicz *et al.*, 1985; Trusk and Crissey, 1987; Allen and Oftedal, 1989). Dissolved calcium in drinking water is an inadequate source of calcium (Fowler, 1978). For example, drinking "extremely" hard water (800 mg $CaCO_3$/liter) would supply only 5% of the daily calcium requirement of captive birds.

Free-ranging wildlife consuming meat, insect, or seed diets or those animals that have very high requirements must actively seek and consume calcium supplements (Fig. 5.3). Many birds ingest snails and their associated calciferous shell to help meet the calcium requirement of egg production (Krapu and Swanson, 1975; Beasom and Pattee, 1978; Ankney and Scott, 1980). Lemming bones and egg shell fragments are essential sources of calcium to arctic sandpipers (MacLean, 1974) and Lapland longspurs (Seastedt and MacLean, 1977). Similarly, adult birds that feed low-calcium fruits, seeds, meat, or insects to their nestlings must also feed calciferous grit, bones, mollusk shells, or eggshell fragments (Mayoh and Zach, 1986; St. Louis and Breebaart, 1991). The consumption of fungi, insects, bones, and other rich calcium sources is essential for free-ranging fox squirrels, because nuts and seeds commonly consumed are inadequate in calcium (Havera, 1978). Osteophagia or bone chewing is often observed in free-ranging mammals and is usually ascribed to a lack of calcium or phosphorus (Krausman and Bissonette, 1977; Sekulic and Estes, 1977; Langman, 1978).

The occasional inability of free-ranging wildlife to ingest adequate calcium has been suggested as an important determinant of their productivity (Dale, 1954; Harper and Labisky, 1964; Kopischke and Nelson, 1966; Cowles, 1967; Anderson and Stewart, 1969, 1973; Kreulen, 1975). One of the better examples of the interaction of ecosystem components in affecting the intake of calcium and subsequent productivity by specific organisms regards the interaction of large predators, particularly hyenas, and vultures (Mundy and Ledger, 1976; Richardson *et al.*, 1986). Breeding white-backed vultures were studied in two wildlife preserves in southern Africa where large mammalian carnivores existed, and cape vultures were studied in a predominant ranching area where large carnivores had been eliminated. Because meat is very deficient in calcium, the altricial nestlings depend on the adults to retrieve and feed appropriate-sized bone fragments in order to meet their calcium requirements. Of the 231 cape vulture chicks examined, 4.8% had broken, mended, or deformed wing bones and 11% had rickets. However, all 35 white-backed vulture chicks examined had completely normal bone formation. White-backed vultures coexisting with large carnivores brought many more bone fragments to the nests than did the cape vultures nesting

Fig. 5.3 A free-ranging Philippine eagle meeting its calcium requirement by ingesting a very large bone. While large bones can be ingested by the adult, one can appreciate the need for small bones and bone fragments in meeting the chick's requirement. The chick (top of downy head just barely visible) died later from asphyxiation as it attempted to ingest too large a bone that became lodged. (Courtesy of Films and Research for an Endangered Environment, Ltd., Suite 1735, 102 N. Wells Street, Chicago, Illinois.)

in the ranching area. The latter brought larger bones and pieces of glass, plastic, china, stones, and teeth in an apparent effort to provide calcium for the growing chicks (Table 5.3). Calcium-deficient birds often exhibit a greater interest in bizarre objects of edible size (Joshua and Mueller, 1979). Creation of vulture "restaurants" in ranching areas where nesting cape vultures could obtain broken bones reduced the occurrence of NSH from approximately 18% of all chicks to about 2%. Complete remission of the problem took as long as eight years in one

TABLE 5.3

Relative Proportions (%) of Main Items Found at Vulture Nests

Item	Cape vulture (no large carnivores)	White-backed vulture (carnivores)
Bone fragments	37	92
Artifacts (glass, china, plastic)	31	0
Whole bones (ribs and phalanges)	18	3
Other (teeth, stones)	14	5
	100	100

Source: Mundy and Ledger, 1976.

area, suggesting a learning-selection process for vultures to seek out the "restaurants" as a source of bone fragments (Richardson *et al.*, 1986).

B. Sodium

1. FUNCTIONS

The terrestrial animal maintains an internal, marine-like environment by bathing all body cells in a saline solution. The chief cation of the marine and extracellular environment is sodium. Physiologically, sodium is important in the regulation of body fluid volume and osmolarity, acid–base balance and tissue pH, muscle contraction, and nerve impulse transmission, and is therefore necessary for growth and reproduction. Although the sodium ion is quite soluble, from 25 to 50% of the total body sodium content can be in a nonionizable, poorly available form in bones (Forbes, 1962; Weeks and Kirkpatrick, 1976; Green, 1978; Christian, 1989).

2. REQUIREMENTS

Most estimates of the sodium requirements for wildlife, such as in Table 5.4 (0.05 to 0.4% of the dry diet), are based entirely on domestic and laboratory animal standards. Although there has not been a thorough study of the sodium requirement of any wild animal, enough data are available to develop interspecific regressions. Minimum intake necessary for sodium balance is 9.0 mg/kg/day (Fig. 5.4). Although only 20% of the sodium ingested at these low dietary levels is retained, 97% of the sodium ingested is absorbed (Fig. 5.4, slope of the regression) with much of it subsequently lost in the urine. Sodium absorption in the intestinal tract occurs concurrent to water absorption and is more efficient when drier feces are produced. The soft, more moist feces of wild rabbits on sodium-poor diets had 2.5 times the sodium concentration of hard feces (Scoggins

TABLE 5.4

Additional Mineral Requirements or Allowances

	Mineral										
	Na	K	Mg	Cl	Fe	Zn	Mn	Cu	I	Se	F
	% of diet				ppm in diet						
Birds											
Pheasants and quail											
Growth	0.15	0.4	0.03	0.2	100	25	90	6	0.3	0.2	—
Egg production	0.15	0.4	0.05	0.15	60	50	70	6	0.3	0.2	—
Ducks and geese (domestic)											
Growth	0.15	—	0.05	0.12	—	60	40	—	—	0.14	—
Egg production	0.15	—	0.05	0.12	—	60	25	—	—	0.14	—
Turkey (domestic)											
Growth	0.17–0.12	0.7–0.4	0.06	0.15–0.12	80–50	75–40	60	8–6	0.4	0.2	—
Egg production	0.15	0.6	0.06	0.12	60	65	60	8	0.4	0.2	—
Mammals											
Guinea pig (growth)	—	0.5–1.4	0.1–0.3	—	50	20	40	6	1.0	0.1	—
Hamster (growth)	0.15	0.6	0.06	—	140	9.2	3.7	1.6	1.6	0.1	0.024
Laboratory mouse (growth and reproduction)	—	0.2	0.05	—	25	30	45	4.5	0.25	—	—
Laboratory rat (growth and reproduction)	0.05	0.36	0.04	0.05	35	12	50	5	0.15	0.1	0.1
Nonhuman primate (growth)	0.2–0.4	0.8	0.15	0.2–0.5	180	10	40	—	2.0	—	—
Rabbit, domestic (growth, maintenance, and reproduction)	0.2	0.6	0.03–0.04	0.3	—	—	8.5	3	0.2	—	—

Sources: NRC, 1977; 1978a,b; 1984.

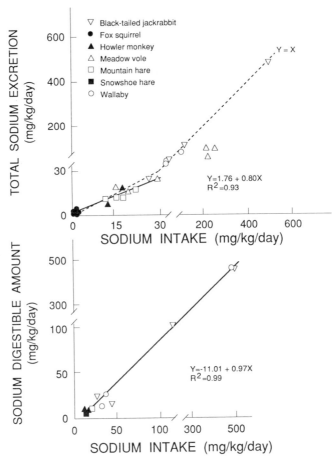

Fig. 5.4 Sodium retention and digestion in captive wildlife. (Data from Nagy *et al.*, 1976; Havera, 1978; Nagy and Milton, 1979; Hume and Dunning, 1979; Pehrson, 1983; Reichardt *et al.*, 1984; Christian, 1989.)

et al., 1970). Environmental pollutants, such as crude oil, can reduce intestinal sodium absorption and thereby contribute to mortality of contaminated wildlife (Crocker *et al.*, 1974).

Sodium retention is primarily controlled by aldosterone, a steroid hormone secreted by the adrenal cortex that stimulates potassium excretion and sodium absorption and retention by the kidney, sweat glands, salivary glands, and gastrointestinal mucosa (Muller, 1971). Glucocorticoids, also secreted by the adrenal cortex during stress with pronounced effects on carbohydrate metabolism, can antagonize the sodium-retaining effects of aldosterone (Uete and Venning, 1962; Geraci, 1972).

Minimum necessary dietary concentrations can be estimated by multiplying 9.0 mg/kg/day by the animal's weight and then dividing by the average daily dry matter intake. These estimates range from 0.006% dietary sodium for prairie voles (Christian, 1989) to 0.008% for mountain hares (Angerbjorn and Pehrson, 1987) to 0.03% for white-tailed deer (Pletscher, 1987). The increasing minimum dietary concentration in larger animals is caused by the interaction of a constant sodium requirement and a decreasing total food intake per unit of body weight in larger animals. If this relationship is correct, then we would expect that larger animals would have more difficulty in meeting a sodium requirement than smaller animals at low dietary sodium concentrations (D. P. Christian, personal communication).

Theoretically, sodium retention can be lessened by excessive water or potassium ingestion, since their excretion could increase urine volumes which would secondarily increase sodium excretion (Rugangazi and Maloiy, 1988). Simultaneous water and potassium loading do occur when herbivores feed on lush spring forages (Bintz, 1969; Scoggins et al., 1970; Weeks and Kirkpatrick, 1976, 1978; Smith et al., 1978; Christian, 1989). For example, early season forbs and grasses can contain more than 80% water on a fresh basis and 2.5% potassium on a dry basis. These conditions are exacerbated in females by the increased sodium demands of gestation and lactation. Ad libitum sodium intake in lactating rabbits increased four-fold over nonproducing animals, although this intake was far in excess of any requirement (Denton and Nelson, 1971). However, sodium appetite in virtually all wild herbivores is highest in spring and summer for the above reasons.

The low sodium content of many plants and allelochemicals that might increase sodium excretion could be important plant defenses that would have the capability to reduce animal populations if they were unable to meet their sodium requirements (Pehrson, 1983; Reichardt et al., 1984; Freeland et al., 1985; Angerbjorn and Pehrson, 1987). While plant phenolics and resins have increased sodium excretion in the above studies, others have found no effect (Mole et al., 1990) or a transitory effect that returned to control levels within 5 to 6 days (Palo, 1987). Because many of the studies reporting increased sodium excretion have been confounded by weight loss caused by low feed intake (Pehrson, 1983; Reichardt et al., 1984), it is difficult to determine if the elevated sodium excretion is due to the direct metabolic effect of the allelochemical on sodium metabolism or is a secondary effect due solely to tissue catabolism and flushing of excess sodium.

3. Deficiencies and Dietary Sources

Few terrestrial plants require sodium, and only halophytes actively concentrate it, even though this element is the sixth most abundant mineral in the earth's crust (Botkin et al., 1973). Therefore, the potential exists, particularly for herbivores, to incur sodium deficiencies. Symptoms of sodium deficiencies are reduced growth, softening of bones, corneal keratinization, gonadal inactivity, loss of appetite, weakness and incoordination, decreased plasma sodium concentration, adrenal hypertrophy, impaired dietary energy and protein utilization, and decreased plasma and fluid volumes producing shock and death.

Carnivores normally would not incur a sodium deficiency as the tissues of even sodium-stressed herbivores have a relatively high sodium content (Blair-West et al., 1968). However, pinnipeds, albatrosses, penguins, and other marine organisms maintained in freshwater pools can develop sodium deficiencies when fed fish or marine invertebrates (Frings and Frings, 1959; Geraci, 1972; Gailey-Phipps and Sladen, 1982). Although the sodium concentration of fish would be adequate for most animals (0.034 to 0.097% on a fresh basis with freshwater species having less sodium than marine species; Thurston, 1958), the deficiency is produced by several interrelated factors. These factors may include: (1) the sodium content of fish is reduced by the common practice of thawing by immersion in tap water (25% sodium loss after 3 hr); (2) marine mammals and birds may be very inefficient at retaining sodium as selection should favor excretion rather than retention; (3) stressing marine birds (such as during forced-feeding or capturing for medical treatment) causes the nasal salt glands to increase their excretion; and (4) parental feeding of hatchlings by regurgitation drains sodium and other minerals from the adult (Gailey-Phipps and Sladen, 1982; Zervanos et al., 1983). Other, more subtle stressors, such as overcrowding, may also increase the sodium requirement (Aumann and Emlen, 1965; Geraci, 1972).

Sodium supplements are easily provided for captive animals by either mixing directly into the diet, providing salt free choice, or, for marine animals, maintaining them in seawater. Dose rates for marine mammals in freshwater pools of 3 g NaCl/kg food (i.e., 0.12% dietary sodium) or higher if necessary are suggested (Geraci, 1972). The practice is not recommended and may be detrimental for marine mammals or birds maintained in seawater. Captive animals having free access to sodium salts may consume more than their minimum daily requirements, but excesses are readily excreted when adequate drinking water is provided. Salt (NaCl) toxicity occurred in pheasants only when the sodium content of the diet reached 2.95%, or about 30 times the estimated daily requirement (Scott et al., 1960). However, desert rats specialized for feeding on halophytes normally consume a diet with as much as 5.6% sodium (Kam and Degen, 1989).

Marine birds and others feeding in highly saline lakes must purposefully seek and feed their nestlings low-sodium foods (e.g., freshwater crayfish). Although the adults feed on high-sodium foods (e.g., fiddler crabs and mollusks), high evaporative water loss and the inability to fly to freshwater can impose severe water restrictions on nestlings. Because water intake is inadequate to excrete excess sodium, nestlings can become dehydrated and die when forced to consume high-sodium foods. Thus, the productivity of marine birds can be closely linked to rainfall and the availability of freshwater foods (Johnston and Bildstein, 1990).

Wildlife ecologists have long been interested in understanding how free-ranging herbivores and granivores meet their sodium requirement and whether low sodium intake might regulate populations. Moose on Isle Royale, caribou in Alaska, deer in Indiana, mountain goats in British Columbia, and fox squirrels in Illinois consumed feeds having from 0.0003 to 0.0251% sodium (Hebert and Cowan, 1971a; Botkin *et al.*, 1973; Weeks and Kirkpatrick, 1976; Havera, 1978; Staaland *et al.*, 1980). Seeds have sodium concentrations ranging from 0.0005 to 0.01% (Cade, 1964). These dietary levels are very low and are not simply the extreme examples. Soils and vegetation of alpine, mountain, and continental areas having moderate to high snow or rainfall are usually sodium depleted, whereas coastal and desert areas are sodium repleted. For example, vegetation of coastal and desert areas of Australia had sodium concentrations from 110 to 130 times higher than in sodium-depleted alpine regions (Scoggins *et al.*, 1970). However, coastal alpine areas with very high rainfall that are behind an initial range of mountains, such as parts of the Olympic Mountains of Washington, can also be quite sodium depleted.

Sodium is easily leached from ecosystems receiving moderate precipitation as it is not accumulated by plants. Ecologically, coastal rainfall and marine aerosols can be very significant sources of sodium. The sodium in rainwater collected 8 km inland from the ocean in New Zealand deposited approximately 1.3 kg of sodium chloride per hectare per centimeter of rainfall (Miller, 1961). Lesser though still very significant amounts of sodium (0.08 kg/ha/cm of rainfall or 4–5 kg/ha/year) were deposited 5–10 km inland in the Santa Yenz Mountains of southern California (Schlesinger and Hasey, 1980).

Animals ingesting foods of minimal sodium content must either conserve sodium or augment sodium intake by actively consuming natural sodium supplements. Sodium-stressed mountain rabbits, kangaroos, and wombats excreted urine almost devoid of sodium (Blair-West *et al.*, 1968), whereas rabbits in sodium-replete grassland and desert areas had urinary sodium concentrations 280 times higher (Scoggins *et al.*, 1970). Sodium-stressed animals had adrenal cortex aldosterone-secreting areas up to 5 times larger than sodium-replete animals (Myers, 1967; Scoggins *et al.*, 1970; Smith *et al.*, 1978). However, investigators should be cautious in interpreting enlarged adrenal cortices and increased aldosterone secretion relative to sodium in that aldosterone's role in increasing potassium excretion may be equally important (Christian, 1989).

Many observations of herbivores, granivores, and carnivores consuming salt or soil or water with a higher than normal sodium content, such as from mineral licks, have been reported (Cade, 1964; Blair-West *et al.*, 1968; Hebert and

Cowan, 1971a; Weir, 1972, 1973; Botkin *et al.*, 1973; Weeks and Kirkpatrick, 1976; Calef and Lortie, 1975; Tankersley and Gasaway, 1983; Coleman *et al.*, 1985; Bennetts and Hutto, 1985; Arthur and Gates, 1988). Use of mineral licks has been attributed to the fact that they often have a higher sodium content than does surrounding vegetation, soil, or water (Fraser *et al.*, 1980). The preference of animals for sodium in sodium-poor environments was eloquently displayed by Blair-West *et al.* (1968), Weeks and Kirkpatrick (1978), and Fraser and Reardon (1980) by observing rabbits, fox squirrels, woodchucks, white-tailed deer, and moose either directly consuming solutions of sodium salts or chewing and licking wooden stakes soaked in either $NaCl$, NaI, or $NaHCO_3$, while largely ignoring stakes soaked in distilled water, $MgCl_2$, $CaCl_2$, $KHCO_3$, KI, and KCl. Similarly, elephants have been observed consuming burned wood and ash in an apparent sodium drive (Weir, 1972, 1973), and other animals, such as porcupines, have damaged buildings where wood was impregnated with salt from evaporated urine (Blair-West *et al.*, 1968).

Mountain goats in the Olympic National Park of Washington avidly consume urine or urine-soaked ground and table salt provided by park visitors. Sodium chloride was as effective a bait in spring and summer as food was during winter for trapping white-tailed deer in the Adirondack Mountains of New York (Mattfeld *et al.*, 1972). Moose and other animals actively seek aquatic plants having from 50 to 500 times higher sodium concentrations than terrestrial plants (Botkin *et al.*, 1973; Fraser, 1979; Fraser *et al.*, 1982, 1984; Pletscher, 1987). Although many of the field observations of food preferences and mineral lick use are difficult to interpret as unequivocally indicating that sodium is the element being sought, the accumulated information collectively indicates that animals in sodium-depleted areas are actively seeking this element (Weeks, 1978).

Thus, although sodium is a ubiquitous element, its acquisition and retention may require extensive effort, particularly in herbivores. Limited availability of sodium in some areas may restrict animal distribution and productivity (Aumann, 1965; Aumann and Emlen, 1965; Weir, 1972, 1973; Weeks and Kirkpatrick, 1978; Belovsky, 1981; Belovsky and Jordan, 1981; Batzli, 1986). Efficient sodium acquisition and retention may require several generations to develop and therefore may limit newly introduced populations from sodium-replete environments. For example, expanding populations of eastern cottontails invading sodium-depleted areas from sodium-repleted areas had higher mortality than did the more adapted resident New England cottontails during cold stress when glucocorticoids would be released and increase sodium excretion (J. Chapman, personal communication).

4. TURNOVER AND ESTIMATES OF FOOD INTAKE

Green (1978) has pioneered the use of sodium turnover to measure food intake of wild animals. Because sodium intake can be predicted from so-

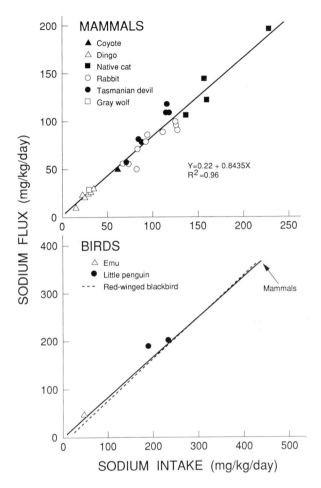

Fig. 5.5 Sodium flux in wildlife as a function of sodium intake. (Data from Green, 1978; Green and Dunsmore, 1978; Green *et al.*, 1978; Green and Eberhard, 1979; Parmenter, 1984; Herd, 1985; Gales, 1989; Gauthier and Thomas, 1990; DelGiudice *et al.*, 1991.) The regression equation for red-winged blackbirds is $Y = -11.3 + 0.90X$, $R^2 = 0.98$ (Gauthier and Thomas, 1990). The regression for mammals is plotted on the graph for birds to illustrate that there are no obvious differences between birds and mammals.

dium turnover (Fig. 5.5), food intake (grams per day) can be predicted if the sodium content of the diet is known. ^{22}NaCl is injected into the animal and blood samples taken after equilibration (several hours) and at the end of the study interval (a week to over a month) to determine sodium kinetics. The method has been used on herbivores (Green *et al.*, 1978; Green and Duns-

more, 1978; Morris and Bradshaw, 1981) and carnivores (Green, 1978; Green
et al., 1978; Green and Eberhard, 1979; Green et al., 1984; Parmenter, 1984;
DelGiudice et al., 1991) and would only be inappropriate when unknown
amounts of sodium are being ingested from nonfood sources (such as seawater or mineral licks) or when reasonable estimates of dietary sodium content
cannot be made.

C. Potassium

Potassium occurs primarily within cells and functions in nerve and muscle
excitability, carbohydrate metabolism and enzyme activation, tissue pH, and
osmotic regulation. The very high potassium content of growing plants and
animals, usually in excess of animal requirements, greatly reduces the chances
of potassium deficiencies occurring in wildlife. The accumulation of potassium
by both aquatic and terrestrial plants has created many terrestrial environments
via biological and geological cycles that are potassium replete (Wilde, 1962).
High concentrations of potassium in some plants, such as early spring grasses,
can reduce the availability and retention of other elements, such as sodium or
magnesium (Rugangazi and Maloiy, 1988; Christian, 1989; Fontenot et al.,
1989). Thus, rather than being toxic, high plant potassium may contribute secondarily to a deficiency of another element.

Symptoms of potassium deficiencies, produced experimentally in many animals, include muscle weakness, poor intestinal tone with intestinal distension,
cardiac and respiratory weakness and failure, retarded growth, and tubular degeneration of the kidneys (McDonald et al., 1973). Potassium may have been
involved in a die-off of sika deer on James Island, Maryland (Christian et al.,
1960; Christian et al., 1964). The deer population decreased from 300 to 100
without apparent, classical starvation. Potassium deficiencies were suggested
from renal pathology at necropsy, even though potassium intake would normally
have been adequate. Stress-induced adrenal hyperplasia and excessive potassium
excretion may have been produced by excessive population levels rather than
by an initial mineral insufficiency (Christian, 1964). However, further studies
of the potassium balance of wildlife consuming cured forages in winter is certainly
warranted.

The diffusion of cellular potassium into the circulatory system, its subsequent
excretion, and, if severe, cardiac and respiratory failure (Wilde, 1962) are also
associated with prolonged stress or trauma in laboratory animals. Potassium
deficiencies may be rare in wildlife, but deficiencies could occur because of a
complex of precipitating factors and should always be suspected in captive
wildlife subjected to stress and prolonged diarrhea (Newberne, 1970).

D. Magnesium

The major portion of body magnesium, approximately 70%, is in bone, with bone ash being 0.31–0.75% magnesium (Morgulis, 1931; Wacker and Vallee, 1964; Hyvarinen et al., 1977b). While magnesium is an essential constituent of bones and teeth, it is of paramount importance in enzyme activation relative to energy metabolism. Like potassium, magnesium is very abundant in both plant and animal dietary sources because magnesium is the chelated metal in chlorophyll.

Deficiency symptoms include vasodilation, hyperirritability, convulsions, reluctance to stand and loss of equilibrium, tetany, increased heat production due to tonic muscular activity, reduced appetite and weight loss, impaired blood clotting, liver damage, soft tissue calcification, defective bones and teeth, and death (Miller et al., 1972; McDonald et al., 1973; Church, 1979). Parathyroid hormone and calcitonin affect renal excretion and bone resorption of magnesium in the same manner as they do calcium, although to a lesser extent (Fontenot et al., 1989). Magnesium deficiencies have been extremely rare in wildlife. Free-ranging pheasants apparently even avoided consuming grit high in magnesium during egg production (Kopischke, 1966). Although magnesium is nontoxic at normal dietary concentrations, it frequently occurs in renal, urethra, or bladder calculi as magnesium ammonium phosphate (struvite) that can be very dangerous if urine flow is impeded (Clark et al., 1982; Nelson, 1983). Because struvite crystallizes in alkaline solutions, urine acidification with various food additives (e.g., phosphoric acid) prevents these calculi (Edfors et al., 1989).

One major pathological magnesium deficiency is grass tetany or grass staggers, which occurs primarily in lactating domestic cows consuming early spring forages grown on fertilized pastures. Such a deficiency apparently occurred in captive deer grazing a heavily fertilized pasture at Washington State University (K. Farrell, personal communication) and may have been a contributing factor to mortality in emaciated reindeer consuming early spring vegetation (Hyvarinen et al., 1977a). Because cattle breeds do differ in their proneness to developing a magnesium deficiency with British and dairy breeds being more susceptible than Brahmans (Greene et al., 1989), wild herbivores may also be far less susceptible than some domestic livestock. Even though the forage may be relatively high in magnesium, the deficiency is apparently produced by dietary factors that affect the absorption or use of magnesium, such as high nitrogen, potassium, aluminum, long-chain fatty acids, or organic acids (Fontenot, 1972; Miller et al., 1972; Wilkinson et al., 1972; Mayland and Wilkinson, 1989; Fontenot et al., 1989). The onset of grass tetany is so rapid that resorption of bone magnesium is insufficient to maintain serum and extracellular magnesium levels (Miller et al., 1972). While magnesium deficiencies have been difficult to understand because of the mineral's occurrence in the diet, the deficiency may be an important mortality factor when animals consume very lush, spring forage.

E. Chloride and Sulfur

Chloride, the principal anion of body fluids, is involved in acid–base relations, gastric acidity (hydrochloric acid), and digestion. Deficiency symptoms may include reduced growth and feed intake, hemoconcentration, dehydration, nervous disorders, and reduced blood chloride levels.

Sulfur is primarily a constituent of the sulfur-containing amino acids (cystine, cysteine, and methionine), with much smaller amounts in biotin, thiamin (two B-complex vitamins), and the hormone insulin (McDonald *et al.*, 1973). Thus, a deficiency of sulfur is synonymous with a deficiency of the sulfur-containing metabolites, particularly the amino acids, and is usually not viewed as a simple deficiency of inorganic sulfur.

II. TRACE ELEMENTS

Trace element research with wildlife has largely been confined to studies of major deficiencies resulting from either improper feeding of captive animals or the inability of free-ranging animals to acquire adequate dietary sources. Trace elements act primarily as catalysts in cellular enzyme systems, although many other functions exist (Table 5.5). Students having a major interest in trace elements should consult Underwood (1977), Bronner and Coburn (1981), and Mertz (1986, 1987).

A. Iron

Iron deficiencies are relatively common in zoological gardens, particularly in young, bottle-raised animals (Wallach, 1970; Flieg, 1973). The iron content of milk is usually highest in very early lactation and decreases as lactation progresses. Because iron is important in the development of the growing neonate's hemoglobin, myoglobin, and iron-containing enzymes and if prenatal liver-storage of iron is inadequate to meet all needs while the neonate is solely dependent on milk, milk can be an important source of iron. However, the iron content of the milk of domestic ungulates is very low (0.2 to 0.5 μg iron/ml). Domestic cow's milk would be very inadequate if used to feed numerous altricial species in which the iron content of mid-lactation milk is much higher [pig—1 to 3 μg/ml, rabbit—2 to 4 μg/ml, rat—4 to 5 μg/ml, dog—5 to 10 μg/ml, cat—3 μg/ml, and quokka (marsupial)—22 μg/ml]. Even the milk of wild equids (zebras and Przewalski horses) has 2 to 13 times more iron than milk from the domestic horse, and the milk of wild ruminants can have 15 times more iron than cow's milk (Baker *et al.*, 1970; Cook *et al.*, 1970a, b; Loh and Kaldor, 1973; Lonnerdal *et al.*, 1981; Schryver *et al.*,

1986; Kaldor and Morgan, 1986). Thus, the anemia in bottle-raised wildlife when fed cow's milk results simply from a deficient diet. Because iron supplements for lactating females are generally ineffective in altering the iron content of the milk produced, iron supplements must be added directly to the milk or injected into the neonate if cow or goat milks are used to raise many species. One must be careful in adding iron to milk as a phosphorus deficiency can be produced by its binding in a nonabsorbable iron complex, and injectable iron dextran can produce a shock-like syndrome in some animals (Schryver and Hintz, 1982).

TABLE 5.5

Functions and Deficiency Signs of Trace Elements[a]

Mineral	Major functions	Deficiency signs
Iron (Fe)	Metal chelate of hemoglobin and myoglobin, component of many enzymes	Anemia, listlessness, weight loss, impaired brain and immune function
Zinc (Zn)	Essential for synthesis of DNA, RNA, and proteins, component or cofactor of many enzyme systems	Enlarged hocks of birds, poor feathering, retarded growth, rough hair coat and hair loss, weight loss, parakeratosis, impaired reproduction, loss of appetite, impaired wound healing, increased susceptibility to infections
Manganese (Mn)	Bone formation, energy metabolism (cofactor in oxidative phosphorylation), enzyme activation	Slipped tendon (perosis), weight loss or reduced growth, impaired reproduction, weakness, nervous disorders, loss of equilibrium, bone malformations
Copper (Cu)	Necessary for hemoglobin and melanin formation, component of several blood proteins and enzyme systems	Anemia, diarrhea, loss of appetite, nervous disorders including posterior ataxia, loss of hair color, reduced hair growth, defective keratinization of hair and hooves, bone deformities and fractures due to osteoporosis, impaired reproduction, cardiovascular disorders and sudden death

(continues)

TABLE 5.5

Continued

Mineral	Major functions	Deficiency signs
Iodine (I)	Hormones thyroxine and triiodothyronine	Reduced growth, goiter, bilateral, posterior alopecia in large carnivores, reduced reproduction and energy metabolism, mental deficiency, dwarfism
Selenium (Se)	Interacts with vitamin E to maintain tissue integrity	Nutritional muscular dystrophy—pale areas in muscles and degeneration of muscle fibers, labored breathing, difficulty in feeding, stiffness and disinclination to move far or fast, diarrhea, liver necrosis, reduced fertility, lung edema, pancreatic atrophy, exudative diathesis, reduced disease resistance
Cobalt (Co)	Vitamin B_{12}	Anemia, wasting away, listlessness, loss of appetite, weakness, fatty degeneration of the liver, reduced hair growth
Molybdenum (Mo)	Component of the enzymes xanthine oxidase, aldehyde oxidase, and sulfite oxidase	Renal calculi, reduced growth
Fluoride (F)	Specific biochemical roles are still uncertain	Reduced rate of growth, infertility, increased susceptibility to dental problems
Chromium (Cr)	Synergism with insulin to promote glucose uptake and metabolism	Reduced rate of growth and longevity, hyperglycemia

[a]Depending on the severity of the deficiency, time span, and species, specific signs may or may not be present.

Red meat and organ tissues are generally rich in iron relative to carnivore requirements. Because chicken, turkey, or quail (i.e., light-meated birds) have approximately one-third the amount of iron as do either birds with dark meat or mammals (NRC, 1982; Garcia *et al.,* 1984), animals consuming high-poultry diets may benefit from iron supplementation (Harvey and Coleman, 1982). However, anemia in captive carnivores fed pure meat diets is probably due to a primary copper deficiency rather than an iron deficiency. With the exception of cereal grains and grasses grown on very sandy soils, adequate amounts of iron are available in most forages (Underwood, 1977). The feeding of high levels of several species of frozen marine fish, such as Atlantic whiting, pollack, and Pacific hake, has induced an iron deficiency called cotton-fur in captive mink. The signs of deficiency include anemia, reduced growth, and a whitish discoloration of the underfur. The deficiency is induced by other dietary factors that reduce iron absorption, as cotton-fur-producing diets have essentially the same iron content as adequate diets (Stout *et al.*, 1960). The deficiency can be cured by injections of iron supplements, but oral supplements are ineffective. While thawed frozen fish produce the deficiency, fresh raw fish do not. Anemias in captive dolphins that cannot be cured by dietary iron supplements may be very similar to the iron-based, fish-induced anemia in mink (Geraci and Aubin, 1980).

Geophagia, or soil consumption not necessarily associated with mineral licks, is commonly observed in wildlife and has been suggested as an important means of meeting trace element requirements, including iron (Arthur and Alldredge, 1979; Arthur and Gates, 1988). Approximately 80% of the iron ingested by pronghorns and black-tailed jackrabbits comes from soil ingestion. Although the minerals of ingested soil may be nutritionally important, clay particles can also effectively chelate metal ions and prevent their absorption. Thus, mineral analyses of soils can be misleading relative to their nutritional interpretation if not combined with availability measurements. Geophagia can be either a useful source of iron or a contributing factor to anemia in wild animals, depending on soil iron content and chelating capacity of soil clay (Underwood, 1977).

Iron toxicity (hemosiderosis and hemochromatosis) is a common problem in many zoo animals (Rehg *et al.*, 1980; Lowenstine and Petrak, 1980; Randall and Patnaik, 1981; Frye, 1982; Taylor, 1984; Dierenfeld and Sheppard, 1989). Iron balance is normally regulated by controlling iron absorption (Morton and Janning, 1982; Gordeuk *et al.*, 1987). Although only a very small fraction (1 to 20%) of dietary iron is absorbed, liver, intestinal, and cardiac damage occur when iron absorption exceeds the body's need and the necessary excretion. The causes of iron overload in zoo animals currently is not understood, although excess dietary iron is suspect.

B. Iodine

The functions of iodine in the animal body are entirely related to the many metabolic controlling mechanisms of the thyroid hormones thyroxine and tri-iodothyronine. If iodine intake is inadequate for necessary thyroxine production, enlargement of the thyroid (goiter) occurs. Iodine deficiencies producing both simple and congenital goiters occur with "astonishing frequency" in captive wildlife because many natural foods, particularly red meats, freshwater fish, fruits, nuts, and seeds, are iodine deficient (Hollander and Riddle, 1946; Wallach,

1970; Russell, 1970; Geraci and Aubin, 1980; Watkins and Ullrey, 1983a, b; Lowenstine, 1986). Iodine deficiencies commonly occur in carnivores fed unsupplemented fresh beef or freshwater fish. Compared to the estimated requirement of 1000 μg/day for a lion, fresh beef at 33 μg/kg and freshwater fish at 30 μg/kg provide only a fraction of the needed intake (Scott, 1968; Brambell and Mathews, 1976; Geraci and Aubin, 1980). Liver may contain as much as 1100 μg of iodine/kg fresh weight, and marine fish 900 μg/kg. The thyroid gland in mammals contains 70 to 80% of the body's iodine and is, thus, a very rich source of this element for a carnivore. Marine plants and animals and iodized salts can be very useful iodine supplements in the formulation of diets for captive wildlife.

Iodine deficiencies also can be produced by plants having goitrogenic compounds (such as nitrates and thiocyanates) that competitively inhibit iodine transport. Examples of goitrogenic plants include cabbage, rape, kale, brussel sprouts, broccoli, cauliflower, turnips, and soybeans. These can be fed if the diet is supplemented with additional iodine or iodine-rich foods. Surprisingly, overdoses of iodine from excessive use of iodine supplements, such as iodide salts or kelp that is rich in iodine, or iodine-containing disinfectants produce goiters and functional iodine deficiencies (Russell, 1977; Jones et al., 1982). Thus, correcting iodine deficiencies can require care and monitoring of iodine intake.

Deficiencies of iodine in free-ranging animals are usually characteristic of areas in which soil iodine and therefore vegetation concentrations are inadequate. Iodine is not required by plants. Thus, the concentration in vegetation can be quite varied and influenced by soil content, chemical form, and soil pH. Areas of low-iodine soils and plants and deficiencies in humans and domestic animals occur on every continent (Kubota and Allaway, 1972; Stanbury and Hetzel, 1980).

C. Copper

Copper deficiencies have occurred in captive carnivores (Wallach, 1971), captive primates (Obeck, 1978), and captive and free-ranging herbivores (Barlow et al., 1964; Terlecki et al., 1964; Flynn et al., 1976, 1977; Zumpt and Heine, 1978; Reid et al., 1980; Dierenfeld et al., 1988; Booth et al., 1989; Gogan et al., 1988, 1989; Wilson, 1989). Red meat is very low in copper, whereas liver (the primary storage site of absorbed copper), heart, brain, and kidney are much higher in copper for animals consuming adequate dietary copper. Liver copper content is frequently highest in neonates and declines with age (Reid et al., 1980; Davis and Mertz, 1987; Leighton et al., 1990). Similarly, copper content of the liver in animals consuming the same diet can differ 10-fold depending on the species. Although cows and sheep frequently have liver copper concentrations of from 100 to 900 μg/g of dry matter, most nonruminants and some wild ruminants have from 10 to 100 μg Cu/g of dry liver (Davis and Mertz, 1987; Freudenberger et al., 1987; Gogan et al., 1989). The copper content of milk varies with stage of lactation (highest in early lactation) and species. Rat milk has 28 times more copper per ml than cow's milk, and the milks of wild artiodactyls have 6 times more copper than cow's milk (Robbins et al., 1987; Davis and Mertz, 1987). Many of the early studies of copper deficiency used laboratory rats fed cow's milk.

Plant copper concentrations are dependent on soil pH and type, content and form of soil copper, concentration of other elements and organic residues, and plant species. Severely leached, sandy soils, alkaline soils, or peat and muck soils often produce plants with a low copper content. Copper absorption tends to be low and is affected by chemical form, copper status of the ingesting animal, and the levels of other metal ions, notably calcium, cadmium, zinc, iron, lead, silver, molybdenum, and sulfur, which may interfere with its absorption (McCullough, 1969; Kubota, 1975; Erdman et al., 1978).

Thus, deficiencies can easily occur in captive carnivores fed unsupplemented red meat diets or adequate diets that have been excessively supplemented with calcium or iron. Anemias and faded coat color are characteristic of copper deficiencies in captive felines fed red meat diets supplemented with excessive calcium (Wallach, 1971). One of the better examples of a copper deficiency induced by the excessive intake of another element (zinc) occurred in nursing rhesus monkeys (Obeck, 1978) (Fig. 5.6). Symptoms of the deficiency were achromotrichia (loss of hair color), alopecia (loss of hair), decreased vigor and activity, anemia with little or no evidence of erythrocyte production, and eventually either cessation of nursing and death or spontaneous recovery. Deficiencies occurred in monkeys in galvanized cages but not in those kept in stainless steel cages. Apparently, because the infants were continually licking and mouthing portions of their caging, they were ingesting enough zinc from the galvanized coating, which had been solubilized by urine, to interfere with dietary copper absorption. Excessive zinc intake produced a copper deficiency from a normally adequate diet. Spontaneous recoveries occurred in those animals who simply stopped mouthing their cages.

Copper deficiencies in wild ruminants (elk, red deer, fallow deer, moose, blesbok, and bontebok) have occurred world-wide with cases in Africa, New Zealand, North America, and England. General symptoms included pale, faded, brittle pelage, osteoporosis and fractures, abnormal hoof and antler growth, weight loss, impaired movement (ataxia), reduced reproduction, and sudden death. Thus, copper-deficient animals in the wild would be highly susceptible to predation. In domestic sheep, liver and serum copper content and susceptibility to deficiencies and toxicities are highly selectable traits that vary with breed (Wiener et al., 1985; Woolliams et al., 1985). Thus, individuals and populations within and between species are likely to differ in copper metabolism and sus-

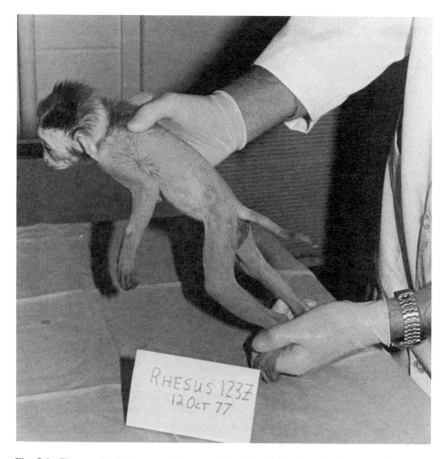

Fig. 5.6 Five-month old rhesus monkey reared in galvanized caging showing severe alopecia as the result of a zinc-induced copper deficiency. [From Obeck (1978), courtesy of the American Association for Laboratory Animal Science.]

ceptibility to deficiencies (Freudenberger *et al.*, 1987; Davis and Mertz, 1987). Of approximately 40 species of hooved mammals maintained on essentially the same diet at the New York Zoological Park, only blesbok are exceedingly prone to copper-deficiency and require heavy copper supplementation (Dierenfeld *et al.*, 1988). The common practice of zoos, wildlife agencies, and private game ranches of translocating wildlife without regard for their mineral requirements and mineral availabilities in new and old ranges will produce unnecessary failures. Although a species may have existed in a particular low-copper area previously, individuals of that species that have lived in a copper-replete area for many generations may not be suitable for reintroduction. Far greater care may be necessary in selecting individuals and populations for transplant programs.

Copper deficiencies can be corrected by (1) altering the diet to include copper-rich foods, such as adding liver to carnivore diets, (2) supplementing the diet with copper sulfate or copper oxide, (3) injecting copper glycinate, or (4) using various forms of slow release copper administered orally (Dierenfeld et al., 1988; Booth et al., 1989; Gogan et al., 1989; Wilson, 1989). Because of the toxicity of copper and variation in the degree of copper deficiency and individual and species responsiveness to copper supplementation, correcting a copper deficiency should be done very carefully with close monitoring of blood or other physiological indices. Just as species vary in their requirement, they also vary in their susceptibility to copper toxicity. Signs of copper toxicity include liver and kidney damage and discoloration, gastroenteritis with a greenish discoloration of intestinal contents, and death (Henderson and Winterfield, 1975).

D. Zinc

Because of zinc's role in protein synthesis and enzyme systems, reduced growth and feed intake are the first signs of a zinc deficiency. Other signs of zinc deficiency, such as parakeratosis (thickening and keratinization of the tongue epithelium or the skin), a rough, unkempt pelage, alopecia, and reduced play and exploratory activity, were observed in squirrel and rhesus monkeys as well as in numerous domestic species (Barney et al., 1967; Macapinlae et al., 1967; Sandstead et al., 1978; Hambidge et al., 1986). The estimated zinc requirements for wild and domestic animals typically range from 10 to 70 ppm in the dry diet (Table 5.4) (Henkin, 1979; Hambidge et al., 1986). Higher requirement estimates do occur, such as 190 ppm for moustached marmosets (Chadwick et al., 1979), but probably represent either errors or a reduced availability of dietary zinc.

Zinc is generally quite available when consumed in animal tissue. Likewise, because the zinc content of animal tissue exceeds the estimated requirements, such as 30–250 ppm in the dry matter of poultry, red meat, milk, and eggs, zinc deficiencies in carnivores and nursing animals are unlikely (Luick et al., 1974; Hall-Martin et al., 1977; Henkin, 1979; Hambidge et al., 1986). The availability of zinc in plants is often less than that in animal tissues because of its complexing with phytate (inositol hexaphosphoric acid), which is most prevalent in seeds. Similarly, high levels of dietary calcium caused by overzealous supplementation of meat or seed diets can further reduce zinc availability. Although the zinc content of liver and bone samples varies seasonally in free-ranging wild granivores and herbivores (Ojanen et al., 1975; Albl et al., 1977; Anke et al., 1980) and zinc deficiencies have occurred in grazing cattle (Legg and Sears, 1960; Dynna and Havre, 1963), zinc deficiencies have not been reported in wild animals. Zinc solubilized from galvanized pails, pipes, and

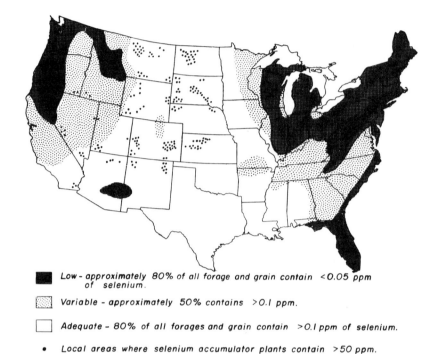

■ Low - approximately 80% of all forage and grain contain <0.05 ppm
of selenium.

▨ Variable - approximately 50% contains >0.I ppm.

□ Adequate - 80% of all forages and grain contain >0.I ppm of selenium.

• Local areas where selenium accumulator plants contain >50 ppm.

Fig. 5.7 Selenium concentration in plants relative to domestic animal needs and areas of toxicity in the Unites States. (Courtesy of J. Kubota, U.S. Plant, Soil and Nutrition Laboratory, Ithaca, New York.)

troughs used for feeding and watering captive wildlife can be an important source of this element (Wallach, 1970). Zinc oxide, carbonate, and sulfate are useful forms if supplementation is warranted. Although zinc is relatively nontoxic, zinc toxicity can occur, and zinc can interfere with copper and iron metabolism.

E. Selenium

Selenium has been of interest because plants in many areas of the world contain concentrations that are either deficient or toxic relative to animal metabolism (Fig. 5.7). Selenium was identified as an essential nutrient in 1957 (Schwarz and Foltz, 1957). One of the major functions of selenium is as a component of the enzyme glutathione peroxidase, which prevents the oxidation of the unsaturated fats in cell membranes. When dietary selenium is inadequate to prevent this oxidation, muscle membranes rupture and leak cellular enzymes into the extracellular circulation. These damaged muscles become nonfunctional and turn white, hence the name white muscle disease. White muscle disease due to a selenium deficiency should not be confused with the similar symptoms of capture myopathy, in which severe exertion or stress of chased or captured animals produces acidosis, destruction of cell membranes, and death (Harthoorn and Young, 1974; Colgrove, 1978). However, stress and exertion due to chasing, trapping, or handling wildlife also can induce the acute signs of white muscle disease (Hebert and Cowan, 1971b).

Selenium deficiencies have been observed in numerous ungulates, small mammals, and birds in North America, Africa, England, and New Zealand (Jarrett *et al.*, 1964; Gandal, 1966; Murray, 1967; Hebert and Cowan, 1971b; Fleming *et al.*, 1977; Stoszek *et al.*, 1980; Dhillon and Winterfield, 1983; Knox *et al.*, 1987; Flueck, 1991). Selenium-supplemented, free-ranging deer in a low-selenium area of California had 83 fawns/100 females in comparison to 32 for non-supplemented females (Flueck, 1989). Selenium deficiencies become more probable as dietary (dry matter basis) or whole blood concentrations drop below 0.05 ppm (Hebert and Cowan, 1971b), although white-tailed deer consuming a diet of 0.04 ppm selenium were not pathologically deficient (Brady *et al.*, 1978). Mountain goats with blood selenium concentrations as low as 0.014 ppm were very susceptible to myopathy during capture (Robbins *et al.*, 1985). Although selenium salts (primarily selenites and selenates) can be injected or incorporated into the feed or free-choice salt supplements, selenium supplementation during wildlife capture programs will not be effective in combating the acute pathological signs because the rapidity of muscle damage (hours) exceeds the time (days to weeks) necessary to convert selenium into glutathione peroxidase and for cellular repair to occur. Because peak glutathione peroxidase activities occur 20 to 30 days following a selenium supplement (Robbins *et al.*, 1985), wildlife capture–transplant programs in areas where selenium deficiencies may occur should begin selenium supplementation (such as free-choice salt blocks) at least a month prior to capture.

Animals do differ in their requirements for selenium and their susceptibility to white muscle disease. Some of this variation between species may be due to differences in the amount of nonselenium-dependent glutathione peroxidase activity (Dhillon and Winterfield, 1983; Butler *et al.*, 1982; Beilstein and Whanger, 1983; Robbins *et al.*, 1985; Samson *et al.*, 1989). Similarly, because high levels of dietary sulfur will reduce selenium availability and chlorinated hydrocarbons interfere with selenium metabolism (Combs and Scott, 1977), necessary dietary concentrations for a particular species will vary.

Selenium was first investigated by nutritionists because of its toxicity when ingested at high levels. Selenium toxicity, also called alkali disease or blind staggers in domestic animals, produces an abundance of symptoms ranging in severity from reduced rates of gain to sloughing of the hoofs, lameness, atrophy of the heart, cirrhosis of the liver, blindness, partial paralysis, and death due to respiratory failure or starvation. Selenium toxicity in free-ranging domestic herbivores has occurred in Ireland, Israel, Australia, Mexico, Canada, Columbia, Soviet Union, Venezuela, China, and South Africa (Levander, 1986). Although wildlife may be able to ingest higher selenium levels than domestic livestock before toxicity occurs (Clemens, 1987), toxicity expressed as embryo mortality and developmental abnormalities has occurred in wild birds at Kesterson National Wildlife Refuge in California (Ohlendorf et al., 1986). Run-off water from agricultural irrigation carried enough selenium into the marsh to ultimately produce plants and invertebrates with 22 to 175 ppm Se (dry weight), or 12 to 130 times normal.

Toxicity is apparently due to the extensive substitution of selenium for sulfur in methionine and cysteine to produce malfunctioning selenoenzymes (Shrift, 1972). Several plants, including milk vetch (Astragalus bisulcatus and A. grayi), poison vetch (A. pectinatus), goldenweed (Haplopappus spp.), woody aster (Machaeranthera spp.), and prince's plume (Stanleya pinnata), are notorious for accumulating toxic selenium concentrations when grown on high-selenium soils. These plants are normally unpalatable to herbivores, but they will be consumed under starvation conditions. More importantly, when these plants drop their leaves or die and decay, readily absorbable selenium is increased in the root area of all adjacent plants. Consequently, plants that are highly palatable but not normally selenium-accumulator species, such as western wheatgrass (Agropyron smithii), blue grama (Bouteloua gracilis), and winter fat (Eurotia lanata), become toxic (Leininger et al., 1977).

F. Cobalt and Fluoride

Although cobalt deficiencies occur in domestic livestock in many areas of the Midwest and eastern United States (Fig. 5.8), white-tailed deer (New York) and ring-necked pheasants (Minnesota) examined in marginal cobalt areas were not deficient in or limited by cobalt (Smith et al., 1963; Nelson et al., 1966). Ingested fluoride is primarily concentrated in bones, teeth, or antlers as calcium fluoride. Although well recognized as an essential trace element, fluoride has been studied in wildlife primarily as a toxic element when ingested in excess of the requirement. Because of fluoride's strong affinity for calcium, excess fluoride and low dietary calcium can lead to an osteomalacia similar to nutritional secondary hyperparathyroidism (Krishnamachari, 1987). Fluorosis has been observed primarily in wild ungulates consuming water from or plants growing in the immediate area of thermal springs or industrial processing plants, particularly aluminum smelters or fertilizer factories (Karstad, 1967; Kay et al., 1975; Newman and Yu, 1976; Kubota et al., 1982; Shupe et al., 1984; Suttie et al., 1987; Walton, 1988). Silver foxes fed a commercial chow have also developed fluorosis when at least one of the ingredients inadvertently contained excess fluoride (Eckerlin et al., 1986). Domestic and wild animals appear equally susceptible to fluorosis, with problems becoming more likely as dietary levels increase above 50 ppm (Suttie et al., 1985; Pattee et al., 1988). Signs of fluoride toxicity include

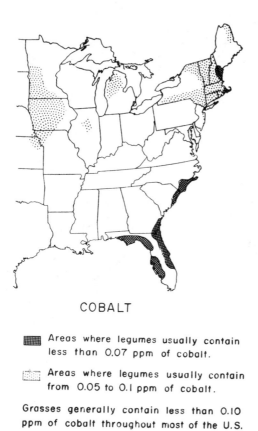

COBALT

▓▓ Areas where legumes usually contain
     less than 0.07 ppm of cobalt.

░░ Areas where legumes usually contain
     from 0.05 to 0.1 ppm of cobalt.

Grasses generally contain less than 0.10
ppm of cobalt throughout most of the U.S.

Fig. 5.8 Geographic distribution of cobalt-deficient areas in the eastern United States relative to domestic livestock and, therefore, possibly wildlife. (Courtesy of J. Kubota, U.S. Plant, Soil and Nutrition Laboratory, Ithaca, New York.)

broken, pitted, blackened teeth; excessive or abnormal wear due to softening of the teeth; fractures of the teeth and jaw bones; anorexia; and impaired milk production and reproduction (Fig. 5.9).

G. Manganese

Manganese concentrations are highest in bone, liver, kidney, and intestine (Hurley and Keen, 1987). The consumption of deficient diets will lower bone manganese content. Because manganese is essential for the proper formation of the cartilaginous matrix of bone, many of the deficiency signs represent improper bone formation and growth.

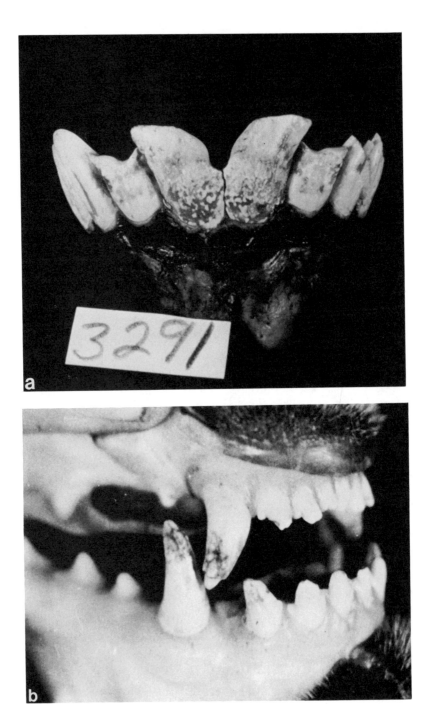

Fig. 5.9 Tooth mottling and abnormal wear due to excessive fluoride intake in (a) an elk and (b) a coyote. (Courtesy of J. L. Shupe, Utah State University.)

The estimated requirements for game birds (Table 5.4) are probably higher than the absolute minimum, but they represent the widespread practice of supplementing poultry diets because manganese salts are relatively inexpensive, manganese has a relatively wide safety margin, and other minerals, such as calcium and phosphorus, can reduce its absorption. Manganese has been largely ignored in studies of free-ranging wildlife (Anke et al., 1979). Pathological manganese deficiencies in free-ranging wildlife have not been observed and probably will seldom occur because manganese is widely distributed in most seeds, forages, and animal tissue in concentrations that are apparently adequate relative to the requirement estimates for domesticated species. A manganese deficiency has occurred in 1 to 2 month old peregrine falcons fed eviserated pigeons. The tibiotarsal bone grew abnormally leading to medial luxation of the Achilles tendon. Manganese content in noneviscerated pigeons varied from 7.1 to 14.2 ppm, while the eviserated birds contained 4.2 to 5.9 ppm (Sykes et al., 1982). The authors suggested that liver consumption is particularly important to young raptors if they are to meet their manganese requirement.

H. Molybdenum

While molybdenum is an essential trace element, it has been studied largely because of its toxicity and complexing potential to induce copper deficiencies (Osman and Sykes, 1989). Molybdenum deficiencies are unlikely for both free-ranging and captive wildlife. Toxicity signs, independent of inducing copper deficiencies, include reduced feed intake, weight loss, and diarrhea. Deer have been able to withstand higher levels of dietary molybdenum than have domestic livestock and have also been able to avoid diets high in molybdenum (Ward and Nagy, 1976). The ability of wildlife to purposefully select low-molybdenum feeds would reduce the chances of toxicity.

III. CONCLUSIONS

The various aspects of mineral requirements and metabolism in wildlife have been studied mainly when acute deficiencies have been observed. The chance observation of numerous mineral deficiencies in captive and free-ranging wildlife and the obvious alterations in the behavior and ecology of many free-ranging animals to cope with potential insufficiencies of minerals suggest a very fruitful area for far more intensive studies. Mineral deficiencies in free-ranging wildlife may become even more prevalent as humans interrupt the various mineral cycles by cropping and removing domestic livestock, wildlife, trees, and forage (Stoszek et al., 1980; Flueck, 1989). One must surely conclude that the entire field of wildlife-related mineral studies will be one of the more interesting and exciting areas of future development in wildlife nutrition and management.

REFERENCES

Albl, P., Boyazoglu, P. A., and Bezuidenhout, J. P. (1977). Observations on the mineral status of springbok (*Antidorcas marsupialis* Zimmerman) in South West Africa. *Madoqua* **10**, 79–83.

Allen, M. E., and Oftedal, O. T. (1982). Calcium and phosphorus levels in live prey. *Northeast. Reg. Proc. Am. Assoc. Zool. Parks Aquar.*, pp. 120–128.

Allen, M. E., and Oftedal, O. T. (1989). Dietary manipulation of the calcium content of feed crickets. *J. Zoo Wildl. Med.* **20**, 26–33.

Anderson, W. L., and Stewart, P. L. (1969). Relationships between inorganic ions and the distribution of pheasants in Illinois. *J. Wildl. Manage.* **33**, 254–270.

Anderson, W. L., and Stewart, P. L. (1973). Chemical elements and the distribution of pheasants in Illinois. *J. Wildl. Manage.* **37**, 142–153.

Angerbjorn, A., and Pehrson, A. (1987). Factors influencing winter food choice by mountain hares (*Lepus timidus* L.) on Swedish coastal islands. *Can. J. Zool.* **65**, 2163–2167.

Anke, M., Kronemann, H., Dittrich, G., and Neumann, A. (1979). The supply of wild ruminants with major and trace elements. II. The manganese content of winter grazing and the manganese status of red deer, fallow deer, roes and mouflons. *Arch. Anim. Nutr.* **29**, 845–858.

Anke, M., Riedel, E., Bruckner, E., and Dittrich, G. (1980). The supply of wild ruminants with major and trace elements. III. The zinc content of winter grazing and the zinc status of red deer, fallow deer, roes and mouflons. *Arch. Anim. Nutr.* **30**, 479–490.

Ankney, C. D., and Scott, D. M. (1980). Changes in nutrient reserves and diet of breeding brown-headed cowbirds. *Auk* **97**, 684–696.

Arnaud, C. D. (1978). Calcium homeostasis: Regulatory elements and their integration. *Fed. Proc.* **37**, 2557–2560.

Arnold, S. A., Kram, M. A., Hintz, H. F., Evans, H., and Krook, L. (1974). Nutritional secondary hyperparathyroidism in the parakeet. *Cornell Vet.* **64**, 37–46.

Arthur, W. J., III, and Alldredge, A. W. (1979). Soil ingestion by mule deer in North central Colorado. *J. Range Manage.* **32**, 67–71.

Arthur, W. J., III, and Gates, R. J. (1988). Trace element intake via soil ingestion in pronghorns and in black-tailed jackrabbits. *J. Range Manage.* **41**, 162–166.

Aumann, G. D. (1965). Microtine abundance and soil sodium levels. *J. Mammal.* **46**, 594–604.

Aumann, G. D., and Emlen, J. T. (1965). Relation of population density to sodium availability and sodium selection by microtine rodents. *Nature (London)* **208**, 198–199.

Baker, B. E., Cook, H. W., and Teal, J. J. (1970). Muskox (*Ovibos moschatus*) milk. I. Gross composition, fatty acid, and mineral constitution. *Can. J. Zool.* **48**, 1345–1347.

Barlow, R. M., Butler, E. J., and Purves, D. (1964). An ataxic condition in red deer (*Cervus elaphus*). *J. Comp. Path.* **74**, 519–529.

Barney, G. H., Macapiniac, M. P., Pearson, W. N., and Darby, J. W. (1967). Parakeratosis of the tongue—a unique histopathologic lesion in the zinc-deficient squirrel monkey. *J. Nutr.* **93**, 511–517.

Batzli, G. O. (1986). Nutritional ecology of the California vole: Effects of food quality on reproduction. *Ecology* **67**, 406–412.

Beasom, S. L., and Pattee, O. H. (1978). Utilization of snails by Rio Grande turkey hens. *J. Wildl. Manage.* **42**, 916–919.

Beilstein, M. A., and Whanger, P. D. (1983). Distribution of selenium and glutathione peroxidase in blood fractions from humans, rhesus and squirrel monkeys, rats and sheep. *J. Nutr.* **113**, 2138–2146.

Belovsky, G. E. (1981). A possible population response of moose to sodium availability. *J. Mammal.* **62**, 631–633.

Belovsky, G. E., and Jordan, P. A. (1981). Sodium dynamics and adaptations of a moose population. *J. Mammal.* **62,** 613–621.

Bennetts, R. E., and Hutto, R. L. (1985). Attraction of social fringillids to mineral salts: An experimental study. *J. Field Ornithol.* **56,** 187–189.

Bernard, J.B., and Ullrey, D.E. (1989). Evaluation of dietary husbandry of marine mammals at two major zoological parks. *J. Zoo Wildl. Med.* **20,** 45–52.

Bernhard, R. (1963). Specific gravity, ash, calcium and phosphorus content of antlers of Cervidae. *Can. Field-Nat.* **90,** 310–322.

Beyers, R. J., Smith, M. H., Gentry, J. B., and Ramsey, L. L. (1971). Standing crops of elements and atomic ratios in a small mammal community. *Acta Theriol.* **16,** 203–211.

Bintz, G. L. (1969). Sodium-22 retention as a function of water intake by *Citellus lateralis. In* "Physiological Systems in Semiarid Environments" (C. C. Hoff and M. L. Riedesel, eds.), pp. 45–52. Univ. New Mexico Press, Albuquerque, New Mexico.

Bird, D.M., Ho, S-K., and Pare, D. (1982). Nutritive values of three common prey items of the American kestrel. *Comp. Biochem. Physiol.* **73A,** 513–515.

Blair-West, J. R., Coghlan, J. P., Denton, D. A., Nelson, J. F., Orchard, E., Scoggins, B. A., Wright, R. D., Myers, K., and Jungueira, C. L. (1968). Physiological, morphological and behavioral adaptations to a sodium deficient environment by wild native Australian and introduced species of animals. *Nature (London)* **217,** 922–928.

Bland Sutton, J. (1888). Rickets in monkeys, lions, bears and birds. *J. Comp. Med. Surg.* **10,** 1–29.

Booth, D. H., Wilson, P. R., and Alexander, A. M. (1989). The effect of oral oxidized copper wire on liver copper in farmed red deer. *N. Z. Vet. J.* **37,** 98–101.

Botkin, D. B., Jordan, P. A., Dominski, A. S., Lowendorf, H. S., and Hutchinson, G. E. (1973). Sodium dynamics in a northern ecosystem. *Proc. Natl. Acad. Sci. U.S.A.* **70,** 2745–2748.

Brady, P. S., Brady, L. J., Whetter, P. A., Ullrey, D. E., and Fay, L. D. (1978). The effect of dietary selenium and vitamin E on biochemical parameters and survival of young among white-tailed deer (*Odocoileus virginianus*). *J. Nutr.* **108,** 1439–1448.

Brambell, M. R., and Mathews, S. J. (1976). Primates and carnivores at Regent's Park. *Symp. Zool. Soc. London* **40,** 147–165.

Bronner, F. (1964). Dynamics and function of calcium. *In* "Mineral Metabolism," Vol. II, Part A (C. L. Comar and F. Bronner, eds.), pp. 341–444. Academic Press, New York.

Bronner, F., and Coburn, J. W. (1981). "Disorders of Mineral Metabolism: Trace Minerals." Academic Press, New York.

Butler, J. A., Whanger, P. D., and Tripp, M. J. (1982). Blood selenium and glutathione peroxidase activity in pregnant women: Comparative assays in primates and other animals. *Am. J. Clin. Nutr.* **36,** 15–23.

Cade, T. J. (1964). Water and salt in granivorous birds. *In* "Thirst" (M. J. Wayner, ed.), pp. 237–254. Pergamon Press, New York.

Cain, J. R., Beasom, S. L., Rowland, L. O., and Rowe, L. D. (1982). The effects of varying dietary phosphorus on breeding bobwhites. *J. Wildl. Manage.* **46,** 1061–1065.

Calef, G. W., and Lortie, G. M. (1975). A mineral lick of the barren-ground caribou. *J. Mammal.* **56,** 240–242.

Case, R. M., and Robel, R. J. (1974). Bioenergetics of the bobwhite. *J. Wildl. Manage.* **38,** 638–652.

Chaddock, T. T. (1940). Chemical analysis of deer antlers. *Wisc. Cons. Bull. (Madison)* **5,** 42.

Chadwick, D. P., May, J. C., and Lorenz, D. (1979). Spontaneous zinc deficiency in marmosets, *Saguinus mystax. Lab. Anim. Sci.* **29,** 482–485.

Chambers, G. D., Sadler, K. C., and Breitenbach, R. P. (1966). Effects of dietary calcium levels on egg production and bone structure of pheasants. *J. Wildl. Manage.* **30,** 65–73.

Christian, D. P. (1989). Effects of dietary sodium and potassium on mineral balance in captive meadow voles (*Microtus pennsylvanicus*). *Can. J. Zool.* **67**, 168–177.

Christian, J. J. (1964). Potassium deficiency: A factor in mass mortality of sika (*Cervus nippon*)? *Wildl. Dis.* **37**, 11 pp.

Christian, J. J., Flyger, V., and Davis, D. E. (1960). Factors in a mass mortality of sika deer. *Chesapeake Sci.* **1**, 79–95.

Church, D. C. (1979). "Digestive Physiology and Nutrition of Ruminants, " Vol. II. O. and B. Books, Corvallis, Oregon.

Clark, W. T., Pass, D., Biddle, J., and Salmon, J. (1982). Urinary calculi composed of magnesium hydrogen phosphate in a kangaroo. *Aust. Vet. J.* **59**, 62–63.

Clemens, E. T., Meyer, K. L., Carlson, M. P., and Schneider, N. R. (1987). Hematology, blood chemistry and selenium values of captive pronghorn antelope, white-tailed deer and American bison. *Comp. Biochem. Physiol.* **87C**, 167–170.

Coleman, J. S., Fraser, J. D., and Pringle, C. A. (1985). Salt-eating by black and turkey vultures. *Condor* **87**, 291–292.

Colgrove, G. S. (1978). Suspected transportation associated myopathy in a dolphin. *J. Am. Vet. Med. Assoc.* **173**, 1121–1123.

Combs, C.F., Jr., and Scott, M. L. (1977). Nutritional interrelationships of vitamin E and selenium. *BioScience* **27**, 467–473.

Conlogue, G. J., Foreyt, W. J., Hanson, A. L., and Ogden, J. A. (1979). Juvenile rickets and hyperparathyroidism in the arctic fox. *J. Wildl. Dis.* **15**, 563–567.

Cook, H. W., Pearson, A. M., Simmons, N. M., and Baker, B. E. (1970a). Dall sheep (*Ovis dalli dalli*) milk. I. Effects of stage of lactation on the composition of the milk. *Can. J. Zool.* **48**, 629–633.

Cook, H. W., Rausch, R. A., and Baker, B. E. (1970b). Moose (*Alces alces*) milk. Gross composition, fatty acid, and mineral constitution. *Can. J. Zool.* **48**, 213–215.

Cowles, R. B. (1967). Fire suppression, faunal changes and condor diets. *Proc. Tall Timbers Fire Ecol. Conf.* **7**, 217–224.

Crocker, A. D., Cronshaw, J., and Holmes, W. N. (1974). The effect of a crude oil on intestinal absorption in ducklings (*Anas platyrhynchos*). *Environ. Pollut.* **7**, 165–177.

Dale, F. H. (1954). Influence of calcium on the distribution of the pheasant in North America. *Trans. North Am. Wildl. Conf.* **19**, 316–323.

Davis, G. K., and Mertz, W. (1987). Copper. In "Trace Elements in Human and Animal Nutrition" (W. Mertz, ed.), pp. 301–364. Academic Press, New York.

DelGiudice, G.D., Duquette, L.S., Seal, U.S., and Mech, L.D. (1991). Validation of estimating food intake in gray wolves by ^{22}Na turnover. *J. Wildl. Manage.* **55**, 59–71.

Denton, D. A., and Nelson, J. F. (1971). Effects of pregnancy and lactation on the mineral appetites of wild rabbits [*Oryctolagus cuniculus* (L.)]. *Endocrinology* **88**, 31–40.

Dhillon, A. S., and Winterfield, R. W. (1983). Selenium-vitamin E deficiency in captive wild ducks. *Avian Dis.* **27**, 527–530.

Dierenfeld, E., and Sheppard, C.D. (1989). Investigations of hepatic iron levels in zoo birds. *Proc. Dr. Scholl Nutr. Conf.* **8**, 101–114.

Dierenfeld, E. S., Dolensek, E. P., McNamara, T. S., and Doherty, J. G. (1988). Copper deficiency in captive blesbok antelope (*Damiliscus dorcas phillipsi*). *J. Zoo Anim. Med.* **19**, 126–131.

Dieterich, R. A., and Van Pelt, R. W. (1972). Juvenile osteomalacia in a coyote. *J. Wildl. Dis.* **8**, 146–148.

Dynna, O., and Havre, G. N. (1963). Interrelationship of zinc and copper in the nutrition of cattle. A complex zinc-copper deficiency. *Acta Vet. Scand.* **4**, 197–208.

Eckerlin, R. H., Krook, L., Maylin, G. A., and Carmichael, D. (1986). Toxic effects of food-borne fluoride in silver foxes. *Cornell Vet.* **76**, 395–402.

Edfors, C.H., Ullrey, D.E., and Aulerich, R.J. (1989). Prevention of urolithiasis in the ferret (*Mustela putorius furo*) with phosphoric acid. *J. Zoo Wildl. Med.* **20**, 12–19.

Erdman, J. A., Ebens, R. J., and Case, A. A. (1978). Molybdenosis: A potential problem in ruminants grazing on coal mine spoils. *J. Range Manage.* **31**, 34–36.

Fleming, W. J., Haschek, W. M., Gutenmann, W. H., Caslick, J. W., and Lisk, D. J. (1977). Selenium and white muscle disease in woodchucks. *J. Wildl. Dis.* **13**, 265–268.

Flieg, G. M. (1973). Nutritional problems in young ratites. *Int. Zoo Yearb.* **13**, 158–163.

Flueck, W.T. (1989). "The Effect of Selenium on Reproduction of Black-tailed Deer (*Odocoileus hemionus columbianus*) in Shasta County, California." Doctoral Dissertation, Univ. Calif. Davis, California.

Flueck, W. T. (1991). Whole blood selenium levels and glutathione peroxidase activity in erthrocytes of black-tailed deer. *J. Wildl. Manage.* **55**, 26–31.

Flynn, A., Franzmann, A. W., and Arneson, P. D. (1976). Molybdenum-sulfur interactions in the utilization of marginal dietary copper in Alaska moose. *In* "Molybdenum in the Environment" (W. R. Chappell and K. K. Petersen, eds.), pp. 115–124. Dekker, New York.

Flynn, A., Franzmann, A. W., Arneson, P. D., and Oldemeyer, J. L. (1977). Indications of copper deficiency in a subpopulation of Alaskan moose. *J. Nutr.* **107**, 1182–1189.

Fontenot, J. P. (1972). Magnesium in ruminant animals and grass tetany. *In* "Magnesium in the Environment" (J. B. Jones, Jr., M. C. Blount, and S. R. Wilkinson, eds.), pp. 131–151. Taylor County Printing Co., Reynolds, Georgia.

Fontenot, J. P., Allen, V. G., Bunce, G. E., and Goff, J. P. (1989). Factors influencing magnesium absorption and metabolism in ruminants. *J. Anim. Sci.* **67**, 3445–3455.

Forbes, G. B. (1962). Sodium. *In* "Mineral Metabolism," Vol. II, Part B (C. L. Comar and F. Bronner, eds.), pp. 1–72. Academic Press, New York.

Fowler, M. E. (1978). Nutritional value of hard water. *J. Zoo Anim. Med.* **9**, 96–98.

Fowler, M. E. (1986). Metabolic bone disease. *In* "Zoo and Wild Animal Medicine" (M. E. Fowler, ed.), pp. 70–90. W. B. Saunders, Philadelphia.

Franzmann, A. W., Oldemeyer, J. L., and Flynn, A. (1975). Minerals and moose. *Proc. Am. Moose Workshop and Conference* **11**, (Mimeo).

Fraser, D. (1979). Aquatic feeding by a woodchuck. *Can. Field-Nat.* **93**, 309–310.

Fraser, D., and Reardon, E. (1980). Attraction of wild ungulates to mineral-rich springs in Central Canada. *Holarctic Ecol.* **3**, 36–40.

Fraser, D., Reardon, E., Dieken, F., and Loescher, B. (1980). Sampling problems and interpretation of chemical analysis of mineral springs used by wildlife. *J. Wildl. Manage.* **44**, 623–631.

Fraser, D., Thompson, B. K., and Arthur, D. (1982). Aquatic feeding by moose: Seasonal variation in relation to plant chemical composition and use of mineral licks. *Can. J. Zool.* **60**, 3121–3126.

Fraser, D., Chavez, E. R., and Paloheimo, J. E. (1984). Aquatic feeding by moose: Selection of plant species and feeding areas in relation to plant chemical composition and characteristics of lakes. *Can. J. Zool.* **62**, 80–87.

Freeland, W. J., Calcott, P. H., and Geiss, D. P. (1985). Allelochemicals, minerals and herbivore population size. *Biochem. Syst. Ecol.* **13**, 195–206.

French, C. E., McEwen, L. C., Magruder, N. D., Ingram, R. H., and Swift, R. W. (1956). Nutrient requirements for growth and antler development in the white-tailed deer. *J. Wildl. Manage.* **20**, 221–232.

Freudenberger, D. O., Familton, A. S., and Sykes, A. R. (1987). Comparative aspects of copper metabolism in silage-fed sheep and deer (*Cervus elaphus*). *J. Agric. Sci.* **108**, 1–7.

Frings, H., and Frings, M. (1959). Observations on salt balance and behavior of Laysan and black-footed albatrosses in captivity. *Condor* **61**, 305–314.

Frye, F. L. (1982). Iron storage disease (hemosiderosis) in an African rock hyrax (*Procavia capensis*). *J. Zoo Anim. Med.* **13**, 152–156.

Gailey-Phipps, J. J., and Sladen, W. J. L. (1982). Survey on nutrition of penguins. *J. Am. Vet. Med. Assoc.* **181**, 1305–1309.

Gales, R. (1989). Validation of the use of tritiated water, doubly labeled water, and ^{22}Na for estimating food, energy, and water intake in little penguins, *Eudyptula minor*. *Physiol. Zool.* **62**, 147–169.

Gandal, C. P. (1966). White muscle disease in a breeding herd of Nyala antelope (*Traglophus angasi*) at New York Zoo. *Int. Zoo Yearb.* **6**, 277–278.

Garcia, F., Ramis, J., and Planas, J. (1984). Iron content in starlings, *Sturnus vulgaris* L. *Comp. Biochem. Physiol.* **77A**, 651–654.

Gauthier, M., and Thomas, D.W. (1990). Evaluation of the accuracy of ^{22}Na and tritiated water for the estimation of food consumption and fat reserves in passerine birds. *Can. J. Zool.* **68**, 1590–1594.

Geraci, J. R. (1972). Hyponatremia and the need for dietary salt supplementation in captive pinnipeds. *J. Am. Vet. Med. Assoc.* **161**, 618–623.

Geraci, J. R., and Aubin, D. J. St. (1980). Nutritional disorders of captive fish-eating animals. *In* "The Comparative Pathology of Zoo Animals" (R. J. Montali and G. Migaki, eds.), pp. 41–49. Smithsonian Inst. Press, Washington, D.C.

Gogan, P.J.P., Jessup, D.A., and Barrett, R.H. (1988). Antler anomalies in tule elk. *J. Wildl. Dis.* **24**, 656–662.

Gogan, P. J. P., Jessup, D. A., and Akeson, M. (1989). Copper deficiency in tule elk at Point Reyes, California. *J. Range Manage.* **42**, 233–238.

Gordeuk, V. R., Bacon, B. R., and Brittenham, G. M. (1987). Iron overload: Causes and consequences. *Annu. Rev. Nutr.* **7**, 485–508.

Gorham, J. R., Peckham, J. C., and Alexander, J. (1970). Rickets and osteodystrophia fibrosa in foxes fed a high horsemeat ration. *J. Am. Vet. Med. Assoc.* **156**, 1331–1333.

Green, B. (1978). Estimation of food consumption in the dingo, *Canis familiaris dingo*, by means of ^{22}Na turnover. *Ecology* **59**, 207–210.

Green, B., and Dunsmore, J. D. (1978). Turnover of tritiated water and ^{22}sodium in captive rabbits (*Oryctolagus cuniculus*). *J. Mammal.* **59**, 12–17.

Green, B., and Eberhard, I. (1979). Energy requirements and sodium and water turnovers in two captive marsupial carnivores: The Tasmanian devil, *Sarcophilus harrisii*, and the native cat, *Dasyurus viverrinus*. *Aust. J. Zool.* **27**, 1–8.

Green, B., Dunsmore, J., Bults, H., and Newgrain, K. (1978). Turnover of sodium and water by free-living rabbits, *Oryctolagus cuniculus*. *Aust. Wildl. Res.* **5**, 93–99.

Green, B., Anderson, J., and Whateley, J. (1984). Water and sodium turnover and estimated food consumption in free-living lions (*Panthera leo*) and spotted hyaenas (*Crocuta crocuta*). *J. Mammal.* **65**, 593–599.

Greene, L. W., Baker, J. F., and Hardt, P. F. (1989). Use of animal breeds and breeding to overcome the incidence of grass tetany: A review. *J. Anim. Sci.* **67**, 3463–3469.

Grimshaw, H. M., Ovington, J. D., Betts, M. M., and Gibb, J. A. (1958). The mineral content of birds and insects in plantations of *Pinus silvestris* L. *Oikos* **9**, 26–34.

Hall-Martin, A. J., Skinner, J. B., and Smith, A. (1977). Observations on lactation and milk composition of the giraffe *Giraffa camelopardalis*. *S. Afr. J. Wildl. Res.* **7**, 67–71.

Hambidge, K. M., Casey, C. E., and Krebs, N. F. (1986). Zinc. *In* "Trace Elements in Human and Animal Nutrition" (W. Mertz, ed.), pp. 1–137. Academic Press, New York.

Harbers, L. H., Callahan, S. L., and Ward, G. M. (1980). Release of calcium oxalate crystals from alfalfa in the digestive tracts of domestic and zoo animals. *J. Zoo Anim. Med.* **11**, 52–56.

Harper, J. A., and Labisky, R. F. (1964). The influence of calcium on the distribution of pheasants in Illinois. *J. Wildl. Manage.* **28,** 722–731.

Harthoorn, A. M., and Young, E. (1974). A relationship between acid-base balance and capture myopathy in zebra (*Equus burchelli*) and an apparent therapy. *Vet. Rec.* **95,** 337–342.

Harvey, J. W., and Coleman, M. W. (1982). Iron deficiency anemia in Siberian lynx. *J. Am. Vet. Med. Assoc.* **181,** 1402–1403.

Havera, S. (1978). "Nutrition, Supplemental Feeding, and Body Composition of the Fox Squirrel, *Sciurus niger*, in Central Illinois." Ph.D. Thesis, Univ. Illinois, Urbana-Champaign, Illinois.

Hebert, D. M., and Cowan, I. McT. (1971a). Natural salt licks as part of the ecology of the mountain goat. *Can. J. Zool.* **49,** 605–610.

Hebert, D. M., and Cowan, I. McT. (1971b). White muscle disease in the mountain goat. *J. Wildl. Manage.* **35,** 752–756.

Henderson, B. M., and Winterfield, R. W. (1975). Acute copper toxicosis in the Canada goose. *Avian Dis.* **19,** 385–387.

Henkin, R. I. (1979). "Zinc." Univ. Park Press, Baltimore.

Herd, R.M. (1985). Estimating food intake by captive emus, *Dromaius novaehollandiae*, by means of sodium-22 turnover. *Aust. Wildl. Res.* **12,** 455–460.

Hollander, W. F., and Riddle, D. (1946). Goiter in domestic pigeons. *Poult. Sci.* **25,** 20–27.

Hume, I. D., and Dunning, A. (1979). Nitrogen and electrolyte balance in the wallabies *Thylogale thetis* and *Macropus eugenii* when given saline drinking water. *Comp. Biochem. Physiol.* **63A,** 135–139.

Hurley, L. S., and Keen, C. L. (1987). Manganese. *In* "Trace Elements in Human and Animal Nutrition" (W. Mertz, ed.), pp. 185–223. Academic Press, New York.

Hyvarinen, H., Helle, T., Nieminen, M., Vayrynen, P., and Vayrynen, R. (1977a). The influence of nutrition and seasonal conditions on mineral status in the reindeer. *Can. J. Zool.* **55,** 648–655.

Hyvarinen, H., Kay, R. N. B., and Hamilton, W. J. (1977b). Variation in the weight, specific gravity and composition of the antlers of red deer (*Cervus elaphus* L.). *Br. J. Nutr.* **38,** 301–311.

Irving, J. T. (1964). Dynamics and function of phosphorus. *In* "Mineral Metabolism," Vol. II, Part A (C. L. Comar and F. Bronner, eds.), pp. 249–313. Academic Press, New York.

Jarrett, W. H. F., Jennings, J. W., Murray, M., and Harthoorn, A. M. (1964). Muscular dystrophy in wild Hunter's antelope. *East Afr. Wildl. J.* **2,** 158–159.

Johnston, J.W., and Bildstein, K.L. (1990). Dietary salt as a physiological constraint in white ibis breeding in an estuary. *Physiol. Zool.* **63,** 190–207.

Jones, R. E., Aulerich, R. J., and Ringer, R. K. (1982). Feeding supplemental iodine to mink: Reproductive and histopathologic effects. *J. Toxicol. Environ. Health* **10,** 459–471.

Joshua, I. G., and Mueller, W. J. (1979). The development of a specific appetite for calcium in growing broiler chicks. *Br. Poult. Sci.* **20,** 481–490.

Justice, K. E. (1985). Oxalate digestibility in *Neotoma albigula* and *Neotoma mexicana*. *Oecologia* **67,** 231–234.

Kaldor, I., and Morgan, E. H. (1986). Iron metabolism during lactation and suckling in a marsupial, the quokka (*Setonix brachyurus*). *Comp. Biochem. Physiol.* **84A,** 691–694.

Kam, M., and Degen, A. A. (1989). Efficiency of use of saltbush (*Atriplex halimus*) for growth by fat sand rats (*Psammomys obesus*). *J. Mammal.* **70,** 485–493.

Karstad, L. (1967). Fluorosis in deer (*Odocoileus virginianus*). *Bull. Wildl. Dis. Assoc.* **3,** 42–46.

Kaufman, D. W., and Kaufman, G. A. (1975). Prediction of elemental content in the old-field mouse. *In* "Mineral Cycling in Southeastern Ecosystems" (F. G. Howell, J. B. Gentry, and M. H. Smith, eds.), pp. 528–535. ERDA Symp. Series Conf. 740513. National Technical Information Service, Springfield, Virginia.

Kaufman, G. A., and Kaufman, D. W. (1975). Effects of age, sex, and pelage phenotype on the elemental composition of the old-field mouse. *In* "Mineral Cycling in Southeastern Ecosystems" (F. G. Howell, J. B. Gentry, and M. H. Smith, eds.), pp. 518–527. ERDA Symp. Series Conf. 740513. National Technical Information Service, Springfield, Virginia.

Kay, C. E., Tourangeau, P. C., and Gordon, C. C. (1975). Industrial fluorosis in wild mule and whitetail deer from western Montana. *Fluoride* **8**, 182–191.

Keiver, K. M., Draper, H. H., Hadley, M., and Ronald, K. (1984). Calcium and phosphorus balance in juvenile harp seals (*Phoca groenlandica*). *Can. J. Zool.* **62**, 777–782.

Knox, D. P., Reid, H. W., and Peters, J. G. (1987). An outbreak of selenium responsive unthriftiness in farmed red deer (*Cervus elaphus*). *Vet. Rec.* **120**, 91–92.

Kopischke, E. D. (1966). Selection of calcium and magnesium-bearing grit by pheasants in Minnesota. *J. Wildl. Manage.* **30**, 276–279.

Kopischke, E. D., and Nelson, M. M. (1966). Grit availability and pheasant densities in Minnesota and South Dakota. *J. Wildl. Manage.* **30**, 269–275.

Korschgen, L. J., Chambers, G. D., and Sadler, K. C. (1965). Digestion rate of limestone force-fed to pheasants. *J. Wildl. Manage.* **29**, 820–823.

Krapu, G. L., and Swanson, G. A. (1975). Some nutritional aspects of reproduction in prairie nesting pintails. *J. Wildl. Manage.* **39**, 156–162.

Krausman, P. R., and Bissonette, J. A. (1977). Bone-chewing behavior of desert mule deer. *Southwest. Nat.* **22**, 149–150.

Kreulen, D. (1975). Wildebeest habitat selection on the Serengeti plains, Tanzania, in relation to calcium and lactation: A preliminary report. *East Afr. Wildl. J.* **13**, 297–304.

Krishnamachari, K. A. V. R. (1987). Fluorine. *In* "Trace Elements in Human and Animal Nutrition" (W. Mertz, ed.), pp. 365–415. Academic Press, New York.

Kubota, J. (1975). Areas of molybdenum toxicity to grazing animals in the western states. *J. Range Manage.* **28**, 252–256.

Kubota, J., and Allaway, W. H. (1972). Geographic distribution of trace element problems. *In* "Micronutrients in Agriculture," (J. J. Mortvedt, P. M. Giordano, and W. L. Lindsay, eds.), pp. 525–554. Soil Sci. Soc. Am., Madison, Wisconsin.

Kubota, J., Naphan, E. A., and Oberly, G. H. (1982). Fluoride in thermal spring water and in plants of Nevada and its relationship to fluorosis in animals. *J. Range Manage.* **35**, 188–192.

Langman, V. A. (1978). Giraffe pica behavior and pathology as indicators of nutritional stress. *J. Wildl. Manage.* **42**, 141–147.

Legg, S. P., and Sears, L. (1960). Zinc sulphate treatment of parakeratosis in cattle. *Nature (London)* **186**, 1061–1062.

Leighton, M.J., Peters, T.J., Hill, R., Smith, G.D., Holt, W., and Jones, D.M. (1990). Subcellular distribution of copper in the liver of fetal deer in the last month of gestation. *Res. Vet. Sci.* **49**, 298–305.

Leininger, W. C., Taylor, J. E., and Wambolt, C. L. (1977). Poisonous range plants of Montana. *Coop. Extension Service, Montana State Univ., Bull.* 348.

Leon, B., and Belonje, P. C. (1979). Calcium, phosphorus, and magnesium excretion in the rock hyrax, *Procavia capensis. Comp. Biochem. Physiol.* **64A**, 67–72.

Levander, O. A. (1986). Selenium. *In* "Trace Elements in Human and Animal Nutrition" (W. Mertz, ed.), pp. 209–279. Academic Press, New York.

Loh, T. T., and Kaldor, I. (1973). Iron in milk and milk fractions of lactating rats, rabbits and quokkas. *Comp. Biochem. Physiol.* **44B**, 337–346.

Lonnerdal, B., Keen, C. L., and Hurley, L. S. (1981). Iron, copper, zinc, and manganese in milk. *Annu. Rev. Nutr.* **1**, 149–174.

Lowenstine, L. J. (1986). Nutritional disorders of birds. *In* "Zoo and Wild Animal Medicine" (M. E. Fowler, ed.), pp. 201–212. W. B. Saunders Co., Philadelphia, Pennsylvania.

Lowenstine, L. J., and Petrak, M. L. (1980). Iron pigment in the livers of birds. *In* "The Comparative Pathology of Zoo Animals" (R. J. Montali and G. Migaki, eds.), pp. 127–135. Smithsonian Inst. Press, Washington, D.C.

Luick, J. R., White, R. G., Gau, A. M., and Jenness, R. (1974). Compositional changes in the milk secreted by grazing reindeer. I. Gross composition and ash. *J. Dairy Sci.* **57**, 1325–1333.

Macapinlae, M. P., Barney, G. H., Pearson, W. N., and Derby, W. J. (1967). Production of zinc deficiency in the squirrel monkey (*Saimisi sciureus*). *J. Nutr.* **93**, 499–510.

MacLean, S. F., Jr. (1974). Lemming bones as a source of calcium for Arctic sandpipers (*Calidris* spp.) *Ibis* **116**, 552–557.

Mahon, C. L. (1969). Mineral deficiencies in desert bighorns and domestic livestock in San Juan County. *Trans. Desert Bighorn Coun.* **13**, 27–32.

Mattfeld, G. F., Wiley, J. E., III, and Behrend, D. F. (1972). Salt versus browse-seasonal baits for deer trapping. *J. Wildl. Manage.* **36**, 996–998.

Mayland, H. F., and Wilkinson, S. R. (1989). Soil factors affecting magnesium availability in plant-animal systems: A review. *J. Anim. Sci.* **67**, 3437–3444.

Mayoh, K. R., and Zach, R. (1986). Grit ingestion by nestling tree swallows and house wrens. *Can. J. Zool.* **64**, 2090–2093.

McCullough, D. R. (1969). The tule elk: It's history, behavior, and ecology. *Univ. Calif. Publ. Zool.* **88**.

McDonald, P., Edwards, R. A., and Greenhalgh, J. F. D. (1973). "Animal Nutrition." Longman, New York.

Mertz, W. (1986). "Trace Elements in Human and Animal Nutrition," Vol. 2. Academic Press, New York.

Mertz, W. (1987). "Trace Elements in Human and Animal Nutrition," Vol. 1. Academic Press, New York.

Miller, R. B. (1961). The chemical composition of rainwater at Taita, New Zealand, 1956–1958. *N. Z. J. Sci.* **4**, 844–853.

Miller, W. J., Britton, W. M., and Ansari, M. S. (1972). Magnesium in livestock nutrition. *In* "Magnesium in the Environment" (J. B. Jones, Jr., M. C. Blount, and S. R. Wilkinson, eds.), pp. 109–130. Taylor County Printing Co., Reynolds, Georgia.

Mole, S., Rogler, J. C., Morell, C. J., and Butler, L. G. (1990). Herbivore growth reduction by tannins: Use of Waldbauer ratio techniques and manipulation of salivary protein production to elucidate mechanisms of action. *Biochem. Syst. Ecol.* **18**, 183–197.

Morgulis, S. (1931). Studies on the chemical composition of bone ash. *J. Biol. Chem.* **93**, 455–466.

Morris, K.D., and Bradshaw, S.D. (1981). Water and sodium turnover in coastal and inland populations of the ash-grey mouse, *Pseudomys albocinereus* (Gould), in western Australia. *Aust. J. Zool.* **29**, 519–533.

Morton, D., and Janning, J. T. (1982). Iron balance in the common vampire bat *Desmodus rotundus*. *Comp. Biochem. Physiol.* **73A**, 421–425.

Muller, J. (1971). Regulation of aldosterone biosynthesis. *Monogr. Endocrinol.* **5**, 1–137.

Mundy, P. J., and Ledger, J. A. (1976). Griffon vultures, carnivores and bones. *S. Afr. J. Sci.* **72**, 106–110.

Murray, M. (1967). The pathology of some diseases found in wild animals in East Africa. *East Afr. Wildl. J.* **5**, 37–45.

Myers, K. (1967). Morphological changes in the adrenal glands of wild rabbits. *Nature (London)* **213**, 147–150.

Nagy, K. A., and Milton, K. (1979). Aspects of dietary quality, nutrient assimilation and water balance in wild howler monkeys (*Alouatta palliata*). *Oecologia* **39**, 249–258.

Nagy, K. A., Shoemaker, V. H., and Costa, W. R. (1976). Water, electrolyte, and nitrogen budgets of jackrabbits (*Lepus californicus*) in the Mojave Desert. *Physiol. Zool.* **49**, 351–363.

National Research Council (NRC). (1971). Atlas of nutritional data on United States and Canadian feeds. Nat. Acad. Sci., Washington, D.C.

National Research Council (NRC). (1977). Nutrient requirements of rabbits. Publ. No. 2607. Nat. Acad. Sci., Washington, D.C.

National Research Council (NRC). (1978a). Nutrient requirements of laboratory animals. Publ. No. 2767. Nat. Acad. Sci., Washington, D.C.

National Research Council (NRC). (1978b). Nutrient requirements of nonhuman primates. Publ. No. 2786. Nat. Acad. Sci., Washington, D.C.

National Research Council (NRC). (1982). Nutrient requirements of mink and foxes. Nat. Acad. Sci., Washington, D.C., 72 pp.

National Research Council (NRC). (1984). Nutrient requirements of poultry. Nat. Acad. Sci., Washington, D.C., 71 pp.

Nelson, G. H. (1983). Urinary calculi in two otters (*Amblyocix sernaria*). *J. Zoo Anim. Med.* **14**, 72–73.

Nelson, M. M., Moyle, J. B., and Farnham, A. L. (1966). Cobalt levels in foods and livers of pheasants. *J. Wildl. Manage.* **30**, 423–425.

Newberne, P. M. (1970). Syndromes of nutritional deficiency disease in nonhuman primates. *In* "Feeding and Nutrition of Nonhuman Primates" (R. S. Harris, ed.), pp. 205–232. Academic Press, New York.

Newman, J. R., and Yu, M. (1976). Fluorosis in black-tailed deer. *J. Wildl. Dis.* **12**, 39–41.

Nielsen, F. H. (1984). Ultratrace elements in nutrition. *Annu. Rev. Nutr.* **4**, 21–41.

Obeck, D. K. (1978). Galvanized caging as a potential factor in the development of the "fading infant" or "white monkey" syndrome. *Lab. Anim. Sci.* **28**, 698–704.

Ohlendorf, H. M., Hothem, R. L., Bunck, C. M., Aldrich, T. W., and Moore, J. F. (1986). Relationships between selenium concentrations and avian reproduction. *Trans. North Am. Wildl. Nat. Res. Conf.* **51**, 330–342.

Ojanen, M., Haarakangas, H., and Hyvarinen, H. (1975). Seasonal changes in bone mineral content and alkaline phosphatase activity in the house sparrow (*Passer domesticus* L.). *Comp. Biochem. Physiol.* **50A**, 581–585.

Osman, N.H.I., and Sykes, A.R. (1989). Comparative effects of dietary molybdenum concentration on distribution of copper in plasma in sheep and red deer (*Cervus elaphus*). *Proc. N. Z. Soc. Anim. Prod.* **49**, 15–19.

Palo, R. T. (1987). "Phenols as Defensive Compounds in Birch (*Betula* spp.): Implications for Digestion and Metabolism in Browsing Mammals." Ph.D. Thesis, Swedish Univ. Agric. Sci., Uppsala.

Parmenter, R. A. (1984). "Food and Energy Intake of Coyotes Determined from Turnover of Tritiated Water and Sodium-22." M.S. Thesis, Colorado State Univ., Fort Collins, Colorado.

Pattee, O.H., Wiemeyer, S.N., and Swineford, D.M. (1988). Effects of dietary fluoride on reproduction in eastern screech-owls. *Arch. Environ. Contam. Toxicol.* **17**, 213–218.

Pehrson, A. (1983). Digestibility and retention of food components in caged mountain hares *Lepus timidus* during the winter. *Holarctic Ecol.* **6**, 395–403.

Pinowski, J., Pinowska, B., Krasnicki, K., and Tomek, T. (1983). Chemical composition of growth in nestling rooks *Corvus frugilegus*. *Ornis Scand.* **14**, 289–298.

Pletscher, D. H. (1987). Nutrient budgets for white-tailed deer in New England with special reference to sodium. *J. Mammal.* **68**, 330–336.

Randall, M. G., and Patnaik, A. K. (1981). Hepatopathy with excessive iron storage in mynah birds. *J. Am. Vet. Med. Assoc.* **179**, 1214.

Ratcliffe, H. L. (1965). Zoological gardens: Institutes of neglected opportunity. *Int. Zoo Yearb.* **5,** 207–209.

Rehg, J. E., Burek, J. D., Strandberg, J. D., and Montali, R. J. (1980). Hemochromatosis in the rock hyrax. In "The Comparative Pathology of Zoo Animals" (R. J. Montali and G. Migaki, eds.), pp. 113–120. Smithsonian Inst. Press, Washington, D.C.

Reichardt, P. B., Bryant, J. P., Clausen, T. P., and Wieland, G. D. (1984). Defense of winter-dormant Alaska paper birch against snowshoe hares. *Oecologia* **65,** 58–69.

Reid, T. C., McAllum, H. J. F., and Johnstone, P. D. (1980). Liver copper concentrations in red deer (*Cervus elaphus*) and wapiti (*C. canadensis*) in New Zealand. *Res. Vet. Sci.* **28,** 261–262.

Richardson, P. R. K., Mundy, P. J., and Plug, I. (1986). Bone crushing carnivores and their significance to osteodystrophy in griffon vulture chicks. *J. Zool.* **210,** 23–43.

Rings, R. W., Doyle, R. E., Hooper, B. E., and Kraner, K. L. (1969). Osteomalacia in the golden-mantled ground squirrel (*Citellus lateralis*). *J. Am. Vet. Med. Assoc.* **155,** 1224–1227.

Robbins, C. T., Parish, S. M., and Robbins, B. L. (1985). Selenium and glutathione peroxidase activity in mountain goats. *Can. J. Zool.* **63,** 1544–1547.

Robbins, C. T., Oftedal, O. T., and O'Rourke, K. I. (1987). Lactation, early nutrition, and hand-rearing of wild ungulates, with special reference to deer. In "Biology and Management of the Cervidae" (C. M. Wemmer, ed.), pp. 429–442. Smithsonian Inst. Press, Washington, D.C.

Romanoff, A. L., and Romanoff, A. J. (1949). "The Avian Egg." Wiley, New York.

Rugangazi, B. M., and Maloiy, G. M. O. (1988). Studies on renal excretion of potassium in the dik-dik antelope. *Comp. Biochem. Physiol.* **90,** 121–126.

Rush, W. M. (1932). "Northern Yellowstone Elk Study." Montana Fish Game Comm., Helena, Montana.

Russell, W. C. (1970). Hypothyroidism in a grizzly bear. *J. Am. Vet. Med. Assoc.* **157,** 656–662.

Russell, W. C. (1977). Iodine-induced goiter in penguins. *J. Am. Vet. Med. Assoc.* **171,** 959–960.

Samson, J., Jorgenson, J. T., and Wishart, W. D. (1989). Glutathione peroxidase activity and selenium levels in Rocky Mountain bighorn sheep and mountain goats. *Can. J. Zool.* **67,** 2493–2496.

Sandstead, H. H., Strobel, D. A., Logan, G. M., Jr., Marks, E. O., and Jacob, R. A. (1978). Zinc deficiency in pregnant rhesus monkeys: Effects on behavior of infants. *Am. J. Clin. Nutr.* **31,** 844–849.

Schlesinger, W. H., and Hasey, M. M. (1980). The nutrient content of precipitation, dry fallout, and intercepted aerosols in the chaparral of southern California. *Am. Midl. Nat.* **103,** 114–122.

Schryver, H. F., and Hintz, H. F. (1982). Trace elements in horse nutrition. *Compend. Continuing Education* **4,** S534–S540.

Schryver, H. F., Oftedal, O. T., Williams, J., Cymbaluk, N. F., Antczak, D., and Hintz, H. F. (1986). A comparison of the mineral composition of milk of domestic and captive wild equids (*Equus przewalski, E. zebra, E. burchelli, E. caballus, E. assinus*). *Comp. Biochem. Physiol.* **85A,** 233–235.

Schwarz, K., and Foltz, C. M. (1957). Selenium as an integral part of factor 3 against dietary necrotic liver degeneration. *J. Am. Chem. Soc.* **79,** 3292–3293.

Scoggins, B. A., Blair-West, J. R., Coghlan, J. P., Denton, D. A., Myers, K., Nelson, J. F., Orchard, E., and Wright, R. D. (1970). The physiological and morphological response of mammals to changes in their sodium status. In "Hormones and the Environment" (G. K. Benson, and J. G. Phillips, eds.), pp. 577–602. Cambridge Univ. Press, Cambridge, England.

Scott, M. L., van Teinhoven, A., Holm, E. R., and Reynolds, R. E. (1960). Studies on the sodium, chlorine and iodine requirements of young pheasants and quail. *J. Nutr.* **71,** 282–288.

Scott, P. P. (1968). The special features of nutrition of cats, with observations on wild felidae nutrition in the London Zoo. *Symp. Zool. Soc. London* **21,** 21–36.

Seastedt, T. R., and MacLean, S. F., Jr. (1977). Calcium supplements in the diet of nestling Lapland longspurs *Calcarius lapponicus* near Barrow, Alaska. *Ibis* **119**, 531–533.

Sekulic, R., and Estes, R. D. (1977). A note on bone chewing in the sable antelope in Kenya. *Mammalia* **41**, 537–539.

Shearer, K. D. (1984). Changes in elemental composition of hatchery-reared rainbow trout, *Salmo gairdneri*, associated with growth and reproduction. *Can. J. Fish Aquat. Sci.* **4**, 1592–1600.

Shrift, A. (1972). Selenium toxicity. *In* "Phytochemical Ecology" (J. B. Harborne, ed.), pp. 145–161. Academic Press, New York.

Shupe, J. L., Olson, A. E., Peterson, H. B., and Low, J. B. (1984). Fluoride toxicosis in wild ungulates. *J. Am. Vet. Med. Assoc.* **185**, 1295–1300.

Skar, H. J., Hagvar, S., Hagen, A., and Ostbye, E. (1975). Food habits and body composition of adult and juvenile meadow pipit (*Anthus pratensis* (L.)). *In* "Fennoscandian Tundra Ecosystems." Ecol. Studies, Vol. 17, Part 2 (F. E. Wielgolaski, ed.), pp. 160–169. Springer-Verlag, New York.

Slusher, R., Bistner, S. I., and Kircher, C. (1965). Nutritional secondary hyperparathyroidism in a tiger. *J. Am. Vet. Med. Assoc.* **147**, 1109–1115.

Smith, M. C., Leatherland, J. F., and Myers, K. (1978). Effects of seasonal availability of sodium and potassium on the adrenal cortical function of a wild population of snowshoe hares, *Lepus americanus*. *Can. J. Zool.* **56**, 1869–1876.

Smith, S. E., Gardner, R. W., and Swanson, G. A. (1963). A study of the adequacy of cobalt nutrition in New York deer. *N. Y. Fish Game J.* **10**, 225–227.

Snyder, S. B., Omdahl, J. L., and Froelich, J. W. (1980). Osteomalacia and nutritional secondary hyperparathyroidism in semi-free-ranging troop of Japanese monkeys. *In* "The Comparative Pathology of Zoo Animals" (R. J. Montali and G. Migaki, eds.), pp. 51–57. Smithsonian Inst. Press, Washington, D.C.

Staaland, H., White, R. W., Luick, J. R., and Holleman, D. F. (1980). Dietary influences on sodium and potassium metabolism of reindeer. *Can. J. Zool.* **58**, 1728–1734.

Stanbury, J. B., and Hetzel, B. S. (eds.). (1980). "Endemic goiter and endemic cretinism: Iodine nutrition in health and disease." John Wiley and Sons, New York.

Stephenson, D. C., and Brown, R. D. (1984). Calcium kinetics in male white-tailed deer. *J. Nutr.* **114**, 1014–1024.

St. Louis, V.L., and Breebaart, L. (1991). Calcium supplements in the diet of nestling tree swallows near acid sensitive lakes. *Condor* **93**, 286–294.

Stoszek, M. J., Willmes, H., and Kessler, W. B. (1980). Trace-mineral metabolism of Idaho pronghorn antelope. *Northwest Sec. Wildl. Soc. Annu. Meeting, Banff, Alberta, Canada.*

Stout, F. M., Oldfield, J. E., and Adair, J. (1960). Aberrant iron metabolism and the "cotton-fur" abnormality in mink. *J. Nutr.* **72**, 46–52.

Strzelewicz, M. A., Ullrey, D. E., Schafer, J. F., and Bacon, J. P. (1985). Feeding insectivores: Increasing the calcium content of wax moth (*Galleria mellonella*) larvae. *J. Zoo Anim. Med.* **16**, 25–27.

Suttie, J. W., Hamilton, R. J., Clay, A. C., Tobin, M. L., and Moore, W. G. (1985). Effects of fluoride ingestion on white-tailed deer (*Odocoileus virginianus*). *J. Wildl. Dis.* **21**, 283–288.

Suttie, J. W., Dickie, R., Clay, A. C., Nielsen, P., Mahan, W. E., Baumann, D. P., and Hamilton, R. J. (1987). Effects of fluoride emissions from a modern primary aluminum smelter on a local population of white-tailed deer (*Odocoileus virginianus*). *J. Wildl. Dis.* **23**, 135–143.

Sykes, G., Hardaswick, V., and Heck, W. (1982). Nutritional deficiency and perosis in peregrine falcons. *Hawk Chalk* **21**, 33–36.

Tankersley, N. G., and Gasaway, W. C. (1983). Mineral lick use by moose in Alaska. *Can. J. Zool.* **61**, 2242–2249.

Taylor, J. J. (1984). Iron accumulation in avian species in captivity. *Dodo* **21**, 126–131.

Terlecki, S., Done, J. T., and Clegg, F. G. (1964). Enzootic ataxia of red deer. *Br. Vet. J.* **120**, 311–321.

Thurston, C. E. (1958). Sodium and potassium content of 34 species of fish. *J. Am. Dietet. Assoc.* **34**, 396–399.

Tomson, F. N., and Lotshaw, R. R. (1978). Hyperphosphatemia and hypocalcemia in lemurs. *J. Am. Vet. Med. Assoc.* **173**, 1103–1106.

Tomson, F. N., Keller, G. L., and Knapke, F. B. (1980). Nutritional secondary hyperparathyroidism in a group of lemurs. *In* "The Comparative Pathology of Zoo Animals" (R. J. Montali and G. Migaki, eds.), pp. 59–64. Smithsonian Inst. Press, Washington, D.C.

Trost, R. E. (1981). Dynamics of grit selection and retention in captive mallards. *J. Wildl. Manage.* **45**, 64–73.

Trusk, A. M., and Crissey, S. (1987). Comparison of calcium and phosphorus levels in crickets fed a high calcium diet versus those dusted with supplement. *Proc. Dr. Scholl Nutr. Conf.* **7**, 93–99.

Uete, T., and Venning, E. H. (1962). Interplay between various adrenal cortical steroids with respect to electrolyte excretion. *Endocrinology* **71**, 768–778.

Underwood, E. J. (1977). "Trace Elements in Human and Animal Nutrition." Academic Press, New York.

Van Pelt, R. W., and Caley, M. T. (1974). Nutritional secondary hyperparathyroidism in Alaskan red fox kits. *J. Wildl. Dis.* **10**, 47–52.

Wacker, W. E. C., and Vallee, B. L. (1964). Magnesium. In "Mineral Metabolism," Vol. II, Part A (C. L. Comar and F. Bronner, eds.), pp. 483–521. Academic Press, New York.

Wallach, J. D. (1970). Nutritional diseases of exotic animals. *J. Am. Vet. Med. Assoc.* **157**, 583–599.

Wallach, J. D. (1971). Nutritional problems in zoos. *Proc. Cornell Nutr. Conf. Feed Manuf.*, 10–19.

Wallach, J. D., and Flieg, G. M. (1967). Nutritional secondary hyperparathyroidism in captive psittacine birds. *J. Am. Vet. Med. Assoc.* **151**, 880–883.

Wallach, J. D., and Flieg, G. M. (1969). Nutritional secondary hyperparathyroidism in captive birds. *J. Am. Vet. Med. Assoc.* **155**, 1046–1051.

Wallach, J. D., and Flieg, G. M. (1970). Cramps and fits in carnivorous birds. *Int. Zoo Yearb.* **10**, 3–4.

Walton, K.C. (1988). Environmental fluoride and fluorosis in mammals. *Mammal. Rev.* **18**, 77–90.

Ward, G. M., and Nagy, J. G. (1976). Molybdenum and copper in Colorado forages, molybdenum toxicity in deer, and copper supplementation in cattle. *In* "Molybdenum in the Environment," Vol. I (W. R. Chappell and K. K. Petersen, eds.), pp. 97–113. Dekker, New York.

Watkins, B. E., and Ullrey, D. E. (1983a). Iodine concentration in plants used by white-tailed deer in Michigan. *J. Wildl. Manage.* **47**, 1220–1226.

Watkins, B. E., and Ullrey, D. E. (1983b). Thyroid iodine and serum thyroid hormone levels in wild white-tailed deer (*Odocoileus virginianus*) from central Michigan. *Can. J. Zool.* **61**, 1116–1119.

Weeks, H. P., Jr. (1978). Characteristics of mineral licks and behavior of visiting white-tailed deer in southern Indiana. *Am. Midl. Nat.* **100**, 384–395.

Weeks, H. P., Jr., and Kirkpatrick, C. M. (1976). Adaptations of white-tailed deer to naturally occurring sodium deficiencies. *J. Wildl. Manage.* **40**, 610–625.

Weeks, H. P., Jr., and Kirkpatrick, C. M. (1978). Salt preferences and sodium drive phenology in fox squirrels and woodchucks. *J. Mammal.* **59**, 531–542.

Weiner, J. G., Brisbin, I. L., Jr., and Smith, M. H. (1975). Chemical composition of white-tailed deer: Whole-body concentrations of macro- and micronutrients. *In* "Mineral Cycling in Southeastern Ecosystems" (F. G. Howell, J. B. Gentry, and M. H. Smith, eds.), pp. 536–541. ERDA Symp. Series Conf. 740513. National Technical Information Service, Springfield, Virginia.

Weir, J. S. (1972). Spatial distribution of elephants in an African National Park in relation to environmental sodium. *Oikos* 23, 1–13.

Weir, J. S. (1973). Exploitation of water soluble sodium by elephants in Murchison Falls National Park, Uganda. *East Afr. Wildl. J.* **11**, 1–7.

Welinder, B.S. (1974). The crustacean cuticle-I. Studies on the composition of the cuticle. *Comp. Biochem. Physiol.* 47A, 779–787.

Widdowson, E. M., and Dickerson, J. W. T. (1964). Chemical composition of the body. *In* "Mineral Metabolism," Vol. II, Part A (C. L. Comar and F. Bronner, eds.), pp. 1–247. Academic Press, New York.

Wiener, G., Woolliams, J. A., Woolliams, C., and Field, A. C. (1985). Genetic selection to produce lines of sheep differing in plasma copper concentrations. *Anim. Prod.* **40**, 465–473.

Wilde, W. S. (1962). Potassium. *In* "Mineral Metabolism," Vol. II, Part B (C. L. Comar and F. Bronner, eds.), pp. 73–107. Academic Press, New York.

Wilkinson, S. R., Stuedemann, J. A., Jones, J. B., Jr., Jackson, W. A., and Dobson, J. W. (1972). Environmental factors affecting magnesium concentrations and tetanigenicity of pastures. *In* "Magnesium in the Environment" (J. B. Jones, Jr., M. C. Blount, and S. R. Wilkinson, eds.), pp. 153–175. Taylor County Printing Co., Reynolds, Georgia.

Wilson, P. R. (1989). Body weight and serum copper concentrations of farmed red deer stags following oral copper oxide wire administration. *N. Z. Vet. J.* **37**, 94–97.

Woolliams, J. A., Wiener, G., Woolliams, C., and Suttle, N. F. (1985). Retention of copper in the liver of sheep genetically selected for high and low concentrations of copper in plasma. *Anim. Prod.* **41**, 219–226.

Zervanos, S. M., McCort, W. D., and Graves, H. B. (1983). Salt and water balance of feral versus domestic hampshire hogs. *Physiol. Zool.* **56**, 67–77.

Zumpt, I. F., and Heine, E. W. P. (1978). Some veterinary aspects of bontebok in the Cape of Good Hope Nature Reserve. *South Afr. J. Wildl. Res.* **8**, 131–134.

6

Vitamins

The scientist is free to ask any question, to doubt any assertion, to seek for any evidence, to correct any error.

ROBERT OPPENHEIMER

Vitamins are organic compounds that usually occur in food in minute amounts and are distinct from carbohydrates, fat, and protein. They are essential for health, maintenance, and production. When vitamins are absent from the diet or are not properly absorbed or used, characteristic deficiency diseases appear. Although many vitamins cannot be synthesized by the animal and therefore must be obtained from the diet, bacterial synthesis of some vitamins in the gastrointestinal tract can reduce the requirement. Free-ranging wildlife must continually adapt their food habits to avoid diets deficient in one or more of the vitamins or precursors.

Vitamins are classified as fat-soluble (vitamins A, D, E, and K) or water-soluble (thiamin, B_1; riboflavin, B_2; nicotinic acid or niacin; pyridoxine, B_6; pantothenic acid; biotin; folic acid; cyanocobalamin, B_{12}; choline; ascorbic acid, C; and *myo*-inositol). Fat-soluble vitamins are absorbed in the intestinal tract with fat and are often stored in large concentrations that can be used during periods of dietary inadequacy. Excesses of fat-soluble vitamins, primarily vitamins A and D, can be highly toxic. Conversely, water-soluble vitamins, with the exception of the liver storage of vitamin B_{12} and riboflavin, are generally not stored in large amounts and thus are needed in a rather constant dietary supply. Because excesses of water-soluble vitamins are readily excreted in the urine, toxic overdoses seldom, if ever, occur.

I. FAT-SOLUBLE VITAMINS

A. Vitamin A

Vitamin A has been of interest to wildlife biologists in North America since Nestler and his co-workers (Nestler, 1946; Nestler *et al.*, 1949a, 1949b) reported on its importance to bobwhite quail. Quail survival, egg production, egg hatch-

TABLE 6.1

Fat-Soluble Vitamin Requirements or Allowances for Growth and Reproduction in Several Wildlife Species per Kilogram of Dry Diet

Species	A[a] (IU)	D₃[b] (IU)	E[c] (IU)	K (mg)	Reference
Birds					
Japanese quail	5,000	1,200	12–25	1.0	NRC, 1984
Ducks and geese (domestic)	4,000	220–500		0.4	NRC, 1984
Pheasant	4,000	900	10–25	1.0	NRC, 1984
Turkey (domestic)	4,000	900	10–25	1.0	NRC, 1984
Mammals					
Fox	2,440				NRC, 1982
Guinea pig	23,000	1,000	50	5.0	NRC, 1978a
Hamster	6,700	2,484	3	4.0	NRC, 1978a
Laboratory mouse	500	150	20	3.0	NRC, 1978a
Laboratory rat	4,000	1,000	30	0.05	NRC, 1978a
Mink	5,930		27		NRC, 1982
Nonhuman primates	10,000	2,000	50		NRC, 1978b

[a] 1 IU = 0.3 μg retinol
[b] 1 IU = 0.025 μg cholecalciferol
[c] 1 IU = 1 mg DL-α-tocopheryl acetate

ability, and growth generally increased as vitamin A was added to a deficient basal diet. Requirement estimates vary widely between species and may reflect true differences between the species or simply differences in experimental conditions or requirement criteria (NAS, 1975) (Table 6.1).

Acute deficiencies of vitamin A produce debilitating signs because of its importance in vision and the maintenance and growth of epithelial derivatives (Table 6.2). Vitamin A deficiencies are far more common in captive than in free-ranging wildlife because of the feeding of inadequate diets. Captive carnivores fed exclusively on eviscerated fish or meat without liver or other internal organs, fat, cod liver oil, or synthetic sources of vitamin A and granivores are prone to deficiencies (Warner, 1961; Heywood, 1967; Scott, 1968; Wallach, 1970; Halliwell and Graham, 1976; O'Sullivan et al., 1977; Lowenstine, 1986; Ghebremeskel et al., 1989). The primary storage site of vitamin A and β-carotene (provitamin A) in animals, and therefore a major dietary source in carnivores, is the liver (Table 6.3) (Dierenfeld et al., 1991). Smaller amounts can be stored in the kidneys, body fat, lungs, and adrenal glands (Thompson and Baumann, 1950; Scott, 1968). Coupled with the inadequacy of a pure meat diet, a higher requirement may also exist for cats, polar bears, and perhaps other specialized carnivores than for other species (Heywood, 1967; Wortman and Larue, 1974;

TABLE 6.2

General Functions and Reported Deficiency Symptoms of Fat-Soluble Vitamins

Vitamin	Major functions	Deficiency signs
A (Retinol, retinal, and retinoic acid)	Major constituent of visual pigment (rhodopsin), maintenance, differentiation and proliferation of epithelial tissue, glycoprotein synthesis	Nervous disorders, reduced fertility or sterility, birth defects, reduced egg hatchability and chick survival, reduced growth or loss of weight, oral and nasal pustules, weakness, night blindness, impaired eyesight because of copious lacrimation or none at all, corneal degeneration, eye infections and eyelid adhesion, bone and teeth abnormalities, lack of alertness, visceral gout, unsteady gait and incoordination, ruffled-droopy appearance
D (D_2-ergocalciferol; D_3-cholecalciferol)	Necessary for active calcium absorption from the gut, calcium metabolism and resorption from bone, HPO_4 resorption from kidney tubules	Rickets, osteomalacia, nervous disorders
E (tocopherol)	Antioxidant	Yellow fat disease (steatitis—orange or brownish yellow discoloration of body fat or body organs), sudden death when subjected to stress, dystrophic lesions of intercostal and myocardial muscles, hypersensitivity, decreased activity and depression, anorexia, fever, lumpiness of subcutaneous fat, severe edema, exudative diathesis or fluid accumulation in the pleural and abdominal cavity and body tissues, nutritional muscular dystrophy, severe hemolytic anemia with blood in urine, weight loss, abnormal pelage molt, unsteady gait, fur discoloration, reproductive failure, ataxia, electrolyte imbalances
K (Phylloquinone and menaquinone)	Necessary for blood clotting	Stillbirth or death of neonates soon after birth, hemorrhaging

Foster, 1981). Yellow corn is one of the few commercially available grains having significant amounts of provitamin A.

Few, if any, cases of acute vitamin A deficiencies have been observed in free-ranging wildlife (Notini, 1941; Cowan and Fowle, 1944; Nestler *et al.*, 1949b). Liver vitamin A levels vary seasonally in free-ranging wildlife as intake and requirements fluctuate. Incipient vitamin A deficiencies based on liver concentrations relative to domestic animal standards were reported in 2–3% of deer killed by cars during winter in Michigan (Youatt *et al.*, 1976). Although Nestler et al. (1949b) suggested that free-ranging game birds might be limited directly by vitamin A, later researchers disagreed (Schultz, 1948, 1959; Jones, 1950; Thompson and Baumann, 1950). Vitamin A sources, primarily green vegetation, were always in sufficient quantities to prevent complete depletion in Gambel's quail in Arizona, even in the driest years (Hungerford, 1964). However, when average body reserves fell below 550 µg/liver or 175 µg/g of liver, sex organs regressed even during the normal breeding period.

Thus, it has often been postulated that vitamin A synchronizes reproduction in desert birds and mammals with rains and the emergence of green vegetation (Hungerford, 1964; Reichman and Van De Graaff, 1975; Kelley *et al.*, 1987). However, Leopold *et al.* (1976) and Labov (1977) suggested that vitamin A was less important than other plant constituents to desert mammals and birds as an actual regulator of reproduction. Phytoestrogens, substances produced by plants having estrogenic effects, were more abundant in the stunted vegetation growing during dry years but were nearly absent in the luxuriant growth of wet years. The reproductive effort of free-ranging quail was inversely proportional to plant estrogen content, and captive feeding trials further demonstrated the inhibitory effects of plant estrogens on quail reproduction (de Man and Peeke, 1982). More recently, a reproductive stimulant (6–methoxybenzoxazolinone) for desert rodents has been identified in sprouting grasses (Berger *et al.*, 1981; Rowsemitt and O'Connor, 1989). Thus, it is unlikely that vitamin A regulates reproduction in free-ranging wildlife.

Vitamin A is not found in plants but does occur in animals. Fortunately, β-carotene and other provitamin A sources are widely distributed in plants (yellow and orange fruits and vegetables and green leaves) and insects and can be hydrolyzed to retinal and subsequently retinol in the intestinal wall (Haugen and Hove, 1960) and liver (McDonald *et al.*, 1973). Retinol and retinal are interchangeable forms of the vitamin that satisfy all requirements. Retinoic acid can meet many of the requirements but cannot function in vision or reproduction. Thus, animals consuming vitamin A–deficient diets supplemented with retinoic acid will be blind and sterile, but otherwise healthy (DeLuca, 1979; Goodman, 1979; Smith and Goodman, 1979). Carotene and other dietary carotenoids also are precursors for the red, pink, orange, and yellow pigments in the feathers and skins of many birds (Brush, 1981).

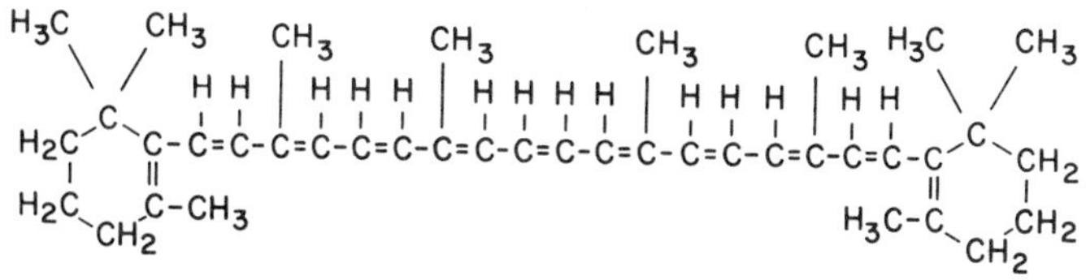

β-Carotene

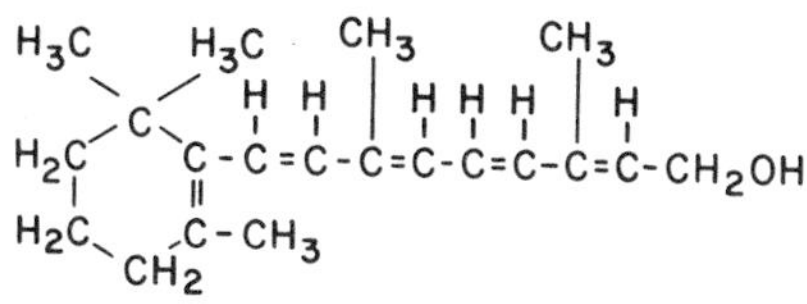

Vitamin A

Fig. 6.1 Chemical structures of β-carotene and vitamin A.

Although it appears theoretically possible to produce two units of vitamin A from each unit of β-carotene (Fig. 6.1), the efficiency of absorption and conversion in herbivores, granivores, and omnivores usually varies from 10 to 50% (Bradford and Smith, 1938; Bassett et al., 1946; Warner et al., 1963; NRC, 1978a, b). Because carnivores normally ingest either retinol or retinyl esters from their prey, metabolic systems for the absorption of carotene and production of vitamin A in carnivores may not exist. Although mink, foxes, and domestic dogs have retained a capability to absorb and convert β-carotene to vitamin A, cats have not and therefore require true vitamin A (Gershoff et al., 1957; Scott, 1968). Many marine birds and mammals may be similar to the cat as their requirements can be met by vitamin A contained in marine invertebrates and other vertebrates (Kon and Thompson, 1949).

One must be very careful in supplementing diets of captive animals with vitamin A because it can be toxic if fed in excess. Carotene is not toxic because the efficiencies of absorption and conversion to vitamin A decrease as intake increases. Martin (1975) suggested that excesses of vitamin A are a relatively common cause of ill health and death in captive wildlife. Typical signs of hypervitaminosis A are internal hemorrhaging, yellow discoloration of the liver and fat deposits, weight loss, deformed embryos and neonates, bone fractures, and reduced reproduction (Friend and Crampton, 1961; Martin, 1975). Because the livers of some carnivores and marine mammals store large amounts of vitamin A (Table 6.3), some of the classical cases of hypervitaminosis A have occurred when humans consumed polar bear and seal livers (Doutt, 1940; Rodahl and Moore, 1943). In general, the livers of carnivores and other vitamin A accu-

TABLE 6.3

Concentrations of Vitamin A in the Liver of Free-Ranging Wildlife

Species	Concentration		References
	μg/g	IU/g	
Polar bear	2,215–10,400	13,000–34,600	Rodahl and Moore, 1943; Rodahl, 1949; Russell, 1967; Leighton et al., 1988
Bearded seal		13,000	Rodahl and Moore, 1943
Arctic fox		12,000	Rodahl, 1949
Whale		4,804	Friend and Crampton, 1961
Adelie penguin	193–1,140		Ghebremeskel et al., 1989
Emperor and chinstrap penguins	37–378		Ghebremeskel et al., 1989
Pronghorn antelope		1,024–2,200	Weswig, 1956
Mule deer		393–1235	Anderson et al., 1972
Psittacine birds		252–1234	Lowenstine, 1986
White-tailed deer	50–143		Youatt et al., 1976
Gambel's quail	52–927		Hungerford, 1964
Bobwhite quail		42–3,668	Schultz, 1959

mulator species (such as whales) should not be fed to other animals unless vitamin A is closely monitored (Friend and Crampton, 1961; Walker et al., 1982).

B. Vitamin D

Vitamin D is well recognized as the antirachitic vitamin necessary for proper calcium absorption and metabolism. Vitamin D is required for the formation of a protein necessary for the active transport of calcium across the intestinal mucosa and into the body (Wasserman et al., 1966). Although very small amounts of dietary calcium can be absorbed by simple diffusion, active transport requiring vitamin D is necessary if calcium homeostasis is to occur. However, abundant vitamin D cannot overcome the effects of excess phosphorus or other elements that reduce the total availability of ionized calcium for absorption. Calcium resorption from bone induced by parathyroid hormone is also a vitamin D–dependent process. Thus, signs of vitamin D deficiency reflect improper or inadequate calcium metabolism (Table 6.2).

The antirachitic vitamin occurs in two major forms (vitamin D_2 = ergocalciferol and vitamin D_3 = cholecalciferol) (Fig. 6.2). Fish, amphibians, reptiles, and birds require vitamin D_3 and cannot utilize vitamin D_2 effectively (Hay and Watson, 1977). While some mammals can utilize either vitamin D_2 or D_3, many

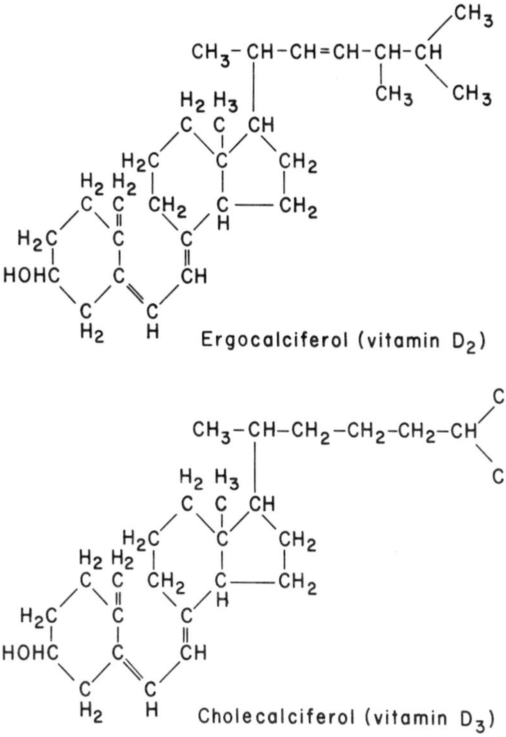

Fig. 6.2 The two major forms of vitamin D.

(such as New World primates, Tasmanian echidna, agouti, lion, tiger, and giant panda) preferentially utilize vitamin D_3. Vitamin D_3 is at least eight times more effective than D_2 in preventing rickets in squirrel monkeys (Lehner et al., 1966). The specificity of the two forms of the vitamin is partially due to the binding capacity and transport by blood proteins.

Transport mechanisms are critical to vitamin D metabolism because several chemical changes must occur before either cholecalciferol or ergocalciferol is effective in calcium metabolism. Vitamin D is the only vitamin that can be produced by the irradiation of a naturally occurring body sterol (7–dehydrocholesterol) on or within the skin surface (Fig. 6.3). The conversion of 7–dehydrocholesterol to cholecalciferol is a two-step process driven initially by ultraviolet radiation (280–320 nm) to form previtamin D_3, which is then slowly converted thermally to vitamin D_3. Because the plasma-binding protein has an affinity for vitamin D that is 1000 times greater than for the previtamin form, the delay in the thermal conversion process provides the means for a very gradual, more

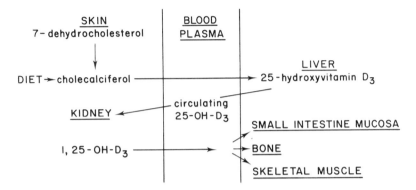

Fig. 6.3 Intermediary metabolism of vitamin D_3. Dietary ergocalciferol (vitamin D_2) must also undergo the same hydroxylations to become metabolically active. [From Fraser and Kodicek (1970), reprinted by permission from *Nature* (*London*) **228**, 764–766. Copyright 1970, Macmillan Journals Limited.]

continuous release of the vitamin following exposure to sunlight and thus may be important in preventing vitamin D toxicity due to prolonged sun exposure (Holick and Clark, 1978). The absorbed cholecalciferol or ergocalciferol must then be transported in succession to the liver and kidney with accompanying molecular alterations before becoming metabolically active. Liver enzymes, and possibly to a lesser extent kidney and small intestine enzymes in some species, convert vitamin D_3 to 25–hydroxyvitamin D_3, which at physiological concentrations is not active in calcium metabolism. The subsequent metabolism of 25–OH-D_3 to 1,25–hydroxyvitamin D_3 by the kidney is stimulated by parathyroid hormone and reduced cellular phosphate levels during hypocalcemia and is the active form of the vitamin stimulating bone resorption and intestinal calcium absorption. Conversely, high dietary calcium reduces the production of 1,25–OH-D_3. Thus, the amount of metabolically active vitamin D is controlled to maintain calcium homeostasis. Metabolic aberrations anywhere within the process will produce a functional vitamin D and calcium deficiency.

The divergence of mammals from the other vertebrate taxa in the utilization of vitamin D_2 has been suggested as an evolutionary response in primitive mammals to being nocturnally active (Hay and Watson, 1977). Diurnal concealment would reduce the opportunities for the production of adequate vitamin D_3 by irradiation, consequently requiring the utilization of a dietary source. Many invertebrates and plants when irradiated contain an antirachitic factor having ergosterol-like activity that may be important to nocturnal, subnivean, and subterranean mammals (Hickie *et al.*, 1982).

Because vitamin D is normally not stored in the body of terrestrial vertebrates, vitamin D deficiencies can appear within days to weeks if dietary or irradiation sources are inadequate (Mann, 1970; Ullrey, 1984). Ring-necked pheasants without dietary vitamin D_3 or exposure to sunlight developed rickets starting the fifth day after hatching (Millar et al., 1977). Although vitamin D deficiencies should be extremely rare in free-ranging animals because of irradiation and dietary intake, captive animals not exposed to direct sunlight or artificial ultraviolet light sources and consuming inadequate diets are very susceptible to this deficiency. Window glass, polyurethane-fiberglass, and acrylic glass do not transmit UV light in the necessary wave bands. Similarly, normal incandescent and fluorescent lights either do not produce UV light or their glass and plastic fixtures prevent UV transmission. Research is currently underway to identify glass and lights that transmit or produce the necessary UV bands. Glass made of vinyl, cellulose triacetate, plexiglass G-UVT, and teflon have the potential to be effective UV transmitters. Sun lamps with high UV intensity permit adequate vitamin D synthesis, although maximum safe exposure must be determined. Lights of medium to low UV intensity, such as Vita-Lite and black light, appear inadequate for vitamin D synthesis (Ullrey, 1984; Bernard et al., 1986; Gehrmann, 1987; Webb and Holick, 1988).

Nonsupplemented domestic cow's milk and, perhaps, the milk of many other species whose young normally experience sunlight shortly after birth are notoriously low in vitamin D (Hollis et al., 1981). The use of these milks requires either dietary supplementation if the animal is bottle-raised or occasional exposure of the young animal to sunlight if maternal-raised. For example, captive maternal-nursed snow leopards, Cape hunting dogs, and Bolivian red howler monkeys developed rickets when not allowed to exercise outside or to consume vitamin D–supplemented foods (Encke, 1962; Wallach, 1970; Ullrey, 1984). The exposure of Cape hunting dogs to an artificial ultraviolet light source for only 3 min per day prevented vitamin D–deficient rickets. Species who normally raise their young in burrows or other dark places must either have moderate levels of vitamin D in their milk or provide adequate body reserves via placental transfer prior to birth.

Although irradiation is probably the main source of vitamin D for most animals, many plants contain ergosterol which becomes ergocalciferol (D_2) when irradiated. Seeds and their by-products are practically devoid of the vitamin. Both phytoplankton and zooplankton contain vitamin D_3 and 7–dehydrocholesterol (Takeuchi et al., 1991). Thus, among the largest naturally occurring sources of vitamin D_3 available for supplementation are marine fish oils, particularly liver oils. While adult, fresh, marine fish frequently have very high levels of vitamin D_3 (Keiver et al., 1988a, b), fish that have been eviserated or frozen for too long will have greatly diminished levels (Nichols et al., 1983). Few other animal products contain any significant quantity of vitamin D, with meat being virtually devoid of the vitamin. Thus, carnivores and granivores are most susceptible to vitamin D deficiency (Lowenstine, 1986).

Vitamin D_2 and D_3 supplements are commercially available, although D_3 is the preferred form for all wildlife. Toxic overdoses must be avoided. Excessive supplementation of vitamin D retards bone growth, increases bone resorption, produces bone deformities, increases fracture susceptibility, and promotes cellular degeneration and calcification of soft tissues, including the urinary, circulatory, and respiratory systems.

Several plants also contain toxic levels of $1,25-OH-D_3$–glycoside. When these plants are consumed, the carbohydrate unit is cleaved in the gastrointestinal tract and the metabolically active form of the vitamin is absorbed. Consequently, when these plants are consumed in conjunction with adequate calcium and phosphorus, the normal vitamin D feedback control at the kidney is bypassed. Calcium and phosphorus absorption and deposition proceed out of control. Of the three plants identified thus far that produce vitamin D toxicity, two are in the Solanaceae (potato family, *Solanum malacoxylon* and *Cestrum diurnum*) and one is in the Graminae (grass family, *Trisetum flavescens*). *S. malacoxylon* occurs in South America; *C. diurnum* occurs in the southeastern United States, Jamaica, and Hawaii; and *T. flavescens* occurs in Germany (Wasserman, 1975; Wasserman *et al.*, 1976). Although free-ranging, fish-eating mammals, such as seals and dolphins, can ingest vitamin D at levels that would be toxic to other mammals, toxicity in these animals is apparently avoided by increasing the rate of vitamin D catabolism and by passive storage in the blubber (Keiver *et al.*, 1988a, b). It is currently unknown if such differences in vitamin D metabolism would increase the minimum requirement in these mammals.

Naked mole rats, blind, hairless, subterranean rodents of Africa, apparently are an exception to the classical vitamin D story (Buffenstein and Yahav, 1991; Skinner *et al.*, 1991). Naked mole rats live quite well without any source of vitamin D. They are never exposed to sunlight; the plant roots and tubers that they consume do not have vitamin D; and there are no detectable vitamin D metabolites in their blood. While they have evolved a very efficient vitamin D–independent calcium metabolism, they have retained the vitamin D–dependent system even though it is never utilized by the free-ranging naked mole rat. However, when captive naked mole rats are fed vitamin D–supplemented diets that activate the vitamin D–dependent system, they die of calcification of the kidneys (nephrocalcinosis).

C. Vitamin E

The primary function of vitamin E is to maintain the functional integrity of cellular and subcellular membranes by preventing lipid peroxidation of unsaturated fatty acids (Machlin, 1980). Although both vitamin E and selenium as glutathione peroxidase function as antioxidants, they are not interchangeable as vitamin E deficiency diseases will occur when selenium intake is within normal

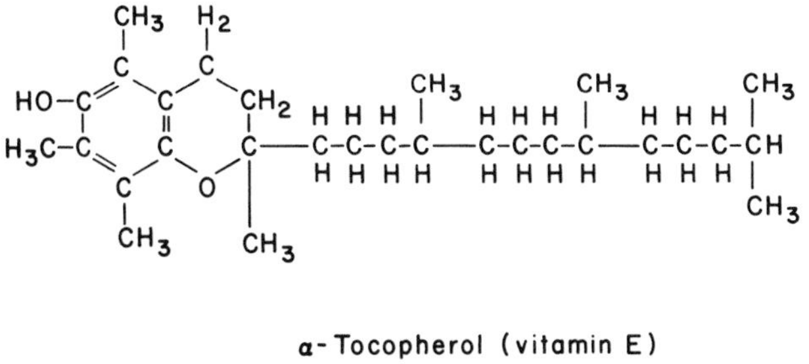

```
   CH3  H2
    |    
HO-C   C   CH2  H H H   CH3   H H H   CH3   H H H   CH3
H3C-C   C   C ——C-C-C-C——C-C-C-C——C-C-C-CH
    C    O       H H H H   H H H H   H H H |
    |    |                                  CH3
   CH3  CH3
```

α-Tocopherol (vitamin E)

Fig. 6.4   Molecular structure of vitamin E.

limits (Dierenfeld, 1989). Two groups of eight compounds (tocopherols and tocotrienols) have vitamin E activity. The most active and widely distributed is α-tocopherol (Fig. 6.4), with the other isomers generally having less than 30% of the activity of α-tocopherol. The natural synthesis of these compounds only occurs in chlorophyll-containing plants, phytoplankton, and microorganisms (Green et al., 1959).

Vitamin E deficiencies have been observed in virtually all taxa of captive wildlife (Liu et al., 1985; Dierenfeld, 1989). This deficiency has occurred most frequently in captive and wild animals consuming fish-based diets (Warner, 1961; Fitch and Dinning, 1963; Bone, 1968; Scott, 1968; Wagner and Dietlein, 1970; Engelhardt, 1974; Campbell and Montali, 1980; Geraci and Aubin, 1980; Gailey-Phipps and Sladen, 1982; Oftedal and Boness, 1983; Citino et al., 1985; Nichols et al., 1986; Bernard et al., 1989). Paradoxically, live or fresh fish in general are very good sources of the vitamin (Helgebostad and Ender, 1973). However, the combination of a relatively high concentration of polyunsaturated fatty acids in marine and coldwater fish, the frozen storage of the fish for several months before being fed, and the evisceration of the fish before freezing contribute to producing the deficiency. These factors are important because (a) the antioxidant role of vitamin E increases the requirement as unsaturated fats or dietary fat rancidity increases; (b) vitamin E in fish is oxidized and inactivated even when stored at very cold temperatures (50% loss after 6 months of storage at $-20°C$); and (c) the viscera of fish are important storage sites of the vitamin (Ackman and Cormier, 1967; Helgebostad and Ender, 1973; Engelhardt and Geraci, 1978). Similarly, the excessive utilization of cod liver oil and other oils high in unsaturated fatty acids and low in vitamin E as a vitamin A or D supplement can contribute to a vitamin E deficiency. Free-ranging great blue herons and other fish-eating birds may be prone to vitamin E deficiencies if feeding on a restricted diet of dead, rancid fish high in polyunsaturated fatty acids (Nichols et al., 1986). Engelhardt and

Geraci (1978) suggested supplementing fish diets with 100 IU of vitamin E per kilogram of fish to offset the oxidative loss of vitamin E during storage and the higher requirement relative to the polyunsaturated fat content of the diet. The sodium requirement of vitamin E–deficient harp seals maintained in fresh water was double the requirement of normal control seals.

Captive raptors fed young quail or a horsemeat-based commercial diet without additional vitamin E have been prone to vitamin E deficiencies (Calle *et al.*, 1989; Dierenfeld *et al.*, 1989). While whole freshly killed prey are commonly considered as nutritionally adequate, reproductive success of captive peregrine falcons doubled as the vitamin E content of the quail was increased. Plasma vitamin E concentration in unsupplemented falcons (3.4 μg/ml) was only 13% of their wild counterparts (26.3 μg/ml; Dierenfeld *et al.*, 1989). Thus, it is unwise to assume that carnivores are adequately nourished when consuming fresh whole prey. Although many animal tissues accumulate the vitamin, fat reserves are normally the site of greatest storage (Engelhardt, 1974; Engelhardt *et al.*, 1975). Protein-rich animal feeds, such as meat or fish meals, skim milk, and bone meal, and fat-extracted plant products are very poor sources (Sorensen, 1973; Kivimae and Carpena, 1973).

Vitamin E deficiencies have also been observed or suspected because of muscle pathology and low plasma concentrations in captive and free-ranging herbivores (Haugen and Hove, 1960; Kakulas, 1961; Anonymous, 1968; Higginson *et al.*, 1973; Decker and McDermid, 1977; Brady *et al.*, 1978; Liu *et al.*, 1985; Dolensek and Combs, 1985; Ghebremeskel *et al.*, 1988; Ghebremeskel and Williams, 1988; Dierenfeld and Dolensek, 1988; Dierenfeld *et al.*, 1988; Dierenfeld, 1989). Although low dietary selenium may have been a contributing factor in many of the older cases, vitamin E deficiencies can occur in herbivores when they are fed hays with a low vitamin E content due to (1) cutting when excessively mature, (2) leaching during the haying process, or (3) storing for too long leading to oxidation of the vitamin. Grass and forb tocopherol levels generally increase during early growth and are higher in leaves than in stems, but they normally decrease dramatically as development approaches seed maturity (Kivimae and Carpena, 1973). Reductions of from 80 to 90% in grasses are common. Tocopherol degradation by gastrointestinal microflora may be important when animals consume the high-grain diets often fed in captivity (Oksanen, 1973; Sorensen, 1973). Destruction of vitamin E increased from 8 to 42% as the dietary content of corn increased from 20 to 80%.

Although poorly understood, black rhinos and elephants are very susceptible to vitamin E deficiencies in captivity (Ghebremeskel *et al.*, 1988; Dierenfeld *et al.*, 1988; Dierenfeld and Dolensek, 1988; Papas *et al.*, 1989). Average vitamin E concentrations in the plasma of wild black rhinos ranged from 0.77 to 1.92 μg/ml as compared to nondetectable levels to 0.18 μg/ml in captives. The browse normally consumed by wild black rhinos is very high in vitamin E as compared to far lower levels in the grass hays commonly fed in captivity (Ghebremeskel *et al.*, 1988). Similarly, the tocopherol molecule of browse may be in a different physical or chemical configuration that is easier to absorb, or other dietary components may stimulate its absorption relative to the diets fed in captivity (Papas *et al.*, 1991).

Requirement estimates frequently range from 10 to 25 IU/kg dry diet (Table 6.1). However, as vitamin E deficiencies have been increasingly recognized in captive wildlife consuming these levels, recent recommendations are for these animals to consume 100–250IU/kg dry diet unless the higher levels produce excessively high serum concentrations (Liu *et al.*, 1984; Dierenfeld and Dolensek, 1988; Dierenfeld, 1989; Calle *et al.*, 1989). Stress and physical exercise can increase the requirement (MacKenzie and Fletcher, 1979; Machlin, 1980; Quintanilha and Packer, 1983; Dierenfeld, 1989). Because dietary vitamin E is poorly absorbed and depleted tissues rapidly absorb the vitamin (Losowsky *et al.*, 1972; Engelhardt, 1977; Eskeland and Rimeslatten, 1979), significant increases in plasma concentrations by dietary supplementation usually require weeks to months. Because tocopherol is very unstable, the most common stable form used in feed supplementation has been tocopheryl acetate. The acetate ester must be hydrolyzed during absorption to produce the free tocopherol. Intramuscular injections can increase plasma levels within minutes (Dierenfeld and Citino, 1989), although the active form of the vitamin (α-tocopherol) should be used. For carnivores, tocopherol can be injected into the prey just prior to feeding or the prey can be raised on vitamin E supplemented diets. A more recently developed form of the vitamin (α-tocopheryl polyethylene glycol 1000 succinate or TPGS) has been effective in quickly raising serum vitamin E levels when fed to black rhinos and elephants (Papas *et al.*, 1989; Kirkwood *et al.*, 1991; Papas *et al.*, 1991).

Deficiency signs can appear within 1 to 4 weeks after an animal begins consuming a deficient diet. Plasma vitamin E levels in peregrine falcons and elephants declined 50% in 4 weeks and 2 weeks, respectively, after stopping vitamin E supplementation (Dierenfeld *et al.*, 1989; Papas *et al.*, 1989). Most deficiency symptoms can be reversed within a similar time span following vitamin E supplementation (West and Mason, 1958; Olson and Carpenter, 1967; Chan and Hegarty, 1977; Dahlin *et al.*, 1978). Hatchability of peregrine falcon eggs increased from 38 to 81% within a single season following vitamin E supplementation (Dierenfeld *et al.*, 1989). Although vitamin E is generally nontoxic with a wide safety margin, excessive supplementation (e.g., 550 to 10,560 IU/kg dry diet for pink-backed pelicans) can produce hemorrhaging and death by reducing blood platelets and clotting time (Nichols *et al.*, 1989). Because these problems can be reversed by reducing vitamin E intake or supplementing with vitamin K, excessive vitamin E antagonizes either the absorption or metabolism of vitamin K (Olson, 1984).

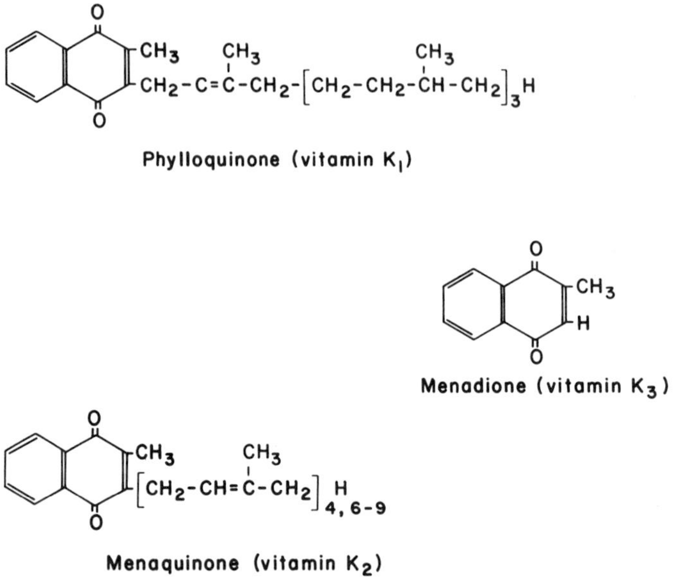

Phylloquinone (vitamin K₁)

Menadione (vitamin K₃)

Menaquinone (vitamin K₂)

Fig. 6.5 Molecular structures of the three major forms of vitamin K. The side chain of vitamin K_2 can range from four to nine isoprene units.

D. Vitamin K

Vitamin K is well known as the antihemorrhagic vitamin necessary for the synthesis of required blood-clotting proteins, although other roles in calcium metabolism and bone development exist (Olson, 1984; Price, 1988). The most important part of the vitamin K molecule is the menadione ring structure (Fig. 6.5) because it, as well as many other molecules of various side chain lengths, is biologically active. The two naturally occurring forms of the vitamin are phylloquinone (K_1), synthesized by green plants, and menaquinone (K_2), synthesized by bacteria. Menadione is available commercially.

Because of the ubiquitous distribution of vitamin K in plants and animals and its synthesis by gastrointestinal bacteria, free-ranging and captive wildlife consuming relatively natural diets probably never suffer a deficiency. However, very purified diets not containing green plant matter, oil seed meals, or animal or fish meals should be supplemented with vitamin K. Similarly, several vitamin K inhibitors, such as the rodenticide warfarin or dicoumarol found in moldy sweet clover, can markedly increase the vitamin K requirement. The excessive consumption of vitamin K inhibitors will produce death due to hemorrhaging. The prolonged use of ingestible drugs that reduce gastrointestinal microbial activity may also require supplemental vitamin K for those species dependent on bacterially produced vitamin K.

Phylloquinone is very nontoxic even in extremely high dosages. Menaquinone and menadione, while more toxic than phylloquinone, must be given in very large doses (such as 1,000 times the dietary requirement if given orally) to produce renal and hepatic toxicosis (Rebhun *et al.*, 1984; NRC, 1987).

Warfarin resistance in wild brown rats is a dominant characteristic controlled by a single gene. Heterozygous and homozygous warfarin-resistant rats have a 2 and 10 times higher vitamin K requirement, respectively, than the more common homozygous susceptible individuals. Microbial synthesis of vitamin K and reingestion of cecal droppings would enable the homozygous susceptible and heterozygous resistant rats to meet their requirements. However, intestinal synthesis is inadequate for the homozygous resistant rats. Thus, depending on the vitamin K intake and bacterial synthesis, homozygous resistant animals may die out when warfarin is withdrawn and leave the more fit homozygous and heterozygous rats (Partridge, 1980).

II. WATER-SOLUBLE VITAMINS

Our understanding of the requirements and metabolism of water-soluble vitamins in wildlife is totally inadequate relative to their importance. The lack of studies is, in part, due to the rarity of water-soluble vitamin deficiencies. Because of synthesis by intestinal microbes and the general availability of dietary sources, water-soluble vitamin deficiencies in free-ranging animals are uncommon, although thiamin and vitamin C deficiencies have occurred in captive wildlife.

A. Thiamin

Thiamin has been studied far more frequently than all other water-soluble vitamins needed by wildlife (Tables 6.4 and 6.5). Thiamin deficiencies have been reported in numerous captive fish-eating carnivores, such as dolphins, polar bears, mink, foxes, sea lions, grebes, and gulls (Rigdon and Drager, 1955; Warner, 1961; Travis, 1963; Hubbard, 1969; Friend and Trainer, 1969; White, 1970; Hess, 1971; Geraci, 1972; Ratti, 1977; Gilman, 1978). Over 35 species of fish and shellfish contain heat-stable or heat-labile compounds that destroy their thiamin prior to its absorption or interfere with its metabolism (NRC, 1982). These compounds are collectively referred to as thiaminase (Geraci, 1974). Thiaminase in fish is normally not found in the muscle but is confined in relatively large concentrations in the viscera and trimmings, including the head, skin, fins, and skeleton (Green *et al.*, 1942). Thiaminase is apparently sequestered in an inactive form in the living animal and stimulated or activated by death and storage (Deolalkar and Sohonie,

1957a, b; White, 1970). Thiamin destruction is virtually complete by 90 min when dead smelt are incubated at 37°C (Geraci, 1972). Thiaminase also occurs in newly hatched chicks and in the heart and spleen of warm-blooded animals. A peregrine falcon developed a thiamin deficiency when fed newly hatched chicks, pigeon and quail muscle, beef, and chicken gizzards and hearts (Ward, 1971). Herbivores can encounter thiaminase by ingesting bracken fern (*Pteris aquilinum*) and horsetail (*Equisetum arvense*) (Harris, 1951). Thiaminase also can be produced by rumen bacteria when high-grain diets are consumed (Brent and Bartley, 1984). Rumen-produced thiaminase can induce a thiamin deficiency even when dietary intake meets recommended standards.

TABLE 6.4

General Functions and Reported Deficiency Signs of Water-Soluble Vitamins[a]

Vitamin	Major functions	Deficiency signs
Thiamin (vitamin B_1)	Necessary coenzyme in carbohydrate metabolism, possibly important in nerve or neuromuscular impulse transmission	Anorexia, weight loss, weakness, lethargy, unsteady gait, ruffled feathers, impaired digestion, diarrhea, seizures and other neurological disorders, liver degeneration, death
Riboflavin (vitamin B_2)	Functions in two coenzymes—flavin adenine dinucleotide (FAD) and flavin mononucleotide	Curled toe paralysis in birds, anorexia, weight loss or reduced growth, perosis, rough hair coat, corneal vascularization, atrophy of hair follicles, diarrhea, leg paralysis, reduced fertility, death
Niacin (nicotinic acid and nicotinamide)	Functions in two coenzymes—nicotinamide adenine dinucleotide (NAD) and nicotinamide adenine dinucleotide phosphate (NADP)	Reduced growth, enlarged hocks, poor feathering, anorexia, diarrhea, dermatitis, drooling and tongue discoloration, death
Vitamin B_6 (pyridoxine, pyridoxamine, and pyridoxal)	Functions in enzyme systems of protein metabolism	Testicular atrophy, sterility, anorexia, retarded growth, roughness and thinning of the hair coat, muscular incoordination, convulsions and neurological disorders, death

TABLE 6.4

Continued

Vitamin	Major functions	Deficiency signs
Pantothenic acid	A component of coenzyme A, necessary for fat, carbohydrate, and amino acid metabolism	Skin lesions, crusty scabs about the beak and eyes, emaciation, weakness, reduced growth, leg disorders, poor feathering, intestinal hemorrhages, enlarged fatty degeneration of the liver, enlarged and congested kidneys, reproductive failure, death
Biotin	Functions as a coenzyme in carbon dioxide fixation and carboxylation	Fur discoloration, hair loss, degenerative changes in the hair follicles, thickened and scaly skin, conjunctivitis, fatty infiltration of the liver, eye infections
Folicin (folic acid)	Transfer of single carbon units in molecular transformations	Anorexia; retarded growth; decreased activity; weakness; diarrhea; profuse salivation; convulsions; adrenal hemorrhages; fatty infiltration of the liver; reduced hemoglobin, hematocrit, and leukocytes; death
Vitamin B_{12} (cyanocobalamin)	Functions as a coenzyme in single carbon metabolism and in carbohydrate metabolism	Anorexia, weight loss, fatty degeneration of the liver, neurological and locomotion disorders
Choline	Nerve functioning (acetylcholine), component of the phospholipid lecithin which is a necessary constituent of cells and tissues throughout the body, methyl donor	Diffuse fatty infiltration of the liver, rupture and hemorrhaging of the liver, enlarged hocks, slipped tendons, reduced growth of the leg bones, awkward gait, growth retardation, muscular weakness, lowered hematocrit, pale kidneys

(continues)

TABLE 6.4

Continued

Vitamin	Major functions	Deficiency signs
Vitamin C (ascorbic acid)	May reduce infections, necessary for phagocytic activity, bone and collagen formation, functions in hydroxylation reactions, antioxidant	Scurvy, severe necrotic stomatitis, anorexia, weight loss, gingivitis, glossitis, pharyngitis, hemorrhages throughout the body, weakness, stiffened hind legs, lowered body temperature, diarrhea, bone fractures, enteritis, retarded growth, death

*a*Deficiency signs vary between species and depend on the severity of the deficiency.

The thiamin requirement of either captive or free-ranging animals ingesting thiaminase can be met by consuming the needed thiamin in a meal or supplement temporally isolated from foods containing thiaminase. Geraci (1974) recommended that captive fish-eating carnivores be fed (1) a varied diet to reduce dietary thiaminase content and (2) a thiamin supplement (35 mg/day/seal) two hours before being fed a thiaminase-containing meal to provide time necessary for thiamin absorption. The inability of free-ranging animals to consume a varied diet may occasionally induce a thiamin deficiency. Nestling gulls raised during a fish die-off may be prone to a thiaminase-induced deficiency if the parents do not occasionally retrieve thiamin-rich foods (Gilman, 1978). Paradoxically, whereas captive gulls fed fresh smelt without a thiamin supplement developed a deficiency, those fed rotten smelt for 10 weeks to simulate feeding during a fish die-off did not develop the deficiency. Thus, either additional thiamin is being produced by bacteria or the anti-thiamin compound is destroyed as decay progresses. Free-ranging nectivorous birds, who normally meet their thiamin requirement by occasionally ingesting insects, can develop a thiamin deficiency if consuming human-provided thiamin-free sugar solutions during the winter when insect availability is greatly reduced (Paton *et al.,* 1983; Bonnin, 1989).

Thiamin deficiencies can usually be rapidly and easily cured even in near terminally sick animals by the addition of adequate thiamin to the diet or by injecting thiamin hydrochloride. The symptoms of thiamin deficiency began disappearing in dolphins and seals 6 to 12 hr after an injection of thiamin (White, 1970; Geraci, 1972). Thiamin-deficient western grebes exhibiting massive neurological disorders completely recovered within 48 hr of oral thiamin supplementation (Ratti, 1977). The daily thiamin requirement is, of course, very de-

TABLE 6.5

Water-Soluble Vitamin Requirements or Allowances for Growth and Reproduction per Kilogram of Dry Diet

Species	Riboflavin (mg)	Niacin (mg)	Choline (mg)	Thiamin (mg)	Biotin (mg)	Folic acid (mg)	Pantothenic acid (mg)	Pyridoxine (mg)	B_{12} (μg)	Ascorbic acid (mg)	References
Birds											
Bobwhite and Japanese quail	3.8–4.0	20–40	1000–2000	2.0	0.15–0.30	1.0	10–15	3.0	—	—	NRC, 1984
Ducks and geese (domestic)	2.5–4.0	20–55	—	—	—	—	10–15	2.6–3.0	—	—	NRC, 1984
Pheasant	3.0–3.5	40–60	1000–1500	—	—	—	10	—	—	—	NRC, 1984
Turkey (domestic)	3.0–4.0	30–70	1000–1900	2.0	0.1–0.2	0.8–1.0	9–16	3.5–4.5	3	—	NRC, 1984
Mammals											
Fox	3.7–5.5	9.6	—	1.0	—	0.2	7.4	1.8	—	—	NRC, 1982
Guinea pig	3.0	10	1000	2.0	0.3	4.0	20	3.0	10	200	NRC, 1978a
Hamster	15.0	90	2000	20.0	0.6	2.0	40	6.0	10	—	NRC, 1978a
Laboratory mouse	7.0	10	600	5.0	0.2	0.5	10	1.0	10	—	NRC, 1978a
Laboratory rat	3.0	20	1000	4.0	—	1.0	8	6.0	50	—	NRC, 1978a
Mink	1.6	20	—	1.3	0.12	0.5	8	1.6	32.6	—	NRC, 1982

pendent on dietary thiaminase activity, temporal sequence of food ingestion, and, particularly, dietary fat content. Since thiamin is necessary for the synthesis of fatty acids, diets high in fats spare thiamin. Animals consuming diets high in fat but deficient in thiamin remain healthier for a much longer period of time than those receiving the same amount of thiamin but less dietary fat. Although the average thiamin requirement of animals consuming diets devoid of thiaminase may be as little as 1–2 mg/kg of diet (Table 6.5), the effective thiamin requirement of seals and foxes consuming thiaminase-containing herring or carp was 25–35 and 147 mg/kg of diet, respectively, with the difference due to thiaminase content (Green et al., 1942; Geraci, 1972).

Infection and nutrition are often closely related processes. Thiamin-deficient herring gulls consuming alewives were highly susceptible to the respiratory fungal disease aspergillosis (Friend and Trainer, 1969). Antifungal agents were generally ineffective in combating the disease. When the diet was supplemented with thiamin rather than the antifungal therapeutic agents, aspergillosis mortality ceased and most of the sick birds immediately recovered.

B. Other B Vitamins

Riboflavin, niacin, pantothenic acid, choline, folacin, and pyridoxine metabolism and requirements have been studied in pheasants and quail (Scott et al., 1959, 1964; Serafin, 1974), mink, foxes, guinea pigs, primates, and virtually all common laboratory animals (data summarized in NRC publications). Riboflavin is not produced to any significant extent by animals and therefore must initially come from plants or microorganisms. Even though animal tissue is a very good source of riboflavin, a riboflavin deficiency was reported in a free-ranging golden eagle (Stauber, 1973). The deficiency may have been precipitated by the consumption of environmental toxicants that interfered with riboflavin metabolism (E. Stauber, personal communication). Although riboflavin can be readily excreted, the biological half-life of the vitamin in well-nourished rhesus monkeys was 3.2 days but lengthened during the deficient state to 9.5 days as the animals responded by conserving body stores (Greenberg, 1970). Riboflavin deficiencies in many captive animals (such as the ostrich) have also been noted (Wallach, 1970). While curled-toe paralysis associated with riboflavin deficiency in birds is a useful diagnostic tool, it is not to be confused with the laterally curled toes produced when birds are maintained simply on smooth surfaces (Wallach, 1970). Biotin deficiencies can occur if the diet is high in raw egg white, which contains a compound called avidin that binds dietary biotin into a nonavailable form, or contains rancid fats or molds that destroy or bind biotin.

C. Vitamin C

Vitamin C, or ascorbic acid, is one of the exceptions to the general definition of vitamins in that it can be produced by many animals and thus is not always a dietary requirement. The development of the synthetic capability and this transition within different organs of the body follows an interesting phylogenetic scale. Invertebrates and fish lack the synthetic capability and are thus dependent on dietary sources. Amphibians, reptiles, most birds, and monotremes synthesize ascorbic acid in the kidney. Approximately one-half of the Passeriformes (particularly numerous Southeast Asian species, such as bulbuls, Asian paradise-flycatcher, black-hooded oriole, pale-billed flowerpecker, crimson sunbird, as well as swallows and some shrikes) are unable to synthesize the vitamin and are therefore totally dependent on a dietary source. The remaining Passeriformes synthesize ascorbic acid in the liver (such as house sparrow, jungle myna, Asian pied starling, and magpie robin) or in both the liver and kidney (Indian house crow and common myna). Most mammals synthesize ascorbic acid in the liver, but a few, including anthropoid primates, bats, guinea pigs, and possibly cetaceans, lack a synthetic ability. Thus, the ability to synthesize ascorbic acid appeared initially in the kidney with the evolution of terrestrial vertebrate life forms and was later either transferred to the liver or lost (Roy and Guha, 1958; Miller and Ridgeway, 1963; Ridgeway, 1965; Elliot et al., 1966; Yess and Hegsted, 1967; Hubbard, 1969; Chaudhuri and Chatterjee, 1969; Chatterjee, 1973; Birney et al., 1976, 1980; Jenness et al., 1984; Pollock and Mullin, 1987).

However, even those species that synthesize ascorbic acid may require a dietary supply at critical times in the life cycle. For example, willow ptarmigan chicks, a species with the ability to synthesize vitamin C in the kidney, fed a commercial poultry diet containing 265 mg vitamin C per kilogram diet developed scurvy and died by 4 weeks of age (Hanssen et al., 1979). The deficiency was cured by vitamin C supplementation or the provision and consumption of blueberry or other plants normally found in the ptarmigan's diet. Although a diet containing 750 mg vitamin C per kilogram diet was adequate, many plants normally consumed by free-ranging ptarmigan contain 2000–5000 mg vitamin C per kilogram. The capability to synthesize vitamin C is sufficient for adult ptarmigan as they thrive in captivity on diets devoid of the vitamin. However, the dietary requirement of the chick is approximately 125–150 mg ascorbic acid per kilogram body weight, which is higher than the natural synthetic capabilities and much higher than the 5 mg/kg body weight required by the newborn guinea pig. Snowshoe hares may be similar in having a synthetic capability but are nevertheless dependent on dietary sources (Jenness et al., 1978). Thus, vitamin C should not be ignored even in those species able to synthesize it, as rapid early growth, stress, or organochloride pesticides may increase the ascorbic acid requirement beyond the capabilities of endogenous synthesis (Scott, 1975; Street and Chadwick, 1975; Chatterjee et al., 1975; Hanssen et al., 1979). Deficiency signs can appear within 2–4 days in ptarmigan chicks, 3 weeks in guinea pigs, to 3–4 months in humans (Chatterjee et al., 1975; Hanssen et al., 1979).

Vitamin C is not as widespread as many of the other water-soluble vitamins. The richest sources are green plants and fleshy fruits, such as rose hips and berries, but it is virtually absent in eggs, seeds, grains, and most bacteria and protozoa. Animal tissues are, in general, poor sources of the vitamin, although the adrenal cortex and liver (300 mg/kg) are relatively good sources.

III. CONCLUSIONS

Even though vitamins are usually found in very minute amounts, they are crucially important to animal health. Deficiencies produce signs that the wildlife nutritionist should recognize. While most of the deficiencies have been detected in captive animals, free-ranging wildlife may also suffer.

REFERENCES

Ackman, R. G., and Cormier, M. G. (1967). α-Tocopherol in some Atlantic fish and shellfish with particular reference to live-holding without food. *J. Fish. Res. Board Can.* **24,** 357–373.

Anderson, A. E., Medin, D. E., and Bowden, D. C. (1972). Carotene and vitamin A in the liver and blood serum of a Rocky Mountain mule deer, *Odocoileus hemionus hemionus,* population. *Comp. Biochem. Physiol.* **41B,** 745–758.

Anonymous. (1968). Avitaminosis E in a white-tailed deer (*Odocoileus virginianus*). *J. Small Anim. Pract.* **9,** 130–131.

Bassett, C. F., Harris, L. E., and Wilke, C. F. (1946). A comparison of carotene and vitamin A utilization in the fox. *Cornell Vet.* **36,** 16–24.

Berger, P. J., Negus, N. C., Sanders, E. H., and Gardner, P. D. (1981). 6–Methoxybenzoxazolinone: A plan derivative that stimulates reproduction in *Microtus montanus. Science* **214,** 67–70.

Bernard, J. B., Watkins, B. E., and Ullrey, D. E. (1986). Artificial lights as a source of vitamin D. *Proc. Dr. Scholl Nutr. Conf.* **6,** 43–47.

Bernard, J. B., Watkins, B. E., and Ullrey, D. E. (1989). Evaluation of dietary husbandry of marine mammals at two major zoological gardens. *J. Zoo Wildl. Med.* **20,** 45–52.

Birney, E. C., Jenness, R., and Ayaz, K. M. (1976). Inability of bats to synthesize L-ascorbic acid. *Nature (London)* **260,** 626–628.

Birney, E. C., Jenness, R., and Hume, I. D. (1980). Evolution of an enzyme system: Ascorbic acid biosynthesis in monotremes and marsupials. *Evolution* **34,** 230–239.

Block, J. A. (1974). Hand-rearing seven-banded armadillos (*Dasypus septemcinctus*) at the National Zoological Park, Washington. *Int. Zoo Yearb.* **14,** 210–214.

Bone, W. J. (1968). Pansteatitis in a lion (*Felis leo*). *J. Am. Vet. Med. Assoc.* **153,** 791–792.

Bonnin, J. M. (1989). Deaths from thiamine deficiency in honeyeaters fed in a suburban garden. *South Aust. Ornithol.* **30,** 190–192.

Bradford, D., and Smith, M. C. (1938). The ability of the dog to utilize vitamin A from plant and animal sources. *Am. J. Physiol.* **124,** 168–173.

Brady, P. S., Brady, L. J., Whetter, P. A., Ullrey, D. E., and Fay, L. D. (1978). The effect of dietary selenium and vitamin E on biochemical parameters and survival of young among white-tailed deer (*Odocoileus virginianus*). *J. Nutr.* **108,** 1439–1448.

Brent, B. E., and Bartley, E. E. (1984). Thiamin and niacin in the rumen. *J. Anim. Sci.* **59,** 813–822.

Brush, A.H. (1981). Carotenoids in wild and captive birds. *In* "Carotenoids as Colorants and Vitamin A Precursors." (J.C. Bauernfeind, ed.). pp. 539–562. Academic Press, New York.

Buffenstein, R., and Yahav, S. (1991). Cholecalciferol has no effect on calcium and inorganic phosphorus balance in a naturally cholecalciferol-deplete subterranean mammal, the naked mole rat (*Heterocephalus glaber*). *J. Endocrinol.* **129**, 21–26.

Calle, P. P., Dierenfeld, E. S., and Robert, M. E. (1989). Serum α-tocopherol in raptors fed vitamin E-supplemented diets. *J. Zoo Wildl. Med.* **20**, 62–67.

Campbell, G., and Montali, R. J. (1980). Myodegeneration in captive brown pelicans attributed to vitamin E deficiency. *J. Zoo Anim. Med.* **11**, 35–40.

Chan, A. C., and Hegarty, P. V. J. (1977). Morphological changes in skeletal muscles in vitamin E-deficient and refed rabbits. *Br. J. Nutr.* **38**, 361–370.

Chatterjee, I. B. (1973). Evolution and biosynthesis of ascorbic acid. *Science* **182**, 1271–1272.

Chatterjee, I. B., Majumder, A. K., Nandi, B. K., and Subramanian, N. (1975). Synthesis and some major functions of vitamin C in animals. *Ann. N. Y. Acad. Sci.* **258**, 24–47.

Chaudhuri, C. R., and Chatterjee, I. B. (1969). L-Ascorbic acid synthesis in birds: Phylogenetic trend. *Science* **164**, 435–436.

Citino, S. B., Montali, R. J., Bush, M., and Phillips, L. G. (1985). Nutritional myopathy in a captive California sea lion. *J. Am. Vet. Med. Assoc.* **187**, 1232–1233.

Cowan, I. McT., and Fowle, C. D. (1944). Visceral gout in a wild ruffed grouse. *J. Wildl. Manage.* **8**, 260–261.

Dahlin, K. J., Chan, A. C., Benson, E. S., and Hegarty, P. V. J. (1978). Rehabilitating effect of vitamin E therapy on the ultrastructural changes in skeletal muscles of vitamin E-deficient rabbits. *Am. J. Clin. Nutr.* **31**, 94–99.

Decker, R. A., and McDermid, A. M. (1977). Nutritional myopathy in a young camel. *J. Zoo Anim. Med.* **8**, 20–21.

DeLuca, H. F. (1979). Retinoic acid metabolism. *Fed. Proc.* **38**, 2519–2523.

de Man, E., and Peke, H.V.S. (1982). Dietary ferulic acid, biochanin A, and the inhibition of reproductive behavior in Japanese quail (*Coturnix coturnix*). *Pharmacol. Biochem. Behav.* **17**, 405–411.

Deolalkar, S. T., and Sohonie, K. (1957a). Studies on thiaminase from fish. I. Properties of thiaminase. *Indian J. Med. Res.* **45**, 571–586.

Deolalkar, S. T., and Sohonie, K. (1957b). Studies on thiaminase from fish. II. Effect of certain compounds on thiaminase activity. *Indian J. Med. Res.* **45**, 587–592.

Dierenfeld, E. S. (1989). Vitamin E deficiency in zoo reptiles, birds, and ungulates. *J. Zoo Wildl. Med.* **20**, 3–11.

Dierenfeld, E. S., and Citino, S. B. (1989). Circulating plasma α-tocopherol following a single injection in a black rhinoceros (*Diceros bicornis*). *J. Wildl. Dis.* **25**, 647–648.

Dierenfeld, E. S., and Dolensek, E. P. (1988). Circulating levels of vitamin E in captive Asian elephants (*Elephas maximus*). *Zoo Biol.* **7**, 165–172.

Dierenfeld, E. S., du Toit, R., and Miller, R. E. (1988). Vitamin E in captive and wild black rhinoceros (*Diceros bicornis*). *J. Wildl. Dis.* **24**, 547–550.

Dierenfeld, E. S., Sandfort, C. E., and Satterfield, W. C. (1989). Influence of diet on plasma vitamin E in captive peregrine falcons. *J. Wildl. Manage.* **53**, 160–164.

Dierenfeld, E.S., Katz, N., Pearson, J. Murru, F., and Asper, E.D. (1991). Retinol and α-tocopherol concentrations in whole fish commonly fed in zoos and aquariums. *Zoo Biol.* **10**, 119–125.

Dolensek, E. P., and Combs, S. B. (1985). Vitamin E deficiency in zoo animals. *Proc. Dr. Scholl Nutr. Conf.* **5**, 171–177.

Doutt, K. (1940). Toxicity of polar bear liver. *J. Mammal.* **21**, 356–357.

Elliot, O., Yess, N. J., and Hegsted, D. M. (1966). Biosynthesis of ascorbic acid in the tree shrew and the slow loris. *Nature (London)* **212**, 739–740.

Encke, W. (1962). Hand-rearing Cape hunting dogs (*Lycaon pictus*) at the Krefeld Zoo. *Int. Zoo Yearb.* **4**, 292–293.

Engelhardt, F. R. (1974). "Aspects of Vitamin E Deprivation in the Harp Seal, *Phoca groenlandica*." Doctoral Dissertation, Univ. Guelph.

Engelhardt, F. R. (1977). Plasma and tissue levels of dietary radiotocopherols in the harp seal, *Phoca groenlandica. Can. J. Physiol. Pharmacol.* **55,** 601–608.

Engelhardt, F. R., and Geraci, J. R. (1978). Effects of experimental vitamin E deprivation in the harp seal, *Pagophilus groenlandicus. Can. J. Zool.* **56,** 2186–2193.

Engelhardt, F. R., Geraci, J. R., and Walker, B. L. (1975). Tocopherol distribution in the harp seal, *Pagophilus groenlandicus. Comp. Biochem. Physiol.* **52B,** 561–562.

Eskeland, B., and Rimeslatten, H. (1979). Studies on the absorption of labelled and dietary α-tocopherol in mink as influenced by some dietary factors. *Acta Agric. Scand.* **29,** 75–80.

Fitch, C. D., and Dinning, J. S. (1963). Vitamin E deficiency in the monkey. *J. Nutr.* **79,** 69–78.

Foster, J. W. (1981). Dermatitis in polar bears—A nutritional approach to therapy. Woodland Park Zoo, Seattle, Washington, unpublished manuscript.

Fraser, D. R., and Kodicek, E. (1970). Unique biosynthesis by kidney of a biologically active vitamin D metabolite. *Nature (London)* **228,** 764–766.

Friend, D. W., and Crampton, E. W. (1961). The adverse effect of raw whale liver on the breeding performance of the female mink. *J. Nutr.* **73,** 317–320.

Friend, M., and Trainer, D. O. (1969). Aspergillosis in captive herring gulls. *Bull. Wildl. Dis. Assoc.* **5,** 271–275.

Gailey-Phipps, J. J., and Sladen, W. J. L. (1982). Survey on nutrition of penguins. *J. Am. Vet. Med. Assoc.* **181,** 1305–1309.

Gehrmann, W. H. (1987). Ultraviolet irradiances of various lamps used in animal husbandry. *Zoo Biol.* **6,** 117–127.

Geraci, J. R. (1972). Experimental thiamin deficiency in captive harp seals, *Phoca groenlandica*, induced by eating herring, *Clupea harengus*, and smelt, *Osmerus mordax. Can. J. Zool.* **50,** 170–195.

Geraci, J. R. (1974). Thiamine deficiency in seals and recommendations for its prevention. *J. Am. Vet. Med. Assoc.* **165,** 801–803.

Geraci, J. R., and Aubin, D. J. St. (1980). Nutritional disorders of captive fish-eating animals. *In* "The Comparative Pathology of Zoo Animals" (R. J. Montali and G. Migaki, eds.), pp. 41–49. Smithsonian Inst. Press, Washington, D.C.

Gershoff, S. N., Andrus, S. B., Hegsted, D. M., and Lentini, E. A. (1957). Vitamin A deficiency in cats. *Lab. Invest.* **6,** 227–240.

Ghebremeskel, K., and Williams, G. (1988). Plasma retinol and alpha-tocopherol levels in captive wild animals. *Comp. Biochem. Physiol.* **89B,** 279–283.

Ghebremeskel, K., Williams, G., Lewis, J. C. M., and DuToit, R. (1988). Serum alpha-tocopherol, all-trans retinol, total lipids and cholesterol in the black rhinoceros (*Diceros bicornis*). *Comp. Biochem. Physiol.* **91A,** 343–345.

Ghebremeskel, K., Williams, G., Keymer, I. F., and Horsley, D. T. (1989). Liver and plasma retinol (Vitamin A) in wild, and liver retinol in captive penguins (*Spheniscidae*). *J. Zool.* **219,** 245–250.

Gilman, A. P. (1978). "Natural and Induced Thiamin Deficiency in the Herring Gull, *Larus argentatus*." Doctoral Dissertation, Univ. Guelph.

Goodman, D. S. (1979). Vitamin A and retinoids: Recent advances. *Fed. Proc.* **38,** 2501–2503.

Green, J., Price, S. A., and Gare, L. (1959). Tocopherols in microorganisms. *Nature (London)* **184,** 1339.

Green, R. C., Carlson, W. E., and Evans, C. A. (1942). The inactivation of vitamin B_1 in diets containing whole fish. *J. Nutr.* **23,** 165–174.

Greenberg, L. D. (1970). Nutritional requirements of Macaque monkeys. *In* "Feeding and Nutrition of Nonhuman Primates" (R. S. Harris, ed.), pp. 117–142. Academic Press, New York.

Halliwell, W. H., and Graham, D. L. (1976). Malnutrition in birds of prey. *In* "Wildlife Diseases" (L. A. Page, ed.), pp. 89–94. Plenum Press, New York.

Hanssen, K., Grav, H. J., Steen, J. B., and Lysnes, H. (1979). Vitamin C deficiency in growing willow ptarmigan (*Lagopus lagopus lagopus*). *J. Nutr.* **109**, 2260–2278.

Harris, R. S. (1951). Thiaminase. *In* "The Enzymes," Vol. I, Part 2, (J. B. Sumner and K. Myrback, eds.), pp. 1186–1206. Academic Press, New York.

Haugen, A. O., and Hove, E. L. (1960). Vitamin A and E in deer blood. *J. Mammal.* **41**, 410–411.

Hay, A. W. M., and Watson, G. (1977). Vitamin D_2 in vertebrate evolution. *Comp. Biochem. Physiol.* **56B**, 375–380.

Helgebostad, A., and Ender, F. (1973). Vitamin E and its function in the health and disease of fur-bearing animals. *Acta Agric. Scand. Suppl.* **19**, 79–83.

Hess, J. K. (1971). Hand-rearing polar bear cubs (*Thalarctos maritimus*) at St. Paul Zoo. *Int. Zoo Yearb.* **11**, 102–107.

Heywood, R. (1967). Vitamin A in the liver and kidney of some felidae. *Br. Vet. J.* **123**, 390–396.

Hickie, J. P., Lavigne, D. M., and Woodward, W. D. (1982). Vitamin D and winter reproduction in the collared lemming, *Dicrostonyx groenlandicus*. *Oikos* **39**, 71–76.

Higginson, J. A., Julian, R. J., and van Drummel, A. A. (1973). Muscular dystrophy in zebra foals. *J. Zoo Anim. Med.* **4**, 24–27.

Holick, M. F., and Clark, M. B. (1978). The photobiogenesis and metabolism of vitamin D. *Fed. Proc.* **37**, 2567–2574.

Hollis, B. W., Ross, B. A., Draper, H. H., and Lambert, P. W. (1981). Vitamin D and its metabolites in human and bovine milk. *J. Nutr.* **111**, 1240–1248.

Hubbard, R. C. (1969). Chemotherapy in captive marine mammals. *Bull. Wildl. Dis. Assoc.* **5**, 218–230.

Hungerford, C. R. (1964). Vitamin A and productivity in Gambel's quail. *J. Wildl. Manage.* **28**, 141–147.

Jenness, R., Birney, E. C., and Ayaz, K. L. (1978). Ascorbic acid and L-gulonolactone oxidase in lagomorphs. *Comp. Biochem. Physiol.* **61B**, 395–399.

Jenness, R., Birney, E. C., Ayaz, K. L., and Buzzell, D. M. (1984). Ontogenetic development of L-gulonolactone oxidase activity in several vertebrates. *Comp. Biochem. Physiol.* **78B**, 167–173.

Jones, G. E. (1950). "A Study of Vitamin A Storage in Bobwhite Quail in Cleveland County, Oklahoma with Comparative Data from Other Counties." Master's Thesis, Univ. Oklahoma.

Kakulas, B. A. (1961). Myopathy affecting the Rottnest quokka (*Setonix brachyurus*) reversed by α-tocopherol. *Nature (London)* **191**, 402–403.

Keiver, K. M., Draper, H. H., and Ronald, K. (1988a). Vitamin D metabolism in the hooded seal (*Cystophora cristata*). *J. Nutr.* **118**, 332–341.

Keiver, K. M., Ronald, K., and Draper, H. H. (1988b). Plasma levels of vitamin D and some metabolites in marine mammals. *Can. J. Zool.* **66**, 1297–1300.

Kelley, J. K., Lochmiller, R. L., Hellgren, E. C., and Grant, W. E. (1987). Vitamin A levels of blood in collared peccaries (*Tayassu tajacu*) from south Texas. *Comp. Biochem. Physiol.* **86A**, 751–753.

Kirkwood, J.K., Markham, J., Hawkey, C.M., and Jackson, S.I. (1991). Plasma vitamin E response in two black rhinoceroses following dietary supplementation. *Vet. Rec.* **128**, 185–186.

Kivimae, A., and Carpena, C. (1973). The level of vitamin E content in some conventional feeding stuffs and the effects of genetic variety; harvesting; processing and storage. *Acta Agric. Scand. Suppl.* **19**, 161–168.

Kon, S. K., and Thompson, S. Y. (1949). Preformed vitamin A in northern krill. *Biochem. J.* **45**, XXXI-XXXII.

Labov, J. B. (1977). Phytoestrogens and mammalian reproduction. *Comp. Biochem. Physiol.* **57A,** 3–9.

Lehner, N. D. M., Bullock, B. C., Clarkson, T. B., and Lofland, H. B. (1966). Biological activity of vitamins D_2 and D_3 fed to squirrel monkeys. *Fed. Proc.* **25,** 533.

Leighton, F. A., Cattet, M., Norstrom, R., and Trudeau, S. (1988). A cellular basis for high levels of vitamin A in livers of polar bears (*Ursus maritimus*): the Ito cell. *Can. J. Zool.* **66,** 480–482.

Leopold, A. S., Erwin, M., Oh, J., and Browning, B. (1976). Phytoestrogens: Adverse effects on reproduction in California quail. *Science* **191,** 98–100.

Liu, S. K., Dolensek, E. P., Tappe, J. P., Stover, J., and Adams, C. R. (1984). Cardiomyopathy associated with vitamin E deficiency in seven gelada baboons. *J. Am. Vet. Med. Assoc.* **185,** 1347–1350.

Liu, S. K., Dolensek, E. P., and Tappe, J. P. (1985). Cardiomyopathy and vitamin E deficiency in zoo animals and birds. *Heart and Vessels,* Suppl. **1,** 288–293.

Lowenstine, L. J. (1986). Nutritional disorders of birds. *In* "Zoo and Wild Animal Medicine" (M. E. Fowler, ed.), pp. 201–212. W. B. Saunders, Philadelphia, Pennsylvania.

Losowsky, M. S., Kelleher, J., Walker, B. E., Davies, T., and Smith, C. L. (1972). Intake and absorption of tocopherol. *Ann. N. Y. Acad. Sci.* **203,** 212–222.

Machlin, L. J. (1980). "Vitamin E: A Comprehensive Treatise." Dekker, New York.

MacKenzie, W. F., and Fletcher, K. (1979). Megavitamin E responsive myopathy in Goodfellow tree kangaroos associated with confinement. *In* "The Comparative Pathology of Zoo Animals" (R. J. Montali and G. Migaki, eds.), pp. 35–39. Smithsonian Inst. Press, Washington, D.C.

Mann, G. V. (1970). Nutritional requirements of *Cebus* monkeys. *In* "Feeding and Nutrition of Nonhuman Primates" (R. S. Harris, ed.), pp. 143–157. Academic Press, New York.

Martin, R. D. (1975). General principles for breeding small mammals in captivity. *In* "Breeding Endangered Species in Captivity" (R. D. Martin, ed.), pp. 143–166. Academic Press, New York.

McDonald, P., Edwards, R. A., and Greenhalgh, J. F. D. (1973). "Animal Nutrition." Longman, New York.

Millar, R. I., Smith, L. T., and Wood, J. H. (1977). The study of the dietary vitamin D_3 requirement of ringnecked pheasant chicks. *Poult. Sci.* **56,** 1739 (abstract).

Miller, R. M., and Ridgeway, S. H. (1963). Clinical experience with dolphins and whales. *Small Anim. Clin.* **3,** 189–193.

National Academy of Sciences (NAS). (1975). The effect of genetic variance on nutritional requirements of animals. Nat. Acad. Sci., Washington, D.C.

National Research Council (NRC). (1978a). Nutrient requirements of laboratory animals. Publ. No. **2767,** Nat. Acad. Sci., Washington, D.C.

National Research Council (NRC). (1978b). Nutrient requirements of nonhuman primates. Publ. No. **2768,** Nat. Acad. Sci., Washington, D.C.

National Research Council (NRC). (1982). Nutrient requirements of mink and foxes. Nat. Acad. Sci., Washington, D.C.

National Research Council (NRC). (1984). Nutrient requirements of poultry. Nat. Acad. Sci., Washington, D.C.

National Research Council (NRC). (1987). Vitamin tolerance of animals. Nat. Acad. Sci., Washington, D.C.

Nestler, R. B. (1946). Vitamin A, vital factor in the survival of bobwhites. *Trans. North Am. Wildl. Conf.* **11,** 176–195.

Nestler, R. B., DeWitt, J. B., and Derby, J. V. (1949a). Vitamin A and carotene content of some wildlife foods. *J. Wildl. Manage.* **13,** 271–274.

Nestler, R. B., DeWitt, J. B., and Derby, J. V. (1949b). Vitamin A storage in wild quail and its possible significance. *J. Wildl. Manage.* **13**, 265–271.

Nichols, D., Montali, R. J., Pickett, C., and Bush, C. (1983). Rickets in double-crested cormorants (*Phalacrocorax auritus*). *J. Zoo Anim. Med.* **14**, 115–124.

Nichols, D. K., Campbell, V. L., and Montali, R. J. (1986). Pansteatis in great blue herons. *J. Am. Vet. Med. Assoc.* **189**, 1110–1112.

Nichols, D. K., Wolff, M. J., Phillips, L. G., and Montali, R. J. (1989). Coagulopathy in pink-backed pelicans (*Pelecanus rufescens*) associated with hypervitaminosis E. *J. Zoo Wildl. Med.* **20**, 57–61.

Notini, G. (1941). Verksamheten vid andkarantanen. *Svensk Jakt.* **79**, 155–159.

Oftedal, O. T., and Boness, D. J. (1983). Fish quality: The net result. *Proc. Am. Assoc. Zoo Vet.*, 47–51.

Oksanen, H. E. (1973). Aspects of vitamin E deficiency in ruminants. *Acta Agric. Scand. Suppl.* **19**, 22–28.

Olson, R. E. (1984). The function and metabolism of vitamin K. *Annu. Rev. Nutr.* **4**, 281–337.

Olson, R. E., and Carpenter, P. C. (1967). Regulatory function of vitamin E. *Adv. Enzyme Regul.* **5**, 325–334.

O'Sullivan, B.M., Mayo, F.D., and Hartley, W.J. (1977). Neurologic lesions in young captive lions associated with vitamin A deficiency. *Aust. Vet. J.* **53**, 187–189.

Papas, A. M., Cambre, R. C., and Citino, S. B. (1989). Vitamin E: Considerations in practical animal feeding and case studies with elephants and black rhinoceros. *Proc. Dr. Scholl Nutr. Conf.* **8**, 59–72.

Papas, A. M., Cambre, R. C., Citino, S. B., and Sokol, R.J. (1991). Efficacy of absorption of various vitamin-E forms by captive elephants and black rhinoceroses. *J. Zoo Wildl. Med.* **22**, 309–317.

Partridge, G. G. (1980). The vitamin K requirements of wild brown rats (*Rattus norvegicus*) resistant to warfarin. *Comp. Biochem. Physiol.* **66A**, 83–87.

Paton, D. C., Dorward, D. F., and Fell, P. (1983). Thiamine deficiency and winter mortality in red wattlebirds, *Anthochaera carunculata* (Aves: Meliphagidae) in suburban Melbourne. *Aust. J. Zool.* **31**, 147–154.

Pollock, J. I., and Mullin, R. J. (1987). Vitamin C biosynthesis in prosimians: Evidence for the anthropoid affinity of Tarsius. *Am. J. Phys. Anthropol.* **73**, 65–70.

Price, P. A. (1988). Role of vitamin-K-dependent proteins in bone metabolism. *Annu. Rev. Nutr.* **8**, 565–583.

Quintanilha, A. T., and Packer, L. (1983). Vitamin E, physical exercise and tissue oxidative damage. In "Biology of Vitamin E," (R. Porter and J. Whelan, eds.), pp. 56–61. Pitman, London.

Ratti, J. T. (1977). "Reproductive Separation and Isolation Mechanisms between Dark and Light-Phase Western Grebes." Doctoral Dissertation, Utah State Univ., Logan.

Rebhun, W. C., Tennant, B. C., Dill, S. G., and King, J. M. (1984). Vitamin K_3–induced renal toxicosis in the horse. *J. Am. Vet. Med. Assoc.* **184**, 1237–1239.

Reichman, O. J., and Van De Graaff, K. M. (1975). Association between ingestion of green vegetation and desert rodent reproduction. *J. Mammal.* **56**, 503–506.

Ridgeway, S. H. (1965). Medical care of marine mammals. *J. Am. Vet. Med. Assoc.* **147**, 1077–1085.

Rigdon, R. H., and Drager, G. A. (1955). Thiamine deficiency in sea lions (*Otaria californiana*) fed only frozen fish. *J. Am. Vet. Med. Assoc.* **127**, 453–455.

Rodahl, K. (1949). Toxicity of polar bear liver. *Nature (London)* **164**, 530.

Rodahl, K., and Moore, T. (1943). The vitamin A content and toxicity of bear and seal liver. *Biochem. J.* **37**, 166–168.

108   6. Vitamins

Rowsemitt, C. N., and O'Connor, A. J. (1989). Reproductive function in *Dipodomys ordii* stimulated by 6–methoxybenzoxazolinone. *J. Mammal.* **70,** 805–809.
Roy, R. N., and Guha, B. C. (1958). Species difference in regard to the biosynthesis of ascorbic acid. *Nature (London)* **182,** 319–320.
Russell, F. E. (1967). Vitamin A content of polar bear liver. *Toxicon* **5,** 61–62.
Schultz, V. B. (1948). Vitamin A as a survival factor of the bobwhite quail (*Colinus v. virginianus*) in Ohio during the winter of 1946–47. *J. Wildl. Manage.* **12,** 251–263.
Schultz, V. B. (1959). Vitamin A and Ohio bobwhite quail during the winter of 1947–48. *J. Wildl. Manage.* **23,** 322–327.
Scott, M. L. (1975). Environmental influences on ascorbic acid requirements in animals. *Ann. N. Y. Acad. Sci.* **258,** 151–155.
Scott, M. L., Holm, E. R., and Reynolds, R. E. (1959). Studies on the niacin, riboflavin, choline, manganese, and zinc requirements of young ring-necked pheasants for growth, feathering, and prevention of leg disorders. *Poult. Sci.* **38,** 1344–1350.
Scott, M. L., Holm, E. R., and Reynolds, R. E. (1964). Studies on the pantothenic acid and unidentified factor requirements of young ring-necked pheasants and bobwhite quail. *Poult. Sci.* **43,** 1534–1539.
Scott, P. P. (1968). The special features of nutrition of cats, with observations on wild felidae nutrition in the London Zoo. *Symp. Zool. Soc. London* **21,** 21–36.
Serafin, J. A. (1974). Studies on the riboflavin, niacin, pantothenic acid and choline requirements of young bobwhite quail. *Poult. Sci.* **53,** 1522–1532.
Skinner, D.C., Moodley, G., and Buffenstein, R. (1991). Is vitamin D₃ esential for mineral metabolism in the Damara mole-rat (*Cryptomys damarensis*)? *Gen. Comp. Endocrinol.* **81,** 500–505.
Smith, J. E., and Goodman, D. S. (1979). Retinol-binding protein and the regulation of vitamin A transport. *Fed. Proc.* **38,** 2504–2509.
Sorensen, P. H. (1973). Basic principles involved in the supplementation of compound feeds with vitamin E. *Acta Agric. Scand.* **19,** 177–180.
Stauber, E. (1973). Suspected riboflavin deficiency in a golden eagle. *J. Am. Vet. Med. Assoc.* **163,** 645–646.
Street, J. C., and Chadwick, R. W. (1975). Ascorbic acid requirements and metabolism in relation to organochloride pesticides. *Ann. N. Y. Acad. Sci.* **258,** 132–143.
Takeuchi, A., Okano, T., Tanda, M., and Kobayashi, T. (1991). Possible origin of extremely high contents of vitamin D₃ in some kinds of fish liver. *Comp. Biochem. Physiol.* **100A,** 483–487.
Thompson, D. R., and Baumann, C. A. (1950). Vitamin A in pheasants, quail, and muskrats. *J. Wildl. Manage.* **14,** 42–49.
Travis, H. F. (1963). Symposium—Speciality feed formulation—Some considerations in the formulation. *Proc. Cornell Nutr. Conf. Feed Manuf.,* pp. 122–126.
Ullrey, D. E. (1984). Do zoo animals need to see the sun? *Proc. Dr. Scholl Nutr. Conf.* **4,** 82–85.
Wagner, J. E., and Dietlein, D. R. (1970). Steatitis in an American white pelican. *Int. Zoo Yearb.* **10,** 174.
Walker, A., Zimmerman, M. R., and Leakey, R. E. F. (1982). A possible case of hypervitaminosis A in *Homo erectus. Nature (London)* **296,** 248–250.
Wallach, J. D. (1970). Nutritional diseases of exotic animals. *J. Am. Vet. Med. Assoc.* **157,** 583–599.
Ward, F. P. (1971). Thiamine deficiency in a peregrine falcon. *J. Am. Vet. Med. Assoc.* **159,** 599–601.
Warner, R. G. (1961). Recent developments in mink nutrition. *Proc. Cornell Nutr. Conf. Feed Manuf.,* pp. 96–100.

Warner, R. G., Travis, H. F., Bassett, C. F., Krook, P., and McCarthy, B. (1963). "Utilization of Carotene by Growing Mink Kits." Mink Farmers Research Foundation Progress Report.

Wasserman, R. H. (1975). Active vitamin D-like substances in *Solanum malacoxylon* and other calcinogenic plants. *Nutr. Rev.* **33,** 1–5.

Wasserman, R. H., Taylor, A. N., and Kallfelz, F. A. (1966). Vitamin D and transfer of plasma calcium to intestinal lumen in chicks and rats. *Am. J. Physiol.* **211,** 419–423.

Wasserman, R. H., Henion, J. D., Haussler, M. R., and McCain, T. A. (1976). Calcinogenic factor in *Solanum malacoxylon:* Evidence that 1,25-dihydroxyvitamin D_3–glycoside. *Science* **194,** 853–855.

Webb, A. R., and Holick, M. F. (1988). The role of sunlight in the cutaneous production of vitamin D_3. *Ann. Rev. Nutr.* **8,** 375–399.

West, W. T., and Mason, K. E. (1958). Histopathology of muscular dystrophy in the vitamin E-deficient hamster. *Am. J. Anat.* **102,** 323–363.

Weswig, P. H. (1956). Vitamin A storage. *Oregon St. Game Bull.* **11,** 7.

White, J. R. (1970). Thiamine deficiency in an Atlantic bottle-nosed dolphin (*Tursiops truncatus*) on a diet of raw fish. *J. Am. Vet. Med. Assoc.* **157,** 559–562.

Wortman, J. D., and Larue, M. D. (1974). Hand-rearing polar bear cubs (*Thalarctos maritimus*) at Topeka Zoo. *Int. Zoo Yearb.* **14,** 215–218.

Yess, N. J., and Hegsted, D. M. (1967). Biosynthesis of ascorbic acid in the acouchi and agouti. *J. Nutr.* **92,** 331–333.

Youatt, W. G., Ullrey, D. E., and Magee, W. T. (1976). Vitamin A concentration in livers of white-tailed deer. *J. Wildl. Manage.* **40,** 172–173.

7

Essential Fatty Acids

Isolation and identification of the vitamins largely occurred between 1840 and the late 1920s (Gurr, 1984). At the end of this exciting time, animals fed vitamin- and mineral-sufficient, fat-free diets developed a characteristic deficiency disease that could be corrected by adding specific polyunsaturated fatty acids to the diet (Burr and Burr, 1929). Because these fatty acids cannot be produced by the animal from any precursor and, thus, must be in the diet, they are known as *essential fatty acids* (EFAs). While there are many polyunsaturated fatty acids, only four have been discussed as essential. These are linoleic, arachidonic, linolenic, and eicosapentaenoic acids.

These acids, particularly linoleic and arachidonic, are essential components of all cell membranes and are precursors to the synthesis of metabolites that regulate the activity of tissues throughout the body. A major group of metabolic regulators that are produced from EFAs are prostaglandins (Fig. 7.1). Prosta- glandins and other EFA-derived metabolites control cyclic AMP production, blood platelet aggregation, vascular tone, inflammatory reactions, and immune responses. Because EFAs are involved in both tissue structure and basic metab- olism, deficiencies affect tissues throughout the body. Deficiency symptoms include alopecia, dermatitis, poor growth even though the appetite is increased, impaired reproduction, hypertrophy and hemorrhaging of the kidneys, failure of wounds to heal, dehydration because the skin becomes very permeable to water, fatty degeneration of the liver, increased susceptibility to infection due to immune system failure, and irritability and hyperactivity.

Many herbivorous and omnivorous animals can produce arachidonic acid from dietary linoleic acid. For these animals, such as the laboratory rat or domestic dog, arachidonic acid is not a dietary requirement as long as linoleic acid is in the diet. However, strict carnivores, such as cats, cannot convert linoleic acid to arachidonic acid and alpha-linolenic acid to eicosapentaenoic acid because the delta-5-desaturase activity (Fig. 7.1) is very low or absent. Thus, cats require both linoleic and arachidonic acids (Rivers *et al.*, 1975, 1976; MacDonald *et al.*, 1983). A classical deficiency of alpha-linolenic acid has been difficult to produce even though one group of prostaglandins must come from alpha-linolenic acid. Rats have been raised successfully for several generations with linoleic acid as the sole dietary EFA. However, alpha-linolenic acid can ameliorate some

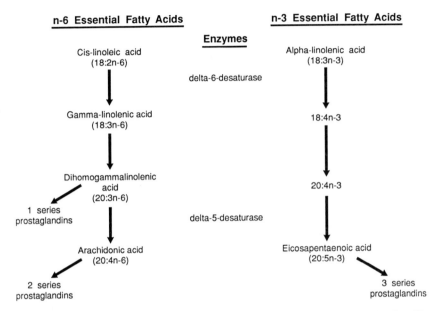

Fig. 7.1 Conversion steps in metabolizing linoleic and linolenic acids into prostaglandins. The two pathways are not interchangeable even though they use the same enzymes and contain forms of linolenic acid. [From Horrobin (1982).]

of the linoleic acid–deficiency symptoms (Neuringer *et al.*, 1988; Gurr, 1989). Recent, more sophisticated studies found that alpha-linolenic acid derivatives are essential in the development and functioning of the retina and brain, with deficiencies impairing vision and learning (Holman, 1987; Neuringer *et al.*, 1988).

Linoleic acid is common in green plants, animal fat, and some seed oils, such as sunflower, safflower, peanut, corn, and soybean oil. However, coconut and palm oil have virtually no linoleic acid, and olive oil and animal organs, such as the liver, have only small amounts. Arachidonic acid is common in meat, liver, milk, and some seafoods, such as shrimp, but does not occur in plants. Thus, cats will develop EFA deficiencies if fed cereal-based dogfood diets that have not been supplemented with meat or other sources of arachidonic acid. Linolenic acid or its derivatives are common in green plants, linseed, soybean, and rapeseed oils, and marine fish oils. Marine vertebrates accumulate linolenic acid because it is synthesized by phytoplankton, the base of the marine food chain (Neuringer *et al.*, 1988). The content of these fatty acids in animals is partially dependent on their total fat content. For example, oily fish, such as sardines, anchovies, and herring, are much better sources of EFAs than nonoily smelt (Gailey-Phipps and Sladen, 1982). Penguins fed dead smelt developed an EFA deficiency that was corrected by injecting corn oil into the smelt prior to feeding (Penny, 1978). All EFAs are easily destroyed by oxidation. Thus, foods and oils that have been stored for too long or at too high a temperature may have little EFA activity.

Two captive female cheetahs fed an animal-based diet (70% beef, 10% horsemeat, 10% donkey, and 5% intact poultry carcasses) developed symptoms of an EFA-deficiency (anestrous, dull hair coat with poor coloration, dry scaly skin with encrusted sores, and dull, staring eyes). If one assumes no desaturase activity to convert linoleic and alpha-linolenic acids into the required metabolites, the EFA content (percentage of total fatty acids) of the beef and chicken was 0% gamma-linolenic, 1.5% arachidonic, and 0.2% eicosapentaenoic acids. Daily supplementation with two 500 mg tablets of fish oil and evening primrose oil containing 4% gamma-linolenic acid, 2% arachidonic, and 8.6% eicosapentaenoic acids cured all deficiency symptoms, including the 2-year anestrus period as both females produced cubs. The deficiency may have been caused by improper or excessively long storage of the carcasses resulting in oxidation of the EFAs or failure to feed internal organs and fat (Davidson et al., 1986).

The requirement for EFAs is 1 to 2% of the total caloric intake. However, the requirement does vary with age. Deficiencies occur most commonly in young, rapidly growing animals. Increased growth and metabolism in young animals may elevate the requirement relative to the nongrowing animal, and the young animal has minimal EFA reserves. Deficiencies are slower to develop in mature, nonproducing animals because of the reserves of EFAs and the lack of a requirement for growth. Because the activity of the enzymes that convert EFA's into the active metabolites decline with age, very old animals could have a functional deficiency even though the diet is theoretically adequate (Horrobin, 1982).

REFERENCES

Burr, G. O., and Burr, M. M. (1929). A new deficiency disease produced by the rigid exclusion of fat from the diet. *J. Biol. Chem.* **82,** 345–367.

Davidson, B. C., Cantrill, R. C., and Varaday, D. (1986). The reversal of essential fatty acid deficiency symptoms in the cheetah. *South Afr. J. Zool.* **21,** 161–164.

Gailey-Phipps, J. J., and Sladen, W. J. L. (1982). Survey on nutrition of penguins. *J. Am. Vet. Med. Assoc.* **181,** 1305–1309.

Gurr, M. I. (1984). "Role of Fats in Food and Nutrition." Elsevier Science Publishing, New York.

Holman, R. T. (1987). Essential fatty acids and nutritional disorders. *In* "Lipids in Modern Nutrition" (M. Horisberger and U. Bracco, eds.), pp. 157–171. Raven Press, New York.

Horrobin, D. F. (1982). Essential fatty acids: A review. *In* "Clinical Uses of Essential Fatty Acids" (D. F. Horrobin, ed.), pp. 3–36. Eden Press, Montreal.

MacDonald, M. L., Rogers, Q. R. and Morris, J. G. (1983). Role of linoleate as an essential fatty acid for the cat independent of arachidonate synthesis. *J. Nutr.* **113,** 1422–1433.

Neuringer, M., Anderson, G. J., and Connor, W. E. (1988). The essentiality of n-3 fatty acids for the development and function of the retina and brain. *Annu. Rev. Nutr.* **8,** 517–541.

Penny, R. L. (1978). Breeding Adelie penguins (*Pygoscelis adeliae*) in captivity. *Int. Zoo Yearb.* **18,** 13–21.

Rivers, J. P. W., Hassam, A. G., Crawford, M. A., and Brambell, M. R. (1976). The inability of the lion, *Panthera leo* L., to desaturate linoleic acid. *FEBS Lett.* **67,** 269–270.

Rivers, J. P. W., Sinclair, A. J., and Crawford, M. A. (1975). Inability of the cat to desaturate essential fatty acids. *Nature (London)* **258,** 171–173.

8

Energy Requirements for Maintenance

The essential continuity between an animal and its environment is revealed most obviously in energy exchanges and transformations.

KING, 1974

Studies of wildlife energy transactions have been popular since the early 1950s because of the recognition that the animal is intimately coupled to its environment via energy flow. While the relative proportion of energetic studies as a percentage of all nutrition studies has remained constant since the 1950s (Fig. 1.1), the focus of these studies has changed with time. From the 1950s through the 1970s, nutritional ecologists most frequently measured the energetics of specific behaviors under controlled laboratory conditions. For example, the energetics of locomotion and thermoregulation have been measured on a large number of species to develop broad interspecific comparisons of costs and efficiencies. In the 1980s, nutritional ecologists began striving to understand the relationships between laboratory and field measurements of energetics and to understand the energetics of free-ranging animals. Such studies have permitted the ecologist to quantify the energetic constraints and strategies that determine the animal's fitness (Gittleman and Thompson, 1988).

The nutritionist is often required to estimate energy and protein requirements of wildlife as a prelude to estimating necessary food intake. Before examining some of the requirement estimates, it is essential to understand the general types of methods employed. For the captive animal in which the ingested food can be easily measured, changes in tissue balance relative to feed intake can be used to estimate requirements for many whole-body processes. For example, if the energy or material state of the animal is constant, the observed intake is the maintenance requirement. Although the maintenance requirement is often defined as the intake at which the animal's weight remains constant, one must be careful in using weight as the only criterion of energy and matter balances as the composition of body tissue can also change. When a range of intakes (X) are graphically compared to the body changes produced (Y), the X-intercept at zero gain or loss is the maintenance requirement while the slope of the line is the gain or loss per unit of additional intake (Fig. 8.1). Intake per animal as well

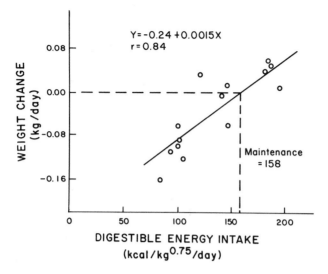

Fig. 8.1 Estimation of maintenance and growth requirements of captive white-tailed deer by feeding many different levels of digestible energy. (From Ullrey *et al.*, 1970, courtesy of the *Journal of Wildlife Management.*)

as the dependent variable are often expressed as a function of body weight, because rarely are the experimental animals perfectly matched and the use of such a common denominator provides a means for extrapolating or comparing the results to other animals of the same or differing species. Additional productive requirements can be determined by feeding at differing levels and measuring the rate (such as milk production) or success (such as reproduction) of the specific process being examined. Thus, all the requirements can be estimated by a direct feeding trial approach, although such estimates may be applicable only to the conditions in which the measurement occurred.

The use of captive animal feeding trials to estimate the requirements of the free-ranging animal poses many problems. As an example, the maintenance energy requirements of captive animals are often below what might be expected under free-ranging conditions because activity and thermoregulatory requirements may be minimized. The captive animal rarely needs to search for food, move between cover and food patches, or flee from predators. For example, energy expenditure of free-ranging ducks was approximately 15% higher than the captive, nonflying bird swimming and feeding in a large pond (Owen, 1969, 1970; Wooley and Owen, 1978). Free-ranging ungulates may expend 25–100% more energy than confined animals (Osuji, 1974; Holleman *et al.*, 1979). The expenditures by wild herbivores may be even higher in heavily grazed areas requiring extensive food searching, in areas where disturbance by humans or predators is extensive, or in severe continental climates requiring an increased thermoregulatory expenditure. Thus, the captive feeding trial approach to estimate energy requirements, while very applicable to understanding other captive animals, may not provide the type of information necessary to understand the free-ranging animal because it simplifies the animal–environment interaction. If one is unable to discern underlying interspecific similarities, a feeding trial approach requires that animals of *n* productive states in *n* environments be used to estimate all possible requirement levels.

The questioning by ecologists of feeding trials using captive animals provided the impetus to examine wildlife requirements from a very basic perspective suitable for predicting requirements under many circumstances. The general approach has been to divide whole-body maintenance and productive processes into their basic components and measure the energetic cost per unit of time. As the relative costs of many of the components are not unique to the species or living state, interspecific comparisons can provide cost estimates for species that have not been studied. The cost per component per unit time is multiplied by its duration in the animal's daily or seasonal life and all of the individual costs are summed to estimate daily or seasonal energy requirements. For maintenance processes, this approach is known as "time-energy budget analyses" (Goldstein, 1988). While the actual measurements of activity costs on captive animals can be very expensive, their application to free-ranging animals can be inexpensive if activity budgets are the only thing being considered. However, because of the large number of biotic and abiotic variables affecting the animal's daily existence, the complexity of predicting total requirements can be formidable (Fig. 8.2). For smaller animals that are very closely coupled to their thermal environment, a good model of thermoregulation is essential when using a time–energy budget analysis to predict daily energy expenditure (Nagy, 1989).

For time–energy budget analyses, maintenance energy expenditure is defined as the necessary chemical energy ingested to meet basal metabolism, activity, and thermoregulation costs. The chemical energy used in these three processes as fats, proteins, or carbohydrates are oxidized is converted to heat. For example, if the animal oxidizes 1 mole of glucose, 6 moles of carbon dioxide and water are produced as 673 kcal of heat is liberated. The stoichiometric relationships between heat production and gas exchanges are constant for the complete oxidation of any organic compound. Therefore, the energy used in the individual maintenance processes can be determined by measuring either heat production (direct calorimetry) or gas production (indirect calorimetry).

Because atmospheric air is a relatively stable 20.94% oxygen, 0.03% carbon dioxide, and 79.03% nitrogen, indirect calorimetry requires only the determination of the expired air volume and composition. Respired air sampling in indirect calorimetry is usually accomplished either by confining the animal to a

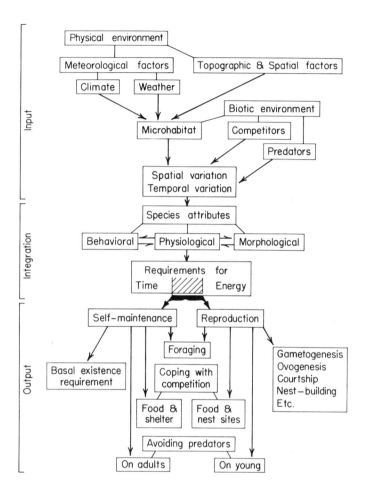

Fig. 8.2 Some of the interactions affecting the energy requirements of free-living birds. (From King, 1974, courtesy of the Nuttall Ornithological Club.)

chamber through which atmospheric air is pumped, by placing on the experimental animal a face mask having a valve system for routing expired air directly into sensors or indirectly via sampling bags, or by surgically providing other gas-collecting ports, such as tracheotomies (Mautz and Fair, 1980). The method of air sampling used depends on specific considerations relative to the animals and hypothesis being examined.

The chamber continues to be popular for birds and small mammals because of the difficulty of placing masks on such animals and the need for visual isolation

TABLE 8.1

Energy Equivalents of Oxygen and Carbon Dioxide and the Corresponding Percentage
of Fat and Carbohydrates Oxidized for Different Nonprotein Respiratory Quotients
in Mammals

Nonprotein RQ	O_2 kcal/liter	CO_2 kcal/liter	kcal/g	Percentage O_2 consumed by Carbohydrates	Fat
0.70	4.686	6.694	3.408	0	100
0.74	4.727	6.388	3.252	11.3	88.7
0.78	4.776	6.123	3.117	24.9	75.1
0.82	4.825	5.884	2.996	38.6	61.4
0.86	4.875	5.669	2.886	52.2	47.8
0.90	4.924	5.471	2.785	65.9	34.1
0.94	4.973	5.290	2.693	79.5	20.5
0.98	5.022	5.124	2.609	93.2	6.8
1.00	5.047	5.047	2.569	100.0	0

Source: Brody, 1945, p. 310.

if many of the animals are to remain calm. The use of a mask depends on considerations of mask weight, air resistance, and dead space, if a passive system, and ease of animal habituation. Although lightweight masks have been used on flying parakeets and gulls (Tucker, 1969), mask use has largely been confined to the larger mammals in which weight and dead space are relatively minor considerations. Because the energy equivalent of consumed oxygen is less variable as different substrates are metabolized (4.69 to 5.05 kcal/liter or ±3.6% of the mean) than the respired carbon dioxide (5.05 to 6.69 kcal/liter or ±16.3% of the mean), the measurement of oxygen consumption and the use of appropriate energy equivalents in indirect calorimetry is preferred to relying solely on carbon dioxide production measurements (Tables 8.1 and 8.2).

TABLE 8.2

Thermal Equivalents of Oxygen and Carbon Dioxide for Various Substrates Metabolized
and the Corresponding Respiratory Quotient in Birds

RQ	Substrate	Thermal equivalents (kcal/liter) O_2	CO_2
0.71	Fat	4.686	6.694
0.72	Protein	4.750	6.597
1.00	Carbohydrate	5.047	5.047

Sources: King and Farner, 1961; Romijn and Lokhorst, 1961.

The stoichiometric ratios between carbon dioxide produced and atmospheric oxygen consumed by the animal are termed the *respiratory quotient* (RQ) and normally range from 0.70 to 1.00. Fats are relatively poor in molecular oxygen and carbohydrates are relatively rich; therefore, the RQ of fats is lower than that of carbohydrates because additional atmospheric oxygen must be respired relative to the carbon dioxide produced (Table 8.1). As the animal fasts, the observed RQ decreases from levels characteristic of carbohydrate metabolism to a nonprotein-corrected RQ of 0.7 associated with fat catabolism (Fig. 8.3). Occasionally, an RQ outside the range 0.7–1.0 occurs. A very high RQ can occur during the initial phases of exercise as carbon dioxide is flushed from the animal, during intense fattening, or during fermentation in the nonfasted ruminant, whereas an RQ lower than 0.7 may be due to the retention of carbon dioxide, excretion of bicarbonates, or the preferential or partial metabolism of long-chain fatty acids. The RQ for protein metabolism is different between birds (0.72) and

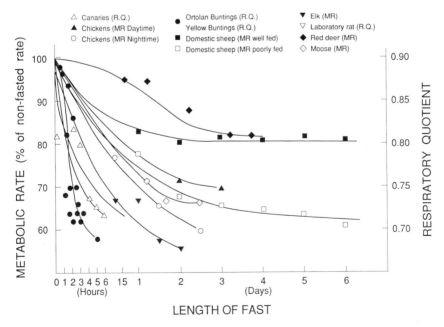

Fig. 8.3 Length of time necessary to reach postabsorptive conditions as indicated by a minimal RQ or stable metabolic rates. (Data from Benedict and Fox, 1933; Barrott *et al.*, 1938; Marston, 1948; Wallgren, 1954; Westerterp, 1977; Robbins, unpublished; Simpson *et al.*, 1978b; Renecker and Hudson, 1986.)

mammals (0.82) and reflects the differences between uric acid and urea excretion (Tables 8.1 and 8.2). The uric acid of bird excreta contains 29% oxygen and 35% nitrogen, whereas urea contains 27% oxygen and 47% nitrogen. Errors in estimating energy expenditure due to failure to correct RQs to a nonprotein basis are always small when using fasted or fed birds and fed mammals (less than 3%), but become more significant when using fasted mammals (Gessaman and Nagy, 1988a).

Indirect calorimetry using face masks, chambers, or other gas collection systems severely restricts measurement opportunities. A newer, indirect calorimetry method called "doubly labeled water" frees the ecologist to measure the energetics of free-ranging wildlife. The method rests on the observation that oxygen atoms in metabolically produced carbon dioxide equilibrate with oxygen atoms in the body's water via the action of carbonic anhydrase in blood (Lifson *et al.*, 1949). Thus, water that is labeled with tritium or deuterium and oxygen-18 (i.e., double-labeled water) is injected into the animal. Because oxygen is lost from the body as both carbon dioxide and water, whereas hydrogen is lost as water only, the difference in the respective biological decay of hydrogen and oxygen isotopes is a measure of carbon dioxide production (Fig. 8.4), and thus energy expenditure (Lifson *et al.*, 1955; Nagy, 1983). Any body water sample

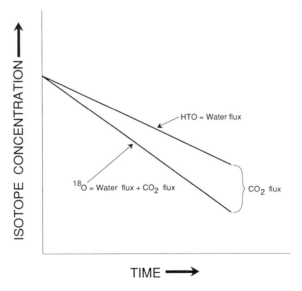

Fig. 8.4 The basis for the use of doubly labeled water to measure CO_2 production and energy expenditure of wild animals. (From Costa, 1988.)

(blood, urine, saliva, or tears) can be used for the measurements, and as few as two post-equilibration samples are necessary to establish the decay curves. Thus, the animal normally must be captured at least twice: once to establish background isotope concentrations, inject the isotope, and take the initial equilibrated sample, and the second time to take the final water sample. Recapture intervals can range from a few hours to 3 days in small mammals and birds, to 7 to 15 days in very large animals. Thus, the method can be used to measure the costs of specific activities, such as flying (Gessaman and Nagy, 1988b), swimming (Costa, 1988), or daily existence (Nagy, 1987). Use of the method was initially restricted to animals weighing less than 2 or 3 kg because of the high cost of doubly labeled water. The development of more sensitive analytical instruments has lessened the amount of labeled water that must be used so the method can be used on animals of any size. However, because hydrogen can be incorporated into new tissue, particularly fat, and methane produced by fermentation in the gastrointestinal tract, the method may require corrections or may not be appropriate for rapidly growing or fattening animals (Klaassen et al., 1989a).

I. BASAL METABOLISM

A. Measurement Criteria

The concept of basal metabolism as some lower level of metabolism necessary for basic body functioning has pervaded thought and studies of energy metabolism for many years. Basal metabolic rate has been defined as the energy expenditure of an animal (a) in muscular and psychic repose although not sleeping; (b) in a thermoneutral environment; and (c) in a postabsorptive state (Brody, 1945; Kleiber, 1961). The values determined are not necessarily minimal because sleeping, prolonged starvation, dehydration, and torpor can further reduce energy expenditure below basal metabolic rate levels (Reese and Haines, 1978; Lyman et al., 1982; Prothero and Jurgens, 1986; Geiser, 1987; Wang and Wolowyk, 1988; Heller, 1988). However, since the animal is not expending energy to thermoregulate, process or metabolize food, or increase the activity state, basal metabolic rate does represent a baseline on which the additional energy expenditures of the active animal can be added. From 36 to 50% of the energy expended as basal metabolic rate comes from the basic service functions of body organs (i.e., kidney filtration, respiration, circulation, nerve and liver function), and from 40 to 56% is expended in the cell maintenance functions of protein and lipid turnover and ion transport (Baldwin et al., 1980).

The postabsorptive state occurs when an animal fasts until it is no longer directly metabolizing ingested feed and is therefore dependent on mobilized body tissue for meeting its energy requirements. Because it is difficult to directly measure emptying of metabolizable material from the gastrointestinal tract, indirect indices—primarily the absence of methane production associated with gastrointestinal fermentation; a stabilized, reduced metabolic rate relative to the fed animal; or a stoichiometric gas relationship indicating fat metabolism—are often used to determine when the animal has reached basal conditions.

The necessary length of fasting to achieve basal conditions is largely dependent on the size of the animal, complexity and type of gastrointestinal tract determining rate of food passage, and the level of previous feeding. Although many small birds and mammals become postabsorptive in 3–6 hr (Stevenson, 1933; Brenner and Malin, 1965; Weathers et al., 1983), shrews began dying after 2 hr of fasting because of their small size and very intense metabolism (Gebczynski, 1971). The required length of fasting increases to more than 40 hr for larger ruminants (Silver, 1968; Wesley et al., 1973; Simpson et al., 1978b; Renecker and Hudson, 1986) (Fig. 8.3).

Unfortunately, the fasting of some animals can make it very difficult to meet the condition of a calm, resting attitude. Hummingbirds often enter torpor when fasted as a physiological and ecological adaptation to reduced energy availability, whereas many rodents and birds become hyperactive as they search for food (Ketterson and King, 1977). The experimental difficulties in achieving the post-absorptive state in a female Indian elephant were described by Benedict (1936 pp. 233–234):

> . . . when she was not fed as frequently as she wished, she became almost frantically restless, moved from side to side, turned not a little, trumpeted, and gave every evidence of extreme discomfort and irritability. . . . At night when the keeper was sleeping and [she] became hungry, she would gather up refuse from the floor and throw it at his cot to wake him to go get hay. If this did not waken him, she would search around until she found a stone. On several occasions stones as large as hens eggs were removed from his bed. . . . One night she actually. . . . crashed through the doors of the barn, went immediately to another building 150 meters away where she knew hay was stored, ate what hay she wanted, and returned to the barn . . . therefore, it was apparent that the measurement of the basal metabolism of the elephant in the true post-absorptive condition was impracticable . . . .

Thus, wildlife present special problems in meeting all conditions of basal metabolic rate measurements. One of the most difficult conditions to judge is whether the animal is in a calm, resting state without excess apprehension and muscle tonus. Extensive training and habituation may be necessary. Similarly, social animals may need the psychophysiological stimulation of adjacent conspecifics to reach basal conditions (Martin et al., 1980). Basal metabolic rate in diurnally active birds can often be measured in the dark to reduce all activity. Avian ecologists have accepted sleeping as a component of basal metabolic rate determinations, while measurements made during the day on quiescent but awake fasted birds in a thermoneutral environment are termed *fasting metabolic rates*.

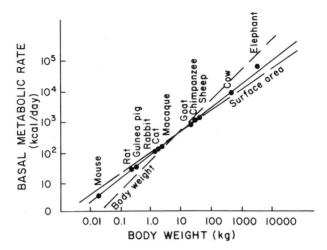

Fig. 8.5 Relationships between basal metabolic rate (0.75 power of body weight), body weight (power of 1), and surface area (0.67 power) in several adult eutherian mammals. (From Kleiber, 1947.)

Thus, additional terminology has arisen, such as *standard metabolic rate* (SMR) and *resting metabolic rate* (RMR). In general, all the metabolic rate terminology has been so "mutilated and confused" (King, 1974, p. 30) that the methodology of each article should be read carefully to determine the conditions of the measurements.

B. Interspecific Comparisons

Basal metabolic rate measurements have been popular because of the fundamental unifying nature of the concept and value to understanding the energy metabolism of diverse biological systems (Brody, 1945; Kleiber, 1961; Schmidt-Nielsen, 1970). Historically, basal metabolic rates of different species have been compared to an exponential function of body weight. Kleiber's (1947) determination that basal metabolic rates of eutherian or placental mammals are a function of the 0.75 power of body weight has been widely accepted (Fig. 8.5):

$$Y = 70X^{0.75}$$

where Y is the basal metabolic rate in kilocalories per day and X is the body weight in kilograms. The nutritional implication of this equation is that the larger animal has an energy requirement for basal metabolism that is less per unit of weight than does the smaller animal. For example, a 0.1 kg mammal has a BMR of 12.4 kcal/day (124 kcal/kg) whereas a 10 kg mammal has a BMR of 394 kcal/day (39.4 kcal/kg). Thus, a population of the smaller species weighing 10 kg (N = 100) would require 1240 kcal/day for basal metabolism, or over 3 times the energy requirement of a population (N = 1) of the larger species with the same biomass.

The Kleiber equation was developed from a very small sample of species heavily biased toward domestic and laboratory animals (Hayssen and Lacy, 1985). A more recent compilation of basal metabolic rates for 272 species of eutherians and 46 marsupials (McNab, 1988a) provides the equations:

$$\text{Eutherians:} \quad Y = 57.2X^{0.716}$$

$$\text{Marsupials:} \quad Y = 46.6X^{0.737}$$

However, many of the basal metabolic rates measured for wild mammals are significantly higher or lower than predicted by these all-inclusive equations. Although variation is lessened when data are grouped by taxonomical categories (Hayssen and Lacy, 1985; McNab, 1988a,b), the most meaningful insights provided thus far are when data are grouped in an ecological and physiological context, particularly by food habits (McNab, 1986a,b; 1988a,b) (Table 8.3). For example, vertebrate-eating carnivores, invertebrate-eating carnivores weighing less than 100 g, nut-eaters, and many grass and forb-eaters have high basal metabolic rates. Invertebrate-eating carnivores weighing more than 100 g, terrestrial and arboreal folivores, frugivores, desert seed-eaters, and large arboreal folivores have low basal metabolic rates. Thus, high metabolic rates frequently occur in mammals that eat foods that are highly digestible and abundant throughout the year, while low metabolic rates occur in species that eat foods that are in relatively short supply, poorly digestible, or heavily defended. Similarly, arboreality can lessen the predation risk and thereby reduce the necessary muscle mass and metabolic rate (McNab, 1986a). While the predictive equations are useful in initial evaluations of energy requirements, species-specific data should always be used when available and appropriate.

Basal metabolic rates are not constant for a species. Mass-specific metabolic rates of young, rapidly growing animals are much higher ($2 \times$) than adult rates (Wesley et al., 1973; Poczopko, 1979; Ashwell-Erckson et al., 1979; McClure and Randolph, 1980; McNab, 1983). Mammalian basal metabolic rates are 16 ± 9% (range: 7–28%) higher than sleeping metabolic rates (Pauls, 1981; Heller, 1988). Because of the daily rhythm in metabolic rates associated with sleep cycles, a systematic bias can occur if the metabolic rates of both nocturnal and diurnal species are measured during the daylight part of the daily cycle (Kenagy and Vleck, 1982; Prothero, 1984). These daily cycles in metabolic rates are superimposed on annual cycles in which basal metabolic rates are frequently lower in large, winter-active mammals than those measured in summer (Chappel and Hudson, 1978b; Newman and Rudd, 1978; Ringberg, 1979; Regelin et al.,

TABLE 8.3

Equations for Basal Metabolic Rate (Y in kcal/day) as a Function of Body Weight (kg) When Mammals are Grouped by Food Habits

Food habits	n	Equation	r^2	Weight range (kg)
Vertebrate eaters	15	$Y = 91.8X^{0.813}$	0.71	0.077–175.0
Invertebrate eaters				
Flying	5	$Y = 47.3X^{0.797}$	0.69	0.009–0.056
Small	20	$Y = 44.1X^{0.597}$	0.78	0.003–0.123
Burrowing	14	$Y = 31.7X^{0.738}$	0.76	0.400–48.0
Large	11	$Y = 43.5X^{0.719}$	0.82	0.206–7.7
Large anteaters	4	$Y = 19.7X^{0.753}$	0.87	1.2–30.6
Frugivores				
Flying	14	$Y = 56.6X^{0.691}$	0.94	0.010–0.598
Arboreal	8	$Y = 50.1X^{0.603}$	0.94	0.300–14.3
Terrestrial	2	$Y = 60.9X^{0.744}$	—	0.498–9.2
Nectarivores	6	$Y = 23.3X^{0.451}$	0.74	0.010–0.052
Seed and nut-eaters	15	$Y = 70.9X^{0.766}$	0.86	0.030–20.2
Desert seed-eaters	13	$Y = 85.8X^{0.873}$	0.21	0.009–0.106
Burrowing seed-eaters	6	$Y = 44.4X^{0.597}$	0.71	0.096–0.600
Grazers				
Small	12	$Y = 62.5X^{0.617}$	0.46	0.025–0.109
Burrowing	12	$Y = 42.5X^{0.799}$	0.87	0.167–6.8
Burrowing-root	16	$Y = 47.2X^{0.663}$	0.87	0.071–2.3
Large	21	$Y = 69.1X^{0.808}$	0.81	0.141–150.0
Folivores				
Small	6	$Y = 42.7X^{0.545}$	0.72	0.047–0.321
Arboreal	9	$Y = 39.9X^{0.657}$	0.65	0.860–7.0
Terrestrial	5	$Y = 52.6X^{0.750}$	0.98	0.801–407.0

[a]Source: McNab, 1988a.

1985; Renecker and Hudson, 1986) and higher in winter than in summer in small- to medium-sized, winter-active mammals (Hinds, 1973; Zervanos, 1975; Wunder et al., 1977, Rogowitz, 1990).

Daily and seasonal metabolic cycles are even more accentuated in species that use torpor to conserve energy. Hibernation, dormancy, and estivation enable animals (e.g., ground squirrels, marmots, hedgehogs, bears) in predictable environments containing abundant, seasonal food supplies to stagger the accumulation and use of energy and, thereby, occupy niches that could not support an active animal year-round. The metabolic rates of hibernators are, in part, dependent on environmental temperature and therefore body temperature (Lyman et al., 1982; Wang and Wolowyk, 1988). Body temperatures of 2° to 5°C are common in small hibernators in very cold environments, although body temperatures as low as $-2.9°C$ can occur (Barnes, 1989). These low body temperatures are associated with heart rates of 3 to 10 beats/minute and maximum intervals between breaths as long as 55 to 150 minutes (Lyman *et al.*, 1982). Body temperatures in larger mammals can be much higher than in the smaller species because increasing fur thickness and decreasing surface area to volume ratios may limit the rate of cooling. For example, the body temperature of bears does not drop below 31°C and heart rates average 16 beats/minute (Morrison, 1960; Kayser, 1961; Watts *et al.*, 1981). The minimal metabolic rates of small hibernators, excluding arousal periods and not correcting for differing body temperatures, are expressed by the equation:

$$Y = 3.2X^{1.03}$$

where Y is the metabolic rate in kilocalories per day and X is the body weight in kilograms (Kayser, 1964). Metabolic rates of hibernating bears are 5 times higher ($Y = 15.2X^{0.99}$) than small hibernators but still far below the nonhibernating bear (Erickson and Youatt, 1961; Watts, 1990).

Thus, unlike basal metabolism, energy expenditure during hibernation is a linear function of body weight. This metabolic rate converges toward the interspecific basal metabolic rate in larger animals as body temperature remains high. Although small animals consume very little energy during the inactive phase of hibernation (as little as 1% of the rate of an active animal [Geiser, 1987]), arousals are very costly. Bats and ground squirrels expended 84 to 90% of all the energy consumed during the total hibernation period in the arousal periods, even though 93 to 99% of the total time was spent in actual hibernation (Wang, 1979; Thomas *et al.*, 1990). Energy savings due to seasonal torpor relative to remaining active range from 88% in small mammals to 66% in bears (Wang and Wolowyk, 1988; Watts and Jonkel, 1988).

Daily torpor occurs in many marsupials, insectivores, bats, primates, and rodents. Minimal body temperatures during daily torpor range from 10° to 22°C. Consequently, energy savings are not as great and range from 18 to 31% depending on depth and duration (Wang and Wolowyk, 1988).

Numerous equations relating basal metabolic rate and weight of adult birds have been proposed (King and Farner, 1961; Lasiewski and Dawson, 1967; Zar, 1968, 1969; Aschoff and Pohl, 1970a; Poczopko, 1971; King, 1974; Kendeigh *et al.*, 1977; Bennett and Harvey, 1987). King and Farner (1961) first suggested that all birds might not be adequately represented by one equation because larger birds (over 125 g) were apparently different from smaller species. Lasiewski and Dawson (1967) later pointed out that it was not purely a question of bird size, but rather that passerines and nonpasserines were represented by differing equations.

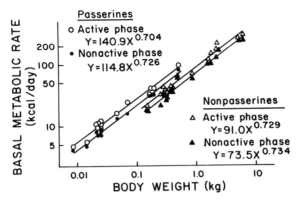

Fig. 8.6   Basal metabolic rates in birds measured during active and nonactive phases of the daily cycle. (From Aschoff and Pohl, 1970b, courtesy of the *Journal fur Ornithologie*.)

Although the basal metabolic rates of larger nonpasserines are indistinguishable from the generalized adult eutherian equation, passerines have metabolic rates 30–70% higher than the generalized mammalian equation (Aschoff and Pohl, 1970b; Calder and King, 1974; Kendeigh *et al.*, 1977; Bennett and Harvey, 1987). As in mammals, some birds have basal metabolic rates significantly different from the interspecific regressions. For example, metabolic rates of tropical birds and nocturnally active birds are lower than temperate and diurnally active birds, whereas marine birds have higher metabolic rates than terrestrial birds (Hails, 1983; Bennett and Harvey, 1987). Similarly, broad patterns occur between the basal metabolic rates of birds and their food habits (McNab, 1988b). Birds that feed primarily on nectar, grass, flying-insects, and vertebrates usually have high metabolic rates.

Avian metabolic rates are not constant within a species. The basal metabolic rates of birds measured during the nonactive phase of the daily cycle are approximately 24% lower than those measured during the active phase (Aschoff and Pohl, 1970a; Kendeigh *et al.*, 1977; Heller *et al.*, 1983; Stahel *et al.*, 1984) (Fig. 8.6). Seasonal differences also occur. Basal metabolic rates in many passerines are significantly higher in winter than in summer (Kendeigh *et al.*, 1977). Seasonal metabolic rates in nonpasserines either do not differ (Kendeigh *et al.*, 1977) or are higher in summer than in winter (West, 1972; Mortensen and Blix, 1986). The mass-specific basal metabolic rate of newly hatched birds is usually low at hatching, rises during the early rapid growth phase, and then declines to a lower adult level (Poczopko, 1979). The initial rate is below the adult level in waterfowl (ranging from 65 to 90% of the predicted adult level) and gallinaceous birds (40–72%), but virtually identical in larids (Dawson *et al.*, 1976).

II. ACTIVITY

Because animals cannot exist indefinitely under basal conditions but must engage in additional energy-demanding activities, the measurement of the energy expenditure for numerous activities is a popular field of investigation. Energy expenditures for activity have been used to answer basic physiological questions, estimate animal requirements, or interpret life strategies.

A. Standing

For virtually all animals, except possibly members of the genus *Equus* which can passively lock the legs to remain upright, standing is energy demanding. Early measurements of the cost of standing relative to lying in domestic cattle, domestic sheep, and humans indicated that standing increased energy expenditure by 9% (summarized by Brody, 1945). While the lowest measurements on wild mammals approach this level if absolutely no movement occurs (White and Yousef, 1977; Regelin *et al.*, 1986), most are higher (Table 8.4). More recent studies on domestic cattle, sheep, and humans have argued that the 9% estimate is too low and will underestimate their energy requirements (Clark *et al.*, 1972; Vercoe, 1973; Summers *et al.*, 1988). Thus, a more reasonable estimate of the incremental cost of standing over lying for mammals that includes very minor position changes is 20%. Although the above measurements on mammals were direct comparisons between lying and standing, no comparable measurements exist for birds. The only data on birds that can be used to estimate standing costs are resting metabolic rates (presumably sitting) and extrapolation of the energy expenditure of birds moving at various speeds on treadmills to zero speed (i.e., the "posture of locomotion" or standing). The cost of standing in the painted quail, bobwhite quail, chukar partridge, guinea fowl, wild turkey, and domestic chickens averages $17.2 \pm 11.0\%$ greater than the cost of sitting (Fedak *et al.*, 1974; Brackenbury and Avery, 1980).

B. Terrestrial Locomotion

1. HORIZONTAL MOVEMENT

The energy costs of terrestrial transport (such as walking, trotting, and running) have been determined for animals exercising on treadmills or outdoors on various surfaces (Fig. 8.7). For most animals, the energetic cost is a linear function of the speed of travel with the Y-intercept corresponding to the energy expenditure while standing (Fig. 8.8). Exceptions to the generalization about linearity do exist and reflect the differing efficiencies of transport by differing gaits and speeds within those gaits (Dawson and Taylor, 1973; Dawson, 1976;

TABLE 8.4

The Energetic Cost of Standing in Several Large Mammals

Species	Weight (kg)	Lying	Standing	Cost of standing versus lying		Sources
		---kcal/kg/min---			%	
Roe deer	23	0.0382	0.0466	0.0084	22	Weiner, 1977
Human	61	0.0181	0.0220	0.0039	22	Bandyopadhyay and Chattopadhyay, 1980; Geissler and Aldouri, 1985
Domestic sheep	62	0.0184	0.0227	0.0043	24	Toutain et al., 1977
Reindeer–caribou	75	0.0319	0.0358	0.0039	12	White and Yousef, 1977; Luick and White, 1983
Bighorn sheep	78	0.0165	0.0196	0.0031	19	Chappel and Hudson, 1979; Gates and Hudson, 1978
Bighorn sheep and mountain goats	—	—	—	—	26	Dailey and Hobbs, 1989
Elk	105	0.0231	0.0287	0.0056	24	Parker et al., 1984; Gates and Hudson, 1978
Domestic cattle	367	0.0124	0.0144	0.0020	16	Vercoe, 1973; Clark et al., 1972
Moose	367	0.0163	0.0201	0.0038	23	Renecker and Hudson, 1986; Regelin et al., 1986
				$\bar{X} = 0.0044$	20	
				$\pm\, 0.0019$	±4	

Fig. 8.7 Different types of gas-collecting procedures used in laboratory and field studies of the energetics of locomotion: (a) White-crowned sparrow running on a treadmill in which air is pumped through the plexiglass box. (Courtesy of D.P. Mack, Washington State University, Pullman.) (b) Mule deer moving through snow while wearing a mask with one-way valves in which air is inspired on the open side and expired through the long tube into a gas sampling bag. (Courtesy of A. Pfister, Washington State University, Pullman.)

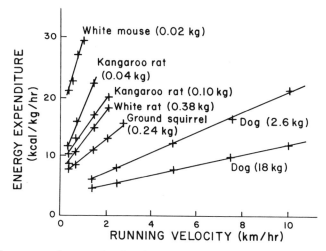

Fig. 8.8   Energy expenditure as a function of speed of locomotion in animals. (From Taylor *et al.*, 1970, courtesy of the American Physiological Society.)

Chassin *et al.*, 1976; Alexander *et al.*, 1980; Williams, 1983; Hoyt and Kenagy, 1988). The most significant deviation from linearity across differing gaits with increasing speed has been that the faster gait (hopping in kangaroos or bounding in mink) has a lower slope and is, thus, more efficient per unit of distance covered than is the slower gait. However, this occurrence is relatively rare and in some animals is due to a lack of adaptation to the treadmill (Thompson *et al.*, 1980; Thompson, 1985). Similarly, the relationship between speed and cost within a gait can be slightly curvilinear (Hoyt and Taylor, 1981) (Fig. 8.9). The animal switches between gaits when the cost of continuing in the same gait is higher than that of moving into the next appropriate gait. However, the error in using the linear expression is so minimal that an assumption of linearity is acceptable for most studies.

The slope of the regression between the energetic cost of horizontal movement and speed is the net cost expressed in kilocalories per kilogram per unit of distance moved and becomes increasingly steep as the weight of the animal decreases (Figs. 8.8 and 8.10). Thus, the same increase in speed produces a far greater rise in the metabolic rate of a mouse than in the larger dog. Earlier studies by Taylor *et al.* (1970) and Fedak *et al.* (1974) of the net cost of locomotion relative to body weight suggested that bipeds and quadrupeds were represented by differing equations. However, later studies (Fedak and Seeherman, 1979; Paladino, 1979) demonstrated that these conclusions were based on inadequate samples and that most bipeds and quadrupeds can be represented by one regression:

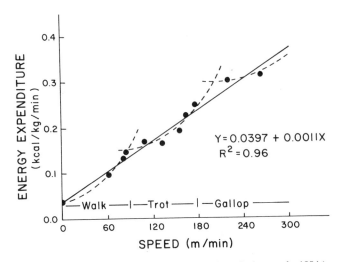

Fig. 8.9 Energetic cost of differing gaits in an elk calf. (From Parker *et al.*, 1984.)

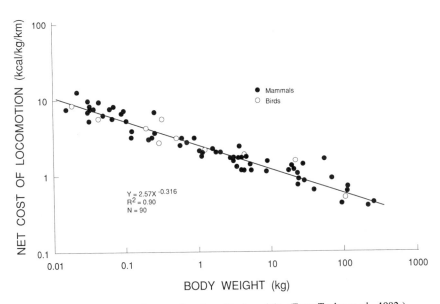

Fig. 8.10 Net cost of locomotion as a function of body weight. (From Taylor *et al.*, 1982.)

$$Y = 2.57X^{-0.316}$$

where Y is kcal/kg/km and X is weight in kg (Taylor et al., 1982). One of the major exceptions is the waddling by penguins and waterfowl which is over twice as costly as terrestrial locomotion in other animals ($Y = 5.57X^{-0.327}$; Pinshow et al., 1977; Dewasmes et al., 1980; Baudinette and Gill, 1985).

The decreasing net cost with increasing body weight occurs because body weight is highly correlated with leg and body length. The longer legs and body of the larger animal increase stride length and decrease stride frequency so a unit distance can be moved with less effort by the larger animal than the smaller animal (Strang and Steudel, 1990). Changes in the anatomical relationships that determine the decreasing cost in larger animals also occur during growth of the individual. For example, the net cost of locomotion in deer and elk decreases with growth in a manner virtually identical to the interspecific regression ($Y = 2.97X^{-0.34}$; Parker et al., 1984). Similarly, the net cost of locomotion for short-legged domestic reindeer (0.8512 kcal/kg/km) is double the cost for longer-legged caribou of a similar weight (0.4105 kcal/kg/km) (Nilssen et al., 1984a,b; Fancy and White, 1987).

The cost for an animal to walk or run 1 km (Y in kcal) can be estimated by summing the net cost of locomotion and the overhead cost of basal metabolism and standing during the time necessary to move that kilometer:

$$\text{Net Cost} + \text{Overhead Cost}$$

$$Y = 2.57X^{0.684} + \frac{1.2(70)X^{0.75}}{1440}\left(\frac{60}{S}\right)$$

where X is body weight in kg, 1.2 is the increment above basal metabolism for standing, 1440 is the minutes per day, 60 is the minutes per hour, and S is the speed in km per hour. If we solve the equation for a 40 kg animal moving at 1 (walk), 7 (trot), and 14 (run) km/hr, the net cost is a constant 32 kcal; but the overhead cost decreases from 56 kcal at 1 km/hr (total cost of 88 kcal) to 8 kcal at 7 km/hr (total cost of 40 kcal) to 4 kcal at 14 km/hr (total cost of 36 kcal). Thus, as speed increases the total cost per unit time increases linearly, but the total cost per unit distance decreases curvilinearly toward the asymptote established by the net cost.

The curvilinear relationship between the decreasing cost per unit distance with increasing speed means that the animal expends about the same amount of energy to trot a kilometer at a leisurely pace as it does to run the kilometer at its top speed. Observations of free-ranging animals suggest that the speed of movement is subjected to an optimization process because individuals of the same species often move within a fairly restricted range of speeds (Pennycuick, 1975; Hoyt and Taylor, 1981; Pyke, 1981; Hoyt and Kenagy, 1988). While this speed might be the minimum speed that approaches the asymptotic net cost (i.e., a fast walk) for a migrating wildebeest or caribou, a much faster speed may be chosen by a predator, such as a Cape hunting dog, that attempts to both minimize the cost per unit distance and maximize prey encounter rate.

Several investigators have noted that the cost of daily movement in nonmigratory, free-ranging mammals is a relatively small part of the total daily energy expenditure (Garland, 1983; Altmann, 1987). For example, the average cost of daily movement ranges from 0.5% of the daily energy expenditure in a 10 g mammal to 4.2% for a 100 kg mammal. Because even a fairly large deviation between the actual cost of locomotion for a particular species and that predicted by the Taylor *et al.* (1982) regression would produce a small error in estimating daily energy expenditure under these conditions, it is increasingly difficult to justify studies of the cost of locomotion if the objective is to merely estimate daily energy expenditure.

However, there are many ecological and evolutionary questions where additional studies of the energetics of locomotion are needed. One example of such an area that developed during the 1980s was in measuring the effect of snow on the cost of locomotion and applying that knowledge to understanding the ecology and management of ungulates. The cost of locomotion through snow increases curvilinearly in deer, elk, caribou, and bighorn sheep as snow depth and snow density increase (Fig. 8.11). The increasing costs occur because deeper and denser snow offers greater physical resistance to movement. While the longer-legged species raise the legs increasingly higher, and ultimately "bound" as snow depth increases, mountain goats and bison "plow" through almost all depths (Dailey and Hobbs, 1989). As long as the snow is light and powdery, plowing is less energy demanding than bounding. Bounding is costly because of the energy expended in elevating the body vertically. The vertical costs are also important when animals walk on crusted snow that will not support the animal's entire weight. Because the animal must lift the body until enough weight is on the foot to break through the surface crust, movement in this type of snow is akin to climbing stairs and costs far more than moving in uncrusted snow (Mattfeld, 1974; Fancy and White, 1987). For social species that follow another animal through deep or crusted snow, the cost for the follower is only a fraction of that experienced by the leader.

Although leg length is an important determinant of the cost of moving through snow, foot area and foot-loading (weight per unit area) are also important in determining sinking depth and energy expenditure. Adult caribou have the lightest foot-loading of North American ungulates; adult mule deer, white-tailed deer, mountain goats, and bighorn sheep have intermediate levels; and adult bison, moose, pronghorn antelope, and elk have the heaviest (Telfer and Kelsall, 1984; Parker *et al.*, 1984; Fancy and White, 1985b; Dailey and Hobbs, 1989). Young

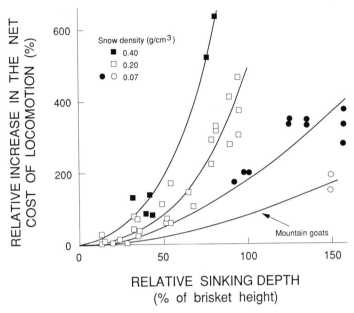

RELATIVE SINKING DEPTH
(% of brisket height)

Fig. 8.11   The relative increase in the net cost of locomotion in ungulates as a function of relative sinking depth in snow. (Data from Mattfeld, 1974; Parker *et al.*, 1984; Fancy and White, 1987; Dailey and Hobbs, 1989.) The three upper lines representing the effect of snow density (g/cm^3) on the cost are composite data from mule deer, white-tailed deer, elk, caribou, and bighorn sheep. A separate line is shown for mountain goats as their method and costs of moving through deep snow are different from the other ungulates.

ungulates have lighter foot-loading than the adults. The behavior of ungulates in snow when threatened by wolves can be explained partially by leg length and foot-loading (Telfer and Kelsall, 1984). Wolves have a light foot-loading similar to caribou but generally shorter legs than most of the ungulates. Thus, caribou tend to flee from wolves through deep, soft snow that would favor their longer legs. Moose, with a much heavier foot-loading but longer legs than the wolf, stand their ground and fight as both wolf and moose are approximately equal in their ability to run through snow. Partial snow-crusting can dramatically alter such relationships between predator and prey. The light foot-loading of wolves and coyotes occasionally enables them to run on crusts that cannot support deer or other ungulates with a heavier foot-loading. Under these conditions, the predator is expending energy at an equivalent rate to running on bare ground while the deer is expending energy at 2 to 4 times that level and, thus, quickly tires.

Unfortunately, modern man occasionally simulates these conditions by using snowmobiles, skis, or snowshoes to observe and unnecessarily frighten ungulates wintering in deep snows. Native North Americans used the advantage of snowshoes to kill moose. "—in the beginning of April following mid-day thaws, (the snow) commonly froze hard at night. The young men took advantage (of this to) run down many moose. A man with a good pair of snowshoes will scarcely make an impression on the snow while moose and deer will break through up to the belly at every step. A good runner will generally tire them in less than a day, and very frequently in 6 or 8 hours, though some Indians continue to chase for two days before they kill the game" (Hearne, 1971).

As an extreme example of animals altering their gate in response to increased costs of moving through snow, penguins change from walking to tobogganing when they encounter soft snow (Wilson *et al.*, 1991). Walking costs would accelerate very rapidly in soft snow because of their short legs and awkward gait whereas tobogganing distributes the weight over a much larger area to reduce locomotion costs by preventing sinking. Tobogganing is also common on smooth ice in which the reduced friction makes walking difficult but tobogganing very efficient. However, the energy savings of tobogganing may be balanced by increased feather wear such that walking is the preferred gait on hard snow.

2. VERTICAL MOVEMENT

Animals often climb up and down hills, trees, or cliffs. Upward movements are costly because of the energy expended in working against gravity, whereas downslope locomotion can be inexpensive because the potential energy stored in moving upslope is recovered as kinetic energy during descent (Taylor *et al.*, 1972). Several different ways are available to express the cost of vertical locomotion. Because we have already estimated horizontal costs, one of the simpler methods is to divide the cost of moving on a slope into its horizontal and vertical vectors. Animals expend 6 kcal/kg/vertical km climbed (Table 8.5). This cost is independent of the species, weight, and angle of ascent for the conditions studied thus far. Because all animals expend the same amount of energy per unit of weight for uphill locomotion while the smaller animal expends more energy per unit of weight for basal metabolism, upslope movement requires a lower relative energy expenditure by the smaller animal than by the larger one. Thus, when different species traverse very rugged terrain in nonfeeding activities, the average angle of ascent decreases with increasing body size. However, as terrain becomes steeper, animals pick steeper ascents because the more vertical path is still less costly than traveling a much greater total distance when using a shallower trail angle (Reichman and Aitchison, 1981; Dailey and Hobbs, 1989). For the feeding animal consuming an evenly distributed resource in steep terrain in which there is no need to be at a different elevation at the end of a feeding bout, horizontal movement should be maximized and vertical displacement minimized in order to maximize the net rate of energy intake (Fig. 8.12).

TABLE 8.5

Mean Energetic Cost for Mammals to Lift One Kilogram of Body Weight One Vertical Kilometer

Species	Body weight (kg)	Angle of slopes (degrees)	Cost (kcal/kg/km)	Reference
Red squirrel	0.25	6, 18, 30, 37	7.69	Wunder and Morrison, 1974
Domestic dog	12.8	4.2, 6.7, 11.5	7.71	Raab et al., 1976
Chimpanzee	17.5	15	3.54	Taylor et al., 1972
Mule deer	19.0	14.3	5.99	Parker et al., 1984
Mountain goats	27.0	3.5, 21.5	6.16	Dailey and Hobbs, 1989
Bighorn sheep	36.0	3.5, 21.5	6.80	Dailey and Hobbs, 1989
Domestic sheep	40.8	2.7, 5.1	6.36	Clapperton, 1964
Lion cubs	53.5	12.6, 17.1	3.27	Chassin et al., 1976
Elk	87.0	14.3	5.73	Parker et al., 1984
Red deer	68.3	7, 14	5.13	Brockway and Gessaman, 1977
Reindeer	96.5	2.9, 5.1	6.04	White and Yousef, 1977
Domestic cattle	155.0	6	6.32	Ribeiro et al., 1977
Burro	253.5	5.7, 9.6	7.20	Yousef et al., 1972

Mean = 6.00 ± 1.37

The efficiency of recovering the potential energy stored during upslope movement depends on both the animal's weight and degree of incline (Table 8.6). Small animals are far more efficient at moving down moderate slopes than are larger animals. As the angle of the slope increases, the larger animal becomes less efficient at a lower slope angle than does the smaller animal. For example, a 1 kg animal reaches 0–efficiency at a slope angle of 27.5°, whereas a 300 kg animal reaches that efficiency at 9°. These relationships are described by the equation:

$$Z = 132 - 4.8X - 0.3Y$$
$$R^2 = 0.76$$

where X equals slope angle in degrees, Y equals body weight in kg, and Z equals efficiency expressed as a percentage. Efficiency can never exceed 100%, although it can become negative. At efficiencies below zero, movement downhill is more costly than moving the same distance horizontally. When animals of different weights descend a hill, the larger animal should either pick a less steep route or should not attempt to control its acceleration and simply run down the hill if it is a relatively short hill. In conducting field studies with tame elk, we have

Fig. 8.12 Trails worn into a mountainside from years of domestic and wild ungulate feeding activities. Note that the very steep vertical profile is turned into a series of horizontal profiles for feeding. The more vertical trail has been worn by nonfeeding animals moving to the top of the hill.

observed that larger elk prefer to run down a relatively steep, short hill that as calves they had routinely walked down.

C. Burrowing

The cost of burrowing per unit time averages 3.8 ± 1.6 (range 1.6 to 5.8) times the resting metabolic rate in eight subterranean rodents and insectivorous moles (Lovegrove, 1989). Burrowing costs involve both shearing soil from the tunnel face and moving that soil to a dumping location. Vleck (1979) proposed the following model to predict the energetics of burrowing per unit distance (E_{seg}) based on the shearing and transporting processes:

$$E_{seg} = K_s(\pi b^2 \rho)(S) + K_p(\pi b^2 \rho)(S)\left(\frac{1}{2S}\right)$$

where K_s is the energy cost of shearing 1 g of soil from the tunnel, ($\pi b^2 \rho$) is the mass of soil removed per centimeter of burrow in which πb^2 is the circumference of the tunnel and ρ is soil density in g/cm^3, S is the length of the tunnel,

TABLE 8.6

Energy Recovered during Downhill Movement in Several Mammals[a]

Species	Body weight (kg)	Incline angle (degrees)	Energy recovered (kcal/kg/km)	Efficiency %	Reference
Mouse	0.03	15	2.05	87	Taylor et al., 1972
Dog	13	4.2	2.63	100	Raab et al., 1976
		6.7	2.32	99	
		11.5	1.43	61	
Chimpanzee	17	15	2.23	95	Taylor et al., 1972
Mule deer	19	14.3	1.76	75	Parker, 1981
Mountain goat	40	21.5	−0.12	−5	Dailey and Hobbs, 1989
Bighorn sheep	47	21.5	0.07	3	Dailey and Hobbs, 1989
Human	70	3	2.34	100	Taylor et al., 1972
		15	0.80	34	
		18	0.00	0	
Reindeer	96	2.9	1.66	71	White and Yousef, 1977
		5.1	1.38	59	
Elk	50	14.3	1.26	54	Parker, 1981
	100	14.3	0.85	35	
	150	14.3	0.66	28	
Burro	253	5.7	1.12	48	Yousef et al., 1972
		9.6	0.23	10	

[a]Per kilometer of vertical movement, 2.34 kcal/kg of potential energy are stored.

and K_p is the energy cost of pushing 1 g soil to a dumping location. Because the K_s and K_p of compact clay soils average 8.1 and 4.7 times those of various sandy soils, respectively, burrowing by pocket gophers in clay averaged 8 times more costly per unit distance than burrowing in sandy soils (Vleck, 1979). Although burrowing is 360 to 3400 times more costly than walking the same distance, burrowing opens a subterranean niche of new food resources, less changeable thermal environment, and lessened predation.

D. Flying

Energy costs of flight vary with type of flight and measurement conditions (Fig. 8.13). Gliding by the herring gull, grey-headed albatross, and wandering albatross costs 2.3 times the resting metabolic rate or 3.4 × BMR; extremely aerial species that are active fliers (such as purple and common house martins, barn and bank swallows, sooty tern, and Wilson's storm petrel) expend energy at 3.4 to 6.4 × BMR; and all other active fliers that do not have the relatively large wings and light wing loading of the extremely aerial species expend energy

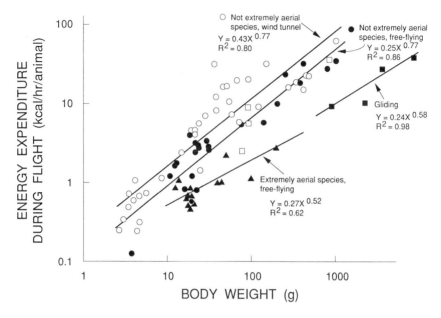

Fig. 8.13   Energy expenditure during gliding in birds and sustained flight in birds and bats. (Data from Thomas and Suthers, 1972; Carpenter, 1975; Thomas, 1975; Baudinette and Schmidt-Nielsen, 1974; Masman and Klaassen, 1987; Obst *et al.*, 1987; Gessaman and Nagy, 1988b; Birt-Friesen *et al.*, 1989.) Bat (□) values are from wind tunnel experiments.

at a rate as high as 14 × BMR (Baudinette and Schmidt-Nielsen, 1974; Hails, 1979; Flint and Nagy, 1984; Masman and Klaassen, 1987; Birt-Friesen *et al.*, 1989). These values for sustained flight may badly underestimate costs for very short flights in which birds expend energy primarily for acceleration and lift and are airborne for less than a second. Energy expenditure during short flights (0.8 sec, 3 m) by European robins averaged 23 × BMR (Tatner and Bryant, 1986). While many of the early measurements used lightweight masks and wind tunnels, such values average 42% higher than measurements on free-flying birds. The additional cost is due to an altered flight pattern and the extra weight and drag of the equipment. Very similar results may occur when birds wear harnesses and transmitters that are commonly used in wildlife field studies. Flight speeds of pigeons wearing a harness or a harness and transmitter weighing 2.5 to 5.0% of body weight were reduced by 15% and 25% and energy expenditure per hour of flight increased approximately 46% (Gessaman and Nagy, 1988b). Energy costs of flight in bats is very similar to that in birds (Fig. 8.13).

While flight costs are very high per unit time, they are very low per unit distance because of the speed. For example, a 10 g bird expends less than 1%

of the energy that a 10 g mouse expends in moving 1 km (Tucker, 1970; Schmidt-Nielsen, 1972). Flight speeds in free-ranging birds are compromises between maintaining a minimum metabolic rate per unit time and per unit distance with the latter being most important (Schnell and Hellack, 1979).

E. Swimming

Surface and submerged swimming for aquatically adapted animals are less expensive per unit distance than are flying and running for other animals (Schmidt-Nielsen, 1972). The energy expended during swimming is largely for thrust with little being expended to work against gravity as occurs during flight and terrestrial locomotion. Although initial studies using animals forced to dive concluded that submerged swimming was largely anaerobic and could occur at the same energy expenditure as that in resting animals (Costello and Whittow, 1975), voluntary dives are predominantly or completely aerobic with the cost being proportional to the effort (Butler, 1988; Woakes, 1988).

The cost of surface swimming increases curvilinearly with speed. As speed increases from 0 to 0.5 m/sec, the energy cost per unit time rises very slowly, such that 0.5 m/sec is the most efficient speed per unit distance for most surface-swimming birds and mammals (Prange and Schmidt-Nielsen, 1970; Baudinette and Gill, 1985; Woakes and Butler, 1986). At faster speeds, a wake of water is pushed in front of the animal and increases cost very rapidly. Faster swimming speeds require submerged swimming where drag or resistance is very small and increases less rapidly as speed increases. The most efficient speeds for submerged swimming increase from 0.6 m/sec for a 1 kg animal to 1.3 m/sec for a 60 kg animal [$Y = 0.57X^{0.21}$, where X is in kg and Y is in m/sec (Baudinette and Gill, 1985; Davis et al., 1985; Feldkamp, 1987; Hui, 1988)].

Energy expenditure by captive mammals and birds swimming either on the surface or submerged at the most efficient speed averages 2.0 ± 0.7 times the resting metabolic rate (Prange and Schmidt-Nielsen, 1970; Woakes and Butler, 1983; Butler and Woakes, 1984; MacArthur, 1984; Baudinette and Gill, 1985; Davis et al., 1985; Woakes and Butler, 1986; Feldkamp, 1987; Hui, 1988; MacArthur and Krause, 1989; Williams, 1989; Williams et al., 1991). However, free-ranging penguins that are pursuing food in high-speed dives expend energy at a rate 3.9 ± 0.6 times higher than observed for captive birds at their most efficient speed (Nagy et al., 1984; Davis et al., 1989; Gales and Green, 1990). For wild penguins in pursuit dives, the cost per unit time (i.e., $7.7 \pm 1.6 \times$ RMR) is within the range reported for flapping flight by other birds.

The cost of swimming per unit distance at the most efficient speed varies with body weight and mode (surface or submerged) (Fig. 8.14). Because the most efficient speed increases with animal size, submerged swimming is the most efficient for larger animals, as the most efficient speed exceeds the rate ($\sim$0.5

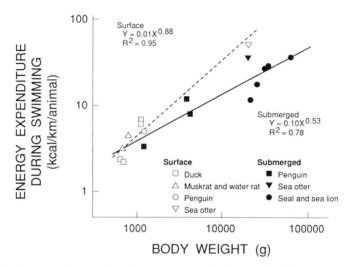

Fig. 8.14 The energetic cost of surface and submerged swimming in birds and mammals at the most efficient speed per unit distance. (Data from Prange and Schmidt-Nielsen, 1970; Fish, 1982; Woakes and Butler, 1983; Butler and Woakes, 1984; MacArthur, 1984; Baudinette and Gill, 1985; Davis *et al.*, 1985; Woakes and Butler, 1986; Feldkamp, 1987; Hui, 1988; MacArthur and Krause, 1989; Williams, 1989; Williams *et al.*, 1991; Culik and Wilson, 1991a.)

m/sec) at which a wake and dramatically increased drag are created by surface swimming. As animal size and, therefore, the most efficient speed decreases, the cost of surface swimming equals that for submerged swimming at a weight of about 700 g.

The rhythmic leaping by penguins and marine mammals at high speeds (porpoising) may either be a strategy to conserve energy by reducing drag or a necessary mechanism for respiration (Au and Weihs, 1980; Hui, 1987). Swimming speeds of free-ranging penguins reflect compromises between drag and energy costs and range from 0.4 m/sec for surface swimming to 2.0 m/sec for underwater swimming, to 3.4 m/sec for porpoising (Wilson and Wilson, 1990; Croxall and Davis, 1990; Kooyman and Ponganis, 1990).

Energy costs for free-ranging penguins and seals can be dramatically increased by fragments of trawl net or plastic debris that are discarded at sea and become lodged on an unsuspecting animal. For example, energy expenditure by a 45 kg sea lion swimming at 2.5 m/sec must be 4.3 times higher if it is dragging a 580 g net fragment than if it is unencumbered by the net. Thus, energy expenditure by the sea lion dragging a net fragment during high-speed chases required for catching prey would have to rise as high as 50 × RMR, an impossibly high cost that can only produce starvation (Feldkamp, 1985). Even the very small, externally mounted instrument packages used by wildlife scientists can increase the energy expenditure of penguins by 25% (Culik and Wilson, 1991b).

F. Other Activities

1. BRACHIATION

One of the remaining forms of locomotion is termed brachiation, which refers to using the arms to swing between objects as occurs in many primates. As with other forms of locomotion, the cost per unit time varies with speed, with the net cost (kcal/kg/km) being 1.5 times higher for brachiation than for normal walking by the spider monkey (Parsons and Taylor, 1977). Hanging motionless increases the resting metabolism of the spider monkey and slow loris by $65 \pm 32\%$ and is, thus, 3 times more costly than the 20% increment for standing over resting in mammals.

2. FEEDING

The energetic cost of feeding is the additional expense of manipulating and ingesting food above the cost of the general activity state, such as standing or perching. The incremental cost of eating is 11% above perching in birds and $36 \pm 16\%$ above standing in ruminants (Table 8.7). The lower increment in birds may be due to their consumption of food without chewing. Because the cost per unit time is quite similar when an animal consumes different diets, the cost per unit of dry matter intake can vary widely with diet because some foods can be consumed faster than others. For example, the cost per unit of intake by ruminants is much higher for hay or pasture than pellets or concentrates because of the differing rates of intake. There are other costs to acquiring food that may need to be quantified for some animals. Caribou, for example, that must paw through snow during the winter to uncover food can expend from 0.29 kcal/kg body weight/hr in light, uncrusted snow to 0.69 kcal/kg body weight/hr in thinly crusted snow (Fancy and White, 1985a).

3. MISCELLANEOUS

Many other energy-demanding activities occur. The energy costs for grooming, fighting, playing, ruminating, sniffing, or other activities may need to be quantified depending on the needs of a particular study (Graham, 1964; Malloy and Herreid, 1979; Weathers et al., 1984; Buttemer et al., 1986; Meyer and Guillot, 1986; Carl and Robbins, 1988; Vehrencamp et al., 1989).

III. THERMOREGULATION

Birds and mammals are able to maintain a relatively high, stable body temperature by balancing heat gains with heat losses. The body temperature of birds

TABLE 8.7

The Actual Cost of Eating above Standing or Swimming in Mammals and Alert
Perching Birds

			Energy expenditure		
Species, diet	Weight (kg)	kcal/ kg$^{0.75}$/hr	Increment of standing or perching (%)	kcal/ animal/kg dry matter ingested	Sources
Birds					
Budgerygahs, millet seeds					
	0.041	0.86	13	—	Buttemer et al., 1986
Loggerhead shrikes, day-old domestic chicks					
	0.045	0.87	10	—	Weathers et al., 1984
Mammals					
Amazonian manatee					
Fresh grass	172	3.19	—	152	Gallivan and Best, 1986
Freshwater hyacinth	172	4.02	—	191	
Bighorn sheep, hay	70	1.27	32	41	Chappel and Hudson, 1978a
Domestic cattle					
Hay	350	1.95	45	75	Adam et al., 1979
Pellets	350	1.77	—	19	
Domestic sheep					
Hay	38	1.34	59	40	Graham, 1964; Young, 1966; Osuji, 1974
Pasture	57	1.51	59	342	
Concentrates	41	1.01	—	18	
Elk, pasture	155	1.13	26	59	Wickstrom et al., 1984
Moose, pellets	87	1.59	20	19	Renecker et al., 1978

is generally regulated between 40° and 44°C and mammals between 36° and 40° (Morowitz, 1968). Temperature gradients between the animal and its environment of up to 100°C are possible in arctic environments. Because heat flux is driven by a temperature gradient, numerous physiological, anatomical, and behavioral mechanisms must exist if endotherms even in less harsh environments are to regulate body temperature without exhausting metabolic capabilities. If the endoderm cannot ultimately balance its heat budget by use of the heat produced in other metabolic processes or absorbed from the environment, a thermoregulatory cost must be added to basal metabolism and activity to estimate the cost of maintenance. Thermoregulation is a very recent field of investigation for wildlife ecologists because many of the ideas and methods originated in a series of papers published in 1950 (Scholander *et al.*, 1950a,b,c). The conceptual definition of thermoregulation as a balancing between heat gain and heat loss necessitates amplification and understanding of both sides of the implied equation in which

$$H_m \pm Q_r \pm Q_c \pm Q_k \pm Q_e = H_s,$$

where H_m is metabolic heat energy; the Q terms represent heat gained or lost by radiation (Q_r), convection (Q_c), conduction (Q_k), and evaporation (Q_e); and H_s is heat stored.

A. Modes of Heat Loss

1. RADIATION

Radiation is the flow of energy as electromagnetic waves through space from all objects above absolute zero ($-273°C$). The wave phenomenon of radiation gives rise to a spectrum of energy levels in biological systems ranging from visible and UV light to invisible infrared heat. These differences are due to the length of the wave in microns (λ_{max}), which is inversely proportional to the absolute temperature (T) of the emitting body, or Wein's law:

$$\lambda_{max} = 2897/T.$$

All living objects are radiating energy in the relatively long wavelength infrared spectrum, while the sun radiates primarily in the infrared and visible spectrums.

Radiant energy striking an object can be absorbed, reflected, or transmitted. Absorption of radiant energy by an animal's surface depends on both the physical characteristics of the surface and the energy wave. For example, the absorptivity of an animal's surface to infrared radiation is virtually 100% irrespective of color or whether it's covered by hair or feathers (Birkebak, 1966), but the absorptivity of shorter wavelengths is quite variable. The plumages of many dark-colored birds reflect 15–25% of the incident solar radiation as compared to over 50% in lighter colored birds (Birkebak, 1966; Walsberg *et al.*, 1978).

The amount of energy radiated by an object is proportional to the fourth power of its absolute temperature:

$$Q_r = \xi\sigma T_s^{\,4}$$

where Q_r is the radiant energy in kilocalories per square meter per hour, ξ is the emissivity ranging from 0 to 1, σ is the Stefan–Boltzmann proportionality constant (4.93 x 10^{-8} kcal/m²/hr), and T_s is the surface temperature in degrees Kelvin. Emissivity is a description of how well the surface of an object emits radiant energy at its characteristic wavelength in comparison to the surface of a theoretically perfect radiator, or "black body." Because emission equals absorption at a specified wavelength when transmission is 0, the emissivity of animal surfaces is virtually 1 since they are emitting in the infrared.

Just as the animal is absorbing and radiating heat, so are all objects in its environment. Consequently, the net radiation exchange describing the quantity and direction of the heat flux is the important quantity. The temperature of the air or space through which the energy is being radiated is unimportant except as it affects the temperature of the radiating surfaces.

2. CONVECTION

Convection is the flow of heat in a moving fluid, which is most often air or water in biological systems. If the movement is due to density or buoyancy differences between particle aggregations in the fluid, the convection is called free convection. However, if the convection is due to the animal moving through the fluid or to pressure differences often quite removed from the animal, such as wind, the heat transfer is called forced convection. Convective heat transfer occurs at the interface of a relatively motionless transitional boundary layer of either air or water surrounding the animal, or within the animal as in the respiratory tract, and can be described in the simplest cases by the equation:

$$Q_c = h_c A(T_s - T_a),$$

where Q_c is the quantity of heat transferred by convection from an object of area A. The direction of the heat flow depends on the temperature gradient between the surface (T_s) and the fluid (T_a). The convection coefficient, h_c, is a mathematical description of the rate at which heat moves across the temperature gradient and depends on the size, shape, and surface qualities of the object; the fluid velocity, viscosity, and turbulence in forced convection; and the magnitude of the temperature gradient in free convection.

Wind velocities above a surface range from zero at the surface as friction impedes molecular movement to a maximum velocity some distance from the surface (Fig. 8.15). Such an orderly progression of wind velocities with height is termed a wind profile. The characteristics of the wind profile largely depend on the roughness of the surface and the speed and turbulence of the fluid. Wind profiles offer an example of the complexity of describing convective heat loss

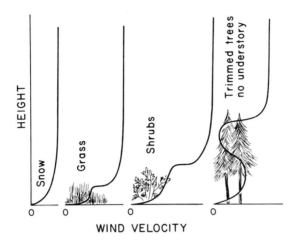

Fig. 8.15   Wind profile over snow or bare ground and different vegetation.

from an animal. While the leading edge of the body of a small passerine might be entirely within a given wind velocity, the larger deer can be within an entire spectrum of wind velocities. Similarly, because objects of small diameter are more efficient convectors of heat than are large ones, the legs of the standing animal have a different convection coefficient than do other body segments.

3. CONDUCTION

Conduction is the flow of heat when oscillating molecules exchange kinetic energy without appreciably changing their position. Because conduction is the only means of heat transfer through opaque solids, it is an important means of transferring heat between an animal and other contacting surfaces, such as the ground, snow, vegetation, or motionless air. Heat flow through still air within the pelage or plumage is usually termed conduction, although conduction, convection, and, to a far lesser extent, radiation are occurring (Cena and Monteith, 1975; Davis and Birkebak, 1975; Walsberg, 1988b). Conduction is expressed by the equation:

$$Q_k = h_k A(T_1 - T_2)L,$$

where Q_k is heat transferred by conduction per unit of time and area (A), $(T_1 - T_2)$ is the temperature gradient, (L) is the length of the conducting path or depth of insulation, and (h_k) is the conductivity coefficient which describes the rate or efficiency that the heat differential described by the temperature gradient can be conducted within or between the contacting surfaces. For the standing animal, conduction may be relatively unimportant as the bottoms of the feet are the only surfaces in which heat is being transferred solely by conduction. However, for the bedded animal, the resting or incubating bird, or the animal in which water of a temperature markedly different from body temperature contacts the skin surface, conduction can be the major route of energy transfer. Conduction losses can also be internal, such as the warming of ingested snow or water to body temperature and its subsequent loss via evaporation or urination (Young and Degen, 1980).

4. EVAPORATION

Evaporative heat loss is the heat removed from the animal as water changes from a liquid to a gas. Although the heat of vaporization depends on the temperature of the water, an average commonly used without significant error for animals is 580 calories per gram of water vaporized at 30°C. The rate of vaporization depends on the absolute humidity gradient, the interacting surface area, and the absolute amount of water available. Evaporation becomes the dominant means of heat loss as ambient temperature approaches or exceeds surface temperature. At very cold ambient temperature, evaporative loss is small because air, even at saturation, can hold very little water. Wind velocity is also important to evaporative heat loss, but its role is in maintaining a vapor pressure gradient across the boundary layer by removing more saturated air closer to the evaporative surface.

B. Surface Area and Insulation Quality

All four modes of heat loss depend on surface area. Methods to measure area have included skinning the animal and measuring the area of the flattened skin, coating the hair or feather surface with various materials that can be subsequently removed and their area measured, or delineating the geometric components of the animal and measuring the necessary linear dimensions to calculate surface area. Problems can arise as the measured surface area must reflect the actual animal-environment interface in which heat exchange is occurring. For example, the area of the detached bird skin has a surface area 20% greater than the interactive surface area of the resting bird (Walsberg and King, 1978). The difference between the two areas is due to the inclusion when the bird is skinned of surfaces that are not external relative to heat exchange (i.e., the undersides of the folded wing and adjoining body surfaces, the skin of the retracted neck, and the upper parts of the legs that are covered by contour feathers). Similarly, surface area of mammals strongly depends on body posture, such as whether the animal is standing or lying and whether the head and legs are stretched out or tucked into the body. Huddling with conspecifics can decrease the animal's exposed surface area and markedly reduce heat loss (LeMeho et al., 1976;

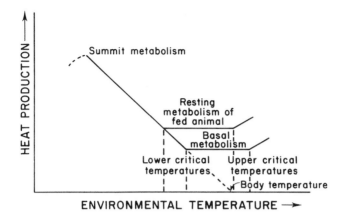

Fig. 8.16   The general Scholander model depicting a characteristic thermoregulatory response.

Chaplin, 1982; Vickery and Millar, 1984; Canals *et al.*, 1989). Huddling is a necessary survival strategy for many birds and mammals. Thus, many observations of subtle postural differences can be understood when interpreted bioenergetically.

Most animals respond metabolically to changes in ambient temperature in a characteristic pattern (Fig. 8.16). The temperature range in which thermoregulation can occur without increasing metabolic heat production is termed the thermoneutral zone and is bounded by the upper (T_{uc}) and lower (T_{lc}) critical temperatures. In the thermoneutral zone, only physical means, such as altering insulation or surface area, are used to balance heat loss and gain. Reductions in environmental temperature below (T_{lc}) require an increased metabolic heat production if body temperature is to remain constant. Eventually, an upper point in metabolic heat production (summit metabolism) is reached where system exhaustion occurs and body temperature begins falling. Similarly, as ambient temperature rises above the upper critical temperature, heat production also increases because of the use of energy-demanding processes to dissipate heat, such as panting or sweating, and the Q_{10} effect on metabolism if body temperature rises. While the vast majority of animals display this pattern, other patterns do occur (Parker and Robbins, 1984; McNab, 1988c).

Insulation quality (thermal conductance in kcal/kg/h/°C) can be estimated either as the slope of the relationship between metabolic heat production and ambient temperature below the lower critical temperature if the line extrapolates to body temperature at zero metabolism or by dividing the animal's metabolic rate by the temperature gradient between the environment and its core body temperature at T_{lc}. Conductance decreases as animal weight increases because

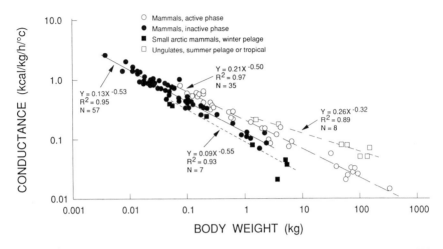

Fig. 8.17   Conductance in mammals as a function of body weight. (Data from Casey *et al.*, 1979; Bradley and Deavers, 1980; Aschoff, 1981; Pauls, 1981; Parker and Robbins, 1985; Nilssen *et al.*, 1984a,b; Renecker and Hudson, 1986; Parker, 1988.) The regression for small, arctic mammals in winter pelage includes data for collared and brown lemmings, red squirrel, snowshoe hare, porcupine, and arctic and red foxes. Although not shown, the regression for the same mammals in summer pelage is $Y = 0.14X^{-0.54}$. Animals weighing more than 10 kg in the "mammals, active phase" are temperate and arctic ungulates in winter pelage.

of increased pelage or plumage thickness and decreasing surface-to-volume ratios (Figs. 8.17 and 8.18). Conductance also has a daily rhythm in which it is 64% higher during the active phase of the daily cycle than during the resting phase (Aschoff, 1981). This daily variation promotes heat conservation during sleep when metabolic rate and body temperature are lessened and heat dissipation during the active phase when metabolic rate and body temperature are elevated. The pelages of marsupials and eutherians are of equal insulation quality (Dawson *et al.*, 1969). Birds have average conductances that are 30% lower than mammals (McNab, 1966). The only mammals that have insulation comparable to birds are arctic mammals. Even though most birds and mammals have seasonal molts, adaptive seasonal changes in conductance are relatively rare (Marsh and Dawson, 1989). The exceptions identified thus far in mammals are temperate and arctic leporids (Rogowitz, 1990) and ungulates, small- to medium-sized arctic mammals, and mammals (such as bears and mountain goats) that have one molt per year in which the summer pelage is a shorter version of the winter pelage. The only well-documented case in birds of seasonal changes in conductance is the willow ptarmigan (West, 1972; Marsh and Dawson, 1989).

Upper (T_{uc}) and lower (T_{lc}) critical temperatures are functionally defined by the interaction of the metabolic rate in the thermoneutral zone, body temperature,

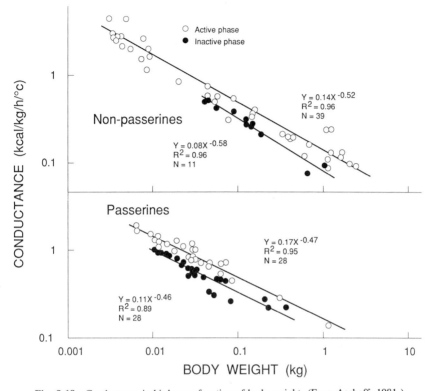

Fig. 8.18 Conductance in birds as a function of body weight. (From Aschoff, 1981.)

and the animal's insulation quality (Calder and King, 1974; Weathers and van Riper, 1982). Many small mammals have very narrow thermoneutral zones bound by T_{uc}'s and T_{lc}'s that average 35 ± 2°C and 27 ± 3°C, respectively (Fig. 8.19). Although many of these animals live in far colder environments than suggested by their T_{lc}'s, animals will select environments with ambient temperatures within their thermoneutral zones if given the chance (Laudenslager and Hamel, 1978). Thus, displaying such animals in zoos at temperatures comfortable to humans (i.e., 21°C) may not be best for the animal (Thompson, 1989). Arctic mammals and temperate and arctic ungulates have lower T_{lc}'s with the most extreme example being adult caribou in winter pelage (T_{lc} = −40°C) (Hart et al., 1961; Nilssen et al., 1984b).

Avian T_{uc}'s average 38 ± 3°C (sources from Aschoff, 1981). T_{lc}'s vary both with activity phase (higher in the active than the inactive phase) and body weight (higher in smaller than larger birds) (Fig. 8.20). The additional variation reflects

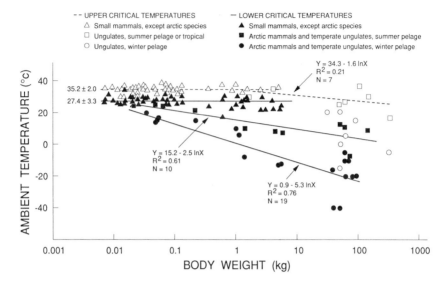

Fig. 8.19 Lower and upper critical temperature for wild mammals. (Data from same sources as Fig. 8.17.)

differences in metabolic rates and conductances due to seasonal adaptations, acclimation and acclimatization temperatures, and numerous other factors.

Water can dramatically reduce insulation quality as the conductance of water is 24 times greater than air (Calder and King, 1974; Webb and King, 1984). Conductance doubles for aquatic birds and mammals swimming in water relative to air (Table 8.8). Much of the increased conductance may be due to heat loss from poorly insulated areas of the body rather than actual penetration of water into the plumage or pelage. For example, the relative heat loss from eider ducklings with only their feet in ice water is very similar to other swimming birds. For mammals, excluding the poorly insulated harbor seal whose absolute heat loss is much higher than for other mammals, conductance Y in water decreases as animal weight (X in kg) increases ($Y = 0.25X^{-0.24}$, $R^2 = 0.91$). Because of the dramatic decrease in insulation quality, T_{lc} in water is higher than T_{lc} in air.

Prolonged rain increased metabolic rates of black-tailed deer only when they were in summer pelage and when air temperature was 10°C or less (Parker, 1988). One hour of rain (4.5 mm/hr) at 10°C increased metabolic rate of the standing deer by 11%; five hours of rain increased metabolic rate by 28%. The longer, denser, oilier winter pelage minimized water penetration and prevented any additional heat loss. The reduced effect of rain relative to submersion by aquatic animals occurs because (1) periodic shaking (7.5 shakes/hr in winter,

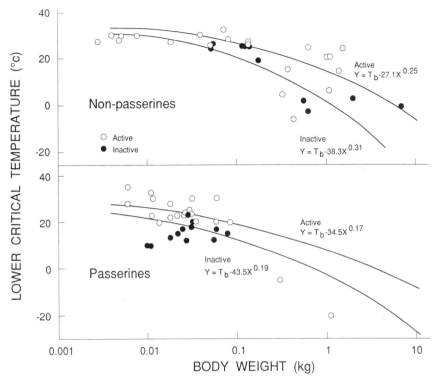

Fig. 8.20 Lower critical temperatures of birds as a function of body weight, the daily cycle of metabolism (Aschoff and Pohl, 1970a), and conductance (Aschoff, 1981). Body temperature (T_b) estimated as 42.2°C (active) and 40.3°C (inactive) for passerines and 41.5°C (active) and 39.6°C (inactive) for nonpasserines (King and Farner, 1961). Derivation of equations as in Weathers and van Riper (1982). Observations from Weathers and van Riper (1982), Thompson and Fritzell (1988), Oberlag *et al.* (1990), and sources in Aschoff (1981).

10.8 in summer) during rain removes excess water from the coat and (2) the less insulated ventral side of the animal remains drier in rain than during sub-mersion.

Metabolic rates of aquatic mammals and birds dramatically increase when the pelage or plumage is contaminated by even small amounts of oil (Hartung, 1967; McEwan and Koelink, 1973; McEwan *et al.*, 1974; Erasmus *et al.*, 1981; Lambert *et al.*, 1982; Costa and Kooyman, 1982; Jenssen and Ekker, 1988; Davis *et al.*, 1988; Jenssen and Ekker, 1991) (Fig. 8.21). Small amounts of oil increase water penetration and mat the pelage or plumage and thereby reduce its insulation and buoyancy. The magnitude of the increased heat production varies with the type and amount of oil, air or water temperature, and the length of time since

TABLE 8.8

Thermal Conductance (kcal/kg/h/°C) at the Lower Critical Temperatures (°C) for Several
Aquatic Mammals and Birds in Air and Water

Species	Body weight (kg)	Thermal conductivity			Incremental increase (water/air)	Lower critical temperature	
		Air	Water	Difference		Air	Water
Mammals							
Water rat	0.78	0.12	0.31	0.19	2.6	24	35
Muskrat	0.93	0.14	0.23	0.09	1.6	10	36
Platypus	1.4	0.11	0.20	0.09	1.8	25	>30
Beaver	12.4	0.05	0.14	0.07	2.8	1	22
Sea otter	17.3	0.06	0.12	0.06	2.0	<−19	5
Harbor seal	27.4	1.10	2.27	1.17	2.1	2	20
Birds, surface swimming							
Common eider (ducklings, feet only in ice water)	0.07	0.45	0.66	0.21	1.5	23	36
Little penguin	0.9	0.15	0.26	0.11	1.7	10	10,35[a]
Common eider	1.7	0.08	0.13	0.05	1.6	0	15

Sources: Hart and Irving, 1959; Hart, 1971; Morrison et al., 1974; Grant and Dawson, 1978; Sherer and Wunder, 1979; Dawson and Fanning, 1981; Stahel and Nicol, 1982; MacArthur, 1984, 1989; Jenssen et al., 1989; Steen et al., 1989; MacArthur and Dyck, 1990.
[a] Heat production in the little penguin increased gradually as water temperature declined from 35°C to 10°C and then sharply at water temperatures below 10°C.

exposure. Heat loss by an oil-contaminated animal remaining in cold water would quickly exceed metabolic capacity. Heavily oiled muskrats remain out of water for weeks, and oiled ducks often rest on shore and become isolated from food resources. If oil contamination is not extensive, the required washing with detergents can increase heat loss even further as the natural oils used to reduce water penetration into the pelage are also removed (Costa and Kooyman, 1982). Because naturally secreted body oils are important in re-establishing insulation quality, animals must be held in thermoneutral conditions for several days before being released (Costa and Kooyman, 1982; Jenssen and Ekker, 1988; Davis et al., 1988). Metabolic rates of sea otters in water did not return to normal until 8 days after washing.

Once one begins working with free-ranging animals, air temperature is no longer an adequate descriptor of the thermal environment (Campbell, 1977; Bakken et al., 1985). Wind, particularly when combined with air temperatures below the thermoneutral zone, markedly increases the metabolic rate necessary to balance heat loss (Goldstein, 1983; Buttemer, 1985; Walsberg, 1986; Stahel et al., 1987; Webster and Weathers, 1988; Bakken, 1990; Parker and Gillingham, 1990). As an indication of the importance of wind to heat loss, free-ranging

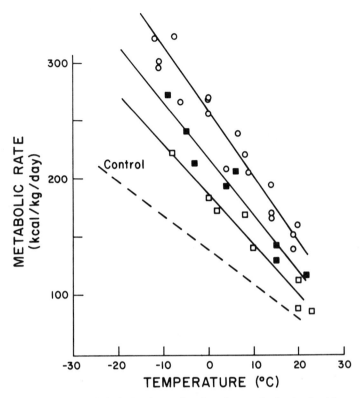

Fig. 8.21   Heat loss in black ducks in air as a function of contamination by 5 g (clear squares), 10 g (darkened squares), and 20 g (clear circles) of lubricating oil in comparison to the noncontaminated bird. (From Hartung, 1967; courtesy of the *Journal of Wildlife Management*.)

animals in cold environments frequently adapt their activity patterns and microenvironment selection to lessen their exposure to wind. Heat gained from solar radiation can minimize thermoregulaory costs in cold environments or increase the cost in hot environments. Solar radiation impinging on the animal can equal 9 to 12 times the heat generated by metabolism (Robertshaw and Finch, 1984). Even though only a fraction of the heat is ultimately absorbed by the animal, T_{lc} of mule deer in winter decreased from $-19°C$ with no solar radiation or wind to $-53°C$ when solar radiation levels are high. Deer that were shivering at T_a's of $-30°C$ in the dark stopped shivering when the first direct beam radiation of sunrise increased skin temperature to what it would be on a 30°C summer day (Parker and Robbins, 1984; Parker and Gillingham, 1990).

The modes of heat loss are not simply independent and additive but are functioning concurrently, with the heat removed by one mode affecting the intensity of another. For example, heat removed by convection can lower the surface temperature and reduce radiant losses. An example of the interaction between radiation and convection in determining animal heat budgets was found by Walsberg *et al.* (1978) who addressed the seemingly paradoxical questions posed by the black plumages in desert birds (such as corvids and vultures) and white plumages in arctic birds and mammals (ptarmigan or polar bear). The intuitive suggestion from human experiences and from animal studies in which wind did not occur is that these coat colors would be thermally maladapted. Nevertheless, the heat load generated by direct solar radiation depended on the interaction of plumage coloration, degree of plumage erection, and wind speed. Black plumages absorbed more radiation at the surface which created a thermal disadvantage at low wind speeds. However, as wind speed increased, the heat load on the erected black plumage fell below that of the white plumage as the radiant energy absorbed at the outer surface of the black plumage was convected away from the animal rather than inward toward the skin surface. Radiation penetrated white plumage much deeper before being absorbed and thereby reduced the effectiveness of wind at removing the heat. Thus, the black vulture and the white ptarmigan are at a thermal advantage in their respective environments if wind is common. Because the animal's insulation has the dual purpose of modifying heat flow both inward and outward, the coat's color, three-dimensional structure, and optical properties and the skin's color must be considered in understanding an animal's thermal budget (Walsberg, 1983; Walsberg, 1988a; Walsberg and Schmidt, 1989; Walsberg, 1990).

Once heat loss has been estimated, one of the major questions relative to thermoregulation is to what extent metabolic heat generated incidental to other activities (such as during locomotion or during digestion and metabolism of food) substitutes for thermoregulatory expenditures below the lower critical temperature. If substitution occurs, then the lower critical temperature of the active or fed animal can be far lower than those estimated relative to basal metabolism (Fig. 8.16). Rubner (1902) first recognized that the heat produced during the processing of food energy could offset thermoregulation costs. Fed guinea pigs and dogs had higher metabolic rates than fasted animals in the thermoneutral zone but virtually identical metabolic rates at very cold temperatures. More recent studies on hamsters, rats, kestrels, and penguins (Baudinette *et al.*, 1986) continue to show that the heat increment of feeding can substitute for the thermoregulatory cost in adult animals (Fig. 8.22). The partial substitution at temperatures only slightly lower than the T_{lc} occurs because the heat increment of feeding exceeds the thermoregulatory cost. Substitution is maximized when the thermoregulatory cost equals or exceeds the heat increment of feeding and may not be 100% if body temperature changes between the fasted and fed states (Masman *et al.*, 1989). A conservative estimate of the maximum substitution is 80%. The heat increment of feeding produced by very young birds (i.e., chicks)

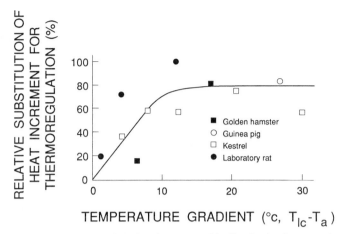

TEMPERATURE GRADIENT (°c, T_{lc}-T_a)

Fig. 8.22 Relative substitution of the heat increment of feeding for the thermoregulatory cost in a bird and several small mammals. (Data from Rubner, 1902; Swift, 1944; Simek, 1975; Masman *et al.*, 1989.)

apparently does not substitute for the thermoregulatory cost (Klaassen *et al.*, 1989b).

The heat increment of feeding may be exceedingly transitory, lasting for only a few hours after a feeding bout. For example, resting metabolism of sea otters increased 54% after consuming meals of either clams or squids before returning to post-absorptive levels 4 to 5 hr after feeding (Costa and Kooyman, 1984). Thus, sea otters could rest during that time in water that normally would be well below their T_{lc} determined under basal conditions without increasing metabolism solely for thermoregulation.

The question of whether heat generated during activity (e.g., standing, walking, running, or flying) substitutes for the thermoregulatory cost below T_{lc} has been exceedingly difficult to answer. The question is critically important because if substitution occurs, the active animal searching for food on very cold days could expend the same amount of energy as the resting animal (i.e., basal metabolism plus activity equalling basal metabolism plus thermoregulation). Theoretically, there are several reasons to argue why complete substitution would not occur and that the active animal could never expend the same amount of energy as the resting animal in the same cold environment. For example, the active animal relative to the resting animal will frequently have a decreased tissue insulation as blood flow is increased to working muscles. Similarly, the active animal has an increased surface area as legs, arms, wings or head and neck are extended, a larger convective and evaporative heat loss due to increased air flow around the body or increased respiration, and increased body and/or skin temperatures leading to a larger heat flow gradient to the environment (McCarron and Dawson, 1984).

For wild mammals, the overwhelming conclusion is that the heat generated during activity does not substitute for the thermoregulatory cost at cold temperatures (Hart, 1950, 1952, 1971; Hart and Heroux, 1955; Hart and Jansky, 1963; Yousef *et al.*, 1970, 1973; Gates and Hudson, 1979; Pauls, 1981; McCarron and Dawson, 1984). Pauls (1981) and McCarron and Dawson (1984) have proposed that activity even creates an additional thermoregulatory cost above that occurring in the resting animal. Although Wunder (1970) initially proposed partial substitution for chipmunks running at high speeds in cold environments, his later model (Wunder, 1975) assumes no substitution with basal metabolism, activity, and thermoregulation being additive. The one remaining study on wild animals (patas monkey; Mahoney, 1980) concluded that the heat generated during activity does substitute for thermoregulation, but the use of a multiple regression as the basis for this claim is very weak.

For birds, conclusions from the various studies have been far more contradictory. Heat produced during walking or hopping substituted for thermoregulatory costs in the white-crowned sparrow (Paladino and King, 1984) and Japanese quail (Nomoto *et al.*, 1983) but did not substitute in the common redpoll (Pohl and West, 1973), chaffinch (Pohl, 1969), and white-throated sparrow (Kontogiannis, 1968) within the same ambient temperature range. Heat produced during flight substituted for thermoregulatory costs in the pigeon (Rothe *et al.*, 1987) and one hummingbird (Berger and Hart, 1972) but did not in other hummingbirds (Schuchmann, 1979). Because of the confusing and contradictory results using captive birds, Webster and Weathers (1990) took the innovative step of testing the idea on small, free-ranging birds (verdins) and concluded that partial substitution does occur. However, they were unable to distinguish between the heat increments of feeding and activity, and the assumptions and variation inherent in using wild birds is still quite large. Continued development of their ideas and methods offer the opportunity to answer this important question in an ecological context.

IV. DAILY AND SEASONAL ENERGY EXPENDITURE FOR MAINTENANCE

Energy expenditures over time in variable environments are rarely constant because of noncompensatory changes in basal metabolism, activity, or thermoregulation. However, because of the predictability of specific energy expenditures as functions of body weight, very general relationships between body weight and energy expenditure for maintenance are expected. Such relationships should be used only as generalizations for interspecific comparisons and not as constants applicable to all members of the group at all times. The overzealous use of such approximations would ignore the rich diversity of life strategies and, consequently, energy expenditures between individuals and species over time. It is not the "average" but the "variation" that determines whether animals reproduce, survive, or die.

Daily energy expenditure (BMR + activity + thermoregulation + heat increment of feeding) by captive wildlife has been measured frequently. Energy expenditure by captive birds at an ambient temperature of 30°C is 31% higher than basal metabolism for passerines and 26% higher for nonpasserines (Kendeigh, 1970). At an ambient temperature of 0°C, energy expenditure of captive birds ranges from 3.2 × BMR for a 10 g passerine to 1.6 × BMR for a 5 kg nonpasserine. At this colder temperature, small birds have a much higher thermoregulatory demand than do larger birds. Daily energy expenditures of captive insectivores and rodents have frequently been measured at a standardized ambient temperature of 20°C (French et al., 1976). Daily metabolic rates (kcal/day) at this temperature average $66.9X_{kg}^{0.43}$ for insectivores [i.e., 2 × BMR ($Y = 32.57X_{kg}^{0.42}$; Hayssen and Lacy, 1985)] and $85.6X_{kg}^{0.54}$ for rodents [i.e., 2.8 to 1.1 × BMR for rodents weighing from 0.007 to 9.2 kg with a BMR of $58.6X_{kg}^{0.67}$; Hayssen and Lacy, 1985)]. For other captive eutherians ranging in size from weasels to moose, the average daily metabolic rate is $141.4X_{kg}^{0.75}$ (N = 14, $R^2 = 0.99$), or approximately 2.0 × BMR (Golley et al., 1965; Jense, 1968; Ullrey et al., 1970; Thompson et al., 1973; Holter et al., 1974; Moors, 1977; Harper et al., 1978; Simpson et al., 1978a; Baker et al., 1979; Ronald et al., 1984; Gallagher et al., 1984; Schwartz et al., 1988; Markussen et al., 1990).

Daily energy expenditure of free-ranging passerines and nonpasserines averages 2.7× the average daily BMR (Aschoff and Pohl 1970a) (Table 8.9). Birds that search and forage during flight expend from 16 to 38% more energy than more sedentary feeders (Williams, 1988). Similarly, nesting seabirds operate at 2.1 × BMR in comparison to those at sea that expend energy at 3.3 × BMR (Birt-Friesen et al., 1989). Seabirds that live in cold waters have daily energy expenditures 70% higher than those living in warm water.

Free-ranging terrestrial eutherians that are not actively breeding or lactating have daily energy expenditures of 2.3 × BMR (Table 8.9), or approximately 15% higher than captive eutherians. The slope of the BMR and daily energy expenditure equations differ in marsupials. Small, insectivorous marsupials expend energy at 6.3 ± 0.7 × BMR whereas larger, herbivorous marsupials operate at 2.5 ± 0.7 × BMR.

One of the major areas of investigation initiated in recent years relative to understanding activity patterns, and therefore variation in daily energy budgets, has been the investigation of animal foraging strategies. The basic assumption in such studies is that activity, and therefore daily energy expenditure, is not a random event or process but is determined by a series of highly predictable interactions between the animal's requirements and its perception of the distri-

TABLE 8.9

Daily Energy Expenditure (Y in kcal/day) for Several Groups of Free-Ranging Wildlife Measured with Doubly Labeled Water

Group	Equation[a]	N	r^2	Weight range (kg)
Mammals				
Terrestrial eutherians	$Y = 160.0\,X^{0.72}$	19	0.97	0.013–32.7
Marsupials	$Y = 145.7\,X^{0.57}$	13	0.98	0.011–44.4
Rodents	$Y = 88.3\,X^{0.54}$	15	0.74	0.013–0.104
Birds				
All birds	$Y = 231.8\,X^{0.66}$	25	0.92	0.004–8.40
Passerines	$Y = 338.9\,X^{0.72}$	10	0.89	0.009–0.079
Nonpasserines	$Y = 222.3\,X^{0.73}$	15	0.92	0.004–8.40
Seabirds, all	$Y = 287.6\,X^{0.67}$	23	0.91	0.043–13.0
Seabirds, nesting	$Y = 161.8\,X^{0.74}$	10	0.93	0.043–6.10
Seabirds, at sea	$Y = 362.3\,X^{0.68}$	15	0.91	0.043–13.0
Seabirds, cold-water	$Y = 322.7\,X^{0.65}$	5	0.94	0.043–6.10
Seabirds, warm-water	$Y = 190.0\,X^{0.65}$	16	0.94	0.045–3.17
High aerial feeders	$Y = 203.8\,X^{0.53}$	7	0.78	0.013–0.05
More sedentary feeders	$Y = 330.1\,X^{0.75}$	11	0.87	0.013–0.09

Sources: Nagy, 1987; Williams, 1988; and Birt-Friesen *et al.*, 1989.
[a]X is body weight in kilograms. Equations differ slightly from those of Nagy (1987) in that multiple values for a particular species were averaged and the *Odocoileus* value was replaced by ones generated in a more extensive study of nine free-ranging deer (Parker, unpublished; body weight = 32.7 kg, DEE = 2242 kcal/day).

bution of resources for meeting those requirements. Since many animals attempt to maximize their net rate of energy intake in optimizing the cost-benefit constraints of the biological system, the energy expenditure for food-searching activities is determined by the cost of different search efforts; prey density, distribution, and energy content; and the efficiency and success rate of capture. Larger predators should use less energy-consuming search methods than should smaller predators if the efficiency of capture and prey size are similar. Small predators should be able to exploit more dispersed food sources than should larger predators when the preceding constraints apply. Because of the higher total energy expenditure per unit of activity in the larger animal, the larger animal will reach a critical threshold of energy expenditure sooner relative to prey energy density than will the smaller animal. As our knowledge of the factors determining the activity patterns of free-ranging animals increases, our estimates and comparisons of daily energy expenditure will become more dependent on a multidimensional analysis. Rather than simply indicating the cost, we will be able to state why and to what extent changes in either the animal, its population, or the environment affect the cost of daily life.

REFERENCES

Adam, I., Young, B. A., and Nicol, A. M. (1979). Energy cost to cattle of ingesting feed. *Agric. For. Bull., Univ. Alberta, Special Issue*, pp. 38–39.

Alexander, R. McN., Jayes, A. S., and Ker, R. F. (1980). Estimates of energy cost for quadrupedal running gaits. *J. Zool.* **190**, 155–192.

Altmann, S. A. (1987). The impact of locomotor energetics on mammalian foraging. *J. Zool.* **211**, 215–225.

Aschoff, J. (1981). Thermal conductance in mammals and birds, its dependence on body size and circadian phase. *Comp. Biochem. Physiol.* **69A**, 611–619.

Aschoff, J., and Pohl, H. (1970a). Rhythmic variations in energy metabolism. *Fed. Proc.* **29**, 1541–1552.

Aschoff, J., and Pohl, H. (1970b). Der Ruheumsatz von Vogeln als Funktion ter Tageszeit und der Korpergrosse. *J. Ornithol.* **111**, 38–47.

Ashwell-Erickson, S., Elsner, R., and Wartzok, D. (1979). Metabolism and nutrition of Bering Sea harbor and spotted seals. *Proc. Alaska Sci. Conf.* **29**, 651–665.

Au, D., and Weihs, D. (1980). At high speeds dolphins save energy by leaping. *Nature (London)* **284**, 548–550.

Baker, D. L., Johnson, D. E., Carpenter, L. H., Wallmo, O. C., and Gill, R. B. (1979). Energy requirements of mule deer fawns in winter. *J. Wildl. Manage.* **43**, 162–169.

Bakken, G. S. (1990). Estimating the effect of wind on avian metabolic rate with standard operative temperature. *Auk* **107**, 587–594.

Bakken, G. S., Santee, W. R., and Erskine, D. J. (1985) Operative and standard operative temperature: Tools for thermal energetic studies. *Am. Zool.* **25**, 933–943.

Baldwin, R. L., Smith, N. E., Taylor, J., and Sharp, M. (1980). Manipulating metabolic parameters to improve growth rate and milk secretion. *J. Anim. Sci.* **51**, 1416–1428.

Bandyopadhyay, B., and Chattopadhyay, H. (1980). Energy metabolism in male college students. *Indian J. Med. Res.* **71**, 961–969.

Barnes, B. M. (1989). Freeze avoidance in a mammal: Body temperatures below 0°C in an arctic hibernator. *Science* **244**, 1593–1595.

Barrott, H. G., Fritz, J. C., Pringle, E. M., and Titus, H. W. (1938). Heat production and gaseous metabolism of young male chickens. *J. Nutr.* **15**, 145–167.

Baudinette, R. V., and Gill, P. (1985). The energetics of "flying" and "paddling" in water: Locomotion in penguins and ducks. *J. Comp. Physiol.* **155B**, 373–380.

Baudinette, R. V., and Schmidt-Nielsen, K. (1974). Energy cost of gliding flight in herring gulls. *Nature (London)* **248**, 83–84.

Baudinette, R.V., Gill, P., and O'Driscoll, M. (1986). Energetics of the little penguin, *Eudyptula minor*: Temperature regulation, the calorigenic effect of food, and moulting. *Aust. J. Zool.* **34**, 35–45.

Benedict, F. G. (1936). "The Physiology of the Elephant." Carnegie Inst. Publ. No. 474, Washington, D.C.

Benedict, F. G., and Fox, E. L. (1933). Der Grundumsatz von kleinen Vogeln (Spatzen, Kanarienvogeln and Sittichen). *Pfluegers Arch.* **232**, 357–388.

Bennett, P. M., and Harvey, P. H. (1987). Active and resting metabolism in birds: Allometry, phylogeny and ecology. *J. Zool.* **213**, 327–363.

Berger, M., and Hart, J. S. (1972). Die Atmung beim Kolibri *Amazilia fimbriata* wahrend des Schwirrfluges bei verschiedenen Umgebungstemperaturen. *J. Comp. Physiol.* **81**, 363–380.

Birkebak, R. C. (1966). Heat transfer in biological systems. *Int. Rev. Gen. Exp. Zool.* **2**, 269–344.

Birt-Friesen, V. L., Montevecchi, W. A., Cairns, D. K., and Macko, S. A. (1989). Activity-specific metabolic rates of free-living northern gannets and other seabirds. *Ecology* **70**, 357–367.

Brackenbury, J. H., and Avery, P. (1980). Energy consumption and ventilatory mechanisms in the exercising fowl. *Comp. Biochem. Physiol.* **66A**, 439–445.

Bradley, S. R., and Deavers, D. R. (1980). A re-examination of the relationship between thermal conductance and body weight in mammals. *Comp. Biochem. Physiol.* **65A**, 465–476.

Brenner, F. J., and Malin, W. F. (1965). Metabolism and survival time of the red-winged blackbird. *Wilson Bull.* **77**, 282–289.

Brockway, J. M., and Gessaman, J. A. (1977). The energy cost of locomotion on the level and on gradients for the red deer (*Cervus elaphus*). *Q. J. Exp. Physiol.* **62**, 333–339.

Brody, S. (1945). "Bioenergetics and Growth." Hafner, New York.

Butler, P. J. (1988). The exercise response and the "classical" diving response during natural submersion in birds and mammals. *Can. J. Zool.* **66**, 29–39.

Butler, P. J., and Woakes, A. J. (1984). Heart rate and aerobic metabolism in Humboldt penguins, *Spheniscus humboldti*, during voluntary dives. *J. Exp. Biol.* **108**, 419–428.

Buttemer, W. A. (1985). Energy relations of roost-site utilization by American gold finches (*Corduelis tristis*). *Oecologia* **68**, 126–132.

Buttemer, W. A., Hayworth, A. M., Weathers, W. W., and Nagy, K. A. (1986). Time budget estimates of avian energy expenditure: Physiological and meteorological considerations. *Physiol. Zool.* **59**, 131–149.

Calder, W. A., and King, J. R. (1974). Thermal and caloric relations of birds. *In* "Avian Biology," Vol. IV (D. S. Farner and J. R. King, eds.), pp. 259–413. Academic Press, New York.

Campbell, G. S. (1977). "An Introduction to Environmental Biophysics." Springer-Verlag, New York.

Canals, M., Rosenmann, M., and Bozinovic, F. (1989). Energetics and geometry of huddling in small mammals. *J. Theor. Biol.* **141**, 181–189.

Carl, G. R., and Robbins, C. T. (1988). The energetic cost of predator avoidance in neonatal ungulates: Hiding versus following. *Can. J. Zool.* **66**, 239–246.

Carpenter, R. E. (1975). Flight metabolism in flying foxes. *In* "Swimming and Flying in Nature, Vol. 2" (T.Y.T. Wu, C.J. Brokaw, and C. Brennen, eds.), pp. 883–890. Plenum Press, New York.

Casey, T. M., Withers, P. C., and Casey, K. K. (1979). Metabolic and respiratory responses of arctic mammals to ambient temperature during the summer. *Comp. Biochem. Physiol.* **64A**, 331–341.

Cena, K., and Monteith, J. L. (1975). Transfer processes in animal coats. I. Radiative transfer. *Proc. R. Soc. Lond. B. Biol. Sci.* **188**, 377–393.

Chaplin, S. B. (1982). The energetic significance of huddling behavior in common bushtits (*Psaltriparus minimus*). *Auk* **99**, 424–430.

Chappel, R. W., and Hudson, R. J. (1978a). Energy cost of feeding in Rocky Mountain bighorn sheep. *Acta Theriol.* **23**, 359–363.

Chappel, R. W., and Hudson, R. J. (1978b). Winter bioenergetics of Rocky Mountain bighorn sheep. *Can. J. Zool.* **56**, 2388–2393.

Chappel, R. W., and Hudson, R. J. (1979). Energy cost of standing in Rocky Mountain bighorn sheep. *J. Wildl. Manage.* **43**, 261–263.

Chassin, P. S., Taylor, C. R., Heglund, N. C., and Seeherman, H. J. (1976). Locomotion in lions: Energetic cost and maximum aerobic capacity. *Physiol. Zool.* **49**, 1–10.

Clapperton, J. L. (1964). The energy metabolism of sheep walking on the level and on gradients. *Br. J. Nutr.* **18**, 47–54.

Clark, R. M., Holter, J. B., Colovos, N. F., and Hayes, H. H. (1972). Effect of postural position and position changes on energy expenditure in fasting dairy cattle. *J. Dairy Sci.* **55**, 257–260.

Costa, D. P. (1988). Methods for studying the energetics of freely diving animals. *Can. J. Zool.* **66**, 45–52.

Costa, D. P., and Kooyman, G. L. (1982). Oxygen consumption, thermoregulation, and the effect of fur oiling and washing on the sea otter, *Enhydra lutris*. *Can. J. Zool.* **60**, 2761–2767.

Costa, D.P., and Kooyman, G. L. (1984). Contribution of specific dynamic action to heat balance and thermoregulation in the sea otter *Enhydra lutris*. *Physiol. Zool.* **57**, 199–203.

Costello, R. R., and Whittow, G. C. (1975). Oxygen cost of swimming in a trained California sea lion. *Comp. Biochem. Physiol.* **50A**, 645–647.

Croxall, J. P., and Davis, R.W. (1990). Metabolic rate and foraging behavior of *Pygoscelis* and *Eudyptes* penguins at sea. *In* "Penguin Biology" (L. S. Davis and J. T. Darby, eds.), pp. 207–228. Academic Press, San Diego.

Culik, B., and Wilson, R. P. (1991a). Energetics of under-water swimming in Adelie penguins (*Pygoscelis adeliae*). *J. Comp. Physiol.* **161B**, 285–291.

Culik, B., and Wilson, R. P. (1991b). Swimming energetics and performance of instrumented Adelie penguins (*Pygoscelis adeliae*). *J. Exp. Biol.* **158**, 355–368.

Dailey, T. V., and Hobbs, N. T. (1989). Travel in alpine terrain: Energy expenditures for locomotion by mountain goats and bighorn sheep. *Can. J. Zool.* **67**, 2368–2375.

Davis, L. B., and Birkebak, R. C. (1975). Convective energy transfer in fur. *In* "Perspectives of Biophysical Ecology" (D. M. Gates and R. B. Schmerl, eds.), pp. 525–548. Springer-Verlag, New York.

Davis, R. W., Williams, T. M., and Kooyman, G. L. (1985). Swimming metabolism of yearling and adult harbor seals (*Phoca vitulina*). *Physiol. Zool.* **58**, 590–596.

Davis, R. W., Williams, T. M., Thomas, J. A., Kastelein, R. A., and Cornell, L. H. (1988). The effects of oil contamination and cleaning on sea otters (*Enhydra lutris*). II. Metabolism, thermoregulation, and behavior. *Can. J. Zool.* **66**, 2782–2790.

Dawson, T. J. (1976). Energetic cost of locomotion in Australian hopping mice. *Nature (London)* **259**, 305–306.

Dawson, T. J., Denny, M. J. S., and Hulbert, A. J. (1969). Thermal balance of the macropodid marsupial *Macropus eugenii* Demerest. *Comp. Biochem. Physiol.* **31**, 645–653.

Dawson,T. J., and Fanning, F. D. (1981). Thermal and energetic problems of semiaquatic mammals: A study of the Australian water rat, including comparisons with the platypus. *Physiol. Zool.* **54**, 285–296.

Dawson, W. R., Bennett, A. F., and Hudson, J. W. (1976). Metabolism and thermoregulation in hatchling ring-billed gulls. *Condor* **78**, 49–60.

Dewasmes, G., LeMaho, Y., Cornet, A., and Groscolas, R. (1980). Resting metabolic rate and cost of locomotion in long-term fasting emperor penguins. *J. Appl. Physiol.* **49**, 888–896.

Erasmus, T., Randall, R. M., and Randall, B. M. (1981). Oil pollution, insulation and body temperatures in the jackass penguin, *Spheniscus demersus*. *Comp. Biochem. Physiol.* **69A**, 169–171.

Erickson, A. W., and Youatt, W. G. (1961). Seasonal variations in the hematology and physiology of black bears. *J. Mammal.* **42**, 198–203.

Fancy, S. G., and White, R. G. (1985a). Energy expenditure by caribou while cratering in snow. *J. Wildl. Manage.* **48**, 987–993.

Fancy, S. G., and White, R. G. (1985b). Incremental cost of activity. *In* "Bioenergetics of Wild Herbivores" (R. J. Hudson and R. G. White, eds.), pp. 143–159. CRC Press, Boca Raton, Florida.

Fancy, S. G., and White, R. G. (1987). Energy expenditures for locomotion by barren-ground caribou. *Can. J. Zool.* **65**, 122–128.

Fedak, M. A., and Seeherman, H. J. (1979). Reappraisal of energetics of locomotion shows identical cost in bipeds and quadrupeds including ostrich and horse. *Nature (London)* **282**, 713–716.

Fedak, M. A., Pinshow, B., and Schmidt-Nielsen, K. (1974). Energy cost of bipedal running. *Am. J. Physiol.* **227**, 1038–1044.

Feldkamp, S. D. (1985). The effects of net entanglement on the drag and power output of a California sea lion, *Zalophus californianus*. *US Natl. Mar. Fish. Serv. Fish. Bull.* **83**, 692–695.

Feldkamp, S. D. (1987). Swimming in the California sea lion: Morphometrics, drag and energetics. *J. Exp. Biol.* **131**, 117–135.

Fish, F. E. (1982). Aerobic energetics of surface swimming in the muskrat *Ondatra zibethicus*. *Physiol. Zool.* **55**, 180–189.

Flint, E. N., and Nagy, K. A. (1984). Flight energetics of free-living sooty terns. *Auk* **101**, 288–294.

French, N. R., Grant, W. E., Grodzinski, W., and Swift, D. M. (1976). Small mammal energetics in grassland ecosystems. *Ecol. Monogr.* **46**, 201–220.

Gales, R., and Green, B. (1990). The annual energetics cycle of little penguins (*Eudyptula minor*). *Ecology* **71**, 2297–2312.

Gallagher, J. F., Varner, L. W., and Grant, W. E. (1984). Nutrition of the collared peccary in South Texas. *J. Wildl. Manage.* **48**, 749–761.

Gallivan, G. J., and Best, R. C. (1986). The influence of feeding and fasting on the metabolic rate and ventilation of the Amazonian manatee (*Trichechus inunguis*). *Physiol. Zool.* **59**, 552–557.

Garland, T., Jr. (1983). Scaling the ecological cost of transport to body mass in terrestrial mammals. *Am. Nat.* **121**, 571–587.

Gates, C. C., and Hudson, R. J. (1978). Energy costs of locomotion in wapiti. *Acta Theriol.* **23**, 365–370.

Gates, C. C., and Hudson, R. J. (1979). Effects of posture and activity on metabolic responses of wapiti to cold. *J. Wildl. Manage.* **43**, 564–567.

Gebczynski, M. (1971). Oxygen consumption in starving shrews. *Acta Theriol.* **16**, 288–292.

Geiser, F. (1987). Hibernation and daily torpor in two pygmy possums (*Cercartetus* spp., *Marsupialia*). *Physiol. Zool.* **60**, 93–102.

Geissler, C. A., and Aldouri, M. S. H. (1985). Racial differences in the energy cost of standardized activities. *Ann. Nutr. Metab.* **29**, 40–47.

Gessaman, J. A., and Nagy, K. A. (1988a). Energy metabolism: Errors in gas-exchange conversion factors. *Physiol. Zool.* **61**, 507–513.

Gessaman, J. A., and Nagy, K. A. (1988b). Transmitter loads affect the flight speed and metabolism of homing pigeons. *Condor* **90**, 662–668.

Gittleman, J. L., and Thompson, S. D. (1988). Introduction to the symposium: Energetics and animal behavior. *Am. Zool.* **28**, 813–814.

Goldstein, D. L. (1983). Effect of wind on avian metabolic rate with particular reference to Gambel's quail. *Physiol. Zool.* **56**, 485–492.

Goldstein, D. L. (1988). Estimates of daily energy expenditure in birds: The time-energy budget as an integrator of laboratory and field studies. *Am. Zool.* **28**, 829–844.

Golley, F. B., Petrides, G. A., Rauber, E. L., and Jenkins, J. H. (1965). Food intake and assimilation by bobcats under laboratory conditions. *J. Wildl. Manage.* **29**, 442–447.

Graham, N. McC. (1964). Energy costs of feeding activities and energy expenditure of grazing sheep. *Aust. J. Agric. Res.* **15**, 969–973.

Grant, T. R., and Dawson, T. J. (1978). Temperature regulation in the platypus, *Ornithorhynchus anatinus*: Production and loss of metabolic heat in air and water. *Physiol. Zool.* **51**, 315–332.

Hails, C. J. (1979). A comparison of flight energetics in Hirundines and other birds. *Comp. Biochem. Physiol.* **63A**, 581–585.

Hails, C. J. (1983). The metabolic rate of tropical birds. *Condor* **85**, 61–65.

Harper, R. B., Travis, H. F., and Glinsky, M. S. (1978). Metabolizable energy requirement for maintenance and body composition of growing farm-raised male pastel mink (*Mustela vison*). *J. Nutr.* **108**, 1937–1943.

Hart, J. S. (1950). Interrelations of daily metabolic cycle, activity and environmental temperature of mice. *Can. J. Res.* **28**, 293–307.

Hart, J. S. (1952). Effects of temperature and work on metabolism, body temperature, and insulation: Results with mice. *Can. J. Zool.* **30**, 90–98.

Hart, J. S. (1971). Rodents. *In* "Comparative Physiology of Thermoregulation" (G. C. Whittow, ed.), pp. 1–149. Academic Press, New York.

Hart, J. S., and Heroux, O. (1955). Exercise and temperature regulation in lemmings and rabbits. *Can. J. Biochem. Physiol.* **33**, 428–435.

Hart, J. S., and Irving, L. (1959). The energetics of harbor seals in air and in water with special consideration of seasonal changes. *Can. J. Zool.* **37**, 447–457.

Hart, J. S., and Jansky, L. (1963). Thermogenesis due to exercise and cold in warm- and cold-acclimated rats. *Can. J. Biochem. Physiol.* **41**, 629–634.

Hart, J. S., Heroux, O., Cottle, W. H., and Mills, C. A. (1961). The influence of climate on metabolic and thermal responses of infant caribou. *Can. J. Zool.* **39**, 845–856.

Hartung, R. (1967). Energy metabolism of oil-covered ducks. *J. Wildl. Manage.* **31**, 798–804.

Hayssen, V., and Lacy, R. C. (1985). Basal metabolic rates in mammals: Taxonomic differences in the allometry of BMR and body mass. *Comp. Biochem. Physiol.* **81A**, 741–754.

Hearne, S. (1971). "A Journey from Prince of Wales's Fort in Hudson's Bay to the Northern Ocean." M.G. Hurtig Ltd., Edmonton, Canada.

Heller, H. C. (1988). Sleep and hypometabolism. *Can. J. Zool.* **66**, 61–69.

Heller, H. C., Graf, R., and Rautenberg, W. (1983). Circadian and arousal state influences on thermoregulation in the pigeon. *Am. J. Physiol.* **245**, R321–R328.

Hinds, D. S. (1973). Acclimatization of thermoregulation in the desert cottontail, *Sylvilagus auduboni*. *J. Mammal.* **54**, 708–725.

Holleman, D. F., Luick, J. R., and White, R. G. (1979). Lichen intake estimates for reindeer and caribou during winter. *J. Wildl. Manage.* **43**, 192–201.

Holter, J. B., Tyler, G., and Walski, T. W. (1974). Nutrition of the snowshoe hare (*Lepus americanus*). *Can. J. Zool.* **52**, 1553–1558.

Hoyt, D. F., and Kenagy, G. J. (1988). Energy costs of walking and running gaits and their aerobic limits in golden-mantled ground squirrels. *Physiol. Zool.* **61**, 34–40.

Hoyt, D. F., and Taylor, C. R. (1981). Gait and the energetics of locomotion in horses. *Nature (London)* **292**, 239–240.

Hui, C. A. (1987). The porpoising of penguins: An energy-conserving behavior for respiratory ventilation? *Can. J. Zool.* **65**, 209–211.

Hui, C. A. (1988). Penguin swimming. II. Energetics and behavior. *Physiol. Zool.* **61**, 344–350.

Jense, G. K. (1968). "Food Habits and Energy Utilization of Badgers." Master's Thesis, South Dakota State Univ., Brookings, South Dakota.

Jenssen, B. M., and Ekker, M. (1988). A method for evaluating the cleaning of oiled seabirds. *Wildl. Soc. Bull.* **16**, 213–215.

Jenssen, B. M., and Ekker, M. (1991). Effects of plumage contamination with crude oil dispersant mixtures on thermoregulation in common eiders and mallards. *Arch. Environ. Contam. Toxicol.* **20**, 398–403.

Jenssen, B. M., Ekker, M., and Bech, C. (1989). Thermoregulation in winter- acclimatized common eiders (*Somateria mollissima*) in air and water. *Can. J. Zool.* **67**, 669–673.

Kayser, C. (1961). "The Physiology of Natural Hibernation." Pergamon, New York.

Kayser, C. (1964). Stoffwechsel und Winterschlaf. *Helgolander wiss. Meeresunters.* **9**, 155–186.

Kenagy, G. J., and Vleck, D. (1982). Daily temporal organization of metabolism in small mammals:

Adaptation and diversity. *In* "Vertebrate Circadian Systems" (J. Aschoff, S. Daan, and G. Groos, eds.), pp. 322–338. Springer, Heidelberg, Germany.

Kendeigh, S. C. (1970). Energy requirements for existence in relation to size of bird. *Condor* **72**, 60–65.

Kendeigh, S. C., Dol'nik, V. R., and Gavrilov, V. M. (1977). Avian energetics. *In* "Granivorous Birds in Ecosystems" (J. Pinowski and S. C. Kendeigh, eds.), pp. 127–204. Cambridge University Press, Cambridge, England.

Ketterson, E. D., and King, J. R. (1977). Metabolic and behavioral responses to fasting in the white-crowned sparrow (*Zonotrichia leucophrys gambelii*). *Physiol. Zool.* **50**, 115–129.

King, J. R. (1974). Seasonal allocation of time and energy resources in birds. *In* "Avian Energetics" (R.A. Paynter, Jr., ed.) pp. 4–85. Nuttall Ornith. Club Publ. No. 15, Cambridge, Massachusetts.

King, J. R., and Farner, D. S. (1961). Energy metabolism, thermoregulation and body temperature. *In* "Biology and Comparative Physiology of Birds," Vol. II (A. J. Marshall, ed.), pp. 215–288. Academic Press, New York.

Klaassen, M., Bech., C., Masman, D., and Slagsvold, G. (1989a). Growth and energetics of arctic tern chicks (*Sterna paradisaea*). *Auk* **106**, 240–248.

Klaassen, M., Bech, C., and Slagsvold, G. (1989b). Basal metabolic rate and thermal conductance in arctic tern chicks and the effect of heat increment of feeding on thermoregulatory expenses. *Ardea* **77**, 193–200.

Kleiber, M. (1947). Body size and metabolic rate. *Physiol. Rev.* **27**, 511–541.

Kleiber, M. (1961). "The Fire of Life." Wiley, New York.

Kontogiannis, J. E. (1968). Effect of temperature and exercise on energy intake and body weight of the white-throated sparrow, *Zonotrichia albicollis*. *Physiol. Zool.* **41**, 54–64.

Kooyman, G. L., and Ponganis, P. J. (1990). Behavior and physiology of diving in emperor and king penguins. *In* "Penguin Biology" (L. S. Davis and J. T. Darby, eds.), pp. 229–242. Academic Press, San Diego.

Lambert, G., Peakall, D. B., Philogene, B. J. R., and Engelhardt, F. R. (1982). Effect of oil and oil dispersal mixtures on the basal metabolic rate of ducks. *Bull. Environ. Contam. Toxicol.* **29**, 520–524.

Lasiewski, R. C., and Dawson, W. R. (1967). A re-examination of the relation between standard metabolic rate and body weight in birds. *Condor* **69**, 13–23.

Laudenslager, M. L., and Hamel, H. T. (1978). Metabolic heat production in the chukar partridge. *Auk* **95**, 592–594.

Le Maho, Y., Delclitte, P., and Chatonnet, J. (1976). Thermoregulation in fasting emperor penguins under natural conditions. *Am. J. Physiol.* **231**, 913–922.

Lifson, N. Gordon, G. B., Vissher, M. B., and Nier, A. O. (1949). The fate of utilized molecular oxygen and the source of the oxygen of respiratory carbon dioxide, studied with the aid of labeled water. *Am. J. Chem.* **180**, 803–811.

Lifson, N., Gordon, G. B., and McClintock, R. M. (1955). Measurement of total carbon dioxide production by means of D_2O^{18}. *J. Appl. Physiol.* **7**, 704–710.

Lovegrove, B. G. (1989). The cost of burrowing by the social mole rats (Bathyergidae) *Cryptomys damarensis* and *Heterocephalus glaber*: The role of soil moisture. *Physiol. Zool.* **62**, 449–469.

Luick, B. R., and White, R. G. (1983). Indirect calorimetric measurements of the caribou calf. *Acta Zool. Fennica* **175**, 89–90.

Lyman, C. P., Willis, J. S., Malan, A., and Wang, L. C. H. (1982). "Hibernation and Torpor in Mammals and Birds." Academic Press, New York.

MacArthur, R. A. (1984). Aquatic thermoregulation in the muskrat (*Ondatra zibethicus*): Energy demands of swimming and diving. *Can. J. Zool.* **62**, 241–248.

MacArthur, R. A. (1989). Energy metabolism and thermoregulation of beaver (*Castor canadensis*). *Can. J. Zool.* **67**, 651–657.

MacArthur, R. A., and Dyck, A. P. (1990). Aquatic thermoregulation of captive and free-ranging beavers (*Castor canadensis*). *Can. J. Zool.* **68,** 2409–2416.

MacArthur, R. A., and Krause, R. E. (1989). Energy requirements of freely diving muskrats (*Ondatra zibethicus*). *Can. J. Zool.* **67,** 2194–2200.

Mahoney, S. A. (1980). Cost of locomotion and heat balance during rest and running from 0 to 55°C in a patas monkey. *J. Appl. Physiol.* **49,** 789–800.

Malloy, L. G., and Herreid, C. F., II. (1979). Energetics of behavior in single and paired mice. *Am. Zool.* **19,** 991.

Markussen, N. H., Ryg., M., and Oritsland, N. A. (1990). Energy requirements for maintenance and growth of captive harbor seals, *Phoca vitulina. Can. J. Zool.* **68,** 423–426.

Marsh, R. L., and Dawson, W. R. (1989). Avian adjustments to cold. *In* "Advances in Comparative and Environmental Physiology, Vol. 4: Animal Adaptation to Cold" (L. C. H. Wang, ed.), pp. 205–253. Springer-Verlag, Berlin.

Marston, H. R. (1948). Energy transactions in the sheep. I. The basal heat production and heat increment. *Aust. J. Sci. Res. B.* **1,** 93–129.

Martin, R. A., Fiorentini, M., and Connors, F. (1980). Social facilitation of reduced oxygen consumption in *Mus musculus* and *Meriones unguiculatus. Comp. Biochem. Physiol.* **65A,** 519–522.

Masman, D., and Klaassen, M. (1987). Energy expenditure during free flight in trained and free-living Eurasian kestrels (*Falco tinnunculus*). *Auk* **104,** 603–616.

Masman, D., Daan, S., and Dietz, M. (1989). Heat increment of feeding in the kestrel, *Falco tinnunculus*, and its natural seasonal variation. *In* "Physiology of Cold Adaptation in Birds" (C. Bech and R. E. Reinertsen, eds.), pp. 123–135. Plenum Press, New York.

Mattfeld, G. F. (1974). "The Energetics of Winter Foraging by White-tailed Deer: A Perspective on Winter Concentration." Doctoral Dissertation, SUNY College of Forestry, Syracuse, NY.

Mautz, W. W., and Fair, J. (1980). Energy expenditure and heart rate for activities of white-tailed deer. *J. Wildl. Manage.* **44,** 333–342.

McCarron, H. C. K., and Dawson, T. J. (1984). Thermoregulatory cost of activity in small dasyurid marsupials. *In* "Thermal Physiology" (J. R. S. Hales, ed.), pp. 327–330. Raven Press, New York.

McClure, P. A., and Randolph, J. C. (1980). Relative allocation of energy to growth and development of homeothermy in the eastern wood rat (*Neotoma floridana*) and hispid cotton rat (*Sigmodon hispidus*). *Ecol. Monogr.* **50,** 199–219.

McEwan, E. H., and Koelink, A. F. C. (1973). The heat production of oiled mallards and scaup. *Can. J. Zool.* **51,** 27–31.

McEwan, E. H., Aitchison, N., and Whitehead, P. E. (1974). Energy metabolism of oiled muskrats. *Can. J. Zool.* **52,** 1057–1061.

McNab, B. K. (1966). An analysis of body temperatures of birds. *Condor* **68,** 47–55.

McNab, B. K. (1983). Energetics, body size, and the limits to endothermy. *J. Zool.* **199,** 1–29.

McNab, B. K. (1986a). The influence of food habits on the energetics of eutherian mammals. *Ecol. Monogr.* **56,** 1–19.

McNab, B. K. (1986b). Food habits, energetics, and the reproduction of marsupials. *J. Zool.* **208,** 595–614.

McNab, B. K. (1988a). Complications inherent in scaling the basal rate of metabolism in mammals. *Q. Rev. Biol.* **63,** 25–54.

McNab, B. K. (1988b). Food habits and the basal rate of metabolism in birds. *Oecologia* **77,** 343–349.

McNab, B. K., (1988c). Energy conservation in a tree-kangaroo (*Dendrolagus matschiei*) and the red panda (*Ailurus fulgens*). *Physiol. Zool.* **61,** 280–292.

Meyer, J. J., and Guillot, A. (1986). The energetic cost of various behaviors in the laboratory mouse. *Comp. Biochem. Physiol.* **83A**, 533–538.

Moors, P. J. (1977). Studies of the metabolism, food consumption and assimilation efficiency of a small carnivore, the weasel (*Mustela nivalis* L.). *Oecologia* **27**, 185–202.

Morowitz, H. J. (1968). "Energy Flow in Biology: Biological Organization as a Problem in Thermal Physics." Academic Press, New York.

Morrison, P. (1960). Some interrelations between weight and hibernation function. *Bull. Harvard Mus. Comp. Zool.* **124**, 75–91.

Morrison, P., Rosenmann, M., and Estes, J. A. (1974). Metabolism and thermoregulation in the sea otter. *Physiol. Zool.* **47**, 218–229.

Mortensen, A., and Blix, A. S. (1986). Seasonal changes in resting metabolic rate and mass-specific conductance in Svalbard ptarmigan, Norwegian rock ptarmigan and Norwegian willow ptarmigan. *Ornis Scand.* **17**, 8–13.

Nagy, K. A. (1983). The doubly labeled water (^{3}H H^{18}O) method: A guide to its use. *UCLA Publ.* No. **12–1417**, University of California, Los Angeles. 45 pp.

Nagy, K. A. (1987). Field metabolic rate and food requirement scaling in mammals and birds. *Ecol. Monogr.* **57**, 111–128.

Nagy, K. A. (1989). Field bioenergetics: Accuracy of models and methods. *Physiol. Zool.* **62**, 237–252.

Nagy, K. A., Siegfried, W. R., and Wilson, R. P. (1984). Energy utilization by free-ranging jackass penguins, *Spheniscus demersus*. *Ecology* **65**, 1648–1655.

Newman, J. R., and Rudd, R. L. (1978). Minimum and maximum metabolic rates of *Sorex sinuosus*. *Acta Theriol.* **23**, 371–380.

Nilssen, K. J., Johnsen, H. K., Rognmo, A., and Blix, A. S. (1984a). Heart rate and energy expenditure in resting and running Svalbard and Norwegian reindeer. *Am. J. Physiol.* **246**, R963–R967.

Nilssen, K. J., Sundsfjord, J. A., and Blix, A. S. (1984b). Regulation of metabolic rate in Svalbard and Norwegian reindeer. *Am. J. Physiol.* **247**, R837–R841.

Nomoto, S., Rautenberg, W., and Iriki, M. (1983). Temperature regulation during exercise in the Japanese quail (*Coturnix coturnix japonica*). *J. Comp. Physiol.* **149B**, 519–525.

Oberlag, D. F., Pekins, P. J., and Mautz, W. W. (1990). Influence of seasonal temperatures on wild turkey metabolism. *J. Wildl. Manage.* **54**, 663–667.

Obst, B. S., Nagy, K. A., and Ricklefs, R. E. (1987). Energy utilization by Wilson's storm-petrel (*Oceanites oceanicus*). *Physiol. Zool.* **60**, 200–210.

Osuji, P. O. (1974). The physiology of eating and the energy expenditure of the ruminant at pasture. *J. Range Manage.* **27**, 437–443.

Owen, R. B., Jr. (1969). Heart rate, a measure of metabolism in blue-winged teal. *Comp. Biochem. Physiol.* **31**, 431–436.

Owen, R. B., Jr. (1970). The bioenergetics of captive blue-winged teal under controlled and outdoor conditions. *Condor* **72**, 153–163.

Paladino, F. V. (1979). "Energetics of Terrestrial Locomotion in White-crowned Sparrows (*Zonotrichia leucophorys gambelii*)." Doctoral Dissertation, Washington State Univ., Pullman.

Paladino, R. V., and King, J. R. (1984). Thermoregulation and oxygen consumption during terrestrial locomotion by white-crowned sparrows *Zonotrichia leucophrys gambelii*. *Physiol. Zool.* **57**, 226–236.

Parker, K. L. (1981). "The Energetics of Survival in Deer and Elk." Unpublished manuscript, Washington State Univ., Pullman.

Parker, K. L. (1988). Effects of heat, cold, and rain on coastal black-tailed deer. *Can. J. Zool.* **66**, 2475–2483.

Parker, K. L., and Gillingham, M. P. (1990). Estimates of critical thermal environments for mule deer. *J. Range Manage.* **43**, 73–81.

Parker, K. L., and Robbins, C. T. (1984). Thermoregulation in mule deer and elk. *Can. J. Zool.* **62**, 1409–1422.

Parker, K. L., and Robbins, C. T. (1985). Thermoregulation in ungulates. *In* "Bioenergetics of Wild Herbivores" (R. J. Hudson and R. G. White, eds.), pp. 161–182. CRC Press, Boca Raton, Florida.

Parker, K. L., Robbins, C. T., and Hanley, T. A. (1984). Energy expenditures for locomotion by mule deer and elk. *J. Wildl. Manage.* **48**, 474–488.

Parsons, P. E., and Taylor, C. R. (1977). Energetics of brachiation versus walking: A comparison of a suspended and an inverted pendulum mechanism. *Physiol. Zool.* **50**, 182–188.

Pauls, R. W. (1981). Energetics of the red squirrel: A laboratory study of the effects of temperature, seasonal acclimatization, use of the nest and exercise. *J. Therm. Biol.* **6**, 79–86.

Pennycuick, C. J. (1975). On the running of the gnu (*Connochaetus taurinus*) and other animals. *J. Exp. Biol.* **63**, 775–799.

Pinshow, B., Fedak, M. A., and Schmidt-Neilsen, K. (1977). Terrestrial locomotion in penguins: It costs more to waddle. *Science* **195**, 592–594.

Poczopko, P. (1971). Metabolic levels in adult homeotherms. *Acta Theriol.* **16**, 1–21.

Poczopko, P. (1979). Metabolic rate and body size relationships in adult and growing homeotherms. *Acta Theriol.* **24**, 125–136.

Pohl, H. (1969). Some factors influencing the metabolic response to cold in birds. *Fed. Proc.* **28**, 1059–1064.

Pohl, H., and West, G. C. (1973). Daily and seasonal variation in metabolic response to cold during rest and forced exercise in the common redpoll. *Comp. Biochem. Physiol.* **45A**, 851–867.

Prange, H. D., and Schmidt-Neilsen, K. (1970). The metabolic costs of swimming in ducks. *J. Exp. Biol.* **53**, 763–777.

Prothero, J. (1984). Scaling of standard energy metabolism in mammals: 1. Neglect of circadian rhythms. *J. Theor. Biol.* **106**, 1–8.

Prothero, J., and Jurgens, K. D. (1986). An energetic model of daily torpor in endotherms. *J. Theor. Biol.* **121**, 403–415.

Pyke, G. H. (1981). Optimal travel speeds of animals. *Am. Nat.* **118**, 475–487.

Raab, J. L., Eng, P., and Waschler, R. A. (1976). Metabolic cost of grade running in dogs. *J. Appl. Physiol.* **41**, 532–535.

Reese, J. B., and Haines, H. (1978). Effects of dehydration on metabolic rate and fluid distribution in the jackrabbit, *Lepus californicus*. *Physiol. Zool.* **51**, 155–165.

Regelin, W. L., Schwartz, C. C., and Franzmann, A. W. (1985). Seasonal energy metabolism of adult moose. *J. Wildl. Manage.* **49**, 388–393.

Regelin, W. L., Schwartz, C. C., and Franzmann, A. W. (1986). Energy cost of standing in adult moose. *Alces* **22**, 83–90.

Reichman, O. J., and Aitchison, S. (1981). Mammal trails on mountain slopes: Optimal paths in relation to slope angle and body weight. *Am. Nat.* **117**, 416–420.

Renecker, L. A., and Hudson, R. J. (1986). Seasonal energy expenditures and thermoregulatory responses of moose. *Can. J. Zool.* **64**, 322–327.

Renecker, L. A., Hudson, R. J., Christophersen, M. K., and Arelis, C. (1978). Effect of posture, feeding, low temperature, and wind on energy expenditures of moose calves. *Proc. 14th Annu. North Am. Moose Conf. Workshop*, pp. 126–140.

Ribeiro, J. M. de C. R., Brockway, J. M., and Webster, A. J. F. (1977). A note on the energy cost of walking in cattle. *Anim. Prod.* **25**, 107–110.

Ringberg, T. (1979). The Spitzbergen reindeer—a winter-dormant ungulate? *Acta Physiol. Scand.* **105**, 268–273.

Robbins, C. T. (unpublished). Basal metabolic rate in elk. Washington State Univ., Pullman, Washington.

Robertshaw, D., and Finch, V. A. (1984). Heat loss and gain in artificial and natural environments. *In* "Thermal Physiology" (J.R.S. Hales, ed.), pp. 243–250. Raven Press, New York.

Rogowitz, G. L. (1990) Seasonal energetics of the white-tailed jackrabbit (*Lepus townsendii*). *J. Mammal.* **71**, 277–285.

Romijn, C., and Lokhorst, W. (1961). Some aspects of energy metabolism in birds. *In* "Symposium on Energy Metabolism" (E. Brouwer and A. J. H. Van Es, eds.), pp. 49–59. European Association for Anim. Prod. Publ. No. 10.

Ronald, K., Keiver, K. M., Beamish, F. W. H., and Frank, R. (1984). Energy requirements for maintenance and fecal and urinary losses of the grey seal (*Halichoerus grypus*). *Can. J. Zool.* **62**, 1101–1105.

Rothe, H. J., Biesel, W., and Nachtigall, W. (1987). Pigeon flight in a wind tunnel. II. Gas exchange and power requirements. *J. Comp. Physiol.* **157B**, 99–109.

Rubner, M. (1902). "The Laws of Energy Consumption in Nutrition." Translated 1982, Academic Press, New York.

Schmidt-Nielsen, K. (1970). Energy metabolism, body size and the problems of scaling. *Fed. Proc.* **29**, 1524–1532.

Schmidt-Nielsen, K. (1972). Locomotion: Energy cost of swimming, flying and running. *Science* **177**, 222–228.

Schnell, G. D., and Hellack, J. J. (1979). Bird flight speeds in nature: Optimized or a compromise. *Am. Nat.* **113**, 53–66.

Scholander, P. F., Walters, V., Hock, R., and Irving, L. (1950a). Body insulation of some arctic and tropical mammals and birds. *Biol. Bull.,* **99**, 225–236.

Scholander, P. F., Hock, R., Walters, V., Johnson, F., and Irving, L. (1950b). Heat regulation in some arctic and tropical mammals and birds. *Biol. Bull.* **99**, 237–258.

Scholander, P. F., Hock, R., Walters, V., and Irving, L. (1950c). Adaptations to cold in arctic and tropical mammals and birds in relation to body temperature, insulation, and basal metabolic rate. *Biol. Bull.* **99**, 259–271.

Schuchmann, K.-L. (1979). Metabolism of flying hummingbirds. *Ibis* **121**, 85–86.

Schwartz, C. C., Hubbert, M. E., and Franzmann, A. W. (1988). Energy requirements of adult moose for winter maintenance. *J. Wildl. Manage.* **52**, 26–33.

Sherer, J., and Wunder, B. A. (1979). Thermoregulation of a semi-aquatic mammal, the muskrat, in air and water. *Acta Theriol.* **24**, 249–256.

Silver, H. (1968). Deer nutrition studies. *In* "White-tailed Deer of New Hampshire" (H. R. Siegler, ed.), pp. 182–196. N. H. Fish and Game Dept., Concord, New Hampshire.

Simek, V. (1975). Specific dynamic action of a high protein diet and its significance for thermoregulation in golden hamsters. *Physiol. Bohemoslov.* **24**, 421–424.

Simpson, A. M., Webster, A. J. F., Smith, J. S., and Simpson, C. A. (1978a). Energy and nitrogen metabolism of red deer (*Cervus elaphus*) in cold environments: A comparison with cattle and sheep. *Comp. Biochem. Physiol.* **60A**, 251–256.

Simpson, A. M., Webster, A. J. F., Smith, J. S., and Simpson, C. A. (1978b). The efficiency of utilization of dietary energy for growth in sheep (*Ovis ovis*) and red deer (*Cervus elaphus*). *Comp. Biochem. Physiol.* **59A**, 95–99.

Stahel, C. D., and Nicol, S. C. (1982). Temperature regulation in the little penguin, *Eudyptula minor*, in air and water. *J. Comp. Physiol.* **148**, 93–100.

Stahel, C. D., Megirian, D., and Nicol, S. C. (1984). Sleep and metabolic rate in the little penguin, *Eudyptula minor*. *J. Comp. Physiol.* **154B**, 487–494.

Stahel, C. D., Nicol, S. C., and Walker, G. J. (1987). Heat production and thermal resistance in the little penguin *Eudyptula minor* in relation to wind speed. *Physiol. Zool.* **60**, 413–423.

Steen, J. B., Grav, H., Borch-Iohnsen, B., and Gabrielsen, G. W. (1989). Strategies of homeothermy in eider ducklings (*Somateria mollissima*). *In* "Physiology of Cold Adaptation in Birds" (C. Bech and R. E. Reinertsen, eds.), pp. 361–370. Plenum Press, New York.

Stevenson, J. (1933). Experiments on the digestion of food by birds. *Wilson Bull.* **45**, 155–167.

Strang, K. T., and Steudel, K. (1990). Explaining the scaling of transport costs: The role of stride frequency and stride length. *J. Zool.* **221**, 343–358.

Summers, M., McBride, B. W., and Milligan, L. P. (1988). Components of basal energy expenditure. *In* "Aspects of Digestive Physiology in Ruminants" (A. Dobson and M. J. Dobson, eds.), pp. 257–285. Cornell Univ. Press, Ithaca, New York.

Swift, R. W. (1944). The effect of feeding on the critical temperature of the albino rat. *J. Nutr.* **28**, 359–364.

Tatner, P., and Bryant, D. M. (1986). Flight cost of a small passerine measured using doubly labeled water: Implications for energetic studies. *Auk* **103**, 169–180.

Taylor, C. R., Schmidt-Nielsen, K., and Raab, J. L. (1970). Scaling of energetic cost of running to body size in mammals. *Am. J. Physiol.* **219**, 1104–1107.

Taylor, C. R., Caldwell, S. L., and Rowntree, V. J. (1972). Running up and down hills: Some consequences of size. *Science* **178**, 1096–1097.

Taylor, C. R., Heglund, N. C., and Maloiy, G. M. O. (1982). Energetics and mechanics of terrestrial locomotion. I. Metabolic energy consumption as a function of speed and body size in birds and mammals. *J. Exp. Biol.* **97**, 1–21.

Telfer, E. S., and Kelsall, J. P. (1984). Adaptation of some large North American mammals for survival in snow. *Ecology* **65**, 1828–1834.

Thomas, D. W., Dorais, M., and Bergeron, J-M. (1990). Winter energy budgets and cost of arousal for hibernating little brown bats, *Myotis lucifugus*. *J. Mammal.* **71**, 475–479.

Thomas, S. P. (1975). Metabolism during flight in two species of bats, *Phyllostomus hastatus* and *Pteropus gouldii*. *J. Exp. Biol.* **63**, 273–293.

Thomas, S. P., and Suthers, R. A. (1972). The physiology and energetics of bat flight. *J. Exp. Biol.* **57**, 317–335.

Thompson, C. B., Holter, J. B., Hayes, H. H., Silver, H., and Urban, W. E., Jr. (1973). Nutrition of white-tailed deer. I. Energy requirements of fawns. *J. Wildl. Manage.* **37**, 301–311.

Thompson, F. R., III, and Fritzell, E. K. (1988). Ruffed grouse metabolic rate and temperature cycles. *J. Wildl. Manage.* **52**, 450–453.

Thompson, S. D. (1985). Bipedal hopping and seed-dispersion selection by heteromyid rodents: The role of locomotion energetics. *Ecology* **66**, 220–229.

Thompson, S. D. (1989). Energy balance in endothermic vertebrates. *Proc. Dr. Scholl Nutr. Conf.* **8**, 27–45.

Thompson, S. D., MacMillen, R. E., Burke, E., and Taylor, C. R. (1980). The energetic cost of bipedal hopping in small mammals. *Nature (London)* **287**, 223–224.

Toutain, P. L., Toutain, C., Webster, A. J. F., and McDonald, J. D. (1977). Sleep and activity, age and fatness, and the energy expenditure of confined sheep. *Br. J. Nutr.* **38**, 445–454.

Tucker, V. A. (1969). The energetics of bird flight. *Sci. Am.* **220**, 70–78.

Tucker, V. A. (1970). Energetic cost of locomotion in animals. *Comp. Biochem. Physiol.* **34A**, 841–846.

Ullrey, D. E., Youatt, W. G., Johnson, H. E., Fay, L. D., Schoepke, B. L., and Magee, W. T. (1970). Digestible and metabolizable energy requirements for winter maintenance of Michigan white-tailed does. *J. Wildl. Manage.* **34**, 863–869.

Vehrencamp, S. L., Bradbury, J. W., and Gibson, R. M. (1989). The energetic cost of display in male sage grouse. *Anim. Behav.* **38**, 885–896.

Vercoe, J. E. (1973). The energy cost of standing and lying in adult cattle. *Br. J. Nutr.* **30**, 207–210.

Vickery, W. L., and Millar, J. S. (1984). The energetics of huddling by endotherms. *Oikos* **43**, 88–93.

Vleck, D. (1979). The energy cost of burrowing by the pocket gopher, *Thomonys bottae*. *Physiol. Zool.* **52**, 122–136.

Wallgren, H. (1954). Energy metabolism of two species of the genus *Emberiza* as correlated with distribution and migration. *Acta Zool. Fennica* **84**, 1–110.

Walsberg, G. E. (1983). Coat color and solar heat gain in animals. *BioScience* **33**, 88–91.

Walsberg, G. E. (1986). Thermal consequences of roost-site selection: The relative importance of three modes of heat conservation. *Auk* **103**, 1–7.

Walsberg, G. E. (1988a). The significance of fur structure for solar heat gain in the rock squirrel, *Spermophilus variegatus*. *J. Exp. Biol.* **138**, 243–257.

Walsberg, G. E. (1988b). Heat flow through avian plumages: The relative importance of conduction, convection, and radiation. *J. Therm. Biol.* **13**, 89–92.

Walsberg, G. E. (1990). Convergence of solar heat gain in two squirrel species with contrasting coat colors. *Physiol. Zool.* **63**, 1025–1042.

Walsberg, G. E., and King, J. R. (1978). The relationship of external surface area of birds to skin surface area and body mass. *J. Exp. Biol.* **76**, 185–189.

Walsberg, G. E., and Schmidt, C.A. (1989). Seasonal adjustment of solar heat gain in a desert mammal by altering coat properties independently of surface coloration. *J. Exp. Biol.* **142**, 387–400.

Walsberg, G. E., Campbell, G. S., and King, J. R. (1978). Animal coat color and radiative heat gain: A re-evaluation. *J. Comp. Physiol.* **126B**, 211–222.

Wang, L. C. H. (1979). Time patterns and metabolic ratees of natural torpor in the Richardson's ground squirrel. *Can. J. Zool.* **57**, 149–155.

Wang, L. C. H., and Wolowyk, M. W. (1988). Torpor in mammals and birds. *Can. J. Zool.* **66**, 133–137.

Watts, P. D. (1990). Comparative weight loss in three species of ursids under simulated denning conditions. *Int. Conf. Bear Res. and Manage.* **8**, 139–141.

Watts, P. D., and Jonkel, C. (1988). Energetic cost of winter dormancy in grizzly bear. *J. Wildl. Manage.* **52**, 654–656.

Watts, P. D., Oritsland, N. A., Jonkel, C., and Ronald, K. (1981). Mammalian hibernation and the oxygen consumption of a denning black bear (*Ursus americanus*). *Comp. Biochem. Physiol.* **69**, 121–123.

Weathers, W.W., and van Riper, C., III. (1982). Temperature regulation in two endangered Hawaiian honeycreepers: The palila (*Psittirostra bailleui*) and the Laysan finch (*Psittirostra cantans*). *Auk* **99**, 667–674.

Weathers, W. W., Weathers, D. L., and van Riper, III, C. (1983). Basal metabolism of the apapane: Comparison of freshly caught birds with longterm captives. *Auk* **100**, 977–978.

Weathers, W. W., Buttemer, W. A., Hayworth, A. M., and Nagy, K. A. (1984). An evaluation of time budget estimates of daily energy expenditure in birds. *Auk* **101**, 459–472.

Webb, D. R., and King, J. R. (1984). Effects of wetting on insulation of bird and mammal coats. *J. Therm. Biol.* **9**, 189–191.

Webster, M. D., and Weathers, W. W. (1988). Effect of wind and air temperature on metabolic rate in verdins, *Auriparus flaviceps*. *Physiol. Zool.* **61**, 543–554.

Webster, M. D., and Weathers, W. W. (1990). Heat produced as a by-product of foraging activity contributes to thermoregulation by verdins, *Auriparus flaviceps*. *Physiol. Zool.* **63**, 777–794.

Weiner, J. (1977). Energy metabolism of the roe deer. *Acta Theriol.* **22**, 3–24.

Wesley, D. E., Knox, K. L., and Nagy, J. G. (1973). Energy metabolism of pronghorn antelopes. *J. Wildl. Manage.* **37**, 563–573.

West, G. C. (1972). Seasonal differences in resting metabolic rate of Alaska ptarmigan. *Comp. Biochem. Physiol.* **42A**, 867–876.

Westerterp, K. (1977). How rats economize—energy loss in starvation. *Physiol. Zool.* **50**, 331–362.

White, R. G., and Yousef, M. K. (1977). Energy expenditure in reindeer walking on roads and on tundra. *Can. J. Zool.* **56**, 215–223.

Wickstrom, M. L., Robbins, C. T., Hanley, T. A., Spalinger, D. E., and Parish, S. M. (1984). Food intake and foraging energetics of elk and mule deer. *J. Wildl. Manage.* **48**, 1285–1301.

Williams, J. B. (1988). Field metabolism of tree swallows during the breeding season. *Auk* **105**, 706–714.

Williams, T. M. (1983). Locomotion in the North American mink, a semi-aquatic mammal. II. The effect of an elongated body on running energetics and gait patterns. *J. Exp. Biol.* **105**, 283–295.

Williams, T. M. (1989). Swimming by sea otters: adaptations for low energetic cost locomotion. *J. Comp. Physiol.* **164A**, 815–824.

Williams, T. M., Kooyman, G.L., and Croll, D.A. (1991). The effect of submergence on heart rate and oxygen consumption of swimming seals and sea lions. *J. Comp. Physiol.* **160B**, 637–644.

Wilson, R. P., and Wilson, M-P. (1990). Foraging ecology of breeding *Spheniscus* penguins. *In* "Penguin Biology" (L.S. Davis and J.T. Darby, eds.), pp. 181–206. Academic Press, San Diego.

Wilson, R. P., Culik, B., and Adelung, D. (1991). To slide or stride: When should Adelie penguins (*Pygoscelis adeliae*) toboggan? *Can. J. Zool.* **69**, 221–225.

Woakes, A. J. (1988). Metabolism in diving birds: Studies in the laboratory and the field. *Can. J. Zool.* **66**, 138–141.

Woakes, A. J., and Butler, P. J. (1983). Swimming and diving in tufted ducks, *Aythya fuligula,* with particular reference to heart rate and gas exchange. *J. Exp. Biol.* **107**, 311–329.

Woakes, A. J., and Butler, P. J. (1986). Respiratory, circulatory and metabolic adjustments during swimming in the tufted duck, *Aythya fuligula. J. Exp. Biol.* **120**, 215–231.

Wooley, J. B., Jr., and Owen, R. B., Jr. (1978). Energy costs of activity and daily energy expenditure in the black duck. *J. Wildl. Manage.* **42**, 739–745.

Wunder, B. A. (1970). Energetics of running activity in Merriam's chipmunk, *Eutamias merriami. Comp. Biochem. Physiol.* **33**, 821–836.

Wunder, B. A. (1975). A model for estimating metabolic rate of active or resting mammals. *J. Theor. Biol.* **49**, 345–354.

Wunder, B. A., and Morrison, P. R. (1974). Red squirrel metabolism during incline running. *Comp. Biochem. Physiol.* **48A**, 153–161.

Wunder, B. A., Dobkin, D. S., and Gettinger, R. D. (1977). Shifts of thermogenesis in the prairie vole (*Microtus ochrogaster*), strategies for survival in a seasonal environment. *Oecologia* **29**, 11–26.

Young, B. A. (1966). Energy expenditure and respiratory activity of sheep during feeding. *Aust. J. Agric. Res.* **17**, 355–362.

Young, B. A., and Degen, A. A. (1980). Ingestion of snow by cattle. *J. Anim. Sci.* **51**, 811–815.

Yousef, M. K., Robertson, W. D., Dill, D. B., and Johnson, H. D. (1970). Energy expenditure of running kangaroo rats *Dipodomys merriami. Comp. Biochem. Physiol.* **36**, 387–393.

Yousef, M. K., Dill, D. B., and Freeland, D. V. (1972). Energetic cost of grade walking in man and burro, *Equus asinus*: Desert and mountain. *J. Appl. Physiol.* **33**, 337–340.

Yousef, M. K., Robertson, W., Dill, D. B., and Johnson, H. (1973). Energetic cost of running in the antelope ground squirrel *Ammospermophilus leucurus*. *Physiol. Zool.* **46,** 139–147.

Zar, J. H. (1968). Standard metabolism comparisons between orders of birds. *Condor* **70,** 278.

Zar, J. H. (1969). The use of the allometric model for avian standard metabolism—body weight relationships. *Comp. Biochem. Physiol.* **29,** 227–234.

Zervanos, S. M. (1975). Seasonal effects of temperature on the respiratory metabolism of the collared peccary (*Tayassu tajacu*). *Comp. Biochem. Physiol.* **50A,** 365–371.

9

Protein Requirements for Maintenance

Mute and still, by night and by day, labor goes on in the workshops of life. Here an animal grows, there a plant, and the wonder of it all is not the less in the smallest being than in the largest.

RUBNER, 1902

Protein requirements as a percentage of the diet decrease with increasing age (Fig. 9.1). The very rapid weight gain during early life requires more protein than does tissue maintenance and replacement by the adult animal. For example, the requirements for galliformes decreases from as much as 30% during very early growth to 12% for adult maintenance. Adult passerines require as little as 4 to 5% dietary protein for maintenance (Martin, 1968; Izhaki and Safriel, 1989). The requirement for adult galliformes increases during egg-laying to approximately 20%. Since these requirement estimates are a qualitative description of the amount of protein necessary to supply both essential and nonessential amino acids, the actual dietary protein requirement will fluctuate depending on dietary protein quality and energy availability (NRC, 1984).

Dietary protein requirements for maximum growth in weaned mammals range from 35% for cats, 25 to 38% for mink and foxes, 19% for rhesus monkeys, 15 to 18% for guinea pigs, voles, and hamsters, to 13 to 20% for deer and other ruminants (Ullrey *et al.*, 1967; Smith *et al.*, 1975; NRC, 1978 a,b; NRC, 1982; Lewis *et al.*, 1987). These requirement estimates do not apply to nursing animals as the dry matter of milk frequently has a much higher protein content. Even though the absolute protein requirement may be similar for both nursing and weaned young animals, the very high concentration of digestible energy in milk lessens total dry matter intake of nursing animals relative to the less digestible diets consumed by weaned animals. Because protein requirements must be met simultaneously with energy requirements, the required dietary protein content must increase as the available energy content increases. The dietary protein requirement for maintenance of adult mammals ranges from 18 to 30% for carnivores, 8 to 10% for ground squirrels, 5 to 9% for wild ruminants, to as little as 1.4% for sugar gliders (Karasov, 1982; Lewis *et al.*, 1987; Schwartz *et al.*, 1987; Smith and Green, 1987). Of all the mammals, cats and perhaps other

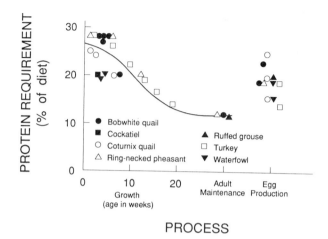

PROCESS

Fig. 9.1   Protein requirements as a percentage of the diet for several processes in birds. (Data from Callenbach and Hiller, 1933; Norris, 1935: Norris *et al.*, 1936; Nestler *et al.*, 1942, 1944; Scott and Reynolds, 1949; Baldini *et al.*, 1950, 1953; Holm and Scott, 1954; Scott *et al.*, 1954; Weber and Reid, 1967; Johnson, 1971; Andrews *et al.*, 1973; Johri and Vohra, 1977; NRC, 1977; Woodard *et al.*, 1976, 1977; Scott, 1977–1978; Yamane *et al.*, 1979; Allen and Young, 1980; Schwartz and Allen, 1981; Serafin, 1982; Warner *et al.*, 1982; Beckerton and Middleton, 1983; Mortensen and Tindall, 1984; NRC, 1984; Roudybush and Grau, 1986.)

strict carnivores have the highest protein requirement. This occurs because much of the protein in a normal meat diet is used to meet the animal's energy requirements. Consequently, liver enzymes that deaminate amino acids in cats have a very high, constant activity rate. Because the activity of these enzymes in omnivores and herbivores is modulated and varies directly with the dietary protein content, these animals will more efficiently use low protein diets than will cats (Rogers *et al.*, 1977).

While the above estimates are useful guidelines in formulating diets for captive wildlife, a more basic approach is necessary to understand the requirements of free-ranging wildlife. As with energy, protein requirements can be estimated by summing the requirements for each maintenance and productive process. Maintenance requirements equal the minimal, constant losses in the feces (metabolic fecal nitrogen, MFN) and urine (endogenous urinary nitrogen, EUN) which must be balanced by intake for nitrogen equilibrium to occur. Very small amounts of nitrogen are also lost in sweat and sloughed skin cells. However, these losses have never been adequately quantified for wildlife and thus are assumed to be negligible. MFN is composed of nonabsorbed digestive enzymes, intestinal cellular debris, undigested bacteria or protozoa associated with fermentation, mucus, and any other nitrogenous product of immediate animal origin excreted in the feces. Theoretically, MFN and EUN could be most easily determined by feeding diets devoid of nitrogen but adequate in energy to prevent the unnecessary loss of catabolized tissue protein. When animals consume nitrogen-free diets, all fecal and urinary nitrogen must be of endogenous origin. When animals are placed on nitrogen-free diets, daily nitrogen excretion decreases over time until a minimal constant level is attained. The number of days required to reach minimal losses ranges from 6 days for rats to 15 days for rabbits (Smuts, 1935). However, because few animals will consume nitrogen-free diets and some dietary nitrogen is essential for fermentation in ruminants (Orskov, 1982), indirect approaches have been used to estimate minimal nitrogen losses.

The most common indirect approach has been to feed animals different levels of the same ration or several rations of different protein content to obtain markedly different nitrogen intakes. The regression between intake (X) and excretion (Y) when extrapolated to zero estimates MFN and EUN because all nitrogen in the urine or feces at a hypothetical zero nitrogen intake must be of animal origin. The use of captive animals to estimate minimal nitrogen losses of free-ranging animals assumes that (a) internal nitrogen metabolism is not altered by confinement and (b) other dietary ingredients that the free-ranging animal may encounter have either no effect or at least a predictable effect on nitrogen loss.

I. MAMMALS

A. Metabolic Fecal Nitrogen

MFN ranges from 1 to 9 g N/kg dry matter ingested (DMI) (Table 9.1). Because a portion of MFN depends on the amount of feces produced and thus the digestibility and fiber content of the food (Schneider, 1935; Meyer, 1956; Williams and Senior, 1978), forage and high-fiber diets produce a higher MFN excretion than do more digestible milk, honey, or grain-based concentrate diets. MFN in forage- and leaf-eating marsupials (4.2 ± 1.4 g N/kg DMI) is similar to that occurring in ruminants (5.1 ± 0.8), although MFN in ruminants consuming only forage varies from 4.4 ± 0.3 in grazers, to 5.4 ± 0.3 in mixed feeders, to 6.2 in browsers (Table 9.1, Robbins et al., 1987). Most (80–90%) of the MFN excretion in grazing ruminants consists of bacterial residues (Virtanen, 1966; Mason, 1969). If the bacterial fecal nitrogen is simply plant nitrogen or very simple forms of endogenous nitrogen, such as urea, then the MFN is largely an excretory process and not a requirement. However, if the bacteria are fermenting complex endogenous substrates, such as gastrointestinal epithelial cells, mucus, or digestive enzymes, then the MFN represents a requirement in the true sense in which additional nitrogen must be ingested, absorbed, and synthesized into the replacement structures (Cheng and Costerton, 1980; Kennedy and Milligan, 1980). Although currently available estimates of MFN in animals

TABLE 9.1

Metabolic Fecal Nitrogen (MFN) Excretion by Mammals

Group or species	Diet	MFN (g N/kg dry matter intake)	Sources
Nonruminant eutherians			
Bears (black, grizzly, and giant panda)	Forage, berries, nuts, or tubers	5.54	Pritchard and Robbins, 1990
Collared peccary	Concentrates and forage	4.52	Gallagher et al., 1984; Carl and Brown, 1985
Lagomorphs			
Black-tailed jackrabbit	Forage	4.61	Nagy et al., 1976
Domestic rabbit	Forage	8.00	Slade and Robinson, 1970
Snowshoe hare	Forage and concentrates	9.10	Holter et al., 1974
Preruminant cervids			
Elk	Milk	1.26	Robbins, unpublished
White-tailed deer	Milk	2.37	Robbins, unpublished
Rhesus monkey	Concentrates	1.04	Robbins and Gavan, 1966
Rock hyrax	Concentrates	3.69	Hume et al., 1980
Rodents	Concentrates	3.18	Meyer and Karasov, 1989
	Forage	8.10	Meyer and Karasov, 1989
Ruminants			
Grazers			
Hartebeest	Concentrates	4.16	Arman and Hopcraft, 1975
Bison	Forage	4.14	Richmond et al., 1977
Yak	Forage	4.57	Richmond et al., 1977

Mixed Feeders			
Eland	Concentrates	3.53	Arman and Hopcraft, 1975
Nilgai antelope	Concentrates	5.66	Priebe and Brown, 1987
Red deer	Forage and concentrates	6.98	Maloiy, 1968
Thomson's gazelle	Concentrates	4.77	Arman and Hopcraft, 1975
Caribou–reindeer	Forage and concentrates	6.26	Robbins et al., 1987
Elk	Forage	5.58	Mould and Robbins, 1981
Nubian ibex	Forage	5.17	Choshniak and Arnon, 1985
Browsers			
Bush duiker	Concentrates	3.63	Arman and Hopcraft, 1975
Moose	Concentrates and sawdust	5.06	Schwartz et al., 1987; Robbins et al., 1987
White-tailed and mule deer	Concentrates	6.38	Robbins et al., 1987
White-tailed and mule deer	Forage	6.19	Robbins et al., 1987
Marsupials			
Omnivores			
Sugar glider	Honey and pollen	0.70	Smith and Green, 1987
Herbivores			
Brushtail possum	Honey and low to high fiber	0.78–3.36	Wellard and Hume, 1981
Euro	Forage and concentrates	3.24	Brown and Main, 1967; Hume, 1974
Koala	Eucalyptus leaves	5.90	Cork, 1986
Parma wallaby	Forage	5.70	Hume, 1986
Quokka	Forage	2.90	Brown, 1968
Red kangaroo	Forage	4.73	Foot and Romberg, 1965; Hume, 1974
Ringtail possum	Eucalyptus leaves	2.38	Chilcott and Hume, 1984
Rufous rat-kangaroo	Grain and oat hulls	3.20	Wallis, 1990
Tammar wallaby	Forage and concentrates	4.80	Barker, 1968; Hume, 1977

with extensive fermentation must be regarded with some skepticism, all nitrogen losses must be balanced by intake if constant weight of both the host and symbiotic microflora is to be attained.

Coprophagy, particularly the selective consumption of cecal droppings (cecotrophy) that are bacterial-rich and more digestible and nutritious than the normal fibrous feces, greatly reduces nitrogen losses in many rodents, lagomorphs, and some marsupials (Kenagy and Hoyt, 1980; Ouellette and Heisinger, 1980; Chilcott and Hume, 1985) The maintenance nitrogen requirement of ringtail possums would be three times higher if cecotrophy did not occur.

B. Endogenous Urinary Nitrogen

Endogenous urinary nitrogen studies were initiated by Folin (1905). He noticed that as dietary protein intake decreased, the relative distribution of urinary nitrogen constituents changed as the total urea excretion decreased, and creatinin excretion remained constant. He suggested that "we are forced to assume that protein catabolism is not all of one kind. . . . There must be at least two kinds . . . which are essentially independent and quite different." He termed the constant form characterized by creatinin, tissue or endogenous metabolism, and the variable form exogenous metabolism. The endogenous form in conjunction with MFN establishes the minimal nitrogen intake necessary for nitrogen equilibrium, whereas the variable form is an inefficiency in the utilization of dietary nitrogen.

EUN is usually expressed as a function of metabolic body weight ($kg^{0.75}$). Earlier studies suggested that mammals excrete 2 mg of EUN per kilocalorie of basal metabolism, or 140 mg $N/kg^{0.75}$/day (Smuts, 1935) However, this relationship would significantly overestimate EUN in many groups of wildlife. EUN decreases from 160 ± 22 mg $N/kg^{0.75}$/day for nonruminant eutherians, to 93 ± 40 for ruminants, to 53 ± 28 for marsupials (excluding eucalyptus diets) (Table 9.2). High terpene eucalyptus, such as *E. radiata* fed to the greater glider, dramatically increases urinary ammonia excretion (Foley, 1991). Because EUN tends to reflect energy metabolism (White *et al.*, 1988), EUN is highest in young animals and lowest during hibernation. Hibernating animals excrete one-tenth or less of the nitrogen excreted by active animals (Kayser, 1961). The hibernating bear does not even urinate during its 3 to 5 months of winter dormancy (Lundberg *et al.*, 1976).

C. Maintenance Nitrogen Requirements

One of the major difficulties in estimating the nitrogen requirement for maintenance is that MFN depends on dry-matter intake, whereas EUN is predicted from metabolic body weight. For the free-ranging animal, body weight is far

TABLE 9.2

Endogenous Urinary Nitrogen Excretion by Mammals

Group or species	EUN (mg N/kg$^{0.75}$/day)	Sources
Nonruminant eutherians		
Antelope ground squirrel	163	Karasov, 1982
Black-tailed jackrabbit	128	Nagy et al., 1976
Collared peccary	177	Carl and Brown, 1985
Fat sand rat	171	Kam and Degen, 1988
Ruminants		
Camel	60	Schmidt-Nielsen et al., 1957
Elk	160	Mould and Robbins, 1981
Moose	56	Schwartz et al., 1987
Red deer	90	Maloiy et al., 1970
Roe deer	78	Eisfeld, 1974b
White-tailed deer	115	Robbins et al., 1975
Marsupials		
Euro	31	Brown and Main, 1967
Greater glider[a]	200	Foley and Hume, 1987
Koala	51	Harrop and Degabriele, 1976; Cork, 1986
Parma wallaby	108	Hume, 1986
Quokka	44	Brown, 1968
Red kangaroo	54	Foot and Romberg, 1965; Hume, 1974
Red-necked pademelon	80	Hume, 1977
Ringtail possum[a]	191	Chilcott and Hume, 1984
Rock wallaby	50	Brown, 1968
Rufous rat-kangaroo	46	Wallis, 1990
Sugar glider	25	Smith and Green, 1987
Tammar wallaby	33	Barker, 1968; Hume, 1977

[a]Eucalyptus diets.

easier to determine than dry matter intake. Consequently, total maintenance nitrogen requirement has frequently been estimated as a function of metabolic body weight (Table 9.3). The average eutherian nitrogen requirement (582 ± 235 mg N/kg$^{0.75}$/day) is approximately 60% higher than the marsupial requirement (356 ± 136).

Unfortunately, the use of metabolic body weight to estimate the total nitrogen requirement for maintenance implies that an animal can meet its requirement at any nitrogen concentration as long as intake is not limited. However, an animal cannot ingest enough food to meet its nitrogen requirement when the dietary nitrogen concentration drops below the critical level of MFN losses. For example,

TABLE 9.3

Average Nitrogen Intake to Achieve Nitrogen Balance

Group or species	Diet	Nitrogen intake (mg $N/kg^{0.75}/day$)	Sources
Nonruminant eutherians			
Antelope ground squirrel	Forage	283	Karasov, 1982
Black-tailed jackrabbit	Forage	950	Nagy et al., 1976
Collared peccary	Concentrates and forage	815	Carl and Brown, 1985
Fat sand rat	Forage	242	Kam and Degen, 1988
Grey-headed flying fox	Fruit, honey, eggs	457	Steller, 1986
Rhesus monkey	Concentrates	680	Robbins and Gavan, 1966
Rock hyrax	Concentrates	311	Hume et al., 1980
Ruminants			
Caribou	Concentrates	820	McEwan and Whitehead, 1970
Moose	Concentrates and sawdust	627	Schwartz et al., 1987
Red deer	Concentrates and forage	680	Eisfeld, 1974a
Roe deer	Concentrates and forage	410	Eisfeld, 1974a,b
White-tailed deer	Concentrates	710	Holter et al., 1979
Marsupials			
Brushtail possum	Honey and low to high fiber	203	Wellard and Hume, 1981
	Eucalyptus	420	Foley and Hume, 1987
Eastern grey kangaroo	—	350	Foley et al., 1980
Eastern wallaroo	—	300	Foley et al., 1980
Euro	Forage and concentrates	290	Brown and Main, 1967
Greater glider	Eucalyptus[a]	560	Foley and Hume, 1987
Koala	Eucalyptus[a]	275	Harrop and Degabriele, 1976; Cork, 1986
Parma wallaby	Forage	566	Hume, 1986
Quokka	—	290	Brown, 1968
Red-necked pademelon	Forage and concentates	600	Hume, 1977
Ringtail possum	Eucalyptus[a]	290	Chilcott and Hume, 1984
Rufous rat-kangaroo	Grain and oat hulls	223	Wallis, 1990
Sugar glider	Honey and pollen	87	Smith and Green, 1987
Tammar wallaby	Forage and concentrates	265	Barker, 1968; Hume, 1977

[a]Based on true digested nitrogen to remove affect of tannins in Eucalyptus.

if an animal loses 5 g N/kg dry matter intake via MFN, the feed must contain at least 3.13% crude protein (5 × 6.25 = 31.3 g/kg) before the maintenance requirement can begin to be met. Of course, the necessary dietary protein concentration will be even higher because not all feed nitrogen is absorbed and retained and the preceding example does not include EUN losses.

Nitrogen requirements and minimal dietary protein concentrations can also be estimated by the following equation:

$$\frac{\text{Dietary Protein}}{\text{Content (\%)}} = [[\text{EUN} + \text{MFN (DMI)} \times 6.25]/\text{DMI}/0.74] \times 100$$

where EUN and MFN are the maintenance nitrogen requirements estimated as functions of body weight and dry matter intake (DMI), 6.25 is the nitrogen to crude protein correction factor, and 0.74 is the usefulness of dietary protein in meeting the maintenance requirements and is composed of digestion (0.93) and retention (0.80) coefficients.

Dietary protein requirements as a percentage of the diet decrease as dry matter intake increases (Fig. 9.2). At low dry matter intake, EUN is the predominant cost. As intake increases, EUN becomes a minimal cost with the asymptote primarily reflecting the constant MFN requirement. The differences in metabolic fecal losses from browsing and grazing ruminants produces minimum dietary protein requirements of 4.5% in the grazer and 6.0% in the browser. While the difference appears insignificant, these levels are very similar to the minimum protein content consumed by these animals with mature grasses having less protein than tree and shrub stems (Owen-Smith, 1982).

II. BIRDS

Separate estimates of MFN and EUN in birds are virtually impossible to make in any simple way because both urine and feces are eliminated together via the cloaca. Attempts have been made to physically separate urinary and fecal nitrogen in birds that eliminate solid excreta by scraping the ureate crystals off the feces or by correcting the total nitrogen excretion for its chemically determined uric acid content (Billingsley and Arner, 1970). Such efforts have been only partially successful because urinary nitrogen in birds is not entirely uric acid and mixing of urine and feces occurs by retrograde peristalsis of urine in the cloaca (Skadhauge, 1976; McNabb et al., 1980). Fermentation of urine in the intestine of herbivorous birds could be an important nitrogen conservation mechanism (Mortensen and Tindall, 1981). Consequently, the combined EUN–MFN losses in birds have been estimated by comparing nitrogen intake to total excretion on a per kilogram metabolic body weight basis (Fig. 9.3). Only values generated for

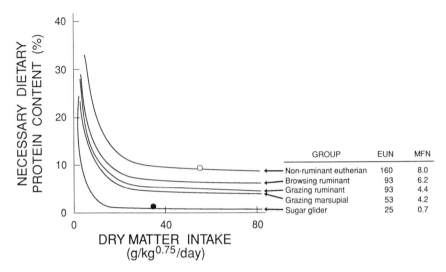

Fig. 9.2   Minimum dietary protein content necessary to meet maintenance requirements for various mammals. EUN is in mg/kg$^{0.75}$/day and MFN is in g/kg dry matter intake/day. Body weights used were 100 g for the nonruminant eutherian, 100 kg for the browsing and grazing ruminants, 10 kg for the grazing marsupial, and 155 g for the sugar glider. Observed dietary requirements for the sugar glider (Smith and Green, 1987) and antelope ground squirrel (Karasov, 1982) are compared to their respective estimates.

birds consuming very low levels of nitrogen but in positive evergy balance are useful in estimating minimal nitrogen requirements as nitrogen retention must be maximized. The combined EUN–MFN losses are 0.27 g N/kg$^{0.75}$/day, and the required maintenance intake level is 0.43g N/kg$^{0.75}$/day. This maintenance estimate is intermediated to eutherians and marsupials, very similar to earlier estimates for domestic poultry, but much lower than the estimate for house sparrows (Weglarczyk, 1981) and much higher than the estimate for the emu (Dawson and Herd, 1983) and hummingbird (Brice and Grau, 1991). The very high value for house sparrows occurs because approximately half of the birds had negative energy balances and, thus, were excreting far more nitrogen than would occur if they were not using body protein to meet their energy needs. Endogenous nitrogen loss (75 mg N/kg$^{0.75}$/day) and minimum dietary protein content for maintenance (1.5%) of the hummingbird is very similar to the sugar glider (Table 9.3, Fig. 9.2) and reflects (1) the lower nitrogen loss when consuming liquid, low-fiber diets and (2) the evolutionary necessity to minimize nitrogen loss when specializing on low nitrogen foods like nectar. One caution in applying these values to free-ranging birds is that cold temperatures that increase energy metabolism tend to also increase protein catabolism and nitrogen

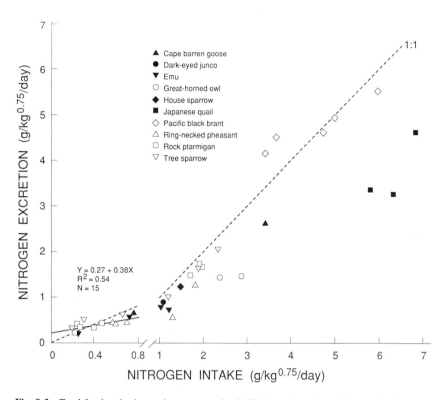

Fig. 9.3 Total fecal and urinary nitrogen excretion in birds as a function of nitrogen intake. (Data from Martin, 1968; Marriott and Forbes, 1970; Duke *et al.,* 1973; Labisky and Anderson, 1973; Moss and Parkinson, 1975; Walsberg, 1975; Parrish and Martin, 1977; Dawson and Herd, 1983; Sedinger *et al.,* 1989.) The regression incorporates only the results for birds consuming less than 0.8 g N/kg$^{0.75}$/day. Points below the 1:1 relationship between intake and excretion represent nitrogen accumulation (such as growth or egg production), whereas those above the line represent a net nitrogen loss (i.e., weight loss).

excretion (Martin, 1968; Aoyagi *et al.,* 1988). Thus, these values are the minimum maintenance requirement to which any additional requirements must be added.

REFERENCES

Allen, N. K., and Young, R. J. (1980). Studies on the amino acid and protein requirements of laying Japanese quail (*Coturnix coturnix japonica*). *Poult. Sci.* **59,** 2029–2037.
Andrews, T. L., Harms, R. H., and Wilson, H. R. (1973). Protein requirement of the bobwhite chick. *Poult. Sci.* **52,** 2199–2201.

Aoyagi, Y., Tasaki, I., Okumura, J.-I., and Muramatsu, T. (1988). Effect of low ambient temperature on protein turnover and heat production in chicks. *Comp. Biochem. Physiol.* **89A**, 433–436.

Arman, P., and Hopcraft, D. (1975). Nutritional studies on East African herbivores. 1. Digestibilities of dry matter, crude fiber and crude protein in antelope, cattle and sheep. *Br. J. Nutr.* **33**, 255–264.

Baldini, J. T., Roberts, R. E., and Kirkpatrick, C. M. (1950). A study of the protein requirements of bobwhite quail reared in confinement in battery brooders to eight weeks of age. *Poult. Sci.* **29**, 161–166.

Baldini, J. T., Roberts, R. E., and Kirkpatrick, C. M. (1953). Low protein rations for the bobwhite quail. *Poult. Sci.* **32**, 945–949.

Barker, S. (1968). Nitrogen balance and water intake in the Kangaroo Island wallaby, *Protemnodon eugenii* (Desmarest). *Aust. J. Exp. Biol. Med. Sci.* **46**, 17–32.

Beckerton, P. R., and Middleton, A. L. A. (1983). Effects of dietary protein levels on body weight, food consumption, and nitrogen balance in ruffed grouse. *Condor* **85**, 53–60.

Billingsley, B. B., Jr., and Arner, D. H. (1970). The nutritive value and digestibility of some winter foods of the eastern wild turkey. *J. Wildl. Manage.* **34**, 176–182.

Brice, A. T., and Grau, C. R. (1991). Protein requirements of Costa's hummingbird *Calypte costae*. *Physiol. Zool.* **64**, 611–626.

Brown, G.D. (1968). The nitrogen and energy requirements of the Euro (*Macropus robustus*) and other species of macropod marsupials. *Proc. Ecol. Soc. Aust.* **3**, 106–112.

Brown, G. D., and Main, A. R. (1967). Studies on marsupial nutrition. V. The nitrogen requirements of the euro, *Macropus robustus*. *Aust. J. Zool.* **15**, 7–27.

Callenbach, E. W., and Hiller, C. A. (1933). The artificial propagation of ring-necked pheasants. *Pa. Agric. Exp. Stn. Bull.* **299**.

Carl, G. R., and Brown, R. D. (1985) Protein requirement of collared peccaries. *J. Wildl. Manage.* **49**, 351–355.

Cheng, K.-J. and Costerton, J. W. (1980). Adherent rumen bacteria—their role in the digestion of plant material, urea and epithelial cells. *In* "Digestive Physiology and Metabolism in Ruminants" (Y. Rickebusch and P. Thivend, eds.), pp. 227–250. MTP Press, Lancaster, England.

Chilcott, M. J., and Hume, I. D. (1984). Nitrogen and urea metabolism and nitrogen requirements of the common ringtail possum, *Pseudocheirus peregrinus*, fed *Eucalyptus andrewsii* foliage. *Aust. J. Zool.* **32**, 615–622.

Chilcott, M. J., and Hume, I. D. (1985). Coprophagy and selective retention of fluid digesta: Their role in the nutrition of the common ringtail possum (*Pseudocheirus peregrinus*). *Aust. J. Zool.* **33**, 1–15.

Choshniak, I., and Arnon, I. (1985). Nitrogen metabolism and kidney function in the Nubian ibex (*Capra ibex nubiana*). *Comp. Biochem. Physiol.* **82A**, 137–139.

Cork, S. J. (1986). Foliage of *Eucalyptus punctata* and the maintenance nitrogen requirements of koalas, *Phascolarctos cinereus*. *Aust. J. Zool.* **34**, 17–23.

Dawson, T. J., and Herd, R. M. (1983) Digestion in the emu: Low energy and nitrogen requirements of this large ratite bird. *Comp. Biochem. Physiol.* **75A**, 41–45.

Duke, G. E., Ciganek, J. G., and Evanson, O. A. (1973). Food consumption and energy, water, and nitrogen budgets in captive great-horned owls (*Bubo virginianus*). *Comp. Biochem. Physiol.* **44A**, 283–292.

Eisfeld, D. (1974a). Protein requirements of roe deer (*Capreolus capreolus* L.) for maintenance. *Int. Congr. Game Biol.* **11**, 133–138.

Eisfeld, D. (1974b). Der Proteinbedarf des Rehes (*Capreolus capreolus* L.) zur Erhaltung. *Z. Jagdwiss* **20**, 43–48.

Foley, W. J. (1991). Nitrogen and energy retention and acid-base status in the common ringtail possum (*Pseudocheirus peregrinus*): Evidence of the effects of absorbed allelochemicals. *Physiol. Zool.* (in press).

Foley, W. J., and Hume, I. D. (1987). Nitrogen requirements and urea metabolism in two arboreal marsupials, the greater glider (*Petauroides volans*) and the brushtail possum (*Trichosurus vulpecula*), fed eucalyptus foliage. *Physiol. Zool.* **60**, 241–250.

Foley, W. J., Hume, I. D., and Taylor, R. (1980). Protein intake and requirements of the eastern wallaroo and the eastern grey kangaroo. *Bull. Aust. Mammal Soc.* **6**, 34–35.

Folin, O. (1905). A theory of protein metabolism. *Am. J. Physiol.* **13**, 117–138.

Foot, J. Z., and Romberg, B. (1965). The utilization of roughage by sheep and the red kangaroo, *Macropus rufus* (Desmarest). *Aust. J. Agric. Res.* **16**, 429–435.

Gallagher, J. F., Varner, L. W., and Grant, W. E. (1984). Nutrition of the collared peccary in south Texas. *J. Wildl. Manage.* **48**, 749–761.

Harrop, C. J. F., and Degabriele, R. (1976). Digestion and nitrogen metabolism in the koala (*Phascolarctos cinereus*). *Aust. J. Zool.* **24**, 201–215.

Holm, E. R., and Scott, M. L. (1954). Studies on the nutrition of wild waterfowl. *N.Y. Fish Game J.* **1**, 171–187.

Holter, J. B., Tyler, G., and Walski, T. W. (1974). Nutrition of the snowshoe hare (*Lepus americanus*). *Can. J. Zool.* **52**, 1553–1558.

Holter, J. B., Hayes, H. H., and Smith, S. H. (1979). Protein requirement of yearling white-tailed deer. *J. Wildl. Manage.* **43**, 872–879.

Hume, I. D. (1974). Nitrogen and sulphur retention and fibre digestion by euros, red kangaroos and sheep. *Aust. J. Zool.* **22**, 13–23.

Hume, I. D. (1977). Maintenance nitrogen requirements of the macropod marsupials *Thylogale thetis*, red-necked pademelon, and *Macropus eugenii*, tammar wallaby. *Aust. J. Zool.* **25**, 407–417.

Hume, I. D. (1986). Nitrogen metabolism in the Parma wallaby, *Macropus parma. Aust. J. Zool.* **34**, 147–155.

Hume, I. D., Rubsamen, K., and Von Engelhardt, W. (1980). Nitrogen metabolism and urea kinetics in the rock hyrax (*Procavia habessinica*). *J. Comp. Physiol.* **138**, 307–314.

Izhaki, I., and Safriel, U. N. (1989). Why are there so few exclusively frugivorous birds? Experiments on fruit digestibility. *Oikos* **54**, 23–32.

Johnson, N. F. (1971). Effects of levels of dietary protein on wood duck growth. *J. Wildl. Manage.* **35**, 798–802.

Johri, T. S., and Vohra, P. (1977). Protein requirements of *Coturnix coturnix japonica* for reproduction using purified diets. *Poult. Sci.* **56**, 350–353.

Kam, M., and Degen, A. A. (1988). Water, electrolyte and nitrogen balances of fat sand rats (*Psammomys obesus*) when consuming the saltbush *Atriplex halimus. J. Zool.* **215**, 453–462.

Karasov, W. H. (1982). Energy assimilation, nitrogen requirement, and diet in free-living antelope ground squirrels *Ammospermophilus leucurus. Physiol. Zool.* **55**, 378–392.

Kayser, C. (1961). "The Physiology of Natural Hibernation." Pergamon Press, New York.

Kenagy, G. J., and Hoyt, D. F. (1980). Reingestion of feces in rodents and its daily rhythmicity. *Oecologica* **44**, 403–409.

Kennedy, P. M., and Milligan, L. P. (1980). Input of endogenous protein into the forestomachs of sheep. *Can. J. Anim. Sci.* **60**, 1029–1032.

Labisky, R. F., and Anderson, W. L. (1973). Nutritional responses of pheasants to corn, with special reference to high lysine corn. *Ill. Nat. Hist. Surv. Bull.* **31**, 87–112.

Lewis, L. D., Morris, M. L., and Hand, M. S. (1987). "Small Animal Clinical Nutrition." Mark Morris Assoc., Topeka, Kansas.

Lundberg, D. A., Nelson, R. A., Wahner, H. W., and Jones, J. D. (1976). Protein metabolism in the black bear before and during hibernation. *Mayo Clin. Proc.* **51**, 716–722.

Maloiy, G. M. (1968). "The Physiology of Digestion and Metabolism in the Red Deer (*Cervus elaphus* L.)." Doctoral Dissertation, Univ. Aberdeen, Scotland.

Maloiy, G. M. O., Kay, R. N. B., and Goodall, E. D. (1970). Digestion and nitrogen metabolism in sheep and red deer given large or small amounts of water and protein. *Br. J. Nutr.* **24,** 843–854.

Marriott, R. W., and Forbes, D. K. (1970). The digestion of lucerne chaff by Cape Barren geese, *Cereopsis novaehollandiae* Latham. *Aust. J. Zool.* **18,** 257–263.

Martin, E. W. (1968). The effects of dietary protein on the energy and nitrogen balance of the tree sparrow (*Spizella arborea arborea*). *Physiol. Zool.* **41,** 313–331.

Mason, V. C. (1969). Some observations on the distribution and origin of nitrogen in sheep feces. *J. Agric. Sci.* **73,** 99–111.

McEwan, E. H., and Whitehead, P. E. (1970). Seasonal changes in the energy and nitrogen intake in reindeer and caribou. *Can. J. Zool.* **48,** 905–913.

McNabb, F. M. A., McNabb, R. A., Prather, I. D., Conner, R. N., and Adkisson, C. S. (1980). Nitrogen excretion by turkey vultures. *Condor* **82,** 219–223.

Meyer, J. H. (1956). Influences of dietary fibre on metabolic and endogenous nitrogen excretion. *J. Nutr.* **58,** 407–413.

Meyer, M. W., and Karasov, W. H. (1989). Antiherbivore chemistry of *Larrea tridentata*: Effects on woodrat *(Neotoma lepida)* feeding and nurtrition. *Ecology* **70,** 953–961.

Mortensen, A., and Tindall, A. R. (1981). Caecal decomposition of uric acid in captive and free-ranging willow ptarmigan (*Lagopus lagopus lagopus*). *Acta Physiol. Scand.* **111,** 129–133.

Mortensen, A., and Tindall, A. (1984). The role of urea in nitrogen excretion and caecal nitrogen metabolism in willow ptarmigan. *J. Comp. Physiol.* **155B,** 71–74.

Moss, R., and Parkinson, J. A. (1975). The digestion of bulbils (*Polygonum viviparum* L.) and berries (*Vaccinium myrtillus* L. and *Empetrum* sp.) by captive ptarmigan (*Lagopus mutus*). *Br. J. Nutr.* **33,** 197–206.

Mould, E. D., and Robbins, C. T. (1981). Nitrogen metabolism in elk. *J. Wildl. Manage.* **45,** 323–334.

Nagy, K. A., Shoemaker, V. H., and Costa, W. R. (1976). Water, electrolyte, and nitrogen budgets of jackrabbits (*Lepus californicus*) in the Mojave desert. *Physiol. Zool.* **49,** 351–363.

National Research Council (NRC). (1977). Nutrient requirements of poultry. Publ. No. 2725, Nat. Acad. Sci., Washington, D. C.

National Research Council (NRC). (1978a). Nutrient requirements of laboratory animals. Publ. No. 2767, Nat. Acad. Sci., Washington, D. C.

National Research Council (NRC). (1978b). Nutrient requirements of nonhuman primates. Publ. No. 2786, Nat. Acad. Sci., Washington, D. C.

National Research Council (NRC) (1982). Nutrient requirements of mink and foxes. Nat. Acad. Press, Washington, D.C.

National Research Council (NRC) (1984). Nutrient requirements of poultry. Nat. Acad. Sci., Washington, D.C.

Nestler, R. B., Bailey, W. W., and McClure, H. E. (1942). Protein requirements of bobwhite quail chicks for survival, growth, and efficiency of feed utilization. *J. Wildl. Manage.* **6,** 185–193.

Nestler, R. B., Bailey, W. W., Llewellyn, L. M., and Rensberger, M. J. (1944). Winter protein requirements of bobwhite quail. *J. Wildl. Manage.* **8,** 218–222.

Norris, L. C. (1935). Nutrition of game birds. *N.Y. Cons. Dept. Annu. Rep.* (1934) **24,** 289–291.

Norris, L. C., Elmore, L. J., Ringrose, R. C., and Bump, G. (1936). The protein requirements of ring-necked pheasant chicks. *Poult. Sci.* **15,** 454–459.

Orskov, O. R., (1982). "Protein Nutrition in Ruminants." Academic Press, San Diego.

Owen-Smith, N. (1982). Factors influencing the comsumption of plant products by large herbivores.

In "The Ecology of Tropical Savannas" (B. J. Huntley and B. H. Walker, eds.), pp. 359–404. Springer–Verlag, Berlin.

Ouellette, D. E., and Heisinger, J. F. (1980). Reingestion of feces by *Microtus pennsylvanicus*. *J. Mammal.* **61**, 366–368.

Parrish, J. W., Jr., and Martin, E. W. (1977). The effect of dietary lysine level on the energy and nitrogen balance of the dark-eyed junco. *Condor* **79**, 24–30.

Priebe, J. C., and Brown, R. D. (1987). Protein requirements of subadult nilgai antelope. *Comp. Biochem. Physiol.* **88A**, 495–501.

Pritchard, G. T., and Robbins, C. T. (1990). Digestive and metabolic efficiencies of grizzly and black bears. *Can. J. Zool.* **68**, 1645–1651.

Richmond, R. J., Hudson, R. J., and Christopherson, R. J. (1977). Comparison of forage intake and digestibility by American bison, yak, and cattle. *Acta Theriol.* **22**, 225–230.

Robbins, C. T., Van Soest, P. J., Mautz, W. W., and Moen, A. N. (1975). Feed analyses and digestion with reference to white-tailed deer. *J. Wildl. Manage.* **39**, 67–79.

Robbins, C. T., Hanley, T. A., Hagerman, A. E., Hjeljord, O., Baker, D. L., Schwartz, C. C., and Mautz, W. W. (1987). Role of tannins in defending plants against ruminants: Reduction in protein availability. *Ecology* **68**, 98–107.

Robbins, R. C., and Gavan, J. A. (1966). Utilization of energy and protein of a commercial diet by rhesus monkeys (*Macaca mulatta*). *Lab. Anim. Care* **16**, 286–291.

Rogers, Q. R., Morris, J. G., and Freedland, R. A. (1977). Lack of hepatic enzymatic adaptation to low and high levels of dietary protein in the adult cat. *Enzyme* **22**, 348–356.

Roudybush, T. E., and Grau, C. R. (1986). Food and water interrelations and the protein requirement for growth of an altricial bird, the cockatiel (*Nymphicus hollandicus*). *J. Nutr.* **116**, 552–559.

Rubner, M. (1902). "The Laws of Energy Consumption in Nutrition." Academic Press, New York.

Schmidt-Neilsen, B., Schmidt-Neilsen, K., Houpt, T. R., and Jarnum, S. A. (1957). Urea excretion in the camel. *Am. J. Physiol.* **188**, 477–484.

Schneider, B. H. (1935). The subdivision of the metabolic nitrogen in the feces of the rat, swine, and man. *J. Biol. Chem.* **109**, 249–278.

Schwartz, C. C., Regelin, W. L., and Franzmann, A. W. (1987). Protein digestion in moose. *J. Wildl. Manage.* **51**, 352–357.

Schwartz, R. W., and Allen, N. K. (1981). Effect of aging on the protein requirements of mature female Japanese quail for egg production. *Poult. Sci.* **60**, 342–348.

Scott, M. L. (1977–1978). Twenty-five years of research in game bird nutrition. *World Pheasant Assoc. J.* **3**, 31–45.

Scott, M. L., and Reynolds, R. E. (1949). Studies on the nutrition of pheasant chicks. *Poult. Sci.* **28**, 392–397.

Scott, M. L., Holm, E. R., and Reynolds, R. E. (1954). Studies on pheasant nutrition. 2. Protein and fiber levels in diets for young pheasants. *Poult. Sci.* **33**, 1237–1244.

Sedinger, J. S., White, R. G., Mann, F. E., Burris, F. A., and Kedrowski, R. A.(1989). Apparent metabolizability of alfalfa components by yearling Pacific black brant. *J. Wildl. Manage.* **53**, 726–734.

Serafin, J. A. (1982). Influence of protein level and supplemental methionine in practical rations for young endangered masked bobwhite quail. *Poult. Sci.* **61**, 988–990.

Skadhauge, E. (1976). Cloacal absorption of urine in birds. *Comp. Biochem. Physiol.* **55A**, 93–98.

Slade, L. M., and Robinson, D. W. (1970). Nitrogen metabolism in nonruminant herbivores. II. Comparative aspects of protein digestion. *J. Anim. Sci.* **30**, 761–763.

Smith, A. P., and Green, S. W. (1987). Nitrogen requirments of the sugar glider (*Petaurus breviceps*), an omnivorous marsupial, on a honey-pollen diet. *Physiol. Zool.* **60**, 82–92.

Smith, S. H., Holter, J. B., Hayes, H. H., and Silver, H. (1975). Protein requirement of white-tailed deer fawns. *J. Wildl. Manage.* **39**, 582–589.

Smuts, D. B. (1935). The relationship between the basal metabolism and the endogenous nitrogen metabolism, with particular reference to the estimation of the maintenance requirement of protein. *J. Nutr.* **9**, 403–433.

Steller, D. C. (1986). The dietary energy and nitrogen requirements of the grey-headed flying fox, *Pteropus poliocephalus (Temminick) (Megachiroptera). Aust. J. Zool.* **34**, 339–349.

Ullrey, D. E., Youatt, W. G., Johnson, H. E., Fay, L. D., and Bradley, B. L. (1967). Protein requirement of white-tailed deer fawns. *J. Wildl. Manage.* **31**, 679–685.

Virtanen, A. I. (1966). Milk production of cows on protein-free feed. *Science* **153**, 1603–1614.

Wallis, I. R. (1990). "The Nutrition, Digestive Physiology and Metabolism of Potoroine Marsupials." Doctoral Dissertation, Univ. New England, Armidale, Australia.

Walsberg, G. E. (1975). Digestive adaptations of *Phainopepla nitens* associated with the eating of mistletoe berries. *Condor* **77**, 169–174.

Warner, R. E., Darda, D. M., and Baker, D. H. (1982). Effects of dietary protein level and environmental temperature stress on growth of young ring-necked pheasants. *Poult. Sci.* **61**, 673–676.

Weber, C. W., and Reid, B. L. (1967). Protein requirements of coturnix quail to five weeks of age. *Poult. Sci.* **46**, 1190–1194.

Weglarczyk, G. (1981). Nitrogen balance and energy efficiency of protein deposition of the house sparrow, *Passer domesticus* L. *Ekol. Pol.* **29**, 519–533.

Wellard, G. A., and Hume, I. D. (1981). Nitrogen metabolism and nitrogen requirements of the brushtail possum, *Trichosurus vulpecula (Kerr). Aust. J. Zool.* **29**, 147–156.

White, R. G., Hume, I. D., and Nolan, J. V. (1988). Energy expenditure and protein turnover in three species of wallabies *(Marsupialia: Macropodidae). J. Comp. Physiol.* **158B**, 237–246.

Williams, V. J., and Senior, W. (1978). The effect of semi-starvation on the digestibility of food in young adult female rats. *Aust. J. Biol. Sci.* **31**, 593–599.

Woodard, A. E., Vohra, P., and Snyder, R. L. (1976). Protein level and growth in the pheasant. *Poult. Sci.* **55**, 2108.

Woodard, A. E., Vohra, P., and Snyder, R. L. (1977). Effect of protein levels in the diet on the growth of pheasants. *Poult. Sci.* **56**, 1492–1500.

Yamane, T., Ono, K., and Tanaka, T. (1979). Protein requirement of laying Japanese quail. *Br. Poult. Sci.* **20**, 379–383.

10

Reproductive Costs

Science: The Endless Frontier
BUSH, 1945

Wildlife reproductive characteristics and success are closely linked to food resources. This interaction has been the basis for innumerable studies by nutritionists, ecologists, and evolutionary biologists. The basis for many of these studies has been the measurement of energy and nutrients necessary for reproduction, including that contained in sperm, egg, fetus, enlarged reproductive organs (testes, ovary–oviduct, uterus, or mammary gland), or milk and the additional heat necessary for incubation in birds. While the reproductive requirements are in addition to normal maintenance processes, maternal or paternal tissues can be mobilized to meet the immediate energy or nutrient requirements of reproduction. However, tissue mobilization does not lessen the requirement, because deficits must eventually be balanced, but it does provide a mechanism to distribute the very high cost over a much longer period of time.

Many other costs or consequences are involved in the total reproductive effort. For example, many birds and mammals do not molt while reproductive demands are high (King, 1973). Increased time and energy expenditures during food searching or territorial defense may predispose reproducing adults to higher mortality (Nur, 1988). Territorial establishment and defense, nest or burrow construction, and courtship are often additional energetic costs. Thus, the ecologist must recognize the far-reaching implications of reproductive demands.

I. BIRDS

A. Gamete Synthesis

Reproductive requirements for tissue synthesis can be estimated by determining energy and matter accumulated on a daily basis.[1] The daily requirement

---

[1]Productive requirement estimates are net energy or protein costs (i.e., the amounts actually retained) and do not include the efficiencies of dietary energy and matter utilization unless otherwise stated.

of males for testicle growth and sperm production are quite minimal [testicle growth: 0.49% of the BMR and 3.5% of the maintenance protein requirement; sperm production: 0.78% of the BMR (Ricklefs, 1974; Robbins, 1981, 1983; Walsberg, 1983)]. Growth of the ovary and oviduct preparatory to egg synthesis increases the daily energy requirement by approximately 4% of BMR and the protein requirement by 28% of the maintenance level (Ricklefs, 1974; Drobney, 1980; Robbins, 1981; Walsberg 1983). Thus, with the potential exception of protein accumulated in the oviduct in preparation for albumen synthesis, the energy and nutrient costs for enlargement of the reproductive organs and sperm production are "negligible" (Walsberg, 1983).

Requirements for egg production are dependent on the number and size of eggs laid, their composition, and the temporal sequence of yolk and albumen synthesis. Average egg size in interspecific comparisons is inversely proportional to body weight—that is, smaller birds generally lay larger eggs relative to body weight than do larger birds (Lack, 1968; Rahn *et al.*, 1975). Although the number and size of eggs laid are characteristic of a species, both do vary with age of the female, time of laying, and food availability (Cody, 1971; Batt and Prince, 1979; Eldridge and Krapu, 1988). Variation in egg composition between species largely reflects the differing stage of embryonic development at hatching (Sotherland and Rahn, 1987) (Table 10.1). The eggs of precocial species have larger yolks than do eggs of altricial birds. Because the yolk contains virtually all of the high-energy lipids, less water, and more protein than the albumen [protein content of fresh yolk = 16.0 ± 2.5%, albumen = 8.6 ± 1.5% (Williams *et al.*, 1982; Roca *et al.*, 1984)], increasing the relative size of the yolk increases the amount of energy and protein per unit of egg available for embryonic development. The differences in available energy are even larger than suggested by relative yolk size because the yolk lipid concentration is 41% higher in the eggs of precocial species (36.5 ± 1.8% of the fresh yolk) than in altricial species (25.8 ± 2.6%) (Ricklefs, 1974; Roca *et al.*, 1982).

The daily requirement for egg production can be estimated by proportioning the energy and protein content of the egg over the number of days required for its synthesis and deposition. Yolk synthesis within the ovary requires from 4 to 26 days, whereas albumen synthesis and deposition occurs during the 1 to 2 days that the ova passes through the oviduct (King, 1973; Ricklefs, 1974; Roudybush *et al.*, 1979; Drobney, 1980; Hirsch and Grau, 1981; Bancroft, 1985; Meijer *et al.*, 1989). The estimated daily energy requirement for egg laying ranges from 29% of the basal metabolic rate in hawks and owls, which lay one egg approximately every third day, to over 200% in waterfowl, which lay a relatively large, high-energy egg each day until the clutch is complete (Table 10.2). These theoretical estimates are quite similar to measurements on individual species within these groups, such as boat-tailed grackles and house sparrows (12 to 47% of BMR) (Bancroft, 1985; Krementz and Ankney, 1986), kestrel (39%)

(Meijer *et al.*, 1989), American coot (121%) (Alisauskas and Ankney, 1985), and wood duck (178%) (Drobney, 1980). The estimated daily protein requirement increases from 72% above the maintenance requirement in hawks and owls to 220% in waterfowl, gulls, and terns. Birds meet these relatively high energy and protein requirements by reducing other non-essential costs, accumulating fat prior to laying, mobilizing fat reserves as well as some protein from internal organs or muscles during laying, increasing food intake, or altering the diet to include more nutritious foods, particularly insects (Jones and Ward, 1976; Fogden and Fogden, 1979; McLandress and Raveling, 1981; Drobney, 1982; Ankney, 1984; Hails and Turner, 1985; Ankney and Afton, 1988).

B. Incubation

The cost of incubation is any excess heat generated to initiate and continue embryonic development within the egg above what would normally be produced by the nonincubating bird. Energy expenditures for incubation in free-ranging birds have been difficult to measure. While doubly labeled water can be used to measure this cost (Williams and Dwinnel, 1990), these measurements will include other costs, such as feeding or flying, if incubation is not continuous. Thus, many of the measurements have used captive birds.

The actual cost of incubation is dependent on adult size, clutch size, quality of nest insulation, and the temperature gradient. Incubation at ambient temperatures within the bird's thermoneutral zone does not impose any additional cost, i.e., normal heat loss through the brood patch is adequate to maintain an appropriate egg temperature (Biebach, 1979; Grant and Whittow, 1983; Brown, 1984; Weathers, 1985; Pettit *et al.*, 1988). Because of differing levels of restlessness, energy expenditure of birds incubating in the thermoneutral zone are frequently even less than resting, nonincubating birds (Brown, 1988). As ambient temperature cools, the T_{lc} for the incubating bird is slightly higher than for the nonincubating bird because of a higher total conductance (Fig. 10.1) (Biebach, 1979; Vleck, 1981; Biebach, 1981; 1984; Weathers, 1985). For example, the T_{lc} for a starling incubating two eggs is 14.1°C and increases to 23.6°C for a starling incubating eight eggs (Biebach, 1984). For birds having a clutch size less than 20% of the adult's weight and nest insulation equal to or greater than the cup or cavity nesters of Fig. 10.1, incubation at temperatures colder than the T_{lc} will not impose an additional energy cost above that occurring in the resting, nonincubating bird. However, birds incubating larger clutches will expend more energy than the resting, nonincubating bird in a similar environment. This additional cost ranges from 3 to 7% per egg in starling and blue tits, and 20 to 30% for an entire starling or zebra finch clutch (Vleck, 1981; Biebach, 1984; Haftorn and Reinertsen, 1985). During late incubation, the developing

TABLE 10.1

Composition of the Avian Egg[a]

Group and representative species	Egg weight (g)	Albumen	Yolk	Shell	Ratio of albumen to yolk	Energy content (kcal/g)	Lipid content	Protein content
		---------(% of fresh weight)---------					- (% of fresh weight) --	
Precocial 1								
Apterygidae (kiwis)	280–414	37.1	57.0	5.9	0.6/1	2.7	—	—
Megapodiidae (mallee fowl and brush turkeys)	169–179	45.8	48.1	6.1	0.9/1	2.4	13.9	15.1
Precocial 2								
Anatidae (ducks and geese)	40–312	49.2	39.7	11.1	1.2/1	1.8	11.0	11.4
Charadriidae (plovers)	14–26	53.3	37.6	9.1	1.4/1	—	—	—
Alcidae (murres, murrelets, razorbills, auklets, puffins, guillemots)	29–120	53.2	36.9	9.9	1.4/1	1.8	11.1	—

Precocial 3								
Phasianidae (junglefowl, quail, pheasant, partridge)	9–112	50.3	38.3	11.4	1.3/1	1.8	11.9	12.1
Numididae (guinea fowl)	31–35	50.4	34.0	15.6	1.5/1	1.7	12.2	10.2
Precocial 4								
Podicipedidae (grebes)	18–40	68.6	22.5	8.9	3.0/1	—	—	—
Rallidae (rails, gallinules, coots)	8–42	63.1	29.1	7.8	2.2/1	—	—	—
Semi-precocial								
Stercorariidae (skuas)	84–102	62.3	27.9	9.9	2.2/1	1.3	8.4	—
Laridae (gulls and terns)	18–116	63.4	28.7	7.9	2.2/1	1.5	8.1	—
Semi-altricial 1								
Ardeidae (herons, egrets, bitterns)	24–50	67.1	23.4	9.5	2.9/1	1.1	7.0	—
Falconidae (falcons)	11–21	67.6	21.1	11.3	3.2/1	1.1	—	—
Accipitridae (kites, hawks, eagles, ospreys)	31–244	71.0	20.0	9.0	3.6/1	—	—	—

(continues)

TABLE 10.1

Continued

Group and representative species	Egg weight (g)	Albumen	Yolk	Shell	Ratio of albumen to yolk	Energy content (kcal/g)	Lipid content	Protein content
		---------- (% of fresh weight) ----------					- (% of fresh weight) --	
Semi-altricial 2								
Spheniscidae (penguins)	60–469	62.4	24.2	13.4	2.6/1	1.3	6.5	9.5
Strigidae (owls)	21–69	70.5	22.2	7.3	3.2/1	—	—	—
Altricial								
Sulidae (gannets and boobies)	53–118	70.2	16.5	13.3	4.2/1	1.0	3.9	—
Pelecanidae (pelicans)	92–204	67.5	19.1	13.4	3.5/1	1.0	4.1	8.9
Phalacrocoracidae (cormorants)	22–51	68.8	18.5	12.7	3.7/1	1.0	6.0	—
Columbidae (doves and pigeons)	6–18	68.0	24.0	8.0	2.8/1	1.2	7.4	7.9
Corvidae (jays, magpies, crows)	6–20	70.8	19.6	9.6	3.6/1	0.8	4.2	—

Muscicapidae (robins, thrushes, bluebirds, flycatchers)	2–8	71.2	21.3	7.5	3.3/1	1.1	6.5	—
Sturnidae (starlings)	6–9	74.9	15.3	9.8	4.9/1	1.0	5.5	—
Icteridae (blackbirds, grackles, cowbirds)	3–8	70.7	19.4	8.7	3.6/1	1.1	5.8	9.0

Offshore and pelagic feeders (characterized by long incubation times, reduced clutch size, and less frequent visits by the parents for feeding of the chick)

Diomedeidae (albatrosses)	242–504	63.7	27.4	8.9	2.3/1	1.5	7.6	—
Procellariidae (petrels, fulmars, shearwaters)	9–258	56.2	34.0	9.5	1.6/1	1.6	9.1	11.2

Sources: Carey et al., 1980; Williams et al., 1982; Warham, 1983; Roca et al., 1984; Sotherland and Rahn, 1987; Muma and Ankney, 1987; Birkhead and Gaston, 1988; Meijer et al., 1989.

[a] Energy and chemical composition are for the entire egg.

10. Reproductive Costs

TABLE 10.2

Average Energy and Protein Costs of Egg Production Estimated for
Various Groups of Birds

Group	Rapid follicle development (days)	Clutch size	Laying interval (days)	Energy requirement (% of BMR)	Protein requirement (% of maintenance)
Raptors	7	5	3	29	72
Passeriformes	4–5	4–5	1	13–41	130
Charadriiformes	8–10	3	2	82–128	209
Galliformes	6–9	10	1	89–162	178
Anseriformes	6–7	5–12	1	101–210	237

Source: Ricklefs, 1974; Robbins, 1981; Walsberg, 1983; Meijer *et al.*, 1989.

embryo also becomes an increasingly important source of heat (Drent, 1970;
Hoyt *et al.*, 1978; Gessaman and Findell, 1979; Vleck *et al.*, 1979, 1980).
Ecologically, one of the main costs of incubation for many birds is the reduced
time available for feeding. Many birds have either very prolonged incubation
shifts or only one parent does all of the incubation (such as petrels, penguins,

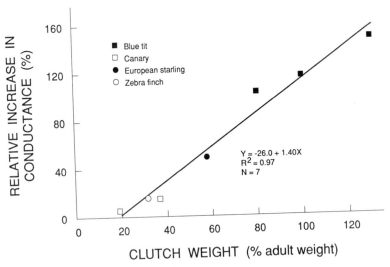

Fig. 10.1   The relative change in conductance of incubating birds in comparison to those that are
not incubating in a similar environment. (Data from Biebach, 1979; Vleck, 1981; Haftorn and
Reinertsen, 1985; Weathers, 1985.)

or geese). In these cases, the incubating bird depends on reserves accumulated prior to nesting. For example, arctic nesting female Canada geese and common eiders lost from 42 to 46% of their peak spring weight between arrival on the nesting ground and hatching of their eggs. Because the females do all of the incubating and therefore can do minimal feeding, the emaciated females feed almost continuously after the eggs have hatched (Raveling, 1979; Parker and Holm, 1990).

II. MAMMALS

A. Gestation

The most significant cost of fetal production in mammals is the direct cost to the female of embryonic development. While the cost of testicle growth and sperm production in males and ovary–oviduct growth in females has not been studied, the costs are undoubtedly quite small in both the absolute and ecological sense. The mammalian oviduct, in contrast to the avian oviduct which enlarges to produce egg albumen and shell, remains quite small. Thus, female gestation requirements largely depend on the amount of energy and matter retained by the gravid uterus and enlarging mammary gland and the increased maintenance costs of these structures.

The fetus represents 80% of the energy retained by the gravid uterus (Robbins and Moen, 1975a; Kurta *et al.*, 1989). Fetal growth during gestation is a cur-vilinear function in which most of the increase in mass occurs after 50–60% of the gestation period has elapsed (Fig. 10.2, Mover *et al.*, 1988). Mammalian gestation periods and birth weights increase as power functions of maternal weight (Table 10.3). Because the average exponent of the relationships between birth weight and maternal weight in mammals is 0.76 ± 0.06 (Table 10.3), birth weight is a reflection of metabolic body weight in which the larger species produce a neonate that represents an increasingly smaller proportion of adult weight. When birth weight is compared to gestation length and those species experiencing delayed implantation or fertilization are excluded in an effort to compare the average rate of fetal growth, primate fetuses grow 76% slower than other mammals (Payne and Wheeler, 1967).

However, comparisons of mass or crude growth rates ignore the important differences in embryonic composition during gestation and between neonates of different species. For example, water content of the developing fetus decreases while the fat, protein, and mineral content increase during gestation (Robbins, and Moen, 1975a; Havera, 1978). The mammalian neonate averages $12.5 \pm 2.3\%$ protein and $2.7 \pm 0.8\%$ ash at birth (Table 10.4). Neonatal fat, water, and energy content do vary between species. Neonatal seals, guinea pigs, and humans contain 4–8 times more fat than do the other mammals, whose body fat

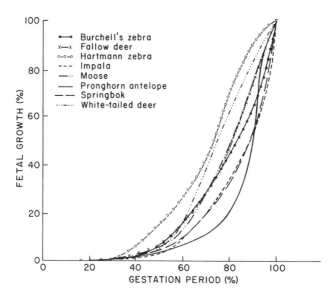

Fig. 10.2   Relative fetal growth (percentage of birth weight) in several ungulate species. (From Robbins and Robbins, 1979, courtesy of The University of Chicago Press.)

content averages 2.1 ± 1.0%. The fat reserves of the guinea pig are catabolized during the first few days postpartum (Widdowson and McCance, 1955; Adolph and Heggeness, 1971), whereas those of the seal are necessary because of the cold environment and short lactation (Blix *et al.*, 1979; Stewart and Lavigne, 1980). The very low fat content of most neonatal mammals occurs irrespective of whether they are precocial or altricial at birth. For example, the white-tailed deer, which is born with a well-developed hair coat and follows its mother shortly after birth, has the same fat content as the very altricial mouse or vole. Because of their low fat content, high metabolism, and, frequently, poor insulation, the survival times of most neonates are only a few hours to days without maternal care.

The energy requirements and food intake of pregnant females are from 17 to 32% higher than nonreproducing females (Mattingly and McClure, 1982; Gebczynski and Gebczynska, 1984; Robbins, 1983; Partridge *et al.*, 1986; Nicoll and Thompson, 1987; Farrell and Christian, 1987; Weiner, 1987; Gittleman and Thompson, 1988; Mover *et al.*, 1988; Thompson, 1991). However, only 10 to 20% of this additional energy is retained as new tissue by the developing uterus with the rest of the energy lost as heat. Because most of the energy metabolized by the gravid uterus is lost as heat, lengthening the gestation period by slowing the growth rate will disproportionately increase the total energy cost per unit of

TABLE 10.3

Relationships between Adult Weight (g), Total Birth or Litter Weight (g), and Gestation Period (days) in Mammals

Group	Birth weight (Y): adult weight (X)	Gestation period (Y): adult weight (X)	References
Placental mammals	$Y = 0.54X^{0.83}$		Leitch *et al.*, 1959
	$Y = 0.34X^{0.83}$		Leutenegger, 1976
	$Y = 0.20X^{0.71}$		Millar, 1977
	$Y = 0.39X^{0.83}$		Kurta and Kunz, 1987
		$Y = 12.0X^{0.25}$	Blaxter, 1964
		$Y = 11.6X^{0.24}$	Zeveloff and Boyce, 1980
Carnivores			
Fissipeds	$Y = 0.39X^{0.66}$		Case, 1978
Pinnipeds	$Y = 5.14X^{0.63}$	$Y = 16.2X^{0.16}$	Case, 1978; Kihlstrom, 1972
Cetaceans		$Y = 201.5X^{0.04}$	Kihlstrom, 1972
Chiropterans	$Y = 0.40X^{0.76}$	$Y = 39.6X^{0.17}$	Case, 1978; Kihlstrom, 1972
	$Y = 0.40X^{0.84}$		Kurta and Kunz, 1987
Insectivores	$Y = 0.12X^{0.80}$	$Y = 16.5X^{0.14}$	Case, 1978; Kihlstrom, 1972
Lagomorphs	$Y = 0.29X^{0.71}$		Millar, 1977
Primates	$Y = 0.41X^{0.78}$	$Y = 31.3X^{0.16}$	Leutenegger, 1973; Kihlstrom, 1972
Rodents	$Y = 0.13X^{0.82}$	$Y = 10.9X^{0.18}$	Case, 1978; Kihlstrom, 1972
Ungulates and sub-ungulates	$Y = 0.89X^{0.79}$	$Y = 29.6X^{0.19}$	Robbins and Robbins, 1979; Kihlstrom, 1972
Up to 400kg	$Y = 0.33X^{0.90}$		Oftedal, 1985
Over 400kg	$Y = 4.65X^{0.68}$		Oftedal, 1985

fetus produced, which may explain why most delays during pregnancy are not via a reduced growth rate but occur prior to the initiation of growth (i.e., delayed fertilization or implantation). Slowing fetal growth rate can be advantageous if dietary protein or minerals are limiting, as might occur for a frugivorous or folivorous primate because of the low available protein content of most fruit and tree leaves (Robbins, 1983; Worthington, 1989; Izhaki and Safriel, 1989).

B. Lactation

The production of milk by the postpartum mammalian female provides a dietary transition between the passive, totally dependent fetus and the weaned, nutritionally independent juvenile. Lactation often enables the neonate to continue growth in an almost embryonic manner anatomically separated from the female, thus freeing her from the locomotory, nutritional, and anatomical con-

TABLE 10.4
Average Weight and Composition of Mammalian Neonates or Full-Term Fetuses

Species	Average weight (g)	Percentage composition				Energy content (kcal/g wet weight)	Reference
		Water	Protein	Fat	Ash		
Harp seal	7267	—	—	—	—	1.73	Worthy and Lavigne, 1983
Ringed seal	3600	61.9	20.3	11.9	—	2.14	Stirling and McEwan, 1975
White-tailed deer	3574	77.7	14.7	2.2	4.0	1.03	Robbins and Moen, 1975a
Human	3564	69.1	11.9	16.1	2.9	2.11	Widdowson, 1950
Reindeer	2850	76.7	18.0	1.4	3.9	1.10	Reimers et al., 1982
Grey seal	—	—	—	9.0	—	—	Widdowson, 1950
Domestic pig	1460	84.1	11.3	1.1	3.5	0.71	Widdowson, 1950
Mink	960.0	82.0	13.1	2.1	1.8	0.97	Oftedal and Gittleman, 1989
Black bear	351.0	83.5	12.0	0.9	2.5	0.73	Oftedal, unpublished
Domestic cat	118.0	80.7	14.9	1.8	2.6	0.97	Widdowson, 1950
Guinea pig	80.1	70.9	14.9	10.1	4.1	1.73	Widdowson, 1950
Domestic rabbit	54.0	84.6	11.1	2.0	2.3	0.78	Widdowson, 1950
European rabbit	35.6	—	—	4.1	—	—	Boyd, 1985
Fox squirrel	22.0	82.4	9.8	—	—	0.86	Havera, 1978
Big brown bat	20.0	—	—	—	—	1.09	Stack, 1985
Laboratory rat	5.85	86.0	10.8	1.0	2.2	0.68	Widdowson, 1950
Bank vole	2.13	84.5	9.8	3.8	1.6	0.88	Sawicka-Kapusta, 1974
Common vole	1.88	83.5	10.6	2.7	2.1	0.82	Sawicka-Kapusta, 1970
Old-field mouse	1.59	82.6	12.2	1.5	2.0	0.82	Kaufman and Kaufman, 1977
Laboratory mouse	1.55	83.3	12.5	2.1	2.1	0.87	Widdowson, 1950

straints of transporting and bearing an excessively large fetus(es) (Pond, 1977). Lactation is 2 to 3 times more costly than gestation. Total energy expenditure (including the milk produced) by lactating females usually ranges form 4 to 7 × BMR, or 65 to 215% higher than the nonlactating female (Robbins et al., 1981; Mattingly and McClure, 1982; Fedak and Anderson, 1982; Sadleir, 1982, 1984; Trillmich, 1986; Nicoll and Thompson, 1987; Kenagy et al., 1990; Kurta et al., 1990; Thompson, 1991).

Although few exceptions exist, mammals are not unique in nourishing their offspring with parental secretions. Pigeons and doves (Vandeputte-Poma, 1980; Blockstein, 1989), penguins (Prévost and Vilter, 1963), and flamingoes (Lang, 1963) feed esophageal or crop secretions to the hatchling. Because of the analogous role of these avian secretions, the pigeon is said to produce crop milk. Pigeon milk is produced by both parents and consists of sloughed, fat-loaded, epithelial cells of the crop wall (Desmeth and Vandeputte-Poma, 1980). Crop milk is the only nourishment for the young pigeon during the first 3 days. Subsequently, the milk is increasingly mixed with grain until milk production stops at 3 to 4 weeks.

1. MILK COMPOSITION

"Of the 4300 species of mammals, the milks of only 176 have been analyzed for protein, fat and carbohydrate and, of these analyses, the figures for only forty-eight species are considered to be reliable" (Widdowson, 1984; citing Oftedal, 1980). Many of the milk samples collected from wildlife have either been the first milk, particularly from zoo animals whose young have died shortly after birth, or milk from very late in the lactation cycle, such as from free-ranging animals killed during fall and winter hunting seasons. Because milk composition changes quite markedly during a lactation cycle, one must be careful in evaluating the meaning of a single milk analysis reported for a particular species.

The first milk produced during each lactation cycle is called colostrum. Because the neonate is born into a very septic environment relative to the sterile uterus, development of an immune system is essential. Colostrum is often noted for its high concentration of maternal antibodies or immunoglobulins, active phagocytic cells,and bacteriocidal enzymes (Cockson and McNeice, 1980). While the phagocytic cells and bacteriocidal enzymes are important to all neonates in countering infection of the gastrointestinal tract, the significance of colostral IgG immunoglobulins in providing circulating, passive immunity is species specific. For example, neonatal primates, guinea pigs, and rabbits acquire all circulating maternal immunoglobulins in utero. For ungulates, marsupials, and mink, colostrum is the sole source of a passive immune system. Intermediate to these groups are rats, mice, cats, and dogs, which acquire maternal immunoglobulins both in utero and from colostrum (Yadav, 1971; Butler, 1974). These differences in *in utero* transfer of immunoglobulins are determined by the number of cellular layers in the placenta that separate fetal and maternal circulations. The secretion of colostral IgG immunoglobulins is practical only as long as the neonatal gut remains permeable to their absorption and upper-tract digestion of these proteins is minimal. The intestine of ungulates remains permeable to the intact immunoglobulin for only 24–36 hr after birth (Lecce and Morgan, 1962; McCoy *et al.*, 1970) but continues in mink for 8 days (Hanson and Johansson, 1970), in mice and rats for 16–20 days (Halliday, 1955; Abrahamson *et al.*, 1979), and in macropod marsupials for 170–200 days (Yadav, 1971). The very prolonged absorption capabilities in marsupials corresponds to the time that the young reside in the pouch. Other types of immunoglobulins, such as IgA, continue to occur in milk after absorption of intact molecules has ceased and are important in protecting the neonatal gut from infection (Hanson and Johansson, 1970; Butler, 1974).

The major constituents of milk are water, minerals, protein (such as casein), fat, and carbohydrates (Table 10.5). Protein concentration ranges from under 10 g/liter in some primates to over 100 g/liter in hares, rabbits, and some carnivores. Fat varies from traces in the milk of rhinoceroses and horses to over 500 g/liter in some seals and whales. The main carbohydrate of placental mammal milk is the disaccharide lactose, a polymer of glucose and galactose. Lactose content ranges from traces in the milk of some marine mammals and marsupials to more than 100 g/liter in some primates. Marsupial milk, nevertheless, can be very high in carbohydrates, but the sugars are primarily oligo- and polysaccharides rich in galactose (Green, 1984).

TABLE 10.5

Composition (%) and Energy Content (kcal/g) of Mammalian Milks for Eutherians at Mid-lactation and for Marsupials While Confined to the Pouch and After Vacating the Pouch

Group or species	Water	Fat	Protein	Sugar	Ash	Energy
Marsupials						
Eastern quoll						
0–9 weeks	83.0	4.5	5.8	5.8	—	0.96
10–22 weeks	68.5	14.2	8.0	4.8	—	1.94
Potoroo						
0–15 weeks	76.0	2.0	6.5	11.0	—	0.84
16–25 weeks	67.5	13.5	12.0	3.5	—	1.73
Red-necked wallaby						
0–33 weeks	80.0	5.0	5.0	9.5	—	0.73
34–57 weeks	73.7	13.2	7.3	3.2	—	1.63
Tammar wallaby						
0–20 weeks	82.0	4.0	4.3	8.0	—	0.93
21–45 weeks	70.0	16.0	10.0	3.0	—	2.14

TABLE 10.5

Continued

Group or species	Water	Fat	Protein	Sugar	Ash	Energy
Tasmanian bettong						
0–18 weeks	76.0	2.0	3.5	10.0	—	0.83
19–24 weeks	65.0	15.0	7.5	2.0	—	1.79
Insectivores						
White-toothed shrew	48.8	31.9	9.7	—	2.6	—
Primates						
Baboons	86.0	4.6	1.5	7.7	0.3	0.80
Human	87.6	4.1	0.8	6.8	0.2	0.69
Lemurs	—	2.3	1.9	6.7	0.3	0.58
Talapoin monkey	87.7	3.0	2.1	7.2	0.3	0.67
Lagomorphs						
Domestic rabbit	68.8	15.2	10.3	1.8	1.8	2.04
Eastern cottontail rabbit	64.8	14.4	15.8	2.7	2.1	2.33
European brown hare	67.8	14.8	10.3	1.6	—	2.00
Rodents						
Brown rat	77.9	8.8	8.1	3.8	1.2	1.43
Chinchilla	—	11.2	7.3	1.7	1.0	1.50
European beaver	65.9	19.0	11.2	1.7	1.1	2.46
Golden hamster	77.4	4.9	9.4	4.9	1.4	1.20
Guinea pig	82.5	5.7	6.3	4.8	0.8	1.08
House mouse	70.7	13.1	9.0	3.0	1.5	1.85
Carnivores—Fissipeds						
Arctic fox	71.4	13.5	11.1	3.0	1.0	1.98
Brown bear	66.4	18.5	8.5	2.3	1.5	2.28
Domestic cat	—	10.8	10.6	3.7	1.0	1.74
Domestic dog	77.3	9.5	7.5	3.8	1.1	1.46
Mink	78.3	7.3	5.6	4.5	1.0	1.18
Racoon dog	81.4	3.4	7.8	—	1.1	—
Red fox	81.9	5.8	6.7	4.6	0.9	1.09
Striped skunk	69.4	13.8	9.9	3.0	—	1.97
Carnivores—Pinnipeds						
California seal-lion	59.0	30.7	8.6	0.3	—	3.30
Harp seal	48.3	42.2	8.7	0.1	0.7	4.34
Hooded seal	30.3	61.0	4.7	1.0	—	5.88
Northern elephant seal	35.6	48.8	7.6	0.3	—	4.88
Northern fur seal	39.0	49.4	10.2	0.1	0.5	5.09
Southern elephant seal	51.2	39.0	9.0	—	—	4.07
Weddell seal	42.8	42.1	15.8	1.0	—	4.08
Proboscideans						
African elephant	82.7	5.0	4.0	5.3	0.7	0.88
Asian elephant	82.3	7.3	4.5	5.2	0.6	1.12
Perissodactyls						
Ass	91.5	0.6	1.4	6.1	0.4	0.38

(continues)

TABLE 10.5

Continued

Group or species	Water	Fat	Protein	Sugar	Ash	Energy
Black rhinoceros	91.2	0.2	1.4	6.6	0.3	0.35
Horse	89.5	1.3	1.9	6.9	0.4	0.51
Artiodactyls						
Bactrian camel	84.8	4.3	4.3	—	0.9	—
Black-tailed deer	—	12.6	7.2	4.8	1.4	1.76
Dall sheep	77.1	9.5	7.2	5.3	0.9	1.48
Domestic cow	87.6	3.7	3.2	4.6	0.7	0.71
Domestic pig	79.9	8.3	5.6	5.0	0.9	1.24
Domestic goat	88.0	3.8	2.9	4.7	0.8	0.69
Domestic sheep	81.8	7.3	4.1	5.0	0.8	1.11
Dorcas gazelle	75.9	8.8	8.8	5.7	1.1	1.53
Eland	78.1	9.9	6.3	4.4	1.1	1.43
Gayal	80.0	7.0	6.3	5.2	—	1.20
Giraffe	85.5	4.8	4.0	4.9	0.8	0.86
Ibex	76.7	12.4	5.7	4.4	1.2	1.62
Moose	78.5	10.0	8.4	3.0	1.5	1.51
North American elk	81.0	6.7	5.7	4.2	1.3	1.10
Red deer	78.9	8.5	7.1	4.5	1.4	1.37
Reindeer	73.7	10.9	9.5	3.4	1.3	1.66
Rocky mountain goat	78.7	8.1	6.4	4.3	0.9	1.27
Tahr	—	7.9	5.4	3.1	—	1.14
Water buffalo	83.2	6.5	4.3	4.9	0.8	1.02
White-tailed deer	77.5	7.7	8.2	4.6	1.5	1.35

Sources: Green *et al.,* 1980, 1983; Messer *et al.,* 1984; Oftedal, 1984a,b; Green *et al.,* 1987; Crowley *et al.,* 1988; Smolenski and Rose, 1988; Merchant *et al.,* 1989.

Variation in milk composition between species reflects numerous compromises between the physiological constraints to milk synthesis and the selective pressures to maximize offspring survival. Most aquatic mammals produce highly concentrated milks (Jenness and Sloan, 1970; Jenness, 1974) (Table 10.5). The reduction in milk water content in aquatic mammals provides a high-energy, low-bulk diet that is useful in offsetting neonatal heat loss in cold environments and conserves water in those mothers, such as the northern elephant seal, that abstain entirely from eating or drinking during a relatively short but intense lactation. Similarly, seals that give birth on pack ice and have very short lactation periods (e.g., hooded seals—4 day lactation) or those that leave the neonate for feeding trips lasting several days produce more concentrated, higher-fat milks than do other seals (Trillmich and Lechner, 1986; Gentry and Kooyman, 1986; Oftedal *et al.,* 1988).

For terrestrial mammals, the largest changes in milk composition over time occur in marsupials (Green, 1984). The embryonic marsupial confined to the pouch consumes a dilute, high-sugar milk that, perhaps, provides nourishment similar to that occurring in the uterus of a eutherian during their longer gestation. Once the young begin leaving the pouch, the milk becomes more concentrated with more fat and protein and less sugar. Most terrestrial eutherians produce milks that are intermediate in concentration to the nutrient-rich milk of aquatic mammals and the very dilute milks of primates and perissodactyls. The milks of domestic cattle, goats, and camels contain about one-half the protein and energy per unit volume that occur in the milks of wild artiodactyls (Robbins *et al.*, 1987). These dilute milks from domestic artiodactyls are more similar to that produced by humans than they are to wild artiodactyls. Because sugars, particularly lactose, and some minerals, such as sodium and potassium, are important regulators of the osmotic potential or water content of milk in the mammary gland, concentrated milks have either a low sugar (such as marine mammals) or mineral content while dilute milks have a higher sugar (such as primates and perissodactyls) or mineral content (Martin, 1984).

The actual composition of the milk fat, protein, and sugar also differ between animals (Table 10.6). For example, the fatty acids of most milks are dominated by palmitic (16:0) and oleic acids (18:1). However, the main fatty acid of lagomorph and elephant milk is capric acid (10:0), which is synthesized in the mammary gland, whereas those of seal milk are long-chain unsaturated fatty acids (18:3 and higher) that are probably derived directly from the diet (Dils *et al.*, 1977; Oftedal *et al.*, 1987). The amino acid taurine appears to be a dietary essential for most neonatal mammals, particularly carnivores. The taurine content of colostrum is usually higher than in mature milk. However, carnivores have much higher concentrations of taurine in the mature milk than do herbivores (cat—287 μmol/100 ml; dog—181, domestic cow—1, guinea pig—17, rabbit—14, sheep—14, and horse 3) (Renner *et al.*, 1989). The sulfur-containing amino acid content of tammar wallaby milk increases sharply at the same time that hair growth begins in the neonate (Renfree *et al.*, 1981). Although not understood chemically, casein composition or structure will determine the hardness of the milk clot formed in the stomach of the neonate and, thus, the rate at which nutrients are digested (Fonty *et al.*, 1979).

2. MILK INTAKE

Measurements of milk composition and intake by maternal-raised neonates provide a basis for estimating maternal requirements and for understanding the processes and requirements of neonatal growth. Methods for determining milk intake include: weighing the neonate or the adult before and after a controlled nursing period, hand milking the lactating female after a controlled period of neonate removal and weighing the milk, or using isotopes of hydrogen or sodium to quantify either the dilution of the neonate's body water or sodium pools by

TABLE 10.6
Fatty Acid Composition of Milk Fats[a]

Group or species	Percentage by weight								
	≤10:0	12:0	14:0	16:0	16:1	18:0	18:1	18:2	≥18:3
Marsupials									
Eastern quoll									
0–6 weeks	—	—	2.5	46.8	7.5	3.8	23.5	12.0	0.9
10–22 weeks	—	—	1.4	24.7	5.6	6.8	36.0	15.9	3.4
Red kangaroo									
0–10 weeks	trace	0.2	3.4	43.5	6.9	3.5	25.2	9.8	3.4
10–52 weeks	trace	0.1	2.0	27.2	5.4	8.6	44.3	6.1	2.2
Tammar wallaby									
0–6 weeks	—	—	2.9	43.2	7.4	5.3	25.9	7.2	1.4
18–45 weeks	—	—	1.1	22.3	4.5	12.9	43.0	6.2	5.3
Primates									
Cottontop marmoset	17.1	15.7	12.1	21.5	2.2	3.4	19.6	8.0	—
Rhesus macaque	12.4	2.4	1.9	20.9	4.7	4.7	30.8	19.7	2.6
Squirrel monkey	11.8	6.0	7.2	29.2	4.2	3.9	30.0	7.8	—
Human	1.3	3.1	5.1	20.2	5.7	5.9	46.4	13.0	1.4

Lagomorphs									
Brown hare	32.3	11.7	7.3	18.2	1.3	3.1	10.0	11.2	2.9
Domestic rabbit	42.5	2.9	1.7	14.2	2.0	3.8	13.6	14.0	4.4
White-tailed jackrabbit	31.1	8.7	4.3	18.7	0.9	3.7	8.8	9.9	14.3
Cottontail rabbit	39.6	4.4	2.2	18.8	1.4	2.3	9.8	16.3	4.6
Rodents									
Deer mouse	0.9	1.5	3.2	19.2	3.1	7.3	38.3	23.4	—
Gerbil	—	—	0.7	13.4	0.7	5.9	24.5	46.8	—
House mouse	6.0	8.1	11.9	23.2	3.9	2.9	25.7	16.3	2.0
Norway rat	11.2	9.5	11.9	30.1	2.2	3.0	18.9	11.4	1.3
White-footed mouse	1.0	1.6	3.8	23.6	4.0	6.4	41.3	17.0	—
Carnivores—Fissipeds									
Badger	—	—	2.8	25.4	5.0	9.2	41.4	16.2	—
Black bear	0.3	0.4	3.4	26.2	4.4	3.0	49.8	11.0	1.4
Grizzly bear	0.5	0.2	3.3	26.8	5.7	3.0	49.8	8.6	1.5
Carnivores—Pinnipeds									
California sea lion	—	—	5.9	17.8	6.8	3.9	17.4	2.0	41.7
Harp seal	—	—	4.9	11.8	19.9	4.2	23.5	1.7	34.0
Northern elephant seal	—	—	2.6	16.8	7.0	3.7	44.1	1.9	24.7
Northern fur seal	—	—	6.3	19.3	9.9	2.0	31.6	2.7	27.1
Weddell seal	—	—	9.8	14.7	12.4	1.8	39.0	2.3	20.2
Proboscideans									
African elephant	74.5	17.4	1.2	2.6	0.5	0.1	3.4	0.1	0.6
Indian elephant	49.6	21.5	3.5	9.1	1.9	0.5	9.8	2.3	1.9

(continues)

TABLE 10.6

Continued

Group or species				Percentage by weight					
	≤10:0	12:0	14:0	16:0	16:1	18:0	18:1	18:2	≥18:3
Perissodactyls									
Donkey	17.9	12.1	6.4	16.9	4.4	1.3	21.0	13.0	5.5
Zebra	23.5	9.2	6.5	13.3	4.2	2.0	20.4	10.1	8.0
Artiodactyls									
Bighorn sheep	6.8	1.9	11.2	24.7	2.2	9.6	36.8	4.7	2.0
Bison	8.8	2.7	8.0	30.8	3.7	14.4	25.5	1.4	1.4
Caribou	7.1	1.4	11.4	34.9	1.3	17.7	18.9	2.0	1.8
Giraffe	11.5	1.9	8.9	23.6	2.6	22.6	23.6	2.3	1.4
Grant's gazelle	14.2	3.1	15.5	33.2	2.7	5.8	15.8	6.4	3.3
Domestic cow	9.2	3.1	9.5	26.3	2.3	14.6	29.8	2.4	0.8
Domestic goat	16.6	3.3	10.3	24.6	2.2	12.5	28.5	2.2	—
Domestic sheep	18.5	5.4	11.8	25.4	3.4	9.0	20.0	2.1	1.4
Mule deer	11.0	0.7	12.7	35.6	1.1	15.0	14.7	1.4	2.1
Pronghorn antelope	8.9	1.6	14.2	42.9	3.7	5.7	16.7	1.6	1.8

Sources: Glass et al., 1967; McCullagh et al., 1969; Glass and Jenness, 1971; Griffiths et al., 1972; Green et al., 1983; Lhuillery et al., 1984; Oftedal et al., 1987; Green et al., 1987.

[a] The fatty acids are represented by the number of carbon atoms in the chain (10 to 18) and the number of double bonds (0 to 3).

ingested milk or the actual transfer of these elements from the mother to the young via milk (Holleman *et al.*, 1975; Oftedal, 1984a; Green *et al.*, 1988). Each method entails various assumptions or experimental and interpretational difficulties. The major difficulty with hand milking is equating observed female production to actual neonatal intake. The interval between milkings, if quite short, may reflect physiological milk production capabilities and overestimate neonatal intake, while if the interval is too long, milk accumulation in the udder can reduce production and thereby underestimate intake (Linzell, 1972). Excitable wild animals often cannot be milked without injections of immobilizers, tranquilizers, or oxytocin (Arman *et al.*, 1974; Mueller and Sadleir, 1977; Arman, 1979).

Investigators weighing the neonate or mother before and after a nursing need to correct for fecal and urine excretion in those species in which the mother stimulates the nursing neonate to void. Red deer calves wore "nappies" to collect the urine and feces when stimulated by the mother or were stimulated by the investigator before rejoining the mother (Arman *et al.*, 1974). As in hand milking, the interval in which the infant is removed from its mother must be very carefully evaluated. For some species —such as the tree shrew, which nourishes its young only once in 48 hr (Martin, 1966), and rabbits and hares, which suckle once in 24 hr (Linzell, 1972; Broekhuizen and Maaskamp, 1980)—the normal frequency can be easily used.

Isotopes provide the greatest promise for determining milk intake of both captive and free-ranging wildlife. Prior to the consumption of free water and preformed water in other feeds, milk is the only external water source. Thus, milk intake can be directly determined from measurements of neonatal water kinetics and milk composition. As other sources of water are ingested, either the mother can be injected with a different water isotope than the neonate to distinguish between the various water sources or, as is often possible with captive animals, consumption of other sources of water can be directly measured (Holleman *et al.*, 1975; Robbins *et al.*, 1981). The major assumptions or requisite determinations of the water isotope methods are that cross-nursing between different neonate–mother combinations does not occur, water cycling between littermates and between neonate and mother is either negligible or measurable if it occurs, and water isotope kinetics reflect body water kinetics (Macfarlane *et al.*, 1969; Holleman *et al.*, 1975; Dove and Freer, 1979). If isotope cycling is a significant problem, one neonate per litter can be left uninjected to serve as a control to correct for isotope cycling.

Milk production generally rises during early lactation to a peak before falling during the weaning process. Because of the changing nature of the lactation curve and the desire of many investigators to understand the maximum stress on the lactating female, peak milk yields by well-fed females have been the main basis for comparison (Fig. 10.3). Peak yields generally increase as a

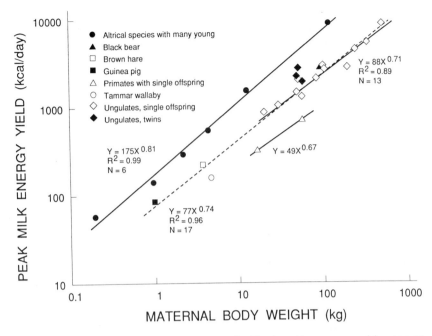

Fig. 10.3   Peak milk production by various mammals. [*Species with many young:* laboratory rat, guinea pig, brown hare, mink, striped skunk, domestic rabbit, domestic dog, domestic pig, and American black bear; *Ungulates with single offspring:* black-tailed deer, domestic sheep, red deer, reindeer, elk, domestic cow, domestic horse, caribou, muskox, mule deer, mountain goat, Dorcas gazelle, and ibex; *Ungulates with twins:* black-tailed deer, mule deer, and domestic sheep; *Primates:* human and baboon; and *Marsupial:* tammar wallaby. (Data from Oftedal, 1984a,b; Lhuillery *et al.*, 1984; Carl and Robbins, 1988; Cork and Dove, 1989; Parker *et al.*, 1990; Farley and Robbins, unpublished.] Regressions are: (1) litter-bearing mammals with altricial young, excluding black bears, brown hares, and guinea pigs; (2) ungulates with single offspring, tammar wallaby, and precocial black bear (den emergence), guinea pig, and brown hare; (3) ungulates with single young; and (4) primates.

function of maternal metabolic body weight [exponents ranging from 0.67 to 0.81 which are not significantly different from 0.75(Oftedal, 1984a)]. Litter-bearing species with altricial young produce at least twice as much milk as do ungulates with a single offspring, American black bears (litter size = 2.5), guinea pigs (3.1), brown hares, and tammar wallabies (1). Although bears and wallabies produce very altricial neonates, their developmental stage at the time of emergence from the den or pouch corresponds to that of a precocial neonate at birth (Renfree *et al.*, 1981; Russell, 1982; Ramsay and Dunbrack, 1986). The guinea pig provisions its young prior to birth with fat that is used to meet some of its energy requirements during lactation. Well-fed ungulates with twins generally produce 67% more milk than do those with a single offspring (Sadleir, 1980a,b; Oftedal, 1985; Carl and Robbins, 1988). The baboon and human produce the least milk, which corresponds with their very slow growth rates (Oftedal, 1984a).

The decline in milk production once the peak has been reached can last for as little as 5 days in mice to many months in large ungulates (White, 1975; Carl and Robbins, 1988; Parker *et al.*, 1990). Although larger species tend to have longer lactation periods, evolutionary constraints create many exceptions. One of the shortest lactation periods occurs in hooded seals (average maternal weight = 179 kg) in which the pup grows from 21.5 to 43.7 kg (70% of the gain being fat) in only 4 days (Bowen *et al.*, 1987). Poorly nourished females and those nursing larger litters often reduce milk production faster than do well-nourished females. The decline in milk intake relative to infant requirements stimulates the young animal to ingest food characteristic of the adult diet. The point at which the offspring is weaned is not solely due to nutritional considerations. Prolonged maintenance of the mother-infant bond in those species in which maternal investment per offspring is already considerable can be of survival benefit, such as in predator avoidance or defense, in development of migration patterns, and in social interactions.

C. Care and Feeding of Orphaned Neonates

Numerous attempts have been made to hand-raise orphaned wildlife, but the successful care of very young animals is still largely an art requiring dedication and perseverance. For example, many neonates do not defecate or urinate unless manually stimulated by rubbing or washing the anal and genital area. Because feces produced from the digestion of milk are normally quite soft and aromatic, their consumption by the lactating female as she licks the infant ensures cleanliness when altricial infants are confined to a nest, den, or pouch (e.g., carnivores, rodents, or marsupials) and reduces the chance of attracting predators even to precocial neonates (e.g., artiodactyls) (Fig. 10.4).

Milk formulation is one of the major concerns in raising orphans. Excess or inappropriate milk sugars or fats can cause diarrhea and digestive upsets (Reineck, 1962; Reuther, 1969; Stephens, 1975). Lactose is a particular problem when using cow's milk or lactose-containing milk replacers to raise neonates of species, such as seals, in which the natural milk is largely devoid of this disaccharide. When lactose is fed to neonates in which the enzyme lactase is inadequate for its digestion, severe diarrhea occurs due to bacterial growth and the osmotic effect of undigested sugar in the intestine. Use of galactose (a component of lactose) or lactose-containing formulas can also produce cataracts in neonates that do not normally encounter these sugars. If cellular enzyme systems are inadequate to metabolize the absorbed galactose, this compound is converted to

Fig. 10.4 A white-tailed deer stimulating her nursing offspring to defecate and urinate. This act must often be simulated when humans bottle-raise wildlife. (Courtesy of Nadine Jacobsen, University of California, Davis.)

a sugar alcohol that is retained in the lens of the eye (Stephens, 1975). Several milk substitutes that are lactose- and galactose-free are available as a formula base for lactose-intolerant species. Many other deficiencies, particularly amino acids in very young mammals, and pathogens can cause cataracts (Vainisi *et al.*, 1980). Disaccharide intolerance and the debilitating consequences also can be produced by feeding other sugars. For example, sucrase, the enzyme necessary to digest common table sugar or corn syrup, is very low or absent in many mammalian neonates (Kerry, 1969; Walcott and Messer, 1980).

Added fats that produce severe diarrhea have been primarily vegetable fats, such as common cooking oils. If fat is to be added, butterfat is usually preferred. Other fats, such as animal tallow or egg yolk, can also be used. Coconut oil has been useful in developing formulas for young elephants as it more closely approximates the high concentration of medium-chain-length fatty acids in elephant milk than does butterfat that is dominated by long-chain fatty acids (McCullagh and Widdowson, 1970). Fats containing medium-chain-length fatty acids are more easily digested than fats containing long-chain fatty acids (Mead *et al.*, 1985). If significant amounts of fat are added or if fat digestion is a problem, the milk fat may need to be emulsified or homogenized to reduce fat droplet size. Although elephant milk contains 2–3 times as much fat as does cow's milk, the fat droplets in elephant milk are one-half the size of those in raw cow's milk.

Although neonates have been successfully fed milk very dissimilar to the composition of the normal maternal milk, most neonates do better when fed milks similar to the normal milk (Oftedal, 1980; Widdowson, 1984; Auestad *et al.*, 1989; Casey, 1989). The once common statement that the gross composition of maternal milk could not be duplicated because of its radical difference from either cow's milk or other common milk replacers is patently incorrect. Because the principal ingredients of milk are available in pure form, milk replacers of any composition can be formulated. However, even far greater sophistication in milk formulation will become necessary as we recognize the importance of the fatty acid, sugar, and amino acid spectra of milk replacers and the normal compositional changes that occur throughout lactation.

After the best milk formula has been determined, the nutritionist must determine the amount to be fed, the method of feeding, and the feeding schedule. The amount fed should be based on a knowledge of neonatal milk intake control, requirements, and efficiencies of nutrient utilization. Many infants have been fed ad libitum quantities of milk with the assumption that the neonate would correctly control its intake. Milk is often ingested in excess of physiological capacities and results in diarrhea, vomiting, listlessness, potbellies, labored breathing, anorexia, and death. Conversely, because of the association between diarrhea and overfeeding, neonates often are purposefully underfed with the only criteria of success being neonatal survival. Both approaches should be rejected and replaced by a thorough understanding of the entire lactation process.

The behaviorist observing nursing interactions has often noted the frequency and duration of nursing bouts and whether the young or the mother behaviorally terminates each bout. For example, well-fed ungulate females during the first week of lactation often allow the offspring seemingly unlimited access to the udder, with the young terminating all nursing bouts by simply moving away voluntarily from the udder. Later, the mother increasingly rebukes advances and behaviorally terminates all nursing bouts by moving away or forcefully rejecting the young before it is willing to relinquish the teat. These observations suggest that the young ungulate is quite capable of controlling its own intake from the beginning, with the mother balancing her needs and resources with those of the neonate once weaning has begun. However, when the same neonatal ungulates are bottle-raised, they are incapable of correctly controlling their intake and, if initially given free access to milk, will drastically overeat and develop acute diarrhea. Thus, if the mother-raised neonatal ungulate is indeed controlling its intake, bottle-raising efforts are not providing the same cues upon which intake can be controlled. For example, the larger hole of most artificial nipples often delivers milk far faster than the maternal teat and may not provide the time cues necessary for the neonate to sense or judge its state of fill.

These paradoxes can be judged in light of milk intake control in young rats. The neonatal rat pup is often attached to the mother's teat for the majority of the day. However, attachment is not synonymous with milk intake and intake control. The 1-day-old pup is indeed incapable of correctly controlling its intake. Neonatal milk intake is controlled by the "continuous duet" between the pup and the mother, which only intermittently lets milk down into the nipple in response to the level of suckling stimulation provided by the pup (Epstein, 1986). The healthy pup will eagerly and almost reflexively consume all milk that the female provides. If the pup is given access to more milk during a sucking bout, such as by cannulating the mother's teat or pup's mouth and artificially providing more milk or inducing additional milk let-down in anesthetized mothers by prolonged, repeated oxytocin injections, milk is consumed until the physical capacity of the stomach forces milk into the intestinal tract as far as the large intestine. Similarly, milk will back up into the nose and mouth, and the pup will simply choke until it has cleared its respiratory tract of milk. Only the 15- to 20-day-old pup is able to control its intake correctly (Hall and Rosenblatt, 1977; Cramer and Blass, 1983).

Mule deer and mountain goats offer another example of the need to understand the animal's basic biology before raising orphans. Neonatal mule deer are "hiders" during their early life as they try to avoid predation by being very secretive. Mother does not stay with the fawn, but returns to the fawn from 2 to 10 times a day for nursing. Goats are "followers" as the mother provides an active defense against predation while nursing the neonate up to 40 times a day. Fawns raised as singles by their mother consume between 150 and 200 g per nursing bout. Mountain goats, because of their more frequent nursing, consume only 50 g per feeding. Although both the composition of the milk and the amount consumed per day are similar for mule deer and mountain goats, bottle-raising protocols that use infrequent feedings (e.g., 4 per day) of large volumes (e.g., 150 ml per feeding) are very successful for mule deer but kill mountain goats. Feeding volumes larger than 90 ml will exceed the capacity of the goat's true stomach and will produce a very sick animal. Thus, mule deer fawns are anatomically and physiologically adapted for ingesting "meals" whereas goat kids have evolved to consume milk in "snack" proportions (Carl and Robbins, 1988).

Many additional studies of the mother-neonate interaction are essential if we are to successfully raise orphaned wildlife. Nutritionists working at zoos should be leaders in this field because of their need to raise many orphans. The pervasive trial-and-error approach to raising orphaned wildlife (e.g., *International Zoo Yearbook*) must be replaced by well-planned, scientifically based efforts (Oftedal, 1980; Robbins *et al.*, 1987). As an indication of our lack of knowledge about lactation and neonatal metabolism, most bottle-raising efforts encounter diarrhea. While some of the diarrhea is primarily pathogenic due to inadequate antibody transfer and totally independent of diet (Kramer *et al.*, 1971), most cases are due to the use of improper milk replacers and feeding schedules that predispose the neonate to gastrointestinal infection (Fonty *et al.*, 1979). Although antibiotics are often used in treating diarrhea, correction of the dietary cause of these diarrheas will be more productive.

REFERENCES

Abrahamson, D. R., Powers, A., and Rodewald, R. (1979). Intestinal absorption of immune complexes by neonatal rats: A route of antigen transfer from mother to young. *Science* **206,** 567–569.

Adolph, E. F., and Heggeness, F. W. (1971). Age changes in body water and fat in fetal and infant mammals. *Growth* **35,** 55–63.

Alisauskas, R. T., and Ankney, C. D. (1985). Nutrient reserves and the energetics of reproduction in American coots. *Auk* **102,** 133–144.

Ankney, C. D. (1984). Nutrient reserve dynamics of breeding and molting brant. *Auk* **101,** 361–370.

Ankney, C. D., and Afton, A. D. (1988). Bioenergetics of breeding northern shovelers: Diet, nutrient reserves, clutch size, and incubation. *Condor* **90,** 459–472.

Arman, P. (1979). Milk from semi-domesticated ruminants. *World Rev. Nutr. Diet.* **33,** 198–227.

Arman, P., Kay, R. N. B., Goodall, E. D., and Sharman, G. A. M. (1974). The composition and yield of milk from captive red deer (*Cervus elaphus* L.). *J. Reprod. Fert.* **37,** 67–84.

Auestad, N., Korsak, R. A., Bergstrom, J. D., and Edmond J. (1989). Milk substitutes comparable to rat's milk; their preparation, composition and impact on development and metabolism in the artificially reared rat. *Br. J. Nutr.* **61,** 495–518.

Bancroft, G. T. (1985). Nutrient content of eggs and the energetics of clutch formation in boat-tailed grackles. *Auk* **102,** 43–49.

Batt, B. D. and Prince, H. H. (1979). Laying dates, clutch size and egg weight of captive mallards. *Condor* **81,** 35–41.

Biebach, H. (1979). Energetik des Brutens beim Star (*Sturnus vulgaris*). *J. Ornithol.* **120,** 121–138.

Biebach, H. (1981). Energetic cost of incubation on different clutch sizes in starlings (*Sturnus vulgaris*). *Ardea* **69,** 141–142.

Biebach, H. (1984). Effect of clutch size and time of day on the energy expenditure of incubating starlings (*Sturnus vulgaris*). *Physiol. Zool.* **57,** 26–31.

Birkhead, T. R., and Gaston, A. J. (1988). The composition of ancient murrelet eggs. *Condor* **90,** 965–966.

Blaxter, K. L. (1964). Protein metabolism and requirements in pregnancy and lactation. *In* "Mammalian Protein Metabolism," Vol. II (H. N. Munro and J. B. Allison, eds.), pp. 173–223. Academic Press, London.

Blix, A. S., Grau, H. J., and Ronald, K. (1979). Some aspects of temperature regulation in newborn harp seal pups. *Am. J. Physiol.* **236,** R188–R197.

Blockstein, D. E. (1989). Crop milk and clutch size in mourning doves. *Wilson Bull.* **101,** 11–25.

Bowen, W. D., Boness, D. J., and Oftedal, O. T. (1987). Mass transfer from mother to pup and

218   10. Reproductive Costs

subsequent mass loss by the weaned pup in the hooded seal, *Cystophora cristata. Can. J. Zool.* **65**, 1–8.

Boyd, I. L. (1985). Investment in growth by pregnant wild rabbits in relation to litter size and sex of offspring. *J. Anim. Ecol.* **54**, 137–147.

Broekhuizen, S., and Maaskamp, F. (1980). Behaviour of does and leverets of the European hare (*Lepus europaeus*) whilst nursing. *J. Zool.* **191**, 487–501.

Brown, C. R. (1984). Resting metabolic rate and energetic cost of incubation in macaroni penguins (*Eudyptes chrysolophus*) and rockhopper penguins (*E. chrysocome*). *Comp. Biochem. Physiol.* **77A**, 345–350.

Brown, C. R. (1988). Energy expenditure during incubation in four species of sub-antarctic burrowing petrels. *Ostrich* **59**, 67–70.

Bush, V. (1945). "Science: The Endless Frontier." U.S. Government Print. Office, Washington, D.C.

Butler, J. E. (1974). Immunoglobulins of the mammary secretions. *In* "Lactation," Vol. III (B. L. Larson and V. R. Smith, eds.), pp. 217–255. Academic Press, New York.

Carey, C., Rahn, H., and Parisi, P. (1980). Calories, water, lipid and yolk in avian eggs. *Condor* **82**, 335–343.

Carl, G. R., and Robbins, C. T. (1988). The energetic cost of predator avoidance in neonatal ungulates: Hiding versus following. *Can. J. Zool.* **66**, 239–246.

Case, T. J. (1978). On the evolution and adaptive significance of postnatal growth rates in the terrestrial vertebrates. *Q. Rev. Biol.* **53**, 243–282.

Casey, C. E. (1989). The nutritive and metabolic advantages of homologous milk. *Proc. Nutr. Soc.* **48**, 271–281.

Cockson, A., and McNeice, R. (1980). Survival in the pouch: The role of macrophages and maternal milk cells. *Comp. Biochem. Physiol.* **66A**, 221–225.

Cody, M. L. (1971). Ecological aspects of reproduction. *In* "Avian Biology," Vol. I (D. S. Farner and J. R. King, eds.), pp. 461–512. Academic Press, New York.

Cork, S. J., and Dove, H. (1989). Lactation in the tammar wallaby (*Macropus eugenii*) II. Intake of milk components and maternal allocation of energy. *J. Zool.* **219**, 399–409.

Cramer, C. P., and Blass, E. M. (1983). Mechanisms of control of milk intake in suckling rats. *Am. J. Physiol.* **245**, R154–R159.

Crowley, H. M., Woodward, D. R., and Rose, R. W. (1988). Changes in milk composition during lactation in the potoroo, *Potorous tridactylus* (Marsupialia: Potoroinae). *Aust. J. Biol. Sci.* **41**, 289–296.

Desmeth, M., and Vandeputte-Poma, J. (1980). Lipid composition of pigeon cropmilk–I. Total lipids and lipid classes. *Comp. Biochem. Physiol.* **66B**, 129–133.

Dils, R., Clark, S., and Knudsen, J. (1977). Comparative aspects of milk fat synthesis. *Symp. Zool. Soc. London* **41**, 43–55.

Dove, H., and Freer, M. (1979). The accuracy of triated water turnover rate as an estimate of milk intake in lambs. *Aust. J. Agric. Res.* **30**, 725–739.

Drent, R. (1970). Functional aspects of incubation in the herring gull. *Behaviour Suppl.* **17**, 1–132.

Drobney, R.D. (1980). Reproductive bioenergetics of wood ducks. *Auk* **97**, 480–490.

Drobney, R. D. (1982). Body weight and composition changes and adaptations for breeding in wood ducks. *Condor* **84**, 300–305.

Eldridge, J. L., and Krapu, G. L. (1988). The influence of diet quality on clutch size and laying pattern in mallards. *Auk* **105**, 102–110.

Epstein, A. A. (1986). The ontogeny of ingestive bahaviors: Control of milk intake by suckling rats and the emergence of feeding and drinking at weaning. *In* "Feeding Behavior. Neural and Humoral Controls" (R. C. Ritter, S. Ritter, and C. D. Barnes, eds.), pp. 1–25. Academic Press, New York.

References   219

Farrell, B. C., and Christian, D. P. (1987). Energy and water requirements of lactation in the North American porcupine, *Erethizon dorsatum*. *Comp. Biochem. Physiol.* **88A**, 695–700.
Fedak, M. A., and Anderson, S. S. (1982). The energetics of lactation: Accurate measurements from a large wild mammal, the grey seal (*Halichoerus grypus*). *J. Zool.* **198**, 473–479.
Fogden, M. P. L., and Fogden, P. M. (1979). The role of fat and protein reserves in the annual cycle of the grey-backed camaroptera in Uganda (Aves: Sylvidae). *J. Zool.* **189**, 233–258.
Fonty, G., Goet, Ph., and Riou, Y. (1979). Effect of milk composition on the gastrointestinal microflora of artificially reared young rabbits. *Ann. Biol. Anim. Bioch. Biophys.* **19**, 567–571.
Gebczynski, M., and Gebczynska, Z. (1984). The energy cost of nesting growth in the European pine vole. *Acta Theriol.* **29**, 231–241.
Gentry, R. L., and Kooyman, G. L. (1986). "Fur Seals: Maternal Strategies on Land and at Sea." Princeton Univ. Press, Princeton, New Jersey.
Gessaman, J. A., and Findell, P. R. (1979). Energy cost of incubation in the American kestrel. *Comp. Biochem. Physiol.* **63A**, 57–62.
Gittleman, J. L., and Thompson, S. D. (1988). Energy allocation in mammalian reproduction. *Am. Zool.* **28**, 863–875.
Glass, R. L., and Jenness, R. (1971). Comparative biochemical studies of milk–VI. Constituent fatty acids of milk fats of additional species. *Comp. Biochem. Physiol.* **38B**, 353–359.
Glass, R. L., Troolin, H. A., and Jenness, R. (1967). Comparative biochemical studies of milks–IV. Constituent fatty acids of milk fats. *Comp. Biochem. Physiol.* **22**, 415–425.
Grant, G. S., and Whittow, G. C. (1983). Metabolic cost of incubation in the Laysan albatross and Bonin petrel. *Comp. Biochem. Physiol.* **74A**, 77–82.
Green, B. (1984). Composition of milk and energetics of growth in marsupials. *Symp. Zool. Soc. London* **51**, 369–387.
Green, B., Griffiths, M., and Leckie, R. M. C. (1983). Qualitative and quantitative changes in milk fat during lactation in the tammar wallaby (*Macropus eugenii*). *Aust. J. Biol. Sci.* **36**, 455–461.
Green, B., Merchant, J., and Newgrain, K. (1988). Milk consumption and energetics of growth in pouch young of the tammar wallaby, *Macropus eugenii*. *Aust. J. Zool.* **36**, 217–227.
Green, B., Newgrain, K., and Merchant, J. (1980). Changes in milk composition during lactation in the tammar wallaby (*Macropus eugenii*). *Aust. J. Biol. Sci.* **33**, 35–42.
Green, B., Merchant, J., and Newgrain, K. (1987). Milk composition in the eastern quoll, *Dasyurus viverrinus* (Marsupialia: Dasyuridae). *Aust. J. Biol. Sci.* **40**, 379–387.
Griffiths, M., McIntosh, D. L., and Leckie, R. M. C. (1972). The mammary glands of the red kangaroo with observations on the fatty acid components of the milk triglycerides. *J. Zool.* **166**, 265–275.
Haftorn, S., and Reinertsen, R. E. (1985). The effect of temperature and clutch size on the energetic cost of incubation in a free-living blue tit (*Parus caeruleus*). *Auk* **102**, 470–478.
Hails, C. J., and Turner, A. K. (1985). The role of fat and protein during breeding in the white-bellied swiftlet (*Collocalia esculenta*). *J. Zool.* **206**, 469–484.
Hall, G. H., and Rosenblatt, J. S. (1977). Suckling behavior and intake control in the developing rat pup. *J. Comp. Physiol. Psychol.* **91**, 1232–1247.
Halliday, R. (1955). The absorption of antibodies from immune sera by the gut of the young rat. *Proc. Roy. Soc. London* **143B**, 408–413.
Hanson, L. A., and Johansson, B. G. (1970). Immunological studies of milk. *In* "Milk Proteins: Chemistry and Molecular Biology," Vol. I (H. A. McKenzie, ed.), pp. 45–123. Academic Press, New York.
Havera, S. P. (1978). "Nutrition, Supplement Feeding, and Body Composition of the Fox Squirrel, *Sciurus niger*, in Central Illinois." Doctoral Dissertation, Univ. of Illinois.
Hirsch, K. V., and Grau, C. R. (1981). Yolk formation and oviposition in captive emus. *Condor* **83**, 381–382.

Holleman, D. F., White, R. G. , and Luick, J. R. (1975). New isotope methods for estimating milk intake and yield. *J. Dairy Sci.* **58**, 1814–1821.

Hoyt, D. F., Vleck, D., and Vleck, C. M. (1978). Metabolism of avian embryos: Ontogeny and temperature effects in the ostrich. *Condor* **80**, 265–271.

Izhaki, I., and Safriel, U. N. (1989). Why are there so few exclusively frugivorous birds? Experiments on fruit digestibility. *Oikos* **54**, 23–32.

Jenness, R. (1974). The composition of milk. *In* "Lactation," Vol. III (B. L. Larson and V. R. Smith, eds.), pp. 3–107. Academic Press, New York.

Jenness, R., and Sloan, R. E. (1970). The composition of milks of various species: A review. *Dairy Sci. Abstr.* **32**, 599–612.

Jones, P. J., and Ward, P. (1976). The level of reserve protein as the proximate factor controlling the timing of breeding and clutch-size in the red-billed quelea, *Quelea quelea*. *Ibis* **118**, 547–574.

Kaufman, D. W., and Kaufman, G. A. (1977). Body composition of the old-field mouse (*Peromyscus polionotus*). *J. Mammal.* **58**, 429–434.

Kenagy, G. J., Masman, D., Sharbaugh, S. M., and Nagy, K. A. (1990). Energy expenditure during lactation in relation to litter size of free-living golden-mantled ground squirrels. *J. Anim. Ecol.* **59**, 73–88.

Kerry, K. R. (1969). Intestinal disaccharidase activity in a monotreme and eight species of marsupials (with an added note on the disaccharidases of five species of sea birds). *Comp. Biochem. Physiol.* **29**, 1015–1022.

Kihlstrom, J. E. (1972). Period of gestation and body weight in some placental mammals. *Comp. Biochem. Physiol.* **43A**, 673–679.

King, J. R. (1973). Energetics of reproduction in birds. *In* "Breeding Biology of Birds" (D.S. Farner, ed.), pp. 78–107. Nat. Acad. Sci., Washington, D.C.

Kramer, T. T., Nagy, J. G., and Barber, T. A. (1971). Diarrhea in captive mule deer fawns attributed to *Escherichia coli*. *J. Wildl. Manage.* **35**, 205–209.

Krementz, D. G., and Ankney, C. D. (1986). Bioenergetics of egg production by female house sparrows. *Auk* **103**, 299–305.

Kurta, A., and Kunz, T. H. (1987). Size of bats at birth and maternal investment during pregnancy. *Symp. Zool. Soc. London* **57**, 79–106.

Kurta, A., Bell, G. P., Nagy, K. A., and Kunz, T. H. (1989). Energetics of pregnancy and lactation in free-ranging little brown bats (*Myotis lucifugus*). *Physiol. Zool.* **62**, 804–818.

Kurta, A., Kunz, T. H., and Nagy, K. A. (1990). Energetics and water flux of free-ranging big brown bats (*Eptesicus fuscus*) during pregnancy and lactation. *J. Mammal.* **71**, 59–65.

Lack, D. (1968). "Ecological Adaptations for Breeding Birds." Methuen, London.

Lang, E. M. (1963). Flamingoes raise their young on a liquid containing blood. *Experientia* **19**, 532–533.

Lecce, J. G., and Morgan, D. O. (1962). Effects of dietary regimen on cessation of intestinal absorption of large molecules (closure) in the neonatal pig and lamb. *J. Nutr.* **78**, 263–268.

Leitch, I., Hytten, F. E., and Billewicz, W. Z. (1959). The maternal and neonatal weights of some mammalia. *Proc. Zool. Soc. London* **133**, 11–28.

Leutenegger, W. (1973). Maternal-fetal weight relationships in primates. *Folia Primat.* **20**, 280–293.

Leutenegger, W. (1976). Allometry of neonatal size in eutherian mammals. *Nature (London)* **263**, 229–230.

Lhuillery, C., Martinent, L., DeMarne, Y., and Lecourtier, M. J. (1984). Food intake in captive leverets before weaning and the composition of the milk of the brown doe-hare (*Lepus europaeus*). *Comp. Biochem. Physiol.* **78A**, 73–76.

Linzell, J. L. (1972). Milk yield, energy loss in milk, and mammary gland weight in different species. *Dairy Sci. Abstr.* **34,** 351–360.

Macfarlane, W. V., Howard, B., and Siebert, B. D. (1969). Tritiated water in the measurement of milk intake and tissue growth of ruminants in the field. *Nature (London)* **221,** 578–579.

Martin, R. D. (1966). Tree shrews: Unique reproductive mechanism of systematic importance. *Science* **152,** 1402–1404.

Martin, R. D. (1984). Scaling effects and adaptive strategies in mammalian lactation. *Symp. Zool. Soc. London* **51,** 87–117.

Mattingly, D. K., and McClure, P. A. (1982). Energetics of reproduction in large-littered cotton rats (*Sigmodon hispidus*). *Ecology* **63,** 183–195.

McCoy, G. C., Reneau, J. K., Hunter, A. G., and Williams, J. B. (1970). Effects of diet and time on blood serum proteins in the newborn calf. *J. Dairy Sci.* **53,** 358–362.

McCullagh, K. G., and Widdowson, E. M. (1970). The milk of the African elephant. *Br. J. Nutr.* **24,** 109–117.

McCullagh, K. G., Lincoln, H. B., and Southgate, D. A. T. (1969). Fatty acid composition of milk fat of the African elephant. *Nature (London)* **222,** 493–494.

McLandress, M. R., and Raveling, D. G. (1981). Changes in diet and body composition of Canada geese before spring migration. *Auk* **98,** 65–79.

Mead, J. F., Alfin-Slater, R. B., Howton, D. R., and Popjak, G. (1985). "Lipids: Chemistry, biochemistry, and nutrition." Plenum Press, New York.

Meijer, T., Masman, D., and Daan, S. (1989). Energetics of reproduction in female kestrels. *Auk* **106,** 549–559.

Merchant, J., Green, B., Messer, M., and Newgrain, K. (1989). Milk composition in the red-necked wallaby, *Macropus rufogriseus banksianus* (Marsupialia). *Comp. Biochem. Physiol.* **93A,** 483–488.

Messer, M., Griffiths, M., and Green, B. (1984). Changes in milk carbohydrates and electrolytes during early lactation in the tammar wallaby, *Macropus eugenii. Aust. J. Biol. Sci.* **37,** 1–6.

Millar, J. S. (1977). Adaptive features of mammalian reproduction. *Evolution* **31,** 370–386.

Mover, H., Hellwing, S., and Ar, A. (1988). Energetic cost of gestation in the white-toothed shrew *Crocidura russula monacha* (Soricidae, Insectivora). *Physiol. Zool.* **61,** 17–25.

Mueller, C. C., and Sadleir, R. M. F. S. (1977). Changes in the nutrient composition of milk of black-tailed deer during lactation. *J. Mammal.* **58,** 421–423.

Muma, K. E., and Ankney, C. D. (1987). Variation in weight and composition of red-winged blackbird eggs. *Can. J. Zool.* **65,** 605–607.

Nicoll, M. E., and Thompson, S. D. (1987). Basal metabolic rates and energetics of reproduction in therian mammals: marsupials and placentals compared. *Symp. Zool. Soc. London* **57,** 7–27.

Nur, N. (1988). The cost of reproduction in birds: An examination of the evidence. *Ardea* **76,** 155–168.

Oftedal, O. T. (1980). Milk composition and formula selection for hand-rearing young animals. *Proc. Dr. Scholl Nutr. Conf.* **1,** 67–83.

Oftedal, O. T. (1984a). Milk composition, milk yield and energy output at peak lactation: A comparative review. *Symp. Zool. Soc. London* **51,** 33–85.

Oftedal, O. T. (1984b). Body size and reproductive strategy as correlates of milk energy output in lactating mammals. *Acta Zool. Fennica* **171,** 183–186.

Oftedal, O. T. (1985). Pregnancy and lactation. *In* "Bioenergetics of Wild Herbivores" (R. J. Hudson and R. G. White, eds.), pp. 215–238. CRC Press, Boca Raton, Florida.

Oftedal, O. T., and Gittleman, J. L. (1989). Patterns of energy output during reproduction in carnivores. *In* "Carnivore Behavior, Ecology, and Evolution" (J. L. Gittleman, ed.), pp. 355–378. Cornell Univ. Press, Ithaca, New York.

222   10. Reproductive Costs

Oftedal, O. T., Boness, D. J., and Tedman, R. A. (1987). The behavior, physiology, and anatomy of lactation in the Pinnipedia. *Current Mammalogy* **1**, 175–245.

Oftedal, O. T., Boness, D. J., and Bowen, W. D. (1988). The composition of hooded seal (*Cystophora cristata*) milk: An adaptation for postnatal fattening. *Can. J. Zool.* **66**, 318–322.

Parker, H., and Holm, H. (1990). Patterns of nutrients and energy expenditure in female common eiders nesting in the high arctic. *Auk* **107**, 660–668.

Parker, K. L., White, R. G., Gillingham, M. P., and Holleman, D. F. (1990). Comparison of energy metabolism in relation to daily activity and milk consumption by caribou and muskox neonates. *Can. J. Zool.* **68**, 106–114.

Partridge, G. G., Lobley, G. E., and Fordyce, R. A. (1986). Energy and nitrogen metabolism of rabbits during pregnancy, lactation, and concurrent pregnancy and lactation. *Br. J. Nutr.* **56**, 199–207.

Payne, P. R., and Wheeler, E. F. (1967). Comparative nutrition in pregnancy. *Nature (London)* **215**, 1134–1136.

Pettit, T. N., Nagy, K. A., Ellis, H. I., and Whittow, G. C. (1988). Incubation energetics of the Laysan albatross. *Oecologia* **74**, 546–550.

Pond, C. M. (1977). The significance of lactation in the evolution of mammals. *Evolution* **31**, 177–199.

Prévost, J., and Vilter, V. (1963). Histologie de la sécrétion oesophagienne du manchot empereur. *Proc. Int. Orithol. Congr.* **13**, 1085–1094.

Rahn, H., Paganelli, C. V., and Ar, A. (1975). Relation of avian egg weight to body weight. *Auk* **92**, 750–765.

Ramsay, M. A., and Dunbrack, R. L. (1986). Physiological constraints on life history phenomena: The example of small bear cubs at birth. *Am. Nat.* **127**, 735–743.

Raveling, D. G. (1979). The annual cycle of body composition of Canada geese with special reference to control of reproduction. *Auk* **96**, 234–252.

Reimers, E., Ringberg, T., and Sorumgard, R. (1982). Body composition of Svalbard reindeer. *Can. J. Zool.* **60**, 1812–1821.

Reineck, M. (1962). The rearing of abandoned sucklings of *Phoca vitulina*. *Int. Zoo Yearb.* **4**, 293–294.

Renfree, M. B., Meier, P., Teng, C., and Battaglia, F.C. (1981). Relationship between amino acid intake and accretion in a marsupial, *Macropus eugenii*. I. Total amino acid composition of the milk throughout pouch life. *Biol. Neonate* **40**, 29–37.

Renner, E., Schaafsma, G., and Scott, K.J. (1989). Micronutrients in milk. *In* "Micronutrients in Milk and Milk Based Food Products" (E. Renner, ed.), pp. 1–70. Elsevier Publ., New York.

Reuther, R.T. (1969). Growth and diet of young elephants in captivity. *Int. Zoo Yearb.* **9**, 168–178.

Ricklefs, R. E. (1974). Energetics of reproduction in birds. *In* "Avian Energetics" (R.A. Paynter, Jr, ed.), pp. 152–297. Publ. Nuttall Ornith. Club No. 15, Cambridge, Massachusetts.

Robbins, C. T. (1981). Estimation of the relative protein cost of reproduction in birds. *Condor* **83**, 177–179.

Robbins, C. T. (1983). "Wildlife Feeding and Nutrition." Academic Press, New York.

Robbins, C. T., and Moen, A. N. (1975a). Uterine composition and growth in pregnant white-tailed deer. *J. Wildl. Manage.* **39**, 684–691.

Robbins, C. T., and Robbins, B. L. (1979). Fetal and neonatal growth patterns and maternal reproductive effort in ungulates and subungulates. *Am. Nat.* **114**, 101–116.

Robbins, C. T., Podbielancik-Norman, R. S., Wilson, D. L., and Mould, E. D. (1981). Growth and nutrient consumption of elk calves compared to other ungulate species. *J. Wildl. Manage.* **45**, 172–186.

Robbins, C. T., Oftedal, O. T., and O'Rourke, K. I. (1987). Lactation, early nutrition, and hand-rearing of wild ungulates, with special reference to deer. *In* "Biology and Management of the Cervidae" (C. M. Wemmer, ed.), pp. 429–442. Smithsonian Inst. Press, Washington, D.C.

Roca, P., Sainz, F., Gonzalez, M., and Alemany, M. (1982). Energetic components in the unincubated egg fractions of several avian species. *Comp. Biochem. Physiol.* **72B**, 439–443.

Roca, P., Sainz, F., Gonzalez, M., and Alemany, M. (1984). Structure and composition of the eggs from several avian species. *Comp. Biochem. Physiol.* **77A**, 307–310.

Roudybush, T. E., Grau, C. R., Peterson, M. R., Ainley, D. G., Kirsch, K. V., Gilman, A. P., and Patten, S. M. (1979). Yolk formation in some charadriiform birds. *Condor* **81**, 293–298.

Russell, E.M. (1982). Patterns of parental care and parental investment in marsupials. *Biol. Rev.* **57**, 423–486.

Sadleir, R. M. F. S. (1980a). Milk yield of black-tailed deer. *J. Wildl. Manage.* **44**, 472–478.

Sadlier, R. M. F. S. (1980b). Energy and protein intake in relation to growth of suckling black-tailed deer fawns. *Can. J. Zool.* **58**, 1347–1354.

Sadlier, R. M. F. S. (1982). Energy consumption and subsequent partitioning in lactating black-tailed deer. *Can. J. Zool.* **60**, 382–386.

Sadlier, R. M. F. S. (1984). Ecological consequences of lactation. *Acta Zool. Fennica* **171**, 179–182.

Sawicka-Kapusta, K. (1970). Changes in the gross body composition and the caloric value of the common vole during their postnatal development. *Acta Theriol.* **15**, 67–79.

Sawicka-Kapusta, K. (1974). Changes in the gross body composition and energy value of the bank vole during their postnatal development. *Acta Theriol.* **19**, 27–54.

Smolenski, A. J., and Rose, R. W. (1988). Comparative lactation in two species of rat-kangaroo (*Marsupialia*). *Comp. Biochem. Physiol.* **90A**, 459–463.

Sotherland, P. R., and Rahn, H. (1987). On the composition of bird eggs. *Condor* **89**, 48–65.

Stack, M.H. (1985). "Energetics of Reproduction in the Big Brown Bat, *Eptesicus fuscus*." Doctoral Dissertation, Boston University.

Stephens, T. (1975). Nutrition of orphan marsupials. *Aust. Vet. J.* **51**, 453–458.

Stewart, R. E. A., and Lavigne, D.M. (1980). Neonatal growth of Northwest Atlantic harp seals, *Pagophilus groenlandicus*. *J. Mammal.* **61**, 670–680.

Stirling, I., and McEwan, E. H. (1975). The caloric value of whole ringed seals (*Phoca hispida*) in relation to polar bear (*Ursus maritimus*) ecology and hunting behavior. *Can. J. Zool.* **53**, 1021–1027.

Thompson, S. D. (1991). Energetics of gestation and lactation in small mammals: Basal metabolic rate and the limits of energy use. *In* "Mammalian Energetics: Interdisciplinary Views of Metabolism and Reproduction" (T. Tomasi and T. Horton, eds.), in press. Cornell Univ. Press, Ithaca, New York.

Trillmich, F. (1986). Are endotherms emancipated? Some considerations on the cost of reproduction. *Oecologia* **69**, 631–633.

Trillmich, F., and Lechner, R. (1986). Milk of the Galapagos fur seal and sea lion, with a comparison of the milk of eared seals (*Otariidae*). *J. Zool.* **209**, 271–277.

Vainisi, S. J., Edelhauser, H. F., Wolf, E. D, Cotlier, E., and Reeser, F. (1980). Nutritional cataracts in timber wolves. *Proc. Dr. Scholl Nutr. Conf.* **1**, 3–21.

Vandeputte-Poma, J. (1980). Feeding, growth and metabolism of the pigeon, *Columba livia domestica*: Duration and role of crop milk feeding. *J. Comp. Physiol.* **135**, 97–99.

Vleck, C. M. (1981). Energetic cost of incubation in the zebra finch. *Condor* **83**, 229–237.

Vleck, C. M., Hoyt, D. F., and Vleck, D. (1979). Metabolism of avian embryos: patterns in altricial and precocial birds. *Physiol. Zool.* **52**, 363–377.

Vleck, C. M., Vleck, D., and Hoyt, D. F. (1980). Patterns of metabolism and growth in avian embryos. *Am. Zool.* **20**, 405–416.

Walcott, P. J., and Messer, M. (1980). Intestinal lactase (β-galactosidase) and other glycosidase activities in suckling and adult tammar wallabies (*Macropus eugenii*). *Aust. J. Biol. Sci.* **33**, 521–530.

Walsberg, G. E. (1983). Avian ecological energetics. *In* "Avian Biology, Vol. VII" (D. S. Farner, J. R. King, and K. C. Parkes, eds.), pp. 161–220. Academic Press, New York.

Warham, J. (1983). The composition of petrel eggs. *Condor* **85**, 194–199.

Weathers, W. W. (1985). Energy cost of incubation in the canary. *Comp. Biochem. Physiol.* **81A**, 411–413.

Weiner, J. (1987). Limits to energy budget and tactics in energy investments during reproduction in the Djungarian hamster (*Phodopus sungorus sungorus Pallas 1770*). *Symp. Zool. Soc. London* **57**, 167–187.

White, J. M. (1975). Milk yield in lines of mice selected for growth or maternal ability. *Can. J. Genet. Cytol.* **17**, 263–268.

Widdowson, E. M. (1950). Chemical composition of newly born mammals. *Nature (London)* **166**, 626–628.

Widdowson, E. M. (1984). Milk and the newborn animal. *Proc. Nutr. Soc.* **43**, 87–100.

Widdowson, E. M., and McCance, R. A. (1955). Physiological undernutrition in the newborn guinea-pig. *Br. J. Nutr.* **9**, 316–321.

Williams, A. J., Siegfried, W. R., and Cooper, J. (1982). Egg composition and hatchling precocity in seabirds. *Ibis* **124**, 456–470.

Williams, J. B., and Dwinnel, B. (1990). Field metabolism of free-living female savannah sparrows during incubation: A study using doubly labeled water. *Physiol. Zool.* **63**, 353–372.

Worthington, A. H. (1989). Adaptations for avian frugivory: Assimilation efficiency and gut transit time of *Manacus vitellinus* and *Pipra mentalis*. *Oecologia* **80**, 381–389.

Worthy, G. A. J., and Lavigne, D. M. (1983). Changes in energy stores during postnatal development of the harp seal, *Phoca groenlandica*. *J. Mammal.* **64**, 89–96.

Yadav, M. (1971). The transmission of antibodies across the gut of pouch-young marsupials. *Immunology* **21**, 839–851.

Zeveloff, S. I., and Boyce, M. S. (1980). Parental investment and mating systems in mammals. *Evolution* **34**, 973–982.

11

Productive Costs

During the last half century there has been a striking change in the study of wild animals and their relation to the environment. Descriptive natural history, however interesting, is increasingly being replaced by quantitative information on animal function. This change to a quantitative approach . . . is essential to a proper understanding . . . of animals in the wild. . . .

SCHMIDT-NIELSEN, 1977

I. BODY GROWTH

Growth is the process whereby an animal incorporates into its molecular structure a portion of the external chemical environment. Growth in all animals, particularly wildlife occupying seasonal environments, has both positive and negative phases. Nutrient requirements for growth are dependent on the rate and composition of the gain. Growth rates per se are not adequate to evaluate the requirement because the composition of the gain or loss varies. Consequently, while many field ecologists have monitored body weights, the nutritionist must also understand body composition.

A. Body Composition

The major components of the ingesta-free animal body are fat, water, protein, and ash or minerals. Although carbohydrates are of immense importance in animal metabolism, their total concentration is always less than 1% even though there is variation with time since feeding, latitude, and animal age and species (Galster and Morrison, 1975; Okon and Ekanem, 1976; Spinage and Shelley, 1981; Blem, 1990). The two major animal carbohydrates are glucose and glycogen. Their concentrations range from 0.08 to 0.18% in sparrows (Farner *et al.*, 1961; Dolnik, 1970) and from 0.06 to 0.56% in ground squirrels (Bintz *et al.*, 1979).

Body lipids function as an energy reserve, as structural elements in cell and

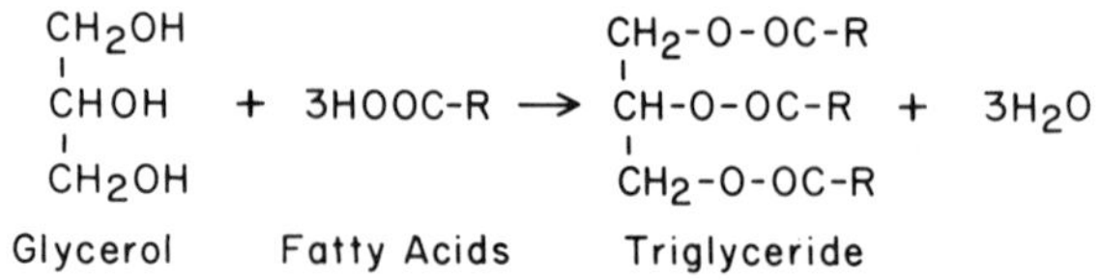

$$CH_2OH \qquad\qquad CH_2-O-OC-R$$
$$|\qquad\qquad\qquad\qquad |$$
$$CHOH \ + \ 3HOOC-R \ \rightarrow \ CH-O-OC-R \ + \ 3H_2O$$
$$|\qquad\qquad\qquad\qquad |$$
$$CH_2OH \qquad\qquad CH_2-O-OC-R$$

Glycerol   Fatty Acids   Triglyceride

Fig. 11.1 Simplistic construction of a triglyceride. R refers to the carbon chain of the fatty acid.

organelle membranes, and as sterol hormones. Because lipids can be stored as relatively nonhydrated adipose tissue containing 2–15% free water (King, 1961; Odum *et al.*, 1965; Worthy and Lavigne, 1983b), eight times more calories per unit of weight can be stored as fat than as hydrated carbohydrates (Allen, 1976). Thus, whereas carbohydrates are a major energy reserve for plants, fat storage is essential for active animals.

Lipid energy reserves are primarily triglycerides. Triglycerides are synthesized from glycerol and three fatty acids (Fig. 11.1; Table 11.1). The energy content of fatty acids increases with molecular weight and degree of saturation. Saturation refers to the absence of internal double bonds and, correspondingly, increased hydrogenation. Thus, stearic acid (18 carbons: 0 double bonds) has a higher energy content (9.48 kcal/g) than either oleic acid (18:1, 9.40 kcal/g) or palmitic acid (16:0, 9.30 kcal/g).

TABLE 11.1

Major Naturally Occurring Fatty Acids Important in Animal Nutrition

Molecular formula	Common name	Molecular formula	Common name	Number of double bonds
Saturated fatty acids		*Unsaturated fatty acids*		
$C_2H_4O_2$	Acetic	$C_{16}H_{30}O_2$	Palmitoleic	1
$C_3H_6O_2$	Propionic	$C_{18}H_{34}O_2$	Oleic	1
$C_4H_8O_2$	Butyric	$C_{18}H_{32}O_2$	Linoleic	2
$C_6H_{12}O_2$	Caproic	$C_{18}H_{30}O_2$	Linolenic	3
$C_8H_{16}O_2$	Caprylic	$C_{20}H_{32}O_2$	Arachidonic	4
$C_9H_{18}O_2$	Pelargonic			
$C_{10}H_{20}O_2$	Capric			
$C_{12}H_{24}O_2$	Lauric			
$C_{14}H_{28}O_2$	Myristic			
$C_{16}H_{32}O_2$	Palmitic			
$C_{18}H_{36}O_2$	Stearic			
$C_{20}H_{40}O_2$	Arachidic			
$C_{22}H_{44}O_2$	Behenic			
$C_{24}H_{48}O_2$	Lignoceric			

The physical and chemical characteristics of triglycerides are determined by the constituent fatty acids. The major fatty acids of body triglycerides are palmitic, stearic, oleic, linoleic, linolenic, and arachidonic acids. However, the fatty acid spectra of the body's triglycerides can be influenced by site of sample, diet, type of gastrointestinal digestion, environmental temperature, photoperiod, and species (Gale *et al.*, 1969; Schultz and Ferguson, 1974; Zar, 1977; Bishop *et al.*, 1983; Reidinger *et al.*, 1985; Blem, 1990). For example, the fatty acid content of triglycerides in the appendages of cold-adapted animals increases in unsaturation distally. Because the melting point and therefore the softness of a fat at a given temperature is dependent on the molecular weight and degree of saturation of its fatty acids (melting points ranging from 70°C for stearic acid [18:0] to −49°C for arachidonic acid [20:4]), increasing unsaturation of the fatty acids in heterothermic appendages is essential for the fats to remain soft and metabolizable.

The concentration of water and fat are inversely proportional to each other in most animals (Fig. 11.2). The inverse proportionality between fat and water is not true of very young animals. Young animals have a water content in the fat-free tissues that is disproportionately higher than that of adults, which subsequently decreases during growth to an asymptotic concentration termed chemical maturity (Moulton, 1923). The water content of the fat-free tissues of young birds and mammals is higher in altricial (85.9 ± 1.8%) than precocial species (77.1 ± 2.4%) (See Table 10.4; Sugden and Harris, 1972; Ricklefs, 1979; Campbell and Leatherland, 1980; Kaminski and Konarzewski, 1984; Tatner, 1984; Williams and Prints, 1986). These differences are related to the differing functional maturity of the muscles at hatching or birth in altricial and procncial neonates. The water content of the fat-free body of chemically mature mammals (72.7%) is higher than in birds (68.3%) (Fig. 11.2). This difference is entirely due to the fact that hair and feathers are included in these whole-body analyses. Because hair and feathers contain very little water and the weight of feathers on birds is at least 60% greater than the weight of hair on mammals, the total fat-free tissue of the bird has a lower water concentration than that of mammals. The remaining dry, fat-free body of the chemically mature mammal contains 81.9 ± 3.6% protein and 18.1% ash ($N = 9$) and the bird 86.0 ± 3.4% protein and 14.0% ash ($N = 10$) (sources from Fig. 11.2). The weight of ash in mammals and birds is not significantly different and can be predicted by the equation $Y = 0.035X^{1.02}$ ($N = 18$, $R^2 = 0.99$), where X is body weight(g) and Y is ash weight(g). The similarity in ash weight between birds and mammals and the exponent slightly greater than 1 are expected, as mammal and bird skeletal weights (Y,g) are also not significantly different and are predicted by an exponent slightly greater than 1 ($Y = 0.063X^{1.08}$ where X is body weight in grams) (Prange *et al.*, 1979). Penguins have a lower body ash content (1.4 to 3.0%; Williams

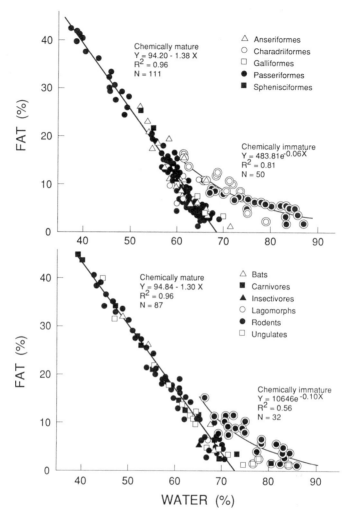

Fig. 11.2 Relationship between body water and fat content in birds and mammals. The circled points in each graph are chemically immature animals (i.e., for precocial birds and mammals — hatchlings and neonates; for altricial birds and mammals — nestlings). (**Birds** — Odum, 1960; Johnston, 1964; Gifford and Odum, 1965; Yarbrough and Johnston, 1965; Zimmerman, 1965; Helms *et al.*, 1967; Helms and Smythe, 1969; Myrcha and Pinowski, 1969; Szwykowska, 1969; Child and Marshall, 1970; Myrcha and Pinowski, 1970; Yarbrough, 1970; Holmes, 1976; Williams *et al.*, 1977; Carey *et al.*, 1978; Ricklefs, 1979; Campbell and Leatherland, 1980; Olson and Kendeigh, 1980; Ricklefs and White, 1981; Thomas and Popko, 1981; Kaminski and Konarzewski, 1984; Dawson and Marsh, 1986; Perry *et al.*, 1986; Jones, 1987; Taylor and Konarzewski, 1989; Hissa *et al.*, 1990; **Mammals** — Hayward, 1965; Baker *et al.*, 1968; Myrcha, 1968; Sawicka-Kapusta, 1968, 1970; Robbins, 1973; Morton *et al.*, 1974; Sawicka-Kapusta, 1974; Holleman and Dieterich, 1975; Schreiber and Johnson, 1975; Stirling and McEwan, 1975; Galster and Morrison, 1976; Fehrenbacher and Fleharty, 1976; O'Farrell and Studier, 1976; Harper *et al.*, 1978; Holleman and Dieterich, 1978; Churchfield, 1981; Huot, 1982; Reimers *et al.*, 1982).

TABLE 11.2

Relationship between Adult Body Weight (X in g) and Growth Rate (Y in g/day) in Neonatal Birds and Mammals

Group	Regression equation	N	R^2
Altricial land birds	$Y = 0.21X^{0.72}$	13	0.97
Precocial land birds	$Y = 0.02X^{0.91}$	4	0.91
Marsupials	$Y = 0.0033X^{0.82}$	4	0.97
Placental Mammals	$Y = 0.0326X^{0.75}$	160	0.94
Cetaceans	$Y = 0.0447X^{0.75}$	3	0.99
Chiropterans	$Y = 0.0526X^{0.65}$	10	0.63
Carnivores			
Fissipeds	$Y = 0.0543X^{0.70}$	23	0.86
Pinnipeds	$Y = 0.0194X^{0.84}$	11	0.48
Insectivores	$Y = 0.0522X^{0.67}$	8	0.76
Lagomorphs	$Y = 0.1262X^{0.61}$	9	0.82
Primates	$Y = 0.2165X^{0.35}$	32	0.66
Rodents	$Y = 0.0408X^{0.71}$	60	0.90
Ungulate and subungulates	$Y = 0.0766X^{0.71}$	22	0.94
Artiodactyls	$Y = 0.0721X^{0.71}$	17	0.76

Sources: Ricklefs, 1968, 1973; Case, 1978; Robbins *et al.,* 1981; Kirkwood, 1985; Pontier *et al.,* 1989.

et al., 1977) than do other birds, which reflects the lessened need of skeletal mass for support and locomotion in water (Reynolds, 1977).

B. Growth Rates

Growth of an individual over time is often described by a sigmoid curve in which most of the growth occurs during a relatively linear intermediate phase. The maximum growth rates of young animals during the linear phase increase as power functions of adult body weight (Table 11.2; Fig. 11.3). Neonates of larger species grow at faster absolute rates but slower relative rates in comparison to adult body weight than do neonates of smaller species. Altricial birds grow at rates twice that of similarly sized precocial birds and placental mammals. Although precocial and altricial mammals grow at approximately the same rates, marsupials and primates have very slow growth rates and pinniped carnivores have very high rates relative to the adult body weight. The maximum growth rates of young animals are apparently established by genetically determined physiological limits to cellular metabolism (Ricklefs, 1968, 1973). Genetically determined growth rates within each species are evolved relative to the selective pressures of infant mortality and nutrient availability.

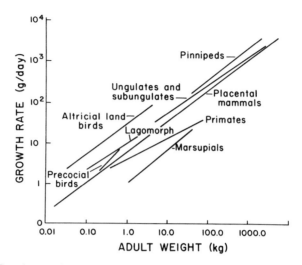

Fig. 11.3 Growth rates of neonatal birds and mammals as a function of adult weight. (Data from sources listed in Table 11.2.)

C. Growth Requirements

Growth requirements are the mathematical description of the rate at which matter and energy are accumulated in the developing organism. Energy requirements are a function of the chemical energy content of the different body constituents. Body water and ash have no available chemical energy (i.e., 0 kcal/g). However, anhydrous body protein and fat average 5.42 ± 0.12 ($N = 15$) and 9.11 ± 0.26 kcal/g ($N = 23$), respectively, in wild birds and mammals (Odum *et al.*, 1965; Baker *et al.*, 1968; Sawicka-Kapusta, 1968; Barrett, 1969; Ewing *et al.*, 1970; Johnston, 1970; Pucek, 1973; Fedyk, 1974; Robbins *et al.*, 1974; Kaufman and Kaufman, 1975; Stirling and McEwan, 1975; Clay et. al., 1979). Consequently, the energy content of the gain or loss can range from 0 (i.e., water or minerals) to 9 kcal/g (fat) depending on the composition of the weight change.

The caloric content of the gain during growth in wildlife increases curvilinearly as body weight increases (Figs. 11.4 and 11.5). Because the body water content decreases and the fat content increases during growth, the caloric content of the gain must also increase. Because few wild animals accumulate large amounts of fat, the energy requirement for growth of young animals tends to be well below the theoretical maximum of 9 kcal/g. The potential for fat accumulation in a species is an evolutionarily determined balancing process between the positive benefits of a reduced chance of starvation when food is not available and the negative energetic costs of maintaining and transporting the extra weight,

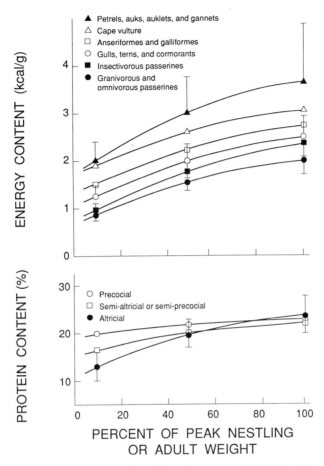

Fig. 11.4 Energy and protein content of the gain in various groups of birds. [Leach's storm-petrel, least auk, South Georgia diving petrel, common diving petrel, little auk, and northern gannet (Ricklefs *et al.*, 1980; Montevecchi *et al.*, 1984; Taylor and Konarzewski, 1989; Roby, 1991); cape vulture (Komen, 1991); arctic tern, common tern, sooty tern, and herring gull (Dunn and Brisbin, 1980; Ricklefs and White, 1981; Klaassen *et al.*, 1989); double-crested cormorant (Dunn, 1975); western bluebird, ash-throated flycatcher, long-billed marsh wren, meadow pipit, house martin, cactus wren, blue-throated bee-eater, Pacific swallow, and white-bellied swiftlet (Kale, 1965; Ricklefs, 1975; Skar *et al.*, 1975; Bryant and Gardiner, 1979; Bryant and Hails, 1983; Mock *et al.*, 1991); lesser snow geese, black-bellied tree duck, lesser scaup, and Japanese quail (Sugden and Harris, 1972; Brisbin and Tally, 1973; Cain, 1976; Aubin *et al.*, 1986); ring dove (Brisbin, 1969); rufous-winged sparrow, European tree-sparrow, house sparrow, starling, savannah sparrow, and jackdaw (Myrcha and Pinowski, 1969; Myrcha *et al.*, 1973; Blem, 1975; Austin and Ricklefs, 1977; Kaminski and Konarzewski, 1984; Williams and Prints, 1986).] Altricial birds include passerines, cape vulture, and double-crested cormorant; semi-altricial and semi-precocial birds include auks, petrels, and terns; and precocial birds include waterfowl and quail. Where standard deviations overlap and would be confusing, only one side is shown.

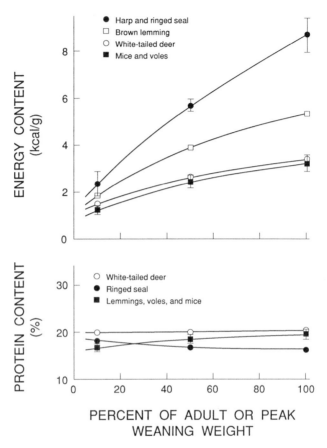

Fig. 11.5 Energy and protein content of the gain in various wild mammals. (Data from Sawicka-Kapusta, 1970; Robbins, 1973; Sawicka-Kapusta, 1974; Stirling and McEwan, 1975; Kaufman and Kaufman, 1975, 1977; Holleman and Dieterich, 1978; Worthy and Lavigne, 1983a.) The X-axis is percentage of adult weight for deer, mice, voles, lemmings, and ringed seals and percentage of peak weaning weight for harp and ringed seals.

therefore increasing the predation risk due either to increased foraging requirements or the reduced efficiency or speed of fleeing from predators (Lima, 1986; Rogers, 1987; Thomas, 1987). Consequently, fat accumulation is highest in species consuming food resources that are unpredictable in their availability. For young birds, the predictability of food post-fledging appears to be as important in determining the level of fat accumulation as food predictability pre-fledging (Bryant and Hails, 1983; Roby, 1991). For example, the energy content of the gain is highest in fish or plankton-feeding seabirds (petrels, auklets, and gannets) whose parents provide no post-fledging care as the young begin feeding on food that may be either difficult to catch or temporarily unavailable due to storms (Ricklefs *et al.*, 1980; Montevecchi *et al.*, 1984; Roby, 1991). Cormorants, gulls, terns, and other seabirds with extensive post-fledging parental care accumulate much smaller lipid reserves and, therefore, have a lower energetic cost of growth than those without parental care (Dunn, 1975; Burger, 1981; Roby, 1991). Amongst aerial-feeding insectivorous birds, lipid storage and the energetic cost of nestling growth are highest in (1) those species feeding in higher aerial strata where insect abundance is the least predictable due to weather and (2) those species with no post-fledging parental care (Bryant and Hails, 1983). Vultures that also feed on an unpredictable food resource (i.e., dead animals) tend to accumulate moderate fat reserves during the nestling period (Komen, 1991). The lowest fat accumulation and energy content of the gain occurs in granivorous and omnivorous passerines that normally have the most predictable, easiest to acquire food resource.

The protein requirement for avian growth depends on the functional maturity of the muscles at hatching (Fig. 11.4). Although the protein content per unit of gain is initially lower in altricial than precocial species, growth during the later nesting stages of altricial species contains the same protein concentration (± 23%) as in precocial birds.

The energy content of growth in young mammals is highest in seals, intermediate in the brown lemming, and least in deer, mice, and voles (Fig. 11.5). Many newborn seals store a great deal of fat during a relatively short but extraordinarily intense lactation (Stirling and McEwan, 1975; Worthy and Lavigne, 1983a; Bowen *et al.*, 1987). Blubber accumulated during lactation is metabolized during a post-weaning fast in which the young seals are completely abandoned by their mothers and must learn to catch their own food, frequently in a relatively cold environment. Thus, the strategy of these seals in provisioning the young prior to a parent-free, post-weaning process is similar to the marine birds that have no post-fledging parental care. White-tailed deer, old-field mice, common voles, and bank voles accumulate relatively little fat during neonatal growth. Thus, the energetic cost of growth ranges from 1.5 to 3.5 kcal/g. For most tropical and temperate mammalian herbivores, granivores, and omnivores that are born during times of seasonal food abundance, the predictability of these food resources minimizes the need for extensive fat deposition. In addition to these changes during early growth, daily and seasonal cycles of fat deposition occur in many wild animals as a prelude to times when energy intake will be less than energy expenditure, such as during daily gain–loss cycles or in preparation for migration, hibernation, or reproduction.

The protein content of growth in terrestrial mammals is similar to that occurring in altricial and precocial birds (Fig. 11.5). For example, the protein content of the gain in the precocial deer starts at 20%, whereas the altricial rodents begin at 16%, but both increase to 23% in the adult. Because of the extensive fat deposition occurring in the ringed seal, the protein content of the gain actually decreased during growth. Thus, for both young birds and mammals, the fat and energy content of the gain are much more variable than the protein deposition.

D. Weight Loss and Starvation

Weight loss during long-term fasting in birds and mammals that accumulate large fat reserves has three phases (Le Maho et al., 1981; Cherel et al., 1987, 1988; Groscolas, 1988). Phase I is a relatively short period characterized by rapid weight loss, emptying of the gastrointestinal tract, very little fat loss, and primarily glycogen and protein utilization to meet energy requirements. Phase II is a very long, constant weight loss that is much slower than in phase I. The reduced rate of weight loss is due to a shift to primarily fat utilization, reduced protein loss (protein-sparing), and energy conservation by reducing basal metabolism and activity. The duration of this phase depends on the initial body fat content as fat represents more than 80% of the energy mobilized (Fig. 11.6A). At the end of phase II, most of the reserve fat stores have been mobilized. Consequently, phase III is a period of increasing protein utilization to meet energy requirements and, therefore, rapid weight loss. Because the energy content of the weight loss can range from over 6 kcal/g when fat is the main energy reserve to as little as 2 kcal/g when protein or glycogen are used (Fig. 11.6B), the composition of the weight loss is a major determinant of the rate of weight loss. Animals can recover from early phase III starvation although later stages become irreversible. Animals that have starved to death will contain a small amount (0.2 to 1.3% of body weight) of nonmobilizable, structural lipids (Newton, 1969; Ward, 1969; Wyndham, 1980; Reimers et al., 1982).

For many small birds and mammals that store very little fat, the three phases of starvation either do not occur or they occur over a very short time span (hours). For example, most nonhibernating small mammals and birds can survive only one to three days of fasting (Gyug and Millar, 1980; Jones, 1987; Jenni and Jenni-Eiermann, 1987; Bronson, 1987; Mutze, 1990; Blem, 1990). In some of these animals, winter night-time survival is enough of a challenge that fasting endurance must be increased by becoming hypothermic to reduce energy expenditure and by feeding just prior to roosting to increase the body's total reserves. For these animals, ice storms, crusted snow, or other vicissitudes that remove the food supply can produce sudden and extensive mortality. Because larger animals generally store more fat, have a lower metabolic rate per unit of weight, and have much colder lower critical temperatures, survival times generally increase with body weight (Lindstedt and Boyce, 1985). Hares and some

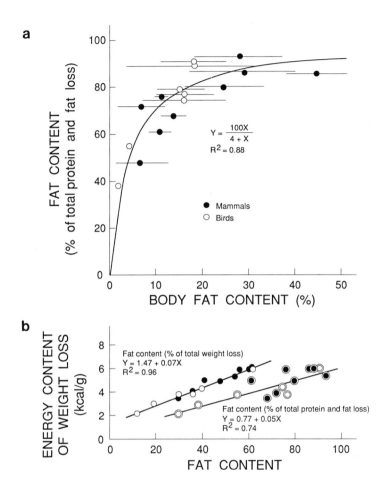

Fig. 11.6 (a) Relative contribution of fat to the combined fat and protein losses during prolonged starvation as a function of total body fat concentration. Because glycogen is readily catabolized during the initial phase of starvation, fat and protein are the only significant sources of energy thereafter. The drop in fat utilization at lower body fat concentrations corresponds to a shift from phase II to phase III starvation. Data are mean and range for body fat content during weight loss in each study. (b) Energy content of the weight loss as a function of the relative contribution of fat to that loss. (Data from Galster and Morrison, 1976; Williams *et al.*, 1977; Bintz and Mackin, 1980; Torbit, 1981; Le Maho *et al.*, 1981; Reimers *et al.*, 1982; Huot, 1982; Dunn et al.,1982; Worthy and Lavigne, 1983a,b; Robin *et al.*, 1988; Groscolas, 1988; DelGiudice *et al.*, 1990; Groscolas *et al.*, 1991.)

grouse can survive fasting for three days to over a week (Whittaker and Thomas, 1983; Mortensen *et al.*, 1983; Thomas, 1987; Hissa *et al.*, 1990).

E. Indirect Indices of Body Composition

Because body composition by whole body grinding is inappropriate for many studies, hundreds of investigators have attempted to develop indirect indices of body composition or condition (Kirkpatrick, 1980). Most of the indices are based on morphometric measurements of the body or its parts or chemical analysis of blood or urine. Many of the studies report regressions with very high coefficients of determination. However, because most have unacceptable high standard errors and frequently are not supported by independent tests on other populations, virtually none of the current indices offer the type of precision necessary for detailed nutritional ecology studies.

The best method to determine body composition in the living animal is tritiated or deuterated water dilution. Fat, protein, and ash can be estimated accurately once body water content is known. Although tritium is radioactive and, thus, requires special permits, deuterium is stable, readily available, relatively cheap, and only slightly more difficult to analyze than tritium. However, because water dilution is not an instantaneous measurement (as it requires blood or urine sampling and later laboratory analyses), there continues to be a need for a fast, but accurate index of body composition. Two of the more recent techniques are bioelectrical impedance analysis (BIA) and total body electrical conductivity (TOBEC) (Fiorotto *et al.*, 1987; Lukaski, 1987; Walsberg, 1988; Hall *et al.*, 1989; Castro *et al.*, 1990). BIA and TOBEC measure the electrical conductivity of the body and are based on the observation that the conductivity of lipids is 4 to 5% that of lean tissue, body fluids, and bone. Thus, the measure of total body conductivity can provide an estimate of body fat content. The equipment is suitable for field use and provides an estimate of body fat content within minutes. While the technique appears very promising, the conductivity value is very sensitive to small changes in animal position and muscle tone and, thus, requires considerable training.

II. PELAGE AND PLUMAGE

Hair and feathers are of interest to the nutritionist because of their role in thermoregulation and the need to quantify the additional nutrients necessary for their growth and replacement. Molt, or the periodic replacement of pelage or plumage, can be partial or complete, with from one to three molts per year occurring in various birds or mammals (Ling, 1970; King, 1973). Single annual molts are most common in aquatic animals in which wear or abrasion are minimal and seasonal variations in environmental temperature are limited. Most animals have two molts per year.

Both hair and feathers are primarily protein. For example, degreased hair is 98.3% protein (Robbins *et al.*, 1974; Torbit, 1981), and feathers are 93–98.5% protein (Nitsan *et al.*, 1981; Murphy and King, 1982, 1986; King and Murphy, 1987; Murphy *et al.*, 1990). The principal protein of these structures is keratin. Keratins are resistant to digestion by vertebrate gastrointestinal enzymes and are insoluble in dilute acids and bases, water, and organic solvents. One of the unique characteristics of many keratins is their high concentration relative to other plant and animal proteins of the sulfur-containing amino acid cystine— 6.7–8.9% in feather keratin, 8.0–9.5% in porcupine quills, and 10.5–15.7% in horn keratins as compared to 0–2.9% in plant proteins and 0–6.3% in other animal proteins (Block and Bolling, 1951; Ward and Lundgren, 1954; Harrap and Woods, 1967; Newton, 1968; Frenkel and Gillespie, 1976; Nitsan *et al.*, 1981; Murphy and King, 1982; Murphy *et al.*, 1990). Degreased feathers and hair average 5.3 kcal/g (Murphy and King, 1982; Robbins, unpublished).

Because feathers and hair grow at relatively constant rates throughout the molt, the requirement can be estimated by dividing the energy and protein retained by the length of the molt. Total feather weight on birds averages 6.3% of body weight [$Y = 0.09X^{0.95}$, where Y is feather weight (g) and X is body weight (g) (Turcek, 1966)], whereas hair weight on mammals averages only 2.0% ($Y = 0.035X^{0.92}$; Smuts *et al.*, 1932; Robbins, 1973; Holleman and Dieterich, 1978; Torbit, 1981). Thus, the lower conductivity of birds relative to mammals (Chapter 8) is, in part, due to more insulation on birds than mammals. While hair weight and composition are probably accurate estimators of the cost of molt in mammals, feathers account for as little as 50% of the nitrogen and 80% of the sulfur retained by the molting bird. Some of the rest of the nitrogen and sulfur are used to synthesize scales of the legs, the horny covering of the beak, and feather sheaths that encase and protect feathers during their growth. Feather sheaths are the most important of these additional structures as they account for approximately 20% of the new plumage mass (Murphy and King, 1986; King and Murphy, 1990).

Molting by birds increases their daily protein requirement from 43 to 76% above the maintenance cost (Murphy and King, 1986; Heitmeyer, 1988). The energetic cost of molting includes both the energy retained in new tissue and any increase in basal metabolism. The actual energy retained in the new feathers of passerines is equivalent to only 5.3% of BMR or 1.8% of the daily energy expenditure (Murphy and King, 1992). The additional heat loss in passerines ranges from 5 to 35% higher than the nonmolting level (King, 1980). Resting metabolism of penguins averages 41% higher in molting than nonmolting birds. Molting in penguins is a very intense process as the birds remain out of water during the entire 12 to 34 days, do not feed, and, therefore, lose from 39 to

45% of their initial body weight (Brown, 1985; Baudinette *et al.*, 1986; Gales *et al.*, 1988; Adams and Brown, 1990). The increased resting metabolism is due to the inefficiency of tissue mobilization and feather synthesis and increased thermoregulatory costs due to the reduced insulation. Feather and probably hair synthesis are very inefficient energetic processes (Murphy and King, 1984). Thus, the total daily energetic cost (energy retained plus elevated metabolism) of feather synthesis averages about 60% of BMR or 20% of the daily energy expenditure (Murphy and King, 1992).

III. ANTLERS

Dead, oven-dried antlers contain 54.0 ± 2.3% ash, 45.0% protein, 1.0% fat, and 2.53 kcal/g (Rush, 1932; Chaddock, 1940; Ullrey *et al.*, 1975; Hyvarinen *et al.*, 1977). Because antlers grow as much as 130 g dry matter/day in moose (Huxley, 1931; Chapman, 1975), large amounts of energy and matter can be accumulated in these structures. However, antler growth occurs at the time when forage resources are most abundant, and thus antlers are probably not a significant ecological cost.

IV. DISEASE AND INJURY

The interaction of nutrition and disease has not been investigated thoroughly in any species (Chandra and Newberne, 1977). While scientists working with domestic animals can often medicate sick animals to minimize the disease process, the ecologist frequently can do little to control or reduce diseases. Since virtually all wildlife carry disease or parasitic organisms throughout life, wildlife nutritionists must increase their attempts to understand the nutritional and ecological implications. Because the additional energy or matter requirements directly associated with the very small weight of most disease organisms are minimal, alterations in host metabolic processes will be far more important. However, some parasitic infections are exceptions as their weight and metabolic demands are significant (Arendt, 1985). In most cases, malnutrition and the course of an infectious disease act synergistically to reduce host resistance and increase the detrimental consequences.

Most disease or injury processes markedly increase energy and nitrogen metabolism. For example, fever is the overt expression of the altered energy metabolism (Richards *et al.*, 1978). Energy expenditure increases from 7 to 33% during the healing of bone fractures and up to 125% following severe burns. Urinary nitrogen and energy excretion are increased and digestibilities decreased by several parasitic and bacterial infections (Arman and Hopcraft, 1971; Seed *et al.*, 1982; Hall and Seed, 1984; Munger and Karasov, 1989). Although such losses are significant, they are often exacerbated by reductions in food intake. Thus, understanding the nutritional impact of a disease process in wildlife is far more complex than simply identifying and quantifying infectious organisms and will require the synergistic expertise of both nutritionists and those studying infectious diseases (Chandra and Newberne, 1977).

REFERENCES

Adams, N. J., and Brown, C. R. (1990). Energetics of molt in penguins. *In* "Penguin Biology" (L. S. Davis and J. T. Darby, eds.), pp. 297–315. Academic Press, San Diego.

Allen, W. V. (1976). Biochemical aspects of lipid storage and utilization in animals. *Am. Zool.* **16,** 631–647.

Arendt, W. J. (1985). *Philornis* ectoparasitism of pearly-eyed thrashers. I. Impact on growth and development of nestlings. *Auk* **102,** 270–280.

Arman, P., and Hopcraft, D. (1971). The effect of disease on nitrogen excretion in the hartebeest. *Proc. Nutr. Soc.* **30,** 65A–66A.

Aubin, A. E., Dunn, E. H., and MacInnes, C. D. (1986). Growth of lesser snow geese on arctic breeding grounds. *Condor* **88,** 365–370.

Austin, G. T., and Ricklefs, R. E. (1977). Growth and development of the rufous-winged sparrow (*Aimophila carpalis*). *Condor* **79,** 37–50.

Baker, W. W., Marshall, S. G., and Baker, V. B. (1968). Autumn fat deposition in the evening bat (*Nycticeius humeralis*). *J. Mammal.* **49,** 314–317.

Barrett, G. W. (1969). Bioenergetics of a captive least shrew, *Cryptotis parva. J. Mammal.* **50,** 629–630.

Baudinette, R. V., Gill, P., and O'Driscoll, M. (1986). Energetics of the little penguin, *Eudyptula minor*: Temperature regulation, the calorigenic effect of food, and moulting. *Aust. J. Zool.* **34,** 35–45.

Bintz, G. L., and Mackin, W. W. (1980). The effect of water availability on tissue catabolism during starvation in Richardson's ground squirrels. *Comp. Biochem. Physiol.* **65A,** 181–186.

Bintz, G. L., Rosebery, H. W., and Bintz, L. B. (1979). Glycogen levels in field and laboratory-acclimated Richardson ground squirrels. *Comp. Biochem. Physiol.* **62A,** 339–342.

Bishop, D. G., Ritz, D. A., Hosie, G. W., Kenrick, J. R., and Olley, J. (1983). Fatty acid composition of the lipids of *Puffinus tenuirostris* (Temminck) in relation to its diet. *J. Exp. Mar. Biol. Ecol.* **71,** 17–26.

Blem, C. R. (1975). Energetics of nestling house sparrows *Passer domesticus. Comp. Biochem. Physiol.* **52A,** 305–312.

Blem, C. R. (1990). Avian energy storage. *Current Ornithology* **7,** 59–113.

Block, J. R., and Bolling, D. (1951). "The Amino Acid Composition of Proteins and Foods: Analytical Methods and Results." Thomas, Springfield, Illinois.

Bowen, W. D., Boness, D. J., and Oftedal, O. T. (1987). Mass transfer from mother to pup and subsequent mass loss by the weaned pup in the hooded seal, *Cystophora cristata. Can. J. Zool.* **65,** 1–8.

Brisbin, I. L., Jr. (1969). Bioenergetics of the breeding cycle of the ring dove. *Auk* **86,** 54–74.

Brisbin, I. L., Jr., and Tally, L. J. (1973). Age-specific changes in the major body components and caloric value of growing Japanese quail. *Auk* **90,** 624–635.

Bronson, F. H. (1987). Susceptibility of fat reserves of mice to natural challenges. *J. Comp. Physiol.* **157B**, 551–554.

Brown, C. R. (1985). Energetic cost of moult in macaroni penguins (*Eudyptes chrysolophus*) and rockhopper penguins (*E. chrysocome*). *J. Comp. Physiol.* **155B**, 515–520.

Bryant, D. M., and Gardiner, A. (1979). Energetics of growth in house martins (*Delichon urbica*). *J. Zool.* **189**, 275–304.

Bryant, D. M., and Hails, C. J. (1983). Energetics and growth patterns of three tropical bird species. *Auk* **100**, 425–439.

Burger, J. (1981). On becoming independent in herring gulls: Parent-young conflict. *Am. Nat.* **117**, 444–456.

Cain, B. W. (1976). Energetics of growth for black-bellied tree ducks. *Condor* **78**, 124–128.

Campbell, R. R., and Leatherland, J. F. (1980). Estimating body protein and fat from water content in lesser snow geese. *J. Wildl. Manage.* **44**, 438–446.

Carey, C., Dawson, W. R., Maxwell, L. C., and Faulkner, J. A. (1978). Seasonal acclimatization to temperature in cardueline finches. II. Changes in body composition and mass in relation to season and acute cold stress. *J. Comp. Physiol.* **125**, 101–113.

Case, T. J. (1978). On the evolution and adaptive significance of postnatal growth rates in the terrestrial vertebrates. *Q. Rev. Biol.* **53**, 243–282.

Castro, G., Wunder, B.A., and Knopf, F.L. (1990). Total body electrical conductivity (TOBEC) to estimate total body fat of free-living birds. *Condor* **92**, 496–499.

Chaddock, T. T. (1940). Chemical analysis of deer antlers. *Wisc. Cons. Bull.* **5**, 42.

Chandra, R. K., and Newberne, P. M. (1977). "Nutrition, Immunity, and Infection: Mechanisms of Interactions." Plenum, New York.

Chapman, D. I. (1975). Antlers—bones of contention. *Mammal. Rev.* **5**, 121–172.

Cherel, Y., Stahl, J-C., and Le Maho, Y. (1987). Ecology and physiology of fasting in king penguin chicks. *Auk* **104**, 254–262.

Cherel, Y., Robin, J-P., Walch, O., Karmann, H., Netchitailo, P., and Le Maho, Y. (1988). Fasting in king penguin. I. Hormonal and metabolic changes during breeding. *Am. J. Physiol.* **254**, R170–R177.

Child, G. I., and Marshall, S. G. (1970). A method of estimating carcass fat and fat-free weight in migrant birds from water content of specimens. *Condor* **72**, 116–119.

Churchfield, S. (1981). Water and fat contents of British shrews and their role in the seasonal changes in body weight. *J. Zool.* **194**, 165–173.

Clay, D. I., Brisbin, I. L. Jr., and Youngstrom, K. A. (1979). Age-specific changes in the major body components and caloric values of growing wood ducks. *Auk* **96**, 296–305.

Dawson, W. R., and Marsh, R. L. (1986). Winter fattening in the American goldfinch and the possible role of temperature in its regulation. *Physiol. Zool.* **59**, 357–368.

DelGuidice, G.D., Mech. L.D., and Seal, U.S. (1990). Effects of winter undernutrition on body composition and physiological profiles of white-tailed deer. *J. Wildl. Manage.* **54**, 539–550.

Dolnik, V. R. (1970). The water storation by the migratory fat deposition in *Passer domesticus bactrianus* Zar. et Kud.—the arid zone migrant. *In* "Productivity, Population Dynamics and Systematics of Granivorous Birds" (S. C. Kendeigh and J. Pinowski, eds.), pp. 103–109. Polish Scientific Publ., Warsaw, Poland.

Dunn, E.H. (1975). Growth, body components and energy content of nestling double-crested cormorants. *Condor* **77**, 431–438.

Dunn, E. H., and Brisbin, I. L., Jr. (1980). Age-specific changes in the major body components and caloric values of herring gull chicks. *Condor* **82**, 398–401.

Dunn, M. A., Houtz, S. K., and Hartsook, E. W. (1982). Effects of fasting on muscle protein turnover, the composition of weight loss, and energy balance of obese and nonobese Zucker rats. *J. Nutr.* **112**, 1862–1875.

Ewing, W. G., Studier, E. H., and O'Farrell, M. J. (1970). Autumn fat deposition and gross body composition in three species of *Myotis*. *Comp. Biochem. Physiol.* **36**, 119–129.

Farner, D. S., Oksche, A., Kamemoto, F. I., King, J. R., and Cheyney, H. E. (1961). A comparison of the effect of long daily photoperiods on the pattern of energy storage in migratory and nonmigratory finches. *Comp. Biochem. Physiol.* **2**, 125–142.

Fedyk, A. (1974). Gross body composition in postnatal development of the bank vole. I. Growth under laboratory conditions. *Acta Theriol.* **19**, 381–401.

Fehrenbacher, L. H., and Fleharty, E. D. (1976). Body composition, energy content, and lipid cycles of two species of pocket gophers (*Geomys bursarius* and *Pappogeomys castonops*) in Kansas. *Southwest. Nat.* **21**, 185–198.

Fiorotto, M., Cochran, W.J., Funk, R.C., Sheng, H-P, and Klish, W. J. (1987). Total body electrical conductivity measurements: Effects of body composition and geometry. *Am. J. Physiol.* **252**, R794–R800.

Frenkel, M. J., and Gillespie, J. M. (1976). The proteins of the keratin component of the bird's beak. *Aust. J. Biol. Sci.* **29**, 467–479.

Gale, M. M., Crawford, M. A., and Woodford, M. (1969). The fatty acid composition of adipose and muscle tissue in domestic and free-living ruminants. *Biochem. J.* **113**, 6P.

Gales, R., Green, B., and Stahel, C. (1988). The energetics of free-living little penguins *Eudyptula minor* (Spheniscidae) during moult. *Aust. J. Zool.* **36**, 159–167.

Galster, W., and Morrison, P. (1975). Carbohydrate reserves of wild rodents from different latitudes. *Comp. Biochem. Physiol.* **50A**, 153–157.

Galster, W., and Morrison, P. (1976). Seasonal changes in body composition of the arctic ground squirrel, *Citellus undulatus*. *Can. J. Zool.* **54**, 74–78.

Gifford, C. E., and Odum, E. P. (1965). Bioenergetics of lipid deposition in the bobolink, a trans-equatorial migrant. *Condor* **67**, 383–403.

Groscolas, R. (1988). The use of body mass loss to estimate metabolic rate in fasting sea birds: A critical examination based on emperor penguins (*Aptenodytes forsteri*). *Comp. Biochem. Physiol.* **90A**, 361–366.

Groscolas, R., Schreiber, L., and Morin, F. (1991). The use of tritiated water to determine protein and lipid utilization in fasting birds: A validation study in incubating great-winged petrels, *Pterodroma macroptera*. *Physiol. Zool.* **64**, 1217–1233.

Gyug, L. W., and Millar, J. S. (1980). Fat levels in a subarctic population of *Peromyscus maniculatus*. *Can. J. Zool.* **58**, 1341–1346.

Hall, J. E., and Seed, J. R. (1984). Increased urinary excretion of aromatic amino acid catabolites by *Microtus montanus* chronically infected with *Trypanosoma brucei gambiense*. *Comp. Biochem. Physiol.* **77B**, 755–760.

Hall, C. B., Lukaski, H. C., and Marchello, M. J. (1989). Estimation of rat body composition using tetrapolar bioeletrical impedance analysis. *Nutr. Rep. Int.* **39**, 627–633.

Harper, R. B., Travis, H. F., and Glinsky, M. S. (1978). Metabolizable energy requirement for maintenance and body composition of growing farm-raised male pastel mink (*Mustela vison*). *J. Nutr.* **108**, 1937–1943.

Harrap, B. S., and Woods, E. F. (1967). Species differences in the proteins of feathers. *Comp. Biochem. Physiol.* **20**, 449–460.

Hayward, J. S. (1965). The gross body composition of six geographic races of *Peromyscus*. *Can. J. Zool.* **43**, 297–308.

Heitmeyer, M.E. (1988). Protein costs of the prebasic molt of female mallards. *Condor* **90**, 263–266.

Helms, C. W., and Smythe, R. B. (1969). Variation in major body components of the tree sparrow (*Spizella arborea*) sampled within the winter range. *Wilson Bull.* **81**, 280–292.

Helms, C. W., Aussiker, W. H., Bower, E. B., and Fretwell, S. D. (1967). A biometric study of major body components of the slate-colored junco, *Junco hyemalis*. *Condor* **69**, 560–578.

Hissa, R., Rinfamaki, H., Virtanen, P., Linden, H., and Vihko, V. (1990). Energy reserves of the capercaillie *Tetrao urogallus* in Finland. *Comp. Biochem. Physiol.* **97A**, 345–351.

Holleman, D. F., and Dieterich, R. A. (1975). An evaluation of the tritiated water method for estimating body water in small rodents. *Can. J. Zool.* **53**, 1376–1378.

Holleman, D. F., and Dieterich, R. A. (1978). Postnatal changes in body composition of laboratory maintained brown lemmings, *Lemmus sibiricus*. *Lab. Anim. Sci.* **28**, 529–535.

Holmes, R. T. (1976). Body composition, lipid reserves and caloric densities of summer birds in a northern deciduous forest. *Am. Midl. Nat.* **96**, 281–290.

Huot, J. (1982). "Body Condition and Food Resources of White-tailed Deer on Anticosti Island, Quebec." Doctoral Dissertation, Univ. of Alaska, Fairbanks, Alaska.

Huxley, J. (1931). The relative size of antlers in deer. *Proc. Zool. Soc. London* **1931**, 819–864.

Hyvarinen, H., Kay, R. N. B., and Hamilton, W. J. (1977). Variation in the weight, specific gravity and composition of the antlers of red deer (*Cervus elephus* L.). *Br. J. Nutr.* **38**, 301–311.

Jenni, L., and Jenni-Eiermann, S. (1987). Body weight and energy reserves on bramblings in winter. *Ardea* **75**, 271–284.

Johnston, D. W. (1964). Ecologic aspects of lipid secretion in some postbreeding arctic birds. *Ecology* **45**, 848–852.

Johnston, D. W. (1970). Caloric density of avian adipose tissue. *Comp. Biochem. Physiol.* **34A**, 827–832.

Jones, G. (1987). Body condition changes of sand martins (*Riparia riparia*) during breeding, and a comparison with fledgling condition. *J. Zool.* **213**, 263–281.

Kale, H. W., II. (1965). Ecology and bioenergetics of the long-billed marsh wren in Georgia salt marshes. *Publ. Nuttall Ornithol. Club* **5**, Cambridge, Massachusetts.

Kaminski, P., and Konarzewski, M. (1984). Changess of body weight, chemical composition and energetic value in the nestlings of the jackdaw, *Corvus monedula* L., during their development in the nest. *Ekol. Pol.* **32**, 125–139.

Kaufman, D. W., and Kaufman, G. A. (1975). Caloric density of the oldfield mouse during postnatal growth. *Acta Theriol.* **20**, 83–95.

Kaufman, G. A., and Kaufman, D. W. (1977). Body composition of the oldfield mouse (*Peromyscus polionotus*). *J. Mammal.* **58**, 429–434.

King, J. R. (1961). The bioenergetics of vernal premigratory fat deposition in the white-crowned sparrow. *Condor* **63**, 128–142.

King, J. R. (1973). Seasonal allocation of time and energy resources in birds. *In* "Avian Energetics" (R. A. Paynter, Jr., ed.), pp. 4–85. *Publ. Nuttall Ornithol. Club* **15**, Cambridge, Massachusetts.

King, J. R. (1980). Energetics of avian molt. *Int. Ornithol. Congr.* **27**, 312–317.

King, J. R., and Murphy, M. E. (1987). Amino acid composition of the calamus, rachis, and barbs of white-crowned sparrow feathers. *Condor* **89**, 436–439.

King, J. R., and Murphy, M. E. (1990). Estimates of the mass of structures other than plumage produced during molt by white-crowned sparrows. *Condor* **92**, 839–843.

Kirkpatrick, R. L. (1980). Physiological indices in wildlife management. *In* "Wildlife Management Techniques Manual" (S. D. Schemnitz, ed.), pp. 99–112. Wildl. Soc., Washington, D.C.

Kirkwood, J. K. (1985). Patterns of growth in primates. *J. Zool.* **205**, 123–136.

Klaassen, M., Bech, C., Masman, D., and Slagsvold, G. (1989). Growth and energetics of Arctic tern chicks (*Sterna paradisaea*). *Auk* **106**, 240–248.

Komen, J. (1991). Energy requirements of nestling cape vultures. *Condor* **93**, 153–158.

Le Maho, Y., Kha, H. Vu Van, Koubi, H., Dewasmes, G., Girard, J., Ferre, P., and Cagnard, M. (1981). Body composition, energy expenditure, and plasma metabolites in long-term fasting geese. *Am. J. Physiol.* **241**, E342–E354.

Lima, S. L. (1986). Predation risk and unpredictable feeding conditions: Determinants of body mass in birds. *Ecology* **67**, 377–385.

Lindstedt, S. L., and Boyce, M. S. (1985). Seasonality, fasting endurance and body size in mammals. *Am. Nat.* **125**, 873–878.

Ling, J. K. (1970). Pelage and molting in wild animals with special reference to aquatic forms. *Q. Rev. Biol.* **45**, 16–54.

Lukaski, H. C. (1987). Methods for the assessment of human body composition: traditional and new. *Am. J. Clin. Nutr.* **46**, 537–556.

Mock, P. J., Khubesrian, M., and Larcheveque, D. M. (1991). Energetics of growth and maturation in sympatric passerines that fledge at different ages. *Auk* **108**, 34–41.

Montevecchi, W.A., Ricklefs, R. E., Kirkham, I. R., and Gabaldon, D. (1984). Growth energetics of nestling northern gannets (*Sula bassanus*). *Auk* **101**, 334–341.

Mortensen, A., Unander, S., Kostad, M., and Blix, A. S. (1983). Seasonal changes in body composition and crop content of Spitzbergen ptarmigan *Lagopus mutus hyperboreus*. *Ornis Scand.* **14**, 144–148.

Morton, M. L., Maxwell, C. S., and Wade, C. E. (1974). Body size, body composition, and behavior of juvenile Belding ground squirrels. *Great Basin Nat.* **34**, 121–134.

Moulton, C. R. (1923). Age and chemical development in mammals. *J. Biol. Chem.* **57**, 79–97.

Munger, J. C., and Karasov, W. H. (1989). Sublethal parasites and host energy budgets: tapeworm infection in white-footed mice. *Ecology* **70**, 904–921.

Murphy, M. E., and King, J. R. (1982). Amino acid composition of the plumage of the white-crowned sparrow. *Condor* **84**, 435–438.

Murphy, M. E., and King, J. R. (1984). Sulfur amino acid nutrition during molt in the white-crowned sparrow. I. Does dietary sulfur amino acid concentration affect the energetics of molt as assayed by metabolizable energy? *Condor* **86**, 314–323.

Murphy, M. E., and King, J. R. (1986). Composition and quantity of feather sheaths produced by white-crowned sparrows during the postnuptial molt. *Auk* **103**, 822–825.

Murphy, M. E., and King, J. R. (1992). Energy and nutrient use during moult by white-crowned sparrows (*Zonotrichia leucophrys gambelii*). *Ornis Scand.* (in press).

Murphy, M. E., King, J. R., Taruscio, T. G., and Geupel, G. R. (1990). Amino acid composition of feather barbs and rachises in three species of *Pygoscelid* penguins: Nutritional implications. *Condor* **92**, 913–921.

Mutze, G. J. (1990). Fat cycles, breeding and population changes in house mice. *Aust. J. Zool.* **38**, 453–464.

Myrcha, A. (1968). Caloric value and chemical composition of the body of the European hare. *Acta Theriol.* **13**, 65–71.

Myrcha, A., and Pinowski, J. (1969). Variations in the body composition and caloric value of nestling tree sparrows (*Passer m. montanus* L.). *Bull. Pol. Acad. Sci. Cl. II Ser. Sci. Biol.* **17**, 475–480.

Myrcha, A., and Pinowski, J. (1970). Weights, body composition and caloric value of postjuvenal molting European tree sparrows (*Passer montanus*). *Condor* **72**, 175–181.

Myrcha, A., Pinowski, J., and Tomek, T. (1973). Variations in the water and ash contents and in the caloric value of nestling starlings (*Sturnus vulgaris* L.) during their development. *Bull. Pol. Acad. Sci. Cl. II Ser. Sci. Biol.* **21**, 649–655.

Newton, I. (1968). The temperatures, weights, and body composition of moulting bullfinches. *Condor* **70**, 323–332.

Newton, I. (1969). Winter fattening in the bullfinch. *Physiol. Zool.* **42**, 96–107.

Nitsan, Z., Dvorin, A., and Nir, I. (1981). Composition and amino acid content of carcass, skin and feathers of the growing gosling. *Br. Poult. Sci.* **22**, 79–84.

O'Farrell, M. J., and Studier, E. H. (1976). Seasonal changes in wing loading, body composition, and organ weights in *Myotis thysanodes* and *M. lucifugus* (Chiroptera: Vespertilionidae). *Bull. South. Calif. Acad. Sci.* **75**, 258–266.

Odum, E. P. (1960). Lipid deposition in nocturnal migrant birds. *Proc. XII Int. Ornithol. Congr.,* Helsinki **2**, 563–576.

Odum, E. P., Marshall, S. G., and Marples, T. G. (1965). The caloric content of migrating birds. *Ecology* **46**, 901–904.

Okon, E. E., and Ekanem, R. T. (1976). Diurnal variations of the glycogen and fat stores in the liver and breast muscle of the insect bat, *Tadarida nigeriae. Physiol. Behav.* **23**, 659–661.

Olson, J. B., and Kendeigh, S. C. (1980). Effect of season on the energetics, body composition, and cage activity of the field sparrow. *Auk* **97**, 704–720.

Perry, M. C., Kuenzel, W. J., Williams, B. K., and Serafin, J. A. (1986). Influences of nutrients on feed intake and condition of captive canvasbacks in winter. *J. Wildl. Manage.* **50**, 427–434.

Pontier, D., Gaillard, J. M., Allaine, D., Trouvilliez, J., Gordon, I., and Duncan, P. (1989). Postnatal growth rate and adult body weight in mammals: A new approach. *Oecologia* **80**, 390–394.

Prange, H. D., Anderson, J. F., and Rahn, H. (1979). Scaling of skeletal mass to body mass in birds and mammals. *Am. Nat.* **113**, 103–122.

Pucek, M. (1973). Variability of fat and water content in two rodent species. *Acta Theriol.* **18**, 57–80.

Reidinger, R. F., Labows, J. N., Fellows, D. P., and Mason, J. R. (1985). Fatty acid composition of adipose tissue as an indicator of diet: A preliminary assessment. *J. Wildl. Manage.* **49**, 170–177.

Reimers, E., Ringberg, T., and Sorumgard, R. (1982). Body composition of Svalbard reindeer. *Can. J. Zool.* **60**, 1812–1821.

Reynolds, W. W. (1977). Skeleton weight allometry in aquatic and terrestrial vertebrates. *Hydrobiologia* **56**, 35–37.

Richards, J. R., Drury, J. K., Goll, C., Besent, R. G., and Al-Shamma, G. A. A. (1978). Energy exchanges and injury. *Proc. Nutr. Soc.* **37**, 39–43.

Ricklefs, R. E. (1968). Patterns of growth in birds. *Ibis* **110**, 419–451.

Ricklefs, R. E. (1973). Patterns of growth in birds. II. Growth rate and mode of development. *Ibis* **115**, 177–201.

Ricklefs, R. E. (1975). Patterns of growth in birds. III. Growth and development of the cactus wren. *Condor* **77**, 34–45.

Ricklefs, R. E. (1979). Patterns of growth in birds. V. A comparative study of development in the starling, common tern, and Japanese quail. *Auk* **96**, 10–30.

Ricklefs, R. E., and White, S. C. (1981). Growth and energetics of chicks of the sooty tern (*Sterna fuscata*) and common tern (*S. hirundo*). *Auk* **98**, 361–378.

Ricklefs, R. E., White, S. C., and Cullen, J. (1980). Energetics of postnatal growth in Leach's storm-petrel. *Auk* **97**, 566–575.

Robbins, C. T. (1973). "The Biological Basis for the Determination of Carrying Capacity." Doctoral Dissertation, Cornell Univ., Ithaca, New York.

Robbins, C. T., Moen, A. N., and Reid, J. T. (1974). Body composition of white-tailed deer. *J. Anim. Sci.* **38**, 871–876.

Robbins, C. T., Podbielancik-Norman, R. S., Wilson, D. L., and Mould, E. D. (1981). Growth and nutrient consumption of elk calves compared to other ungulate species. *J. Wildl. Manage.* **45**, 172–186.

Robin, J-P., Frain, M., Sardet, C., Groscolas, R., and Le Maho, Y. (1988). Protein and lipid utilization during long-term fasting in emperor penguins. *Am. J. Physiol.* **254**, R61–R68.

Roby, D. D. (1991). Diet and postnatal energetics in convergent taxa of plankton-feeding seabirds. *Auk* **108**, 131–146.

Rogers, C. M. (1987). Predation risk and fasting capacity: Do wintering birds maintain optimal body mass? *Ecology* **68**, 1051–1061.

Rush, W. M. (1932). "Northern Yellowstone Elk Study." Montana Fish and Game Comm, Helena, Montana.

Sawicka-Kapusta, K. (1968). Annual fat cycle of field mice *Apodemus flavicollus* (Melchoir, 1834). *Acta Theriol.* **13**, 329–339.

Sawicka-Kapusta, K. (1970). Changes in the gross body composition and the caloric value of the common voles during their postnatal development. *Acta Theriol.* **15**, 67–79.

Sawicka-Kapusta, K. (1974). Changes in the gross body composition and energy value of the bank voles during their postnatal development. *Acta Theriol.* **19**, 27–54.

Schmidt-Nielsen, K. (1977). The physiology of wild animals. *Proc. R. Soc. London* **199B**, 345–360.

Schreiber, R. K., and Johnson, D. R. (1975). Seasonal changes in body composition and caloric content of Great Basin rodents. *Acta Theriol.* **20**, 343–364.

Schultz, T. D., and Ferguson, J. H. (1974). Influence of dietary fatty acids on the composition of plasma fatty acids in tundra wolf *(Canis lupus tundrarum)*. *Comp. Biochem. Physiol.* **49A**, 575–581.

Seed, J. R., Hall, J. E., and Sechelski, J. (1982). Phenylalanine metabolism in *Microtus montanus* chronically infected with *Trypanosoma brucei gambiense*. *Comp. Biochem. Physiol.* **71B**, 209–215.

Skar, H. J., Hagvar, S., Hagen, A., and Ostbye, E. (1975). Food habits and body composition of adult and juvenile meadow pipit [*Anthus pratensis* (L.)]. *In* "Fennoscandian Tundra Ecosystems. Part 2. Animals and Systems Analysis" (F. W. Wielgolaski, ed.), pp. 160–173. Springer-Verlag, New York.

Smuts, D. B., Mitchell, H. H., and Hamilton, T. S. (1932). The relation between dietary cystine and the growth and cystine content of hair in the rat. *J. Biol. Chem.* **95**, 283–295.

Spinage, C. A., and Shelley, H. J. (1981). Tissue carbohydrate reserves in adult and foetal Grant's gazelles and wildebeest. *Comp. Biochem. Physiol.* **70A**, 87–89.

Stirling, I., and McEwan, E. H. (1975). The caloric value of whole ringed seals *(Phoca hispida)* in relation to polar bear *(Ursus maritimus)* ecology and hunting behavior. *Can. J. Zool.* **53**, 1021–1027.

Sugden, L. G., and Harris, L. E. (1972). Energy requirements and growth of captive lesser scaup. *Poult. Sci.* **51**, 625–633.

Szwykowska, M. M. (1969). Seasonal changes of the caloric value and chemical composition of the partridge *(Perdix perdix)*. *Ekol. Polska, Ser. A.* **17**, 795–809.

Tatner, P. (1984). Body component growth and composition of the magpie *Pica pica*. *J. Zool.* **203**, 397–410.

Taylor, J. R. E., and Konarzewski, M. (1989). On the importance of fat reserves for the little auk *(Alle alle)* chicks. *Oecologia* **81**, 551–558.

Thomas, V. G. (1987). Similar winter energy strategies of grouse, hares and rabbits in northern biomes. *Oikos* **50**, 206–212.

Thomas, V. G., and Popko, R. (1981). Fat and protein reserves of wintering and prebreeding rock ptarmigan from south Hudson Bay. *Can. J. Zool.* **59**, 1205–1211.

Torbit, S. C. (1981). "In vivo Estimation of Mule Deer Body Composition." Doctoral Dissertation, Colorado State Univ., Fort Collins, Colorado.

Turcek, F. J. (1966). On plumage quantity in birds. *Ekol. Pol., Ser. A* **14**, 617–634.

Ullrey, D. E., Youatt, W. G., Johnson, H. E., Cowan, A. B., Fay, L. D., Covert, R. L., Magee, W. T., and Keahey, K. K. (1975). Phosphorus requirements of weaned white-tailed deer fawns. *J. Wildl. Manage.* **39**, 590–595.

Walsberg, G. E. (1988). Evaluation of a nondestructive method for determining fat stores in small birds and mammals. *Physiol. Zool.* **61,** 153–159.

Ward, P. (1969). Seasonal and diurnal changes in the fat content of an equitorial bird. *Physiol. Zool.* **42,** 85–95.

Ward, W. H., and Lundgren, H. P. (1954). The formation, composition and properties of the keratins. *In* "Advances in Protein Chemistry" (M. T. Anson, K. Bailey, and J. T. Edwall, eds.), pp. 243–297. Academic Press, New York.

Whittaker, M. E., and Thomas, V. G. (1983). Seasonal levels of fat and protein reserves of snowshoe hares in Ontario. *Can. J. Zool.* **61,** 1339–1345.

Williams, A. J., Siegfried, W. R., Burger, A. E., and Berruti, A. (1977). Body composition and energy metabolism of molting eudyptid penguins. *Comp. Biochem. Physiol.* **56A,** 27–30.

Williams, J. B., and Prints, A. (1986). Energetics of growth in nestling savannah sparrows: A comparison of doubly labeled water and laboratory estimates. *Condor* **88,** 74–83.

Worthy, G. A. J., and Lavigne, D. M. (1983a). Changes in energy stores during postnatal development of the harp seal, *Phoca groenlandica. J. Mammal.* **64,** 89–96.

Worthy, G. A. J., and Lavigne, D. M. (1983b). Energetics of fasting and subsequent growth in weaned harp seal pups, *Phoca groenlandica. Can. J. Zool.* **61,** 447–456.

Wyndham, E. (1980). Total body lipids of the budgerigar *Melopsittacus undulatus* (Psittaciformes: Platycericidae) in inland mid-eastern Australia. *Aust. J. Zool.* **28,** 239–247.

Yarbrough, C. G. (1970). Summer lipid levels of some subarctic birds. *Auk* **87,** 100–110.

Yarbrough, C. G., and Johnston, D. W. (1965). Lipid deposition in wintering and premigratory myrtle warblers. *Wilson Bull.* **77,** 175–191.

Zar, J. H. (1977). Fatty acid composition of emporer penguin (*Aptenodytes forsteri*) lipids. *Comp. Biochem. Physiol.* **56B,** 109–112.

Zimmerman, J. L. (1965). Carcass analysis of wild and thermal stressed dickcissels. *Wilson Bull.* **77,** 55–70.

12

Food Composition

Biology is by far a more difficult subject than physics. It is much more complex, and it has more variables. It is more difficult to do a controlled experiment and to understand the basic laws of nature which apply in biology than it is in physics. The complexity of problems in biology means that the subject should be attacked with all the skills and tools available.

GATES, 1962

The animal's nutritional environment is a vast array of chemical compounds conveniently ordered by scientists into aggregations from species to ecosystems. While countless food habit studies have indicated the relative importance of plant or animal species in the nutritional environment of many animals, our increasing knowledge of food selection and metabolism dictates that far more basic and analytical studies are needed if we are to understand the food–animal interaction. While the simple listing of species ingested by animals is a first step in understanding an animal's natural history, such studies provide only the slightest glimmer of a nutritional understanding.

Latin binomials (animals) simply do not eat other latin binomials (plant or animal)(Janzen, 1979). Food selection by free-ranging animals is not based on the anatomical characteristics used by plant or animal taxonomists, but rather on the animal's perception of cost–benefit constraints imposed when different foods are sought and ingested. Therefore, our quantification of the nutritional environment must be based on the animal's perception of that environment. The animal is linked to its nutritional environment by (a) olfactory, visual, and taste cues enabling food selection and (b) digestion–metabolism processes enabling absorption, distribution, and utilization of the specific chemicals within the ingested food. The integration of these processes in which external cues are associated with internal metabolic events provides the framework within which the animal can constantly evaluate its nutrient environment.

I. CARBOHYDRATES

Most plant carbohydrates are polymers of five- and six-carbon monosaccharides. Plant carbohydrates can be divided into nonstructural and structural cat-

TABLE 12.1

Carbohydrate Content of Plant Tissues

		Content (% of dry matter)				
Component	Function	Fruits	Seeds	Legumes	Grasses	Tree and shrub twigs and leaves
Soluble sugars	Nonstructural	17–77	0–1	2–16	5–15	5–15
Starch	Nonstructural	0–3	80	1–7	1–5	—
Pectin	Structural	5–17	0–1	5–10	1–2	6–12
Hemicellulose	Structural	2–7	7–15	3–10	15–40	8–12
Cellulose	Structural	3–17	2–5	7–35	20–40	12–30

Sources: Bailey and Ulyatt, 1970; Mould and Robbins, 1981; Van Soest, 1981; Englyst, 1981.

egories based on their composition, position, and function. Nonstructural carbohydrates range from soluble mono- and disaccharides, such as sucrose in plant
sap, to large polysaccharides, such as starch in seeds and roots. Nonstructural
carbohydrates are important reserves for plant growth and respiration. They are
used to initiate new growth and maintain plant respiration when photosynthesis
is inadequate. Daily and seasonal rhythms in nonstructural carbohydrates represent a balancing between photosynthesis and respiration. For example, nonstructural carbohydrates are lowest in the early morning after night respiration
and prior to active photosynthesis and increase during the day as photosynthetic
production exceeds respiration. On a seasonal basis, nonstructural carbohydrates
within the vegetative structures decrease during rapid spring growth and during
seed production, but often increase during late fall preparatory to plant dormancy
(McConnell and Garrison, 1966). The annual cycle of reserve carbohydrates is
extremely important in determining plant vigor, health, and regeneration after
foliage removal. Although nonstructural carbohydrates occur in all living plant
parts, the highest concentrations occur in fruits, seeds, stem bases and roots of
grasses, stems of legumes, and roots of most trees and shrubs (Kramer and
Kozlowski, 1960; McConnell and Garrison, 1966; Smith, 1973; White, 1973).
    The two main structural carbohydrates of plant cell walls are cellulose and
hemicellulose (Table 12.1). Cellulose, the predominant carbohydrate of higher
plants, is a glucose polymer linked by β 1,4 bonds. Unlike starch, which can
be a highly digestible glucose polymer, cellulose cannot be digested by vertebrates without symbiotic gastrointestinal microflora. Hemicelluloses are predominantly polymers of five-carbon sugars, although six-carbon sugars such as glucose, also occur (Bailey, 1973; Wilkie, 1979). Because of the diversity of
monosaccharide components and linkages, hemicelluloses are poorly understood.
Hemicelluloses are hydrolyzed by both acid and alkaline solutions and thus are

partially digested by stomach acidity. Cellulose and hemicellulose are occasionally grouped as holocellulose.

Pectin is the remaining structural carbohydrate and occurs primarily in the middle lamella between adjacent cell walls. Pectins are more prevalent in fruits and dicotyledonous plants than in grasses (Table 12.1). It is primarily composed of galacturonic acid linked α 1,4, with smaller amounts of arabinose and galactose (Van Soest, 1981). Pectins are readily digested by symbiotic bacteria and protozoa (Bonhomme-Florentin, 1988). Thus, pectin digestibility can vary depending on the extent of gastrointestinal fermentation. For animals without significant gastrointestinal fermentation, pectin is termed soluble fiber as it adds bulk to the feces even though it is soluble. Because of the difficulty in definitively separating hemicelluloses and pectins on the basis of either their solubility or carbohydrate fractions, they are occasionally grouped as noncellulosic polysaccharides.

II. PROTEIN

Dietary crude protein is usually determined by the Kjeldahl procedure in which a weighed sample is boiled in a concentrated sulfuric acid–catalyst solution until all organic matter is destroyed and the nitrogen converted to ammonium sulfate. The solution is subsequently cooled, sodium hydroxide is added, and the ammonia is volatilized. The ammonia is captured in a weak acid solution and back-titrated with a known normality acid to determine the amount of nitrogen in the original sample. As discussed earlier, nitrogen times 6.25 provides a crude estimate of dietary protein content.

True protein frequently accounts for 75–90% of the nitrogen in herbage and animal products, with the remainder being inorganic nitrogen, free amino acids, low-molecular-weight peptides, nucleic acids, and other nonprotein nitrogen compounds (Lyttleton, 1973; Luick et al., 1974; Sedinger, 1984). Most plant protein is found within the cytoplasm of the cell, with only small amounts associated with the cell wall (Lyttleton, 1973; Albersheim, 1975). Plant protein increases during growth or regeneration when active anabolic processes are occurring, but then it decreases with increasing vegetative maturity as greater emphasis is placed on the production of nitrogen-free cell wall components for structural support (Greenwood and Barnes, 1978). For example, early growth in grasses, forbs, and browses can be as high as 20–30% protein on a dry-weight basis, but the protein subsequently falls to as little as 3–4% at maturity (Dietz et al., 1962; Cowan et al., 1970; Kubota et al., 1970; Lyttleton, 1973; Cogswell and Kamstra, 1976).

The one exception to the generally decreasing protein content in plants with increasing maturity are relatively high levels in many seeds. For example, seeds consumed by ruffed grouse in New York contained 9.5–33.8% crude protein

(Bump *et al.*, 1947). However, many commercial grains, such as wheat or corn, have relatively low levels of crude protein (generally 8–15%) because the high levels of endosperm carbohydrates dilute the higher protein concentrations in the germ. In contrast to seeds, fruits usually contain even less protein. Most fruits are 80–90% water, and even the dry matter usually has less than 10% crude protein, with some fruits having as little as 2% crude protein (Johnson *et al.*, 1985; Sakai and Carpenter, 1990). Many seeds and fruits also contain digestion inhibitors or toxins that reduce the amount of available protein or minimize their total intake (Bullard and Elias, 1979; McKey, 1979; Seigler, 1979; Mack, 1990).

Animal tissues are generally higher in total protein content on a dry weight basis than are plants because the cell walls of animal tissue are largely protein while those of plants are largely carbohydrate; and animal protein is generally either more available or more useful because of its amino acid spectra than is plant protein. For example, the dry matter of fish, birds, and mammals contains 60% crude protein (range: 22–91%), and the dry, ash-free matter of terrestrial and aquatic invertebrates averages 65% crude protein (range: 30–88%) (Driver *et al.*, 1974; Thompson and Sparks, 1978; Redford and Dorea, 1984; Montevecchi *et al.*, 1984; Vlieg, 1984; Heath and Randall, 1985; Jorde and Owen, 1988; Pritchard and Robbins, 1990). Ash-free comparisons are necessary for invertebrates because some have calciferous shells or have large amounts of soil in their gastrointestinal tract. The range in protein concentration largely reflects differences in fat accumulation as affected by species, season, or stage in the life cycle.

III. FATS

Total dietary lipids have traditionally been estimated by extracting a dried sample with an organic solvent, such as anhydrous ethyl or petroleum ether. While nonspecific lipid extractions of animal tissue generally indicate useable fat, similar extractions of plants often have little nutritional meaning. Plant ether extract is a very heterogeneous mixture of generally high-energy compounds, such as glycerides, phospholipids, sterols, pigments, waxes, volatile oils, and resins. Very high concentrations of triglycerides are confined in plants to oil-bearing seeds and fruits, such as 75% of the dry weight in pecans, 62% in walnuts, and 64% in pinyon pine seeds (Kramer and Kozlowski, 1960). Conversely, the predominant glycerides of plant leaves and stems have a lower caloric content than a triglyceride (Lough and Garton, 1968; Hawke, 1973; Karis and Hudson, 1974). Rather than the three fatty acids of triglycerides, plant glycerides often have either one or two galactose units replacing the fatty acids of a triglyceride. Because galactolipids are most prevalent in actively metabolizing leaves, their concentration decreases with increasing leaf maturity and increasing stem to leaf ratios (Van Soest, 1981). Waxes, which are fatty acid esters of alcohols, are common throughout the marine foodweb. Wax, whether of the marine form or as beeswax, is highly digestible in animals adapted to its consumption (Roby *et al.*, 1986; Diamond and Place, 1988).

Lipid analyses are confounded by their propensity to oxidize, volatilize, or form insoluble soaps. Unsaturated lipids are particularly prone to oxidation during storage to form insoluble, indigestible resins and gels. The aromatic fragrances of evergreens and sagebrush are volatile oils that can easily be lost during drying. Lipids in feces are often underestimated because they commonly form calcium or magnesium soaps (Van Soest, 1981).

IV. PROTECTIVE AND DEFENSIVE AGENTS

Because many plant carbohydrates, proteins, and lipids are easily degraded, the development of protective and defensive agents has been an important step in plant evolution. Major evolutionary emphasis has been at the chemical level. Plants contain substances that physically impede digestive enzymes or microorganisms as well as a far more diverse and active chemical defense arsenal of secondary plant compounds. Lignin, cutin, suberin, and biogenic silica are the main structural agents that physically prevent degradation. Secondary plant constituents are a heterogeneous mixture of over 33,000 compounds of relatively small molecular weight that can interfere with growth, neurological and tissue functioning, reproduction, and digestion of organisms that ingest them.

A. Lignin

Lignin is a high-molecular-weight, aromatic, nonsaccharide polymer that adds rigidity to the plant cell-wall (Harkin, 1973). Structural rigidity is probably lignin's most important evolutionary function as it is confined to the higher plants and does not occur in algae, fungi, and mosses. Lignin concentrations increase with advancing cellular maturity and can reach as much as 15–20% of the cell wall.

Lignin is resistant to enzymatic and acid hydrolysis by bacteria, protozoa, and vertebrates and is therefore largely indigestible. However, some fungal digestion may occur in the gastrointestinal tract of birds and mammals (Akin and Barton, 1983). Although lignin is the main factor limiting the digestibility of cell-wall polysaccharides, its mode of action is poorly understood. The most plausible explanation is that lignin–carbohydrate bonds throughout the cell wall physically impede enzymatic hydrolysis (Rhoades, 1979) because delignified cell walls are highly digestible (Darcy and Belyea, 1980).

B. Cutin–Suberin

Cutin, an aliphatic polymer, and suberin, a mixed aromatic–aliphatic polymer, are closely related chemical compounds (Kolattukudy, 1977). Cutin is the structural component of the plant cuticle and is thus extracellular at the plant surface. Suberin occurs between the cell wall and cytoplasm and is a major constituent of bark (Martin and Juniper, 1970). Cutin and suberin are important to the plant in wound healing, reducing water loss, and physically preventing entry by microorganisms.

Cutin and suberin, as a percentage of plant dry matter, are quantitatively insignificant in grasses. However, tree and shrub cell walls contain up to 15% cutin–suberin (Robbins and Moen, 1975). Although cutin–suberin are slightly digestible (Brown and Kolattukudy, 1978), they may physically block the digestibility of more readily available cell-wall polysaccharides.

C. Biogenic Silica

Silica can occur in plants as distinct concretions that reduce cell-wall digestibility, increase tooth wear, and promote the formation of siliceous urinary calculi. Grasses, sedges, and many of the lower plants, such as ferns and *Equisetum*, can accumulate silica, whereas dicotyledonous plants generally do not. Frequently, the silica content of grasses varies from 3 to 5% of the dry matter, although grasses can respond to grazing by increasing the silica content of the regrowth (Jones and Handreck, 1967; Van Soest and Jones, 1968; McNaughton and Tarrants, 1983; McNaughton *et al.*, 1985; Brizuela *et al.*, 1986).

D. Secondary Plant Compounds

Secondary plant compounds are an extremely diverse assemblage of antiherbivory chemicals. Their effects can range from feeding deterrence to toxicity. They have been labeled "secondary" because few have primary metabolic functions within the plant and at one time they were viewed as end products of other metabolic systems. They include alkaloids, pyrethrins, rotenoids, cyanogenic glycosides, long-chain unsaturated isobutylamides, cardenolides and saponins, sesquiterpene lactones, nonprotein amino acids, glucosinolates and isothiocyanates, oxalates, fluoro fatty acids, selenoamino acids, tannins, phenolic resins, proteinase inhibitors, and phytohemagglutinins (Harborne, 1972; Richardson, 1977; Rhoades, 1979). While most of these compounds have a broad spectrum of activity in providing defense against all consumers, selective toxicities do occur. For example, the pyrethrins are potent insecticides with minimal mammalian toxicity (Mabry and Gill, 1979).

Because plants and their varied consumers are "involved in an incessant evolutionary struggle," evolution will favor the continued development of molecular uniqueness in secondary plant constituents (Levin, 1976b). Plants must constantly evolve new defenses as their consumers evolve more elaborate detoxification pathways (Brattsten, 1979). Because many of these compounds are also toxic to plants, they must be either isolated in plant organelles or stored as inactive forms that are released or activated when consumed. For example, inactive cyanogenic glycosides occur in over 1000 plant species and are activated upon consumption to hydrogen cyanide. Both the glycoside and the activating glycosidase occur within the plant but are brought into contact only when the plant tissue is mascerated (Conn, 1979).

Although secondary plant compounds are invariably viewed as antinutrients, some may have beneficial roles in animal nutrition. Tannins can reduce the infectivity of viruses or other pathogens by binding with them in the gastrointestinal tract (Keating et al., 1988). 6–MBOA, a cyclic carbamate found in highest concentrations in sprouting grasses, stimulates reproduction in both male and female grazing rodents (Rowsemitt and O'Connor, 1989). 6–MBOA was recently identified in bamboo, a type of grass (Rowsemitt, unpublished). Consequently, the dietary absence of newly emerging bamboo shoots high in 6–MBOA may be a cause of reproductive failures in many captive giant pandas.

The concentrations of these compounds vary in both space and time within and between plants (Feeny, 1976; Rhoades and Cates, 1976; Mattson, 1980). For example, defensive compounds in woody plants can either increase or decrease following browsing. This response depends on the physiological age of the plant, the degree of damage, and the plant's physiological and resource constraints (Bryant et al., 1991). Similarly, although many unripened fruits contain very high levels of secondary plant compounds, plants that depend on vertebrate ingestion for seed scattering detoxify these compounds in the ripening fruit while continuing to concentrate them in the seed itself. Thus, the fruit is ingested only after the seed has matured and will pass undigested through the gastrointestinal tract. The three most prevalent groups of plant secondary compounds are soluble phenolics, alkaloids, and terpenoids.

1. SOLUBLE PHENOLICS

Soluble plant phenolics include over 8000 flavonoids, isoflavonoids, and hydrolyzable and condensed tannins (Harborne, 1991). Flavonoids are particularly well known for the brilliant flower, fruit, and leaf colors that they confer. Flavonoids usually occur as soluble nontoxic glycosides in the plant. Isoflavonoids are best known as phytoestrogens. Excessive consumption of these nonsteroidal estrogenic compounds can produce abortions, sterility, or liver damage. Although estrogenic isoflavonoids have been identified in over 200 different plant species, major problems in animal health and reproduction have occurred when captive wildlife consumed some soybean-based feeds or certain types of clover (Farnsworth *et al.*, 1975; NRC, 1982). Carnivores, such as mink and foxes, are very susceptible to infertility produced by isoflavonoid phytoestrogens in soybeans. Similarly, current problems in breeding cheetahs in the United States, where only 9 to 12% of sexually mature females produce live cubs as compared to 60 to 80% at the DeWildt Cheetah Research Center in South Africa, may be due to the use of soybeans that contain phytoestrogens in the commercial feline diets in the United States as compared to phytoestrogen-free carcasses in Africa (Setchell *et al.*, 1987).

The term *tannin* derives from the ability of these soluble polyphenols to tan animal hides into leather. Tannins are the most ancient, widespread, and successful generalized defensive plant compound (Swain, 1979). They occur in about 17% of the nonwoody annuals, 14% of herbaceous perennials, 79% of deciduous woody perennials, and 87% of evergreen woody perennials (Rhoades and Cates, 1976). Because tannins are nonspecific in their ability to precipitate proteins, they are equally effective in preventing fungal, viral, and bacterial attacks as well as herbivory by both vertebrates and invertebrates. Some tannins are absorbed by vertebrates that ingest them and thereby produce internal physiological damage (McLeod, 1974). The deterrence of soluble phenolics to herbivory depends on either innate or acquired association of their astringent taste with the incurred metabolic aberrations when ingested (Rhoades, 1979).

2. ALKALOIDS

Alkaloids differ from the other secondary plant compounds by having one or more nitrogen atoms in a heterocyclic ring (Culvenor, 1973; Levin, 1976b; Robinson, 1979). The term *alkaloid* was derived at a time when plant compounds were considered as either neutral or acidic from the observation that these nitrogen-containing compounds had alkaline properties (Wasacz, 1981). Approximately 10,000 different alkaloids have been identified, and they occur in about 20% of the flowering plants (Harborne, 1991). The alkaloids include many of the plant-derived pharmacological and hallucinogenic drugs used by humans. Examples of well-known alkaloids are nicotine and various morphine drugs, delphinine of larkspur, conine of poison hemlock, tomatine of tomato plants, atropine of deadly nightshade, and lupinine of lupine. Plant alkaloid concentrations vary during the day. For example, opium sap has been collected for centuries during the morning because the sap has its highest morphine content between 9 and 10 A.M. (Wasacz, 1981).

The prevalence of secondary plant compounds, and particularly alkaloids, also increases from arctic to tropical latitudes. Just as plant diversity and abundance increase as the tropics are approached, so do the pressures from plant pests that dictate the need for more extensive plant defenses. For example, the percentage of alkaloid-bearing plants increases from approximately 15% at 40° north or south latitude to 40% at the equator (Levin, 1976a; Moody, 1978;

Robinson, 1979). Alkaloids also are more common in plants growing in nitrogen-rich environments (Mattson, 1980).

3. TERPENOIDS

Terpenoids are one of the largest classes of plant secondary constituents with between 15,000 to 20,000 having been characterized (Harborne, 1991). They are all low molecular weight, generally cyclic compounds that are soluble in organic solvents. They are all structurally related through their repeating isopentenoid units, $[CH_2=C(-CH3)-CH=CH_2]$. Examples of commonly encountered terpenes include the volatile, aromatic oils of sagebrush and evergreens, carotenes and vitamin A, the insecticide pyrethrin from *Chrysanthemum*, eucalyptol of eucalyptus, peel oils of citrus fruits, and gossypol of cottonseed.

Terpenoids are best known for their insecticidal, antimicrobial, and toxic effects. Terpenoid toxicity to gastrointestinal bacteria in which small amounts can be tolerated is dose dependent. However, cellulolytic rumen bacteria are more susceptible to terpenoid toxicity than are starch-digesting bacteria (Oh *et al.*, 1967; Schwartz *et al.*, 1980a). Because many of the terpenoids are either volatile or bitter in taste and thus can be readily associated with the metabolic aberrations, they are effective feeding deterrents (Morrow *et al.*, 1976; Mabry and Gill, 1979; Schwartz *et al.*, 1980b; Reichardt *et al.*, 1984).

V. ENERGY CONTENT

The caloric or gross energy content of a food is dependent on its composition and the caloric content of the different constituents. Mammals and birds consumed whole by carnivores vary from less than 1 kcal/g fresh weight in very lean animals to as much as 5 kcal/g in very fat animals like ringed seal weanlings (Robbins, 1983). However, the energy content of most wild birds or mammals that do not accumulate large fat reserves rarely exceeds 2.5 kcal/g. Consequently, the weight or number of prey consumed to meet a carnivore's energy requirement could vary several fold depending on the energy content of the prey. Similarly, selective feeding on only portions of prey can alter the energy content of the diet. For example, the selective feeding by polar bears on the fat deposits of ringed seals dramatically increases the average energy content of their diet (Stirling and McEwan, 1975).

Whole fish range from 0.8 kcal/g fresh weight to 2.5 kcal/g (MacKinnon, 1972; Jensen, 1979; Ashwell-Erickson and Elsner, 1981; Montevecchi *et al.*, 1984; Heath and Randall, 1985). The higher energy levels occur in the more oily fish, such as mackerel, or in egg-laden females. The energy content of insects ranges from 0.6 kcal/g fresh weight to 2.2 kcal/g, with egg-laden females, advancing prepupal stages, and those that accumulate fat for seasonal dormancy having the highest levels (Driver *et al.*, 1974; Norberg, 1978; Graber and Graber, 1983). Other invertebrates have similar energy contents with the exception of very low levels (such as 0.1 kcal/g) in those that accumulate minerals, such as mollusks in which the calciferous shell is a large percentage of their weight (Thompson and Sparks, 1978; Montevecchi *et al.*, 1984; Heath and Randall, 1985; Jorde and Owen, 1988). Thus, the energy content of animals generally ranges from 0.6 to 2.5 kcal/g with the variation largely due to factors regulating fat accumulation.

The gross energy content of plants varies by plant part, plant growth form, season, and latitude or elevation (Golley, 1961; Jordan, 1971; Baruch, 1982). Alpine and arctic woody plants that are slow growing and well-defended by high energy resins, waxes, or oils have a higher energy content (5.4 kcal/g) than the trees of a tropical rain forest (3.8 kcal/g). Similarly, conifers have a higher energy content (5.4 kcal/g) than deciduous, broadleaf trees (4.9 kcal/g for an oak woodland). The energy content of plant seeds increases from averages of 4.5 kcal/g for grass seeds, to 5.0 kcal/g for deciduous tree and shrub seeds, to 6.1 kcal/g for coniferous tree seeds (Kendeigh and West, 1965; Johnson and Robel, 1968; Grodzinski and Sawicka-Kapusta, 1970; Robel *et al.*, 1979a, b). The increasing energy content of the seeds is directly related to their fat content.

VI. FIBER

Nutritionists have long attempted to develop analytical systems to predict the nutritive value of plant matter. Because plant cytoplasmic proteins, carbohydrates, and fats are usually highly digestible, much of the emphasis has been on understanding plant cell wall composition and digestibility. Plant cell wall digestibility depends on its chemical composition, the internal molecular configuration of each component, the three-dimensional relationships of all components, and the digestive system of the ingesting animal.

A. Sample Preparation

Care of samples during collection, storage, and analysis is of the utmost importance in the development of analyses that reflect the nutritive value of the animal's diet. Sample care and subsequent analysis must ensure maximum accuracy in component extraction and identification, as well as practicality. Food samples are routinely dried and ground prior to analysis. Such procedures are justifiable only as long as chemical composition is unaltered.

The effects of drying are dependent on temperature and the forage chemical composition. Drying of forages above 50°C often increases the lignin content because proteins and carbohydrates complex in the nonenzymatic browning or

Maillard reaction to form insoluble lignin-like complexes. Conversely, air drying of forages can increase cell-wall content as cell solubles are metabolized during the time the fresh plant sample continues respiration. Thus, the preferred drying temperature for forages that are not defended by secondary plant compounds, such as grasses, is 40°C, which is rapid and hot enough to minimize cell soluble catabolism yet cool enough to minimize artifact lignin formation (Goering *et al.*, 1973; Culberson *et al.*, 1977; Acosta and Kothmann, 1978; Mould and Robbins, 1981).

Forages that contain significant levels of soluble phenolics, volatile terpenoids, or unsaturated lipids often need special care before or during drying. Because the analyses of these compounds in the dried sample will underestimate their content in the original sample due to volatilization, formation of insoluble complexes, or oxidation, freeze-drying, immediate extraction of the fresh sample, or analyses of frozen samples may be necessary. Volatile oils are commonly obtained through steam distillation of fresh or frozen samples, and nonvolatile terpenoids and soluble phenolics by organic or aqueous-organic solvent extraction of fresh samples (Swain, 1979; Schwartz *et al.*, 1980a, b; Hagerman and Butler, 1989).

B. Fiber Analyses

Fiber analyses have attempted either to quantify chemically discrete components, such as cellulose, hemicellulose, or lignin, or to separate digestible from nondigestible fractions. The two aims of fiber analyses are not synonymous because cellulose and hemicellulose are partially digestible. Attempts to develop simple chemical procedures to quantify the nondigestible fraction have been futile.

First attempts at fiber analyses for nutritional purposes began in 1803, when plant samples were merely washed with water. Subsequently, alcohol, ether, and weak acid and alkaline solutions were used in attempts to remove digestible fractions more thoroughly while retaining fiber (Tyler, 1975). Further development and standardization of methods to define nutritional entities in the 1850s and 1860s led to what is now known as the proximate system of analysis (Fonnesbeck, 1977; Van Soest, 1981). It consists of the following steps;

1. Determine dry matter at 100°C.
2. Extract with ether the dried sample to estimate lipid content.
3. Reflux the ether-extracted residue for 30 min in 1.25% sulfuric acid, followed by a similar boiling in 1.25% sodium hydroxide. The insoluble organic residues are reported as crude fiber.
4. Determine nitrogen by the Kjeldahl method and multiply by 6.25 to estimate crude protein content.

5. Determine ash content at 500°C.

6. Subtract the percentage of ether extract, crude fiber, crude protein, and ash from 100 to estimate the nitrogen-free extract (NFE).

Such analyses are definitive because the method of isolation arbitrarily defines the residue. The components at each extraction are not purified and identified on the basis of their chemical properties. Such analyses are useful only if the method of isolation depends on a unique molecular property that allows a quantitatively discrete chemical determination relatively free of interfering compounds or provides the ability to predict the outcome of a specific nutritional interaction, such as digestion.

Because each step in the proximate analysis determines the content of a heterogeneous mixture, the value of proximate analysis must rest on its ability to predict the sample's nutritive value. Crude fiber has been considered the least digestible fibrous matter, and NFE has been considered to be highly digestible carbohydrates. However, the digestibilities of crude fiber range from 0 to 90% in ruminants (Maynard and Loosli, 1969). Because lignin is partially soluble in alkaline solutions and hemicellulose in both acid and alkali (Van Soest, 1969), NFE can have a lower digestibility than does crude fiber. Thus, the two major components of proximate analysis have neither a uniform composition nor a predictable digestibility. Although crude fiber–NFE analyses continue to be used because of their simplicity and sizable data base generated during the last 100 years, further progress in understanding the role of fiber in animal nutrition depends on the development of better analytical procedures.

Detergent analyses were proposed during the early 1960s as a replacement for crude fiber–NFE determinations (Van Soest, 1963a, b, 1965, 1967; Goering and Van Soest, 1970). The plant sample is theoretically divided into cell wall–cell soluble fractions on the basis of solubility in detergent solutions of differing acidity. Detergents are used to emulsify and bind cell solubles (cytoplasm), particularly protein that must be removed to minimize artifact lignin formation. The residual cell wall can be further partitioned into its components—hemicellulose, cellulose, lignin, and cutin–suberin. The basic steps in detergent analyses are

1. Reflux a plant sample in neutral detergent to obtain the cell wall or neutral detergent fiber residue (NDF). Cell solubles or neutral detergent solubles (NDS) are equal to the weight loss between the original sample and the NDF. The NDF contains hemicellulose, cellulose, lignin, and cutin–suberin. Separate amylase treatments are necessary when high levels of starch occur, as in seeds or vegetables (McQueen and Nicholson, 1979).

2. Reflux the NDF in acid detergent to remove hemicellulose and determine acid detergent fiber (ADF) by difference.

3. Treat ADF with saturated potassium permanganate to oxidize and remove lignin and determine lignin by difference.

4. Treat the delignified ADF with 72% sulfuric acid to solubilize cellulose and determine cellulose by difference.

5. Ash the sulfuric acid residue to gravimetrically determine cutin–suberin. When the samples contain minimal cutin–suberin, step 3 can be omitted, as the final ashing will determine the combined lignin–cutin–suberin content.

6. Biogenic silica is determined by treating an ashed separate ADF residue with hydrobromic acid.

Detergent analysis does not attempt in itself to determine the nutritive value or digestibility of the various plant components. However, it does provide a useful definitive separation of the plant sample into its basic components, which ultimately may be related to nutritive value through statistical comparison. While detergent analyses are appealing after decades of stagnation in forage analyses, intriguing difficulties still remain because of the chemical complexity of plants relative to the use of definitive methods.

Detergent analyses have changed significantly since their inception. For example, sodium sulfite, which was initially added to the neutral detergent solution to improve protein removal, is no longer used for low-tannin forages because it also removed some lignin (Van Soest and Robertson, 1980, 1981; Mould and Robbins, 1981). However, sodium sulfite should be used when analyzing tannin-containing forages as the error produced by lignin removal is small when compared to the error in fiber and lignin caused by the retention of tannin complexes (Hanley *et al.*, 1992). Neutral detergent fiber and ADF were originally isolated from separate samples of the intact plant material rather than sequentially as outlined here. However, it was not uncommon to obtain higher ADF than NDF, resulting in negative hemicellulose estimates by subtraction. The use of sequential analyses eliminates the potential for negative hemicellulose values, but it does not necessarily provide an accurate hemicellulose estimate (Mould and Robbins, 1981). Similarly, pectins are removed by neutral detergent (Bailey and Ulyatt, 1970; Bailey *et al.*, 1978; Mould and Robbins, 1981). Because pectins are a major structural carbohydrate of the plant cell wall, neutral detergent fiber and cell wall are not synonyms.

The removal of soluble fiber by neutral detergent is an unacceptable error when analyzing feeds consumed by animals with minimal gastrointestinal fermentation. For these animals, enzymatic analyses have been developed for the determination of total dietary fiber, i.e., both soluble and insoluble fiber (Asp *et al.*, 1983; Prosky *et al.*, 1984). The basic steps are

1. Remove fat from sample with petroleum or ethyl ether.

2. Incubate sample in phosphate buffer (pH 7.5) with α-amylase to break down starch to maltose and dextrins.

3. Incubate acidified (pH 4.5) sample with protease to remove protein.

4. Continue incubation with amyloglucosidase to complete removal of starch and small sugars.

5. Add 95% ethanol to precipitate soluble fiber.

6. Filter, wash, dry, and weigh residue and express total dietary fiber as a percentage of the original sample.

Current fiber analyses should be viewed with a healthy degree of skepticism. Although detergent and enzymatic analyses offer far greater potential for understanding the nutritional value of foods than did crude fiber–NFE analyses (Pritchard and Robbins, 1990; Hanley *et al.*, 1992), further development is necessary. Ultimately, it is unrealistic to expect that one analytical scheme will be suitable for all feeds and all animals.

REFERENCES

Acosta, R. A., and Kothmann, M. M. (1978). Chemical composition of esophageal-fistula forage samples as influenced by drying method and salivary leaching. *J. Anim. Sci.* **47**, 691–698.

Akin, D. E, and Barton, F. E., II. (1983). Forage ultrastructure and the digestion of plant cell walls by rumen microorganisms. *In* "Wood and Agricultural Residues" (E.J. Soltes, ed.), pp. 33–57. Academic Press, New York.

Albersheim, P. (1975). The walls of growing plant cells. *Sci. Am.* **232**, 80–95.

Ashwell-Erickson, S., and Elsner, R. (1981). The energy cost of free existence for Bering Sea harbor and spotted seals. *In* "The Eastern Bering Sea Shelf Oceanography and Resources" (D. W. Wood and J. A. Calder, eds.), pp. 869–899. Univ. Washington Press, Seattle.

Asp, N-G., Johansson, C. G., Hallmer, H., and Siljestrom, M. (1983). Rapid enzymatic assay of insoluble and soluble dietary fiber. *J. Agric. Food Chem.* **31**, 476–482.

Bailey, R. W. (1973). Structural carbohydrates. *In* "Chemistry and Biochemistry of Herbage," Vol. I (G. W. Butler and R. W. Bailey, eds.), pp. 157–211. Academic Press, New York.

Bailey, R. W., and Ulyatt, M. J. (1970). Pasture quality and ruminant nutrition. II. Carbohydrate and lignin composition of detergent-extracted residues from pasture grasses and legumes. *N. Z. J. Agric. Res.* **13**, 591–604.

Bailey, R. W., Chesson, A., and Munroe, J. (1978). Plant cell wall fractionation and structural analysis. *Am. J. Clin. Nutr.* **31**, S77–S81.

Baruch, Z. (1982). Patterns of energy content in plants from the Venezuelan Paramos. *Oecologia* **55**, 47–52.

Bonhomme-Florentin, A. (1988). Degradation of hemicellulose and pectin by horse caecum contents. *Br. J. Nutr.* **60**, 185–192.

Brattsten, L. B. (1979). Biochemical defense mechanisms in herbivores against allelochemicals. *In* "Herbivores: Their Interaction with Secondary Plant Metabolites" (G.A. Rosenthal and D.H. Janzen, eds.), pp. 199–270. Academic Press, New York.

Brizuela, M. A., Detling, J. K., and Cid, M. S. (1986). Silicon concentration of grasses growing in sites with different grazing histories. *Ecology* **67**, 1098–1101.

Brown, A. J., and Kolattukudy, P. E. (1978). Evidence that pancreatic lipase is responsible for the hydrolysis of cutin, a biopolyester present in mammalian diet, and the role of bile salt and colipase in this hydrolysis. *Arch. Biochem. Biophys.* **190**, 17–26.

Bryant, J. P., Kuropat, P. J., Reichardt, P. B., and Clausen, T. P. (1991). Controls over the allocation of resources by woody plants to chemical antiherbivore defense. *In* "Plant Defenses Against Mammalian Herbivory" (R. T. Palo and C. T. Robbins, eds.), pp. 83–102. CRC Press, Boca Raton, Florida.

Bullard, R. W., and Elias, D. J. (1979). Sorghum polyphenols and bird resistance. *Proc. Inst. Food Technol.* **36**, 43–49.

Bump, G., Darrow, R. W., Edminster, F. C., and Crissey, W. F. (1947). "The Ruffed Grouse: Life History, Propagation, Management." New York Cons. Dept., Albany, New York.

Cogswell, C., and Kamstra, L. D. (1976). The stage of maturity and its effect upon the chemical composition of four native range species. *J. Range Manage.* **29**, 460–463.

Conn, E. E. (1979). Cyanide and cyanogenic glycosides. In "Herbivores: Their Interaction with Secondary Plant Metabolites" (G. A. Rosenthal and D. H. Janzen, eds.), pp. 387–412. Academic Press, New York.

Cowan, R. L., Jordan, J. S., Grimes, J. L., and Gill, J. D. (1970). Comparative nutritive values of forage species. *Range and Wildlife Habitat Evaluation, U.S.D.A. Misc. Publ.* **1147**, 48–56.

Culberson, C. R., Culberson, W. L.., and Johnson, A. (1977). Thermally induced chemical artifacts in lichens. *Phytochemistry* **16**, 127–130.

Culvenor, C.C. (1973). Alkaloids. In "Chemistry and Biochemistry of Herbage," Vol. I (G. W. Butler and R. W. Bailey, eds.), pp. 375–446. Academic Press, New York.

Darcy, B. K., and Belyea, R. L. (1980). Effect of delignification upon in vitro digestion of forage cellulose. *J. Anim. Sci.* **51**, 798–803.

Diamond, A. W., and Place, A. R. (1988). Wax digestion by black-throated honey-guides *Indicator indicator. Ibis* **130**, 558–561.

Dietz, D. R., Udall, R. H., and Yeager, L. E. (1962). Chemical composition and digestibility by mule deer of selected forage species, Cache la Poudre Range, Colorado. *Colo. Game Fish Tech. Publ.* **14**.

Driver, E. A., Sugden, L. G., and Kovach, R. J. (1974). Calorific, chemical and physical values of potential duck foods. *Freshwater Biol.* **4**, 281–292.

Englyst, H. (1981). Determination of carbohydrate and its composition in plant materials. In "The Analysis of Dietary Fiber in Food" (W. P. T. James and O. Theander, eds.), pp. 71–91. Marcel Dekker, New York.

Farnsworth, N. R., Bingel, A. S., Cordell, G. A., Crane, F. A., and Fong, H. H. S. (1975). Potential value of plants as sources of new antifertility agents. II. *J. Pharm. Sci.* **64**, 717–754.

Feeny, P. (1976). Plant apparency and chemical defenses. *Recent Adv. Phytochem.* **10**, 1–42.

Fonnesbeck, P. V. (1977). Estimating nutritive value from chemical analyses. *Proc. Int. Symp. Feed Composition, Animal Nutr. Reg., and Computerization of Diets* **1**, 219–227.

Gates, D. M. (1962). "Energy Exchange in the Biosphere." Harper, New York.

Goering, H. K., and Van Soest, P. J. (1970). Forage fiber analyses (apparatus, reagents, procedures, and some applications). *U.S.D.A. Agric. Handbook* **379**.

Goering, H. K., Van Soest, P. J., and Hemken, R. W. (1973). Relative susceptibility of forages to heat damage as affected by moisture, temperature and pH. *J. Dairy Sci.* **56**, 137–143.

Golley, F. B. (1961). Energy values of ecological materials. *Ecology* **42**, 581–584.

Graber, J. W., and Graber, R. R. (1983). Feeding rates of warblers in spring. *Condor* **85**, 139–150.

Greenwood, D. J., and Barnes, A. (1978). A theoretical model for the decline in the protein content of plants during growth. *J. Agric. Sci.* **91**, 461–466.

Grodzinski, W., and Sawicka-Kapusta, K. (1970). Energy values of tree-seeds eaten by small mammals. *Oikos* **21**, 52–58.

Hagerman, A. E., and Butler, L. G. (1989). Choosing appropriate methods and standards for assaying tannin. *J. Chem. Ecol.* **15**, 1795–1810.

Hanley, T. A., Robbins, C. T., Hagerman, A. E., and McArthur, C. (1992). Predicting digestible protein and digestible dry matter in tannin-containing forages consumed by ruminants. *Ecology* **73**, 537–541.

Harborne, J. B. (1972). "Phytochemical Ecology." Academic Press, London.

Harborne, J. B. (1991). The chemical basis of plant defense. *In* "Plant Defenses Against Mammalian Herbivory" (R. T. Palo and C. T. Robbins, eds.), pp. 45–59. CRC Press, Boca Raton, Florida.

Harkin, J. M. (1973). Lignin. *In* "Chemistry and Biochemistry of Herbage," Vol. I (G. W. Butler and R. W. Bailey, eds.), pp. 323–373. Academic Press, New York.

Hawke, J. C. (1973). Lipids. *In* "Chemistry and Biochemistry of Herbage," Vol. I (G. W. Butler and R. W. Bailey, eds.), pp. 213–263. Academic Press, New York.

Heath, R. G. M., and Randall, R. M. (1985). Growth of jackass penguin chicks (*Spheriscus demersus*) hand reared on different diets. *J. Zool.* **205**, 91–105.

Janzen, D. H. (1979). New horizons in the biology of plant defenses. *In* "Herbivores: Their Interaction with Secondary Plant Metabolites" (G. A. Rosenthal and D. H. Janzen, eds.), pp. 331–350. Academic Press, New York.

Jensen, A. J. (1979). Energy content analysis from weight and liver index measurements of immature pollock (*Pollachius virens*). *J. Fish. Res. Bd. Can.* **36**, 1207–1213.

Johnson, R. A., Willson, M. F., Thompson, J. N., and Bertin, R. I. (1985). Nutritional value of wild fruits and consumption by migrant frugivorous birds. *Ecology* **66**, 819–827.

Johnson, S. R., and Robel, R. J. (1968). Caloric values of seeds from four range sites in northeastern Kansas. *Ecology* **49**, 956–961.

Jones, L. H. P., and Handreck, K. A. (1967). Silica in soils, plants, and animals. *Adv. Agron.* **19**, 107–149.

Jordan, C. F. (1971). A world pattern in plant energetics. *Am. Sci.* **59**, 425–433.

Jorde, D. G., and Owen, R. B, Jr. (1988). Efficiency of nutrient use by American black ducks wintering in Maine. *J. Wildl. Manage.* **52**, 209–214.

Karis, I. G., and Hudson, B. J. F. (1974). Effect of crop maturity on leaf lipids. *J. Sci. Food Agric.* **25**, 885–886.

Keating, S. T., Yendal, W. G., and Schultz, J. C. (1988). Relationship between susceptibility of gypsy moth larvae (*Lepidoptera: Lymantriidae*) to a baculovirus and host plant foliage constituents. *Environ. Entomol.* **17**, 952–958.

Kendeigh, S. C., and West, G. C. (1965). Caloric values of plant seeds eaten by birds. *Ecology* **46**, 553–555.

Kolattukudy, P. E. (1977). Lipid polymers and associated phenols, their chemistry, biosynthesis, and role in pathogenesis. *In* "The Structure, Biosynthesis, and Degradation of Wood. Recent Advances in Phytochemistry," Vol. II (F. A. Loewus and V. C. Runeckles, eds.), pp. 185–246. Plenum, New York.

Kramer, P. J., and Kozlowski, T. T. (1960). "Physiology of Trees." McGraw-Hill, New York.

Kubota, J., Rieger, S., and Lazer, V. A. (1970). Mineral composition of herbage browsed by moose in Alaska. *J. Wildl. Manage.* **34**, 565–569.

Levin, D. A. (1976a). Alkaloid-bearing plants: An ecogeographic perspective. *Am. Nat.* **110**, 261–284.

Levin, D. A. (1976b). The chemical defenses of plants to pathogens and herbivores. *Annu. Rev. Ecol. Syst.* **7**, 121–159.

Lough, A. K., and Garton, G. A. (1968). Digestion and metabolism of feed lipids in ruminants and non-ruminants. *Symp. Zool. Soc. London* **21**, 163–173.

Luick, J. R., White, R. G., Gau, A. M., and Jenness, R. (1974). Compositional changes in the milk secreted by grazing reindeer. I. Gross composition and ash. *J. Dairy Sci.* **57**, 1325–1333.

Lyttleton, J. W. (1973). Proteins and nucleic acids. *In* "Chemistry and Biochemistry of Herbage," Vol. I (G. W. Butler and R. W. Bailey, eds.), pp. 63–103. Academic Press, New York.

Mabry, T. J., and Gill, J. E. (1979). Sesquiterpene lactones and other terpenoids. *In* "Herbivores: Their Interaction with Secondary Plant Metabolites" (G. A. Rosenthal and D.H. Janzen, eds.), pp. 501–537. Academic Press, New York.

Mack, A. L. (1990). Is frugivory limited by secondary compounds in plants? *Oikos* **57**, 135–138.

MacKinnon, J. C. (1972). Summer storage of energy and its use for winter metabolism and gonad maturation in American plaice (*Hippoglossoides platessoides*). *J. Fish. Res. Bd. Can.* **29,** 1749–1759.

Martin, J. T., and Juniper, B. E. (1970). "The Cuticles of Plants." St. Martin's, New York.

Mattson, W. J., Jr. (1980). Herbivory in relation to plant nitrogen content. *Annu. Rev. Ecol. Syst.* **11,** 119–161.

Maynard, L. A., and Loosli, J. K. (1969). "Animal Nutrition" McGraw-Hill, New York.

McConnell, B. R., and Garrison, G. A. (1966). Seasonal variations of available carbohydrates in bitterbrush. *J. Wildl. Manage.* **30,** 168–172.

McKey, D. (1979). The distribution of secondary compounds within plants. *In* "Herbivores: Their Interaction with Secondary Plant Metabolites" (G. A. Rosenthal and D. H. Janzen, eds.), pp. 55–133. Academic Press, New York.

McLeod, M. N. (1974). Plant tannins-their role in forage quality. *Nutr. Abstr. Rev.* **44,** 803–815.

McNaughton, S. J., and Tarrants, J. L. (1983). Grass leaf silicification: Natural selection for an inducible defense against herbivores. *Proc. Natl. Acad. Sci. USA* **80,** 790–791.

McNaughton, S. J., Tarrants, J. L., McNaughton, M. M., and Davis, R.H. (1985). Silica as a defense against herbivory and a growth promoter in African grasses. *Ecology* **66,** 528–535.

McQueen, R. E., and Nicholson, J. W. (1979). Modification of the neutral-detergent fiber procedure for cereals and vegetables by using α-amylase. *J. Assoc. Off. Anal. Chem.* **62,** 676–680.

Montevecchi, W. A., Ricklefs, R. E., Kirkman, I. R., and Gabaldon, D. (1984). Growth energetics of nestling northern gannets (*Sula bassanus*). *Auk* **101,** 334–341.

Moody, S. (1978). Latitude, continental drift, and the percentage of alkaloid-bearing plants in floras. *Am. Nat.* **112,** 965–968.

Morrow, P. A., Bellas, T. E., and Eisner, T. (1976). Eucalyptus oils in the defensive oral discharge of Australian sawfly larvae (*Hymenoptera: Pergidae*). *Oecologia* **24,** 193–206.

Mould, E. D., and Robbins, C. T. (1981). Evaluation of detergent analysis in estimating nutritional value of browse. *J. Wildl. Manage.* **45,** 937–947.

National Research Council (NRC). (1982). Nutrient requirements of mink and foxes. Nat. Acad. Sci., Washington, D.C.

Norberg, R. A. (1978). Energy content of some spiders and insects on branches of spruce (*Picea abies*) in winter; prey of certain passerine birds. *Oikos* **31,** 222–229.

Oh, H. K., Sakai, T., Jones, M. B., and Longhurst, W. M. (1967). Effects of various essential oils isolated from Douglas fir needles upon sheep and deer rumen microbial activity. *Appl. Microbiol.* **15,** 777–784.

Pritchard, G. T., and Robbins, C. T. (1990). Digestive and metabolic efficiencies of grizzly and black bears. *Can. J. Zool.* **68,** 1645–1651.

Prosky, L., Asp, N-G., Furda, I., DeVries, J. W., Schweizer, T. F., and Harland, B. F. (1984). Determination of total dietary fiber in foods, food products, and total diets: Interlaboratory study. *J. Assoc. Off. Anal. Chem.* **67,** 1044–1051.

Redford, K. H., and Dorea, J. G. (1984). The nutritional value of invertebrates with emphasis on ants and termites as food for mammals. *J. Zool.* **203,** 385–395.

Reichardt, P. B., Bryant, J. P., Clausen, T. P., and Wieland, G. D. (1984). Defense of winter dormant Alaska paper birch against snowshoe hares. *Oecologia* **65,** 58–69.

Rhoades, D. F. (1979). Evolution of plant chemical defense against herbivores. *In* "Herbivores: Their Interaction with Secondary Plant Metabolites" (G. A. Rosenthal and D. H. Janzen, eds.), pp. 3–54. Academic Press, New York.

Rhoades, D. F., and Cates, R. G. (1976). Toward a general theory of plant antiherbivore chemistry. *In* "Recent Advances in Phytochemistry, Vol. 10. Biochemical Interaction Between Plants and Insects" (J. W. Wallace and R. L. Mansell, eds.), pp. 168–213. Plenum, New York.

Richardson, M. (1977). The proteinase inhibitors of plants and microorganisms. *Phytochemistry* **16,** 159–169.

Robbins, C. T. (1983). "Wildlife Feeding and Nutrition." Academic Press, New York.

Robbins, C. T., and Moen, A. N. (1975). Composition and digestibility of several deciduous browses in the Northeast. *J. Wildl. Manage.* **39,** 337–341.

Robel, R. J., Bisset, A. R., Clement, T. M., Jr., and Dayton, A.D. (1979a). Metabolizable energy of important foods in bobwhites in Kansas. *J. Wildl. Manage.* **43,** 982–987.

Robel, R. J., Bisset, A. R., Dayton, A. D., and Kemp, K. E. (1979b). Comparative energetics of bobwhites on six different foods. *J. Wildl. Manage.* **43,** 987–992.

Robinson, T. (1979). The evolutionary ecology of alkaloids. *In* "Herbivores: Their Interaction with Secondary Plant Metabolites" (G. A. Rosenthal and D. H. Janzen, eds.), pp. 413–448. Academic Press, New York.

Roby, D. D., Place, A. R., and Ricklefs, R. E. (1986). Assimilation and deposition of wax esters in planktivorous seabirds. *J. Exp. Zool.* **238,** 29–41.

Rowsemitt, C. N., and O'Connor, A. J. (1989). Reproductive function in *Dipodomys ordii* stimulated by 6–methoxybenzoxazolinone. *J. Mammal.* **70,** 805–809.

Sakai, H. F., and Carpenter, J. R. (1990). The variety and nutritional value of foods consumed by Hawaiian crow nestlings, an endangered species. *Condor* **92,** 220–228.

Schwartz, C. C., Nagy, J. G., and Regelin, W. L. (1980a). Juniper oil yield, terpenoid concentration, and antimicrobial effects on deer. *J. Wildl. Manage.* **44,** 107–113.

Schwartz, C. C., Regelin, W. L., and Nagy, J. G. (1980b). Deer preference for juniper forage and volatile oil treated foods. *J. Wildl. Manage.* **44,** 114–120.

Sedinger, J. S. (1984). Protein and amino acid composition of tundra vegetation in relation to nutritional requirements of geese. *J. Wildl. Manage.* **48,** 1128–1136.

Seigler, D. S. (1979). Toxic seed lipids. *In* "Herbivores: Their Interaction with Secondary Plant Metabolites" (G. A. Rosenthal and D. H. Janzen, eds.), pp. 449–470. Academic Press, New York.

Setchell, K. D. R., Gosselin, S. J., Welch, M. B., Johnston, J. O., Balistreri, W. F., Kramer, L. W., Dresser, B. L., and Tarr, M. J. (1987). Dietary estrogens: A probable cause of infertility and liver disease in captive cheetahs. *Gastroenterology* **93,** 225–233.

Smith, D. (1973). The nonstructural carbohydrates. *In* "Chemistry and Biochemistry of Herbage," Vol. I (G. W. Butler and R. W. Bailey, eds.), pp. 105–155. Academic Press, New York.

Stirling, I., and McEwan, E. H. (1975). The caloric value of whole-ringed seals (*Phoca hispida*) in relation to polar bear (*Ursus maritimus*) ecology and hunting behavior. *Can. J. Zool.* **53,** 1021–1027.

Swain, T. (1979). Tannins and lipids. *In* "Herbivores: Their Interaction with Secondary Plant Metabolites" (G. A. Rosenthal and D. H. Janzen, eds.), pp. 657–682. Academic Press, New York.

Thompson, C. M., and Sparks, R. E. (1978). Comparative nutritional value of a native fingernail clam and the introduced Asiatic clam. *J. Wildl. Manage.* **42,** 391–396.

Tyler, C. (1975). Albrecht Thaer's hay equivalents: Fact or fiction. *Nutr. Abstr. Rev.* **45,** 1–11.

Van Soest, P. J. (1963a). Use of detergents in the analysis of fibrous feeds. I. Preparation of fiber residues of low nitrogen content. *J. Assoc. Off. Agric. Chem.* **46,** 825–829.

Van Soest, P. J. (1963b). Use of detergents in the analysis of fibrous feeds. II. A rapid method for the determination of fiber and lignin. *J. Assoc. Off. Agric. Chem.* **46,** 829–835.

Van Soest, P. J. (1965). Non-nutritive residues: A system of analysis for the replacement of crude fiber. *J. Assoc. Off. Agric. Chem.* **49,** 546–551.

Van Soest, P. J. (1967). Development of a comprehensive system of feed analysis and its application to forages. *J. Anim. Sci.* **26,** 119–128.

Van Soest, P. J. (1969). The chemical basis for the nutritive evaluation of forages. *Proc. Natl. Conf. Forage Qual. Eval. Util.*

Van Soest, P. J. (1981). "Nutritional Ecology of the Ruminant." O and B Books, Inc., Corvallis, Oregon.

Van Soest, P. J., and Jones, L. H. P. (1968). Effect of silica in forages upon digestibility. *J. Dairy Sci.* **51,** 1644–1648.

Van Soest, P. J., and Robertson, J. B. (1980). Systems of analysis for evaluating fibrous feeds. *In* "Standardization of Analytical Methodology for Feeds" (W. J. Pigden, C. C. Balch, and M. Graham, eds.), pp. 49–60. Int. Develop Center and Int. Union Nutr. Sci., Ottawa, Canada.

Van Soest, P. J., and Robertson, J. B. (1981). The detergent system of analysis and its application to human foods. *In* "Analysis of Dietary Fiber in Food" (P. James and O. Theander, eds.), pp. 123–158. M. Dekker, New York.

Vlieg, P. (1984). Proximate composition of some New Zealand squid species. *N. Z. J. Sci.* **27,** 145–150.

Wasacz, J. (1981). Natural and synthetic narcotic drugs. *Am. Sci.* **69,** 318–324.

White, L. M. (1973). Carbohydrate reserves of grasses: A review. *J. Range Manage.* **26,** 13–18.

Wilkie, K. C. B. (1979). The hemicellulose of grasses and cereals. *Adv. Carbohydr. Chem. Biochem.* **36,** 215–264.

13

Gastrointestinal Anatomy and Function

The field of nutrition has advanced significantly in recent years because of experimental work conducted on a broad spectrum of animal species.
CHANDRA AND NEWBERNE, 1977

Knowledge of the morphology and functioning of the gastrointestinal tract is essential for understanding nutrient utilization. Digestive systems provide many diverse examples of adaptive radiation in form and function that correspond to observed diets and nutritional strategies. All birds and mammals are dependent on the hydrolysis of ingested organic molecules by gastrointestinal digestive enzymes and the subsequent absorption of small fragments. The following discussion is largely based on the extensive reviews of Ziswiler and Farner (1972), Hume (1982), Vonk and Western (1984), Stevens (1988), and Langer (1988).

I. BUCCAL CAVITY

The buccal cavity is the first structure of the generalized digestive tract. Major differences between species occur in the teeth and lips of mammals, the bills of birds, and tongues, tastebuds, and saliva of both birds and mammals. For example, the tongues of birds can be long and sticky, as in woodpeckers, or tubular or semitubular, as in hummingbirds; or they can contain posterior-directed horny hooks for holding food tightly, as in penguins, or filtering processes, as in ducks and geese. Mammalian teeth are particularly important in the prehension of food and in reducing particle size for swallowing and digestion.

Saliva's major roles include lubricating food for swallowing, providing nutrients and buffers for foregut fermentation in many herbivores, solubilizing water-soluble food components for tasting, and initiating digestion through salivary enzymes. Saliva is produced primarily by the parotid, mandibular, and sublingual glands. Species that ingest slippery aquatic food or those that do little chewing because they ingest relatively moist food in large chunks, such as many carnivores, secret little saliva, whereas those, such as ruminant and nonruminant herbivores, that ingest drier fibrous food needing both mastication and lubrication secrete large volumes. Large ruminants can secrete from tens to hundreds of liters of saliva daily (Chauncey and Quintarelli, 1961). Many mammals (e.g., humans, laboratory rats, bears, moose, and mule deer) that are adapted for consuming tannin-containing foods secrete tannin-binding salivary proteins. Because free tannins can impede digestion and can be toxic if absorbed, these animals synthesize salivary proteins with a high tannin-binding affinity that neutralizes tannins as they are ingested (Robbins et al., 1991).

The identification of salivary enzymes is often difficult because of the contamination of saliva samples by food remnants, bacteria and protozoa, and oral tissue debris. However, several digestive enzymes do occur in saliva and include amylase and lipase. Salivary amylase occurs widely in herbivorous and omnivorous mammals but is absent from strict carnivores, such as cats (Vonk and Western, 1984). Because the results regarding salivary amylase in birds are very conflicting (Bhattacharya and Ghose, 1971; Jerrett and Goodge, 1973), salivary amylase is either minimal or absent in birds (Ziswiler and Farner, 1972). Taste and, consequently, food selection may be affected by salivary amylase as it hydrolyzes starch and glycogen to maltose and small oligosaccharides. Although salivary amylase is inactivated by the acidity of the mammalian glandular stomach, the enzyme can remain active in food boluses in which the interior is not immediately exposed to stomach acidity and in the more neutral pH of nonglandular stomach compartments of many herbivorous mammals (Karn and Malacinski, 1978).

Salivary and gastric lipase are the predominant enzymes for the digestion of milk fat (Hamosh, 1979; Abrams et al., 1988). Although fat digestion in adult animals is primarily by pancreatic and small intestine lipases, the activities of these enzymes are very low in nursing animals. The low levels of the normal, adult lipases in nursing mammals contrasts with the very high levels of fat in the milk of most wild animals (49 $\pm$ 8% of the dry matter of mature marsupial milk, 30 $\pm$ 5% for primates, 45 $\pm$ 4% for lagomorphs, 39 $\pm$ 13% for rodents, 39 $\pm$ 12% for terrestrial carnivores, 79 $\pm$ 5% for seals and sea lions, 38 $\pm$ 6% for artiodactyls, and a low of 7 $\pm$ 5% for perissodactyls) [Table 10.5]. Consequently, fat digestion in the newborn occurs in the stomach where the milk clot entraps both milk lipids and salivary lipase (Hamosh, 1979).

II. AVIAN CROP AND ESOPHAGUS

The esophagus conducts food from the mouth to the stomach. Passage can be delayed in those birds where food is stored in an expandable, nondifferentiated portion of the esophagus (e.g., grebes, penguins, gulls, owls, and woodpeckers) or in an expandable, differentiated portion called a crop. Although the crop usually protrudes ventrally to the vertebral column, the crop of several hummingbirds extends dorsally (Hainsworth and Wolf, 1972). However, some birds (such as frugivorous manakins) do not have a crop or any other esophageal storage capacity (Worthington, 1989).

The functions of the crop include storing food, softening and swelling of hard food particles by water absorption, providing nourishment for nestlings, and possibly initiating digestion. The storage capacity of the crop enables birds to consume more food than the stomach could handle efficiently at one time and thereby minimizes the frequency of feeding. Stored food is regurgitated from the esophagus or crop to nourish the young in such diverse groups as hawks, storks, penguins, pelicans, doves, pigeons, and parrots. Digestion in the crop is probably minimal in most birds as the crop does not secrete digestive enzymes. However, because crop pH (4.5 to 7.5 with an approximate mean of 6.0) is suitable for many plant and microbial enzymes, some hydrolysis may occur. Thus far, only one bird, the hoatzin, which is a 750 arboreal folivore of South America, has a crop and esophagus morphologically adapted for extensive microbial fermentation (Grajal et al., 1989).

III. STOMACH

A. Forestomach

Because vertebrates do not secrete enzymes to digest plant cell wall carbohydrates, symbiotic relationships with fiber-digesting bacteria and protozoa enable herbivores to utilize otherwise nondigestible plant fiber. Bacteria occur in both aerobic and anaerobic forms. Symbiotic relationships with aerobic bacteria would yield only bacterial cells and oxidized end products, primarily carbon dioxide and water. However, anaerobic fermentation in which oxidation is limited by the molecular oxygen content of ingested organic matter yields bacterial cells, reduced bacterial end products (such as volatile fatty acids that can be further oxidized by the host), oxygen-depleted and easily digestible food components (such as long-chain saturated fatty acids of dietary fat that cannot be metabolized by anaerobic bacteria), and carbon dioxide, methane, and hydrogen gas. The major volatile fatty acids produced during fermentation are acetic, propionic, and butyric acids. The complete oxidation of 1 mole of glucose from cellulose yields 38 moles of high-energy ATP. Because anaerobic bacteria fermenting glucose can capture only 2–6 moles of ATP (Van Soest, 1981), the residual 32–36 moles are available to the host via oxidative metabolism of the volatile fatty acids.

Animals with forestomach fermentation include the cervids; giraffes; bovids; tragulids or mouse deer; camels; peccaries and hippopotamuses; macropod marsupials, such as kangaroos and wallabies; leaf-eating monkeys, such as langurs; numerous herbivorous rodents; hyraxes; and leaf-eating tree sloths. The anatom-

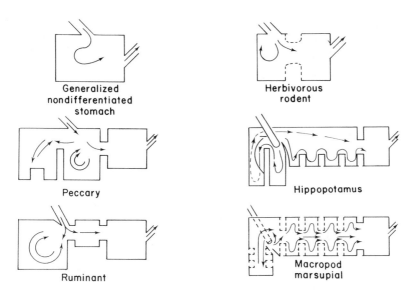

FIG. 13.1 Schematic diagram of several stomach types, indicating flow, general compartments, and separations. The folds of the macropod stomach are changeable and therefore drawn with broken lines. The division in the herbivorous rodent stomach is indicated with broken lines because stomach specialization can range from a unilobular stomach with minimal differentiation to complex, multichambered stomachs having cornified epithelium and papillae in areas removed from the glandular stomach by constrictions or folds. The compartment on the right of each herbivore stomach diagram is the true stomach, or abomasum. The rumen and reticulum of the ruminant stomach are illustrated as a single fermentation chamber. (Adapted from Langer, 1979; Verlag Paul Parey.)

ical complexity of the forestomach fermentation pouches ranges from a single diverticulum with minimal specialization communicating directly with the true stomach (as in many rodents), to the four-chambered, highly specialized ruminant stomach (Fig. 13.1). Very extensive forestomach pouches also occur in many cetaceans (whales, porpoises, and dolphins) and several small marsupials (honey possum, rufous rat-kangaroo, and long-nosed potoroo) (Gaskin, 1978; Chivers and Hladik, 1980; Richardson *et al.*, 1986; Hume *et al.*, 1988). Although volatile fatty acids occur in the contents of these sacculations, their mere presence does not indicate that these are important fermentation sites, particularly when the diet is highly digestible without fermentation. While some of these pouches are undoubtedly analogous to the avian crop in which food storage is their primary role (Richardson *et al.*, 1986; Hume *et al.*, 1988), bacterial and VFA concentrations in the forestomach of baleen whales, which can contain as much as 550 kg of food in a large fin whale, increasingly suggest that fermentation is an

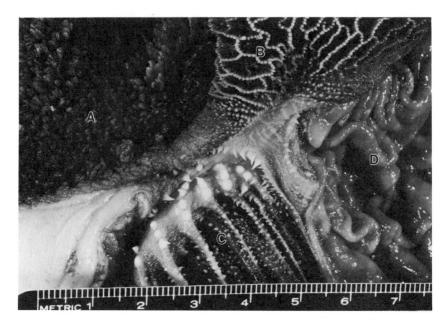

FIG. 13.2   Cross-section of a ruminant stomach showing the interior surfaces of the (A) rumen, (B) reticulum, (C) omasum, and (D) abomasum. (From Ullrey, 1980; O and B Books, Corvallis, Oregon.)

important digestive process in these animals (Herwig *et al.*, 1984). Only ruminants, camels, and macropod marsupials regurgitate the contents of the fermenting stomach in order to reduce particle size through further mastication. This process is called rumination in the ruminant and merycism in nonruminants.

The four chambers of the ruminant stomach are the rumen, reticulum, omasum, and abomasum (Fig. 13.2). The rumen is a large, thin-walled, saclike structure lined with papillae. The papillae increase the absorptive surface area from 16- to 38-fold relative to the theoretically nonpapillated rumen wall (Hoppe *et al.*, 1977). Finer food particles and microorganisms pass into the reticulum, which has a honey-combed, reticulated epithelium. The omasum is a finely partitioned, weirlike structure that (a) separates the highly acidic abomasal contents from the fermenting contents of the rumen–reticulum; (b) provides for the passage of smaller food particles into the abomasum while retaining less digested, larger particles in the rumen–reticulum; and (c) absorbs water and soluble food and microbial products (Prins *et al.*, 1972). Microbial cells, small food particles, and previously nonabsorbed metabolites pass into the abomasum, or true stomach, for enzymatic and acid hydrolysis.

The extensive evolution of forestomach fermentation in artiodactylas is associated with the development of widespread grass and forb plant communities (Langer, 1974, 1979; Janis, 1976; Van Soest, 1981; Demment and Van Soest, 1985). Fermentation enabled these animals to meet their energy requirements from previously nondigestible plant fiber. Perhaps equally important, because the Perissodactyla (horses, rhinoceroses, and other odd-toed ungulates) and many other animals had already developed an extensive lower-tract fermentation capable of digesting plant fiber, was the capability to conserve and synthesize microbial protein from nonprotein nitrogen, to synthesize vitamins, and to detoxify many secondary plant compounds *anterior* to the normal site of host enzymatic digestion and absorption. However, the benefits of forestomach fermentation can be balanced by a reduced rate of food passage and microbial losses of easily digestible, plant cellular contents.

The volumes of forestomach fermentation chambers as a percentage of total stomach volume in large adult herbivores average approximately 90%, ranging from 98% in the llama and guanaco, 95% in the hippopotamus, 92% in macropod marsupials, 90% in wild ruminants, to 87% in peccaries (Short, 1964; Vallenas *et al.*, 1971; Arman and Field, 1973; Hofmann, 1973; Robbins and Moen, 1975; Langer, 1974, 1978, 1979). However, the volume and functionality of the compartments change as the animal grows. For example, the relative forestomach fermentation volume in white-tailed deer increases from approximately 10% of the stomach at birth to 90% in the adult (Short, 1964).

The neonatal stomach of forestomach fermenters functions as if the animal were a simple-stomached animal. Because milk is totally digested by enzymes of the true stomach and small intestine, fermentation of milk would be both unnecessary and detrimental. Consequently, a necessity of advanced forestomach fermenters has been the concomitant evolution of a mechanism to pass milk directly from the esophagus into the acidic stomach. This mechanism is called the reticular groove in ruminants. The reticular groove is a bilipped channel passing along the reticulum wall from the esophageal orifice to the omasal orifice (Figs. 13.3 and 13.4). As milk passes down the esophagus, the lips of the groove close reflexively to form a rumen–reticulum bypass, which continues to function as long as milk is ingested. The groove will close even when milk is consumed from a bucket (Matthews and Kilgour, 1980). Such a bypass does not occur in rodents and hyraxes because of the close juxtaposition of the esophageal opening to the acidic stomach (Kinnear *et al.*, 1979; Leon, 1980). Although a gastric sulcus (groove) occurs in some macropod marsupials but is absent in others, a milk bypass is apparently unnecessary in very young marsupials as the stomach is undifferentiated and has a classical acid proteolysis throughout. Once the young leave the pouch and begin ingesting forage and developing areas of fermentation, the gastric sulcus may become important as a milk bypass mechanism (Hume, 1982).

Rumen development is dependent on the ingestion and fermentation of plant

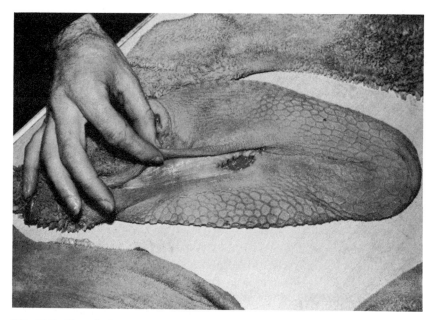

FIG. 13.3   The reticular groove, which in young ruminants conveys milk from the esophogeal orifice (left) to the omasal orifice (right), traversing the reticulum of an adult elk.

matter. Bacterial inoculation of the rumen is normally not a problem, with suitable bacteria potentially being transmitted in maternal saliva during licking of the neonate, on feed mouthed but not consumed by the mother, and on maternal feces touched or consumed by the neonate. Young deer and elk removed from the mother 6–18 hr after birth and raised in isolation develop normally functioning rumens. Thus, either inoculation is occurring very shortly after birth or suitable bacteria are being encountered throughout the environment. Papillary growth is stimulated by the metabolic products of fermentation, particularly volatile fatty acids. Butyrate, because of its metabolism by the rumen epithelium, provides the greatest stimulant to papillary growth, followed by propionate and acetate. Reduced milk intake increases the rate of rumen development by stimulating dry-feed intake and therefore fermentation (Tamate *et al.*, 1962; Poe *et al.*, 1971).

Many anatomical and functional differences occur among the stomachs of ruminants. Hofmann (1973, 1989) has done more than any other author to clarify these differences. Stomach structure, volume, mouth anatomy, and feeding habits are interrelated. On the basis of stomach characteristics and diet, Hofmann divided the ruminants into three major groups: concentrate selector (fruit and

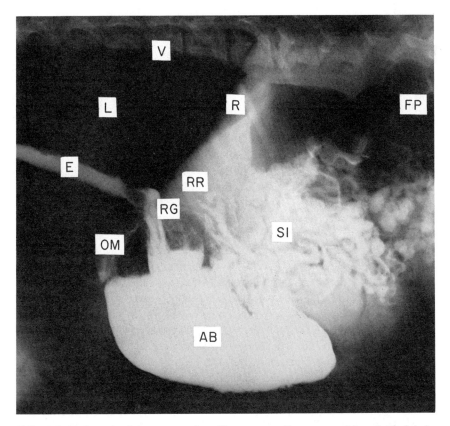

FIG. 13.4 Radiograph of the passage of a milk-contrast medium consumed by a bottle-fed, 3-week-old elk calf. The mixture, consumed approximately 20–30 min prior to the radiograph exposure, can be seen as it moves into the small intestine. Structures indicated are the esophagus (E), reticular groove (RG), omasum (OM), abomasum (AB), small intestine (SI), rumen–reticulum (RR), fecal pellets in the large intestine (FP), lungs (L), ribs (R), and vertebral column (V).

dicotyledonous foliage eaters), grass/roughage feeders, and intermediate types (mixed feeders). Grass/roughage feeders and intermediate feeders have rumen–reticulum volumes that are 53% and 22% greater, respectively, than those of concentrate selectors. However, Robbins *et al.* (1987) argued that concentrate selector is an inappropriate term when used to describe tree and shrub leaf and twig eaters (i.e., browsers). The digestibility of tree and shrub leaves (range: 35–62%) is not higher than the digestibility of grasses (29–73%) (Mould and Robbins, 1982; Chilcott and Hume, 1984; Foley and Hume, 1987; Robbins *et al.*, 1987). However, browsers can have a smaller rumen if leaves can be digested and passed faster than grasses. This can occur as (1) browsers have a less complex, more open omasum than grazers that is less of an impediment to particle flow (Hofmann, 1989) and (2) tree, shrub and forb leaves are more readily comminuted than grasses (Spalinger *et al.*, 1986; Baker and Hobbs, 1987). The failure of those feeding captive wildlife to recognize that very basic differences in gastrointestinal anatomy and function prevent the feeding of standardized diets to all members of a group (e.g., grass and legume hays to all ruminants) has killed many animals (Schoonveld *et al.*, 1974; Chivers and Hladik, 1980; Schwartz *et al.*, 1985; Hofmann and Matern, 1988).

Fluid from the rumen or the forestomach of marsupials contains from 11 to 760 billion bacteria per milliliter (McBee *et al.*, 1969; Pearson, 1969; Hume, 1982). These bacteria secrete cellulase into an immediately adjacent, extracellular zone to digest plant cell wall carbohydrates (Fig. 13.5). Monosaccharides are absorbed by the bacteria and metabolized to volatile fatty acids, 50 to 80% of which is acetic acid. Volatile fatty acids absorbed from the forestomach account for 21–75% of the digestible energy intake in ruminants and macropod marsupials (Stewart *et al.*, 1958; Gray *et al.*, 1967; Faichney, 1968; Leng *et al.*, 1968; Hume, 1977; Van Hoven and Boomker, 1981).

The pH of the forestomach contents is dependent on the balance between the production of volatile fatty acids, their rate of absorption or outflow, salivary buffering capacity, and the completeness of separation between the forestomach and the true stomach. For example, rumen pH in red deer decreased from 6.5 prior to feeding to 5.5 ninety minutes after feeding when the rate of acid production exceeded buffering and absorption capacities (Maloiy *et al.*, 1968). Forestomach pH has generally varied from 5.4 to 6.9 in wild ruminants, macropod marsupials, and hippopotamuses (Prins and Geelen, 1971; Dean *et al.*, 1975; Hoppe *et al.*, 1977; Van Hoven, 1978; Kinnear *et al.*, 1979; Kreulen and Hoppe, 1979; Leon, 1980; Van Hoven and Boomker, 1981; Clemens and Maloiy, 1982).

Plant nitrogen in the rumen or forestomach following a meal decreases as bacterial, protozoal, and soluble nitrogen increase. Bacteria largely degrade feed amino acids into their respective organic acid and ammonia elements, but subsequently resynthesize amino acids relative to their needs from the same precursors. From 64 to 85% of the plant nitrogen is incorporated into microbial nitrogen in the ruminant and marsupial forestomach (Weller *et al.*, 1962; Pilgrim *et al.*, 1970; Lintern-Moore, 1973). Fortunately, the synthesis of amino acids balances or even exceeds the degradation rate if nonprotein nitrogen, such as urea, is consumed. Thus, despite differences in true protein intake and its amino acid composition, forestomach bacteria tend to have a leveling effect on both dietary protein quality and quantity (Gray *et al.*, 1958; Purser, 1970; Leibholz, 1972; Storm and Orskov, 1983).

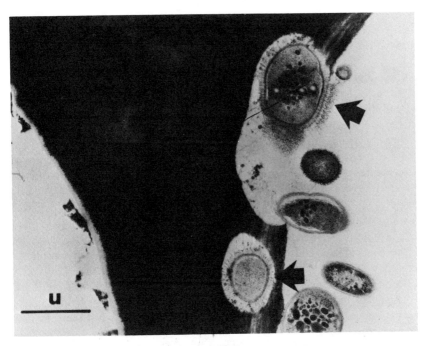

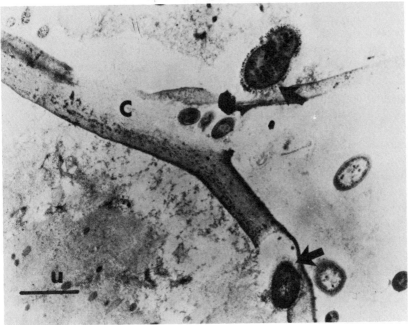

FIG. 13.5 Electron micrograph of rumen bacteria degrading plant cell walls. Sharp zones of degradation are noted around the bacteria. (From Akin and Amos, 1975; American Society of Microbiology.)

B. Mammalian Abomasum and Avian Proventriculus–Gizzard

Acidic digestion occurs in the abomasum of mammals and the proventriculus and gizzard of birds. The avian proventriculus primarily secretes hydrochloric acid and digestive enzymes, while the muscular stomach mechanically reduces particle size concurrently with enzymatic and acid hydrolysis. The gizzard can have a very strong musculature for efficient grinding, such as in granivores, or it can be very weak, in which case digestion is entirely chemical, such as in hawks, vultures, pelicans, and loons (Ziswiler and Farner, 1972; Houston and Cooper, 1975). The acidic stomach of both mammals and birds can also be a storage organ even though digestion is occurring. Many carnivores are well known for their rapid ingestion of very large quantities of food that require many hours of digestion. The stomach can also be a filter in which bones, hairs, and feathers are retained and often regurgitated, as in hawks and owls, while the more digestible components move into the small intestine.

The pH of pure gastric acid in both birds and mammals ranges from 0.2 to 1.2 (Ziswiler and Farner, 1972). However, the observed pH of the stomach contents generally ranges from 1.0 to 3.0 in birds and from 1.6 to 4.0 in mammals (Moir et al., 1956; Ziswiler and Farner, 1972; Schoonveld et al., 1974; Duke et al., 1975; Houston and Cooper, 1975; Rhoades and Duke, 1975; Van Hoven, 1978; Kinnear et al., 1979; Clemens and Phillips, 1980; Leon, 1980; Clemens and Maloiy, 1981; Knight-Eloff and Knight, 1988). The higher pH of stomach contents than of pure gastric acid is due to the dilution and neutralization by food or ingested fluids, the internal regulation or optimization of gastric pH, and, in some species, the retrograde flow of more alkaline small-intestinal contents into the stomach (LePrince et al., 1979). Acid secretion is often minimal in neonatal mammals, but it increases during the first few hours or days of life until stomach pH approaches the adult level. Although many of the differences in stomach pH of adult animals are simply due to the method of measurement, significant differences between species do occur. For example, the pH of the stomach contents in Falconiformes (hawks, falcons, and eagles; average of 1.6) is much lower than in the Strigiformes (owls; average of 2.3) (Duke et al., 1975; Rhoades and Duke, 1975). Because pH is a logarithmic function of hydrogen ion concentration, Falconiformes have a hydrogen ion concentration six times that of Strigiformes. These differences are reflected in higher dry matter digestibilities in Falconiformes versus Strigiformes due to the more extensive corrosion of bones in the Falconiformes' stomach. However, because the differences in dry matter digestibility are largely due to the absorption of bone ash, energy digestibilities are virtually identical in hawks and owls (Kirkwood, 1979).

Digestion in the acidic stomach is primarily proteolysis. Pepsin is the primary gastric proteolytic enzyme occurring in both mammals and birds. Pepsin occurs in the abomasum, proventriculus, and, possibly, the gizzard mucosa in an inactive form called pepsinogen. When pepsinogen is secreted into the gastric lumen in the presence of hydrochloric acid at a pH below 5, a low-molecular-weight polypeptide is cleaved to form active pepsin. Below pH 4, the conversion of pepsinogen to pepsin is catalyzed by pepsin; thus, the reaction is autocatalytic. Pepsin activity is generally strongest between pH 1 and 2, although a second peak may occur between pH 3.5 and 4.0. The acidic environment of the stomach generally denatures ingested protein, which exposes the bonds to enzymatic hydrolysis. Pepsins preferentially split peptide bonds involving phenylalanine, tyrosine, leucine, and glutamic acid.

An additional enzyme, rennin, occurs in the gastric juice of nursing mammals and has an optimum activity at pH 4.0. Both pepsin and rennin readily coagulate milk casein in nursing animals. The digestion of the milk clot provides a continuous, prolonged flow of nutrients into the small intestine of the young animal and avoids flow surges or the excessive passage of fermentable substrates into the intestinal tract.

Chitinase, an enzyme capable of hydrolyzing the carbohydrate exoskeleton of invertebrates, occurs in the stomach of some birds and mammals. It probably occurs most commonly in those animals where insects are a significant part of the diet (Le Prince *et al.*, 1979; Vonk and Western, 1984). Gastric lipase also occurs in some animals (Abrams *et al.*, 1988).

Many other enzymes have been identified as being of gastric origin, particularly in birds. Because it is now recognized that digestion in birds involves the movement of digesta back and forth between the stomach and small intestine (Le Prince *et al.*, 1979; Sklan, 1980), one cannot use the mere presence of an enzyme in stomach contents as an indicator of its origin. The reversible flow of digesta between the stomach and small intestine in birds maximizes digestive efficiency while minimizing intestinal weight and length.

IV. SMALL INTESTINE

The small intestine is the primary site of enzymatic digestion and absorption. The mammalian small intestine is morphologically divided into a proximal duodenum looping around the pancreas, intermediate jejunum, and distal ileum. The avian small intestine is divided only into the duodenum and ileum, with no major histological differences between the two segments. The length of all intestinal segments in both mammals and birds relative to body weight are longest in herbivores, intermediate in granivores and frugivores, and shortest in carnivores and insectivores. Relative intestinal length, weight, and volume within each species varies with sex, age, seasonal food habits, and level of intake as determined by changing requirements or food quality (Leopold, 1953; Chivers and

Hladik, 1980; Green and Millar, 1987; Kehoe *et al.*, 1988; Robel *et al.*, 1990; Sibly *et al.*, 1990; Bozinovic *et al.*, 1990; Hammond and Wunder, 1991). Digestive secretions enter the small intestine from the liver (bile salts: glycocholates and taurocholates), pancreas (buffering bicarbonate ion; proteases, including trypsinogen, chymotrypsinogen, and procarboxypeptidase; amylase; lipase; lecithinase; and nuclease), intestinal mucosa (primarily peptidases and saccharidases), and duodenal glands (alkaline fluid for pH regulation). The secretion of the various enzymes and buffering solutions is stimulated by the passage of stomach contents, called chyme, into the duodenum. Liver and pancreas ducts carrying digestive secretions open near the duodenal–abomasal orifice in mammals and more distally in the duodenum in birds (Sklan, 1980). The initial response must be to neutralize the chyme because intestinal enzymes function optimally between pH 6 and 8. The pH of intestinal tract contents posterior to the stomach in both birds and mammals range from 5.2 to 7.5, with a mean of approximately 6.5 (Farner, 1942; Moir *et al.*, 1956; Johnson and McBee, 1967; Hoover and Clarke, 1972; Houston and Cooper, 1975; Clemens and Phillips, 1980; Clemens and Maloiy, 1981, 1982; Knight-Eloff and Knight, 1988).

The pancreatic proteases are secreted as inactive proenzymes. The proenzymes are converted to active enzymes by a series of reactions beginning with the activation of trypsinogen by enterokinase, an enzyme produced by the intestinal mucosa. Trypsin in turn activates chymotrypsinogen and procarboxypeptidase. Each pancreatic protease preferentially hydrolyzes specific peptide bonds. For example, trypsin hydrolyzes bonds involving lysine and arginine, and chymotrypsin hydrolyzes bonds involving aromatic amino acids. These enzymes are termed endopeptidases because they hydrolyze the interior peptide bonds. Carboxypeptidase is an exopeptidase that hydrolyzes peptide bonds in sequence from the end of the chain. The additional intestinal mucosal proteases complete protein digestion and produce free amino acids for absorption.

The absorption of colostral immunoglobulins is contrary to the general mosaic of protein digestion because the molecule must be absorbed intact by pinocytosis. Important mechanisms enabling the passage and absorption of intact immunoglobulins include (a) the time lag in acid and enzyme production by the neonatal stomach and small intestine and (b) the incorporation of enzyme inhibitors in maternal colostrum. Because colostral immunoglobulins are relatively resistant to chymotrypsin but are destroyed by trypsin, trypsin inhibitors occur in the colostrum of many species. Trypsin inhibitors protect the immunoglobulin without completely inhibiting the digestion of other milk proteins by pancreatic and intestinal proteases (Morris, 1968; Canwell, 1977; Corring *et al.*, 1978; Esparza and Brock, 1978; Brown and Perry, 1981).

Numerous saccharidases are produced by the pancreas and intestinal mucosa. These include amylase, which hydrolyzes starch and glycogen; maltase, which hydrolyzes the glucose disaccharide maltose; sucrase, which hydrolyzes the glucose–fructose dissaccharide of plants; isomaltase, which hydrolyzes dextrans linked α 1,6; and lactase, which hydrolyzes the galactose–glucose disaccharide of milk. The occurrence of these enzymes is related to the age of the animal and the composition of the food entering the small intestine. For example, those species in which the milk does not contain lactose normally do not produce lactase. Even though marsupial milk in its natural form contains only traces of lactose, the pouch young do produce lactase equal to that occurring in eutherian neonates, apparently because the cleavage of the galactose-rich oligo- and poly-saccharides produces a lactose unit that must be further digested (Walcott and Messer, 1980). In lactose-producing species, lactase is the first disaccharidase to develop and remains high while milk is consumed, but it subsequently falls after weaning as amylase, maltase, sucrase, and other saccharidases needed to digest the adult diet increase. Because the carbohydrate composition of the food and intestinal contents are the same in animals with simple stomachs, the intestinal saccharidases reflect the carbohydrate composition of the normally ingested food. For example, hummingbirds that pollinate flowers rich in sucrose have sucrase activities 2 to 188 times higher than several passerines that pollinate flowers in which the sugars, glucose and fructose, are in the monosaccharide form rather than the disaccharide (Martinez del Rio, 1990a,b). However, the intestinal disaccharidases of forestomach fermenters often do not reflect food composition, but rather the carbohydrate spectra of the fermentation products. For example, although ruminants and macropod marsupials consume plant sucrose, sucrase does not occur in these animals. The ingested sucrose is readily fermented to volatile fatty acids, obviating any need for intestinal sucrase (Semenza, 1968; Kerry, 1969; Walcott and Messer, 1980).

Fat digestion is due to pancreatic lipase and emulsifying bile salts. Pancreatic lipase in simple-stomached animals preferentially hydrolyzes the 1 and 3 position fatty acids of a triglyceride to produce two free fatty acids and a 2–monoglyceride. Pancreatic lipase in forestomach fermenters can be less important than in simple-stomached animals as the microbes have often already hydrolyzed the fatty acids of ingested glycerides and fermented the glycerol component. The bile salts and hydrolyzed fats form micelles whose diameter relative to the fat droplet is reduced 100-fold and the surface area increased 10,000-fold. The micelle is the functional unit of fat absorption at the intestinal epithelium. The intestinal reabsorption of bile salts and their transport to the liver, termed the enterohepatic circulation, is important because bile salts are often secreted in excess of hepatic production (Johnston, 1968; Weiner and Lack, 1968; Patton and Carey, 1979; Sklan, 1980).

V. CECUM AND LARGE INTESTINE (HINDGUT)

Ceca are blind, intestinal diverticula usually occurring at the junction of the small and large intestine. They are usually paired in birds (ceca) and unilateral

TABLE 13.1

Hindgut Contents (Wet Weight) as a Percentage of Body Weight and the Energy Derived
from Their Fermentation

Species	Contents (% body weight)	Energy (%BMR)	Sources
Predominantly foregut fermenters			
Ruminants and Macropods			
Black-tailed deer	0.5	1	Allo et al., 1973
Black wildebeest	0.9	5–7	Van Hoven and Boomker, 1981
Domestic sheep	1.1–4.9	5–15	Allo et al., 1973; Hume 1977
Red-necked pademelon	1.3	7	Hume 1977
Red-necked wallaby	0.5	3	Hume, 1977
Hindgut fermenters			
Birds			
Rock ptarmigan	1–3	15–24	Gasaway, 1976a
Sharp-tailed grouse	1.4	14	Gasaway, 1976b
Willow ptarmigan	1.2	4–19	Gasaway, 1976b
Mammals			
Beaver	3.6	19	Hoover and Clarke, 1972
Cape porcupine	8	33	Knight-Eloff and Knight, 1988
Domestic horse	8.2	72–77	Elsden et al., 1946; Glinsky et al., 1976
Domestic rabbit	2–8	10–38	Hoover and Hietmann, 1972; Parker, 1976; Marty and Vernay, 1984
Elephant	10	122	Van Hoven et al., 1981
Fat jird	—	22–35	Yahav and Choshniak, 1990
Guinea pig	5	31	Sakaguchi et al., 1985
Laboratory rat	1.8–2.4	9	Yang et al., 1969, 1970
Levant vole	—	9–15	Yahav and Choshniak, 1990
Naked mole-rat	6–8	12–59	Buffenstein and Yahav, 1991
North American porcupine	4.4	16	Johnson and McBee, 1967
Rock hyrax	9.2–12.6	68–87	Elkoff and Van Hoven, 1985

in mammals. The most extensive cecal development in birds occurs in the Te-
traonidae, or grouse and ptarmigan, although ducks and geese also have very
functional ceca. Rudimentary, nondigestive ceca occur in many carnivorous and
insectivorous birds (McLelland, 1989). Functional digestive ceca in mammals
are largely confined to ruminant and nonruminant herbivores and frugivores.

The large intestine extends from the ileo-cecal juncture to the rectum of
mammals and the cloaca of birds. The cloaca in birds is a common route for
the passage of feces, urine, and reproductive products. The relative length of
the large intestine is dependent on the dietary regimen of the species. For ex-

ample, the length of the large intestine relative to the small intestine averages 6% in small carnivorous mammals, 33% in omnivores, and 78% in herbivores as fiber digestion, bulk, and a reduced rate of passage become more important (Barry, 1977). The functions of the ceca and large intestine include the fermentation of plant fiber and soluble plant or endogenous matter; the absorption of water and therefore small water-soluble nutrients, such as electrolytes, ammonia, volatile fatty acids and amino acids; and bacterial vitamin synthesis (Table 13.1). The large intestine and ceca work as a unit to selectively pass coarse food residues in the feces while separating and retaining the liquids, very small food residues, and bacteria for further fermentation (Sperber *et al.*, 1983; Bjornhag, 1989a,b). For example, only 18% of the dry matter passing the ileocecal–colic junction of rock ptarmigan entered the ceca as compared to 96% of liquid digesta (Gasaway *et al.*, 1975; Gasaway, 1976c). Similarly, more than 70% of the liquid–small particle phase digesta entered the cecum of white-tailed deer (Mautz, 1969). The ceca–large intestine is an even more important site of water, nitrogen and electrolyte conservation in birds than in mammals as urine moves from the cloaca into the large intestine and ceca by antiperistalsis where digestion and reabsorption can occur (Braun and Campbell, 1989; Mead, 1989; Obst and Diamond, 1989).

REFERENCES

Abrams, C. K., Hamosh, M., Lee, T. C., Ansher, A. F., Collen, M. J., Lewis, J. H., Benjamin, S. B., and Hamosh, P. (1988). Gastric lipase: Localization in the human stomach. *Gastroenterology* **95**, 1460–1464.

Akin, D. E., and Amos, H. E. (1975). Rumen bacterial degradation of forage cell walls investigated by electron microscopy. *Appl. Microbiol.* **29**, 692–701.

Allo, A. A., Oh, J. H., Longhurst, W. M., and Connolly, G. E. (1973). VFA production in the digestive systems of deer and sheep. *J. Wildl. Manage.* **37**, 202–211.

Arman, P., and Field, C. R. (1973). Digestion in the hippopotamus. *East Afr. Wildl. J.* **11**, 9–17.

Baker, D. L., and Hobbs, N. T. (1987). Strategies of digestion: Digestive efficiency and retention time of forage diets in montane ungulates. *Can. J. Zool.* **65**, 1978–1984.

Barry, R. E., Jr. (1977). Length and absorptive surface area apportionment of segments of the hindgut for eight species of small mammals. *J. Mammal.* **58**, 419–420.

Bhattacharya, S., and Ghose, K. C. (1971). Influence of food on the amylase system in birds. *Comp. Biochem. Physiol.* **40B**, 317–320.

Bjornhag, G. (1989a). Sufficient fermentation and rapid passage of digesta. A problem of adaptation in the hindgut. *Acta Vet. Scand. Suppl.* **86**, 204–211.

Bjornhag, G. (1989b). Transport of water and food particles through the avian ceca and colon. *J. Exp. Zool. Suppl.* **3**, 32–37.

Bozinovic, F., Novoa, F. F., and Veloso, C. (1990). Seasonal changes in energy expenditure and digestive tract of *Abrothrix andinus* (*Cricetidae*) in the Andes range. *Physiol. Zool.* **63**, 1216–1231.

Braun, E. J., and Campbell, C. E. (1989). Uric acid decomposition in the lower gastrointestinal tract. *J. Exp. Zool. Suppl.* **3**, 70–74.

Brown, J. J., and Perry, T. W. (1981). Trypsin and chymotrypsin development in the neonatal lamb. *J. Anim. Sci.* **52,** 359–362.

Buffenstein, R., and Yahav, S. (1991). The effect of diet on microfaunal population and function in the caecum of a subterranean naked mole-rat, *Heterocephalus glaber. Br. J. Nutr.* **65,** 249–258.

Canwell, P. D. (1977). Acid and pepsin secretion in young pigs reared solely by the sow or supplemented with solid food and weaned at 21 d. *Proc. Nutr. Soc.* **36,** 142A.

Chandra, R. K., and Newberne, P. M. (1977). "Nutrition, Immunity, and Infection: Mechanisms of Interactions." Plenum, New York.

Chauncey, H. H., and Quintarelli, G. (1961). Localization of acid phosphatase, nonspecific esterases and *B*-D-galactosidase in parotid and submaxillary glands of domestic and laboratory animals. *Am. J. Anat.* **108,** 263–294.

Chilcott, M. J., and Hume, I. D. (1984). Digestion of *Eucalyptus andrewsii* foliage by the common ringtail possum, *Pseudocheirus peregrinus. Aust. J. Zool.* **32,** 605–614.

Chivers, D. J., and Hladik, C. M. (1980). Morphology of the gastrointestinal tract in primates: Comparisons with other mammals in relation to diet. *J. Morphol.* **166,** 337–386.

Clemens, E., and Phillips, B. (1980). Organic acid production and digesta movement in the gastrointestinal tract of the baboon and Sykes monkey. *Comp. Biochem. Physiol.* **66A,** 529–532.

Clemens, E. T., and Maloiy, G. M. O. (1981). Organic acid concentration and digesta movement in the gastrointestinal tract of the bushbaby (*Galago crassicaudatus*) and Vervet monkey (*Cercopithecidae pygerythrus*). *J. Zool.* **193,** 487–497.

Clemens, E. T., and Maloiy, G. M. O. (1982). The digestive physiology of three East African herbivores: The elephant, rhinoceros and hippopotamus. *J. Zool.* **198,** 141–156.

Corring, T., Aumaitre, A., and Durand, D. (1978). Development of digestive enzymes in the piglet from birth to 8 weeks. *Nutr. Metab.* **22,** 231–243.

Dean, R. E., Strickland, M. D., Newman, J. L., Thorne, E. T., and Hepworth, W. G. (1975). Reticulo-rumen characteristics of malnourished mule deer. *J. Wildl. Manage.* **39,** 601–604.

Demment, M. W., and Van Soest, P. J. (1985). A nutritional explanation for body-size patterns of ruminant and nonruminant herbivores. *Am. Nat.* **125,** 641–672.

Duke, G. E., Jegers, A. A., Loff, G., and Evanson, O. A. (1975). Gastric digestion in some raptors. *Comp. Biochem. Physiol.* **50A,** 649–656.

Eloff, A. K., and Van Hoven, W. (1985). Volatile fatty acid production in the hindgut of *Procavia capensis. Comp. Biochem. Physiol.* **80A,** 291–295.

Elsden, S. R., Hitchcock, M. W. S., Marshall, R. A., and Phillipson, A. T. (1946). Volatile acid in the digesta of ruminants and other animals. *J. Exp. Biol.* **22,** 191–202.

Esparza, I., and Brock, J. H. (1978). Inhibition of rat and bovine trypsins and chymotrypsins by soybean, bovine basic pancreatic, and bovine colostrum trypsin inhibitors. *Comp. Biochem. Physiol.* **61B,** 347–350.

Faichney, G. J. (1968). The production and absorption of volatile fatty acids from the rumen of the sheep. *Aust. J. Agric. Res.* **19,** 791–802.

Farner, D. S. (1942). The hydrogen ion concentration in avian digestive tracts. *Poult. Sci.* **21,** 445–450.

Foley, W. J., and Hume, I. D. (1987). Digestion and metabolism of high-tannin *Eucalyptus* foliage by the brushtail possum (*Trichosurus vulpecula*) (Marsupialia: Phalangeridae). *J. Comp. Physiol.* **157B,** 67–76.

Gasaway, W. C. (1976a). Seasonal variation in diet, volatile fatty acid production and size of the cecum of rock ptarmigan. *Comp. Biochem. Physiol.* **53A,** 109–114.

Gasaway, W. C. (1976b). Volatile fatty acids and metabolizable energy derived from cecal fermentation in the willow ptarmigan. *Comp. Biochem. Physiol.* **53A,** 115–121.

Gasaway, W. C. (1976c). Cellulose digestion and metabolism by captive rock ptarmigan. *Comp. Biochem. Physiol.* **54A,** 179–182.

Gasaway, W. C., Holleman, D. F., and White, R. G. (1975). Flow of digesta in the intestine and cecum of the rock ptarmigan. *Condor* **77,** 467–474.

Gasaway, W. C., White, R. G., and Holleman, D. F. (1976). Digestion of dry matter and absorption of water in the intestine and cecum of rock ptarmigan. *Condor* **78,** 77–84.

Gaskin, D. E. (1978). Form and function in the digestive tract and associated organs in cetacea, with a consideration of metabolic rates and specific energy budgets. *Oceanogr. Mar. Biol.* **16,** 313–345.

Glinsky, M. J., Smith, R. M., Spires, H. R., and Davis, C. L. (1976). Measurement of volatile fatty acid production rates in the cecum of the pony. *J. Anim. Sci.* **42,** 1465–1470.

Grajal, A., Strahl, S. D., Parra, R., Dominguez, M. G., and Neher, A. (1989). Foregut fermentation in the hoatzin, a neotropical leaf-eating bird. *Science* **245,** 1236–1238.

Gray, F. V., Pilgrim, A. F., and Weller, R. A. (1958). The digestion of foodstuffs in the stomach of the sheep and the passage of digesta through its compartments. *Br. J. Nutr.* **12,** 413–420.

Gray, F. V., Weller, R. A., Pilgrim, A. F., and Jones, G. B. (1967). Rates of production of volatile fatty acids in the rumen. V. Evaluation of fodders in terms of volatile fatty acid produced in the rumen of the sheep. *Aust. J. Agric. Res.* **18,** 625–634.

Green, D. A., and Millar, J. S. (1987). Changes in gut dimensions and capacity of *Peromyscus maniculatus* relative to diet quality and energy needs. *Can. J. Zoo.* **65,** 2159–2162.

Hainsworth, F. R., and Wolf, L. L. (1972). Crop volume, nectar concentration and hummingbird energetics. *Comp. Biochem. Physiol.* **42A,** 359–366.

Hammond, K. A., and Wunder, B. A. (1991). The role of diet quality and energy need in the nutritional ecology of a small herbivore, *Microtus ochrogaster. Physiol. Zool.* **64,** 541–567.

Hamosh, M. (1979). A review. Fat digestion in the newborn: Role of lingual lipase and preduodenal digestion. *Pediatr. Res.* **13,** 615–622.

Herwig, R. P., Staley, J. T., Nerini, M. K., and Braham, H. W. (1984). Baleen whales: Preliminary evidence for forestomach microbial fermentation. *Appl. Environ. Microbiol.* **47,** 421–423.

Hofmann, R. R. (1973). "The Ruminant Stomach." *East Afr. Monogr. in Biol., Vol. II.* E. Afr. Lit. Bureau, Nairobi.

Hofmann, R. R. (1989). Evolutionary steps of ecophysiological adaptation and diversification of ruminants: A comparative view of their digestive system. *Oecologia* **78,** 443–457.

Hofmann, R. R., and Matern, B. (1988). Changes in gastrointestinal morphology related to nutrition in giraffes *Giraffa camelopardalis:* A comparison of wild and zoo specimens. *Int. Zoo Yearb.* **27,** 168–176.

Hoover, W. H., and Clarke, S. D. (1972). Fiber digestion in the beaver. *J. Nutr.* **102,** 9–16.

Hoover, W. H., and Heitmann, R. N. (1972). Effects of dietary fiber levels on weight gain, cecal volume and volatile fatty acid production in rabbits. *J. Nutr.* **102,** 375–380.

Hoppe, P. P., Qvortrup, S. A., and Woodford, M. H. (1977). Rumen fermentation and food selection in East African Zebu cattle, wildebeest, Coke's hartebeest and topi. *J. Zool.* **181,** 1–9.

Houston, D. C., and Cooper, J. E. (1975). The digestive tract of the whiteback griffon vulture and its role in disease transmission among wild ungulates. *J.Wildl. Dis.* **11,** 306–313.

Hume, I. D. (1977). Production of volatile fatty acids in two species of wallaby and in sheep. *Comp. Biochem. Physiol.* **56A,** 299–304.

Hume, I. D. (1982). "Digestive Physiology and Nutrition of Marsupials." Cambridge Univ. Press, Cambridge, England.

Hume, I. D., Carlisle, C. H., Reynolds, K., and Pass, M. A. (1988). Effects of fasting and sedation on gastrointestinal tract function in two Potoroine marsupials. *Aust. J. Zool.* **36,** 411–420.

Janis, C. (1976). The evolutionary strategy of the Equidae and the origins of rumen and cecal digestion. *Evolution* **30**, 757–774.

Jerrett, S. A., and Goodge, W. R. (1973). Evidence for amylase in avian salivary glands. *J. Morphol.* **139**, 27–46.

Johnson, J. L., and Mcbee, R. H. (1967). The porcupine cecal fermentation. *J. Nutr.* **91**, 540–546.

Johnston, J. M. (1968). Mechanism of fat absorption. *In* " Alimentary Canal, Section 6. Handbook of Physiology" (C. F. Code, ed.), pp. 1353–1375. Am. Physiol. Soc., Washington, D.C.

Karasawa, Y. (1989). Ammonia production from uric acid, urea, and amino acids and its absorption from the ceca of the cockerel. *J. Exp. Zool. Suppl.* **3**, 75–80.

Karn, R. C., and Malacinski, G. M. (1978). The comparative biochemistry, physiology, and genetics of animal α-amylases. *Adv. Comp. Physiol. Biochem.* **7**, 1–103.

Kehoe, F. P., Ankney, C. D., and Alisauskas, R. T. (1988). Effects of dietary fiber and diet diversity on digestive organs of captive mallards (*Anas platyrhynchos*). *Can. J. Zool.* **66**, 1597–1602.

Kerry, K. R. (1969). Intestinal disaccharidase activity in a monotreme and eight species of marsupials (with an added note on the disaccharidases of five species of sea birds). *Comp. Biochem. Physiol.* **29**, 1015–1022.

Kinnear, J. E., Cockson, A., Christensen, P., and Main, A. R. (1979). The nutritional biology of the ruminants and ruminant-like mammals—A new approach. *Comp. Biochem. Physiol.* **64A**, 357–365.

Kirkwood, J. K. (1979). The partition of food energy for existence in the kestrel (*Falco tinnunculus*) and the barn owl (*Tyto alba*). *Comp. Biochem. Physiol.* **63A**, 495–498.

Knight-Eloff, A. K., and Knight, M. H. (1988). Volatile fatty acid production in the cape porcupine. *South Afr. J. Wildl. Res.* **18**, 157–159.

Kreulen, D. A., and Hoppe, P. P. (1979). Diurnal trends and relationship to forage quality of ruminal volatile fatty acid concentration, pH and osmolarity in wildebeest on dry range in Tanzania. *Afr. J. Ecol.* **17**, 53–63.

Langer, P. (1974). Stomach evolution in the Artiodactyla. *Mammalia* **38**, 295–314.

Langer, P. (1978). Anatomy of the stomach of the collared peccary, *Dicotyles tajacu* (L. 1758) (Artiodactyla: Mammalia). *Z. Saugetierkunde* **43**, 42–59.

Langer, P. (1979). Phylogenetic adaptation of the stomach of the Macropodidae Owen, 1839, to food. *Z. Saugetierkunde* **44**, 321–333.

Langer, P. (1988). "Mammalian Herbivore Stomach. Comparative Anatomy, Function and Evolution." Verlag, Stuttgart.

Leibholz, J. (1972). Nitrogen metabolism in sheep. II. The flow of amino acids into the duodenum from dietary and microbial sources. *Aust. J. Agric. Res.* **23**, 1073–1083.

Leng, R. A., Corbett, J. L., and Brett, D. J. (1968). Rates of production of volatile fatty acids in the rumen of grazing sheep and their relation to ruminal concentrations. *Br. J. Nutr.* **22**, 57–68.

Leon, B. (1980). Fermentation and the production of volatile fatty acids in the alimentary tract of the rock hyrax, *Procavia capensis*. *Comp. Biochem. Physiol.* **65A**, 411–420.

Leopold, S. A. (1953). Intestinal morphology of gallinaceous birds in relation to food habits. *J. Wildl. Manage.* **17**, 197–203.

LePrince, P., Dandrifosse, G., and Schoffeniels, E. (1979). The digestive enzymes and acidity of the pellets regurgitated by raptors. *Biochem. Syst. Ecol.* **7**, 223–227.

Lintern-Moore, S. (1973). Incorporation of dietary nitrogen into microbial nitrogen in the forestomach of the Kangaroo Island wallaby *Protemnodon eugenii* (Desmarest). *Comp. Biochem. Physiol.* **44A**, 75–82.

Maloiy, G. M. O., Kay, R. N. B., and Goodall, E. D. (1968). Studies on the physiology of digestion and metabolism of the red deer (*Cervus elaphus*). *Symp. Zool. Soc. London* **21**, 101–108.

Martinez del Rio, C. (1990a). Sugar preferences in hummingbirds: The influence of subtle chemical differences on food choice. *Condor* **92**, 1022–1030.

Martinez del Rio, C. (1990b). Dietary, phylogenetic, and ecological correlates of intestinal sucrase and maltase activity in birds. *Physiol. Zool.* **63**, 987–1011.

Marty, J., and Vernay, M. (1984). Absorption and metabolism of the volatile fatty acids in the hind-gut of the rabbit. *Br. J. Nutr.* **51**, 265–277.

Matthews, L. R., and Kilgour, R. (1980). Learning and associated factors in ruminant feeding behavior. *In* "Digestive Physiology and Metabolism in Ruminants" (Y. Ruckebusch and P. Thivend, eds.), pp. 123–144. MTP Press, Lancaster, England.

Mautz, W. W. (1969). "Investigation of Some Digestive Parameters of the White-tailed Deer Using the Radioisotope ^{51}Chromium." Doctoral Dissertation, Michigan State Univ., East Lansing, Michigan.

McBee, R. H., Johnson, J. L., and Bryant, M. P. (1969). Ruminal microorganisms from elk. *J. Wildl. Manage.* **33**, 181–186.

McLelland, J. (1989). Anatomy of the avian cecum. *J. Exp. Zool. Suppl.* **3**, 2–9.

Mead, G. C. (1989). Microbes of the avian cecum: Types present and substrates utilized. *J. Exp. Zool. Suppl.* **3**, 48–54.

Moir, R. J., Somers, M., and Waring, H. (1956). Studies on marsupial nutrition. I. Ruminant-like digestion in a herbivorous marsupial (*Setonix brachyurus* Quoy and Gaimard). *Aust. J. Biol. Sci.* **9**, 293–304.

Morris, I. G. (1968). Gamma globulin absorption in the newborn. *In* "Alimentary Canal, Section 6. Handbook of Physiology" (C. F. Code, ed.), pp. 1491–1512. Am. Physiol. Soc., Washington, D.C.

Mould, E. D., and Robbins, C. T. (1982). Digestive capabilities in elk compared to white-tailed deer. *J. Wildl. Manage.* **46**, 22–29.

Obst, B. S., and Diamond, J. M. (1989). Interspecific variation in sugar and amino acid transport by the avian cecum. *J. Exp. Zool. Suppl.* **3**, 117–126.

Parker, D. S. (1976). The measurement of production rates of volatile fatty acids in the caecum of the conscious rabbit. *Br. J. Nutr.* **36**, 61–70.

Patton, J. S., and Carey, M. C. (1979). Watching fat digestion. *Science* **204**, 145–148.

Pearson, H. A. (1969). Rumen microbial ecology in mule deer. *Appl. Microbiol.* **17**, 819–824.

Pilgrim, A. F., Gray, F. V., Weller, R. A., and Belling, C. B. (1970). Synthesis of microbial protein from ammonia in the sheep's rumen and the proportion of dietary nitrogen converted into microbial nitrogen. *Br. J. Nutr.* **24**, 589–598.

Poe, S. E., Ely, D. G., Mitchell, G. E., Jr., Glimp, H. A., and Deweese, W. P. (1971). Rumen development in lambs. II. Rumen metabolite changes. *J. Anim. Sci.* **32**, 989–993.

Prins, R. A., and Geelen, M. J. H. (1971). Rumen characteristics of red deer, fallow deer, and roe deer. *J. Wildl. Manage.* **35**, 673–680.

Prins, R. A., Hungate, R. E., and Prast, E. R. (1972). Function of the omasum in several ruminant species. *Comp. Biochem. Physiol.* **43A**, 155–163.

Purser, D. B. (1970). Nitrogen metabolism in the rumen: Micro-organisms as a source of protein for the ruminant animal. *J. Anim. Sci.* **30**, 988–1001.

Rhoades, D. D., and Duke, G. E. (1975). Gastric function in a captive American bittern. *Auk* **92**, 786–792.

Richardson, K. C., Wooller, R. D., and Collins, B. G. (1986). Adaptations to a diet of nectar and pollen in the marsupial *Tarsipes rostratus* (Marsupialia: Tarsipedidae). *J. Zool.* **208**, 285–297.

Robbins, C. T., and Moen, A. N. (1975). Milk consumption and weight gain of white-tailed deer. *J. Wildl. Manage.* **39**, 355–360.

Robbins, C. T., Mole, S., Hagerman, A. E., and Hanley, T. A. (1987). Role of tannins in defending plants against ruminants: Reduction in dry matter digestion? *Ecology* **68**, 1606–1615.

Robbins, C. T., Hagerman, A. E., Austin, P. J., McArthur, C. and Hanley, T. A. (1991). Variation in mammalian physiological responses to a condensed tannin and its ecological implications. *J. Mammal.* **72**, 480–486.

Robel, R. J., Barnes, M. E., Kemp, K. E., and Zimmerman, J. L. (1990). Influences of time postmortem, feeding activity, and diet on digestive morphology of two emberizids. *Auk* **107**, 669–677.

Sakaguchi, E., Becker, G., Rechkemmer, G., and Engelhardt, W. V. (1985). Volume solute concentrations and production of short chain fatty acids in the caecum and upper colon of the guinea pig. *Z. Tierphysiol. Tierernahr. Futtermittelkd.* **54**, 276–285.

Schoonveld, G. G., Nagy, J. G., and Bailey, J. A. (1974). Capability of mule deer to utilize fibrous alfalfa diets. *J. Wildl. Manage.* **38**, 823–829.

Schwartz, C. C., Regelin, W. L., and Franzmann, A. W. (1985). Suitability of a formulated ration for moose. *J. Wildl. Manage.* **49**, 137–141.

Semenza, G. (1968). Intestinal oligosaccharidases and disaccharidases. *In* "Alimentary Canal, Section 6. Handbook of Physiology" (C. F. Code, ed.), pp. 2543–2566. Am. Physiol. Soc., Washington, D.C.

Short, H. L. (1964). Postnatal stomach development of white-tailed deer. *J. Wildl. Manage.* **28**, 445–458.

Sibly, R. M., Monk, K. A., Johnson, I. K., and Trout, R. C. (1990). Seasonal variation in gut morphology in wild rabbits (*Oryctolagus cuniculus*). *J. Zool.* **221**, 605–619.

Sklan, D. (1980). Site of digestion and absorption of lipids and bile acids in the rat and turkey. *Comp. Biochem. Physiol.* **65A**, 91–95.

Spalinger, D. E., Robbins, C. T., and Hanley, T. A. (1986). The assessment of handling time in ruminants: The effect of plant chemical and physical structure on the rate of breakdown of plant particles in the rumen of mule deer and elk. *Can. J. Zool.* **64**, 312–321.

Sperber, I., Bjornhag, G., and Ridderstrale, Y. (1983). Function of proximal colon in lemming and rat. *Swed. J. Agric. Res.* **13**, 243–256.

Stevens, C.E. (1988). "Comparative Physiology of the Vertebrate Digestive System." Cambridge Univ. Press, Cambridge, England.

Stewart, W. E., Stewart, D. G., and Schultz, L. H. (1958). Rates of volatile fatty acid production in the bovine rumen. *J. Anim. Sci.* **17**, 723–736.

Storm, E., and Orskov, E. R. (1983). The nutritional value of rumen micro-organisms in ruminants. 1. Large scale isolation and chemical composition of rumen micro-organisms. *Br. J. Nutr.* **50**, 463–470.

Tamate, H., McGilliard, A. D., Jacobson, N. L., and Getty, R. (1962). Effect of various dietaries on the anatomical development of the stomach in the calf. *J. Dairy Sci.* **45**, 408–420.

Ullrey, D. E. (1980). The nutrition of captive wild ruminants. *In* "Digestive Physiology and Nutrition of Ruminants. Vol. 3. Practical Nutrition" (D.C. Church, ed.), pp. 306–320. O. and B. Books, Corvallis, Oregon.

Vallenas, A., Cummings, J. F., and Munnell, J. F. (1971). A gross study of the compartmentalized stomach of two new-world camelids, the llama and guanaco. *J. Morphol.* **134**, 399–424.

Van Hoven, W. (1978). Digestion physiology in the stomach complex and hindgut of the hippopotamus (*Hippopotamus amphibius*). *South Afr. J. Wildl. Res.* **8**, 59–64.

Van Hoven, W., and Boomker, E. A. (1981). Feed utilization and digestion in the black wildebeest (*Connochaetes gnou*, Zimmerman, 1780) in the Golden Gate Highlands National Park. *South Afr. J. Wildl. Res.* **11**, 35–40.

Van Hoven, W., Prins, R. A., and Lankhorst, A. (1981). Fermentative digestion in the African elephant. *South Afr. J. Wildl. Res.* **11**, 78–86.

Van Soest, P. J. (1981). "Nutritional Ecology of the Ruminant." O. and B. Books, Corvallis, Oregon.

Vonk, H. J., and Western, J. R. H. (1984). "Comparative Biochemistry and Physiology of Enzymatic Digestion." Academic Press, New York.

Walcott, P. J., and Messer, M. (1980). Intestinal lactase (B-galactosidase) and other glycosidase activities in suckling and adult tammar wallabies. *Aust. J. Biol. Sci.* **33,** 521–530.

Weiner, I. M., and Lack, L. (1968). Bile salt absorption: Enterohepatic circulation. *In* "Alimentary Canal, Section 6. Handbook of Physiology" (C. F. Code, ed.), pp. 1439–1455. Am. Physiol. Soc., Washington, D.C.

Weller, R. A., Pilgrim, A. G., and Gray, F. V. (1962). Digestion of foodstuffs in the rumen of the sheep and the passage of digesta through its compartments. *Br. J. Nutr.* **16,** 83–90.

Worthington, A. H. (1989). Adaptations for avian frugivory: Assimilation efficiency and gut transit time of *Manacus vitellinus* and *Pipra mentalis*. *Oecologia* **80,** 381–389.

Yahav, S., and Choshniak, I. (1990). Response of the digestive tract to low quality dry food in the fat jird (*Meriones crassus*) and in the levant vole (*Microtus guentheri*). *J. Arid Environ.* **19,** 209–215.

Yang, M. G., Manoharan, K., and Young, A. K. (1969). Influence and degradation of dietary cellulose in cecum of rats. *J. Nutr.* **97,** 260–264.

Yang, M. G., Manoharan, K., and Michelsen, O. (1970). Nutritional contribution of volatile fatty acids from the cecum of rats. *J. Nutr.* **100,** 545–550.

Ziswiler, V., and Farner, D. S. (1972). Digestion and the digestive system. *In* "Avian Biology," Vol. II (D. S. Farner and J. R. King, eds.), pp. 343–430. Academic Press, New York.

14

Digestion and Nutrient Metabolism

One thing I have learned in a long life: that all our science, measured against reality, is primitive and childlike—and yet it is the most precious thing we have.

ALBERT EINSTEIN

Ingested food must be digested, absorbed, and metabolized if the animal is to meet its requirements. The amount of food that an animal must ingest to meet a fixed requirement is directly proportional to the losses in digestion and metabolism. For example, if an animal requires 250 nutritional units (such as kilocalories of energy, grams of protein, or milligrams of mineral or vitamin) and the ingested food contains five units per gram, 50 g of food must be consumed if all five units are available. However, if only 40% of the five units are available because of losses in digestion and metabolism, then 125 g must be consumed [250 ÷ (5 × 0.4) = 125].

Efficiencies of nutrient utilization are not random quantities but can be understood by their dependence on the interaction of food composition and digestive and metabolic capabilities of the ingesting animal. For example, animals with fermenting gastrointestinal bacteria can utilize plant cell-wall carbohydrates more efficiently than can animals without such bacteria. Losses of most nutrients include fecal and urinary excretion. Two additional losses, gas and excess heat production, are relevant in determining energy efficiencies. Consequently, the quantification and understanding of the efficiencies of nutrient utilization are necessary to relate requirements to available food resources.

I. DIGESTION

A. Methods and Terminology

Digestibility coefficients are broadly defined as the relative amount of ingested matter or energy that does not appear in the feces. Digestibilities determined by feeding the live animal and collecting the feces are termed *in vivo*. *In vivo* digestion trials typically use captive animals because of the ease with which feed and feces can be quantified. An underlying assumption in using captive animals is that the basic physiological processes of digestion are comparable between free-ranging and captive states. The assumption has never been adequately tested because of the difficulty in conducting digestion trials on unrestrained animals. Training or habituation of wildlife to accept the confinement imposed by *in vivo* digestion trials may be necessary.

Most *in vivo* digestion trials use the total balance method in which all feed ingested and feces produced are weighed and analyzed. Usually, the animal is confined to a crate in which the only food available is that provided by the experimenter. Urine and feces separation is necessary because digestibilities refer only to the efficiencies of processes occurring within the digestive tract and do not include the internal losses represented by urine. Urinary contamination of feces will often reduce digestibility estimates, particularly of nitrogen and minerals. While stanchioning or fitting fecal bags to male animals can ensure total separation of feces and urine, many wild animals will not accept such restraint or manipulation. Consequently, most wildlife digestion crates are large enough that the animal can turn around as it walks on a porous metal screen through which both urine and feces fall (Fig. 14.1). Feces in such crates are collected on a second screen just below the floor, and urine runs down plastic or metal sheeting to collection jars. Digestion trials can not be conducted on birds without surgical manipulation because urine and feces mix in the cloaca and large intestine and therefore are physically inseparable.

Total collection trials typically have a 3- to 10-day pretrial period followed by the 5- to 7-day trial. The pretrial adaptation period provides time for (a) the microbial and enzymatic digestion processes to equilibrate with the diet; (b) the residues from previous diets to be eliminated; and (c) the feces to equilibrate quantitatively with the feed. Short pretrial and trial periods are characteristic of small, simple-stomached animals that pass food very quickly through the gastrointestinal tract as compared to longer periods for the large ruminant and nonruminant herbivores.

Total balance trials with small mammals are relatively inexpensive but become increasingly expensive and laborious with larger animals. Collection of the few grams of feed consumed by a small rodent or carnivore may be a trivial problem when compared to collecting the hundreds of kilograms of small twigs or leaves consumed by large browsers. Because of the time, labor, and cost necessary for total balance trials using captive animals and the desire by many field ecologists to estimate directly the digestibility of mixed diets consumed by free-ranging animals, several attempts have been made to estimate digestibility by using nondigestible feed markers, such as plant lignin, silica, or various minerals (Fadely *et al.*, 1990). For example, the dry-matter digestibility of a diet could

Fig. 14.1 Internal view of a deer digestion crate. Notice the expanded metal floor on which the deer walks and through which feces and urine fall to lower collection screens or funnels. Feeder and urine collection funnel are also visible (From Cowan *et al.*, 1969, courtesy of the *Journal of Wildlife Management.*)

be determined by only two analyses of representative feed and fecal samples using the following equation:

$$\text{Dry matter, digestibility (\%)} = \left(1 - \frac{\text{Feed marker concentration}}{\text{Fecal marker concentration}}\right) \times 100.$$

If the feed marker concentration is 10% in a given diet, fecal concentrations of 20 and 30% indicate dry matter digestibilities of 50 and 67%, respectively. Unfortunately, the perfect marker is yet to be found. Many of the so-called nondigestible plant markers (such as lignin) are not completely recoverable in the feces. The excretion of added markers, such as chromium, can vary diurnally, and the marker may not move with the nutrient being examined (Gasaway *et al.*, 1975, 1976; Ruggiero and Whelan, 1977).

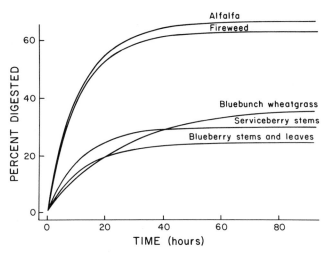

Fig. 14.2   Rate of *in vitro* dry matter digestion of five forages using mule deer inocula. (From Milchunas *et al.*, 1978, courtesy of the Colorado Division of Wildlife.)

Such problems have stimulated the development of additional digestion procedures, particularly *in vitro*. *In vitro* refers to the use of a laboratory digestion procedure that may only remotely be related to animal functioning. *In vitro* digestion trials are most popular in estimating ruminant digestibilities because they attempt to simulate the fermentation and acid protease hydrolysis occurring *in vivo*. The ingredients in the fermentation step are (a) a carefully weighed 0.5– 1.0 g food sample; (b) 40 ml of a buffer–nutrient solution; (c) 10 ml of rumen fluid obtained from a fistulated or recently killed animal; (d) a small flask or vial within which the above components are mixed; (e) bottled carbon dioxide, which is used to purge the flasks of all oxygen; and (f) a water bath or oven within which the *in vitro* fermentation can be maintained at 38–40°C. The general philosophy of the *in vitro* fermentation procedure is to maximize digestion opportunity such that the limitation imposed by the plant–microbial interaction establishes the end point and not an unfavorable pH shift or limiting nutrient.

Fermentation generally lasts for 48 hr as particles are often retained in the rumen for prolonged periods and the *in vitro* digestive process normally has reached an end point because of either toxic end-product accumulation or substrate exhaustion (Fig. 14.2). The contents of the fermentation flask can either be acidified with hydrochloric acid and incubated with pepsin for 24 to 48 hr (Tilley and Terry, 1963) or refluxed in neutral detergent (Goering and Van Soest, 1970). The acid–pepsin hydrolysis attempts to simulate abomasal digestion, while refluxing in neutral detergent removes microbial cells and soluble plant debris. The residues of either procedure are filtered, washed, dried, and weighed. The amount of dry matter disappearance is an estimate of digestibility, although rarely are *in vivo* and *in vitro* digestibilities the same, as there is extensive interlaboratory variation in techniques and results.

A hybrid of both the *in vivo* and *in vitro* procedures that takes advantage of the rumen environment is the nylon bag technique. A 0.5–1.0 g sample is carefully weighed and placed in a small-pore nylon bag that is subsequently suspended in the rumen of a fistulated animal. A major value of the nylon bag technique is that it provides a mechanism to examine the rate of rumen digestion. For example, while forbs and shrubs have a very rapid initial disappearance, with rumen digestion being completed in 48 hr, digestion of mature grasses is much slower and can continue in excess of 96 hr (Short *et al.,* 1974; White and Trudell, 1980). The major problem with the nylon bag technique is correcting for the passage of fine rumen or sample particles through the pores of the bag (Johnson *et al.,* 1982).

Digestibilities are termed either *apparent* or *true*. The two terms refer not to the accuracy of a digestion measurement but to whether the digestibility coefficient is a gross (apparent) or net (true) function. For example, apparent digestibilities are determined by the following equation:

$$\frac{\text{Apparent digestibility}}{(\%)} = \frac{\text{Amount consumed} - \text{Fecal excretion}}{\text{Amount consumed}} \times 100.$$

However, fecal losses include both nondigested feed residues as well as metabolic products. True digestibilities are determined by correcting the total fecal loss for the metabolic losses:

$$\frac{\text{True digestibility}}{(\%)} = \frac{\text{Amount consumed} - (\text{Total fecal excretion} - \text{Metabolic losses})}{\text{Amount consumed}} \times 100.$$

True and apparent digestibilities differ for only those food constituents in which the animal adds a metabolic fecal component. For example, fecal protein, lipids, minerals, or vitamins can be either from the feed or from the animal. When apparent digestibilities include a metabolic loss, true digestibility coefficients will always be higher than the apparent coefficient. For highly digestible feed components in which a constant metabolic loss occurs, the apparent digestibility is a curvilinear function of dietary concentration (Fig. 14.3; Table 14.1). However, the apparent digestible amount is always a linear function when the same assumptions prevail. Note that the equations for both the linear and curvilinear lines describing apparent digestive functions are composed of the true digestibility coefficient and the metabolic fecal loss. Negative apparent digestibilities occur when metabolic and nondigested fecal losses exceed the amount of intake.

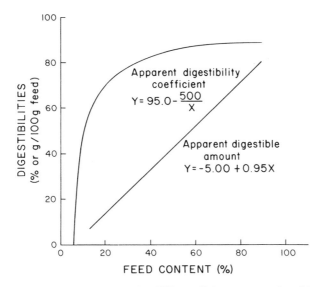

FEED CONTENT (%)

Fig. 14.3 Relationship between apparent digestibility coefficients, apparent digestible amount (feed content times apparent digestibility) and feed content for the example in Table 14.1.

TABLE 14.1

Relationships between Feed Content and True and Apparent Digestibilities of a Highly Digestible Feed Fraction whose Ingestion Produces a Constant Metabolic Fecal Loss

Feed content (g/100 g feed)	True digestible amount[a] (g/100 g feed)	Nondigested amount (g/100 g feed)	Metabolic loss (g/100 g feed)	Apparent digestible amount[b] (g/100 g feed)	Apparent digestibility coefficient[c] (%)
0.0	0.00	0.00	5.0	−5.00	−∞
5.0	4.75	0.25	5.0	−0.25	−5.0
10.0	9.50	0.50	5.0	4.50	45.0
20.0	19.00	1.00	5.0	14.00	70.0
30.0	28.50	1.50	5.0	23.50	78.3
100.0	95.00	5.00	5.0	90.00	90.0

[a]True digestibility is 95%.
[b]Apparent digested amount is intake minus total fecal excretion.
[c]Apparent digestibility coefficient is apparent digested amount divided by feed content.

B. Digestibilities

1. PROTEIN

The true digestibility of dietary protein averages 92.0 ± 4.8% with no significant differences between animals or diets (Table 14.2). Thus, the numerous protease enzymes of wildlife or their symbiotic microflora extensively digest plant and animal proteins, excluding keratinized hair, feathers, or hoof-type structures (Jense, 1968; Davison, 1975; Pritchard and Robbins, 1990). Because of the high true digestibility of dietary protein and constant metabolic loss (Table 9.1), apparent digestibilities are curvilinear functions of dietary protein content. As dietary protein content increases, the apparent digestibility of protein increases from negative to very high positive values (Mould and Robbins, 1982). Thus, discussions in which apparent protein digestibilities are compared in order to identify those feeds in which protein is more available are almost always misleading because the food with the most protein will always have the highest apparent digestibility coefficient even though the actual availability of feed protein (i.e., true digestibility) is the same.

One group of plant defenses, tannins, can dramatically reduce apparent protein digestibilities (Robbins *et al.*, 1987a; Hanley *et al.*, 1992). The magnitude of the reduction varies depending on the animal's ability to minimize or neutralize the tannin's protein-binding capacity. For example, apparent protein digestibilities are reduced much less in animals that secrete tannin-binding salivary proteins (such as mule deer, black bears, and laboratory rats) than in those that do not (prairie voles or domestic sheep) (Robbins *et al.*, 1991). The arboreal folivores of Australia, such as the koala and ringtail possum, that consume eucalyptus leaves having moderate to low levels of protein and moderate to high levels of tannins may have very different mechanisms for neutralizing tannins. Because eucalyptus tannins apparently reduce protein digestion very minimally (Cork, 1986; McArthur, 1988), extensive hindgut fermentation and long retention of digesta in these animals may permit either the degradation of tannins and/or the recovery of tannin-bound proteins.

2. PLANT NEUTRAL DETERGENT SOLUBLES AND FIBER

The true digestibility of neutral detergent solubles (excluding soluble plant defensive compounds) ranges from 98 to 100% (Van Soest, 1967; Parra, 1978; Mould and Robbins, 1982; Robbins *et al.*, 1987b). As with protein, apparent digestibilities of the solubles will range from negative to highly positive depending on feed content, although tannins do reduce the apparent digestibility of neutral detergent solubles (Hanley *et al.*, 1992).

Digestibilities of neutral detergent fiber are functions of the relative concentration of structural digestion inhibitors, particularly lignin, cutin, and silica;

type of gastrointestinal tract; and rate of passage. For example, the digestibility of the NDF decreases in ruminants as the lignin and cutin concentration increases (Fig. 14.4). Silica reduces the NDF digestibility of grasses by three units per unit of silica (Van Soest and Jones, 1968). In general, large or grazing ruminants with slower rates of passage digest slightly more of the fiber than do small, browsing ruminants and macropod marsupials (Forbes and Tribe, 1970; Hume, 1974; Mould and Robbins, 1982; Baker and Hansen, 1985; Baker and Hobbs, 1987). At low lignin and cutin concentrations where much of the cellulose and hemicellulose are available for microbial digestion, large hindgut fermenters (e.g., rhinoceros and emu) digest more of the fiber than do small hindgut fermenters but often less than ruminants. At high lignin and cutin concentrations where little of the fiber is actually available, the differences in fiber digestion due to rate of passage or site of fermentation are greatly reduced. For animals like the giant panda that have very fast passage and no major sites of fermentation, fiber digestion is restricted to acid hydrolysis of the hemicellulose (Dierenfeld

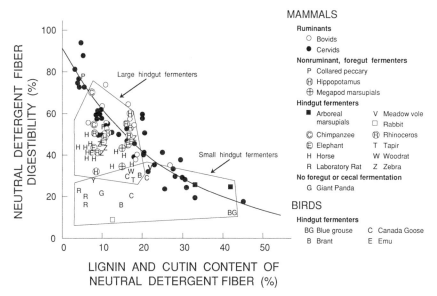

Fig. 14.4 The effect of lignin, cutin, and type of gastrointestinal tract on fiber digestion. (Data from Fonnesbeck, 1968; Keys and Van Soest, 1970; Keys *et al.*, 1970; Ullrey *et al.*, 1971, 1972; Milchunas *et al.*, 1978; Dierenfeld *et al.*, 1982; Mould and Robbins, 1982; Foose, 1982; Uden and Van Soest, 1982; Cork *et al.*, 1983; Herd and Dawson, 1984; Baer *et al.*, 1985; Baker and Hansen, 1985; Karasov *et al.*, 1986; Carl and Brown, 1986; Buchsbaum *et al.*, 1986; Baker and Hobbs, 1987; Foley and Hume, 1987; Robbins *et al.*, 1987b; Ullrey *et al.*, 1987; Milton and Demment, 1988; Sedinger *et al.*, 1989; Remington, 1989; Domingue *et al.*, 1991; Hanley *et al.*, 1992.) Hindgut fermenters are encircled. The line ($Y = 90.1e^{-0.0377X}$, $N = 38$, $R^2 = 0.84$) is for cervids only.

TABLE 14.2

True Digestibility (%) of Dietary Protein

Group or species	Diet	Digestibility coefficient	Sources
Nonruminant eutherians			
Carnivores			
Black bear, grizzly bear, and giant panda	Forage, fruit, grain	88.1	Pritchard and Robbins, 1990
Bears, canids, mustelids, and seals	Meat, fish, whole mammals and birds	100.0	Pritchard and Robbins, 1990
Lagomorphs			
Black-tailed jackrabbit	Forage	98.5	Nagy et al., 1976
Domestic rabbit	Fish meal, almond hulls, oat hay	92.0	Slade and Robinson, 1970
Snowshoe hare	Twigs and concentrates	91.3	Holter et al., 1974; Walski and Mautz, 1977
Primates			
Rhesus monkey	Pelleted diet	87.4	Robbins and Gavan, 1966
Rodents			
Guinea pig, mice, rats, squirrels, and voles	Concentrates	94.0	Meyer and Karasov, 1989
	Forage	94.0	
Ruminants and pseudo-ruminants			
Bovids			
Bison	Hay	96.8	Richmond et al., 1977
Bush duiker	Pelleted diet	83.5	Arman and Hopcraft, 1975
Eland	Pelleted diet	83.2	Arman and Hopcraft, 1975
Hartbeest	Pelleted diet	87.4	Arman and Hopcraft, 1975

Nilgai antelope	Pelleted diet	95.8	Priebe and Brown, 1987
Nubian ibex	Forage	95.4	Choshniak and Arnon, 1985
Thomson's gazelle	Pelleted diet	84.7	Arman and Hopcraft, 1975
Cervids			
Caribou and reindeer	Silage and grain	92.4	Robbins et al., 1987a
Elk	Forage	98.0	Mould and Robbins, 1981
Moose	Pelleted diet	92.5	Robbins et al., 1987a
Mule and white-tailed deer	Forage	92.8	Robbins et al., 1987a
	Pelleted diet	93.2	
	Twigs	93.6	
Red deer	Pelleted diet	96.0	Maloiy et al., 1970
Suiformes			
Collard peccary	Pelleted diet and forage	95.3	Gallagher et al., 1984; Carl and Brown, 1986
Marsupials			
Brushtail possum	Concentrates	95.5	Wellard and Hume, 1981
Euro	Forage and grain	91.5	Brown and Main, 1967; Hume, 1974
Grey and red kangaroos	Forage	84.3	Foot and Romberg, 1965; Forbes and Tribe, 1970; Hume, 1974; Dellow and Hume, 1982
Tammar and parma wallabies	Forage	85.7	Barker, 1968; Hume, 1977; Hume and Dunning, 1979; Dellow and Hume, 1982; Hume, 1986

et al., 1982). Tannins can reduce fiber digestion in species that are not evolutionarily adapted for their consumption (i.e., grazing ruminants) (Robbins *et al.*, 1991).

3. DRY MATTER AND ENERGY

The understanding of factors determining digestible dry matter is basic to predicting digestible energy. For most plant-based diets, dry matter and energy digestibility coefficients are virtually identical (Table 14.3). Digestibilities of dry matter and energy of meat (95.1 ± 2.2% and 95.5 ± 1.9%), fish (90.5 ± 2.2% and 95.3 ± 2.4%), and invertebrate larvae (90.5 ± 6.7% and 91.2 ± 5.3%) fed to carnivores are very high (Jense, 1968; Litvaitis and Mautz, 1976, 1980; Davison *et al.*, 1978; Hackenburger and Atkinson, 1983; Robbins, 1983; Powers *et al.*, 1989; Pritchard and Robbins, 1990). However, digestibilities of dry matter (76.2 ± 5.0%, range: 68.3 to 85.6) and energy (85.3 ± 4.7%, range: 77.3 to 91.6) for carnivores consuming whole birds or mammals are less than meat diets because of the nondigestible hair, feathers, and other residues. Because of the consumption of high-energy fat deposits when animals are consumed whole that are normally not part of meat diets, digestible energy is higher than digestible dry matter. Similarly, adult insects are less digestible (DEC = 76.7 ± 1.7%) than larvae (Barclay *et al.*, 1991).

The digestibility of plant-based diets can range from 89.5 ± 5.0% for the dry matter and energy of agricultural seeds (barley, oats, corn, wheat, and sunflowers) and nuts (acorns, walnuts, hazelnuts, and beechmast, excluding hulls) fed to rodents to as little as 12% for bamboo leaves and stems consumed by giant pandas (Robbins, 1983; Schaller *et al.*, 1985). The range in digestibilities is caused by increasing levels of nondigestible fiber. Consequently, in order to predict the digestibility of plant-based diets, one has to develop equations that incorporate the food's chemical composition with the animal's ability to digest those fractions. In doing this, the equations must be based on an *a priori* understanding of the digestive process and not on abiological multiple correlations.

One of the simplest equations to understand has been developed for bears (Pritchard and Robbins, 1990). Because bears digest very little fiber (i.e., only acid hydrolysis of hemicellulose; Dierenfeld *et al.*, 1982), dry matter digestibility can be predicted from total dietary fiber content (Fig. 14.5). For nontannin-containing diets, fiber accounts for 98% of the variation in digestibility. The one exception in the above study was a diet that contained yams. The raw, very crystalline, large starch granules of yams and potatoes are very difficult for animals without significant gastrointestinal fermentation to digest (Panigrahi and Francis, 1982). Consequently, zoos that feed potatoes to bears must cook the potatoes in order to open the starch granules for digestion.

TABLE 14.3

Relationship between Apparent Digestible Dry Matter (X) and
Apparent Digestible Energy (Y)

Animals	Diet	Equation	Sources
Ruminants	Forage, browse, pelleted diets	$Y = -0.49 + 0.99X$ $R^2 = 0.96, N = 73$	Drozdz and Osiecki, 1973; Robbins et al., 1975; Milchunas et al., 1978; Mould and Robbins, 1982
Rodents	Forage, grains, nuts, pelleted diets	$Y = -0.13 + 1.01X$ $R^2 = 0.98, N = 33$	Drozdz, 1968; Smith and Follmer, 1972; Hanson and Cavender, 1973; Batzli and Cole, 1979; Hammond and Wunder, 1991
Carnivores	Meat	$Y = 1.12 + 0.99X$ $R^2 = 0.94, N = 6$	Pritchard and Robbins, 1990
	Whole mammals, birds, fish	$Y = 25.15 + 0.78X$ $R^2 = 0.98, N = 16$	Pritchard and Robbins, 1990

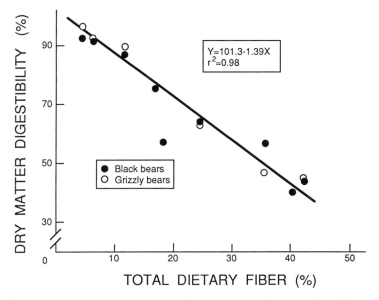

Fig. 14.5 Relationship between total dietary fiber content and dry matter digestibility of meat (deer, beef, ground squirrels, and trout) and plant (blueberries, clover, pine nuts, alfalfa, and grain) diets. A diet that contained yams (TDF = 18.1, dry matter digestibility = 57.8) was not included in the regression. (From Pritchard and Robbins, 1990.)

A more complex predictive equation has been developed for North American deer (Robbins *et al.*, 1987b; Hanley *et al.*, 1992):

Neutral Detergent Solubles   +   Neutral Detergent Fiber

$$Y = [(-16.03 + 1.02 \text{ ND}) - 2.8 \text{ } P] + [(0.9231^{-0.0451A} - 0.03B)(\text{NDF})]$$

where

Y = digestible dry matter (g/100 g feed or %)
A = lignin and cutin content as a percentage of the NDF,
B = biogenic silica content (%) of monocots,
NDF = neutral detergent fiber (%),
NDS = neutral detergent solubles (%), and
P = reduction in protein digestion (g/100 g feed) due to tannins.

Unlike bears, ruminants are capable of digesting much of the plant fiber. Consequently, the overall equation combines two independent equations to estimate and sum the digestible units originating from the neutral detergent solubles and fiber. These equations are called *summative equations*. For a plant containing 44% NDS, 56% NDF, 3.5% lignin and cutin, and no biogenic silica or tannins, 28.9 g/100 g of feed are digestible NDS [i.e., $Y = -16.03 + 1.02(44.0)$] and 39.0g/100g of feed are digestible NDF [i.e., for a lignin and cutin to NDF ratio of 6.25%[(3.5 ÷ 56)100], NDF digestibility is 69.6% (0.696 × 56 = 39.0)]. Thus, the digestibility of the dry matter of this feed is 67.9% (i.e., 28.9 + 39.0). One of the major benefits of this type of summative equation is that each factor controlling digestibility is accounted for separately and functionally. For animals that digest more fiber than bears but less than large ruminants (i.e., many hindgut and foregut fermenters with rapid passage), the fiber digestibility component of a summative equation must incorporate expressions describing the interaction between rate of passage and rate of digestion (Milton and Demment, 1988).

One of the underlying, theoretical problems in conducting digestion trials and predicting digestibility of herbivore diets is whether components or characteristics of one ingested food affect the digestibility of other feeds in a mixed diet (Table 14.4). Because of the complexity of the problem, few wildlife studies have attempted to determine if associative effects occur (Dietz *et al.*, 1962; Mould and Robbins, 1982; Robbins *et al.*, 1987a, b; Baker and Hobbs, 1987; Pritchard and Robbins, 1990; Bjorndal, 1991). Two recent studies found major associative effects that suggest the need for further study. In the first example, shrub stems added to a grass diet consumed by wild ruminants increased food retention time and thereby increased fiber digestion (Baker and Hobbs, 1987). In the second example, insect larvae added to a duckweed diet consumed by yellow-bellied slider turtles improved both fiber and protein digestion (Bjorndal, 1991).

II. METABOLISM OF ABSORBED NUTRIENTS

A. Metabolizable Energy

Digestible energy must be further partitioned to determine the amount of food energy that can be used to meet maintenance and production requirements. Losses of urinary and gaseous energy must be subtracted from the digestible energy consumed by mammals to estimate metabolizable energy. Because of the difficulty in separating urine and feces in birds, metabolizable energy coefficients in birds combine losses of fecal, urinary, and gaseous energy to produce an assimilation efficiency as a function of gross energy.

Mammals:

$$\frac{\text{Metabolizable}}{\text{energy}} = \frac{\text{Digestible energy} - \text{Urinary energy} - \text{Gaseous energy}}{\text{Digestible energy}} \times 100$$

Birds:

$$\frac{\text{Metabolizable}}{\text{energy}} = \frac{\text{Gross energy} - \text{Urinary and fecal energy} - \text{Gaseous energy}}{\text{Gross energy}} \times 100$$

1. URINARY ENERGY

Excretion of urinary energy largely depends on diet and increases from fruit, grain, and nut diets to forage, meat, and tree and shrub twigs and leaves (Table 14.5). Forage ingestion increases urinary energy excretion because plant foliage contains many high-energy compounds that, although absorbed, cannot be oxidized. For example, the benzene ring contained in many plant compounds is excreted in the urine as a conjugate of the amino acid glycine called hippuric acid. Browses produce the greatest loss of urinary energy because of the necessary excretion of absorbed terpenoids, phenols, and many other secondary plant compounds. The volatile, high-energy oils of conifers and eucalyptus are 96 to 97% digestible even though they can not be used and are excreted in the urine (Foley *et al.*, 1987).

2. GASEOUS ENERGY

Methane is produced in the gastrointestinal tract during fermentation. Methane, propionate, and, to a lesser extent, unsaturated fatty acids are hydrogen sinks because their production or hydrogenation enable gastrointestinal fermentation to continue without producing significant amounts of free hydrogen. However, methane, unlike propionate and saturated fatty acids, cannot be oxidized by mammals or birds and is therefore an energy loss when it is eructed, exhaled, or passed.

TABLE 14.4

Potential Effect and Direction of Associative Digestion in Herbivores with Forestomach Fermentation

Item	Mode of action	Potential result	
		Single-component diet	Mixed diet
Secondary plant compounds Terpenoids	Toxicity to microorganisms at a threshold level	Reduced NDF and dry matter digestion	When diluted below the threshold level, increased NDF and dry matter digestion
Tannins and other soluble phenolics	Precipitation of protein or toxicity	Reduced protein, dry matter and potentially NDF digestion	No associative effect, further reductions if complete precipitation has not occurred in the single-component diet, or increased digestion if toxicity has occurred in the single-component diet
Grinding and pelleting	Increased rate of passage	Reduced digestibility of all components	When diluted with feeds in a long form capable of slowing the rate of passage of the fine pelleted particles, increased digestibilities of all components

Increasing level of intake	Increased rate of passage	Reduced NDF and dry matter digestion above a threshold level	Reduced NDF and dry matter digestion above a threshold level
	Reduced metabolic excretion per unit of feed	Increased apparent dry matter digestion	Increased apparent protein and dry matter digestion
Inadequate intake of protein or other essential nutrient	Reduced secretion of digestive enzymes, reduced microbial populations	Reduced digestion of all components	When mixed with other forages containing adequate quantities of deficient nutrient, increased digestion of all components
High levels of grain added to fibrous diets	Increased microbial emphasis on digestion of readily available carbohydrates		Reduced digestion of NDF and dry matter because of inefficient cellulose digestion
Increased fiber	Reduced rate of passage	Rapid passage and incomplete digestion	Increased digestion of all plant fiber

303

TABLE 14.5

Urinary Energy as a Percentage of Apparent Digestible Energy

Diet	Urinary energy (%ADE)	N
Fruit (blueberries)	2.5	1
Grains and nuts (oats, wheat, acorns, beechmast, hazelnuts, pinyon pine nuts)	2.8 ± 1.3	10
Herbage (grasses, legumes, forbs, saltbush leaves)	5.8 ± 3.1	10
Meat or whole vertebrates	8.0 ± 3.5	26
Deciduous, winter browse stems (witchhobble, apple, mountain maple, red maple, striped maple)	11.0 ± 4.4	8
Conifer browse (hemlock and balsam fir)	18.9 ± 0.7	4
Eucalyptus	27.3 ± 14.0	3

Sources: Colovos *et al.*, 1954; Colovos, 1955; Greeley, 1956; Silver and Colovos, 1957; Golley *et al.*, 1965; Drozdz, 1968; Jense, 1968; Rogerson, 1968; Barrett, 1969; Gebczynski *et al.*, 1972; Davison, 1975; Gorecki and Grygielska, 1975; Shoemaker *et al.*, 1976; Moors, 1977; Stueck *et al.*, 1977; Simpson *et al.*, 1978; Nagy and Milton, 1979; Mould and Robbins, unpublished; Rau, 1981; Ashwell-Erickson and Elsner, 1981; Cork *et al.*, 1983; Chilcott and Hume, 1984; Keiver *et al.*, 1984; Foley, 1987; Degen *et al.*, 1988; Kam and Degen, 1989; Pritchard and Robbins, 1990.

Wild ruminants produce significant amounts of methane (Table 14.6) and only very small amounts of free hydrogen (less than 1% of the methane produced; Van Hoven and Boomker, 1981). The reduction in methane production as concentrates are added to hay diets is indicative of the increasing production of propionate and its role as a hydrogen acceptor. The fermentation of browse produces even less methane.

Animals with primarily lower-tract fermentation, such as the rock ptarmigan, greater glider, and snowshoe hare, do not produce significant amounts of methane (Table 14.6). The chemical pathways and efficiencies of lower-tract fermentation may be far different from those occurring in ruminants because only 4–12% of the chemical energy fermented by the ptarmigan ends up as methane as compared to 19% in the ruminant (Gasaway, 1976). Similarly, even though macropod marsupials have forestomach fermentation, methane production by macropods is far less than in ruminants. Passage of food through the macropod stomach may simply be too fast for the establishment of slow-growing methanogenic bacteria (Hume, 1982).

3. METABOLIZABLE ENERGY COEFFICIENTS

Apparent metabolizable energy coefficients for mammals decrease from the highest efficiencies in nonruminants consuming fruit, grain, or nuts to the lowest

TABLE 14.6

Methane Production as a Percentage of Apparent Digestible Energy in Mammals and Apparent Metabolizable Energy in Birds

Species or group	Diet	Methane production (%)
Ruminants		
Eland, moose, red deer, white-tailed	Legume and grass hay	12.1 ± 0.2
deer, wildebeest	Hay and grain	9.5 ± 2.0
	Grain	9.0 ± 1.4
	Tree and shrub twigs	5.4 ± 0.3
	Tree and shrub twigs and grain	2.5 ± 1.0
Nonruminants		
Mammals		
Macropod marsupials	Legume and grass hay	1.0 ± 0.6
Greater glider	Eucalyptus foliage	0.7
Snowshoe hare	Tree and shrub twigs and grain	0.6 ± 0.1
Birds		
Rock ptarmigan	Commercial poultry diet	0.3

Sources: Colovos *et al.,* 1954; Greeley, 1956; Silver, 1963; Rogerson, 1968; Thompson *et al.,* 1973; Holter *et al.,* 1974; Mautz *et al.,* 1975; Gasaway, 1976; Kempton *et al.,* 1976; Simpson *et al.,* 1978; von Engelhardt *et al.,* 1978; Regelin *et al.,* 1981; Foley, 1987.

efficiencies in ruminants and arboreal marsupials consuming conifers and eucalyptus leaves (Table 14.7). For birds, the efficiencies are less and the order is slightly different than in mammals because of the inclusion of fecal losses. Within each group, the species of consumer is far less important than the composition of the food (Sibbald, 1976; Castro *et al.,* 1989; Karasov, 1990). However, amount of intake does affect the apparent metabolizable energy coefficient, particularly in birds. When very little food is consumed, the constant urinary and fecal (birds) losses are disproportionately high relative to the ingested energy (Sibbald, 1975, 1982; Miller and Reinecke, 1984). When this occurs, the apparent metabolizable energy coefficient will be low even though the food energy is well utilized. Because of this problem, energy intake during metabolizable energy trials should be at maintenance level or higher where food composition becomes the predominant factor determining the metabolizable energy coefficient.

Occasionally, metabolizable energy coefficients are corrected to nitrogen balance because urinary energy is, in part, dependent on total nitrogen metabolism. If an animal consuming a test diet is in negative nitrogen balance due to inadequate energy intake, a portion of the urinary energy is being derived from tissue catabolism and is thus not solely a property of the efficiency of food utilization.

TABLE 14.7

Apparent Metabolizable Energy Coefficients (AMEC) as a Percentage of Apparent
Digestible Energy in Mammals and as a Percentage of Gross Energy in Birds

Group	Diet	AMEC(%)	N
Nonruminant eutherians	Fruit	97.5	1
	Grains and nuts	97.2 ± 1.3	9
	Herbage	92.7 ± 3.2	8
	Meat or whole vertebrates	91.3 ± 3.0	25
Ruminants	Concentrates	86.9	1
	Hay and concentrates	84.1 ± 2.6	3
	Hay	81.8 ± 0.2	3
	Deciduous, winter browse stems	80.6 ± 3.9	8
	Conifer browse	76.4 ± 1.9	4
Arboreal marsupials	Eucalyptus	72.7 ± 15.9	3
Birds	Nectar	98 ± 1	10
	Agricultural seeds	80 ± 17	26
	Insects	77 ± 8	7
	Vertebrates	75 ± 7	20
	Wild seeds	67 ± 12	36
	Fruit (pulp and skin)	64 ± 15	31
	Bulbs and rhizomes	56 ± 18	4
	Fruit (pulp, skin, and seed)	51 ± 15	22
	Herbage	36 ± 12	16

Sources: Colovos et al., 1954; Colovos, 1955; Greeley, 1956; Silver and Colovos, 1957; Drozdz, 1968; Jense,
1968; Rogerson, 1968; Gebczynski et al., 1972; Thompson et al., 1973; Davison, 1975; Gorecki and Grygielska,
1975; Litvaitis and Mautz, 1976; Mautz et al., 1976; Shoemaker et al., 1976; Moors, 1977; Stueck et al., 1977;
Simpson et al., 1978; Ashwell-Erickson and Elsner, 1981; Rau et al., 1981; Regelin et al., 1981; Cork et al.,
1983; Chilcott and Hume, 1984; Keiver et al., 1984; Foley, 1987; Degen et al., 1988; Kam and Degen, 1989;
Pritchard and Robbins, 1990; (Birds): Worthington, 1989; Castro et al., 1989; Karasov, 1990.

The correction of metabolizable energy to nitrogen balance is accomplished by
adding 7.45 kcal/g of nitrogen deficit in mammals and 8.73 kcal/g deficit in
birds and, conversely, subtracting when in positive nitrogen balance (Sibbald,
1981; Wolynetz and Sibbald, 1984).

B. Net Energy Coefficients

Heat is produced during the many digestive and metabolic processes that
ultimately convert ingested gross energy to mechanical or tissue energy. The
work of digestion, including mastication, peristalsis, secretion, and active transport, and all aspects of fermentation and absorbed nutrient metabolism produce
heat because of the inefficiency of metabolic pathways. The net energy coefficient
is the estimate of the efficiency to which metabolizable energy can be used in
maintenance and productive processes.

Of all the efficiency estimates, the net energy coefficient has been the most difficult to estimate and understand because it varies with diet and productive state (Reid *et al.*, 1980). Net energy coefficients for maintenance and production are usually determined by feeding animals housed in thermoneutral environments several different levels of intake. Energy balance or heat production is plotted against metabolized energy intake (Fig. 14.6). When the regression involves energy balance as the dependent variable, the slope of the regression is the net energy coefficient. However, when heat production is the dependent variable, one minus the slope is the efficiency estimate.

The net energy coefficient measured below energy balance is the efficiency with which metabolizable energy substitutes for tissue energy in meeting maintenance requirements. Because heat increments at increasing intake are a slightly curvilinear function, the linear expression is often used, as it provides an average efficiency estimate (Fig. 14.6) (Blaxter, 1974; Holter *et al.*, 1979). Net energy

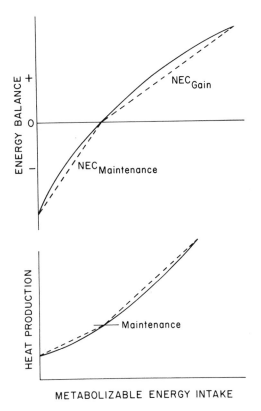

Fig. 14.6 Relationship between metabolizable energy intake, heat production, and energy balance and the linear approximations used to estimate net energy coefficients.

TABLE 14.8

Apparent Net Energy Coefficients (ANEC) as a Percentage of Apparent Metabolizable Energy

Species or group	Diet	Process	ANEC(%)	Sources
Mammals				
Carnivores				
Fisher	Meat	Maintenance	77.2	Davison, 1975
Harbor seal	Fish	Maintenance	91.2	Ashwell-Erickson and Elsner, 1981
Harp seal	Fish	Maintenance	81.3	Gallivan and Ronald, 1981
Sea otter	Squid	Maintenance	81.7	Costa and Kooyman, 1984
	Clams	Maintenance	86.1	
Mink	Meat and grain	Gain	71.3	Harper et al., 1978
Rodents and lagomorphs				
Common vole	Hazelnuts and grains	Gain	88.8	Jagosz et al., 1979
Dormice	Hazelnuts and carrots	Gain	43.7	Gebczynski et al., 1972
Fat sand rat	Saltbush leaves	Gain	30.8	Degen et al., 1988; Kam and Degen, 1989
Gray squirrel	Commercial diet	Gain	51.2	Ludwick et al., 1969
Snowshoe hare	Browse and concentrates	Gain	78.6	Holter et al., 1974
Ruminants				
Eland	Hay and concentrates	Maintenance	72.7	Rogerson, 1968
Moose	Sawdust–grain pellet	Maintenance	71.1	Regelin et al., 1981; Hubbert, 1987
White-tailed deer	Browse	Maintenance	63.9	Robbins, 1973
	Browse	Maintenance	48.3	Mautz et al., 1975

Animal	Diet	Process	Value	Reference
Wildebeest	Hay and concentrates	Maintenance	70.8	Rogerson, 1968
Pronghorn antelope	Milk and concentrates	Maintenance and gain	73.0	Wesley et al., 1970
White-tailed deer	Pelleted diet	Maintenance and gain	81.1	Thompson et al., 1973
Eland	Hay and concentrates	Gain	52.4	Rogerson, 1968
Red deer	Hay and concentrates	Gain	47.0	Simpson et al., 1978
Wildebeest	Hay and concentrates	Gain	59.3	Rogerson, 1968
Birds				
Brant	Alfalfa pellets	Maintenance	77.0	J. S. Sedinger, personal communication
Kestrel	Mice	Maintenance	83.4	Masman et al., 1989
Bobolink	Commercial diet	Gain, fat	64.0	Gifford and Odum, 1965
Brant	Alfalfa pellets	Gain	82.0	J. S. Sedinger, personal communication
Brown honeyeater	Sucrose solutions	Gain, fat	87.5	Collins et al., 1980
Bobwhite quail	Commercial diet	Egg synthesis	71.2	Case and Robel, 1974
Zebra finch	Commercial diet	Egg synthesis	75.0	El-Wailly, 1966
Granivorous birds	Seeds	Feather molt	4.9	Kendeigh et al., 1977; Dolnik and Gavrilov, 1979; King, 1980
Carnivorous and insectivorous birds	Animal tissue	Feather molt	9.1	Kendeigh et al., 1977
White-crowned sparrows	Semisynthetic diet	Feather molt	6.4	Murphy and King, 1984

coefficients for gain, feather and hair growth, egg and milk production, and fetal growth are simply the efficiencies to which metabolizable energy of feed or tissue can be converted into the gross energy of these products.

In general, the net energy coefficient of a feed for maintenance is higher than the net energy coefficient for gain. For example, the average net energy coefficient of diets fed to ruminants is 68.7 ± 10.3% for maintenance and 52.9 ± 6.2% for gain (Table 14.8). Net energy coefficients also tend to increase as the fiber content of the diet decreases and the metabolizable energy content increases (Blaxter, 1974; Blaxter and Boyne, 1978; Kam and Degen, 1989). For example, the highest net energy coefficients for maintenance are for carnivorous mammals (83.5 ± 5.3%) and birds (83.4%) in which the diet has minimal fiber and a very high metabolizable energy content. Net energy coefficients will also be reduced by secondary plant compounds that are absorbed and must be metabolized prior to their excretion (Thomas et al., 1988). Net energy coefficients for gain will vary depending on the composition of the gain. For example, growth that is largely protein has an average efficiency of 44% as compared to 74% for fat deposition (Webster, 1988). Similarly, the efficiency for fat synthesis will be very high if the fats are coming directly from the diet (such as the enormous fat deposition in nursing hooded seals) as compared to diets requiring complete synthesis of the fat from carbohydrate or protein precursors. Feather synthesis is the least efficient process (6.5%) apparently due to a dramatically increased protein turnover in molting birds (Murphy and King, 1984).

C. True versus Apparent Energy Utilization Schemes

Several schematic pathways have been used by nutritionists to visualize the various losses of energy relative to its progression from ingested gross energy to usable net energy (Fig. 14.7). The two systems used have been termed apparent and true relative to the steps where energy losses are subtracted. The most significant difference between the two systems is in the recognition of metabolic fecal and endogenous urinary energy as simply excretory losses similar to non-digested food residues in the apparent scheme versus a requirement in the true scheme. One cannot interchange the various steps in the schemes, such as to multiply apparent digestible energy by a true metabolizable or net coefficient.

D. Protein Metabolism

Protein utilization efficiencies have been studied less by wildlife nutritionists than have similar energy efficiencies. The lack of studies on protein efficiencies is in part due to the preoccupation of wildlife nutritionists in understanding energy flow and the fact that protein utilization is not an independent observation but is dependent on many other animal, dietary, and environmental parameters, including energy. However, only one additional efficiency estimate beyond digestible protein is needed to quantify the utilization of absorbed nitrogen, as urine is the primary route of digested nitrogen loss (Fig. 14.8). Absorbed nitrogen not appearing in the urine is used for maintenance and production.

The efficiency of utilization of absorbed dietary nitrogen is termed biological value (Mitchell, 1924). Several different equations have been used to calculate biological values and include:

$$\frac{\text{Biological}}{\text{value (\%)}} = \frac{NI - (FN - MFN) - (UN - EUN)}{NI - (FN - MFN)} \times 100,$$

where NI is nitrogen intake, FN is total fecal nitrogen, MFN is metabolic fecal nitrogen, UN is total urinary nitrogen, and EUN is endogenous urinary nitrogen. All components of the equation must be in the same units, such as grams per day or grams per kilogram per day. Since NI − (FN − MFN) is the true digestible amount of dietary nitrogen, the equation can also be expressed as:

$$\frac{\text{Biological}}{\text{value (\%)}} = \frac{NI\ (TD) - (UN - EUN)}{NI\ (TD)} \times 100,$$

where TD is the true digestibility of dietary nitrogen. The final form of the equation commonly seen is:

$$\frac{\text{Biological}}{\text{value (\%)}} = \frac{NB + MFN + EUN}{ADN + MFN} \times 100,$$

where NB is the nitrogen balance and ADN is apparent digestible nitrogen. The numerator of this equation represents the maintenance (MFN and EUN) and production (nitrogen balance or retention) requirements, while the denominator is simply another way to express true digestible nitrogen.

Biological values are not constant but rather vary with protein source and its amino acid composition, animal age and productive state, digestible energy intake relative to energy requirements, total protein requirement, and internal physiological means of conserving absorbed nitrogen. A deficiency of one essential amino acid relative to its requirement would lower the biological value of the total protein. Because various productive processes require amino acids in differing concentrations, such as the sulfur-containing amino acid requirement for feather keratin synthesis, biological value will vary depending upon the specific process. Similarly, protein metabolism is inseparably related to energy metabolism. Absorbed amino acids can be used for energy as the carbon and hydrogen are oxidized when dietary energy is lacking, thus lowering the biological value. Consequently, the classical determination of biological value always requires that dietary energy be adequate to prevent excessive protein catabolism.

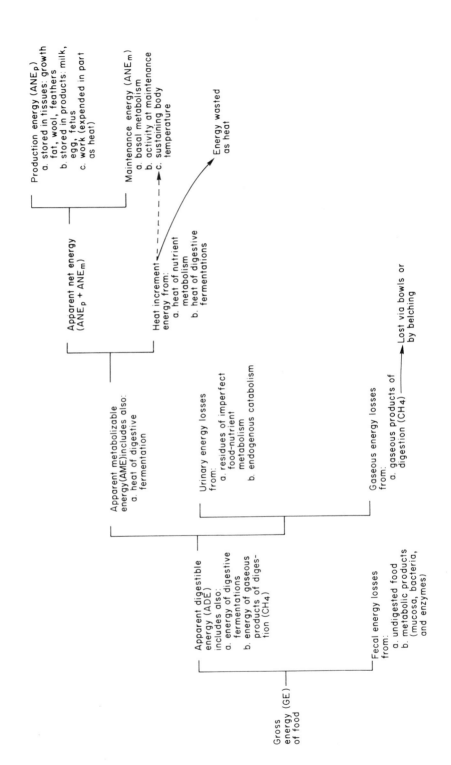

312

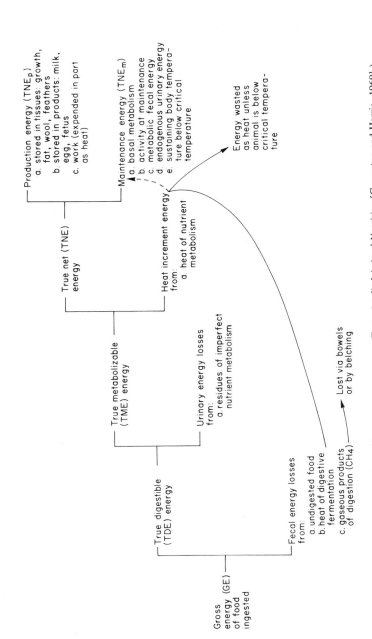

Fig. 14.7 Apparent and true partition of ingested gross energy. (From *Applied Animal Nutrition* [Crampton and Harris, 1969].)

313

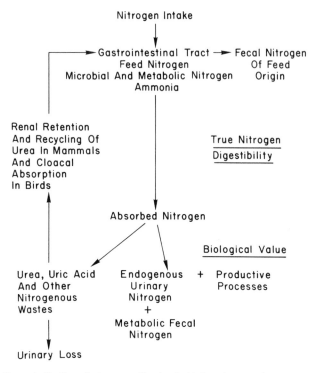

Fig. 14.8   Conceptualization of nitrogen utilization in birds and mammals.

Biological values decrease as dietary protein content increases (Fig. 14.9). Marsupial and eutherian herbivores utilize absorbed protein with equal efficiency. However, mink are not as efficient as herbivores and averaged 17% less efficient than the omnivorous rat when consuming the same protein (Glem-Hansen and Eggum, 1974). The lower efficiency in mink probably reflects the lack of protein conservation through the modulation of hepatic enzyme activity in strict carnivores (Rogers *et al.*, 1977).

REFERENCES

Arman, P., and Hopcraft, D. (1975). Nutritional studies on East African herbivores. 1. Digestibilities of dry matter, crude fiber and crude protein in antelope, cattle and sheep. *Br. J. Nutr.* **33**, 255–264.

Ashwell-Erickson, S., and Elsner, R. (1981). The energy cost of free existence for Bering Sea harbor and spotted seals. *In* "The Eastern Bering Sea Shelf: Oceanography and Resources" (D. W. Hood and J. A. Calder, eds.), pp. 869–899. Univ. of Washington Press, Seattle.

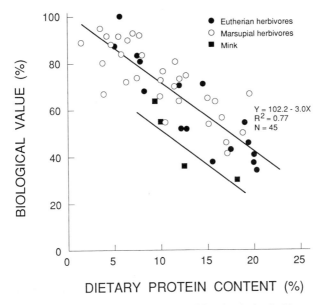

Fig. 14.9 Biological value of dietary protein to marsupial and eutherian herbivores and one carnivore. (Data from Ullrey *et al.*, 1967; Brown and Main, 1967; McEwan and Whitehead, 1970; Hansen and Jorgensen, 1973; Glem-Hansen and Eggum, 1974; Robbins *et al.*, 1974; Hume, 1974, 1977; Kennedy and Hume, 1978; Hume and Dunning, 1979; Hume *et al.*, 1980; Mould and Robbins, 1981; Wellard and Hume, 1981; Chilcott and Hume, 1984; Hume, 1986; Cork, 1986; Foley and Hume, 1987; Smith and Green, 1987; Kam and Degen, 1988; Wallis, 1990.)

Baer, D. J., Oftedal, O. T., and Fahey, G. C., Jr. (1985). Food selection and digestibility by captive giraffe. *Zoo Biol.* **4,** 57–64.

Baker, D. L., and Hansen, D. R. (1985). Comparative digestion of grass in mule deer and elk. *J. Wildl. Manage.* **49,** 77–79.

Baker, D. L., and Hobbs, N. T. (1987). Strategies of digestion: Digestive efficiency and retention time of forage diets in montane ungulates. *Can. J. Zool.* **65,** 1978–1984.

Barclay, R. M. R., Dolan, M-A., and Dyck, A. (1991). The digestive efficiency of insectivorous bats. *Can. J. Zool.* **69,** 1853–1856.

Barker, S. (1968). Nitrogen balance and water intake in the Kangaroo Island wallaby, *Protemnodon eugenii* (Desmarest). *Aust. J. Exp. Biol. Med. Sci.* **46,** 17–32.

Barrett, G. W. (1969). Bioenergetics of a captive least shrew, *Cryptotis parva. J. Mammal.* **50,** 629–630.

Batzli, G. O., and Cole, F. R. (1979). Nutritional ecology of microtine rodents: Digestibility of forage. *J. Mammal.* **60,** 740–750.

Bjorndal, K. A. (1991). Diet mixing: Nonadditive interactions of diet items in an omnivorous freshwater turtle. *Ecology* **72,** 1234–1241.

Blaxter, K. L. (1974). Metabolisable energy and feeding systems for ruminants. *In* "Seventh Nutrition Conference for Feed Manufacturers, University of Nottingham" (H. Swan and D. Lewis, eds.), pp. 3–25. Avi Publishing Co., Westport, Connecticut.

Blaxter, K. L., and Boyne, A. W. (1978). The estimation of the nutritive value of feeds as energy sources for ruminants and derivation of feeding system. *J. Agric. Sci.* **90**, 47–68.

Brown, G. D., and Main, A. R. (1967). Studies on marsupial nutrition. V. The nitrogen requirements of the euro, *Macropus robustus*. *Aust. J. Zool.* **15**, 7–27.

Buchsbaum, R., Wilson, J., and Valiela, I. (1986). Digestibility of plant constituents by Canada geese and Atlantic brant. *Ecology* **67**, 386–393.

Carl, G. R., and Brown, R. D. (1986). Comparative digestive efficiency and feed intake of the collared peccary. *Southwest. Nat.* **31**, 79–85.

Case, R. M., and Robel, R. J. (1974). Bioenergetics of the bobwhite. *J. Wildl. Manage.* **38**, 638–652.

Castro, G., Stoyan, N., and Myers, J. P. (1989). Assimilation efficiency in birds: A function of taxon or food type? *Comp. Biochem. Physiol.* **92A**, 271–278.

Chilcott, M. J., and Hume, I. D. (1984). Digestion of *Eucalyptus andrewsii* foliage by the common ringtail possum, *Pseudocheirus peregrinus*. *Aust. J. Zool.* **32**, 605–613.

Choshniak, I., and Arnon, I. (1985). Nitrogen metabolism and kidney function in the Nubian ibex (*Capra ibex nubiana*). *Comp. Biochem. Physiol.* **82A**, 137–139.

Collins, B. G., Cary, G., and Packard, G. (1980). Energy assimilation, expenditure and storage by the brown honeyeater, *Lichmera indistincta*. *J. Comp. Physiol.* **137**, 157–163.

Colovos, N. F. (1955). The nutritive evaluation of some forage rations for deer. *N.H. Fish Game Dept. Proj. FW-2-R-3* (Mimeo).

Colovos, N. F., Keener, H. A., Davis, H. A., and Terri, A. E. (1954). The nutritive evaluation of some forage rations for deer. *N.H. Fish Game Dept. Proj. FW-2-R-2* (Mimeo).

Cork, S. J. (1986). Foliage of *Eucalyptus punctata* and the maintenance nitrogen requirements of koalas, *Phascolarctos cinereus*. *Aust. J. Zool.* **34**, 17–23.

Cork, S. J., Hume, I. D., and Dawson, T. J. (1983). Digestion and metabolism of a natural foliar diet (*Eucalyptus punctata*) by an arboreal marsupial, the koala (*Phascolarctos cinereus*). *J. Comp. Physiol.* **153**, 181–190.

Costa, D. P., and Kooyman, G. L. (1984). Contribution of specific dynamic action to heat balance and thermoregulation in the sea otter *Enhydra lutris*. *Physiol. Zool.* **57**, 199–203.

Cowan, R. L., Hartsook, E. W., Whelan, J. B., Long, T. A., and Wetzel, R. S. (1969). A cage for metabolism and radioisotope studies with deer. *J. Wildl. Manage.* **33**, 204–208.

Crampton, E. W. and Harris, L. E. (1969). "Applied Animal Nutrition." W. H. Freeman, San Francisco.

Davison, R. P. (1975). "The Efficiency of Food Utilization and Energy Requirements of Captive Female Fishers." Master's thesis, Univ. of New Hampshire, Durham, New Hampshire.

Davison, R. P., Mautz, W. W., Hayes, H. H., and Holter, J. B. (1978). The efficiency of food utilization and energy requirements of captive female fishers. *J. Wildl. Manage.* **42**, 811–821.

Degen, A. A., Kam, M., and Jurgrau, D. (1988). Energy requirements of fat sand rats (*Psammomys obesus*) and their efficiency of utilization of the saltbush *Atriplex halimus* for maintenance. *J. Zool.* **215**, 443–452.

Dellow, D. W., and Hume, I. D. (1982). Studies on the nutrition of macropodine marsupials. I. Intake and digestion of lucerne hay and fresh grass, *Phalaris aquatica*. *Aust. J. Zool.* **30**, 391–398.

Dierenfeld, E. S., Hintz, H. F., Robertson, J. B., Van Soest, P. J., and Oftedal, O. T. (1982). Utilization of bamboo by the giant panda. *J. Nutr.* **112**, 636–641.

Dietz, D. R., Udall, R. H., and Yeager, L. E. (1962). Chemical compostion and digestibility by mule deer of selected forage species, Cache la Poudre range, Colorado. *Colo. Game Fish Dept. Tech. Publ. No.* **14**.

Dolnik, V. R., and Gavrilov, V. M. (1979). Bioenergetics of molt in the chaffinch (*Fringilla coelebs*). *Auk* **96**, 253–264.

Domingue, B. M. F., Dellow, D. W., Wilson, P. R., and Barry, T. N. (1991). Comparative digestion in deer, goats, and sheep. *N. Z. J. Agric. Res.* **34,** 45–53.

Drozdz, A. (1968). Digestibility and assimilation of natural foods in small rodents. *Acta Theriol.* **13,** 367–389.

Drozdz, A., and Osiecki, A. (1973). Intake and digestibility of natural foods by roe-deer. *Acta Theriol.* **13,** 81–91.

El-Wailly, A. J. (1966). Energy requirements for egg-laying and incubation in the zebra finch, *Taeniopygia castanotis. Condor* **68,** 582–594.

Fadely, B. S., Worthy, G. A. J., and Costa, D. P. (1990). Assimilation efficiency of Northern fur seals determined using dietary manganese. *J. Wildl. Manage.* **54,** 246–251.

Foley, W. J. (1987). Digestion and energy metabolism in a small arboreal marsupial, the greater glider (*Petauroides volans*), fed high-terpene *Eucalyptus* foliage. *J. Comp. Physiol.* **157B,** 355–362.

Foley, W. J., and Hume, I. D. (1987). Digestion and metabolism of high-tannin *Eucalyptus* foliage by the brushtail possum (*Trichosurus vulpecula*) (Marsupialia: Phalangeridae). *J. Comp. Physiol.* **157B,** 67–76.

Foley, W. J., Lassak, E. V., and Brophy, J. (1987). Digestion and absorption of *Eucalyptus* essential oils in greater glider (*Petauroides volans*) and brushtail possum (*Trichosurus vulpecula*). *J. Chem. Ecol.* **13,** 2115–2130.

Fonnesbeck, P. V. (1968). Digestion of soluble and fibrous carbohydrate of forage by horses. *J. Anim. Sci.* **27,** 1336–1344.

Foose, T. J. (1982). "Trophic Strategies of Ruminants versus Nonruminant Ungulates." Doctoral Dissertation, Univ. Chicago.

Foot, J. Z., and Romberg, B. (1965). The utilization of roughage by sheep and the red kangaroo, *Macropus rufus* (Desmarest). *Aust. J. Agric. Res.* **16,** 429–435.

Forbes, D. K., and Tribe, D. E. (1970). The utilization of roughages by sheep and kangaroos. *Aust. J. Zool.* **18,** 247–256.

Gallagher, J. F., Varner, L. W., and Grant, W. E. (1984). Nutrition of the collared peccary in south Texas. *J. Wildl. Manage.* **48,** 749–761.

Gallivan, G. J., and Ronald, K. (1981). Apparent specific dynamic action in the harp seal (*Phoca groenlandica*). *Comp. Biochem. Physiol.* **69A,** 579–581.

Gasaway, W. C. (1976). Methane production in rock ptarmigan (*Lagopus mutus*). *Comp. Biochem. Physiol.* **54A,** 183–185.

Gasaway, W. S., White, R. G. and Holleman, D. F. (1975). Flow of digesta in the intestine and cecum of the rock ptarmigan. *Condor* **77,** 467–474.

Gasaway, W. C., White, R. G., and Holleman, D. F. (1976). Digestion of dry matter and absorption of water in the intestine and cecum of rock ptarmigan. *Condor* **78,** 77–84.

Gebczynski, M., Gorecki, A., and Drozdz, A. (1972). Metabolism, food assimilation and bio-energetics of three species of dormice (*Gliridae*). *Acta Theriol.* **17,** 271–294.

Gifford, C. E., and Odum, E. P. (1965). Bioenergetics of lipid deposition in the bobolink, a trans-equatorial migrant. *Condor* **67,** 383–403.

Glem-Hansen, N., and Eggum, B. O. (1974). A comparison of protein utilization in rats and mink based on nitrogen balance experiments. *Z. Tierphysiol., Tierernahrg. u. Futtermittelkde.* **33,** 29–34.

Goering, H. K., and Van Soest, P. J. (1970). Forage fiber analyses. U.S.D.A. Agric. Handbook **379.**

Golley, F. B., Petrides, G. A., Rauber, E. L., and Jenkins, J. H. (1965). Food intake and assimilation by bobcats under laboratory conditions. *J. Wildl. Manage.* **29,** 442–447.

Gorecki, A., and Grygielska, M. (1975). Consumption and utilization of natural foods by the common hamster. *Acta Theriol.* **20,** 237–246.

Greeley, F. (1956). Nutritive evaluation of some forage rations of deer. *N.H. Fish Game Dept. Proj. FW-2-R* (Mimeo).

Hackenburger, M. K., and Atkinson, J. L. (1983). The apparent diet digestibilities of captive tigers (*Panthera tigris* spp.). *Proc. Dr. Scholl Nutr. Conf.* **3**, 70–83.

Hammond, K. A., and Wunder, B. A. (1991). The role of diet quality and energy need in the nutritional ecology of a small herbivore, *Microtus ochrogaster*. *Physiol. Zool.* **64**, 541–567.

Hanley, T. A., Robbins, C. T., Hagerman, A. E., and McArthur, C. (1992). Predicting digestible protein and digestible dry matter in tannin-containing forages consumed by ruminants. *Ecology* **73**, 537–541.

Hansen, N. G. and Jorgensen, G. 1973. Determination of the metabolic fecal nitrogen and the endogenous urinary nitrogen in mink. *Acta Agric. Scand.* **23**, 34–38.

Hanson, R. M., and Cavender, B. R. (1973). Food intake and digestion by black-tailed prairie dogs under laboratory conditions. *Acta Theriol.* **18**, 191–200.

Harper, R. B., Travis, H. F., and Glinsky, M. S. (1978). Metabolizable energy requirement for maintenance and body composition of growing farm-raised male pastel mink (*Mustela vison*). *J. Nutr.* **108**, 1937–1943.

Herd, R. M., and Dawson, T. J. (1984). Fiber digestion in the emu, *Dromaius novaehollandiae*, a large bird with a simple gut and high rates of passage. *Physiol. Zool.* **57**, 70–84.

Holter, J. B., Tyler, G., and Walski, T. (1974). Nutrition of the snowshoe hare (*Lepus americanus*). *Can. J. Zool.* **52**, 1553–1558.

Holter, J. B., Urban, W. E., Jr., and Hayes, H. H. (1979). Predicting energy and nitrogen retention in young white-tailed deer. *J. Wildl. Manage.* **43**, 880–888.

Hubbert, M. E. (1987). "The Effect of Diet on Energy Partitioning in Moose." Doctoral Dissertation, Univ. of Alaska, Fairbanks.

Hume, I. D. (1974). Nitrogen and sulfur retention and fibre digestion by euros, red kangaroos and sheep. *Aust. J. Zool.* **22**, 13–23.

Hume, I. D. (1977). Maintenance nitrogen requirements of the macropod marsupials *Thylogale thetis*, red-necked pademelon, and *Macropus eugenii*, Tammar wallaby. *Aust. J. Zool.* **25**, 407–417.

Hume, I. D. (1982). "Digestive Physiology and Nutrition of Marsupials." Cambridge Univ. Press, Cambridge.

Hume, I. D. (1986). Nitrogen metabolism in the Parma wallaby *Macropus parma*. *Aust. J. Zool.* **34**, 147–155.

Hume, I. D., and Dunning, A. (1979). Nitrogen and electrolyte balance in the wallabies *Thylogale thetis* and *Macropus eugenii* when given saline drinking water. *Comp. Biochem. Physiol.* **63A**, 135–139.

Hume, I. D., Rubsamen, K., and Engelhardt, W. V. (1980). Nitrogen metabolism and urea kinetics in the rock hyrax (*Procavia habessinica*). *J. Comp. Physiol.* **138B**, 307–314.

Jagosz, J., Gorecki, A., and Pozzi-Cabaj, M. (1979). The bioenergetics of deposit and utilization of stored energy in the common vole. *Acta Theriol.* **24**, 391–397.

Jense, G. K. (1968). "Food Habits and Energy Utilization of Badgers." Master's Thesis. South Dakota St. Univ., Brookings.

Johnson, M. K., Wofford, H., and Mitchell, W. (1982). Contamination during nylon-bag digestion trials. *J. Wildl. Manage.* **46**, 253–255.

Kam, M., and Degen, A. A. (1988). Water, electrolyte and nitrogen balances of fat sand rats (*Psammomys obesus*) when consuming the saltbush *Atriplex halimus*. *J. Zool.* **215**, 453–462.

Kam, M., and Degen, A. A. (1989). Efficiency of use of saltbush (*Atriplex halimus*) for growth by fat sand rats (*Psammomys obesus*). *J. Mammal.* **70**, 485–493.

Karasov, W. H. (1990). Digestion in birds: Chemical and physiological determinants and ecological implications. *Stud. Avian Biol.* **13**, 391–415.

Karasov, W. H., Petrossian, E., Rosenberg, L., and Diamond, J. M. (1986). How do food passage rate and assimilation differ between herbivorous lizards and nonruminant mammals? *J. Comp. Physiol.* **156B**, 599–609.

Keiver, K. M., Ronald, K., and Beamish, F. W. H. (1984). Metabolizable energy requirements for maintenance and fecal and urinary losses for juvenile harp seals (*Phoca groenlandica*). *Can. J. Zool.* **62**, 769–776.

Kempton, T. J., Murray, R. M., and Leng, R. A. (1976). Methane production and digestibility measurements in the grey kangaroo and sheep. *Aust. J. Biol. Sci.* **29**, 209–214.

Kendeigh, S. C., Dolnik, V. R., and Gavrilov, V. M. (1977). Avain energetics. *In* "Granivorous Birds in Ecosystems" (J. Pinowski and S.C. Kendeigh, eds.), pp. 127–204. Cambridge Univ. Press, London.

Kennedy, P. M., and Hume, I. D. (1978). Recycling of urea nitrogen to the gut of the tammar wallaby (*Macropus eugenii*). *Comp. Biochem. Physiol.* **61A**, 117–121.

Keys, J. E., Jr., and Van Soest, P. J. (1970). Digestibility of forages by the meadow vole (*Microtus pennsylvanicus*). *J. Dairy Sci.* **53**, 1502–1508.

Keys, J. E., Jr., Van Soest, P. J., and Young, E. P. (1970). Effects of increasing dietary cell wall content on the digestibility of hemicellulose and cellulose in swine and rats. *J. Anim. Sci.* **31**, 1172–1177.

King, J. R. (1980). Energetics of avian moult. *Proc. Int. Ornithol. Congr.* **17**, 312–317.

Litvaitis, J. A., and Mautz, W. W. (1976). Energy utilization of three diets fed to a captive red fox. *J. Wildl. Manage.* **40**, 365–368.

Litvaitis, J. A., and Mautz, W. W. (1980). Food and energy use by captive coyotes. *J. Wildl. Manage.* **44**, 56–61.

Ludwick, R. L., Fontenot, J. P., and Mosby, H. S. (1969). Energy metabolism of the eastern gray squirrel. *J. Wildl. Manage.* **33**, 569–575.

Maloiy, G. M. O., Kay, R. N. B., Goodall, E. D., and Topps, J. H. (1970). Digestion and nitrogen metabolism in sheep and red deer given large or small amounts of water and protein. *Br. J. Nutr.* **23**, 843–854.

Masman, D., Daan, S., and Dietz, M. (1989). Heat increment of feeding in the kestrel, *Falco tinnunculus*, and its natural seasonal variation. *In* "Physiology of Cold Adaptation in Birds" (C. Bech and R. E. Reinertsen, eds.), pp. 123–135. Plenum, New York.

Mautz, W. W., Silver, H., and Hayes, H. H. (1975). Estimating methane, urine, and heat increment for deer consuming browse. *J. Wildl. Manage.* **39**, 80–86.

Mautz, W. W., Walski, T. W., and Urban, W. E., Jr. (1976). Digestibility of fresh frozen versus pelleted browse by snowshoe hares. *J. Wildl. Manage.* **40**, 496–499.

McArthur, C. (1988). "Influences of Tannins on Digestion of Eucalypt Foliage in Common Ringtail Possums (*Pseudocheirus peregrinus*), and an Analysis of Some Chemical Assays in the Presence of Condensed Tannins." Doctoral Dissertation, Monash University, Clayton, Australia.

McEwan, E. H., and Whitehead, P. E. (1970). Seasonal changes in the energy and nitrogen intake in reindeer and caribou. *Can. J. Zool.* **48**, 905–913.

Meyer, M. W., and Karasov, W. H. (1989). Antiherbivore chemistry of *Larrea tridentata*: Effects on woodrat (*Neotoma lepida*) feeding and nutrition. *Ecology* **70**, 953–961.

Milchunas, D. G., Dyer, M. I., Wallmo, O. C., and Johnson, D. E. (1978). *In vivo/in vitro* relationships of Colorado mule deer forages. *Colo. Div. Wildl. Spec. Rep.* **43**.

Miller, M. R., and Reinecke, K. J. (1984). Proper expression of metabolizable energy in avian energetics. *Condor* **86**, 396–400.

Milton, K., and Demment, M. W. (1988). Digestion and passage kinetics of chimpanzees fed high and low fiber diets and comparison with human data. *J. Nutr.* **118**, 1082–1088.

Mitchell, H. H. (1924). A method of determining the biological value of protein. *J. Biol. Chem.* **58**, 873–903.

Moors, P. J. (1977). Studies of the metabolism, food consumption and assimilation efficiency of a small carnivore, the weasel (*Mustela nivalis* L.). *Oecologia* **27**, 185–202.

Mould, E. D., and Robbins, C. T. (1981). Nitrogen metabolism in elk. *J. Wildl. Manage.* **45**, 323–334.

Mould, E. D., and Robbins, C. T. (1982). Digestive capabilities in elk compared to white-tailed deer. *J. Wildl. Manage.* **46**, 22–29.

Murphy, M. E., and King, J. R. (1984). Sulfur amino acid nutrition during molt in the white-crowned sparrow. I. Does dietary sulfur amino acid concentration affect the energetics of molt as assayed by metabolizable energy? *Condor* **86**, 314–323.

Nagy, K. A., and Milton, K. (1979). Energy metabolism and food consumption by wild howler monkeys (*Alouatta palliata*). *Ecology* **60**, 475–480.

Nagy, K. A., Shoemaker, V. H., and Costa, W. R. (1976). Water, electrolyte, and nitrogen budgets of jackrabbits (*Lepus californicus*) in the Mojave desert. *Physiol. Zool.* **49**, 351–363.

Panigrahi, S., and Francis, B. (1982). Digestibility and possible toxicity of the yam *Dioscorea alata*. *Nutr. Rep. Int.* **26**, 1007–1013.

Parra, R. (1978). Comparison of foregut and hindgut fermentation in herbivores. *In* "The Ecology of Arboreal Folivores" (G. G. Montogomery, ed.), pp. 205–229. Smithsonian Inst. Press, Washington, D.C.

Powers, J. G., Mautz, W. W., and Pekins, P. J. (1989). Nutrient and energy assimilation of prey by bobcats. *J. Wildl. Manage.* **53**, 1004–1008.

Priebe, J. C., and Brown, R. D. (1987). Protein requirements of subadult nilgai antelope. *Comp. Biochem. Physiol.* **88A**, 495–501.

Pritchard, G. T., and Robbins, C. T. (1990). Digestive and metabolic efficiencies of grizzly and black bears. *Can. J. Zool.* **68**, 1645–1651.

Rau, J., Murua, R., and Rosenmann, M. (1981). Bioenergetics and food preferences in sympatric southern Chilean rodents. *Oecologia* **50**, 205–209.

Regelin, W. L., Schwartz, C. C., and Franzmann, A. W. (1981). Energy expenditure of moose on the Kenai National Wildlife Refuge. *Kenai Alaska Field Station, Ann. Prog. Rep. Proj. W-17-11*.

Reid, J. T., White, O. D., Anrique, R., and Fortin, A. (1980). Nutritional energetics of livestock: Some present boundaries of knowledge and future research needs. *J. Anim. Sci.* **51**, 1393–1415.

Remington, T. E. (1989). Why do grouse have ceca? A test of the fiber digestion theory. *J. Exp. Zool. Suppl.* **3**, 87–94.

Richmond, R. J., Hudson, R. J., and Christopherson, R. J. (1977). Comparison of forage intake and digestibility by American bison, yak and cattle. *Acta Theriol.* **22**, 225–230.

Robbins, C. T. (1973). "The Biological Basis for the Determination of Carrying Capacity." Doctoral Dissertation, Cornell Univ., Ithaca, New York.

Robbins, C. T. (1983). "Wildlife Feeding and Nutrition." Academic Press, New York.

Robbins, C. T., Prior, R. L., Moen, A. N., and Visek, W. J. (1974). Nitrogen metabolism of white-tailed deer. *J. Anim. Sci.* **38**, 186–191.

Robbins, C. T., Van Soest, P. J., Mautz, W. W., and Moen, A. N. (1975). Feed analyses and digestion with reference to white-tailed deer. *J. Wildl. Manage.* **39**, 67–79.

Robbins, C. T., Hanley, T. A., Hagerman, A. E., Hjeljord, O., Baker, D. L., Schwartz, C. C., and Mautz, W. W. (1987a). Role of tannins in defending plants against ruminants: Reduction in protein availability. *Ecology* **68**, 98–107.

Robbins, C. T., Mole, S., Hagerman, A. E., and Hanley, T. A. (1987b). Role of tannins in defending plants against ruminants: Reduction in dry matter digestion? *Ecology* **68**, 1606–1615.

Robbins, C. T., Hagerman, A. E., Austin, P. J., McArthur, C., and Hanley, T. A. (1991). Variation in mammalian physiological responses to a condensed tannin and its ecological implications. *J. Mammal.* **72,** 480–486.

Robbins, R. C., and Gavan, J. A. (1966). Utilization of energy and protein of a commercial diet by rhesus monkeys (*Macaca mulatta*). *Lab. Anim. Care* **16,** 286–291.

Rogers, Q. R., Morris, J. G., and Freedland, R. A. (1977). Lack of hepatic enzymatic adaptation to low and high levels of dietary protein in the adult cat. *Enzyme* **22,** 348–356.

Rogerson, A. (1968). Energy utilization by the eland and wildebeest. *Symp. Zool. Soc. London* **21,** 153–161.

Ruggiero, L. F., and Whelan, J. B. (1977). Chromic oxide as an indicator of total fecal output in white-tailed deer. *J. Range Manage.* **30,** 61–63.

Schaller, G. B., Jinchu, H., Wenshi, P., and Jing, Z. (1985). "The Giant Pandas of Wolong." Univ. Chicago Press, Chicago, Illinois.

Sedinger, J. S., White, R. G., Mann, F. E., Burris, F. A., and Kedrowski, R. A. (1989). Apparent metabolizability of alfalfa components by yearling Pacific black brant. *J. Wildl. Manage.* **53,** 726–734.

Shoemaker, V. H., Nagy, K. A., and Costa, W. R. (1976). Energy utilization and temperature regulation by jackrabbits (*Lepus californicus*) in the Mojave Desert. *Physiol. Zool.* **49,** 364–375.

Short, H. L., Blair, R. M., and Segelquist, C. A. (1974). Fiber composition and forage digestibility by small ruminants. *J. Wildl. Manage.* **38,** 197–209.

Sibbald, I. R. (1975). The effect of level of feed intake on metabolizable energy values measured with adult roosters. *Poult. Sci.* **54,** 1990–1997.

Sibbald, I. R. (1976). The true metabolizable energy values of several feedingstuffs measured with roosters, laying hens, turkeys and boiler hens. *Poult. Sci.* **55,** 1450–1463.

Sibbald, I. R. (1981). Metabolic plus endogenous energy and nitrogen losses of adult cockerels; The correction used in the bioassay for true metabolizable energy. *Poult. Sci.* **60,** 805–811.

Sibbald, I. R. (1982). Measurement of bioavailable energy in poultry feeding stuffs: A review. *Can. J. Anim. Sci.* **62,** 983–1048.

Silver, H. (1963). Deer nutrition studies. Laboratory analyses of fish and game and their foods. *N.H. Fish Game Dept. Proj. FW-2-R-11* (Mimeo).

Silver, H., and Colovos, N. F. (1957). Nutritive evaluation of some forage rations of deer. *N.H. Fish Game Dept. Tech. Circ. No. 15* (Mimeo).

Simpson, A. M., Webster, A. J. F., Smith, J. S., and Simpson, C. A. (1978). The efficiency of utilization of dietary energy for growth in sheep (*Ovis ovis*) and red deer (*Cervus elaphus*). *Comp. Biochem. Physiol.* **59A,** 95–99.

Slade, L. M., and Robinson, D. W. (1970). Nitrogen metabolism in nonruminant herbivores. II. Comparative aspects of protein digestion. *J. Anim. Sci.* **30,** 761–763.

Smith, A. P., and Green, S. W. (1987). Nitrogen requirements of the sugar glider (*Petaurus breviceps*), an omnivorous marsupial, on a honey-pollen diet. *Physiol. Zool.* **60,** 82–92.

Smith, C. C., and Follmer, D. (1972). Food preferences of squirrels. *Ecology* **53,** 82–91.

Stueck, K. L., Farrell, M. P., and Barrett, G. W. (1977). Ecological energetics of the golden mouse based on three laboratory diets. *Acta Theriol.* **22,** 309–315.

Thomas, D. W., Samson, C., and Bergeron, J-M. (1988). Metabolic costs associated with the ingestion of plant phenolics by *Microtus pennsylvanicus*. *J. Mammal.* **69,** 512–515.

Thompson, C. B., Holter, J. B., Hayes, H. H., Silver, H., and Urban, W. E., Jr. (1973). Nutrition of white-tailed deer. I. Energy requirements of fawns. *J. Wildl. Manage.* **37,** 301–311.

Tilley, J. M. A., and Terry, R. A. (1963). A two-stage technique for in vitro digestion of forage crops. *J. Br. Grassl. Soc.* **18,** 401–411.

Uden, P., and Van Soest, P. J. (1982). Comparative digestion of timothy (*Phleum pratense*) fibre by ruminants, equines and rabbits. *Br. J. Nutr.* **47**, 267–272.

Ullrey, D. E., Youatt, W. G., Johnson, H. E., Fay, L. D., and Bradley, B. L. (1967). Protein requirement of white-tailed deer fawns. *J. Wildl. Manage.* **31**, 679–685.

Ullrey, D. E., Youatt, W. G., Johnson, H. E., Fay, L. D., Purser, D. B., Schoepke, B.L., and Magee, W. T. (1971). Limitations of winter aspen browse for the white-tailed deer. *J. Wildl. Manage.* **35**, 732–743.

Ullrey, D. E., Youatt, W. G., Johnson, H. E., Cowan, A. B., Covert, R. L., and Magee, W. T. (1972). Digestibility and estimated metabolizability of aspen browse for white-tailed deer. *J. Wildl. Manage.* **36**, 885–891.

Ullrey, D. E., Nellist, J. T., Duvendeck, J. P., Whetter, P. A., and Fay, L. D. (1987). Digestibility of vegetative rye for white-tailed deer. *J. Wildl. Manage.* **51**, 51–53.

Van Hoven, W., and Boomker, E. A. (1981). Feed utilization and digestion in the black wildebeest (*Connochaetes gnou*, Zimmerman, 1780) in the Golden Gate Highlands National Park. *S. Afr. J. Wildl. Res.* **11**, 35–40.

Van Soest, P. J. (1967). Development of a comprehensive system of feed analyses and its application to forages. *J. Anim. Sci.* **26**, 119–128.

Van Soest, P. J., and Jones, L. H. P. (1968). Effect of silica in forages upon digestibility. *J. Dairy Sci.* **51**, 1644–1648.

von Engelhardt, W., Wolter, S., Lawrenz, H., and Hemsley, J. A. (1978). Production of methane in two non-ruminant herbivores. *Comp. Biochem. Physiol.* **60A**, 309–311.

Wallis, I. R. (1990). "The Nutrition, Digestive Physiology and Metabolism of Potoroine Marsupials." Doctoral Dissertation, Univ. of New England, Armidale, Australia.

Walski, T. W., and Mautz, W. W. (1977). Nutritional evaluation of three winter browse species of snowshoe hares. *J. Wildl. Manage.* **41**, 144–147.

Webster, A. J. F. (1988). Comparative aspects of the energy exchange. *In* "Comparative Nutrition" (K. Blaxter and I. McDonald, eds.), pp. 37–54. John Libbey, London.

Wellard, G. A., and Hume, I. D. (1981). Nitrogen metabolism and nitrogen requirements of the brushtail possum, *Trichosurus vulpecula* (Kerr). *Aust. J. Zool.* **29**, 147–156.

Wesley, D. E., Knox, K. L., and Nagy, J. G. (1970). Energy flux and water kinetics in young pronghorn antelope. *J. Wildl. Manage.* **34**, 908–912.

White, R. G., and Trudell, J. (1980). Habitat preference and forage consumption by reindeer and caribou near Atkasook, Alaska. *Arct. Alp. Res.* **12**, 511–529.

Wolynetz, M. S., and Sibbald, I. R. (1984). Relationship between apparent and true metabolizable energy and the effects of a nitrogen correction. *Poult. Sci.* **63**, 1386–1399.

Worthington, A. H. (1989). Adaptations for avian frugivory: Assimilation efficiency and gut transit time of *Manacus vitellinus* and *Pipra mentalis*. *Oecologia* **80**, 381–389.

15

Food Intake Regulation

The efficient exploitation of available food is a vital requirement of all animals.

EMLEN, 1966

Food intake is one of the best regulated of all homeostatic mechanisms. Intake regulation occurs at several levels. For example, the animal must balance nutrient acquisition to meet daily and seasonal metabolic demands by regulating the incidence and intake during individual meals. Such a system must monitor numerous environmental conditions (e.g., photoperiod and food availability), gut fill and nutrient absorption, fat stores, and whole-body energy and nutrient needs. These monitoring and control mechanisms must incorporate hierachical, fail-safe redundancy that permits the maintenance of energy balance in diverse nutritional environments (Leibowitz and Stanley, 1986).

I. PHYSIOLOGICAL REGULATION

Although early studies sought an overriding intake control mechanism, a multitude of neurotransmitters (e.g., norepinephrine, epinephrine, dopamine, serotonin, and gamma-aminobutyric acid) and hormones (e.g., insulin, cholecystokinin, neurotensin, glucagon, calcitonin, and growth hormone-releasing factor) respond to nutrient balances and food intake (Ritter *et al.*, 1986). These compounds affect various sites in the brain (e.g., hypothalamus, brainstem, autonomic nervous system, and hindbrain) that ultimately regulates food intake. For wildlife that have seasonal gain–loss cycles independent of food availability, the brain also varies the set-point in its response to these compounds.

II. PHYSICAL REGULATION

The physical and physiological capacity of the gastrointestinal tract to hold and process food can limit intake when foods of either low nutrient density, low digestibility, or intermittent availability are ingested. Examples of each are the crop storage limitations to the ingestion of dilute nectar solutions by humming-birds (Hainsworth and Wolf, 1972), forestomach and crop–gizzard limitations when herbivores ingest poorly digested forages (Montgomery and Baumgardt, 1965; Sedinger and Raveling, 1988), and stomach or crop capacities when predators gorge on large or temporarily abundant prey (Kaufman *et al.,* 1980). Another meal cannot be ingested until gastrointestinal bulk is reduced by either digestion and absorption or passage. Complete digestion can be as rapid as a few minutes for small birds or as slow as many days for some mammalian herbivores.

A. Rate of Passage

Passage is defined as the flow of material within or through the entire gastrointestinal tract per unit time. Consequently, the interval between the ingestion of a food and the excretion of its nondigested residues must be timed. Passage has been studied by adding inert, nonabsorbable markers to the feed and collecting ingesta samples at various sites along the gastrointestinal tract, in feces, or in oral pellets in such species as hawks and owls that void most nondigestible residue orally rather than anally. Of all the decisions to be made in studying passage rate, none is more important than the choice of the marker(s).

Markers of the solids have included dyes, nail polish or paint, glass beads, pieces of plastic, rubber, aluminum or steel, radioactive and stable isotopes, rare earth elements, cotton threads, brine shrimp eggs, and charcoal. Liquid markers, i.e., those that are soluble and move with the fluid, include chromium chloride, Cr-EDTA, cobalt-EDTA, and polyethylene glycol. While all of these markers have been used, a marker provides useful nutritional data only if it moves with specific fluids or non-digested residues. A marker, such as glass beads, that moves independently of all other gastrointestinal contents has no value unless it is an important dietary constituent. For example, one early investigator that consumed 300 g of glass beads noted "a serious case of constipation" as they moved 60% slower than other markers (Hoelzel, 1930). Markers that work in one species may not be useful in another. Although pieces of plastic have been used successfully in humans, that does not mean that plastic is a useful marker for all other primates (Clemens and Phillips, 1980; Clemens and Maloiy, 1981; Milton, 1981). Useful markers in many primates and other animals with either forestomach fermentation or large, functional ceca that regulate particle entry or exit based on particle size or density must either be part of the food (such as seeds if studying seed dispersal) or bind with the food and, thereby, reflect the particle distribution created by chewing. Plastic particles meet neither criteria.

The most significant marker development in recent years has been the ob-

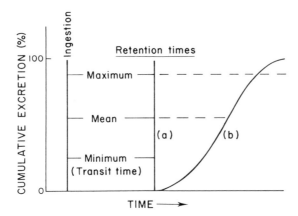

Fig. 15.1 Excretion characteristics of a meal fed to hypothetical animals in which (a) no mixing or pooling occurs as food moves through the gastrointestinal tract and (b) pooling and mixing occur.

servation that certain rare earth elements, such as samarium, cerium, ytterbium, and lanthanum, bind to plant fiber in nondissociable complexes when properly prepared (Allen, 1982). Similarly, chromium can be mordanted to plant fiber (Uden *et al.*, 1980). Thus, there are now several methods for tightly binding markers to food to ensure that marker kinetics reflect food passage. Unfortunately, many of the early investigators using rare earth elements poured ruthenium solutions directly into the stomach or onto the food without the washings necessary to ensure complete adhesion of the marker. Under these conditions, the marker may move between particles and disproportionately mark very fine particles (Cork and Warner, 1983; Cork and Foley, 1991).

Passage phenomena would be easy to understand if the gastrointestinal tract were simply a tube through which food moved as a unit in discrete pulses (Fig. 15.1). Raptors and several other birds are one of the few groups in which excretion occurs in pulses that are readily relatable to the time of ingestion. The nondigested matter in these birds is orally cast at regular intervals (Duke, 1977; Below, 1979). Meal-to-pellet intervals average 11–12 hr in owls and 22 hr in hawks and falcons (Smith and Richmond, 1972; Duke *et al.*, 1976; Fuller *et al.*, 1979; Fuller and Duke, 1979; Duke *et al.*, 1980). However, the precise interval is affected by the amount and temporal sequence of food eaten, food composition, level of hunger, occurrence of additional prey, and external cues, such as dawn. When pooling and mixing occur anywhere within the gastrointestinal tract, such as in the crop, gizzard, ceca, and large intestine of birds and in the stomach, cecum, and large intestine of mammals, passage can be prolonged and diffused.

Passage rate terminology includes turnover rate, transit time or minimum retention time, mean retention time, and maximum retention time (Fig. 15.1). Turnover usually refers to the rate at which food passes from either an individual gastrointestinal segment or the entire tract by both digestion and passage. Transit time is the time between feeding and first appearance of the marker in the feces. Mean retention time is the integrated average time between marker ingestion and excretion. Transit time and mean retention time would be identical if mixing did not occur and marker excretion was complete at one defecation. As mixing occurs, mean retention time and transit time become increasingly different. Maximum retention time is the interval between feeding and the last excretion of the marker. Maximum retention time in animals with extensive gastrointestinal mixing is almost meaningless because it incorporates both the time necessary for physical breakdown and, more importantly, simply the mathematical probability that the last particle has of being diluted and washed out of a specific gastrointestinal pool.

Mean retention time (MRT) increases as animal weight increases (Figs. 15.2, 15.5, 15.6). MRTs in mammals are longest in ruminants, macropod marsupials with complex forestomachs, and arboreal folivores with cecal and large intestine fermentation; they are shortest in carnivores and insectivores. Fluids and the very small particles (<1.2 mm; Martz and Belyea, 1986) of some pelleted diets move through the gastrointestinal tract of ruminants and macropods approximately twice as fast as long forages. Larger particles (5 mm; Schaefer et al., 1978; Sanchez-Hermosillo and Kay, 1979), even when pelleted, move at the slower rates of long forages. Residence time in the rumen accounts for 55 to 65% of the total retention time in ruminants (Hubbert, 1987; Baker and Hobbs, 1987). Although early studies comparing mean retention times and digestive efficiencies of kangaroos and domestic sheep concluded that the ruminant has a longer mean retention time and therefore, higher dry matter and fiber digestive efficiencies (Foot and Romberg, 1965; Forbes and Tribe, 1970), the sheep used in those studies ranged from 1.9 to 3.5 times larger than the kangaroos. Because ruminants and macropods of similar size have similar rates of passage (Fig. 15.2), the observed differences in digestive efficiency may have been entirely due to body size differences and not due to type of gastrointestinal tract. The digestive efficiencies of euros and domestic sheep more similar in size were not significantly different (Hume, 1974). Thus, based on current data, there is no convincing evidence independent of body size that the ruminant and the macropod digestive systems differ in either mean retention times or digestive efficiencies.

Liquid–small particle flow and, therefore, the rate at which large particles can be degraded to small particles are important determinants of digestion and retention time in ruminants. The rate of large particle breakdown is not a constant between foods but varies with the resistance to chewing provided by mean cell-wall thickness (Lees et al., 1982; Lees, 1984; Spalinger et al., 1986). Similarly, rumination rarely exceeds 10 hr/day (Fig. 15.3; Renecker and Hudson, 1989).

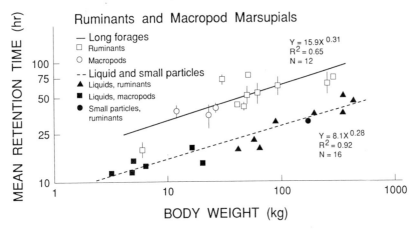

Fig. 15.2 Mean retention time of liquids and small particles (i.e., finely ground, pelleted diets) and long forages (hay, leaves, stems or coarse [5mm] pelleted diets) in the gastrointestinal tract of wild ruminants and macropod marsupials. Liquid passage was measured using chromium chloride, Cr-EDTA, and cobalt-EDTA. Small particles and long forages were either stained or marked with the rare earth elements ytterbium, cerium, or samarium. Mean and range are shown for species fed different diets [*ruminants*: bison, elk, Japanese sika deer, moose, mountain sheep, mule deer, red deer, reindeer, suni antelope, and white-tailed deer (Cowan *et al.*, 1970; Mautz and Petrides, 1971; Thorne and Dean, 1973; Milchunas *et al.*, 1978; Schaefer *et al.*, 1978; Hoppe and Gwynne, 1978; Sanchez-Hermosillo and Kay, 1979; Valtonen *et al.*, 1983; Holleman *et al.*, 1984; Baker and Hobbs, 1987; Hubbert, 1987; Schwartz *et al.*, 1988; Jenks and Leslie, 1989; Katoh *et al.*, 1991) and *macropod marsupials*: eastern wallaroo, grey kangaroo, red kangaroo, red-necked pademelon, and tammar wallaby (Foot and Romberg, 1965; Forbes and Tribe, 1970; Warner, 1981a; Dellow, 1982)]. Regressions for ruminants and macropods are not significantly different; and, therefore, data are combined.

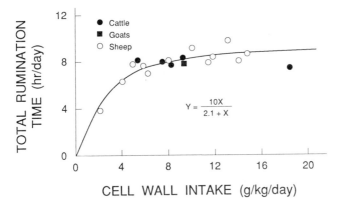

Fig. 15.3 Rumination time as a function of neutral detergent fiber intake. (Data from Welch and Smith, 1969a,b, 1971; Bae *et al.*, 1979; Welch, 1982.)

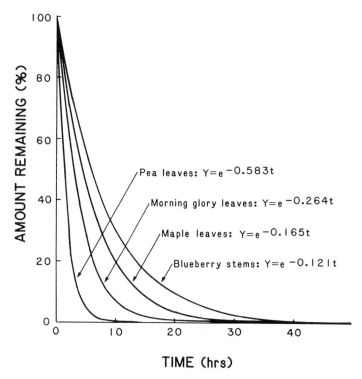

Fig. 15.4 The relative breakdown rates of large particles of four plants in the rumen of mule deer and elk. (From Spalinger *et al.*, 1986.)

Thus, because young forb or shrub leaves with thin cell walls are more easily fractured into small particles that can be digested and passed more quickly from the rumen than are mature shrub leaves, stems, or grasses (Fig. 15.4), the relative nutritional value of the young forb or shrub leaf in a herbivore's diet is much higher than indicated by differences in digestibility alone.

Small, eutherian hindgut fermenters that are primarily cecal fermenters (e.g., rodents and rabbits [Hume, 1982]) have long retention times relative to their body weight because of the entrapment of liquids and small particles in the cecum (Fig. 15.5). Cecal retention accounts for 75% of the total mean retention time in rodents (Yahav and Choshniak, 1990). The longer retention of liquids and small particles than large particles in cecal fermenters (Fig. 15.5) is opposite of that in the ruminant (Fig. 15.2). While the cecum retains small particles and excludes large particles for more rapid excretion, the rumen retains large particles and passes small particles produced by rumination. Large, eutherian hindgut fermenters that are primarily colon fermenters (e.g., zebra, elephant or rhinoc-

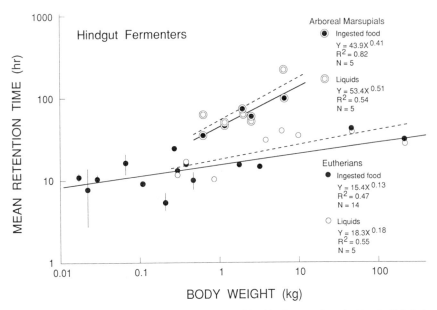

Fig. 15.5 Mean retention time of liquids and ingested food in the gastrointestinal tract of hindgut-fermenting eutherians and arboreal marsupials. Liquid passage was measured using polyethylene glycol, Co-EDTA, and Cr-EDTA. Ingested food by eutherians was either stained, mordanted with chromium, or marked with the rare earth element lanthanum. The food marker for the arboreal marsupials was the rare earth element ruthenium. Mean and range are shown for species fed different diets [*primates — liquids only*: baboon, bushbaby, vervet and sykes monkey (Clemens and Phillips, 1980; Clemens and Maloiy, 1981); *liquids and solids*: chimpanzee (Milton and Demment, 1988); *rodents*: bank vole, common vole, deer mouse, fat jirds, field vole, golden-mantled ground squirrel, guinea pig, hamster, laboratory rat, levant vole, nutria, snow vole, water vole (Gill and Bieguszewski, 1960; Kostelecka-Myrcha and Myrcha, 1964a,b; Sakaguchi *et al.*, 1987; Cork and Kenagy, 1989; Woodall, 1989; Yahav and Choshniak, 1990); *rabbit and domestic horse:* (Warner 1981b; Uden *et al.*, 1982; Sakaguchi *et al.*, 1987); *arboreal marsupials:* brushtail possum, common ringtail possum, greater glider, koala (Wellard and Hume, 1981; Cork and Warner, 1983; Chilcott and Hume, 1985; Foley and Hume, 1987)].

eros) have mean retention times that are only slightly longer than the smaller hindgut fermenters and, therefore, approximately one-third of those occurring in similar-sized ruminants. Faster passage in the eutherian hindgut fermenters relative to ruminants leads to a reduced digestive efficiency of plant fiber (Fig. 14.4). However, because passage is faster, large hindgut fermenters are able to ingest more total food to overcome the reduced digestive efficiency. Large hindgut fermenters have a competitive advantage over the ruminant system when consuming very abundant but very fibrous, low-nutrient foods (Foose, 1982). Therefore, free-ranging ruminants tend to be more selective and choose less fibrous, more digestible foods than do zebras, elephants, and other large hindgut-fermenting herbivores (Bell, 1971; Janis, 1976). However, when food abundance is limited, the ruminant system is advantageous because it maximizes digestive efficiency.

Two additional groups of hindgut fermenters (primates and arboreal, folivorous marsupials) have been studied (Fig. 15.5). Liquid and food passage rates are two to five times longer in arboreal marsupials than in eutherians. Unfortunately, two very questionable particulate markers (plastic for the primates and ruthenium for the marsupials) have been used in many of these studies. Mean retention times of the solids have ranged from 16 to 65 hr in primates and 35 to 100 hr in marsupials. The very long retention times in marsupials (e.g., 100 hr in the koala) have been difficult to understand because they exceed the time necessary for complete fiber digestion, although they might be useful in nitrogen or mineral absorption or a slow degradation of secondary plant compounds. However, as an indication that ruthenium is either measuring small particle passage or is moving between particles, mean retention time of Cr-mordanted large particles (23 ± 2 hr) in the greater glider is half the value (50 hr) determined for food passage with ruthenium (Foley and Hume, 1987). These differences indicate that cecal fermenters can control passage rate by altering the size of particles produced by chewing.

Mean retention times are generally shortest in carnivores and insectivores because they have relatively tubular, noncomplex digestive systems (Fig. 15.6). Meat diets do not require symbiotic microflora for complete digestion. Even when the omnivorous bear consumes plants, passage rates are actually increased (MRT = 7 hr when ingesting white clover) relative to meat diets (MRT = 13 hr) (Pritchard and Robbins, 1990). Such rapid rates of passage enable the herbivorous giant panda with its carnivore-type gastrointestinal tract to meet its nutritional requirements by ingesting large quantities of poorly digestible bamboo (Dierenfeld et al., 1982; Schaller et al., 1985). Because small mammals have much higher energy requirements per unit of weight than the panda, there are limits to the amount of fiber that frugivorous bats and shrews can ingest and still meet their energy requirements. Thus, frugivorous bats and shrews take small bites, chew and suck the fruit, swallow the juice and some very soft pulp, and spit out fiber, seeds, and skins (Morrison, 1980; Emmons, 1991). Thus, they are able to use a nutrient-poor food by consuming the most digestible, least fibrous components that move through the digestive system very quickly.

Mean retention times in birds are generally short (Fig. 15.7). However, there are major differences due to diet and gastrointestinal specializations. Hard seeds require 100% more time than herbage. The delay in seed passage is due primarily to increased crop and stomach residence times (Karasov, 1990). Frugivorous birds have the fastest passage rates, with transit times being as short as 7 minutes

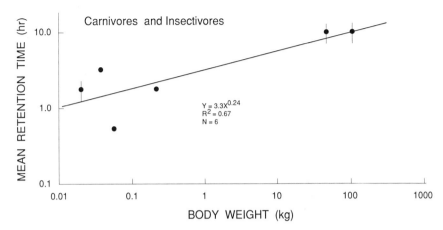

Fig. 15.6 Mean retention times of food ingested in the gastrointestinal tract of the black bear, Cape Rock elephant shrew, grizzly bear, old world water shrew, and tree shrew. Foods were either stained or mordanted with chromium. (Data from Kostelecka-Myrcha and Myrcha, 1965; Woodall and Currie, 1989; Pritchard and Robbins, 1990; Emmons, 1991.)

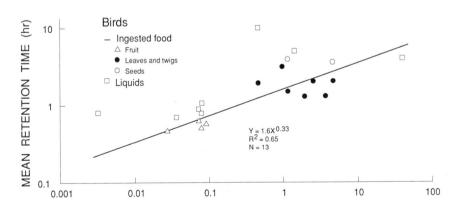

Fig. 15.7 Mean retention time of liquids and ingested food in the gastrointestinal tract of birds. Liquid passage was measured using chromium chloride, Cr-EDTA, or polyethylene glycol. Ingested food was either stained, marked with cerium, or could be identified from fragments. (Data from Karasov and Levey, 1990; Karasov, 1990.)

(Walsberg, 1975; Herrera, 1984; Worthington, 1989; Karasov and Levey, 1990). Liquid passage rates are quite variable with very long mean retention times in the herbivorous ptarmigan and pheasant due to fluid retention in the ceca (Duke *et al.*, 1968; Gasaway *et al.*, 1975).

B. Digestion versus Passage

Digestion and passage are interacting, competing processes. Increasing rates of passage will reduce digestibility if insufficient time is available for complete hydrolysis and absorption. Reduced digestibilities due to faster passage occur in comparisons between species (e.g., browsing and grazing ruminants, domestic sheep and kangaroos, ruminants and equids, or frugivorous and granivorous birds) and within species (Foot and Romberg, 1965; Forbes and Tribe, 1970; Hume, 1974; Milne *et al.*, 1978; Harlow, 1981; Foose, 1982; Mould and Robbins, 1982; Karasov and Levey, 1990). Faster passage rates within a species are usually caused by increased intake. Thus, slightly reduced digestive efficiencies are not necessarily maladapted if they result in increased total nutrient absorption.

Because the ability of an animal to meet its requirements when gastrointestinal capacity is limiting is a function of the rate of digestion, rate of passage, and volume of the limiting gastrointestinal compartment, very general relationships between these three parameters are expected. The capacity of several limiting gastrointestinal compartments, such as the rumen–reticulum of ruminants, cecum and large intestine of nonruminant herbivores, crops of hummingbirds, and cheek pouches of herbivorous heteromyid rodents, are linear functions of body weight (i.e., $W^{1.0}$) (Hainsworth and Wolf, 1972; Parra, 1978; Morton *et al.*, 1980; Chivers and Hladik, 1980; Van Soest, 1981; Moss, 1983). Correspondingly, energy expenditures are generally a function of metabolic body weight (i.e., $W^{0.75}$). Thus, the larger animal or species will be in a more favorable energetic state than the smaller species when low-quality food is abundant because more food can be gathered, transported, and processed relative to energy requirements (Parra, 1978; Case, 1979; Morton *et al.*, 1980; Van Soest, 1981; Demment and Van Soest, 1985). Similarly, the difference between the exponents of capacity and requirements (W $^{1.0}/W^{0.75} = W^{0.25}$) suggests that the larger animal with the relatively slower rate of passage can afford to consume more fibrous, slower digesting forage than can the smaller species (Milton, 1979; Hanley, 1980). The slopes of the regressions between body weight and mean retention times of food for ruminants and macropods (0.31, Fig. 15.2), carnivores and insectivores (0.24, Fig. 15.6), and birds (0.33, Fig. 15.7) agree with the theoretical estimate that mean retention time should be a function of body weight to the 0.25 power (Demment and Van Soest, 1985).

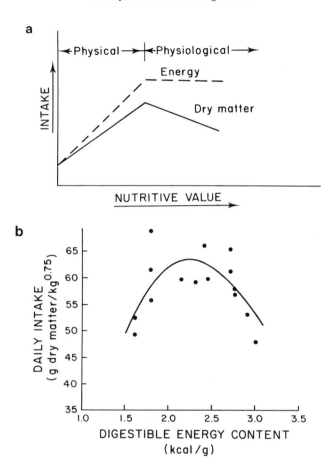

Fig. 15.8   (a) Generalized relationship between nutritive value and intake. (From Montgomery and Baumgardt, 1965, courtesy of the *Journal of Dairy Science*.) (b) Dry matter intake as a function of digestible energy content in deer. (From Spalinger, 1980.)

III. SYNTHESIS: INTAKE REGULATION

Intake regulation changes from primarily physical to physiological as food nutritive value increases (Fig. 15.8A). At very low nutritive values, limited gastrointestinal capacities and passage rates prevent an animal from meeting its energy requirements. As nutritive value increases, the animal is ultimately able to ingest enough dry matter to meet its energy requirements. Once nutritive value is high enough to overcome physical limitations, physiological regulation maintains a constant energy intake at increasing nutritive values by decreasing dry matter intake.

Numerous examples supporting such a generalized theory of intake regulation are available. For example, hummingbirds increased meal size from 0.03 g to 0.16 g as nectar concentration decreased from 1.2 to 0.4 molar (Collins and Cary, 1981), and frugivorous birds increase intake rate as much as 5-fold as fruit energy content decreases (Worthington, 1989). Dry matter intake in deer is a bell-shaped function decreasing on either side of approximately 2.2 kcal apparent digestible energy per gram dry matter (Fig. 15.8B). Since many forage diets consumed by deer contain approximately 4.4 kcal/g of dry matter, intake is physically regulated in this example below approximately 50% apparent digestible energy and physiologically regulated above this level (Ammann et al., 1973). However, the critical level of nutritive quality determining the switch from physical to physiological intake regulation should be an inverse function of body size and will vary with animal requirements and digestive and metabolic capabilities.

IV. FORAGING STRATEGIES

The wildlife nutrition and ecology literature is replete with observations of food habits. However, only in recent years has the focus of these studies shifted from purely descriptive to analytical as attempts to understand the cause–effect basis of foraging are increased (Stephen and Krebs, 1986; Hughes, 1990). Food habits, foraging patterns, energy and time expenditures, and individual well-being depend on the animal's perception of its energy and nutrient requirements relative to the spatial and temporal distribution of its nutritional environment. The optimal foraging strategy is determined by the simultaneous solution of various cost–benefit functions. For example, foraging costs may include energy and time expenditures for pursuit, handling, and ingestion of food, increased thermoregulatory costs, the risk of predation, reduced reproduction or territorial maintenance activities, or the potential consumption of toxic or inhibitory compounds. Benefits of food acquisition range from short-term satiety to long-term reproductive success. Ultimately, the solution of the cost–benefit functions determine the biological fitness of the forager.

A. Food Selection

Food habits are commonly determined by direct observation of captive or wild animals, analyses of identifiable food residues or fragments, measurement of utilization plots or transects, or measurements of carbon and nitrogen isotopes unique to different food resources. While it is rarely difficult to simply list foods ingested, quantification of the relative amounts can be extremely difficult.

Investigators compiling reported food habits, particularly for generalist herbivores, are often struck by the diversity of foods consumed. Food habits determined for a particular species–habitat interaction are potentially different from all other species–habitat interactions (Nudds, 1980). Thus, if one is simply interested in descriptions of food habits, an infinite number of studies are possible (i.e., N mammal and bird species $\times$ N past nutritional histories $\times$ N environments $\times$ . . .). Thus, we must recognize that, while data on food habits are important, listings of food habits in themselves are only a superficial facade of nutritional understanding. Knowledge and understanding of the animal–food–environment interactions determining the observed food habits must ultimately take precedence over ad infinitum listing.

Early attempts to explain food habits of herbivores revolved around correlations between the preference ranking of a food and its nutrient or chemical content. Significant correlations have been reported between preference and soluble carbohydrates, protein or amino acids, energy, plant fiber, ether extract, many minerals and vitamins, secondary plant compounds, and organic acids (Westoby, 1974). Such correlations relative to herbivore food habits are almost impossible to evaluate because many plant chemical components are reflections of each other. For example, plant parts high in protein are often low in fiber and high in digestible dry matter and energy. Because of the molecular complexity of plants, it is not surprising that significant correlations between animal preference and different plant constituents are virtually as numerous as the number of authors attempting such analyses. Thus, statistically significant correlations between preference and feed components often have no biological or ecological meaning.

In further evaluations of food habits as a component of the overall foraging strategy, most investigations have used energy as the currency of the various cost–benefit functions. The preoccupation with energy occurs because it is a measurable requirement of all animals, it is often in limited supply, and the body is replete with sensory and regulatory systems for energy intake monitoring. Energy optimization models have often predicted food habits that agreed quite closely with field observations. However, models based solely on energy considerations will be inadequate for many species without the inclusion of other constraints, such as protein, minerals, plant cell walls, toxins, and digestion inhibitors. When nutrient constraints and secondary plant compounds are included in foraging models, the complexity mushrooms because the value of each food item is no longer independent of all others, but rather each food item subsequently has an absolute value as well as a relative value that is dependent on the composition of all other dietary components.

The selection of foods on the basis of their nutrient content requires a perception of one's requirements and an internal recognition of a food's value in meeting rather specific requirements, but not necessarily a taste or smell for each nutrient. For example, even though sodium is one of the few nutrients that is tasted, animals given free access in a cafeteria-style experiment to the 30 or 40 purified, required nutrients are able to select a diet that enables growth about equal to that of animals consuming balanced laboratory diets (Richter, 1955). Birds can select the best diet for meeting specific amino acid requirements within 16 hr of the initial choice (Murphy and King, 1987). Rozin (1976) has suggested that food selection is based on a categorization of foods as (a) novel and of unknown nutritional value; (b) familiar–dangerous; (c) familiar–safe; and (d) familiar–beneficial. For animals exposed to many different foods, the avoidance of toxins while meeting the necessary requirements could be accomplished by:

1. Treating new foods with extreme caution (i.e., neophobic).
2. Being able to learn quickly to eat or reject particular foods and needing to ingest only minute quantities to do so.
3. Having the capacity to seek out and eat plants containing highly specific classes of nutrients and to balance nutrient ingestion relative to the spectra of nutrient requirements.
4. Having to ingest a number of different staple foods over a short period of time and to indulge simultaneously in a continuous food sampling program.
5. Preferentially feeding on the foods with which they are familiar and continuing to feed on them for as long as possible.
6. Preferring to feed on foods that contain only minor amounts of toxic secondary plant compounds (Freeland and Janzen, 1974).

Thus, generalist plant consumers must continuously sample a broad spectrum of available foods in order to monitor changes in essential nutrients, fiber content, secondary plant compounds, and availability. It is not uncommon to see herbivore diets in which 90% of the ingesta is composed of 3 or 4 species capable of meeting all immediate nutrient requirements while in the remaining 10% are 10–15 species that are either being sampled or have a very limited availability.

B. Foraging Costs and Efficiencies

If feeding and the search for food are the predominant activities of most animals, then activity patterns, daily energy expenditures, and overall fitness should reflect the costs and efficiencies with which foods can be gathered. Foraging costs are most easily measured in units of time and energy. The efficient animal will minimize time and energy expenditures for food gathering while maximizing digestible energy intake. Because necessary minimum foraging times and energy expenditures are inverse curvilinear functions of food availability, foraging efficiency when defined as energy intake per unit of energy expenditure will increase as food availability increases (Homewood, 1978; Hainsworth and Wolf, 1979; Spalinger *et al.,* 1988). At high levels of food availability, foraging efficiency becomes asymptotic because food availability no longer limits intake per unit of foraging effort.

As food density decreases, foraging effort must increase. Although the animal can alter foraging strategies by selecting larger prey (Schoener, 1979; Kaufman *et al.*, 1980; Kaufman, 1980), becoming less selective (Nudds, 1980), or choosing more favorable food patches in the total environment (MacArthur and Pianka, 1966; Charnov, 1976; Tinbergen, 1981), foraging efficiency must ultimately decrease as the animal is forced to expend more time and energy acquiring the necessary food. The critical threshold of decreasing food density and, therefore, bite size at which foraging effort must increase is a function of body weight (Fig. 15.9). For example, limited food availability to a moose is a superabundance to a prairie dog. Ultimately, food availability becomes so low that requirements cannot be met because continued foraging would simply increase requirements faster than intake. At this point, animals can either hibernate, emigrate, or reduce foraging effort to conserve body reserves.

An inadequate understanding of foraging strategies has been a major weakness of many wildlife biologists. It has often been assumed that if a moderate amount of food is available, almost irrespective of its density or distribution, the animal will effectively consume it. A classical example of the error in this assumption can be seen each winter in Yellowstone National Park. The northern winter range in the park is about 100,000 ha and contains 120,918 × 10³ kg of forage (Houston, 1982). Using daily consumption rates of captive elk to predict the requirements of free-ranging elk, Barmore (1972) suggested that a wintering population of 10,000 elk would consume only 5% of the forage and thus were not food limited. However, 47% of the winter range is composed of vegetation types having standing crops of 337 kg or less per hectare, and 54% had 673 kg or less per hectare. These forage measurements did not include the effect of snow (which at times can be several feet deep), very poor palatability and digestibility of many of the forages, and animal social interactions that can reduce the useful forage density to a fraction of that measured. Intake rates in elk decrease when forage density drops below 1000 kg/ha (Collins *et al.*, 1978; Wickstrom *et al.*, 1984.). To the contrary of Barmore's conclusion, forage availability relative to the energy requirements of elk living in an exceedingly harsh environment is the major determinant of elk survival in Yellowstone during winter.

A seemingly contradictory observation to this conclusion is that wintering elk spend less time feeding in the park during winter than during any other season (Craighead *et al.*, 1973). While this observation might be interpreted as suggesting that elk are having no problem in meeting their food requirements, the more appropriate conclusion is that (1) they are simply in that portion of the foraging efficiency curve where nutrient availability is so low compared to foraging costs that the only feasible approach is to reduce costs and conserve limited

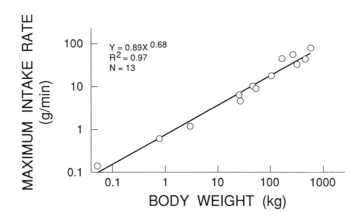

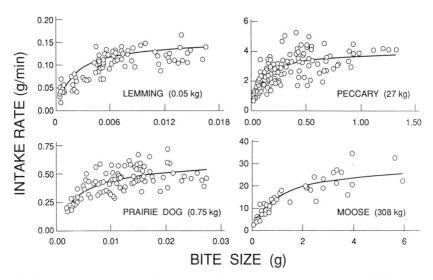

Fig. 15.9 Maximum intake rate (top) and individual response curves in mammals of different size consuming various distributions of alfalfa (L.A. Shively and D.E. Spalinger, personal communication). Species used were lemming (0.05 kg), prairie dog, domestic rabbit (3 kg), peccary, white-tailed deer (46 kg), axis deer (53 kg), caribou (100 kg), grizzly bear (160 kg), elk (265 kg), moose (308 kg), domestic horse (430 kg), and domestic cattle (500 kg).

body reserves and (2) the very fibrous foods consumed in winter require more rumination than the succulent foods of summer (Gates and Hudson, 1979; Renecker and Hudson, 1989).

REFERENCES

Allen, M. S. (1982). "Investigations into the Use of Rare Earth Elements as Gastrointestinal Markers." M. S. Thesis, Cornell Univ. Ithaca, New York.

Ammann, A. P., Cowan, R. L., Mothershead, C. L., and Baumgardt, B. R. (1973). Dry matter and energy intake in relation to digestibility in white-tailed deer. *J. Wildl. Manage.* **37,** 195–201.

Bae, D. H., Welch, J. G., and Smith, A. M. (1979). Forage intake and rumination by sheep. *J. Anim. Sci.* **49,** 1292–1299.

Baker, D. L., and Hobbs, N. T. (1987). Strategies of digestion: Digestive efficiency and retention time of forage diets in montane ungulates. *Can. J. Zool.* **65,** 1978–1984.

Barmore, W. J. (1972). A computer simulation model of elk distribution, habitat use, and forage consumption on winter range in Yellowstone National Park. Yellowstone National Park, Mammoth.

Bell, R. H. V. (1971). A grazing ecosystem in the Serengeti. *Sci. Am.* **225,** 86–93.

Below, T. H. (1979). First reports of pellet ejection in 11 species. *Wilson Bull.* **91,** 626–628.

Case, T. J. (1979). Optimal body size and an animal's diet. *Acta Biotheor.* **28,** 54–69.

Charnov, E. L. (1976). Optimal foraging: The marginal value theorem. *Theor. Pop. Biol.* **9,** 129–136.

Chilcott, M. J., and Hume, I. D. (1985). Coprophagy and selective retention of fluid digesta: Their role in the nutrition of the common ringtail possum, *Pseudocheirus peregrinus. Aust. J. Zool.* **33,** 1–15.

Chivers, D. J., and Hladik, C. M. (1980). Morphology of the gastrointestinal tract in primates: Comparisons with other mammals in relation to diet. *J. Morphol.* **166,** 337–386.

Clemens, E. T., and Maloiy, G. M. O. (1981). Organic acid concentrations and digesta movement in the gastrointestinal tract of the bushbaby (*Galago crassicaudatus*) and Vervet monkey (*Cercopithecidae pygerythrus*). *J. Zool.* **193,** 487–497.

Clemens, E. T., and Phillips, B. (1980). Organic acid production and digesta movement in the gastrointestinal tract of the baboon and Sykes monkey. *Comp. Biochem. Physiol.* **66A,** 529–532.

Collins, B., and Cary, G. (1981). Short-term regulation of food intake by the brown honeyeater, *Lichmera indistincta. Comp. Biochem. Physiol.* **68A,** 635–640.

Collins, W. B., Urness, P. J., and Austin, D. D. (1978). Elk diets and activities on different lodgepole pine habitat segments. *J. Wildl. Manage.* **42,** 799–810.

Cork, S. J., and Foley, W. J. (1991). Digestive and metabolic strategies of arboreal mammalian folivores in relation to chemical defenses in temperate and tropical forests. *In* "Plant Defenses Against Mammalian Herbivory" (R. T. Palo and C. T. Robbins, eds.), pp. 133–166. CRC Press, Boca Raton, Florida.

Cork, S. J., and Kenagy, G. J. (1989). Rates of gut passage and retention of hypogeous fungal spores in two forest-dwelling rodents. *J. Mammal.* **70,** 512–519.

Cork, S. J., and Warner, A. C. I. (1983). The passage of digesta markers through the gut of a folivorous marsupial, the koala *Phascolarctos cinereus. J. Comp. Physiol.* **152,** 43–51.

Cowan, R. L., Jordan, J. S., Grimes, J. L., and Gill, J. D. (1970). Comparative nutritive values of forage species. *In* "Range and Wildlife Habitat Evaluation—A Research Symposium," pp. 48–56. U.S.D.A. Misc. Publ. 1147.

Craighead, J. J., Craighead, F. C., Jr., Ruff, R. L., and O'Gara, B. W. (1973). Home ranges and activity patterns of nonmigratory elk of the Madison drainage herd as determined by biotelemetry. *Wildl. Monogr.* **33**, 50 pp.

Dellow, D. W. (1982). Studies on the nutrition of macropodine marsupials III. The flow of digesta through the stomach and intestine of macropodines and sheep. *Aust. J. Zool.* **30**, 751–765.

Demment, M. W., and Van Soest, P. J. (1985). A nutritional explanation for body-size patterns of ruminant and nonruminant herbivores. *Am. Nat.* **125**, 641–672.

Dierenfeld, E. S., Hintz, H. F., Robertson, J. B., Van Soest, P. J., and Oftedal, O. T. (1982). Utilization of bamboo by the giant panda. *J. Nutr.* **112**, 636–641.

Duke, G. E. (1977). Pellet egestion by a captive chimney swift (*Chaetura pelagica*). *Auk* **94**, 385.

Duke, G. E., Petrides, G. A., and Ringer, R. K. (1968). Chromium-51 in food metabolizability and passage rate studies with the ring-necked pheasant. *Poult. Sci.* **47**, 1356–1364.

Duke, G. E., Evanson, O. A., and Jegers, A. (1976). Meal to pellet intervals in 14 species of captive raptors. *Comp. Biochem. Physiol.* **53A**, 1–6.

Duke, G. E., Fuller, M. R., and Huberty, B. J. (1980). The influence of hunger on meal to pellet intervals in barred owls. *Comp. Biochem. Physiol.* **66A**, 203–207.

Emlen, J. M. (1966). The role of time and energy in food preference. *Am. Nat.* **100**, 611–617.

Emmons, L. H. (1991). Frugivory in tree shrews (Tupaia). *Am. Nat.* **138**, 642–649.

Foley, W. J., and Hume, I. D. (1987). Passage of digesta markers in two species of arboreal folivorous marsupials—the greater glider (*Petauroides volans*) and the brushtail possum (*Trichosurus vulpecula*). *Physiol. Zool.* **60**, 103–113.

Foose, T. J. (1982). "Trophic Strategies of Ruminants Versus Nonruminant Ungulates." Doctoral Dissertation, Univ. of Chicago.

Foot, J. Z., and Romberg, B. (1965). The utilization of roughage by sheep and the red kangaroo, *Macropus rufus* (Desmarest). *Aust. J. Agric. Res.* **16**, 429–435.

Forbes, D. K., and Tribe, D. E. (1970). The utilization of roughages by sheep and kangaroos. *Aust. J. Zool.* **18**, 247–256.

Freeland, W. J., and Janzen, D. H. (1974). Strategies in herbivory by mammals: The role of plant secondary compounds. *Am. Nat.* **108**, 269–289.

Fuller, M. R., and Duke, G. E. (1979). Regulation of pellet egestion: The effects of multiple feedings on meal to pellet intervals in great horned owls. *Comp. Biochem. Physiol.* **62A**, 439–444.

Fuller, M. R., Duke, G. E., and Eskedahl, D. L. (1979). Regulation of pellet egestion: The influence of feeding time and soundproof conditions on meal to pellet intervals of red-tailed hawks. *Comp. Biochem. Physiol.* **62A**, 433–438.

Gasaway, W. C., Holleman, D. F., and White, R. G. (1975). Flow of digesta in the intestine and cecum of the rock ptarmigan. *Condor* **77**, 467–474.

Gates, C. C., and Hudson, R. J. (1979). Effects of posture and activity on metabolic responses of wapiti to cold. *J. Wildl. Manage.* **43**, 564–567.

Gill, J., and Bieguszewski, H. (1960). Die Durchgangszeiten de Nahrung durch den Verdauungskanal der Nutria, *Myocastor coypus* Molina 1782. *Acta Theriol.* **4**, 11–26.

Hainsworth, F. R., and Wolf, L. L. (1972). Crop volume, nectar concentration, and hummingbird energetics. *Comp. Biochem. Physiol.* **42**, 359–366.

Hainsworth, F. R., and Wolf, L. L. (1979). Feeding: An ecological approach. *Adv. Study Behav.* **9**, 53–96.

Hanley, T. A. (1980). "Nutritional Constraints on Food and Habitat Selection by Sympatric Ungulates." Doctoral Dissertation, Univ. of Washington, Seattle.

Harlow, H. J. (1981). Effect of fasting on rate of food passage and assimilation efficiency in badgers. *J. Mammal.* **62**, 173–177.

Herrera, C. M. (1984). Adaptation to frugivory of Mediterranean avian seed dispersers. *Ecology* **65**, 609–617.

Hoelzel, F. (1930). The rate of passage of inert materials through the digestive tract. *Am. J. Physiol.* **92**, 466–497.

Holleman, D. F., White, R. G., Frisby, K., Jourdan, M., Henrichsen, P., and Tallas, P. G. (1984). Food passage rates in captive muskoxen as measured with non-absorbed radiolabeled markers. *Biol. Pap. Univ. Alaska Spec. Rep.* **4**, 188–192.

Homewood, K. M. (1978). Feeding strategy of the Tana mangabey (*Cercocebus galeritus galeritus*) (Mammalia: Primates). *J. Zool.* **186**, 375–391.

Hoppe, P. P., and Gwynne, M. D. (1978). Food retention times in the digestive tract of the suni antelope (*Nesotragus moschatus*). *Saugetierkundliche Mitteilungen* **26**, 236–237.

Houston, D. B. (1982). "The Northern Yellowstone Elk." Macmillan Publ., New York.

Hubbert, M. E. (1987). "The Effect of Diet on Energy Partitioning in Moose." Doctoral Dissertation, Univ. of Alaska, Fairbanks.

Hughes, R. N. (ed.) (1990). "Behavioural Mechanisms of Food Selection." Springer-Verlag, New York.

Hume, I. D. (1974). Nitrogen and sulfur retention and fibre digestion by euros, red kangaroos and sheep. *Aust. J. Zool.* **22**, 13–23.

Hume, I. D. (1982). "Digestive Physiology and Nutrition of Marsupials." Cambridge Univ. Press, Cambridge, England.

Janis, C. (1976). The evolutionary strategy of the Equidae and the origins of rumen and cecal digestion. *Evolution* **30**, 757–774.

Jenks, J. A., and Leslie, D. M., Jr. (1989). Digesta retention of winter diets in white-tailed deer (*Odocoileus virginianus*) fawns in Maine, U.S.A. *Can. J. Zool.* **67**, 1500–1504.

Karasov, W. H. (1990). Digestion in birds: Chemical and physiological determinants and ecological implications. *Stud. in Avian Biol.* **13**, 391–415.

Karasov, W. H., and Levey, D. J. (1990). Digestive system trade-offs and adaptations of frugivorous passerine birds. *Physiol. Zool.* **63**, 1248–1270.

Katoh, K., Kajita, Y., Odashima, M., Ohta, M., and Sasaki, Y. (1991). Passage and digestibility of lucerne (*Medicago sativa*) hay in Japanese sika deer (*Cervus nippon*) and sheep under restricted feeding. *Br. J. Nutr.* **66**, 399–405.

Kaufman, L. W. (1980). Foraging cost and meal patterns in ferrets. *Physiol. Behav.* **25**, 139–141.

Kaufman, L. W., Collier, G., Hill, W. L., and Collins, K. (1980). Meal cost and meal patterns in an uncaged domestic cat. *Physiol. Behav.* **25**, 135–137.

Kostelecka-Myrcha, A., and Myrcha, A. (1964a). The rate of passage of foodstuffs through the alimentary tracts of certain Microtidae under laboratory conditions. *Acta Theriol.* **9**, 37–53.

Kostelecka-Myrcha, A., and Myrcha, A. (1964b). Rate of passage of foodstuffs through the alimentary tract of *Neomys fodiens* (Pennant, 1771) under laboratory conditions. *Acta Theriol.* **9**, 371–373.

Kostelecka-Myrcha, A., and Myrcha, A. (1965). Effect of the kind of indicator on the results of investigations of the rate of passage of foodstuffs through the alimentary tract. *Acta Theriol.* **10**, 229–232.

Lees, G. L. (1984). Cuticle and cell wall thickness: Relation to mechanical strength of whole leaves and isolated cells from some forage legumes. *Crop Sci.* **24**, 1077–1081.

Lees, G. L., Howarth, R. E., and Goplen, B. P. (1982). Morphological characteristics of leaves from some legume forages: Relation to digestion and mechanical strength. *Can. J. Bot.* **60**, 2126–2132.

Leibowitz, S. F., and Stanley, B. G. (1986). Neurochemical controls of appetite. *In* "Feeding Behavior. Neural and Humoral Controls" (R. C. Ritter, S. Ritter, and C. D. Barnes, eds.), pp. 191–234. Academic Press, San Diego.

MacArthur, R. H., and Pianka, E. R. (1966). On optimal use of a patchy environment. *Am. Nat.* **100**, 603–609.

Martz, F. A., and Belyea, R. L. (1986). Role of particle size and forage quality in digestion and passage by cattle and sheep. *J. Dairy Sci.* **69**, 1996–2008.

Mautz, W. W., and Petrides. G. A. (1971). Food passage rate in the white-tailed deer. *J. Wildl. Manage.* **35**, 723–731.

Milchunas, D. G., Dyer, M. I., Wallmo, O. C., and Johnson, D. E. (1978). *In vivo/in vitro* relationships of Colorado mule deer forages. *Colo. Div. Wildl. Spec. Rep.* **43**.

Milne, J. A., Macrae, J. C., Spence A. M., and Wilson, S. (1978). A comparison of voluntary intake and digestion of a range of forages at different times of the year by the sheep and the red deer (*Cervus elaphus*). *Br. J. Nutr.* **40**, 347–357.

Milton, K. (1979). Factors influencing leaf choice by howler monkeys: A test of some hypotheses of food selection by generalist herbivores. *Am. Nat.* **114**, 362–378.

Milton, K. (1981). Food choice and digestive strategies of two sympatric primate species. *Am. Nat.* **117**, 496–505.

Milton, K., and Demment, M. W. (1988). Digestion and passage kinetics of chimpanzees fed high and low fiber diets and comparison with human data. *J. Nutr.* **118**, 1082–1088.

Montgomery, M. J., and Baumgardt, B. R. (1965). Regulation of food intake in ruminants. I. Pelleted rations varying in energy concentration. *J. Dairy Sci.* **48**, 569–574.

Morrison, D. W. (1980). Efficiency of food utilization by fruit bats. *Oecologia* **45**, 270–273.

Morton, S. R., Hinds, D. S., and MacMillen, R. E. (1980). Cheek pouch capacity in heteromyid rodents. *Oecologia* **46**, 143–146.

Moss, R. (1983). Gut size, body weight and digestion of winter food by grouse and ptarmigan. *Condor* **85**, 185–193.

Mould, E. D., and Robbins, C. T. (1982). Digestive capabilities in elk compared to white-tailed deer. *J. Wildl. Manage.* **46**, 22–29.

Murphy, M. E., and King, J. R. (1987). Dietary discrimination by molting white-crowned sparrows given diets differing only in sulfur amino acid concentrations. *Physiol. Zool.* **60**, 279–289.

Nudds, T. D. (1980). Forage preference: Theoretical considerations of diet selection by deer. *J. Wildl. Manage.* **44**, 735–740.

Parra, R. (1978). Comparison of foregut and hindgut fermentation in herbivores. *In* "The Ecology of Arboreal Folivores" (G. G. Montgomery, ed.), pp. 205–229. Smithsonian Inst. Press, Washington, D.C.

Pritchard, G. T., and Robbins, C. T. (1990). Digestive and metabolic efficiencies of grizzly and black bears. *Can. J. Zool.* **68**, 1645–1651.

Renecker, L. A., and Hudson, R. J. (1989). Seasonal activity budgets of moose in aspen-dominated boreal forests. *J Wildl. Manage.* **53**, 296–302.

Richter, C. P. (1955). Self-regulatory functions during gestation and lactation. *Trans. Conf. Gestation* **2**, 11–93.

Ritter, R. C., Ritter, S., and Barnes, C. D. (eds.). (1986). "Feeding Behavior. Neural and Humoral Controls." Academic Press, San Diego.

Rozin, P. (1976). The selection of foods by rats, humans, and other animals. *Adv. Study Behav.* **6**, 21–76.

Sakaguchi, E., Itoh, H., Uchida, S., and Horigome, T. (1987). Comparison of fiber digestion and digesta retention time between rabbits, guinea pigs, rats and hamsters. *Br. J. Nutr.* **58**, 149–158.

Sanchez-Hermosillo, M., and Kay, R. N. B. (1979). Retention time and digestibility of milled hay in sheep and red deer (*Cervus elaphus*). *Proc. Nutr. Soc.* **38**, 123A.

Schaefer, A. L., Young, B. A., and Chimwano, A. M. (1978). Ration digestion and retention times of digesta in domestic cattle (*Bos taurus*), American bison (*Bison bison*), and Tibetan yak (*Bos grunniens*). *Can. J. Zool.* **56**, 2355–2358.

Schaller, G. B., Jinchu, H., Wenshi, P., and Jing, Z. (1985). "The Giant Pandas of Wolong." Univ. of Chicago Press, Chicago, Illinois.

Schoener, T. W. (1979). Generality of the size-distance relation in models of optimal feeding. *Am. Nat.* **114**, 902–914.

Schwartz, C. C., Regelin, W. L., Franzmann, A. W., White, R. G., and Holleman, D. F. (1988). Food passage rate in moose. *Alces* **24**, 97–101.

Sedinger, J. S., and Raveling, D. G. (1988). Foraging behavior of cackling Canada goose goslings: Implications for the roles of food availability and processing rate. *Oecologia* **75**, 119–124.

Smith, C. R., and Richmond, M. E. (1972). Factors influencing pellet egestion and gastric pH in the barn owl. *Wilson Bull.* **84**, 179–186.

Spalinger, D. E. (1980). "Mule Deer Habitat Evaluation Based upon Nutritional Modeling." Master's Thesis, Univ. of Nevada, Reno.

Spalinger, D. E., Robbins, C. T., and Hanley, T. A. (1986). The assessment of handling time in ruminants: The effect of plant chemical and physical structure on the rate of breakdown of plant particles in the rumen of mule deer and elk. *Can. J. Zool.* **64**, 312–321.

Spalinger, D. E., Hanley, T. A., and Robbins, C. T. (1988). Analysis of the functional response in foraging in the Sitka black-tailed deer. *Ecology* **69**, 1166–1175.

Stephens, D. W., and Krebs, J. R. (1986). "Foraging Theory." Princeton Univ. Press, Princeton, New Jersey.

Thorne, T., and Dean, R. (1973). Evaluation of pelleted alfalfa hay as winter feed for elk. *Wyo. Game Fish Dept., Proj. FW-3-R20.*

Tinbergen, J. M. (1981). Foraging decisions in starlings (*Sturnus vulgaris* L.). *Ardea* **69**, 1–67.

Uden, P., Colucci, P. E., and Van Soest, P. J. (1980). Investigation of chromium, cerium and cobalt as markers in digesta rates of passage studies. *J. Sci. Food Agric.* **31**, 625–632.

Uden, P., Rounsaville, T. R., Wiggans, G. R., and Van Soest, P. J. (1982). The measurement of liquid and solid digesta retention in ruminants, equines and rabbits given timothy (*Phleum pratense*) hay. *Br. J. Nutr.* **48**, 329–339.

Valtonen, M. H., Uusi-Rauva, A., and Salonen, J. (1983). Rate of digesta passage in reindeer and sheep. *Acta Zool. Fennica* **175**, 65–67.

Van Soest, P. (1981). "Nutritional Ecology of the Ruminant." O and B Books, Corvallis, Oregon.

Walsberg, G. E. (1975). Digestive adaptations of *Phainopepla nitens* associated with the eating of mistletoe berries. *Condor* **77**, 169–174.

Warner, A. C. I. (1981a). The mean retention times of digesta markers in the gut of the tammar, *Macropus eugenii*. *Aust. J. Zool.* **29**, 759–771.

Warner, A. C. I. (1981b). Rate of passage of digesta through the gut of mammals and birds. *Nutr. Abst. Rev.* **51**, 789–820.

Welch, J. G. (1982). Rumination, particle size and passage from the rumen. *J. Anim. Sci.* **54**, 885–894.

Welch, J. G., and Smith, A. M. (1969a). Influence of forage quality on rumination time in sheep. *J. Anim. Sci.* **28**, 813–818.

Welch, J. G., and Smith, A. M. (1969b). Effects of varying amount of forage intake on rumination. *J. Anim. Sci.* **28**, 827–830.

Welch, J. G. and Smith, A. M. (1971). Effect of beet pulp and citrus pulp on rumination activity. *J. Anim. Sci.* **33**, 472–475.

Wellard, G. A., and Hume, I. D. (1981). Digestion and digesta passage in the brush-tail possum, *Pseudocheirus peregrinus*. *Aust. J. Zool.* **29**, 157–166.

Westoby, M. (1974). An analysis of diet selection by large generalist herbivores. *Am. Nat.* **108**, 290–304.

Wickstrom, M. L., Robbins, C. T., Hanley, T. A. Spalinger, D. E., and Parish, S. M. (1984). Food intake and foraging energetics of elk and mule deer. *J. Wildl. Manage.* **48,** 1285–1301.

Woodall, P. F. (1989). The effects of increased dietary cellulose on the anatomy, physiology, and behaviour of captive water voles, *Arvicola terrestris* (L.). *Comp. Biochem. Physiol.* **94A,** 615–621.

Woodall, P. F., and Currie, G. J. (1989). Food consumption, assimilation and rate of food passage in the Cape Rock elephant shrew, *Elephantulus edwardii. Comp. Biochem. Physiol.* **92A,** 75–79.

Worthington, A. H. (1989). Adaptations for avian frugivory: Assimilation efficiency and gut transit time of *Manacus vitellinus* and *Pipra mentalis. Oecologia* **80,** 381–389.

Yahav, S., and Choshniak, I. (1990). Response of the digestive tract to low quality dry food in the fat jird (*Meriones crassus*) and in the levant vole (*Microtus guentheri*). *J. Arid. Environ.* **19,** 209–215.

16

Computer Models of the Nutritional Interaction

Because of the multiplicity of factors involved, the possible variations in each factor and the interactions among the parameters, a synthesis of the whole process to show energy [or matter] flow through a population . . . , the consequent impact on the ecosystem, (and the possible effects of various management strategies) can best be accomplished through use of computer simulation models.

KENDEIGH ET AL., 1977

The applications of a knowledge of wildlife nutrition are very broad and basic to understanding many facets of animal ecology. Many field studies of the interaction between wildlife populations and their food resources have been conducted. Only through understanding of the animal and its interaction with the ecosystem is manipulation and control of the system possible. Although a comprehensive review of these studies is beyond the role of this text, several general findings indicating the importance of the nutritional interaction in ecosystem functioning are warranted.

Although small mammals and birds generally consume less than 5% of the primary productivity of temperate and tropical ecosystems, selective feeding on seeds and seedlings can alter plant distribution, abundance and form (Weins and Dyer, 1977; Ryszkowksi and French, 1982). More significant consumption rates and impacts by small mammals can occur in less complex ecosystems, such as arctic ecosystems, agricultural fields, and forestry plantations (Batzli, 1975). Ungulates frequently consume between 5 and 30% of the primary productivity, although consumption as high as 90% can occur (Sinclair, 1974; Ryszkowski and French, 1982).

Predation by insectivores and carnivores can also be significant. For example long-billed marsh wrens and red-winged blackbirds consumed 30–50% of the insect standing crop (Kale, 1965; Brenner, 1968). Fish-eating birds consumed 10–30% of the annual fish production (Wiens and Scott, 1975; Furness, 1978; Guillet and Furness, 1985). Large, mammalian carnivores frequently kill more than 50% of the young ungulates born each year (Barrett, 1981; Spinage, 1982;

Gasaway *et al.,* 1983). Thus, the ecosystem effect of animal food consumption can range from minor or subtle to a major determinant of energy and matter flow. Most bird and mammal populations are food limited (Boutin, 1990). However, food is not the only factor controlling animal populations. Social interactions, disease, pesticides, pollution, and competition for other resources, such as nest sites, can be equally important.

An intimate understanding of ecosystem functioning relative to the nutritional interaction, even in the most simple system, often must utilize computer modeling as a tool because of the very complex, dynamic, and subtle nature of living systems. Computers provide an essential tool for physically processing the data and equations necessary to evaluate a complex set of nutritional interactions. The development of a computer model follows a logical sequence in which the conceptual idea is transferred from the investigator's thoughts to a mathematical model appropriate for computer interfacing. The mechanistic model describing the efficiencies and magnitude of energy or matter flow within each nutritional process is developed from the types of data discussed in preceding chapters. Although the individual bits of information are often generated from basic research, their compilation and use in applied analyses is relevant to such diverse topics as diet formulation for captive animals and the evaluation of various field management programs. The computer model must be continuously refined as goals are redefined and critical experiments are conducted to provide more specific information or to test the model's biological validity.

Computer models, even if in a very simplified form relative to our recognition of the complexity of living systems, can be extremely helpful via component or error analyses in indicating the net effect of variability in any single parameter. Such analyses can indicate where more precision in understanding is needed or where existing information, irrespective of the error or variability associated with the measurement, is adequate. Modeling efforts and sensitivity analyses are essential if we are to avoid the innumerable studies whose goal is merely to "add another brick to the temple of science" (Platt, 1964) irrespective of their value to increasing our collective understanding of wildlife nutrition and ecology.

Several computer models have been developed that incorporate current nutritional knowledge of specific wildlife (Furness, 1978; Barkley *et al.,* 1980; Hobbs, 1989). In most of these models, the various nutritional requirements and digestive and metabolic efficiencies interact to estimate food intake, survival, or productivity. Rather than offering definitive answers, many of the models have reemphasized the poorly understood, immense complexity of the natural world. While this may be frustrating to the individual investigator, continued progress in understanding wildlife nutrition will be immensely rewarding relative to understanding the productivity of wildlife populations and implementing meaningful management programs.

REFERENCES

Barkley, S. A., Batzli, G. O., and Collier, B. D. (1980). Nutritional ecology of microtine rodents: A simulation model of mineral nutrition for brown lemmings. *Oikos* **34**, 103–114.

Barrett, M. W. (1981). Environmental characteristics and functional significance of pronghorn fawn bedding sites in Alberta. *J. Wildl. Manage.* **45**, 120–131.

Batzli, G. O. (1975). The role of small animals in arctic ecosystems. *In* "Small Mammals: Their Productivity and Population Dynamics" (F. B. Golley, K. Petrusewicz, and L. Ryszkowski, eds.), pp. 243–268. Cambridge Univ. Press, London.

Boutin, S. (1990). Food supplementation experiments with terrestrial vertebrates: Patterns, problems and the future. *Can. J. Zool.* **68**, 203–220.

Brenner, F. J. (1968). Energy flow in two breeding populations of red-winged blackbirds. *Am. Midl. Nat.* **79**, 289–310.

Furness, R. W. (1978). Energy requirements of seabird communities: A bioenergetics model. *J. Anim. Ecol.* **47**, 39–53.

Gasaway, W. C., Stephenson, R. O., Davis, J. L., Shepherd, P. E. K., and Burris, D. E. (1983). Interrelationships of wolves, prey, and man in interior Alaska. *Wildl. Monogr.* **84**, 50 pp.

Guillet, A., and Furness, R. W. (1985). Energy requirements of a great white pelican (*Pelecanus onocratalus*) population and its impact on fish stocks. *J. Zool.* **205**, 573–583.

Hobbs, N. T. (1989). Linking energy balance to survival in mule deer: Development and test of a simulation model. *Wildl. Monogr.* **101**, 39 pp.

Kale, H. W., II. (1965). Ecology and bioenergetics of the long-billed marsh wren in Georgia salt marshes. *Publ. Nuttall Ornithol. Club* **5**.

Kendeigh, S. C., Wiens, J. A., and Pinowski, J. (1977). Epilogue. *In* "Granivorous Birds in Ecosystems" (J. Pinowski and S. C. Kendeigh, eds.), pp. 341–344. Cambridge Univ. Press, London.

Platt, J. R. (1964). Strong inference. *Science* **146**, 347–353.

Ryszkowksi, L., and French, N. R. (1982). Trophic impact of mammals in terrestrial ecosystems. *Acta Theriol.* **27**, 3–24.

Sinclair, A. R. E. (1974). The natural regulation of buffalo populations in East Africa. IV. The food supply as a regulating factor, and competition. *East Afr. Wildl. J.* **12**, 291–311.

Spinage, C. A. (1982). "A Territorial Antelope: The Uganda Kob." Academic Press, New York.

Wiens, J. A., and Dyer, M. I. (1977). Assessing the potential impact of granivorous birds in ecosystems. *In* "Granivorous Birds in Ecosystems" (J. Pinowski and S. C. Kendeigh, eds.), pp. 205–266. Cambridge Univ. Press, London.

Wiens, J. A., and Scott, J. M. (1975). Model estimation of energy flow in Oregon coastal seabird populations. *Condor* **77**, 439–452.

Index

Index